Professional
Construction
Management

McGRAW-HILL SERIES IN CONSTRUCTION ENGINEERING AND PROJECT MANAGEMENT

Raymond E. Levitt, *Consulting Editor*

Barrie and Paulson: PROFESSIONAL CONSTRUCTION
  MANAGEMENT
Douglas: CONSTRUCTION EQUIPMENT POLICY
Koerner: CONSTRUCTION AND GEOTECHNICAL METHODS
  IN FOUNDATION ENGINEERING
Parker and Oglesby: METHODS IMPROVEMENT FOR CONSTRUCTION
  MANAGERS
Shuttleworth: MECHANICAL AND ELECTRICAL SYSTEMS FOR
  CONSTRUCTION

Professional Construction Management

Second Edition

Donald S. Barrie
Vice President
Raymond Kaiser Engineers

Boyd C. Paulson, Jr.
Professor of Civil Engineering
Stanford University

McGraw-Hill Book Company

New York St. Louis San Francisco Auckland Bogotá Hamburg
Johannesburg London Madrid Mexico Montreal New Delhi
Panama Paris São Paulo Singapore Sydney Tokyo Toronto

PROFESSIONAL CONSTRUCTION MANAGEMENT

Copyright © 1984, 1978 by McGraw-Hill, Inc. All rights reserved. Printed in the
United States of America. Except as permitted under the United States Copyright Act
of 1976, no part of this publication may be reproduced or distributed in any form or by
any means, or stored in a data base or retrieval system, without the prior written
permission of the publisher.

34567890HALHAL898765

ISBN 0-07-003847-3

This book was set in Times Roman by Black Dot, Inc.
The editors were Kiran Verma and Madelaine Eichberg;
the production supervisor was Marietta Breitwieser.
New drawings were done by J & R Services, Inc.
Halliday Lithograph Corporation was printer and binder.

Library of Congress Cataloging in Publication Data

Barrie, Donald S.
  Professional construction management.

  (McGraw-Hill series in construction engineering and
project management)
  Bibliography: p.
  Includes index.
  1. Construction industry—Management. I. Paulson,
Boyd C. II. Title. III. Series.
TH438.B23 1984   624'.068   83–11287
ISBN 0–07–003847–3

Contents

2
PROFESSIONAL CONSTRUCTION
MANAGEMENT IN PRACTICE

3

METHODS IN PROFESSIONAL
CONSTRUCTION MANAGEMENT

Preface to the
Second Edition

In the years since this book's first edition was published, professional construction management has become a generally accepted alternative to traditional construction contracting procedures. It is by no means a panacea, but there are a variety of conditions where this is the best way of meeting an owner's project objectives. It is therefore important for owners, contractors, and architect/engineers to understand all of the main alternatives and to be able to select and apply the ones that best fit the needs of each project.

Although the original emphasis of the first edition was on the professional construction management approach, it mainly used this perspective to explain almost all major alternatives and described the advantages and disadvantages of each. The majority of sections in the book dealt with methods and procedures that applied to any form of construction contracting.

In response to suggestions from readers of the first edition, several new sections and chapters have been included in the second edition. First, Chapter 2 adds a description of program management which is another contract administration alternative gaining wider acceptance. Chapter 9 adds a new section on marketing. For readers needing a review of basic critical-path network-scheduling techniques, Appendix E has been added to supplement the applications-oriented topics in Chapter 12. Chapters 17 and 19 broaden project planning and control methods to include material on computer applications and industrial relations. Chapter 20 is also new, and provides guidelines for implementing concepts covered in the book.

Together with revisions and updates to the original material, this book now provides both broad coverage and practical details for students and working professionals seeking to improve their management of future construction projects.

The following reviewers have been helpful in giving constructive suggestions for improved continuity and accuracy: George Blessis, North Carolina State University; Stephen Nunnally, North Carolina State University; and Jerald L. Rounds, Iowa State University.

Donald S. Barrie
Boyd C. Paulson, Jr.

Preface to the
First Edition

In the years ahead, the construction industry will be challenged by increasingly difficult and complex problems in both engineering and management. This book offers its readers and the industry a challenge of another sort: to aspire to a still higher degree of professionalism in construction and, particularly in the management of construction, to overcome what otherwise might become insurmountable obstacles to the industry's continued prosperity.

In the past decade, professional construction management has in many applications emerged as a strong alternative to traditional construction contracting procedures. Toward this end, we address this subject on two levels. First, in a narrow sense, "professional construction management" means a three-party team, consisting of an owner, an architect/engineer, and a professional construction manager, united in a nonadversary contractual relationship to best serve the needs of the owner's project. In this case, considerable practical, experience-based guidance is given for the appropriate applications and limitations of this contractual arrangement as an alternative to more traditional approaches. Part 2, in particular, focuses on this alternative. Second, on a broader level, both the philosophy inherent in professional construction management and most of the methods and procedures that are discussed herein can enhance almost all the available contractual approaches, including design followed by competitively bid general contracts, "design-construct" or "turn-key" projects, "separate contracts," "design-manage," and even an owner's in-house "force-account" work, as well as professional construction management itself. Industry needs all these options to accomplish the challenging projects in its future. Part 3 of this book therefore goes into some detail on several of the basic management planning and control tools that apply in all these alternative contracting methods.

In both organization and content, this book has been designed to provide students and practitioners with a practical, in-depth introduction and orientation to this challenging subject and to further acquaint them with the major engineering and management techniques used in the professional construction management approach. A major feature of the book is the extensive use of examples related to a hypothetical project that is based on the senior author's own successful experience with professional construction management in the construction of several real projects.

As a college text, this book is written to be effective on several levels. First, it can serve as the text for a self-contained survey introduction to construction engineering and management. Such a course is often included in conventional undergraduate civil engineering and architecture programs. In this case, the main prerequisite is a major in such a related field. On a higher level, the student may gain even more from the text in a course that focuses more directly on construction administration or on construction planning and controls. In this case, it will be helpful, though not essential, for the student to have first had courses in either or both (1) construction specifications, contracts, and law; and (2) construction planning and scheduling. In either case, the example project that is introduced in Chapter 4 and amplified in Appendix A will provide realistic data for assignments designed to reinforce the student's understanding of new concepts as they are introduced. Appendix A also gives information on how to obtain reproducible copies of the original drawings and specifications.

Several other people contributed to the preparation of this book. In particular, we would like to thank Leo Rosenthal, registered architect and engineer in Denver, Colorado, for preparing the drawings that are reproduced in Appendix A. We are grateful to the American Society of Civil Engineers for permission to draw extensively upon some of our own earlier papers published by the Society, and for permission to reproduce in Chapter 16 the quality assurance drawings referenced therein. Kaiser Engineers also granted us permission to use several of its figures and reports. We are also indebted to our families for their patience and support while we worked evenings, weekends, and holidays that would have been more enjoyable spent together. Finally, we acknowledge the following persons for their helpful comments upon reading the manuscript: Professor Joseph E. Bowles, Bradley University; Professor Keith C. Crandall,

University of California at Berkeley; Professor Ben C. Gerwick, Jr., University of California at Berkeley; Dr. Thomas C. Kavanaugh, Iffin, Kavanaugh, and Waterbury of New York City; Professor Walter L. Meyer, University of Colorado at Boulder; Mr. James J. O'Brien, Professional Engineer; and Professor C. H. Oglesby, Stanford University.

Donald S. Barrie
Boyd C. Paulson, Jr.

Part One

Construction Industry and Practice

Professional Construction Management in the Engineering and Construction Industry

From architects' and engineers' dreams to the final coat of paint, construction is responsible for many of our noblest works—and for some of our most humble. Designers and constructors from history left us the Mayan and Egyptian pyramids, the Gothic cathedrals, the Great Wall of China, and, quite literally, the physical as well as the technological foundations upon which many of our modern structures are built. The scope of the industry today is immense: from suburban homes to 100-story skyscrapers; from city sidewalks to dams and tunnels for irrigation and hydroelectric power; from recreational marinas to complete harbors and even structures in the deep open sea; from bicycle shops to aircraft factories; nuclear power plants, petroleum refineries, and mining developments; bridges, highways, and rapid transit systems that not only span physical spaces, but bring people together in their social, political, and economic endeavors. For better or worse, the constructed environment is among the most ubiquitous and pervasive factors in our lives.

CONSTRUCTION'S FUTURE

The most profound recent developments in construction are the increasing size of many of its projects and organizations, the increasing technological complexity of such projects, more complex interdependencies and variations in the relationships among its organizations and institutions, and proliferating regulations and demands from government. At the project level, management has just

3

begun to integrate design, procurement, and construction into one total process. There are now, and will continue to be, shortages of resources, including materials, equipment, skilled workers, and technical and supervisory staff. There will be more and more governmental regulation of the safety of design and of field construction methods, environmental consequences of projects, and personnel policies at all levels. Management must also cope with new economic and cultural realities resulting from inflation, energy shortages, changing world development patterns, and new societal standards. These trends have been accelerating and will probably continue into the future. Figure 1-1 summarizes some of the elements that are involved.

Clearly, economic difficulties and increasing shortages of materials and other resources play a major role in the problems now facing today's projects. But this is not to say that engineers and managers must sit hopelessly by while urgently needed projects run out of control or are abandoned altogether. On the contrary, it is all the more critical that the skills of project engineers and managers improve, and that they have better tools with which to work, so they can optimize the planning and control of available resources and better cope with challenging realities imposed by new economic constraints. In spite of continuing economic problems, there is an ongoing need for the construction industry to expand and improve its capabilities and its scope of operations to meet changing and, in the long run, growing demands for its services.

The potential benefits from improved methods of accomplishing the management of future projects are worth seeking. For example, knowledgeable sources have estimated that the costs of delay on a major two-unit nuclear power plant exceed $200,000 per day. Consider this in view of current 10- to 11-year design and construction times for such projects, and multiply it by the 50-plus power plants in the active concept, design, or construction phases at any one time. The potential savings thus derived are for just one segment of the industry. Similar conclusions may be drawn when looking at urban rapid transit systems, refinery and chemical plants, pipelines, mineral resource developments, and the design and construction of projects to implement the advanced technologies that will be required even to maintain, let alone improve, our standard of living.

Time, money, equipment, technology, people, materials. These are resources. Organize them into activities, perform the activities in a logical sequence, and one has a project. Whether it is to construct a cottage at the beach or to design and construct a billion-dollar rapid transit system, the pattern is the same. Practice has been to assign total responsibility for all these factors to one person: a project manager. Over the years, this has proven to be a good approach. Intelligent, competent, experienced project managers have succeeded in "putting it all together." Can they continue? Why the past decade's failures? Now, more than ever, planning and control of the resources required to successfully accomplish today's increasingly complex projects remain among the most difficult and perplexing management responsibilities. Success will require the fullest understanding of all facets of the construction industry.

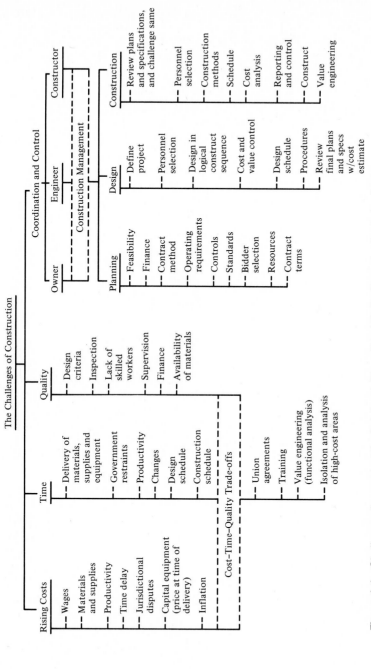

Figure 1-1 Challenges in construction's future. *(From Boyd C. Paulson, Jr., Goals for Basic Research in Construction, Technical Report No. 202, Stanford University, Dept. of Civil Engineering, The Construction Institute, Stanford, Calif., July 1975.)*

THE NATURE OF THE CONSTRUCTION INDUSTRY

The construction industry is a paradox in many ways. In its roughly 10 percent, $200-billion-plus share of the United States's gross national product, it is the largest industry, but the vast majority of its hundreds of thousands of participants are small businesses. There are over half a million construction firms in the United States alone. These firms are intensely competitive among themselves in the best traditions of the free enterprise system, yet, compared with other industries, construction's technological advances sometimes appear trivial.

Construction has many characteristics common to both manufacturing and service industries. Certainly, as in other manufacturing, there are physical products, and often these are of mind-boggling size, cost, and complexity. But in other ways, construction is more like a service industry because it does not accumulate significant amounts of capital when compared with industries such as steel, transportation, petroleum, and mining. One sees this in comparative financial surveys, such as the *Forbes* and *Fortune* magazines' listings of the "top 500" businesses. Although several of construction's largest firms are listed each year on the basis of sales (cumulative annual contract awards or revenues), and sometimes on the basis of profits, few, if any, are even near the "top 500" on the basis of assets. Also, as in other service industries, success or failure in construction is by far more dependent on the qualities of its people than it is on technologies protected by patents or by the sheer availability of capital facilities, though the latter, in particular, is often also very important.

Construction is highly fragmented and sometimes divisive, yet in response to pressing national needs, such as a major war effort, few industries can mobilize resources more quickly. Each of its elements—designers, constructors, regulators, consumers, suppliers, crafts—can be highly skilled in its own area, yet there is little general perspective on how all the pieces fit together. There really is no central focus.

Indeed, there is no clear definition as to just what the construction industry is. Certainly it must include the hundreds of thousands of general and specialty construction contractors. But really to understand the industry, one must extend its scope to include designers of facilities, materials suppliers, and equipment manufacturers. Labor organizations add still another dimension, as do public and private consumers of construction services, many of whom have considerable construction expertise of their own. Government regulatory agencies in such areas as safety, health, employment practices, and fair trade also play an increasingly important role.

The construction industry is very custom-oriented; there is a strong feeling that if something is unique, it is better. Yet, this orientation also means that the industry has been slow to respond to the benefits of mass production. Its structure is highly specialized and layered, with complex interlocking interests and traditions. Its character makes it highly effective on practical or project matters, yet often ineffective on general or program matters.

Research and development fall in the latter category of the less practical and more general and speculative. Accurate data are not available, but it is generally assumed that only a fraction of 1 percent of the industry's gross revenues is invested even in applied research, let alone basic research. This is in strong contrast to industries, such as electronics, where an estimated 10 to 20 percent of revenues goes into research and development. This investment, in turn, at least partially accounts for the quantum leaps the high-technology industries have taken in recent years.

It has been observed that the construction industry is almost completely incentive-oriented. If there is little programmatic activity, it is likely that there is little incentive for investing in it. This reluctance to invest probably results in part because advances in construction tend to develop from innovations, or "better ideas." Most of these cannot be protected by either secrecy or patents, and therefore disseminate rapidly through the industry. Thus, there is little incentive for one firm to invest heavily in new developments that can soon be expected to benefit its competitors equally.

Owing to the comparatively large numbers and small sizes of its business-es, its fragmentation and divisiveness, and its service characteristics, the construction industry, as a whole, cannot significantly influence the demand for its output or control the supply. The consequent instability of demand thus dominates everything. For example, seasonality is chronic, and construction has an amplified reaction to basic business and economic cycles. Other economic problems in the industry relate to the lack of mobility of resources. Consequently, there is often too much work in some regions at the same time that others are suffering localized recessions. Major problems recur in funding both large and small projects, and these difficulties can be aggravated by government competition for and manipulation of the finite funds that are available. Construction also is often placed in the forefront of government fiscal and social policy.

To illustrate these economic problems, in early 1974 there seemed to be an insatiable need for more nuclear power plants, and the industry was hard-pressed to fill it. Six months later, largely as a result of short-run financial problems in the utilities industries, plus the impact on overall projected energy demands caused by higher prices resulting from the Arab oil boycott, there were postponements and cancellations of projects and pending layoffs of the skilled people the industry was so recently struggling to find. Little is known about the long-run consequences of such events for the construction industry and for the national and international economies.

TYPES OF CONSTRUCTION PROJECTS

Construction intersects almost all fields of human endeavor, and this diversity is reflected in its projects. Designers of hospitals interact closely with medical professionals best to serve the needs of patients. Educational philosophies and practices take shape in the architecture of schools and colleges, while governments and corporations express their "images" with structures that house their offices and production facilities. The design and construction of refineries, factories, and power plants generally require that the builders be more knowledgeable of the related industrial technologies than the manufacturers and utilities that operate them. Builders of dams, tunnels, bridges, and other civil works today must be geologists, ecologists, and sociologists as well as architects, engineers, and managers. And most of us, in our homes, recognize how intimately the design and quality of our constructed environment either enhance or frustrate our personal lives.

It is difficult, if not impossible, neatly to categorize so great a spectrum of projects. The exceptions, the ones that transcend the boundaries, often seem to outnumber those that are clearly recognizable. What follows, nevertheless, are four somewhat arbitrary but generally accepted major types of construction. In large measure, these categories parallel the general specialties into which designers and constructors tend to group themselves.

Residential Construction

Residential construction includes single-family homes, multiunit town houses, garden apartments, high-rise apartments, and condominiums. The latter, in particular, are technologically less closely related to residences than to certain types of nonresidential building construction, described below, and are sometimes incorporated as part of multipurpose commercial developments. They are classified here from the user's point of view.

Residential construction accounts for about 30 to 35 percent of construction expenditures in an average year. Although largely financed by the private sector, the supply and demand for residential construction are heavily impacted by governmental regulation and fiscal policy. There are a few very large firms, but as a rule the low capital and technology requirements in this sector of the industry mean that it is characterized by large numbers of very small firms. Demand instability, among other things, causes a high rate of business failures among them. Designs are generally done by either architects, home designers, or the builders themselves, and construction is usually handled by either independent contractors or developer-builders. Whether in single units or in large developments, traditional construction has been field-labor–intensive, with on-site hand fabrication and installation of literally thousands of pieces per dwelling unit. In recent years, however, there has been a small but growing trend toward industrialization and factory mass production of at least some major components, and even of complete modular homes.

Building Construction

Building construction produces structures ranging from small retail stores to urban redevelopment complexes, from grade schools to complete new universities, hospitals, churches, commercial office towers, theaters, government buildings, recreation centers, light manufacturing plants, and warehouses. For most of us, these structures form our nonresidential environment during our commercial, educational, institutional, governmental, social, religious, and recreational activities. Economically, this sector typically accounts for 35 to 40 percent of the construction market. Though labor- and materials-intensive like residential construction, the scope and technology of these buildings are generally much larger and more complex.

Most of these structures are financed and built by the private sector of the economy. Design is typically coordinated by architects working together with engineering specialists for the structural, mechanical, and electrical subsystems. Construction is usually coordinated by general contractors or construction managers, who, in turn, subcontract substantial portions of the work to specialty firms. In some cases, such as hospitals and schools, design requires a good working knowledge of the activities to take place within them. In others, such as commercial office space, an in-depth knowledge of the tenants' businesses is less important.

Heavy Engineering Construction

Though accounting for only some 20 to 25 percent of the market, heavy engineering construction includes many of the structures for which the industry is best known. Dams and tunnels provide hydroelectric power, flood control, and irrigation; bridges range from footpaths to internationally famous landmarks such as that spanning San Francisco's Golden Gate; other transportation structures include interstate railways, airports, highways, and urban rapid transit systems; ports and harbor structures fall into this category, as do many of those in the deep open sea. Pipelines, like the one recently completed in Alaska, are included here, as are some of our more utilitarian structures, such as water treatment and distribution systems, sewage and stormwater collection, treatment and disposal systems, power lines, and communication networks.

Both the design and construction phases of heavy construction are primarily the domain of civil engineers, though almost all disciplines play important roles. The construction phase is much more equipment-intensive, characterized by fleets of large earthmovers, cranes, and trucks, working with massive quantities of basic materials such as earth, rock, steel, concrete, timber, and pipe. Another major distinction is that many, if not most, heavy construction projects are publicly financed, and this fact in turn limits the alternative contractual arrangements in this sector. Typically, design is done either by, or under contract with, a public agency, and construction is by competitive open bidding. Construction contractors here usually require much greater expertise in engineering and geology than do those in building and residential construction.

Industrial Construction

Industrial construction represents only about 5 to 10 percent of the market, but it has some of the largest projects and is dominated by some of the largest engineering and construction firms. These projects include petroleum refineries and petrochemical plants; synthetic fuel plants; fossil-fuel and nuclear power plants; mine developments, smelters, steel mills, and aluminum plants; large heavy-manufacturing plants; and other facilities essential to our utilities and basic industries.

Both design and construction require the highest levels of engineering expertise, from not only civil, but also chemical, electrical, mechanical, and other disciplines, and typically all phases of the project are handled by the same firm on a negotiated design-construct or "turnkey" contractual arrangement, with considerable overlap between design, procurement, and construction. The design-constructors must be intimately familiar with the technology and operations of the facility from the owner's point of view, and often they hold some of the key patents for advanced process technologies needed therein. In the Western free enterprise countries, most of this work is privately financed.

In contrast with the basic materials characteristic of heavy engineering construction, the major factors in industrial construction generally consist of large amounts of highly complex mechanical, electrical, process piping, and instrumentation work. This work tends to be much more labor-intensive, though some of the largest hoisting and materials-handling equipment is also required.

EVOLUTION OF PROFESSIONAL CONSTRUCTION MANAGEMENT

In recent decades, traditional construction practices fell under increasing economic pressures from three separate, broad groups: (1) owners who wanted to achieve the best value for their expenditures; (2) contractors (and subcontractors) desiring to bid low enough to get the work but high enough to realize a fair profit on investment; and (3) workers hoping to achieve increasingly better living standards and working conditions. Although a significant amount of negotiated work existed in various forms, the basic interactions in determining prices and in negotiating wage rates continued along classic economic lines. On the other hand, the architect and the consulting engineer were professionals who, to a significant degree, were dissociated from the economic interests of the three groups.

Owing primarily to the rapid economic growth that took place in the United States in the 1950s and 1960s, the demand for construction accelerated rapidly. The effect upon the traditional methods in each component of the construction industry is worth reviewing.

Modification of Traditional Concepts

In heavy construction, the demand took the form of multimillion-dollar projects of a complexity never before undertaken. Spurred by this growing market, contractors enlarged their scope of operations so that intense competition prevailed in spite of the demand. In fact, it was a profitless prosperity for a large number of construction firms which expanded rapidly to acquire major contracts through competitive bidding, only to find that profits on some jobs were difficult to achieve. The missile program of the United States government, encompassing Atlas, Titan, and Minuteman, is but one example where expanding demand for new technology, under extremely competitive conditions, brought disappointment to many contractors.

In building and light industrial work, private owners increasingly realized the importance of the time value of money in the construction process. The emergence of the design-construct engineer-contractor, and the negotiated contract with a selected general contractor for architect-designed projects, were two developments that fulfilled a need to shorten the overall elapsed time from concept to occupancy. Public and institutional work, until recently, clung to the traditional method, employing a separate designer and a lump-sum contractor.

However, it was in the industrial field that the design-construct concept, often on a cost-plus-fixed-fee contract, became particularly attractive to owners. Once demand for a new plant was established, the design-constructor's combination of process know-how and construction, and its ability to shorten the project duration through simultaneous design and construction, was clearly advantageous to industrial owners when compared with traditional methods. One year saved in overall time, compared with competitors, could mean the difference between economic survival, increased market penetration, increased profits—or bankruptcy. This design-construction ability helped increase the stature of the engineer-constructors constituting the National Constructors Association, which represents most of the larger firms that have captured the major share of this type of work.

Briefly summarized, influential trends included the following: heavy and highway construction continued with traditional methods; building and industrial work tended more and more toward design-construct or negotiated contracts to shorten the overall design-construct period; general contractors adopted or fought the inroads upon traditional methods; and owners tried to maximize investment returns. Add to these influences the increasing demands of labor for better working conditions and higher pay; and further, add the unfamiliarity of many architects, engineers, and owners with the basic conflicts and postures inherent within the industry. An erosion of traditional values and concepts was inevitable.

The Partial Breakdown

It is beyond the scope of this book to describe further the many problems facing the construction industry. Labor blames the contractor; the contractor blames labor and the designer; and the owner blames them all. Declining productivity almost defies solutions in certain sections of the country, while in others a reasonable balance has been maintained or restored. Too often, however, labor has been just a scapegoat for poor designs and bad field management.

Under traditional methods, there was a major economic incentive for contractors to protect their potential profits in collective bargaining with labor. Historically, the Associated General Contractors or other local general and specialty contractor associations bargained with unions for wage and working conditions largely without outside interference. Owners generally included "force majeure" (unforeseen event) or extension clauses in contracts to cover strikes and labor disputes. Many contracts between contractors and labor organizations included full protection against unanticipated wage increases in all work started during the contract period. Future wage increases would apply only to work started after the new collective bargaining agreement went into effect. Owners remained aloof from the economic bargaining. A reasonable balance was maintained, but it was better in some sections of the country than in others.

When owners discovered that design-construction and negotiated contracts in various forms could significantly reduce project durations, they intensified pressures on contractors to get facilities into production or occupancy at the earliest possible moment to maximize returns on invested capital. Construction was increasingly programmed to proceed simultaneously with design in the industrial and building fields.

Since substantial work was performed under some form of negotiated cost-reimbursable basis, owners began to exercise more control over the work. The sweeping acceptance of the critical path method (CPM) pointed out the importance of scheduling; through "crashing," segments of the work could be accelerated to make up delays or shorten completion times. Crashing could normally be performed in two ways: by working substantial overtime; or by adding more workers and equipment.

Contractors increasingly applied both methods to maintain schedules. As work volume increased, labor shortages on many projects became critical. Good craftworkers could be attracted from other areas only by offering scheduled overtime premiums, such as workweeks of six 10-hour days. Thus, the dominant goal of shortening overall design-construct periods became counterproductive on many individual projects.

The Long Road Back

The basic laws of economics continue to operate in construction as they do in other industries, although the results may not always be as readily apparent. For the reasons just given, industrial and building owners were primarily responsible for the emergence of the negotiated contract. As long as escalating costs could be offset by increased revenues from early utilization, the problems created by the growing power of the labor unions, and by the weakening stature of construction contractors and their local bargaining committees, were tolerated.

However, as the nation's economic climate deteriorated, excessive construction costs started to outweigh early returns from facilities. Demand for manufactured products began to suffer from skyrocketing prices, and owners began to see that the forecast market returns from some new facilities would not be realized. In other areas, such as electric power, new capacity was not to be required as soon as had been contemplated. This realization had a sweeping effect on the industry. Overtime was curtailed; site labor demand slackened; and contractor and owner organizations actively started to publicize the evils that had crept into the industry.

Many owners reappraised the advantages of negotiated contracts. A return to traditional fixed-price, competitively bid contracts, with a single lump-sum general contractor following a completed design, became more attractive, provided that sufficient lead time was available. In numerous other cases, shortening the design-construct period remained a paramount objective to achieve expected economic benefits. In the latter situation, utilization of professional construction management gained increasing consideration.

WHAT IS PROFESSIONAL CONSTRUCTION MANAGEMENT?

At this stage it is appropriate to define the contractual alternative upon which this book is based. The bibliography lists sources of numerous definitions that have already been published, and there have also been several books and articles on the subject. But many of the existing official definitions too greatly reflect the special interests of the organizations that proposed them.

In contrast, the definitions given below are not intended to include or exclude any particular party or organization. Indeed, they are not intended to describe a specific type of business, but to define an approach to contracting that is available to any organization having the necessary qualifications. Nor should the definitions imply that this is the "best" approach. They simply define one of many possible alternatives for the procurement of constructed facilities. Professional construction management may have advantages in some circumstances, but be inappropriate in others.

Professionalism

Before continuing, the word "professional" deserves further explanation. The *Official Register* of the American Society of Civil Engineers defines and amplifies "profession" as follows:

> A profession is the pursuit of a learned art in a spirit of public service . . . [and] is a calling in which special knowledge and skill are used in a distinctly intellectual plane in the service of mankind, and in which the successful expression of creative ability and application of professional knowledge are the primary rewards. There is implied the application of the highest standards of excellence in the educational fields prerequisite to the calling, in the performance of services, and in the ethical conduct of its members. Also implied is the conscious recognition of the profession's obligation to society to advance its standards and to prescribe the conduct of its members.[1]

This quality of professionalism is vital in the practice of professional construction management. For this reason it was incorporated into the terms defined below.

[1]American Society of Civil Engineers, *Official Register, 1981,* New York, p. 294.

Professional Construction Management[2]

Professional construction management is one effective method of satisfying an owner's construction needs. It treats the project planning, design, and construction phases as integrated tasks. Tasks are assigned to a project management team consisting of the owner, the professional construction manager, and the design organization. A prime construction contractor and/or funding agency may also be part of the team. The team works together from the beginning of design to project completion, with the common objective of best serving the owner's interests. Contractual relationships among members of the team are intended to minimize adversary relationships and contribute to greater responsiveness within the management group. Interactions relating to construction cost, environmental impact, quality, and completion schedule are carefully examined by the team so that a project of maximum value to the owner is realized in the most economical time frame.

Professional Construction Manager

A professional construction manager is a firm or an organization specializing in the practice of professional construction management, or practicing it on a particular project, as a part of a project management team. As the primary construction professional on the team, the professional construction manager provides the following services, or such portion thereof, as may be appropriate to the specific project in question.

1 The professional construction manager works with the owner and the design organization from the beginning of design through completion of construction, providing leadership to the construction team on all matters relating to construction, keeping the project management team informed, and making recommendations on design improvements, construction technology, schedules, and construction economies.

2 The professional construction manager proposes construction and design alternatives to be studied by the project management team during the planning phase, and analyzes the effects of these alternatives on the project cost and schedule.

3 Once the project budget, schedule, and quality requirements have been established, the professional construction manager monitors subsequent development of the project in order that these targets are not exceeded without the knowledge of the owner.

4 The professional construction manager advises on and coordinates procurement of material and equipment and the work of all construction contractors; the firm may monitor payments to contractors, changes, claims, and inspection for conformance to design requirements; it provides current

---

[2]The definitions for "professional construction management," and "professional construction manager," and the rationale that follows are based on the work of the American Society of Civil Engineers' (ASCE's) Task Committee on the Management of Construction Projects. They were published in D.S. Barrie and B.C. Paulson Jr., "Professional Construction Management," *Journal of the Construction Division,* ASCE, vol. 102, no. CO3, September 1976, pp. 425-436.

cost and progress information as the work proceeds; and it performs other construction-related services as required by the owner.

In keeping with the nonadversary relationship of the team members, the professional construction manager does not normally perform significant design or construction work with its own forces, although it may provide the general conditions of the site.

Rationale

Comments on the originally published definitions reflected the general confusion and inconsistency in the use of the terms "construction management," or "CM," in the industry. Some thought that design should be a part of the professional construction manager's job. Others seemed to think that the definitions were intended to exclude qualified general contractors. The definitions therefore deserve some further clarification.

The term "professional construction manager" is certainly not intended to exclude qualified general contractors or any other qualified organization. To quote from the definition given earlier, "A professional construction manager is a firm or organization specializing in the practice of professional construction management, or practicing it on a particular project. . . ." This definition thus might include a qualified general contracting organization, a qualified design-construct or design firm, or a qualified construction management firm. Many qualified general contractors have been providing construction management services for years under a negotiated contract with the owner in which they perform certain portions of the work with their own forces. Many design-construct firms have also prepared the design and performed construction management services utilizing a number of independent contractors to do the actual construction.

But professional construction management in its pure form was defined to consist of three independent parties: owner, designer, and construction manager. Possible alternative relationships are discussed further in Chapter 2. To summarize, when the construction manager performs significant work with his own forces, one of the more traditional methods is generally being utilized. Such methods may include a competitive or negotiated general contract, design-manage, design-build, etc. These are all legitimate approaches that have their own advantages and appropriate applications, but they do not fit the definitions above. The terms "professional construction management" and "professional construction manager" are intended to define both another alternative for the procurement of constructed facilities and the interrelationships among the three parties while practicing this form of construction management.

In practice, of course, general contractors proposing to manage construction under a negotiated contract will compete with other general contractors acting as professional construction managers, as well with construction management consultants, designers, and design-constructors who have obtained the necessary construction skills—skills that can probably best be learned by working as a general and specialty contractor. Professional construction management thus actually adds another option for qualified and progressive general contracting organizations, design-constructors, and others, and does not exclude them from the rapidly growing field. Later chapters of this book will deal with responsibilities and planning and execution requirements for any of these organizations wishing to practice professional construction management.

The professional construction management team approach is a truly new and different form of organization concept in which (utilizing all the existing industry tools) construction-oriented knowledge can be supplied for the benefit of an owner without the necessity of appraising the short-term effect of economic consequences of such actions and decisions upon the economic survival of the construction manager or contractor. In summary, professional construction management differs from conventional design-construct and traditional separate contractor and designer approaches in that there are, by definition, three separate and distinct members of the team (owner, designer, manager), and in that the professional construction manager does not perform significant design or construction work with his own forces.

Professional construction management is not necessarily better or worse than other methods of procuring constructed facilities. However, the three-party team approach is certainly a viable alternative to more traditional methods in many applications, as its increasing use is proving.

SUMMARY

Construction faces challenging projects in the future, including work of unprecedented scope and technical complexity. Problems accompanying these projects include the need for improved organization and management structures; increasing social, economic, and environmental constraints; and antiquated customs, interrelationships, and interests inherent in the underlying nature of the industry. One of the most basic obstacles is that fragmentation and divisiveness among its participants inhibits the type of programmatic efforts that can help improve the industry's long-term prospects.

Present and future construction projects have been divided into four main categories: (1) residential construction; (2) building construction; (3) heavy engineering construction; and (4) industrial construction. Each of these, and the many subdivisions within them, has its own special needs, characteristics, participants, and clientele; each will be important to the future development of our constructed environment.

Of the many contractual alternatives for the procurement of constructed facilities, professional construction management is relatively new, having evolved in response to the changing needs and constraints in construction. Since it is new, there remains much confusion about its definition and appropriate applications and limitations. In this book, professional construction management refers to a three-party team consisting of an owner, an architect/engineer, and a professional construction manager, united in a nonadversary contractual relationship to best serve the needs of the owner's project.

This book does not advocate professional construction management as the best alternative for all projects, nor is it limited to just a few types of organizations. Rather, the approach is simply an alternative, an addition to the list of contractual methods that in some circumstances can best serve the needs of an owner. The alternative can be used by a wide range of construction organizations, including those that normally work primarily as design consultants, general contractors, or design-constructors on other projects. Professional construction management is a new and uniquely different approach that has justifiably established its place on the construction scene.

Chapter 2

Development and Organization of Projects

From concept to implementation, the stages in the development of construction projects fall into broadly consistent patterns, but in timing and degree of emphasis each project takes on its own unique character. Depending upon circumstances, the basic stages can occur sequentially in the traditional approach, or they can overlap to varying degrees as a part of a phased construction program. Based upon the degree of overlap desired or permitted, alternative contractual and organizational structures are available to provide the means best to achieve the owner's cost, time, and quality objectives.

This chapter first describes six major stages that compose the "life cycle" of a typical project, then introduces the principal types of contractual and organizational arrangements employed on today's construction projects. Together, these subjects provide a broad perspective within which subsequent chapters can focus on the professional construction management approach.

THE LIFE CYCLE OF A CONSTRUCTION PROJECT

Six basic phases contribute to developing a project from an idea to reality:

Concept and feasibility studies
Engineering and design
Procurement
Construction
Start-up and implementation
Operation or utilization

Figure 2-1 is a bar chart showing a typical chronology for these steps.

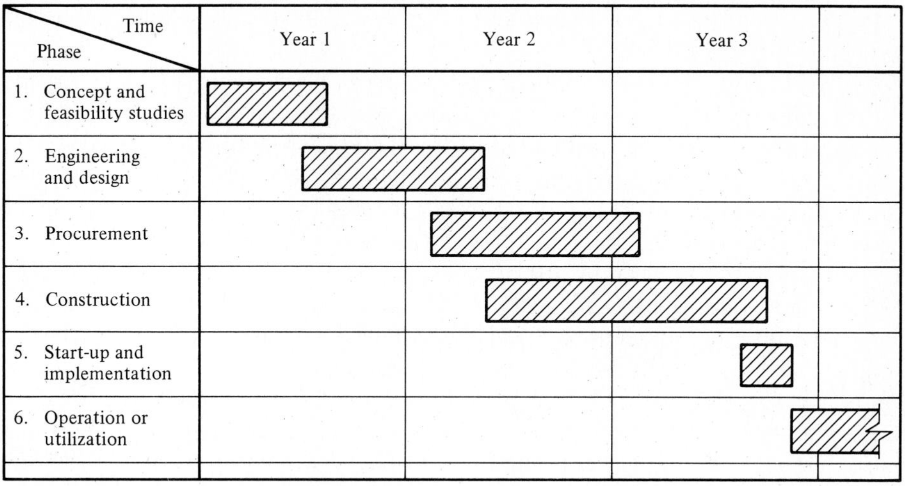

Phase \\ Time	Year 1	Year 2	Year 3	
1. Concept and feasibility studies	▨			
2. Engineering and design	▨			
3. Procurement		▨		
4. Construction		▨		
5. Start-up and implementation			▨	
6. Operation or utilization			▨	

Figure 2-1 The life cycle of a construction project.

In practice, of course, the degree of overlap among phases, in both time and operations performed, varies widely from one project to another, as does the distribution of responsibilities.

This section describes each phase and shows how they all fit together. Functions, responsibilities, and interrelationships of the key parties involved are also briefly introduced. Part 2, Chapters 4 through 9, will develop these subjects in much more detail for the professional construction management approach.

Concept and Feasibility Studies

Most construction projects begin with recognition of a need for a new facility. Long before designers start preparing drawings, and certainly well before field construction can commence, considerable thought must go into broad-scale planning. Elements of this phase include conceptual analyses, technical and economic feasibility studies, and environmental impact reports.

For example, location is fundamental to planning for a new industrial plant. Where can the plant be located to provide desirable, nearby employment for an adequate supply of skilled, productive workers? What are the present and projected costs and customs associated with the labor force? Depending on the nature of its raw-materials input and its products, will the plant have access to the most appropriate and economical forms of transportation, be they air, water, highway, rail, or pipeline? Does the location provide access to raw materials and to markets? Are there adequate sources for energy, including gas, oil, and electricity; and are there convenient communication facilities? What political or institutional factors may ease or impede the development and operation of the facility? What will be the sociological and economic impact of this plant on the community? What will be the environmental impact? What do all these factors, taken as a whole, mean for the technical and economic feasibility of the project?

To illustrate, one might wonder why there is a large aluminum plant on the north shore of Norway's Hardanger Fjord. Norway does not produce the raw material; rather, bauxite comes from Africa, Jamaica, or elsewhere. Nor does this country of 4 million people provide a large market. The location nonetheless makes technical and economic sense. Technically, the production of aluminum requires vast amounts of electric energy. The west coast of Norway is mountainous and has one of the highest average annual rainfalls in the world. When these facts are taken together, it is no coincidence that a hydroelectric power station sits adjacent to the aluminum plant. For transportation, once the bauxite is loaded into ocean freighters, the cheapest form of long-distance transport for bulk materials, the geologic nature of a fjord provides for an ideal receiving harbor that requires no expensive dredging and only minimal berthing structures, thus making transshipment an economical proposition. Although Norway's population is small, it is highly educated and productive, thus providing an excellent skilled labor pool for a technologically complex facility. Finally, the nearby European industrial populations to the south provide a vast market for the plant's output.

Similar forethought must go into the planning for any new project. Transportation facilities, such as highways, bridges, airports, and rapid transit systems, need not only forecasts of future demands, but also analyses of how the existence or nonexistence of these structures will actually affect social, economic, and demographic patterns and thus influence the demands the structures are intended to create or fulfill. The same applies to water supply systems, wastewater treatment plants, and new or more economical sources of energy.

Traditionally, these early stages are handled by the owner alone, or by the owner working with consultants knowledgeable of the most important factors affecting the situation. Considerable amounts of "free" information are available from, or offered by, public and private organizations that may benefit from, or be adversely impacted by, a new facility. To some extent, architect/engineer consultants, design-constructors, or professional construction managers can become involved in this early activity, but normally they are not brought in at least until the latter stages, if at all.

Engineering and Design

Engineering and design have two main phases: (1) *preliminary* engineering and design; and (2) *detailed* engineering and design. These phases are traditionally the domain of architects and design-oriented engineers. Increasingly, however, the owner's operations and utilization knowledge and the field constructor's experience are being more strongly injected at this stage through both direct participation and stringent review procedures. This involvement should be the case especially with professional construction management, and it is one of the strong points of the approach.

Preliminary Engineering and Design Preliminary engineering and design stress architectural concepts, evaluation of technological process alternatives, size and capacity decisions, and comparative economic studies. To a great extent, these steps evolve directly from the concept and feasibility stage, and it is sometimes difficult to see where one leaves off and the other begins.

To illustrate, in a high-rise building the preliminary design determines the number and spacing of the stories, the general layout of the service and occupied floor spaces, general functional allocations (parking, retail, office space, etc.), and the overall design approach. The last-mentioned factor involves decisions such as the choice between a bolted structural-steel frame or a reinforced-concrete structure. Further refinements determine whether the structure will be precast or cast-in-place concrete. In building construction, the architect has the primary responsibility for preliminary design.

In heavy construction, engineers are responsible for the preliminary design, but they often need substantial input from geologists, hydrologists, and increasingly from ecologists and other professionals in the natural sciences. For example, in designing a dam for flood control, hydroelectric power, recreation, or water storage for agricultural, domestic, or industrial uses or for regulating water quality, preliminary design requires analysis of the watershed's hydrologic characteristics as they relate to the purpose of the structure to determine the necessary reservoir storage characteristics; the geologic nature of the foundation and abutments determines the precise location of the dam on its site; the geology, size, shape, and availability of materials influence the choice among basic structural types, such as concrete, earth-fill, or earth-rock. A concrete structure might be further specified to be a gravity, arch, or buttress design, and an earth-fill might require decisions on the type of impermeable barrier, filters, and foundation cutoffs. These and succeeding decisions result in a set of preliminary plans and specifications that are first subject to review and refinement, and then serve as the departure point for the detailed engineering and design process.

Preliminary engineering and design in industrial construction involve input and output capacity decisions, choices between basic process alternatives, general site layout, and often the preparation of overall process flowsheets. In a mining and ore-processing operation, engineers and geologists work out the mine development scheme, choose between alternative ore benefication methods, and specify other related processes. In a nuclear power plant, it is necessary to decide between the types of reactor, such as a two-cycle boiling water reactor or a three-cycle pressure water reactor. An oil refinery or petrochemical plant often involves decisions between licensing several alternative patented processes. These decisions demand close cooperation among specialists from several engineering disciplines, and they require considerable interaction between the owner's staff and the design-constructor's personnel.

Once preliminary engineering and design are essentially complete, there is generally an extensive review process before detailed work is allowed to proceed. In private work, such as industrial construction and commercial building, the review focuses mainly on seeking approval from higher levels of management and from sources of external financing, where required. But increasingly this review involves regulatory bodies that look for compliance with zoning regulations, building codes, licensing procedures, safety standards, environmental impact, etc. In public works, agencies are providing more and more opportunities for direct involvement of the general public. There are also complicated funding cycles in legislative and executive bodies, and most of the constraints from regulatory bodies and others also apply much as they do in private construction.

Detailed Engineering and Design   Detailed engineering and design involve the process of successively breaking down, analyzing, and designing the structure and its elements so that it complies with recognized standards of safety and performance while rendering the design in the form of a set of explicit drawings and specifications that will tell the constructors exactly how to build the structure in the field.

This detailed phase is the traditional realm of design professionals, including architects, interior designers, landscape architects, and several engineering disciplines, including chemical, civil, electrical, mechanical, and other engineers as needed. The types of design professionals involved vary by type of work (building, heavy, or industrial) and are much the same as in the preliminary design phase, but the staffs become much larger and are generally augmented by various people at the technician and technology level, such as draftsmen and soils testers. In addition to designing the structure itself, the design professional often conducts detailed field studies to get good engineering information on foundation conditions, slope stability, and structural properties of natural materials. Such studies can require further input from experts in other disciplines, such as geologists, economists, and environmental scientists.

Again, it is becoming increasingly common for field construction methods and cost knowledge to be injected into the detailed engineering and design process. This is especially true in the design-construct and professional construction management approaches.

Procurement

Procurement involves two major types of activities. One is contracting and subcontracting for services of general and specialty construction contractors. The other is obtaining materials and equipment required to construct the project. Allocation of responsibilities for these two functions varies widely, and it is especially dependent on the contractual approach taken for a particular project.

The traditional form for procuring construction services as well as most of the materials and equipment required for a project is to solicit competitive bids for a single general contract. This takes place soon after the detailed engineering and design phase has produced a comprehensive set of plans and specifications. The general contractor then handles all subcontracting, plus the procurement of materials and equipment. In design-construct projects, the contractor also handles all these services, but awarding of subcontracts and procurement of major equipment and materials items can proceed incrementally and can considerably overlap the design phase. In professional construction management, the professional construction manager often coordinates all these functions, including the letting of several prime contracts instead of subcontracts, while acting as the agent of the owner.

Construction

Construction is the process whereby designers' plans and specifications are converted into physical structures and facilities. It involves the organization and coordination of all the resources for the project—labor, construction equipment, permanent and temporary materials, supplies and utilities, money, technology and methods, and time—to complete the project on schedule, within the budget, and according to the standards of quality and performance specified by the designer.

The key roles at this stage are played by the contractors and subcontractors and their employees from the building trades. There is also considerable input for inspection and interpretation from the architect/engineer. Supporting roles are played by suppliers of materials and equipment, specialty consultants, shipping and transport organizations, etc.

Since much of this book focuses on construction, we will not discuss it further at this stage.

Start-up and Implementation

Most structures and facilities of any significance involve a start-up and implementation phase. In both simple and complex cases, much testing of components is done while the project is underway. Nevertheless, as the project nears completion, it is important to be sure that all components function well together as a total system. In some cases, this mainly involves testing, adjusting, and correcting the major electrical and mechanical systems so that they perform at their optimum level. Often this phase also involves a warranty period during which the designer and the contractors can be called back to correct problems that were not immediately evident upon initial testing and to make adjustments to better suit the facility to the owner's needs after he has had a chance to try it out.

In many projects, especially large industrial facilities such as power plants, refineries, and factories, start-up is a highly complex process that pushes the facility to its technological limits, as well as seeing that it operates efficiently under "normal" conditions. In this case, start-up is a project in its own right; it requires months of careful advance planning and demands good coordination and supervision, once underway. Often, spares for critical components will be kept on hand just in case something goes wrong.

Operation and Utilization

The functional value of the project will depend upon the decisions and implementation of the objectives developed during the preceding phases. With a projected operational life of 20 to 25 years or more, it is evident that the overall cost and value to the owner throughout the operating life are determined largely during the period from conception through start-up.

Parties involved at this stage range from homeowners doing weekend maintenance, through janitors and equipment specialists in buildings, to public works staffs maintaining highways and operating dams and bridges, and on to the skilled engineers and technicians who operate factories, refineries, power plants, and mines. In the case of major alterations or expansions, the operations phase can also involve recycling through the first five phases of a project mentioned above, whether the work is done in-house or by contract.

ORGANIZATIONS AND CONTRACTS

There are numerous alternative contractual and organizational approaches to the design and construction of a project. The principal categories addressed in this section will include the traditional approach, the owner-builder, turnkey (design-construct or design-manage), and professional construction management. Each has its advantages and disadvantages for a particular application, and each has developed a certain degree of flexibility so that, in reality, many of the individual alternatives overlap one another; in practice, it is sometimes difficult to categorize any one particular arrangement precisely.

The following descriptions outline major differences among approaches and explore some of their variations, advantages, and disadvantages, as well as their similarities. Figure 2-2 gives a simplified chart of each major form. Figure 2-3 illustrates several organizational approaches applicable with minor variations to each of the project management concepts.

The Traditional Approach

Members of the Associated General Contractors of America (AGC) have generally advocated and operated under the traditional method. Here the owner employs a designer (architect, architect/engineer, or engineer) who first prepares the plans and specifications, then exercises some degree of inspection, monitoring, or control during construction. Construction itself is the responsibility of a single general contractor under contract to the owner. Much of the work may actually be performed by individual trade contractors under subcontract to the general contractor. Although the subcontractors normally bid upon a portion of the owner's plans and specifications, their legal contractual relationships are directly with the general contractor; the latter, in turn, is responsible to the owner for all the work, including that which is subcontracted.

Traditional

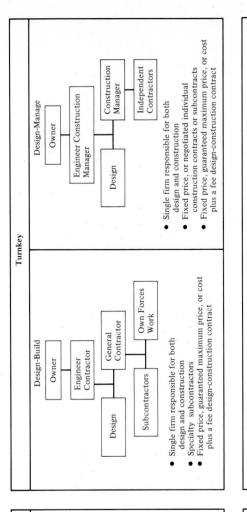

Owner — Designer — General Contractor — Subcontractors — Own Forces Work

- Separate designer
- Single general contractor
- Numerous subcontractors
- Fixed price, unit price, guaranteed maximum, or cost plus a fixed fee construction contract
- Negotiated professional fee for design services

Owner-Builder

Owner — Design Department — Construction Department — Contractors and Subcontractors — Optional Own Forces Work

- Owner responsible for design and construction
- Optional own forces work contractors and subcontractors
- Fixed price, unit price, or negotiated construction contracts

Turnkey

Design-Build

Owner — Engineer Contractor — General Contractor — Design — Subcontractors — Own Forces Work

- Single firm responsible for both design and construction
- Specialty subcontractors
- Fixed price, guaranteed maximum price, or cost plus a fee design-construction contract

Design-Manage

Owner — Engineer Construction Manager — Construction Manager — Design — Independent Contractors

- Single firm responsible for both design and construction
- Fixed price, or negotiated individual construction contracts or subcontracts
- Fixed price, guaranteed maximum price, or cost plus a fee design-construction contract

Professional Construction Manager

General Contractor

Owner — General Contractor Acting as Construction Manager — Design — Subcontractors

- Three-party team of owner, separate designer, and general contractor acting as a construction manager
- Fixed price or negotiated independent subcontractors
- Construction manager usually acting as agent for owner
- Negotiated professional fee for construction management services with cost reimbursement for subcontractors
- Negotiated professional fee for design services

Construction Manager

Owner — Construction Manager — Design — A Number of Independent Contractors

- Three-party team of owner, designer and construction manager
- Fixed price or negotiated individual construction contracts directly with owner
- Construction manager may act as owner's agent to extent delegated
- Negotiated professional fee for construction management services
- Negotiated professional fee for design services

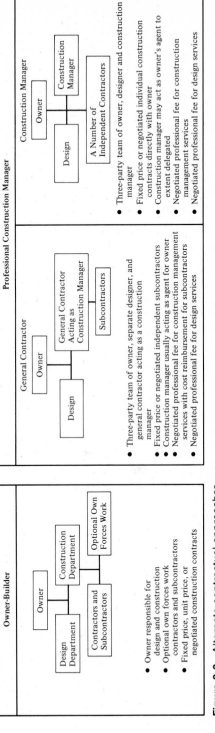

Figure 2-2 Alternate contractual approaches.

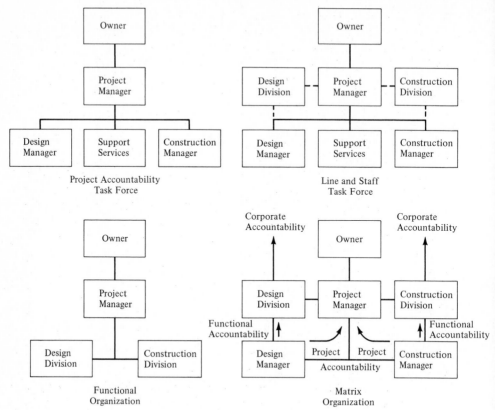

Figure 2-3 Organizational concepts.

Types of Contracts The traditional approach can be implemented using the single fixed-price or lump-sum contract, a unit-price contract, a negotiated cost–plus–fixed-fee contract, or a guaranteed maximum-price arrangement. Other variations or combinations are, of course, also utilized.

Advantages and Disadvantages To compare it with other forms, the traditional approach must first be further subdivided into the different types of contracts just mentioned. The contracts will be explained in some detail here under the traditional method, but the same facts will apply in discussing the other categories.

Single Fixed-Price Contracts In the fixed-price form, the contractor agrees to perform the work for a predetermined price that includes profit. This method has long been the traditional form of the competitively bid (sometimes negotiated) general contract. Usually most of the work is subcontracted to specialty contractors under fixed-price subcontracts incorporating plans, specifications, and terms and conditions from the general contract.

Unit-price contracts are similar, except that the prices of specified units of work are fixed, and the total cost to the owner will vary with the actual quantities of units put in place. This type of contract applies best where the details and general character of the work are known but the quantities are subject to variation within reasonable limits.

Advantages from the owner's position include the following:

1 These systems are accepted and historically supported with well-established legal and contractual precedents.

2 The lump-sum type permits overall cost to be determined before the construction contract is let.

3 Minimal involvement of the owner is required in the construction process.

4 The owner may benefit from price competition in a competitive situation.

Disadvantages from the owner's viewpoint are as follows:

1 Design usually does not benefit from construction expertise.

2 Overall design-construct time is usually the longest.

3 The owner is usually in an adversary position with the general contractor.

4 The designer is often in an adversary position with the general contractor, and the owner may be required to be the referee.

5 Changes to the work or unforeseen difficulties will often end in disputes and litigation that can drive up costs in spite of the fixed-price concept.

Negotiated Cost-Plus-A-Fee Contract   In negotiated cost-plus contracts, the contractor agrees to perform the work for a fixed or variable fee covering profit and home-office costs, with all field costs being reimbursable at actual cost. Common variations will include a fixed fee to cover profit and general and administrative costs only, with both direct home-office costs and field costs being reimbursable. Incentive fees, where some or all of the fee is dependent upon achieving certain cost or schedule goals, are becoming increasingly popular. Cost-plus-percentage-fee contracts are generally not favored, except for extra work or for minor work where the scope is indeterminate.

Fees are usually based upon the size and complexity of the project; they may be expressed as a flat dollar sum, as a percentage of a "definitive estimate" prepared at a specific point, or as a sliding scale tied to cost or estimated cost. Fees will usually involve a detailed understanding and agreement on cost-accounting methods, reimbursable items, and nonreimbursable items.

A variation on negotiated contracts, the guaranteed maximum price, has some of the features of competitively bid lump-sum work. In this form, the contractor agrees, for a fixed fee, to complete a project at a cost not to exceed a preestablished maximum or upset price. Costs above the guarantee are absorbed by the contractor. Savings where the final cost is under the guarantee may revert entirely to the owner or be divided in a previously agreed-upon proportion with the contractor.

Advantages from the owner's point of view include those below:

1 These contract systems are also accepted and historically supported.
2 They permit reduction of design-construct time by utilizing phased construction.
3 This approach enables the contractor to react quickly to major design changes and unforeseen conditions, and, in part, minimizes the adversary position.

Disadvantages from the owner's position are the following:

1 Cost plus a fixed fee may not be the most economical alternative in a competitive market.
2 Disreputable contractors can abuse this arrangement if the owner is not careful in selection.
3 The guaranteed maximum, while theoretically setting a ceiling, may not stand up in the event of changed conditions or numerous change orders.
4 Owner involvement (or that of the designer) is increased over the lump-sum method in view of the necessity for controls on expenditures, audits, approvals, and other administrative requirements that are considered good practice when this form of contract is employed.

The Owner-Builder

Historically, many city, county, and state public works departments, federal government agencies such as the Tennessee Valley Authority, and private companies such as DuPont and Coors have performed both their own design work and some or all of the actual construction with their own forces. This approach is often referred to as "force account." Other owners (or owners' representatives), such as the Army Corps of Engineers, the Bureau of Reclamation, the Public Building Service of the General Services Administration, and Proctor & Gamble in the private sector, while retaining many of the management and conceptual design responsibilities, have utilized consultants for some or all of the detail design, and have depended upon construction contractors for the actual hiring and supervision of the labor force.

Types of Contracts Owner-builders have utilized many of the contractual forms discussed above for the traditional approach, and they are increasingly moving to professional construction management methods. Actually, the owner-builder can be likened to the design-constructor, except that the ultimate product is utilized in-house rather than developed for an outside owner. Many of the owner-builders have developed design-construct divisions that are of a size comparable with those of many of the larger turnkey builders.

Advantages and Disadvantages The circumstances of each individual owner determine the advantages and disadvantages of the owner-builder approach. However, it appears that this method of performing design and construction can be best justified when the volume of work is relatively large and relatively constant over a long period of time, and where project management can be separated from operational management.

The owner-builder can employ all the techniques of the design-constructor, the professional construction manager, and the traditional approach. However, the advantages of this type of approach are best suited to a relatively few, favorably situated companies or agencies. Further discussion is beyond the scope of this book, but would generally include components of all the other concepts, altered as necessary to fit the owner-builder's objectives.

As a sideline to their basic business, some successful construction companies have themselves turned into owner-builders, constructing apartment houses, office buildings, and other rental or lease-back facilities. In a few instances their success as developers has minimized or eliminated the general contracting or design-construct parent company.

Design-Construct or Design-Manage (Turnkey)

Some authorities differentiate between "design-construct" and "turnkey." General usage, however, treats them interchangeably. In this method, all phases of a project, from concept through design and construction, are handled by the same organization.

In the case of design-construct, the constructor acts as a general contractor with single-firm control of all subcontractors. Usually, but not always, there is some form of negotiated contract between design-constructor and owner. In the case of design-manage, construction is performed by a number of independent contractors in a manner similar to the professional construction management concept. Under either design-construct or design-manage, construction can readily be performed under a phased construction program to minimize project duration. This form of completing projects has been used for the majority of process-oriented heavy industrial projects constructed in the United States in the last few decades. Reference to *Engineering News-Record*'s annual list of the 500 largest designers shows that the design-constructors are heavily represented in the top 20.

Types of Contract The turnkey approach can be utilized under just about any form of contract, including lump sum, cost plus a fixed fee, cost plus an incentive fee, and guaranteed maximum price. Unit-price contracts do not generally lend themselves to the turnkey approach. However, most of the turnkey work performed in recent years has been through some form of negotiated cost-plus-a-fee type of arrangement.

Advantages and Disadvantages Advantages and disadvantages of the turnkey approach depend upon the individual owner, the importance of the process in an industrial project, and the skill of the design-construct firm. The choice between design-construct and design-manage is usually one of minimizing the overall project cost (including benefits of shortening the schedule); it is dependent upon the location of the project, the skill and availability of local contractors, the contemplated number of potential changes, factors pertinent to the economic climate, availability of competition, and other considerations.

Advantages to the owner include the following:

1   There is but one overall contract for the owner, with design, construction, and often process know-how furnished by a single organization.

2   Minimal owner coordination is needed between construction, design, and other project elements. This can be of great benefit to an unknowledgeable owner.

3   Design-construct time can be reduced through phased construction.

4   There is considerable opportunity for construction expertise to be incorporated during the design phase.

5   Implementation of changes is simplified throughout the construction program.

Disadvantages from the owner's viewpoint are these:

1   Usually no firm project cost is established until construction is well underway.

2   If performed under a lump-sum or guaranteed maximum-price contract, overall quality and performance may be subordinated to ensure profitable operation by the design-constructor.

3   There are few checks and balances, and the owner is sometimes not advised or aware of design or construction problems that may greatly affect cost or schedule.

4   Because of the minimum involvement of the owner, the final result may not fully comply with expectations.

5   Successful integration of design and construction functions and avoidance of changes are largely left up to the design-construct firm; the owner may not be aware of weaknesses that interfere with economical and timely project completion.

6   Insistence by the owner's personnel on making major decisions, the consequences of which (such as working unreasonable overtime) may not be understood, can prejudice the overall economic result.

7   Other disadvantages are similar to those listed for the negotiated contract under the traditional method.

Professional Construction Management

Professional construction management unites a three-party team consisting of owner, designer, and construction manager in a nonadversary relationship, and it provides the owner with an opportunity to participate fully in the construction process. It is competitive in overall design-construct time with a negotiated contract under the traditional method and with the turnkey approach. It usually features a number of separate lump-sum or unit-price construction contracts which, under certain circumstances, may prove more competitive than either the general contract or the cost-plus-a-fee approach. If phased construction is used, it, like phased construction under other methods, involves the owner in some degree of risk in overrunning budgets.

Type of Contracts   Both the Associated General Contractors (AGC) and the American Institute of Architects have developed model contracts along the lines of a negotiated construction contract; the principal difference is the guaranteed maximum-price alternative included in the AGC document. Both these documents are reproduced in Appendix C.

Usually, professional construction management contracts with the owner will provide for full reimbursement of field costs, plus a fixed fee to cover home-office costs and profit. An alternative form preferred in certain situations is to provide for reimbursement of home-office costs plus a fixed fee for profit only. This arrangement can also include a guaranteed maximum price for home-office costs, and sometimes also for the field costs incurred by the manager's forces.

Advantages and Disadvantages   Advantages from the owner's position are as follows:

1   Special construction skills may be utilized at all stages of the project with no conflicts of interest between the owner and the designer.

2   Independent evaluation of costs, schedules, and overall construction performance, including similar evaluation for changes or modifications, helps assure decisions in the best interest of the owner.

3   Full-time coordination between design and the construction contractors is available.

4   Minimum design-construction time can be achieved through use of phased construction.

5   The professional construction manager approach allows price competition from local contractors akin to the traditional lump-sum or unit-price methods.

6   Significant opportunities are provided for value engineering in the design, bidding, and award phases.

Disadvantages from the owner's position are as follows:

1   If the professional construction manager recommends phased construction, the owner begins the project before the total price is established. Early completion may not provide a sufficient trade-off for this risk.

2   If the owner has only a fixed amount to spend, and would not build the project if its cost would exceed this amount, the traditional method would be preferable in such a go–no-go situation.

3   The owner has certain responsibilities and obligations that must be fulfilled in a timely manner.

4   Success of the program depends greatly upon the planning, scheduling, estimating, and management skills of the professional construction manager.

5   The professional construction manager does not usually guarantee either the overall price or the quality of the work; this situation contrasts with that of the general contractor in the traditional lump-sum approach.

PROGRAM MANAGEMENT

Program management (sometimes called project management) is an emerging concept being used on some of the very largest projects. Program management services may include no design or direct construction but could handle overall management of a number of individual projects related to an overall program. Program management has been applied on several major projects where the owner has participated heavily in managing the program in an integrated program management team utilizing owner top management personnel and management and specialized personnel from a CM firm, architect/engineer, or other consultant.

The Program management concept as now emerging is in some ways similar to the project management concept generally favored by the design-construction companies. Here, the project manager is in overall charge of the firm's design, administrative, and construction functions, with the task force a favorite operational method. The program management concept utilizes an overall management organization that may manage a number of design firms, construction contractors, material and equipment suppliers, and other participants in the building program. See Figure 2-4 for alternate program management concepts.

Program management concepts have been applied to a number of rapid transit systems, to a $1.6 billion municipal sewerage project for the city of Milwaukee, to a number of nuclear power projects, and to major private undertakings.

One interesting innovation being discussed for a billion dollar manufacturing upgrading and renovation program is for the owner to employ a program manager who will assist in developing common programs and standards for the execution of the individual projects. This particular program consists of four major multimillion dollar projects, each contemplated to be managed by a construction management firm reporting to the owner's program management organization, which is assisted by a program management consultant.

SUMMARY

The life cycle of a construction project can be classified into the following six major identifiable phases:

- Concept and feasibility studies
- Engineering and design
- Procurement
- Construction
- Start-up and implementation
- Operation or utilization

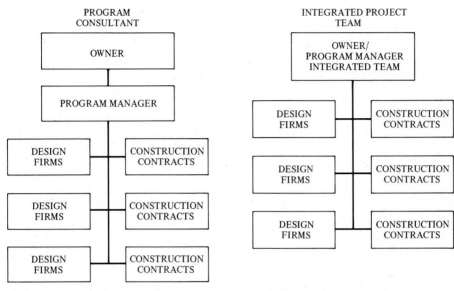

PROGRAM MANAGEMENT

PROGRAM CONSULTANT

OWNER

PROGRAM MANAGER

| DESIGN FIRMS | CONSTRUCTION CONTRACTS |

| DESIGN FIRMS | CONSTRUCTION CONTRACTS |

| DESIGN FIRMS | CONSTRUCTION CONTRACTS |

INTEGRATED PROJECT TEAM

OWNER/ PROGRAM MANAGER INTEGRATED TEAM

| DESIGN FIRMS | CONSTRUCTION CONTRACTS |

| DESIGN FIRMS | CONSTRUCTION CONTRACTS |

| DESIGN FIRMS | CONSTRUCTION CONTRACTS |

- SEVERAL DESIGN FIRMS
- PROGRAM MANAGER RESPONSIBLE FOR OVERALL PROJECT
- PROGRAM MANAGER USUALLY ACTS AS CONSTRUCTION MANAGER
- FIXED, UNIT PRICE OR NEGOTIATED CONSTRUCTION CONTRACTS

- SEVERAL DESIGN FIRMS
- INTEGRATED TEAM RESPONSIBLE FOR OVERALL PROJECT
- INTEGRATED TEAM USUALLY ACTS AS CONSTRUCTION MANAGER
- FIXED, UNIT PRICE OR NEGOTIATED CONSTRUCTION CONTRACTS

Figure 2-4 Program management.

Owners often handle the concept and feasibility studies themselves, with assistance from specialized consultants as required. This phase includes broad-scale planning, conceptual analysis, and technical and economic feasibility studies; it culminates in defining the general location and components of the project. The other construction phases can usually be performed sequentially, as they are in traditional methods, or be subject to overlapping in a phased construction or "fast-track" program.

Alternative contractual and organizational approaches include traditional design followed by a general construction contract, owner-builder, design-construction (turnkey), professional construction management, and the emerging program management concept. Each method has its advantages and disadvantages for a particular application. In practice, each approach has developed certain degrees of flexibility so that, in reality, many of the alternatives overlap one another; it is thus sometimes difficult to neatly categorize one particular situation.

Chapter 3

Organization for Professional Construction Management

Professional construction management has emerged as one of several time-tested methods for organizing a construction project. Like other approaches, however, its advantages and limitations depend upon its specific applications. Each of the three parties—owner, designer, and manager—has relationships and responsibilities to each of the other team members, to others in the construction industry, and to the public. To succeed, professional construction management must create a nonadversary team relationship involving all three parties. Just as the designer must have a sound organization with proven qualifications and skills, the professional construction manager must have the personnel, qualifications, and applicable construction experience to develop and implement a well thought-out program for successful accomplishment of the project.

This chapter will first explore some of the applications as well as the limitations of professional construction management. It will then examine key relationships among, and responsibilities of, the team members. Finally, it will specify some of the important planning and execution requirements that are assumed by a qualified professional construction manager.

APPLICATIONS AND LIMITATIONS

Most construction projects are unique, with plans and specifications developed on an individual basis. However, one can at least perceive certain broad classifications of owner objectives that in turn influence the most appropriate contractual and organizational arrangements for a particular job. Although professional construction management can operate successfully in almost all these areas, certain situations are generally more suitable than others. Factors that should be considered in selecting the best approach include budget, geographic location, technical and managerial characteristics of the project itself, and the needs and capabilities of the owner. Each of these will be discussed in this section.

Budget Considerations

The knowledgeable owner is interested in achieving lowest overall project costs commensurate with maximum return on investment while maintaining required value. Capital costs for a project with a typical distribution would include, but not be limited to, the following:

Property acquisition	5%
Preliminary planning	3%
Design	7%
Construction	54%
Construction administration	6%
Financing	20%
Owner's internal costs	5%
Total capital cost	100%

When shortest elapsed design-construction time is of sizable economic importance, the professional construction management approach, combined with a phased construction program, should receive serious consideration. However, an owner might find other ways of organizing the project to be more advantageous when other influences are more important. A few of these are discussed below.

Little- or No-Risk Situations   One situation where a professional construction management program, combined with phased construction, may not be suitable occurs when the project definitely must be constructed within a fixed sum of money; some form of construction cost guarantee is then required. The tightest guarantee, of course, is the traditional single-contract method, where no award is made if the low bid is over budget. Other possible answers to this situation include negotiating a lump-sum or guaranteed maximum-price contract with a design-constructor to produce a structure with the desired design and performance standards, or negotiating a similar contract with a qualified developer who would obtain his own design services to achieve the same result.

In fact, a construction manager who is indeed a professional would recommend these alternatives in a go–no-go situation of this type.

Early Completion Economically Significant   When the owner can assume some risk regarding the project's ultimate construction cost and when earliest completion is required, it is still both feasible and prudent for the owner to approach choosing the method of construction and the individual companies involved with an underlying goal of minimizing not only time, but also risk and overall project costs. Here, the owner has a number of time-tested general methods for consideration, all featuring simultaneous design and construction. He may:

Employ a design-construct firm as both designer and general contractor on the basis of cost plus a fee, or cost plus an incentive fee, utilizing lump-sum contractors.

Employ a separate architect, negotiate a contract with a qualified general contractor on a cost-plus-a-fee or incentive-fee basis, and use lump-sum subcontractors.

Employ a design-manage firm to prepare the design and to administer and manage a phased construction program with lump-sum bid packages.

Employ a separate designer coupled with a professional construction manager to develop, administer, and manage a phased construction program with lump-sum bid packages.

Figure 3-1 shows representative overall design-construct schedules for the

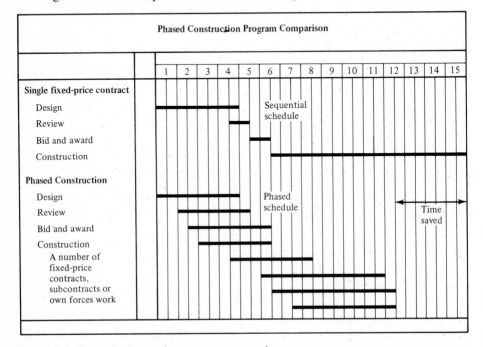

Figure 3-1 Phased construction program comparison.

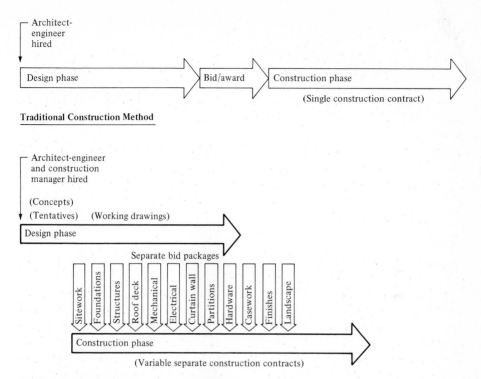

Figure 3-2 Traditional versus phased construction. (*From* The GSA System for Construction Management, *General Services Administration, Public Buildings Service, Washington, D.C., rev. ed., April 1975.*)

above methods; it further compares these methods' phased-construction program with a single fixed-price contract based upon complete documents. Figure 3-2, developed by the General Services Administration, also compares phased construction with traditional methods.

Long-lead Planning with Minimum Risk When advance planning and/or project completion requirements permit the design to be completed before beginning construction, and without significant economic penalty, the traditional approach, with a separate designer and a lump-sum general construction contract, remains attractive. However, in special situations, each of the methods previously outlined may also prove advantageous, depending upon the special qualifications of the firms involved and upon the geographic location of the project.

Owner Evaluation Each of the mentioned classifications of firms is actively promoting its concepts as the best solution to the owner's problems. The owner must evaluate the anticipated overall costs, financial risks, and the advantages and disadvantages of each method and each firm involved in order to choose the best method and firm for the individual project under consideration.

Geographic Considerations

When an owner is evaluating which method to use in today's complex business environment, geographic or location factors can influence the choice of the best-qualified individual firms and further assist in comparing alternative methods. Two important points to be discussed here include the owner's location and organization, and conditions and practices at the job site.

Owner Location and Organization   Many owners who have a continuing annual volume of new construction (such as a rapidly expanding food chain may have) prefer to centralize conceptual planning, budget responsibilities, designer and constructor selection, and administration and financial control in one or more central offices. Project sites : over North America and even in foreign countries will be controlled and a   ed from the home or branch office.

In this situation, a typical project may   e the owner's project manager located in one city, an architect in another, general contractor in still a third, a construction site in yet another, and possi   associate architect in the city where the project is being constructed. C   the vastly different communication problems present in this situation hen compared with a project constructed in the owner's home city with   al architect and a local general contractor.

Considering only a professional cor   management program, similar geographic separation will introduce a   complexities and communication difficulties. Again, each construct   ct is unique. The intelligent and economical construction managemen   will ake full advantage of area location and familiarity when significant, a   ill develop individual methods consistent with overall project economy.

For example, an owner who has developed a strong central construction and design control group over the years, and who has a reasonably level or accelerating volume, may well find it advantageous to use a professional construction manager with offices located near the same central location. In this way, face-to-face analysis of recommendations and problems, and joint determination of solutions affecting the remote site are more easily handled.

On the other hand, a one-time or infrequent owner who delegates procurement action to a professional construction manager may well prefer that such a firm be located in the same city as the job site to facilitate on-the-spot decisions, especially if the architect is also located in the same area. Or, alternatively, the project office can perform all work with minimal reliance upon a remote home office.

Job-Site Construction Practice   A professional construction management program must take into account existing conditions at the job site. This factor is increasingly important when the designer is located some distance away, since practices differ in various sections of the country. Specifications may require particular brand-name products that are not readily available, or other peculiar methods may be called for that will result only in excessive costs. Designers cannot be expected to understand construction trade jurisdictions in a multiplicity of locations, or to analyze construction craft productivity, or to be knowledgeable about continuing local jurisdictional or other labor disputes among different crafts.

One of the major contributions that a professional construction manager can make in minimizing construction costs under any method of construction is to influence the design and specifications to take full advantage of proven local methods and materials understood by all potential bidders. Equally important is the development of work packages, under a phased- or multiple-contract program, that generally fit into the prevailing method of doing business in the area. Conforming to trade jurisdiction in work packages, avoiding continuing jurisdictional squabbles, using locally favored materials and methods, and planning construction packages best fitted to local weather conditions and labor availability and contractor workload in the area can materially reduce the construction cost as well as expedite earlier completion.

It is, of course, helpful—although not necessary—for key personnel in the manager's organization to have worked in a responsible capacity in the job-site area. Although the cited factors may be unique in a particular area, their general existence is known to any construction professional qualified to develop a plan for managing the program. Pure logic, coupled with design and estimating experience, no matter how well performed, cannot discharge the professional construction manager's planning and value-engineering functions unless accompanied by a sound knowledge of job-site conditions.

An apprenticeship in "hard-dollar" estimating, and in profit-and-loss responsibility for lump-sum general and specialty contractors, is by far the best way to gain an appreciation for the importance of this phase of planning and value-engineering review. This kind of background will enable a team of qualified construction professionals quickly to grasp essential project needs and constraints while visiting the area and meeting with representatives of the local building trades council, individual labor unions, contractor associations, individual local contractors, subcontractors, and other local contacts. By comparing answers to questions and listening to the knowledgeable local representatives, a competent construction professional can develop a reasonably accurate picture of local conditions affecting design and contract package preparations in the area in a surprisingly short time. The importance of a job-site visit by qualified personnel prior to design review and bid package development cannot be overemphasized.

Type of Project and Approach

Broad categories in the construction industry were listed in Chapter 1 as follows:

1 Heavy engineering construction
2 Building construction
3 Industrial construction
4 Residential construction

Each category has its own special demands that influence the advantages and disadvantages of alternative organizational and contractual approaches.

Heavy Engineering Construction   Is there a future for construction management and the emerging program management on heavy construction projects? To date, the approach, or variations on it, has been applied frequently to airports, including those at Dallas–Fort Worth, Newark, Salt Lake City, and Cincinnati. A modified form of construction management has also been practiced for many years by certain design-construct firms. One major project is the Bay Area Rapid Transit facility in San Francisco. Here, a joint venture of Parsons-Brinckerhoff-Tudor-Bechtel supplied construction consultation during design; packaged the work into a number of phased lump-sum and unit-price contracts; provided cost and management control, planning, and programming; supplied field coordinating and inspection services; and provided other functions supplied by a construction manager in addition to design. Variations of this approach have also been applied on new rapid transit projects in Washington, D.C., Atlanta, Baltimore, Miami, Montreal, and other cities. The Alaska pipeline is of course one of the largest projects which utilized construction management principles as well as program management concepts.

A smaller but similar earlier example was a new water supply and treatment project constructed for the City of Vallejo, California, in the early 1950s. On this project, Kaiser Engineers acted as consulting engineer for the City of Vallejo, The project included phased construction packages including a lump-sum water treatment plant, a 30-mile pipeline under a unit-price contract, a reservoir under a unit-price contract, and a pumping station constructed on a lump-sum contract. While the on-site representative was called a "resident engineer" on this project, all the functions usually supplied by a professional construction manager, plus design and feasibility studies, were provided by Kaiser.

It is believed that professional construction management does have a bright future on sizable heavy construction projects. Through phased construction, separate lump-sum and unit-price bid packages can be developed using a number of individual designers and can be bid by several general or trade contractors, all managed and coordinated by a professional construction manager responsible to the owner. Although the preponderance of projects will undoubtedly continue in the traditional manner, in certain circumstances a carefully planned professional construction management program can be of substantial benefit to an owner in achieving earliest completion as well as additional economies of increased competition on separately bid packages.

Building Construction Professional construction management has received its widest acceptance by private owners in building construction, and it is indeed becoming the predominant way of doing business in this sector. As in other types of construction, however, the value of professional construction management will depend upon individual project and owner considerations. Some of the situations for which construction management should receive consideration, with or without a phased construction program, will include the following:

Unknowledgeable Owner Where the owner is neither capable nor desirous of performing value engineering and of coordinating and adjudicating differences between the designer and contractor, he may wish to consider delegation of this responsibility to a professional construction manager.

Overloaded Owner Where an owner is staffed to handle value engineering and overall coordination and management for a level workload, he may wish to engage a professional construction manager to perform this function for individual major projects or peaks in the total program. In this case, the owner uses the professional construction manager as an extension to his own way of working.

Knowledgeable Owner In some cases, an owner may recognize the potential savings possible through fresh design review and overall program planning, even though he is himself also capable of performing these functions. Here, the professional construction manager can prove useful for a wide variety of spot consulting services at all stages of the program, but especially in the value-engineering and design criteria development.

Industrial Construction Much of the discussion regarding building construction is also applicable to industrial construction, but there are certain additional considerations that are largely due to the importance of the project's industrial process. First, when drawings are completely finished because of far-sighted planning, the lump-sum single contract, with or without separate bidding for mechanical, electrical, or other significant specialties, is generally preferable. In this case, the process itself is the significant contribution of the designer. The opportunity for outside professional construction manager consultation during the design phase is considerably minimized. The typical solution, preferable in most cases, is to employ a design-constructor with process skills for the design work, and assign to him construction control or resident engineering services during the construction phase, using the single lump-sum contract, or a modified version of it with separate electrical, mechanical, or other specialties. In this situation, contracts can either be assigned to the prime contractor for coordination and control or be handled by the resident engineer.

On the other hand, where drawings and specifications cannot be completed before construction begins, the owner generally has the choice of adopting a phased construction program utilizing a design-constructor skilled in process know-how, or of proceeding on a negotiated construction contract either with the design-constructor or a separate general contractor. When earliest completion is economically significant, and where the process is complicated and forms the basis of the success or failure of the entire project, justification of a separate professional construction manager becomes more difficult. It appears that the use of a three-party professional construction management team in this situation may have the least potential advantage to the owner.

Residential Construction Again, much of the discussion of building construction should apply also in residential work, especially on larger developments. Many developers are in fact skilled professional construction managers performing all the basic functions and duties while hiring a separate designer and completing construction using lump-sum, phased packages, or in the conventional manner as a general contractor.

Other Considerations

Other considerations would include the different objectives, policies, and organizations of owners in the following three basic categories:

One-time owner with a single project
Owner with a continuing level of workload with a reasonably predictable number of projects over a given time period
Owner with a fluctuating workload with major peaks and valleys over a given time period

Single Project Most owners with a single project to build are not equipped with internal staffing or internal controls geared to performance of construction work. The professional construction manager can serve as a knowledgeable representative for such an owner while being free to recommend the method as well as prequalification of individual firms most qualified to achieve the objectives of a particular project. However, the design-constructor, the separate designer–general contractor combination, and the developer all perform work for this class of owner with varying degrees of success. The principal advantage of the qualified professional construction manager is the freedom from economic conflict with the owner that is present to some degree in other forms. However, the single most important factor is choosing a firm, whichever method is employed, that is thoroughly qualified and of unquestionable integrity.

Level Continuing Workload The owner with a level continuing workload has great flexibility in choosing the methods to be employed for a particular project. He can, by developing his own organization, achieve a significant degree of in-house construction management or even construction capability. His benefits from use of a professional construction manager will depend upon his realistic appraisal of the strengths and weaknesses of his own organization. This class of owner has the opportunity to develop a staff of knowledgeable people who can analyze each project for its unique objectives, then choose the performance method as well as the individual firms that offer the greatest potential. He can develop technical skills and resources that will make him capable of handling construction management functions ranging from entire projects to specialization in one or more technical or process-oriented major portions of typical installations. The outside professional construction manager, performing on selected projects, can supplement his own forces under relatively set procedures, or inject new ideas, techniques, or knowledge of local area practices that can prove advantageous.

Fluctuating Workload Major peaks and valleys superimposed on a continuing workload create a greater need for outside planning and control services for certain individual projects, coupled with parallel development of in-house capabilities for the level portion of the workload. Assignment of management and control responsibilities for major peaks, as well as the choice of the particular method, can again upgrade the basic organization through cross-fertilization from knowledgeable outsiders. Furthermore, this type of owner must be able to develop house capacity to analyze and choose the proper course for the major consistent with his own capabilities and requirements.

An Added Thought Many owner organizations become specialized. Their construction management personnel are constantly being exposed to only one side—that of the owner—of the complex problems and interactions within the industry. Use of a professional construction manager, one who is up to date and knowledgeable about the forms and latest techniques of contractors, subcontractors, labor unions, and other groups, helps the owner's forces to adapt to a sometimes chaotic and constantly changing construction environment.

RELATIONSHIPS AND RESPONSIBILITIES

The functions of the professional construction manager are to plan, administer, and control an overall construction program objectively and conscientiously, in a manner best suited to the individual project objectives of the owner, while maintaining a fair and businesslike relationship with others involved in the program. Objectives of the owner will include minimum overall project cost, involving the economic benefits of minimum design-construction time, compliance with recognized owner administrative and control requirements, and assurance of specified quality and utility in the finished product.

Responsibilities to the Owner

The professional construction manager's duties and responsibilities toward the owner include faithful and professional representation and advice, free from economic conflict. This advice and representation will be objectively handled within the framework of the delegations of responsibilities that the owner may elect to assign the manager. The manager should keep the owner fully informed at all times regarding the current status of the project in comparison with the overall plan.

Responsibilities to the Designer

The manager's relationship with the designer must be thoroughly professional; to succeed, he must obtain full cooperation from the architect or engineer designing the project. Only by working together can the full benefit of a design-phase value-engineering program be achieved; credit for successful reduction of project cost while preserving value must be equally shared with the designer if the relationship is to survive and prosper. The manager provides his economic knowledge of the construction industry as a resource for the designer in furthering the overall objectives of the owner. If, in turn, the continuing design responsibilities of the designer to the owner are preserved and acknowledged by the professional construction manager, he will then have a valuable partner. By working together to attain their mutual economic interests, the designer, owner, and manager will aid in achieving the owner's objectives.

Responsibilities to the Contractors

The manager's relationship with the project contractors must be equally professional. He must accurately interpret plans and specifications and promptly request clarification from the designer when necessary. Many years ago, resident engineers interpreted plans and specifications in an impartial manner and decided questions of fact and conflicts between owner and contractor. Today, the professional construction manager must fully discharge this same responsibility to the contractors. He must insist upon compliance with plans and specifications to ensure achieving the owner's objectives, but he must equally insist upon fair compensation to contractors for changes and modifications initiated by the owner or designer, or caused by his own omissions.

Responsibilities to Others

The manager also has a duty toward labor. He must recognize the collective bargaining agreements under which contractors and labor unions operate, and must have a reasonable knowledge of craft jurisdiction as practiced in the project area. In open-shop areas he has similar, though different, responsibilities.

The professional construction manager has a duty to the industry and to the general public. If qualified, he is aware of the many problems facing the industry. He should act as a knowledgeable professional in advising the owner and in fulfilling his own responsibilities to assist in solving the underlying problems and economic conflicts that are always present to some degree in a particular project area.

REQUIREMENTS OF THE PROFESSIONAL CONSTRUCTION MANAGER

The professional construction manager must first obtain the facts, then develop a sound plan and implement the plan during construction.

Planning Requirements

The success of a professional construction management program depends on sound planning. The plan forms the standard upon which the project control system is based and by which future performance is judged.

For best results, the professional construction manager should be appointed prior to the beginning of detailed design. Sufficient preliminary planning by the owner and his designer should be available so that the general scope of the project is apparent at that time.

Depending upon the owner's method of selection, some preliminary planning may have been accomplished in a proposal submitted by the prospective manager. In any event, the manager's preliminary and final planning is performed during the design stage of the project.

The professional construction manager's initial planning is divided into several major stages:

Fact Finding   This step is often neglected but represents a major key to unlock the essential facts and information necessary to construct a successful project. Each construction project is unique in terms of both structures and geographic and economic factors prevalent at the work site. If, by virtue of long-time associations, the manager is familiar with the project area and its local economic conditions, fact finding for a particular project can be confined to visiting the work site itself and becoming familiar with the planned structures, and understanding the objectives, needs, and requirements of the owner and designer. Fact finding will include the following considerations:

Owner's Objectives and Requirements   The professional construction manager will meet with the owner's representatives to understand his objectives and requirements. The professional manager, among other things, will:

Determine project duration, completion priorities, and other scheduling information

Obtain preliminary cost estimates, cost criteria, appropriations, and other budget considerations

Obtain owner's drawings, specifications, and preferred construction techniques

Obtain owner's operating procedures, including contractual requirements, bidder qualifications, bonding requirements, and other internal procedures required or preferred by the owner

Define responsibilities of owner, designer, and construction manager, as well as the extent of delegation to each

Determine specific functions the owner intends to perform for himself, and the extent to which supplementary assistance may be required

Define responsibilities of key individuals on the staffs of both the owner and the professional construction manager

Designer Objectives and Requirements   The professional construction manager will meet with the designer's representatives in order to understand his objectives and requirements and to establish ground rules for a mutually rewarding professional relationship. The purposes of these meetings will be to:

Review design criteria, conceptual planning, and detail design to date

Review or develop a preliminary design schedule; this will be significant in developing a phased construction program

Develop the basic understandings necessary to commence a partnership value-engineering program utilizing the manager, designer, and owner

Determine designer experience in the area and his understanding of job-site economic factors relating to the construction work

Review overall completion requirements and agree on preliminary scheduling

Establish the type of professional relationship that will enhance the standing of the designer with the owner by giving him a new resource for planning, implementing, and controlling the program

Establish a meeting of the minds with the designer on his construction responsibilities to both the owner and the manager, and with the manager on his responsibilities to the designer

Review the delegation of authority to each party by the owner

Define responsibilities of key individuals in both organizations

Area and Site Visit   The professional construction manager will spend sufficient time at the job site and surrounding area to appreciate local factors and requirements. He will:

Review local work practices and jurisdiction

Ascertain local craft productivity and availability

Obtain collective bargaining agreements

Determine locally favored methods and materials

Ascertain key local prices for standard items

Obtain climate information for use in developing weather constraints

Screen local contractor capabilities, workload, and interests

Visit key local contractors, trade associations, labor union representatives, and other knowledgeable local industry representatives

Determine building-permit requirements and local agency jurisdiction and permit requirements

Development of Preliminary Program   After determination of owner and designer objectives and requirements, and on the basis of a thorough knowledge of the job site and its surrounding area, a "Preliminary Program" for the project can be developed. This program will include some or all of the following items, depending upon information available:

Development of criteria and conclusions from the site and surrounding area investigation

Development of a proposed "Work Plan," setting forth in detail the recommended approach to the project, including:

- Overall approach
- Home-office services
- Field management services
- List of proposed work packages
- List of proposed contractors for further screening
- Preliminary design schedule and package procurement schedule
- Value-engineering program
- Preliminary construction schedule
- Preliminary CPM precedence diagram
- Bar-chart schedule

Submission of preliminary magnitude estimate of project cost for preliminary control purposes and for prequalifying selective bidders

Submission of a detailed estimate of professional construction management costs, if not already presented as a part of the proposal

Assignment of key personnel and submission of schedules for contemplated future personnel to be assigned

Development of Final Program   After review of the preliminary plans with the owner and with the designer, the "Project Plan" is completed and issued to all three partners in the overall project for use in controlling the actual progress. Final planning will include the following:

Breakdown of design schedule by contemplated construction contract packages

List of proposed contract packages, including detailed scope of each

Completion and issuance of overall project CPM schedule

Establishment of project control systems

Beginning of value-engineering program

Issuance of a procedures manual for the project, setting forth key duties and responsibilities

Implementation Requirements

Execution of the plan is divided into two equally important objectives. The job must be "bought out" at a price within the budget, that is, firm prices must be obtained for materials and construction contracts; and it must be completed as designed and on schedule.

Bidding and Award Phase   In a phased construction program, the first packages must be developed shortly after commencement of detail design, and will proceed simultaneously with the detail design work. Items to be considered during this phase will include the steps necessary to:

Finalize preliminary contractor bid lists by contract package
Prequalify selected contractors based upon qualifications criteria
Issue final invited bidder list by contract package
Prepare bid packages
Review bid packages
Issue "Requests for Quotation"
Prepare detailed fair-cost estimate for each bid package
Review and analyze bids
Recommend contract awards
Issue "Notices to Proceed with Field Work"

Construction Phase   The field construction phase will begin prior to the award of the first contract. Home-office management and control will parallel the field effort. On certain large projects, the two may be combined in the field location through choice of proper personnel. The manager's function during the construction phase will include responsibilities to:

Establish the field office
Hire testing laboratory and surveyor
Obtain necessary permits
Manage, coordinate, and inspect the work of individual contractors
Maintain job diaries, drawing register, and other records
Prepare and approve progress-payment requests
Maintain progress records and photographs
Prepare input for project control system
Prepare field reports and schedules
Prepare contract closeout and acceptance documents

Controls   The development and implementation of a comprehensive project control system are essential if the full potential of a professional construction management program is to be realized. The controls must be based upon realistic goals developed during the planning and design phase. The control system, by itself, will not manage the project, but it will, if properly designed, measure the current status against programmed goals, so that corrective management action can be applied when warranted. Features of a comprehensive project control system will include:

An updated and current CPM network
A design and procurement schedule showing actual progress compared with that scheduled
CPM summary schedule showing actual contract progress compared with scheduled progress for each contract

Cost report comparing forecast-at-completion costs, including committed and estimated contract costs to complete, compared with budget estimates

Value-engineering summary showing results of program to date

Weekly progress reports listing significant progress, lack of progress, current problems, proposed solutions, and other pertinent information

Monthly progress reports summarizing pertinent information developed from the above control information

Special studies developing recommended solutions or alternate solutions to current or anticipated problems

SUMMARY

Professional construction management is one of many methods for organizing a construction program. Each of these time-tested methods has certain advantages and disadvantages in individual cases, depending upon the owner's objectives. The qualifications of an individual firm, represented by its management and technical personnel actively assigned to the project, may in many cases be more important than the particular method chosen.

The three-party professional construction management team has the advantage of freedom from the adversary relationship prevalent in older, more traditional methods. If all parties of the team are knowledgeable, technically proficient, and professional, this combination of efforts can often result in achieving minimum costs while preserving phased construction's reduced design-construction time schedules.

Part 2

Professional Construction Management in Practice

Chapter 4

Introduction to an Example Project[1]

This chapter introduces an example project that will help explain practical implications of concepts and procedures described in the chapters that follow. The project is large enough to illustrate all the main procedures and tools associated with professional construction management, yet small enough to emphasize overall concepts without obscuring them in the maze of detail associated with large projects. Many of the schedules, estimates, reports, and other exhibits in this and later chapters are also based on the example project better to illustrate the interrelationships in an integrated approach to project planning and control.

To describe the example in sufficient detail, this chapter begins with a technical description of the project and an overview of its life cycle. To illustrate more realistically the project's objectives, organization, and administration, the chapter's format then shifts to a summary of the actual professional construction management proposal, followed by a copy of the procedure outline.

THE EASYWAY WAREHOUSE PROJECT

With some 150,000 square feet under roof, the Easyway Food Company's new warehouse in Mountaintown, Westamerica, will provide storage for grocery

[1]This example is based on a real project, but names, dates, and places have been changed for confidentiality.

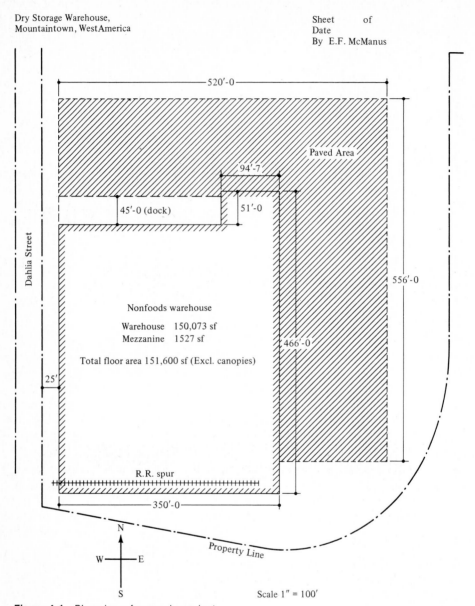

Dry Storage Warehouse,
Mountaintown, WestAmerica

Sheet   of
Date
By E.F. McManus

Figure 4-1   Plan view of example project.

and nonfood items. Although primarily equipped with pallet racks for storage of items handled by forklift trucks, it also includes flow racks that permit individual items to be packed in assortments for shipment to retail stores.

Figure 4-1 gives a simplified plan view of the new warehouse.

Initial nonfoods storage is shown in flow racks (lower tiers) and pallet racks above.

Dry storage warehouse has a nominal floor area of 150,000 square feet and is used to warehouse a large variety of nonperishable items.

Figure 4-2 Photographs from a similar project.

Figure 4-2 shows photographs from a similar project.

Other principal features are:

Heavy-duty concrete yard paving
Loading-dock-high floor slab
Special hardened topping on floor slab
Double-tee precast concrete walls
Structural steel framing with metal roof deck
Sprinklered throughout
Built-up roof
Required utilities, including domestic water, fire water, storm sewer, sanitary sewer, and natural gas
Natural gas unit heaters
Mercury vapor lighting
Rail spur for incoming items
Usual appurtenances

Six working drawings were prepared to describe the new warehouse. A comprehensive set of technical specifications was also required. The following drawings were prepared by the architect.[2]

Drawing SI-1: Plot Plan and Utility Plan
Drawing A-1: Foundation and Floor Plans, and Finish Schedule
Drawing A-2: Roof Framing, Plan and Details
Drawing A-3: Elevations and Roof Plan
Drawing PH-1: Plumbing and Heating Plan
Drawing E-1: Electrical Plan

Included in Appendixes A and B are a simplified specification, a CPM precedence diagram, fair-cost estimates, and a sample-bid package for one of the construction contracts.

PROJECT LIFE CYCLE

Chapter 2 separated the life cycle for a new project into the following key phases:

Concept and feasibility studies
Engineering and design
Procurement
Construction
Start-up and implementation

This section will summarize what each involved for the Easyway Warehouse.

---

[2]Instructions for obtaining full-size reproducible copies of these drawings are also given in Appendix A.

Concept and Feasibility Studies

The Design and Construction Department of the Easyway Food Company, an expanding grocery chain with regional distribution and retail outlets, did the initial feasibility studies, then prepared a conceptual drawing based upon overall requirements obtained from the Operating Division. The Operating Division specified that the new warehouse cover approximately 150,000 square feet, that it provide for incoming shipments by both truck and rail, and that the storage-rack layout conform to existing standards. Other standards were set by Easyway's insurance underwriter, the Mountaintown local building department, and other agencies. The Operating Division also required that the occupancy date coincide with the anticipated need for the new facilities. The conceptual drawing, accompanied by company standard details and specifications, gave sufficient detail to enable an architect to prepare detailed drawings and specifications.

Easyway's Design and Construction Department had to choose the architect, develop a preliminary schedule for achieving the required completion date, and select the method of designing and constructing the project.

In the case of this new warehouse, Easyway prepared a comparison between a sequential schedule (traditional lump-sum single contract) and a phased schedule. Figure 4-3 shows this comparison.

Sequential Schedule If time available for completion was 12 months or

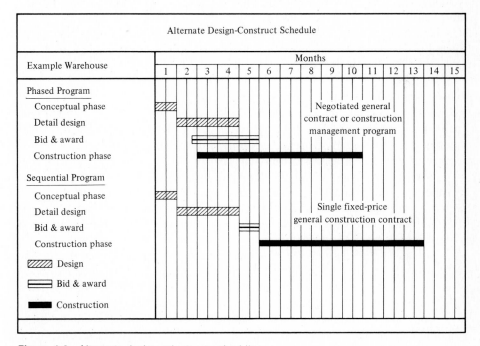

Figure 4-3 Alternate design-construct schedules.

more, the traditional approach would probably be chosen. This method would include plans and specifications prepared by a local architect, followed by construction performed under a single lump-sum contract. Design would take 3 months; 1 month would be allowed for bidding and award, and 8 months for construction. Barring changes after award, the cost of the project would be fully known before construction begins.

Phased Schedule   In this example, only 10 months were available for design and construction if required completion dates were to be met. Therefore, the owner's choice narrowed to turnkey, traditional with a negotiated construction contract, and professional construction management. All these methods could phase the construction program and, if successful, would complete the facility by the required occupancy date.

The owner reviewed the three methods, the capabilities of firms in the area, and Easyway's own internal qualifications and objectives. The company determined that, for this particular project, professional construction management offered advantages of lump-sum contracts coupled with completion by the required date.

Because of the tight schedule, Easyway immediately negotiated a contract with a local architect and selected a professional construction manager in accordance with established procedures.

For the new warehouse it took about 2 weeks for achievement of conceptual agreement with the architect, Rushmore, Owens and Peril (ROP), and another 2 weeks for the selection of Construction Management and Control, Inc. (CMC) as the professional construction manager. With the manager thus selected, the project moved to the engineering and design phase.

Engineering and Design

The professional construction manager and the architect met and reviewed the proposal previously submitted to the owner. After making required modifications, they reached a basic understanding, and CMC prepared and issued for approval a "Procedure Outline" spelling out the relationships between the owner, architect, and construction manager.

Early in this phase CMC developed a procurement schedule, finalized the number of bid packages, and the team agreed that, with the professional construction manager's review, the architect would put out the bid packages. Bids were received by the owner, and an evaluation and recommendation for award was prepared by CMC.

Several value-engineering alternates were reviewed during the design phase. Some, chosen as being clearly most economical, were included in the final plans and specifications, while others were included as alternates in the bidding documents to enable contractors to determine the least costly solution.

Construction Management and Control, Inc. developed the CPM control schedule, prepared the fair-cost estimates during the design phase, and set up the project control system to monitor the actual performance against the budget estimate and project schedule.

Procurement

Since the project was built using phased construction, procurement overlapped both design and construction. For this project a total of 10 contracts were chosen as a compromise between scheduling requirements, engineering design schedules, and local contractor interests and capabilities. These contracts are summarized as follows:

1 *Site earthwork* Includes cut and fill required for site grading, imported fill for the dock-high warehouse pad, fencing, and other work shown on the drawings.

2 *Foundation and slab concrete* Includes concrete foundations complete with structural excavation and backfill. Also includes exterior concrete slabs to make the overall package more attractive to better-qualified contractors. Includes installation of anchor bolts, frames, and other embedded items furnished by the structural steel contractor.

3 *Structural steel* Includes furnishing and erection of all structural steel, including the metal roof deck. Does not include miscellaneous steel that is not fully designed at this time.

4 *Precast concrete walls* Includes furnishing and erection of double-tee wall system.

5 *Fire protection* Includes design and construction of an overhead dry-type sprinkler system to performance specifications. Includes interior sprinkler system and exterior fire mains as indicated on the drawings.

6 *Plumbing, heating, ventilating, and air conditioning* The mechanical contract includes rough and finish plumbing, gas-fired unit heaters, gravity roof ventilation, and office air conditioning. Also included are sheet metal flashings required for the roofing in conformance to trade practices in the area, and site underground utilities, such as domestic water, storm sewer, and gas.

7 *Electrical* Includes all power wiring, lighting, and electrical controls.

8 *Roofing* Includes roof insulation, built-up roof, and required accessories.

9 *Special floors* Includes the base slab and $3/4$-inch-topping wear surface for the warehouse interior.

10 *Building Finish* This contract includes balance of specialty items, such as remaining concrete, concrete block, drywall, painting, tile, glazing, finish carpentry, dock hardware, and items not otherwise covered.

Construction

On-site work began with award of the site earthwork contract. CMC appointed a field construction manager and hired a clerk typist. Initial layout was handled by a local professional surveyor, and a testing laboratory was chosen for soils, concrete, and other specialized inspection and testing. The local architect visited the project frequently in accordance with his overall responsibilities during the construction phase. All contractors were directed through the job-site office. The "Procedure Outline," given later in this chapter, describes significant features during the construction phase, along with key forms and reports utilized in managing the project.

Start-up and Implementation

For the new warehouse the owner handled moving in of the stock and initial operations. Since the owner performed such functions with the company's own forces, start-up responsibilities of the professional construction manager were limited to initial owner familiarization with operating equipment, and to troubleshooting throughout the start-up phase.

THE SUCCESSFUL PROPOSAL

The successful proposal was submitted generally in accordance with established methods. In this example, the owner also requested proposals from two local general contractors. After evaluating the proposals, the owner chose the professional construction management approach as being best suited to the requirements of this particular project.

A summary of the successful construction management (CM) proposal is set forth on the following pages. The proposal consists of a letter that outlines proposed services and quotes a fixed fee for home office services, general overhead, and profit. The following key exhibits, illustrating preliminary planning which has been performed as a part of the proposal, are also included at the end of the proposal.

Preliminary Schedule (Figure 4-4)
Preliminary Cost Estimate (Figure 4-5)
Estimate of Construction Management Costs (Figure 4-6)
Proposed Organization Chart (Figure 4-7)
Preliminary CPM Diagram (Figure 4-8)

CM PROPOSAL
Easyway Dry Storage Warehouse
CONSTRUCTION MANAGEMENT & CONTROL, INC.
September 1, 1984

Proposal No. 84-17

Mr. Peter J. Cleaveland
Manager, Design & Construction Department
Easyway Food Company
200 Madison Street
Mountaintown, WestAmerica 99999

Subject: Professional Construction Management Proposal
Mountaintown Dry Storage Warehouse

Dear Mr. Cleaveland:

In accordance with your request we are pleased to submit this proposal to furnish Professional Construction Management services for construction of the Mountaintown Dry Storage Warehouse.

Construction Management & Control, Inc. proposes to provide a management services program structured to meet the objective of achieving warehouse completion in ten calendar months from this date while preserving the benefits of fixed-price construction contracts. Through use of the "Fast Track" (or phased construction) approach, fixed-price construction contracts will be developed, bid, and awarded to permit building closure at the earliest possible date. This will enable interior work to continue during the winter months in order to permit owner occupancy on schedule next spring.

We propose herein that Construction Management & Control, Inc. will provide the following services:

1 *Prepare Control Schedule* Prepare a master control schedule showing the contemplated bid packages and the required construction duration for achieving project objectives.

2 *Develop Bid Packages* With the assistance of owner and architect, develop a detailed scope of the separate bid packages applicable for lump-sum bidding.

3 *Prepare Bidders List* Handle prequalification of prospective bidders having the specialized skills necessary for accomplishing the work. A bid list will be prepared in consultation with architect and owner.

4 *Prepare Fair-Cost Estimates* A fair-cost estimate for each bid package will be prepared for use in evaluating bids.

5 *Receive, Review, and Evaluate Bids* Bid openings will be conducted, bids evaluated, and recommendations prepared for contract award by Easyway Food Company, Inc.

6 *Manage, Coordinate, and Inspect the Work* It is our understanding that a representative of Easyway Food Company, Inc. will visit the work periodically, and that the architect will also make periodic visits as required. Construction Management & Control, Inc. will provide a full-time Field Construction Manager who will be assigned to the site for managing, coordinating, and inspecting all work performed on the project. His duties will include coordination of contracts; monitoring the schedule of individual phases of the work; making recommendations for adjusting the work to accommodate changing and unforeseen conditions if applicable; preparation of reports on the progress of the work; reviewing and recommending progress payments; obtaining required shop drawings and forwarding them to the architect for approval; obtaining testing laboratory services as required; inspecting the quality of materials and workmanship; maintaining daily logs and records; and such other services as are customarily required in order to manage the work in accordance with the owner's objectives.

7 *Provide Home-Office Support Services* Construction Management & Control, Inc., will designate one individual in the office who will be responsible to the owner's Project Manager for all work, and who will be utilized on an "as required" basis to the extent necessary for this purpose. In addition the resources of Construction Management & Control, Inc.'s management and technical personnel will be available for assistance to the owner throughout the project in the event of special need.

Attached for your review and consideration are the following exhibits illustrating the preliminary program that we have developed in an effort to achieve your overall objectives:

Preliminary Schedule
Preliminary Construction Cost Estimate
Estimate of Construction Management Costs (General Conditions)
Proposed Organization Chart
Preliminary CPM Diagram

We propose to provide the Professional Construction Management services for a fixed fee to cover home office services, with all field costs to be reimbursable. Our fixed fee will be One Hundred Thousand Dollars ($100,000.00). Reimbursable costs are set forth in exhibit A.

Our proposal is subject to the negotiation of a mutually satisfactory agreement.

We greatly appreciate the opportunity to provide our proposal for Professional Construction Management services for your Mountaintown project. Since our proposal has been developed on the basis of preliminary information, we would be pleased to discuss the program further, and incorporate modifications if required, in order to more fully comply with your overall objectives.

Very truly yours,
CONSTRUCTION MANAGEMENT & CONTROL, INC.
JWH:mp   J. Walter Harrington
Attach.   President

EXHIBIT A
REIMBURSABLE COSTS

In addition to the fixed fee covering home office costs, general corporate overhead, and profit, the costs and expenses to be reimbursed to Construction Management & Control, Inc. shall consist generally of the following:

1 Field Costs
   A All salary and wage costs for Construction Management & Control, Inc. personnel assigned to the project field office for time expended in the performance of services, including salaries and wages, payroll taxes, vacation allowances, sick leave, welfare benefits, pensions, retirement benefits, and all other benefits pursuant to employee benefit programs.
   B The cost of any outside consultants retained for performance of necessary services.
   C All amounts paid or incurred by Construction Management & Control, Inc. under or in connection with any contracts, subcontracts, or purchase orders let or issued for the project.
   D Sales, use, turnover, gross receipts, or other taxes paid in connection with the project which are not measured by net corporate income.
   E All costs of the project field office. These costs include but are not

limited to rental costs, furniture, fixtures, and utilities and telephone services.

F All insurance and bond premiums paid or incurred in connection with field services.

G All costs of incidental purchased labor and services.

H All costs of long distance calls, telegrams, cables, postage, duplicating, photostating, teletype, and other similar items of expense directly connected with the services.

I The cost of travel, transportation, moving, and living expenses (including relocation subsistence) incurred by construction management and supervisory staff personnel directly connected with the services.

J All other direct costs and expenses incurred in connection with the performance of the services.

2 Special Services

A The fixed fee for home-office costs, general overhead, and profit will include all normal home-office expenses associated with the anticipated program. In the event that changes to the work initiated by owner or architect result in additional planning or estimating costs in the home office, such work will be performed at Construction Management & Control, Inc.'s standard rates for such services, subject to prior approval of the owner.

B Should expediting services for owner-furnished equipment be required, Construction Management & Control, Inc. will perform such services in an effort to maintain project schedules at Construction Management & Control, Inc.'s standard rates for such services, subject to prior approval by the owner.

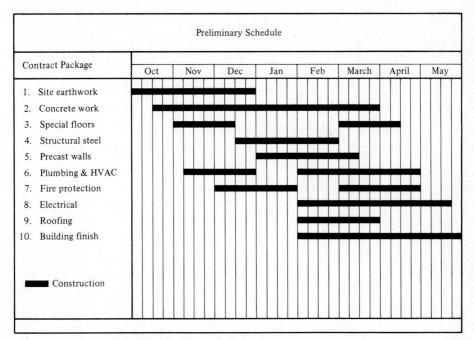

Figure 4-4 Preliminary schedule for example project.

Preliminary Cost Estimate
Easyway Food Co.   **Location Mtntown**
Dry Storage Warehouse
(From Preliminary Drawings)

Job No.
Date   9-15
By   DSB
Sheet   1   **Of 1**

Code	Description	Quantity	Unit Cost	Amount	Total
1	Site earthwork	46,000CY	4.50		208,000
2	Structural concrete	450CY	350.00	158,000	
	Yard paving	3,500CY	110.00	396,000	
	Fencing	4,700LF	13.00	62,000	
	Struct. & yard concrete	Total			616,000
3	Structural steel	500T	1700.00	850,000	
	Metal roof deck	165,000SF	1.20	198,000	
	Structural steel	Total			1,048,000
4	Double tee walls	60,000SF	8.00		480,000
5	Fire protection	150,000SF	2.00		300,000
6	Plumbing	150,000SF	.60	90,000	
	Sheet metal	2,000LF	20.00	40,000	
	Heat—vent.—air cond.	150,000SF	1.00	150,000	
	Yard utilities	Lot	Allow	100,000	
	Mechanical	Total			380,000
7	Electrical	150,000SF	2.20		330,000
8	Roofing & insulation	165,000SF	1.80		298,000
9	Special floors	144,000SF	3.80		548,000
10	Doors, windows, carpets	150,000SF	1.00	150,000	
	Painting	150,000SF	.80	120,000	
	Dock hardware	Lot	Allow	140,000	
	Block, part, glass & misc.	150,000SF	1.20	180,000	
	Building finish	Total			590,000
	Estimated total cost	150,000SF	32.00		4,798,000
	Contingency	4,798,000	10%		482,000
	Total construction cost	150,000SF	35.20		5,280,000

Figure 4-5   Preliminary cost estimate—work items.

Preliminary Cost Estimate			Job No.		
			Date	9-15	
Easyway Food Co. Location Mtntown			By	DSB	
CM & General Conditions			Sheet	1	Of 1

Code	Description	Quantity	Unit Cost	Amount	Total
	Field Construction Mgr	8 mos	4600	36,800	
	Clerk	7 mos	1600	11,200	
	Subtotal			48,000	
	Payroll taxes, ins., benefits		30%	14,400	
	Subtotal field labor				62,400
	Office trailer rent	8 mos	500	4,000	
	Telephone	8 mos	600	4,800	
	Reproduction	8 mos	200	1,600	
	Office equipment	Lot		4,000	
	Safety equip. & supp.	Lot		1,000	
	Utility bills—office	8 mos	400	3,200	
	Move in expense	Allow		10,000	
	Job pickup truck	8 mos	600	4,800	
	Travel & misc. exp.	Allow		2,200	
	Subtotal field expense				35,600
	Sanitary toilets	8 mos	240	2,000	
	Trash removal	8 mos	500	4,000	
	Guards (by owner)				
	Testing lab (by owner)				
	Surveyor (initial layout)	Allow		10,000	
	Temporary lighting	Allow		10,000	
	Final cleanup	Allow		16,000	
	Utility bills—field	8 mos	1500	12,000	
	Subtotal general cond.				54,000
	Estimated total				152,000
	Escalation	152,000	3%		4,000
	Contingency	156,000	10%		16,000
					172,000
	Est. reimb. cost	5,280,000	3.25%		
	Fixed fee (home office, profit, general o'head)	5,280,000	3.80%		200,000
	Total CM & general cond.	5,280,000	7.05%		372,000

Figure 4-6 Preliminary cost estimate—administration and general conditions.

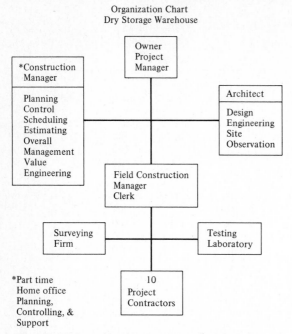

Figure 4-7   Organization chart for example project.

THE PROCEDURE OUTLINE

In a three-party professional construction management program, it is extremely important that the duties and responsibilities of each of the three team members be clearly set forth. The Procedure Outline, however, is not intended to define fully the design relationships between the owner and the architect. Rather, it illustrates the duties and responsibilities during the planning, procurement, and construction phases. The document serves as a general guide, and can be easily modified or added to throughout the course of the project.

For Easyway's Mountaintown dry storage warehouse, the professional construction manager met with both the architect and the owner immediately upon notification of his selection. After this meeting, a draft of the Procedure Outline was prepared and submitted to both the architect and the owner for review, modification, and approval. A summary of the Procedure Outline prepared for the Mountaintown project follows.

Mountaintown Warehouse Milestone CPM

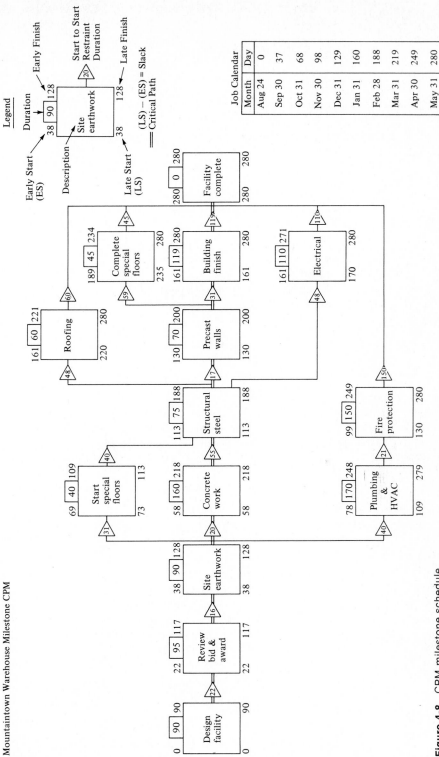

Figure 4-8 CPM milestone schedule.

PROCEDURE OUTLINE
for
PROFESSIONAL CONSTRUCTION MANAGEMENT SERVICES
to
EASYWAY FOOD COMPANY, INC.
on
MOUNTAINTOWN DRY STORAGE WAREHOUSE
by
CONSTRUCTION MANAGEMENT AND CONTROL, INC.

TABLE OF CONTENTS

I. GENERAL

A. <u>PURPOSE</u>

The purpose of this Procedure Outline is to establish standing administration procedures for guidance in the performance by the Professional Construction Manager (CM) of Professional Construction Management services for the Mountaintown Dry Storage Warehouse. This document does not supersede the Contract.

The Professional Construction Manager names as its home-office representative, _____, Project Manager. The Owner names _____.

B. <u>NAMES AND ADDRESSES OF KEY PERSONNEL</u>

    1. Owner

                                            — Address
                            Field Office — None
                      Project Personnel — _____
                                      Project Manager
                          Key Personnel — _____, Manager
                                      Design and Construction
                                    Department

    2. Construction Manager

                                            — Address
                            Field Office — Address
                      Project Personnel — _____
                                      CM Project Manager

                                       — _____
                                       Field Construction Manager
                                     — _____, Vice-President

3. Architect

— Address

Project Personnel — _____

_____

Mechanical Consultant — _____

Electrical Consultant — _____

C. CORRESPONDENCE

Official correspondence on all subjects between Owner and Professional Construction Manager shall be between _____ and _____.

All correspondence between Field Construction Manager and the Architects or Job-site Contractors shall be by Field Transmittal Memorandum (FTM). One copy of all FTM's shall be sent to Owner's Project Manager and to _____, Project Manager.

Job-site transmittal and other information requested by Owner shall be sent by FTM to _____ with a copy to _____.

Information or correspondence originating from Owner pertaining to field activity shall be sent directly to the Field Construction Manager with a copy to _____, Project Manager.

Important instructions received by telephone or determined in meetings shall be confirmed in writing by the Professional Construction Manager.

D. REPORTS TO OWNER

1. Monthly Progress Report

The CM Project Manager shall prepare and issue by the 15th calendar day of the following month a monthly progress report covering significant phases of the monthly activity.

A. The report shall include the following:

1   A short narrative covering the professional construction management activities during the period.

2   A summary of requests for quotations received, bids evaluated, recommendations for procurement by Owner, and contracts awarded to date.

3   A graphic (bar chart) schedule showing scheduled and actual progress during the month, and cumulative progress to date.

4   A summary cost report showing status to date, covering both contract awards status, and recorded and estimated costs at completion.

B. Distribution of the report will be as follows:

The Professional Construction Manager will distribute three copies to Owner's Project Manager, and one copy to the Architect.

Internal copies will also be distributed by the Professional Construction Manager as follows:

One copy CM Project Manager
One copy CM Field Construction Manager
One copy CM Vice President

2. Weekly Field Activity Report

The Field Construction Manager will prepare and issue a Weekly Field Activity Report listing significant items accomplished during the week.

    A. The report will be typed on interoffice-memo forms, and shall include the following:

        1 Significant progress or lack of progress achieved during the week

        2 General description of weather conditions and their effect on progress

        3 Job visitors, including inspections by City and County personnel

        4 Status of schedule

        5 Construction problems

        6 Summary Force Report

    B. Distribution of the report will be as follows: Same as Monthly Progress Report.

3. Weekly Force Report

The Field Construction Manager will prepare and issue a Weekly Force Report listing number of CM and contractor personnel on the job.

Distribution will be the same as above.

4. Contract Status Report

The Field Construction Manager will prepare and issue a Monthly Contract Status Report.

    A. The report shall include the following:

        1 Contractor and description

        2 Original contract price

        3 Change orders

        4 Revised estimated contract price

        5 Percent complete

        6 Contract completion date

        7 Estimated completion date

    B. Distribution of the report will be as follows:

Owner Project Manager

CM Project Manager

Architect

5. Other Reports

Other reporting requirements are discussed in Section IV, Field Responsibilities. No other monthly or weekly reports will be issued except at the request of Owner, unless approved in advance by the CM Project Manager.

II. RELATIONSHIP WITH ARCHITECTS AND OWNER

The following items are listed in order to clarify relationships and responsibilities:

    1. **Special Conditions and General Conditions** Typical copies of general and special conditions for contracts, notice to bidders, and other standard documents were given to the Professional Construction Manager by Owner. The Professional Construction Manager made certain modifications to fit the professional construction management concept; these have been reviewed and approved by Owner's Project Manager and by the Architect. This package will be used as a model for remaining packages.

2. Drawings and Specifications Drawings and Specifications for all work will be developed by the Architect, who will furnish the required number of plans and specifications for all bid packages as per a predetermined bid list, and for contract revisions. All revisions prepared after contract packages have been prepared shall be accompanied by a description of the change and shall show revision numbers and dates.

3. Substitution Policy In general, "or equals" are not specified. Value Engineering alternates are encouraged to be set forth in the original proposal. Alternates are generally given consideration for 30 days after award. All proposed modifications or alternates should be reviewed by the Professional Construction Manager and then be submitted directly to the Architect. A joint recommendation will be made to the Owner if found desirable.

4. Shop Drawings All shop drawings shall be submitted directly to the Architect by the CM Field Construction Manager. After approval, four copies will be required for distribution as follows:

One copy Owner
One copy Architect
One copy Field Construction Manager
One copy Contractor

Additional copies may be requested as required. One additional copy will be held at field office during the approval period.

5. Modification and Changes The Professional Construction Manager is not authorized to commit the Owner. In the case of changes as well as in original contracts, the Professional Construction Manager will make recommendation to the Owner's Project Manager. All commitments will be made by the Owner unless specifically authorized in advance. The Professional Construction Manager will prepare fair-cost estimates as required in order to review and evaluate changes.

6. Building Permit The Architect (or Professional Construction Manager) will contact the proper authorities to obtain the Building Permit. The Architect has confirmed that earthwork can proceed in advance of obtaining the overall permit, and that a phased construction schedule is satisfactory.

7. Survey and Testing Laboratories The Architect will request proposals from qualified firms. A joint recommendation for award will be submitted to the Owner by the Architect and Professional Construction Manager.

8. Proposed Bid Packages One week's review period has been allowed in the Procurement Schedule. Copies of prepared bid packages shall be submitted for approval by the Architect as follows:

Field Construction Manager   one copy
CM Project Manager   one copy
Owner Project Manager   two copies

9. Approved Bid List Plans and specifications will not be issued to any prospective bidder unless prior approval of the Owner is obtained. Proposed bid lists shall be submitted to Owner by the CM Project Manager in sufficient time to permit full evaluation of bidders financial qualifications by the Owner prior to issuing requests for quotations.

In general, all potential bidders will initially be screened by the Field Construction Manager. Potential bidders will be requested to supply the following information for use in the prequalification:

(a) Filled out contractor's reference form, setting forth general experience, annual volume, and other pertinent information.

(b)   Current financial statement

(c)   Certification, signed by a responsible officer or accounting firm, that financial statement is true.

10.   Approved Bid Documents   The Professional Construction Manager will submit recommended bid documents to the Owner's Project Manager. After approval, forms will be printed by the Architect. Deviation from the approved form is not authorized unless prior approval of both Owner and Professional Construction Manager is obtained.

11.   On-Site Inspection   The Professional Construction Manager will perform day-to-day construction inspection as required, under the direction of the Architect, and with the assistance of the Testing Laboratory and Surveyor. In addition, periodic visits by the Architect will be required. The Architect shall be kept fully informed at all times of the status of job and of the status of problems or required action.

12.   Plan Interpretation   All design questions or determination of "or equals" shall be submitted to the Architect by the Professional Construction Manager.

III. HOME-OFFICE RESPONSIBILITIES

Home-office responsibilities will be directed and coordinated by the CM Project Manager. These responsibilities will include the following:

A.   OVERALL JOB SCHEDULE

An overall job CPM network similar to the one included in Proposal No. 17 will be developed and updated as required. From this network, individual contract summary schedules will be developed for inclusion in bidding documents and for use in measuring actual progress. An overall summary schedule suitable for measuring job progress against scheduled progress as described in the Monthly Progress Report will be prepared and updated monthly.

B.   FAIR-COST ESTIMATES

Fair-Cost or Engineer's Estimates will be prepared for each contract package, then will be transmitted to the Owner's Project Manager in advance of the bid due date for each contract.

These estimates will be prepared in a format similar to normal fair-cost estimates. In the event of unusual discrepancies between the fair-cost estimate and bids, the estimate may be useful in negotiations with the low bidder or bidders.

C.   GENERAL HOME-OFFICE SUPERVISION

Home-office supervision and support services will be kept to a minimum consistent with the needs of the project, unless other services are requested by Owner's Project Manager. Home-office supervision and support services will include duties set forth in the Agreement and summarized as follows:

1.   Develop, with the assistance of the Owner and Architect, a detailed scope and bidding document for each proposed bid package, suitable for lump-sum bidding. Obtain the Owner's approval of above, and prepare necessary number of copies of documents not furnished by the Architect.

2. Assist the Owner in the Prequalification of proposed bidders, and present proposed bid lists for the Owner's approval or modification.
3. Evaluate bids, prepare recommendations for award by the Owner, and develop recommended Contract Format. All contracts will be prepared using Standard Owner Forms as approved for the Project.
4. Issue Monthly Progress Report.
5. Provide general home-office supervision of field activity, and maintain liaison with the Owner and Architect.

IV. FIELD RESPONSIBILITIES

Responsibility for the performance of all work at the job site will be delegated to the Field Construction Manager. He will establish a local trailer office and will hire a field clerk.

A. DUTIES AND RESPONSIBILITIES WILL INCLUDE:

1. Assist in the prequalification of prospective bidders and in the preparation of bid lists.
2. Assist in evaluation of bids and recommendations for award.
3. Manage, coordinate, and inspect all work performed by contractors on the project as set forth in the Agreement.
4. Administer and direct the Testing Lab and Surveying contracts jointly with the Architect.

B. SUPPLEMENTARY REPORTING AND RECORDS REQUIREMENTS

In addition to reporting requirements set forth in I-D, the following additional reporting and recording requirements will be followed when indicated:

1. Maintain job diaries for each contract package on a daily basis. These diaries shall be open to inspection by the Owner's Project Manager and the Architect (or his representatives) at all times.
2. Maintain drawing register and records.
3. Document all correspondence by FTM (Field Transmittal Memorandum).
4. Initiate *Force Majeure* Delay Reports when required, reflecting effect on each contractor. Distribution will be as follows:

Owner Project Manager
CM Project Manager

5. Review, document, and recommend for payment or disapproval all Contractor Proposals and Requests for Change Order using Owner forms. All Change Order Requests shall be forwarded to the CM Project Manager with full documentation attached. A copy of the

transmittal only shall go to the Owner's Project Manager. Recommendation regarding acceptance will be prepared by the CM Project Manager.

6. Review, modify, or approve all Contractor Monthly Progress Payment Reports, and forward them to the Owner's Project Manager for approval and payment using specified forms. Distribution will be as follows:

> Owner Project Manager
> CM Project Manager

7. Initiate completion and final acceptance procedure per Owner requirements.
8. Maintain progress and record photographs at the job site. No distribution will be made unless requested by the Owner's Project Manager.
9. Maintain liaison with the Architect in order to document and expedite approval of shop drawings, drawing preparation, clarify construction or materials requirements, or handle other significant items.
10. Maintain one record set of "as-built" drawings at the job site, marked up to show all field changes, locations of buried utilities, and other significant items. This information shall be turned over to the Architect for preparation of final record drawings.
11. Request architectural clarification or design interpretation from the Architect.

V. REPORTS AND CORRESPONDENCE SUMMARY

Attachment 1 summarizes the above-referenced reporting and correspondence procedures.

INDEX OF STANDARD FORMS

1. Notice to Proceed
2. Progress-Payment Report
3. Proposal and/or Request for Change Order
4. Sample Force Report
5. Contract Status Report
6. Contract Closeout Procedure
   (a) Final Progress Payment Report
   (b) Release and Waiver of Lien
   (c) Contract Completion and Acceptance Certificate

NOTE: Examples of the standard forms referenced above are further explained or set forth as exhibits in the following chapters.

Table 4-1 Document Distribution List (not complete; for example only)

Codes O – Originator R – Review I – Information A – Action	Owner	Arch./Engineer	Contractors	Others	Professional Const. Mgr.	
					Field Office	Home Office
Correspondence, CM to:						
Owner	A	I			I	O
Arch/Engineer (FTM)	I	A			I	O
Contractors	I	I	A		O	I
Others	I	I		A	O	I
Reports						
Monthly Progress	I	I			I	O
Weekly Field Activity	I	I			O	I
Weekly Force	I	I			O	I
Contract Status	I	I			O	I
Force Majeure	I	I			O	I
Progress Payment Request	A	I			O	I

Table 4-1 Document Distribution List (not complete; for example only)

Codes O – Originator R – Review I – Information A – Action	Owner	Arch./Engineer	Contractors	Others	Professional Const. Mgr.	
					Field Office	Home Office
Contract Documents						
Bid Documents	R	O				R
Bid Packages	R	R	A		R	O
A/E Drawings, Specs.	R	O			R	R
A/E Revisions	R	O	A		A	I
Shop Drawings	I	R	O		I	
Change Requests	A	I	O		R	I
Change Approvals	O	I	A		A	I

SUMMARY

The example project described in this chapter establishes a common data base for estimates, schedules, reports, procedures, and other tools which in later chapters will illustrate interrelationships among the methods utilized in professional construction management. The drawings included in Appendix A were prepared by a practicing architect to present a simplified version of a project actually designed for a knowledgeable owner. These project management and control examples, although based upon the fictitious example project, will illustrate the degree of accuracy achieved in similar real projects managed with the professional construction management concepts set forth in this book. This example project, which shows the interrelationship among the various exhibits, will help convey the importance of integrating all the specialty components into the overall project plan and management control system.

The example project also has one other major objective. Its exhibits, reports, and other illustrations are indicative of the level of detail needed in a real-world compromise between the theoretical optimization of the component parts covered in Part 3, Methods in Professional Construction Management, and the time, financial, and resource limitations imposed by the profit-oriented marketplace. This device will thus enable the reader to understand the simplified approaches that must be adopted by successful firms in order to preserve the overall relationships among all components of the management system. Overoptimization of a few components, accompanied by neglect of the integrated relationship of all components to the overall project, generally results in a lack of overall control, and this in turn results in cost overruns, delays and owner dissatisfaction with the construction project.

Chapter 5

Preconstruction Site Investigation, Planning, Scheduling, Estimating, and Design

Planning aims at a workable program that will achieve project goals and serve as a standard against which actual progress can be measured. The importance of fact finding at this stage of professional construction management cannot be overemphasized. The manager must first understand the designer's objectives and operating methods, but, above all, he must thoroughly investigate, and become expert on, the local job-site conditions and area construction practices important to developing proposed contract packages, fair-cost estimates, realistic schedules, and the value-engineering program.

After the professional construction manager has obtained a thorough knowledge of job-site conditions that will affect performance of the work, preparation of the *work plan* for the project can begin. An early work plan for overall project execution is important in creating a team effort among the designer, owner, and professional construction manager, and it forms the basis for planning that will continue throughout the project as additional information becomes available. Approaches to initial planning will vary with project objectives, but the component parts of a project work plan will generally include the following items or their equivalents:

Preliminary estimate
Summary schedules
Work packages

Value-engineering program
Construction planning

Each of these will be discussed in the following sections.

CONSTRUCTION SITE CONDITIONS

Successful contractors and subcontractors native to the area are fully cogni-
zant of factors affecting performance of construction work at the job site;
those who are not soon fail. The professional construction manager must also
become knowledgeable of these factors if he is to offer his services to the
owner and the designer. Programs and bid packages that have worked well in
one section of the country will not necessarily work as well in another. This
section examines information that must be obtained before a meaningful and
realistic program for completing the project can be developed.

Representatives of the professional construction manager must visit the
site of the work. Their investigation is similar to that of a contractor planning to
bid a project or a portion of a project, and likewise must be conducted by
experienced construction professionals who can translate information obtained
into the best way to minimize construction costs which will later be evaluated
by the bidders. The professional construction manager who does not develop
his program in this manner is not fulfilling his obligation to the owner, nor is he
enhancing his own position.

The items to investigate on the site are many and varied. A knowledgeable
general contractor or specialty contractor will have developed his own method
of appraising site conditions. The selection of items for investigation and the
conclusions drawn are the result of many years of experience in managing and
estimating construction work. Individuals may approach the investigation from
different directions, but the overall conclusions must be similar. The items in
the subsection below have been chosen to illustrate the importance of the site
visit. The visit itself will turn up numerous other factors that must play a
significant part in the overall project plan. As a guide to illustrate some of the
items that should be investigated, Table 5-1 shows a checklist for the site
investigation for the example project in Chapter 4.

Table 5-1   Area Investigation Guidelines

1. Site Description
   (Vegetation, trees, terrain, depth of topsoil, drainage, existing structures,
   existing utilities, access, etc.)

2. Utilities Serving Site
   (Electricity, gas, water, sanitary sewer, storm sewer, railroad, highway, railroad
   siding, etc.)

3. Building Department
   (Contact, telephone number, building code, plan check time, fees, zoning,
   licensing, etc.)

4. Labor Unions
   (Membership, manpower shortages, manpower surplus, current agreements, wage rates, expiration dates, etc.)

5. Recommended Contractors
   (List recommended general and trade contractors for further consideration.)

6. Materials and Methods
   (List favored local materials and methods including current quoted price for readi-mix concrete, lumber, imported granular base, plywood, masonry, and other key items.)

7. Equipment Rental
   (List local prices or key local quotations.)

8. Climatological Data
   (List average maximum and average minimum temperature, precipitation, and other significant data by months.)

9. Other Projects
   (Visit other projects noting productivity, favored methods, favored materials, subcontractors, etc.)

10. General Appraisal
    (Summarize results of site and area visit and recommend significant conclusions to be taken into account during the planning of the program.)

Foundation and Earthwork Conditions

The knowledgeable construction manager first obtains an overall plot plan of the new facility, along with a copy of the soil's report and other information that may be available. Noting the soils engineer's proposed foundation recommendations, he can then approach the earthwork phase to determine the desirability of a separate earthwork contract and the broad scope and extent of the contract, and to make a preliminary judgment as to methods that should prove most economical. In addition, he should determine the extent of stripping or removal of top soil or other unsuitable materials shown in the soils report, and should confirm this information by surface inspection and hand excavation. He should also observe unusual conditions, such as the presence of surface rocks or water, peculiar drainage patterns, and other factors. In short, he should approach the investigation as if he were a potential bidder. If he is not aware of the potential problems and difficulties, he cannot prepare a meaningful estimate for the work, nor can he frame a bid package that will minimize uncertainties, unneeded risks, and hence the contingencies that would be included by bidders in their prices.

On one professional construction management project involving substantial fill, the earthwork bid package was developed by a local architect with a standard specification requiring the bidders to strip top soil and unsuitable material up to 18 inches. Because of the rush nature of the project, the professional construction manager was not able to visit the job site or review the specifications until the bids were received. Upon visiting the site later, the manager determined that the indicated stripping depths were more probably of the order of 6 inches. Bidders were requested to reappraise their positions assuming an average stripping depth of 6 inches, with additional stripping to be paid by the owner at quoted unit prices. Every bidder reduced his quotation substantially, reflecting the decreased risk. As it turned out, the 6-inch stripping estimated by the professional construction manager proved sufficient, and the owner received a 10 percent decrease in the originally estimated contract price for this item. Had the manager been able to visit the site prior to requesting bids, the specifications could have been amended in the first place to achieve identical results. The saving would not have been quite so obvious to the owner, but it would have been just as significant.

General Planning

By visiting the site, the professional construction manager can see access roads, railroads, and other factors firsthand. He can then choose areas for locating temporary facilities, develop a preliminary plan for contractor storage areas, and later allow for existing electrical, water, or other service utilities in developing or evaluating bid packages and in reviewing owner-furnished items. He can observe interferences with existing facilities and develop a plan for site security. The investigator should also be alert for conditions on the site that may necessitate changes from preliminary design information that he may have. Again, the professional construction manager will approach his investigation of general conditions exactly as would a general contractor planning to bid the work.

On one professional construction management project, the manager visited the site a second time after preliminary earthwork drawings were received. These drawings had been prepared by a local architect on the basis of a contour survey prepared as a part of the property acquisition several years before. It immediately became obvious that someone had dumped a significant amount of loose fill on the site, completely changing the site conditions from those shown on the previous survey. All this material had to be removed so that unsuitable top soil could be stripped. Through a resurvey and modification of the plans and specifications prior to bidding, a lump-sum bid for the actual conditions was awarded. In comparing unit prices for additional work as actually bid by the low bidder, it was clear that the owner received a substantial saving over performance of the added work by the unit prices originally contemplated.

Site visits are generally the only way that items of the type described here can be taken into account in the overall program. As the project evolves, the professional construction manager must continue to be fully informed of new developments peculiar to the site, and he must be able to communicate his on-site knowledge to the designer, the owner, and his own personnel.

AREA CONSTRUCTION PRACTICE

Equally important to the job-site investigations, or even more important, is the investigation of the normal method of doing business in the project locale.

Even if the manager is familiar with the area, he should systematically review the local conditions and practices. If he is operating in a new area, the investigation is of paramount importance. Some of the significant items that must be investigated in order to develop a suitable program are outlined in the following subsections.

Local Work Practices and Jurisdiction

Each area is unique in the local practices and jurisdictions which have evolved over the years. The professional construction manager handling a phased construction program is constantly faced both with fitting his construction packages to the design schedule and with tailoring them to the optimum size that will attract qualified contractors. In order to achieve this objective while making bid packages attractive to potential bidders, he must know the prevailing practices in the area.

For example, in some parts of the country, storm and sanitary sewer pipes outside the building lines are installed by utility contractors using laborers. In other sections, this work is customarily performed by plumbers. In still others, work outside the building lines can be performed by laborers if it is a part of the sitework, but must be performed by plumbers if it is included in the overall building plumbing. The manager must be aware of these practices so that he can develop his work packages in the best manner to fit the project objectives.

In certain areas, sheet-metal flashing is customarily furnished and installed by the roofing contractor. In other locations, flashings are furnished by a separate sheet-metal contractor, with the roofing contractor supplying only the built-up roof.

The general and specialty contractors operating in the area are fully familiar with these types of area practices. The professional construction manager must become equally well informed to be able to define the work packages in the most expedient and economical manner.

Labor Costs, Productivity, and Availability

Determination of craft productivity is difficult since it varies considerably from contractor to contractor and from trade to trade. Any conclusions by necessity must be subjective. Nevertheless, in discussions with local contractors and labor union personnel, numerous relevant facts will be obtained. Inspection of several projects in the area can also be helpful.

In some areas, key contractors and subcontractors employ a substantial number of workers on a year-round basis; depending on their business volume, they will obtain additional workers for seasonal peaks or for increased workload. Framing work packages to utilize the relatively permanent craft-workers can thus sometimes have a significant economic benefit to the owner.

Other large projects will have a completely different outlook, since substantial manpower must be recruited by all contractors involved. Productivity will also generally follow the extent to which contractor management has retained control over the labor force. Estimating construction costs in areas where extensive coffee breaks, long lunch hours, early quitting, and similar practices are uniformly tolerated is completely different from estimating similar work in areas where contractor management has good control over the work force.

Determination of labor availability is also significant. One simple way for an outsider to develop his own conclusions is to meet with key business agents of each trade, ascertain the size of the local union, and observe the number of workers on the bench. Key design decisions can sometimes be influenced to change specifications from those requiring chronically scarce craftsmen to alternate methods for which sufficient manpower is available.

Collective bargaining agreements for all crafts should always be obtained by the manager as early as possible. The agreements, of course, will be used in determining wage rates to be used in the estimate, and they can also help in forecasting productivity by revealing the presence or absence of restrictive work practices. Agreement expiration dates, anticipated strikes, and anticipated wage increases not yet negotiated are also significant.

Locally Favored Methods and Materials

Many designers habitually specify methods or name-brand items, with equals to be proposed by the bidder only as an alternate. If the designer is unfamiliar with local conditions, investigation of locally favored methods and materials, and their subsequent utilization where possible in the specifications, can significantly reduce project costs. It is unreasonable to require bidders to specify and price numerous alternates when a thorough investigation of locally favored and more economical items can result in specifications tailored to the use of more economical local materials and methods.

Key Local Prices

Local prices for standard items can be readily obtained, and they are of significant value in comparing alternative methods as well as in making the fair-cost estimates. Such local prices can include readi-mix concrete, sand and gravel, lumber, reinforcing steel, concrete blocks, precast concrete, pipe and fittings, cement, and other items.

In certain areas, precast concrete plants have developed standard sections that are very economical when compared with other methods. In other areas, no precast plant is readily available.

Local Contractors

The professional construction manager must develop a representative list of qualified, interested contractors for each proposed bid package. The list should be large enough to ensure competition, yet small enough to create significant interest in all bidders. By far the best procedure is to invite only fully qualified bidders to submit proposals, so that the award can be made to the lowest responsive bidder.

Some owners will require strict—sometimes overly strict—financial qualifications. One major owner, with a continuing, reasonably level, repetitive workload of upward of $150 million per year, insists upon a certified financial statement. This owner requires net quick assets of 20 percent of the estimated cost of the contract, or the contractor will not be allowed to submit a proposal. In addition, this owner requires a 100 percent payment and performance bond for every contract.

Other owners will depend upon the professional construction manager to screen potential bidders. Here the question of whether or not bonds shall be required is always present.

Preliminary lists of prospective bidders should generally be developed prior to financial screening. A knowledgeable professional construction manager, even if initially unfamiliar with the project area, will have developed local contacts who can give valuable information. Union representatives, contractor associations, local architects and engineers, and many others can give valuable assistance in prescreening available contractors.

One method that offers significant fringe benefits to a professional construction manager relatively unfamiliar in the project area is initially to develop a preliminary list for further screening, as discussed above. Then, several days early in the planning stage can be allowed for scheduling short individual meetings with all interested contractors. These meetings can be preplanned and conducted in 20 to 30 minutes to accomplish the following:

1   Explain the overall program for the project, including the approximate scope and number of individual bid packages.
2   Review the preliminary procurement schedule, discussing the approximate periods when packages of possible mutual interest will be put out to bid.
3   Determine the interests of the potential bidder, and specifically the package for which he is interested in being considered for the invited list.
4   Discuss trade jurisdiction as applied to the particular contractor. Request his advice regarding inclusion of certain items in various work packages.
5   Obtain required information on previous jobs completed by the contractor; if possible, determine his present workload; and, if necessary, obtain required financial information.

A skilled professional construction manager will stimulate local interest with the above technique. By comparing answers to questions from similar contractors, he will also obtain in a surprisingly short time a reasonably accurate picture of how the construction business is conducted in the area.

Particular emphasis should be placed on meeting with reputable and leading general contractors. Many professional construction management jobs cannot be successfully managed unless certain phases of the work, such as a building finish package, are handled by a knowledgeable and skilled general contractor. If the program is properly explained, many leading general contractors, who may or may not be interested themselves, can and do offer suggestions for scoping work packages or for using local methods or materials that can be worth considerable savings to the owner upon implementation.

Operating from a hotel room, on one project the senior author met with over 35 prospective contractors for early bid packages for a phased construction program; appointments were scheduled every 20 minutes over a day and a half. Almost all the contractors arrived on time, most offered valuable suggestions, and all were very appreciative of the opportunity to hear about the project.

Other Key Local Contacts

In most areas, the local chamber of commerce can furnish economic data, discuss weather and climate conditions, confirm local business licenses, assist with tax information, and offer considerable other assistance.

The local building department is in many areas a key factor to a successful, early start for a phased construction program. Some areas require all plans and specifications to be approved before construction can begin. Others require special licenses for the professional construction manager's field construction manager who is in direct charge of the job-site work. All areas have special permits and fees required at various stages in the program, such as sewer and water connections. In some areas, these contacts are best handled by the designer, especially if he represents a local firm; but in others, the designer needs input from the professional construction manager.

Local utilities should be contacted so that an early determination of the method of supplying construction power, water, and other required temporary utilities can be made.

A large amount of local business information is often available. In any relatively unfamiliar area, the ingenuity of the professional construction manager is challenged by the need quickly to gain an understanding that will serve as a base for the planning phase.

Establishment of Project Field Office

The information developed in the early site visits is by nature preliminary. It is important to build upon this base continuously throughout the planning, design, and procurement phases so that new or revised information may be incorporated into the program.

Ideally, the field office should be established in advance of the award of the first contract so that potential bidders can be shown the work site and so that a local contact with other potential bidders, agencies, and others is maintained. The field construction manager will be the key representative in all dealings with local people; the earlier he assumes this position, the better for all concerned.

PRELIMINARY ESTIMATE

When the overall scope and conceptual design have evolved to the point where the manager has a reasonable idea of the requirements of the owner and the implementation program of the designer, preparation of a preliminary estimate can proceed. Figure 4-5 in Chapter 4 gave an example of the document prepared in this vital step.

The preliminary estimate initially serves to check the design against the owner's original budget or appropriation estimate. If costs appear to be over budget, alternative concepts can be explored through the value-engineering program before anyone launches into a significant amount of detail design.

The preliminary estimate is also necessary for preparing a realistic overall project schedule that forecasts occupancy dates and specifies completion schedules for individual construction contracts. The preliminary estimate forms the basis for cost control during design and procurement and is extremely useful in determining the proper size of individual contract packages that will stimulate maximum competition and interest among selected bidders.

SUMMARY SCHEDULES

Three separate but distinct summary schedules are important for effective control on most multiple-facility projects. These include a design and procurement schedule, a construction schedule summarized by individual contracts, and a construction schedule summarized by individual facilities.

Design and Procurement Schedules

For best results, a schedule for each proposed bid package must be prepared showing the detailed design and specification period, package review and approval period, bidding period, and evaluation and award period. This schedule must be developed early and must be used by the designer, owner, and manager in performing their assigned tasks. The schedule will form the control standard for monitoring actual performance during the planning and design and the procurement phases, since the construction schedule is wholly dependent upon award contracts by the required dates.

In general, most designers will prepare an overall design schedule. The manager must take the proposed bid packages and, with the designer, develop a control design schedule by bid package. Depending upon construction schedule requirements, adjustments can be made with the designer to schedule an orderly design completion that fits the needs of the critical path.

A period for owner and manager review of the preliminary bid packages is a necessity if the designer is preparing bidding documents under the manager's general instruction regarding scope. If the manager prepares the bid packages from plans and specifications furnished by the designer, a review period by owner and designer is equally important. This review period is generally the last chance to avoid errors, take advantage of recent knowledge, and avoid later plan changes which will result in additional costs if made after contract award.

Reasonable bid periods should be scheduled by the manager, taking into account his knowledge of the present bidding volume in the area. If sufficient time is planned from the beginning, schedules can be more easily met, and more competitive bids will normally be received.

The professional construction manager has a unique opportunity to solicit alternate quotations, either by specifying clear choices in the contract document or by encouraging the ingenuity of the bidders. Evaluation of alternates, whether requested or volunteered, takes time; a reasonable period for evaluation and award of each bid package should therefore be included in the schedule. See Figure 5-1 for a design and procurement schedule summary.

Summary Construction Schedules

When a preliminary estimate and a design schedule by contract package have been finalized, a CPM precedence diagram (or arrow diagram)[1] can be prepared setting forth the logic of the contemplated program in sufficient detail to determine the critical path and to develop key contract milestones. This diagram will enable adjustments to be made to the design and procurement schedule so that critical items are taken into account by the designer, owner, and manager. See Figure 4-8 in Chapter 4 for an example of a preliminary CPM diagram. A more detailed diagram is included in Appendix A.

After the planning is complete and the CPM logic is developed and reviewed, working summary bar-chart schedules can be prepared showing early- and late-start dates, early and late completion dates, the anticipated duration of each contract package, and also the interrelationships between the separate packages. Monitoring of actual performance when compared to early-

[1]Chapter 12 will provide more detail on these and other scheduling tools.

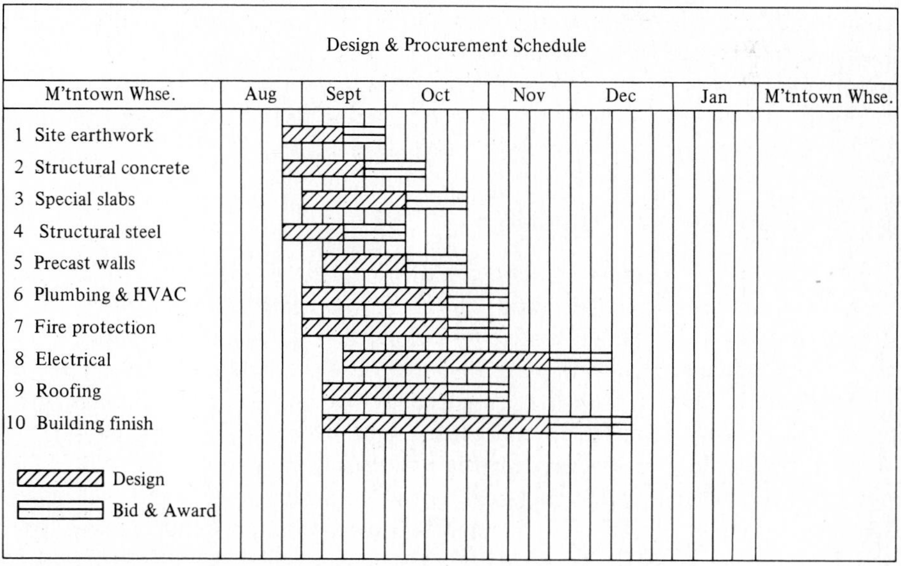

Figure 5-1 Design and procurement schedule.

and late-start scheduled performance will show status of schedule at all times, and is an integral part of the project control system. Figure 8-8 in Chapter 8 shows a project schedule summarized by contract.

On a multiple-feature project, a similar bar chart can be prepared, fully consistent with early- and late-start schedules, showing relationships of the separate facilities, and with provision for monitoring actual performance by facility in a similar manner.

WORK PACKAGES

After the professional construction manager has become thoroughly familiar with the project locale, after the preliminary design schedule is developed, and after the preliminary estimate is complete, he can define proper work packages and develop a reasonably detailed scope. Two of many important factors that should influence this process are construction economy and design constraints.

Construction Economy

Bid package development is one of the most significant contributions of the professional construction manager. The scope of packages should be designed to be of a size that will prove most economical by stimulating competition, that will minimize overall costs by avoiding unnecessary tiers of contractors and subcontractors, and yet that will take advantage of the coordination skills of the various general and trade contractors in the area.

Design Constraints

The packages must be scoped to fit a reasonable design schedule when earliest completion is important. Design constraints will modify the content of bid packages in balance with overall objectives. A successful phased construction program is wholly dependent upon the care and skill that go into defining work packages in order to balance economic considerations with completion requirements to achieve maximum overall benefit to the owner.

VALUE-ENGINEERING PROGRAM

Practical value engineering as defined and practiced by the successful professional construction manager sheds much of the methodology that has to a degree obscured the significant contributions that an organized program can make. The value-engineering program must be enthusiastically accepted and practiced by all members of the project team—owner, designer, and manager. All savings result from the team effort, and should be so acknowledged. Approaching value engineering in this way can eliminate most or all of the natural resistance many designers display when design review and alternative suggestions are proposed. The manager's function is to provide an organized program and to stimulate creative analysis during all phases of the program, but especially in the planning and design, bidding, and award phases.

Value-engineering considerations in three of these phases will be discussed below.

Conceptual Phase

Early in the program, the manager and the designer can explore basic concepts and list possible alternative solutions. If the professional construction manager's historical cost data are properly tabulated, alternative comparable cost estimates can be prepared quickly and economically. If suggested alternates are indicated to be less expensive while preserving basic value, a refined, detailed estimate can be developed. Proposed savings can be presented to the owner for approval, or for consideration as a joint effort between professional construction manager and designer. For example, alternative evaluations of basic wall specifications for industrial and warehouse buildings can be developed easily and cheaply, using basic materials, prices, and labor estimates for the particular area in question. On one project, a simple low-cost study of precast double-tee wall sections, tilt-up concrete slabs, and concrete-block walls showed decidedly that the precast double-tee walls were less expensive, structurally equivalent, and architecturally more pleasing. See Figure 5-2 for a value-engineering study of those alternative wall systems. Without the study, a different wall system would have been specified. Significant opportunities of this type are available for an alert owner-designer-manager team to produce substantial cost savings at the conceptual stage.

Detail Design Phase

Similar opportunities are available during the detail design phase. A well-organized professional construction manager will keep an up-to-date book, indexed by standard architectural specifications sections, listing numerous alternative materials and methods, together with cost comparisons from previous jobs. As each new project is value-engineered, the book becomes more valuable. The professional construction manager can review proposed items and, when alternatives look promising, recost the alternatives for the individual project area. This kind of construction-cost–oriented advice greatly benefits designers by allowing them to stay within budgets. If properly handled, such recommendations are usually well accepted by the designers, and the cost advantages are realized by the owner.

Procurement Phase

Within limits, alternate quotations can be received in a phased construction program much more readily than under a lump-sum, single contract let under competitively bid conditions. If bidders are requested to price two alternates on a 15-contract phased construction management project, no unreasonable effort is required from any one bidder, and the owner receives the opportunity to achieve significant savings. Imagine the impracticality of asking for the same alternates for a single lump-sum bid assembled by general contractors accepting last-minute telephone quotations just prior to bid time.

Title Value-Engineering Study   **Job No.**

Client Easyway Food Co.   Location Mountaintown   Date 9-15

Subject Alternate Wall Systems   **By DSB**

Comparative Costs   **Sheet 1   Of 1**

Code	Description	Quantity	Unit Cost	Amount	Total
1	7½ in. concrete tilt up				
	Panel size 20 × 36 × 7.5″	720SF			
	Casting slab	240SF	1.00	240	
	Panel concrete	17CY	100.00	1,700	
	Reinforcing steel	1,440LB	.60	864	
	Embedded steel	360LB	1.20	432	
	Bond breaker	480SF	.10	48	
	Edge forms	112LF	3.00	336	
	Bracing & lifting inserts	720SF	.20	144	
	Finish trowell	720SF	.50	360	
	Winter protection & cure	17CY	20.00	340	
	Erect panels	720SF	1.20	864	
	Caulking	36LF	3.00	108	
	Subtotal	720SF		5,436	
	Overhead & profit	12.5%		680	
	Estimated total cost	720SF	8.50	6,116	8.50/SF
2	12 in. concrete block				
	Est. cost 720 SF				
	12 in. block—quote	814EA	4.00	3,256	
	Mortar	36CF	2.50	90	
	Grout	108CF	2.50	270	
	Scaffold	720SF	.40	288	
	Clean	1,440SF	.20	288	
	Waterproofing	720SF	.40	288	
	Wall truss reinf.	550LF	.20	110	
	Reinforcing steel	500	.50	250	
	Winter protection & cure	720SF	.80	576	
	Subtotal			5,416	
	Overhead & profit	12.5%		678	
	Estimated total cost	720SF	8.46	6,094	8.50/SF
3	Precast double tees				
	Local quote—furnish	720SF	6.00	4,320	
	Erection	720SF	1.20	864	
	Caulking	90LF	3.00	270	
	Overhead & profit	6.125%		344	
	Estimated total cost	720SF	8.06	5,798	8.00/SF

Figure 5-2   Value-engineering study.

An often overlooked but important resource for value-engineering savings consists of the bidding contractors themselves. To tap these ideas, specifications can encourage bidders to submit original cost-saving modifications as an alternate. If bidding contractors are aware of the possibilities of receiving an award through a voluntary submission of an equally desirable alternate, many will develop additional options for consideration.

A helpful technique is to list each agreed value-engineering saving by number and to make a complete record of the overall result of the program for an individual project. The record is then available to the manager, architect, and owner for use on future similar projects where applicable. Figure 8-7 in Chapter 8 tabulates value-engineering savings for Chapter 4's example warehouse project.

CONSTRUCTION PLANNING

Basic construction planning during or before the detail design phase will include an organization chart, project staffing schedule, temporary facility requirements of the construction manager, selection of the particular individuals to be assigned, and delineation of their responsibilities. A complete cost estimate to serve as the manager's budget can be readily prepared if initial planning is sound.

Temporary Facilities

An important phase of construction planning is the analyzing of temporary utility and general conditions requirements for the project; this analysis is similar to a general contractor's appraisal. Temporary utilities can be furnished by the owner, be built into individual contract packages, or be obtained from others based upon local practice and job-site conditions. Utility bills can be paid for by the owner, or individual contractors can be billed or required to furnish their own utilities. Again, the best solution depends upon the professional construction manager's knowledge of the area.

Much of the construction planning can be best accomplished from the job site. Sending in the field construction manager at an early date and depending upon him to develop construction planning details under job-site conditions is usually most productive.

Successful general contractors have developed the knowledge and skills necessary to plan temporary facility requirements and perform general conditions items in a manner most economical for the project. A qualified professional construction manager must have similar knowledge and skills. You may wish to refer back to Figure 4-6 for an estimate of general conditions costs.

Procedure Outline

Each project is unique. One of the greatest advantages of a professional construction management program is its flexibility. The manager must be able to assess the conditions and problems as they develop and to react without delay to further the interests of the project.

However, with three parties involved in the management of the project, it is important that each understand the responsibilities and duties of the others. This was one of the main purposes of the procedure outline given in Chapter 4, and it is very important to construction planning.

Cash-Flow Requirements

An estimate of cash-flow requirements for the project can be readily prepared from the preliminary estimate and from the summary schedule. Some owners require more accurate cash-flow projections than others. A simple cash-flow projection based upon prior planning can be prepared as a part of the control package. If warranted, actual requirements can be tabulated monthly and compared with earlier forecast requirements. See Figure 5-3 for a cash-flow projection.

SUMMARY

Planning must be based upon facts if project goals are to be achieved. To start, the professional construction manager must understand the overall objectives of the owner, and he must know the overall concepts and operating methods of the designer. However, the implementation of the owner's objectives and the designer's concepts must be done in the particular locality where the project is to be built.

Each area and locality has its own construction peculiarities. Programs, methods, and materials developed for certain sections of the country are totally inappropriate for other localities because of the vastly different local conditions which will affect the work. The professional construction manager recognizes that he must become fully acquainted with local conditions as well as with owner objectives, design concepts, and operating methods, if he is to develop a planned program which will be both realistic and capable of serving as a standard against which actual project accomplishment can be measured.

In the planning stage, all portions of the project are developed in a straightforward and logical manner consistent with project knowledge and anticipated conditions. This development of a logical program will form the basis of the project control system that will assist in managing the project throughout the construction period.

Planning during the planning and design phase of a construction project will include the preparation of preliminary estimates and design, procurement, and construction schedules. From this information, construction contract packages can be chosen in a logical manner. A formal plan for a value-engineering program and initial construction phase planning complete the overall work plan to be used as a standard in measuring project performance at all stages.

As unanticipated events impact upon the project, the plan must be changed if it is to fulfill its primary function. In this event, replanning will occur

Cash-Flow Schedule Mountaintown Warehouse

	Estimated cost	% Complete Period	Cumul	Payments period	Payments cumulative
Design & observation	$ 130,000				
October		15	15	39,000	39,000
November		15	30	39,000	78,000
December		20	50	52,000	130,000
January		20	70	52,000	182,000
February		10	80	26,000	208,000
March		10	90	26,000	234,000
April		10	100	26,000	260,000
				260,000	
Construction (all costs)	$2,800,000				
October		2	2	112,000	112,000
November		9	11	504,000	616,000
December		9	20	504,000	1,120,000
January		12	32	672,000	1,792,000
February		21	53	1,176,000	2,968,000
March		27	80	1,512,000	4,480,000
April		16	96	896,000	5,376,000
May		4	100	224,000	5,600,000
				5,600,000	
Equipment & owners	$ 270,000				
October		5	5	27,000	27,000
November		5	10	27,000	54,000
December		5	15	27,000	81,000
January		5	20	27,000	108,000
February		5	25	27,000	135,000
March		25	50	135,000	270,000
April		25	75	135,000	405,000
May		25	100	135,000	540,000
				540,000	
Total project cost	$3,200,000				
October		3	3	178,000	178,000
November		9	12	570,000	748,000
December		9	21	583,000	1,331,000
January		12	33	751,000	2,082,000
February		19	52	1,229,000	3,310,000
March		26	78	1,673,000	4,958,000
April		17	95	1,057,000	6,041,000
May		5	100	359,000	6,400,000
				6,400,000	

Figure 5-3 Cash-flow schedule (Mountaintown Warehouse).

throughout the construction phase of the project. If the management control system is to have any effect at the project level, such replanning must be reflected in the control system so that actual results are being compared with a realistic plan.

Chapter 6

Bidding and Award

There are two basic requirements that must be met for a professional construction management project to be meaningful: First, the project must be "bought out" within budget; and second, it must be completed on schedule and in accordance with the plans and specifications.

The bidding and award phase, which will be explained in this chapter, establishes the foundation for the project and offers an excellent opportunity for designer, owner, and professional construction manager to learn to work together while enhancing their mutual respect and confidence. The initial planning process described in the previous chapter continues into the bidding and award phase. Here, again, the importance of owner and designer review, input, and acceptance of the plan cannot be overemphasized. All members of the construction management team must carry out their assignments in keeping with project schedules. As new problems are encountered, new solutions must be fed into the overall plan if the project is to achieve its initial objectives.

DEVELOPING CONSTRUCTION PACKAGES

Proposed contract packages outlined in the overall plan can be developed in detail by either the professional construction manager with designer review, or by the designer with manager review. The choice will depend in part upon the requirements of the owner and the location and procedures of both the designer and the professional construction manager. Each method will have advantages and disadvantages for a particular project. Setting forth the required scope in a straightforward manner, so that the bidder understands what is required, is of paramount importance. Ambiguities or alternative interpretations in the scope of work are the forerunners of misunderstandings, claims, and litigation, so the qualified professional construction manager will pay particular attention to avoiding such problems. The manager's close communication and cooperation with the designer are essential; each must contribute in his own area of primary responsibility and act as a helpful advisor and counselor in the other's area.

For purposes of scoping construction contract packages, it is assumed here that all plans and specifications are prepared by, and are the responsibility of, the designer. No changes to plans and specifications can be made by the professional construction manager without the prior consent and approval of the designer. Within these guidelines, two different and distinct methods of preparing construction contract packages are commonly applied by an experienced manager. He may:

1 Prepare individual contract packages from relatively standard specifications and drawings similar to those prepared for a single general-contract project.
2 Prepare individual contract packages from individual specifications and drawings prepared with the overall scope of the desired contract packages clearly in mind.

Each approach will be discussed in more detail in the following sections.

Standard Drawings and Specifications

Many design firms update or modify standard specifications they have developed over many years; these firms have geared their individual designers and specification writers to conform to the standard specifications. Many design firms also standardize construction details in a similar manner. The routine and smooth working methods of the design office in many instances depend upon use of such established standards.

When this situation is encountered, it is often preferable that the professional construction manager prepare the detailed scope sections of the construction contract package, and designate those drawings to be included as contract drawings and those to be included for reference and general information. Properly handled, assumption of this responsibility by the manager will avoid additional difficulties and possible added costs for the designer, and will contribute greatly to the partnership philosophy.

Neglecting for the moment the standard documents common to each work package, one method found to be successful in outlining the detailed scope is summarized thus:

1 The manager adopts all the specification sections pertinent to the work package in question and includes them in that package.

2 The manager writes a general scope of the work to be included, describing in general terms the work to be performed under the contract.

3 The manager prepares two summary schedules, setting forth each item by specification number and subnumber under "Work Included in Contract" or "Work Not Included in Contract." All included standard specification sections and subsections are covered in one or the other of the two schedules.

4 In the event of conflict between the standard specification provisions and the requirements of the work package, an addendum, written jointly with the designer, makes the required modifications. Thus, the standard specifications as developed by the designer are never changed, and any modifications are clearly specified either in the schedules or in the addendum.

5 The manager lists by number all drawings to be included as contract drawings and identifies drawings to be included as reference drawings.

6 Before the manager incorporates the package into the bidding documents, the designer reviews the entire scope of the work package as just described. Owner review is also performed at this time if desired.

Individually Developed Drawings and Specifications

Other designers commonly develop plans and specifications to fit phased construction programs or multiple-contract projects. In this case, it is often more expedient and more economical for the designer to prepare the plans and specifications to fit the requirements of the program. One method found to be successful is outlined here:

1 In addition to the preliminary scope for each contract package, the manager prepares a detailed scope of individual items and describes the overall intent covering the scope of each work package.

2 The manager carefully reviews this overall intent and detailed scope with the designer and modifies it as required. The designer is encouraged to offer additional suggestions or modifications to fit his design schedules better as the design work progresses.

3 Prior to requesting bids, the manager blocks out a definite period for his detailed review of the completed packages. Owner review is accomplished simultaneously.

PREPARATION OF BIDDING DOCUMENTS

Bidding documents for a professional construction management project must be developed as a joint effort of the designer, owner, and manager. Bid package makeups will vary depending on owner requirements and on designer and manager procedures. A typical bid package might consist of the following items:

Invitation to bid
Bid form

Bid breakdown
Construction contract
General conditions
Special conditions
Work included in contract (optional)
Work not included in contract (optional)
Specifications, addendums, and drawings
Supplemental provisions
Owner-furnished items
Construction schedule

Each will be discussed in more detail in the following paragraphs. An example bid package is also included in Appendix B.

Invitation to Bid   Generally, the invitation to bid states the requirements and procedures for a responsive bid and gives additional information pertaining to the contract itself.

Bid Form   The bid form is completed and signed by the bidder and states the terms of his offer. Information commonly submitted in the bid form may include:

A statement that the bidder has examined plans, specifications, and the job-site location
The amount of compensation to be received for the work performed or offered by the bidder
The amount of liquidated damages if applicable
A statement that the bidder agrees to execute a contract if his bid is accepted
An agreement to submit a performance and payment bond, if required
Overhead and profit percentages applicable to extra work
Bid alternates, if applicable
Contract completion requirements, or number of days to complete the work
Special provisions that may be applicable

Bid Breakdown   The bid breakdown is filled in by the bidder, and it gives the individual price components that sum to the total contract price. This breakdown may later guide progress payments.

Construction Contract   A sample contract is included to inform prospective bidders of the type of contract each will be expected to sign if his executed proposal form is accepted by the owner.

General Conditions   The general conditions usually are part of the specifications; they state conditions applicable to all contracts to be awarded.

Special Conditions The special conditions generally are a part of the specifications, and they set forth specific conditions applicable to the particular contract or group of contracts to be awarded.

Work Included in Contract (Optional) This section may designate provisions of a standard specification applicable to the particular contract to be awarded.

Work Not Included in Contract (Optional) This section may exclude provisions of a standard specification not applicable to the particular contract to be awarded.

Specifications, Addendums, and Drawings These items provide technical requirements of the contract; taken together, they fully define the scope, extent, and quality of the work.

Supplemental Provisions Supplemental provisions may include additional items not suited for inclusion in the special conditions, such as a definition of the status of the professional construction manager, and prevailing wage rates, if applicable.

Owner-Furnished Items This section describes all items to be furnished to the contractor by others. It may include varied items such as materials and equipment, temporary utilities, storage areas, water and sanitation facilities, and survey controls.

Construction Schedule This section shows scheduled milestones and overall completion requirements for the particular contract being bid, and provides an overall schedule showing general relationships between work packages and design activities.

CONTRACTOR QUALIFICATION, BIDDING, AND AWARD

Development of Bidders List

Prescreening techniques were discussed in Chapter 5. The success of any professional construction management program depends upon utilization of reputable, skilled, and financially sound contractors. Prequalification of all contractors prior to issuing bidding documents is by far the best way to achieve this objective. Methods and techniques used to prequalify prospective bidders will vary, but they should include obtaining evidence of capability from previous projects and of financial strength sufficient to handle the project. Owner approval of the bidders list is often required, and many owners are quite specific about the financial qualifications they expect potential contractors to have.

The best way to ensure fair prices as well as performance for the owner is to receive competitive bids from a reasonable number of prescreened, prequalified bidders. The inclusion of too many bidders, while promoting competition, will reduce the attraction for many of the best-qualified contractors, and the use of too few bidders will generally increase prices because of lack of competition. The manager must strike a reasonable balance to stimulate high interest while assuring reasonable competition. Six to eight bidders is normally about right. With prequalification, the award can almost always be made to the one evaluated as the lowest responsive bidder. See Figure 6-1 for a sample bid tabulation.

Fair-Cost Estimates

There are many advantages to preparing a fair-cost estimate from the same bid package submitted to the bidders. It shows within reasonable limits a fair price for the work, and gives the professional construction manager a chance to spot inconsistencies or conflicts in the detailed drawings or specifications that may have escaped his notice in earlier reviews. In this event, an addendum can be issued correcting the discrepancy before bid date.

In the event of widespread differences between estimate and bids,

Mountaintown Warehouse

Special Floors	Palmer Floors, Inc.	Curt Flooring Co.	Rutherford Floor Co.	Fair cost estimate
1. Base slab	380,000	404,000	370,000	340,000
2. ¾ in. topping	160,000	150,000	150,000	144,000
3. Joints & other	32,000	40,000	50,000	52,000
Subtotal	572,000	594,000	570,000	536,000
Bond	3,600	4,000	4,000	incl.
Total bid price	575,600	598,000	574,000	536,000
Alternate Bids				
1. Expansive cement	(15,600)	—	6,000	
Addenda acknowledged	2	2	2	
Completion	165 days	170 days	per schedule	5½ mos.
Bid bond	yes	yes	yes	
Exclusions	none	none	based on availability of area by 11-1	
Evaluated bid	560,000	598,000	574,000	

Remarks: Award is recommended to Palmer Floors, Inc., based upon lowest price after architect approval of expansive cement alternate.

Figure 6-1 Bid tabulation (Mountaintown Warehouse).

discussions with the low bidder can often pinpoint reasons for the difference, especially if the manager has prepared his estimate as carefully as the bidder.

Records of actual manpower employed on the contract are normally kept during the construction phase. Comparisons with estimated manpower can provide quantitative productivity measurements.

Often, in preparing the estimate, the manager's estimator will spot alternate materials or methods that have escaped prior consideration. Exploration of these alternatives with the low bidder prior to award can often significantly add to savings developed in the value-engineering program.

One of the principal benefits from preparing a detailed fair-cost estimate is that of placing the professional construction manager on a par with the successful bidder. Through this estimate, detailed job-site scheduling is encouraged, review of modifications or changes is facilitated, and in general the manager is able to deal with the successful contractor from a position of knowledge, strength, and mutual respect.

Analyses of Bids and Value Engineering

Once all proposals have been received, the professional construction manager first prepares a spread sheet tabulating all quotations and notes other pertinent factors such as qualifications, omissions, unit prices, and completion times. He then reviews alternates requested or proposed by the bidder.

If they are encouraged prior to bid and dealt with fairly in the bid evaluation, alternates proposed by the bidders themselves form an excellent value-engineering opportunity. Proposed alternates, either volunteered or requested, should always be reviewed jointly with the designer, and ideally, a joint recommendation should be made to the owner. In some cases, only the owner can evaluate the desirability of a saving resulting from a proposed modification.

One method of assuring that bidders are treated fairly in the evaluation of volunteered alternates provides the following guidelines:

1 When a bidder who is not low under the basic bid volunteers an alternate judged by the designer to be equal to the specified requirements, and thus becomes the new low bidder, the award will be made to that bidder; both the bidder and the owner gain from the bidder's ingenuity.

2 When, under similar conditions, a bidder submits an alternate that represents a sizable monetary saving but is not equal to the specified product, and if in this event the proposed substitution is acceptable to the owner because of the magnitude of the cost saving, all bidders in contention should be given an opportunity to quote on the acceptable but lower-quality alternate, and the award should be made to the subsequent low bidder.

3 When an alternate is volunteered by a high bidder who would not be low even after taking the alternate into account, and if the alternate is acceptable to the designer and the owner, the low bidder may be contacted and requested to quote on the proposed modification.

In all these proceedings, the professional construction manager must apply fairness and good judgment to avoid any practices bordering on unethical "bid shopping." Where alternates will be accepted, guidelines of the type given here must be clearly stated in the bidding documents.

Recommendation for Award

After evaluation of the bids, including alternates, a recommendation for award is made to the owner. After approval by the owner, actual award can be made either by the manager or directly by the owner.

In the event that the award is recommended to other than the low bidder, a full explanation of the reasons for such a recommendation should be made to the owner, and his approval should be obtained. Under an invited, prequalified bid list, the award should normally go to the low initial bidder unless schedule demands or other equally significant considerations indicate that the award should go to a bidder whose volunteered alternates or other qualifications make him a more cost-effective choice overall.

Some companies follow a policy of opening all bids in the presence of the bidders. Others will advise all bidders of the bid results for the base bid. Where the owner is in the continuing-workload classification, such policies can benefit the owner as well as the bidders.

Negotiating Contracts

Occasionally it is necessary to contact bidders to obtain clarification in order to evaluate the bids properly. At other times, drawing revisions approved shortly after the receipt of bids may require price changes. The manager must be thoroughly aware of the practices within the industry. When further discussions or negotiations are required, the manager must pay particular attention to conducting such discussions in an ethical manner. The manager is responsible to the industry and to the owner to avoid any taint of "bid shopping," as pointed out earlier. No rules can be laid down to cover all situations, but a qualified professional construction manager must know what is right.

APPLICATION OF CONTROLS

Controls during the bidding and award phase will include the following two main areas:

Procurement Schedule Control

The initial planning schedule specified the design, review, bidding, and award periods for each construction package. Actual progress can be monitored against the planning schedule so that current status is immediately apparent and planning can be revised where required to take care of delays or other revisions. If schedules are to be met, construction contracts must be awarded as required by the overall construction schedule. This simple, updated control schedule, showing actual accomplishments compared with programmed accomplishments, can be of great value in assuring timely procurement. See Figure 6-2 for an updated procurement schedule.

Construction Cost Control

As contracts are awarded for a phased construction program, the actual cost at completion becomes more certain. Comparing actual award prices with the preliminary and fair-cost estimates is important for both feedback and control. A similar cumulative comparison of all awards to date will indicate the current status of the project.

    On individual contracts, any significant difference between the fair-cost estimate and the bids is cause for further investigation. Through review of the fair-cost estimate and discussions with the low bidder, this difference can be accounted for in many instances. In other cases, specifications can be modified. As a last resort, packages can be modified and rebid.

    After the "buy out" is complete, the sum of the individual contract costs

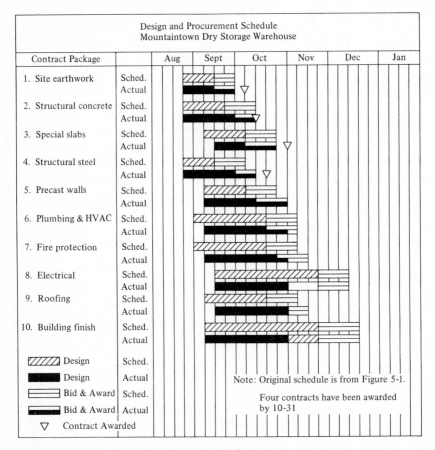

Figure 6-2 Design and procurement schedule.

becomes a committed cost to the owner. Almost all jobs will require change orders due to changes, drawing errors, and other modifications. A contingency allowance for changes and minor omissions should thus be developed so that an overall estimated cost at completion can be determined. Allowances for changes will vary depending on the nature of the project, the requirements of the owner, and the accuracy of the designer. A contingency of 2 to 5 percent added to the sum of the individual contracts is normally sufficient for minor changes. Major modifications, if contemplated, should be separately evaluated.

SUMMARY

The bidding and award phase establishes the framework for project construction; by encouraging contractor ingenuity, it can offer another major opportunity for improvements and cost savings on the project. Here, again, participation of the owner and designer with the professional construction manager is important for review and decision making.

Success in this phase depends first upon clear and unambiguous development of construction work packages. The complete set of plans and specifications must be subdivided and categorized in such a way that no items are omitted, none is duplicated, and all contractors bidding on a given package are indeed bidding on the same scope of work. The professional construction manager's contractor-type knowledge of area and trade work practices is essential to this step.

Development of work packages is followed by preparation of bidding documents, which is again a joint effort of the designer, owner, and manager. Items typically included are the invitation to bid; bid form; bid breakdown; construction contract; general conditions; special conditions; specifications, addendums, and drawings; supplemental provisions; owner-furnished items, and construction schedules.

The selection of the best contractors will be aided by prequalification and by keeping the number of contractors small enough so that the best contractors will know they have a sufficiently reasonable chance of obtaining the work to make bidding worthwhile. The professional construction manager should also prepare his own fair-cost estimates; these help him to evaluate bids more knowledgeably and to find previously undiscovered errors in the contract documents. By specifying fair and reasonable procedures for evaluation, the professional construction manager can also encourage bidders to submit worthwhile value-engineering proposals and volunteered alternates.

Application of controls in the bidding and award phase falls in two main areas: procurement schedule control, and construction cost control. Important documents for control at this stage include an updated procurement schedule and the preliminary and fair-cost estimates. Once the "buy out" is completed, the project is committed to construction.

Chapter 7

Construction

Once the planning, design, bidding, and award phases have been accomplished, the success of a professional construction management project depends on completing the field construction phase on schedule and in compliance with plans and specifications. The initial planning for this phase forms the basis of the construction program. With this as a point of departure, the basic plan must be made current, and detailed planning to accomplish overall objectives must begin. Detailed planning at the field office will continue throughout the project.

The initial planning was based upon broad assumptions, many of which will prove to be either incorrect or oversimplified as the project develops. Detailed field planning must both anticipate and overcome possible problems in advance and help provide satisfactory solutions to current problems and delays if overall objectives and schedules are to be met.

OVERALL PLANNING AND CONTROL

The field construction manager and his staff are the keys to successful construction. Procedures, guidelines, rules, handbooks, and other aids can never replace the ingenuity of qualified construction professionals in anticipating and avoiding problems and in reacting to minimize the effects of unexpected developments.

If he is to understand, manage, and coordinate the project properly, the field construction manager must plan and coordinate each of the major initial operations almost as though he were performing the work as a general contractor.

For example, structural steel erection is usually on the critical path, and it is often the source of potential delays. The alert field construction manager will know the fabrication status in the vendor's plant long before the first deliveries are expected. If potential delays become apparent, all resources at the manager's disposal can be brought to bear before significant delays are experienced. The professional will have planned well enough to be able to monitor early performance and react while a satisfactory solution can still be achieved. The nonprofessional will blame and threaten the fabricator long after the damage is done, and he will use such nonperformance as an excuse for not achieving project schedules.

Home Office Management Services

The basic requirement for home-office organization throughout construction is control. Field offices can be staffed to provide all, or a major part of, the necessary services during construction, and the home office must depend upon the field construction manager to manage the project in accordance with the predetermined plan. However, the overall responsibility and accountability to the owner for developing and monitoring a proper control system are at the top; they cannot be delegated entirely to the field construction manager.

Once the professional construction manager has chosen a sound, qualified on-site construction team and has developed a plan for achieving the objectives of the owner, his remaining duty is to know at all times whether the project is proceeding according to plan so that he can react quickly when necessary to modify, assist, and correct prior planning.

Apart from control responsibilities and accountability to the owner, most or all construction-phase management tasks can be delegated to the field construction manager and his assistants. On small- and medium-sized jobs, the minimum home-office staff will thus generally consist only of a part-time project manager or construction executive qualified to oversee project accomplishment, accept control responsibilities, and retain overall accountability to the owner. The home-office staff can, in addition, provide the field construction manager with part-time services that cannot economically be staffed at the job site. On the other hand, on certain large projects located in remote areas, many of the responsibilities for the preplanning, planning and design, and bidding and award phase outlined in preceding chapters can be best handled from the field construction site.

The extent of detailed work performed in the home office during construction will dictate organization requirements. Each project is unique, and for optimum results each will require different planning and assignment of responsibilities between the home office and the field construction office. The location of the owner, designer, and sources of supply will affect the balance for an individual project, as will the extent of delegation by the owner to the manager and the designer. As a general observation, for a project requiring full-time personnel, it is probably more economical and satisfactory to staff the project site than it is to perform the functions in the home office.

Certain services are commonly performed in whole or in part from the home office of the professional construction manager. They may include services that:

1 Provide management-level reporting to the owner through a straightforward quantitative description of project status.
2 Keep the owner informed of current and anticipated problems and their proposed or planned solutions.
3 Provide general supervision to assist, counsel, and direct field activity when necessary.
4 Monitor or administer project control systems; initiate remedial action when warranted.
5 Provide special assistance to the field construction manager where desirable. Such assistance may include preparation of schedules, estimates at completion, fair-cost estimates for extra work, claims negotiations, and expediting critical materials or equipment.

Field Management Services

Services normally performed in the field office will include the following:

1 Establishing field office, including provisions for general conditions items such as sanitary services, water supply, and temporary electrical and other items to be furnished to the contractors by the owner.
2 Hiring the testing laboratory and surveyor either jointly with, or with the approval of, the designer. Services needed include soils engineering, concrete inspection and testing, and other specialized requirements. On major projects, surveying and inspection normally are provided directly by the professional construction manager. On medium-sized and smaller projects, it is often more economical to contract for such services on a part-time basis.
3 Obtaining necessary permits on behalf of the owner. Depending on project conditions, the designer or owner can share some or all of this responsibility.
4 Managing, coordinating, and inspecting the work of contractors to help achieve project cost, schedule, and quality objectives. Weekly contractor meetings with written minutes are often worthwhile.
5 Performing schedule, progress, and cost-control functions as needed for a particular project. Requesting home-office assistance for specialty items where indicated.
6 Maintaining job diaries, drawing registers, and other records fully to document the development of the project and promote a businesslike relationship with all contractors. These records will further assist in evaluating change-order requests and claims.
7 Initiating notice to proceed for individual contracts, preparing or

approving progress-payment requests, and developing final contract closeout in accordance with owner and local requirements.

8 Maintaining progress-and-record photographs as part of progress and schedule controls, and to document potential claims, accidents, or similar occurrences.

9 Preparing input for the project control system by evaluating progress of each individual contract.

10 Maintaining job safety in accordance with contract and legal requirements. While safety is primarily the responsibility of each individual contractor, the manager has the duty to assist and to insist upon compliance with contract provisions. Recent legislative and judicial precedents have given the professional construction manager greater responsibilities in this area.

11 Maintaining liaison with the designer, requesting his assistance to interpret plans and specifications, and keeping him fully informed of the status of the project.

12 Obtaining or developing information for "as built" drawings, including maintenance of a current set of working drawings at the job site, available for all contractors and showing all current revisions and field changes.

13 Preparing field reports, including weekly progress reports, force reports, delay (or *force majeure*) reports, contract status reports, evaluation of claims, evaluation of requests for change orders, and reports covering other significant and periodic requirements.

TYPICAL ORGANIZATIONS

Each project is physically different, has different objectives, and is constructed under different local conditions. Depending upon project size, location, and other factors, certain functions can be performed in either the home office or the field project location. To illustrate a range of professional construction management approaches, additional organization charts are included here showing a phased construction program for a $3-million dry storage warehouse, a $13-million meat plant, a $60-million airport expansion program, a $60-million hospital, a $100-million industrial project constructed under professional construction management, the same project constructed by the traditional general-contractor method, and a typical project for the United States General Services Administration.

$6-Million Dry Storage Warehouse

Figure 4-7 in Chapter 4 shows an organization chart for the example warehouse project. The owner and the professional construction manager's home offices are in one city, and the architect and the job location are in another.

$25-Million Meat Plant

Figure 7-1 shows an organization chart for a meat processing plant. The owner and the job site are located in one city, and the architect and professional construction manager in another. The manager also handled overall cost accounting for the owner.

Organization Chart
Meat Processing Plant

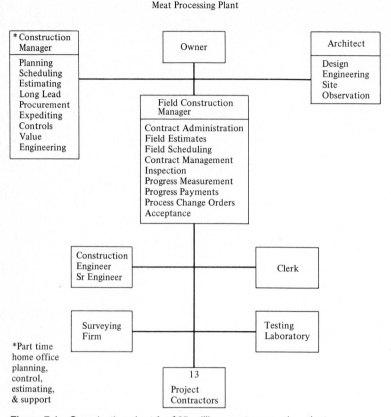

Figure 7-1   Organization chart for $25-million meat processing plant.

$100-Million Airport Expansion

Figure 7-2 shows an organization chart for an airport expansion program featuring a runway addition, a new terminal building, and appurtenant facilities.

$100-Million Hospital

Figure 7-3 shows an organization chart for a $100-million hospital complex built for a nongovernmental owner. Construction is planned to utilize a separate foundation contract, a building construction contract, and separate mechanical and electrical contracts.

$200-Million Industrial Project

Figure 7-4 shows a typical professional construction management organization for a major project where essentially all work except initial planning is performed in the field.

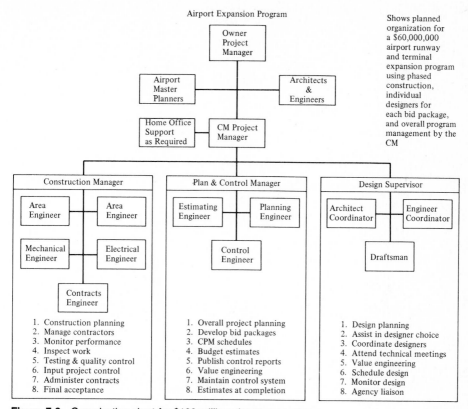

Figure 7-2   Organization chart for $100-million airport expansion.

$200-Million Industrial Project

By way of comparison, Figure 7-5 shows an organization chart for the preceding industrial project as it could be constructed with a traditional general contract approach.

Typical General Services Administration Project

Figure 7-6 shows typical organizations for construction management projects performed for the General Services Administration. Almost all project functions are performed from the field office.

SAFETY RESPONSIBILITIES

While legal ramifications of the 1970 federal Occupational Safety and Health Act may be debated for some time to come, the wise professional construction manager will endeavor to set up a program similar to one he would need if he were acting as a general contractor. He will also require each individual

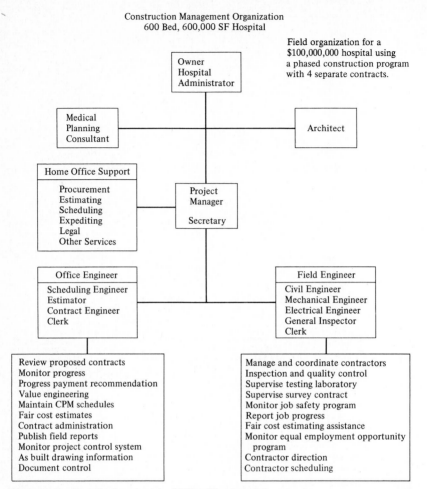

Figure 7-3   Organization chart for $100-million hospital.

contractor to live up to his obligations under both the contract and the law. Weekly safety meetings, frequent job inspections, and implementation of a job safety program should be the responsibility of the manager.

The manager must be especially alert to handle areas where clear responsibility cannot be practically or economically transferred to individual contractors. Typical examples include guard rails around openings or roofs when the contractor responsible for their construction has completed his work, and adequate provision for temporary lighting in areas where a number of contractors are working.

A prudent rule for the professional construction manager to follow is that if there is any doubt about who should take care of a potential problem, the manager should see that it is done. Budgets and the contractual agreement with the owner should contemplate a reasonable sum to cover safety measures so that the gray-area responsibilities are handled before accidents happen.

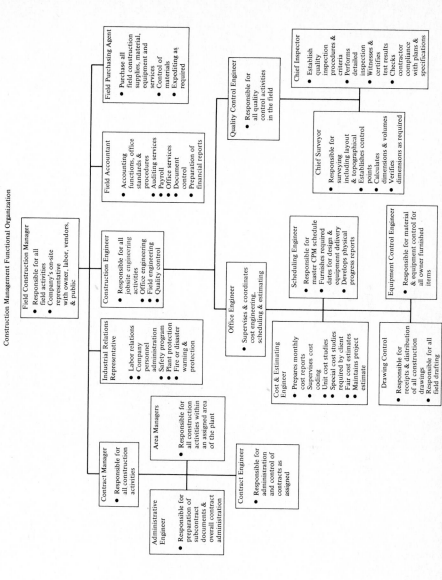

MAJOR INDUSTRIAL PROJECT
Construction Management Functional Organization

Field Construction Manager
- Responsible for all field activities
- Company's on-site representative with owner, labor, vendors, & public

Contract Manager
- Responsible for all construction activities

Industrial Relations Representative
- Labor relations
- Company personnel administration
- Safety program
- Plant protection
- Fire or disaster warning & protection

Construction Engineer
- Responsible for all jobsite engineering activities
- Office engineering
- Field engineering
- Quality control

Field Accountant
- Accounting functions, office standards & procedures
- Auditing services
- Payroll
- Office services
- Document control
- Preparation of financial reports

Field Purchasing Agent
- Purchase all field construction supplies, material, equipment and services
- Control of materials
- Expediting as required

Quality Control Engineer
- Responsible for all quality control activities in the field

Chief Inspector
- Establish quality inspection procedures & criteria
- Performs detailed inspection
- Witnesses & certifies test results
- Checks contractor compliance with plans & specifications

Chief Surveyor
- Responsible for surveying including layout & topographical
- Establishes control points
- Calculates dimensions & volumes
- Verifies dimensions as required

Scheduling Engineer
- Responsible for master CPM schedule
- Furnishes required dates for design & equipment delivery
- Develops physical progress reports

Equipment Control Engineer
- Responsible for material & equipment control for all owner furnished items

Office Engineer
- Supervises & coordinates cost engineering, scheduling & estimating

Area Managers
- Responsible for all construction activities within an assigned area of the plant

Administrative Engineer
- Responsible for preparation of subcontract documents & overall contract administration

Contract Engineer
- Responsible for administration and control of contracts as assigned

Cost & Estimating Engineer
- Prepares monthly cost reports
- Supervises cost coding
- Unit cost studies
- Special cost studies required by client
- Fair cost estimates
- Maintains project estimate

Drawing Control
- Responsible for receipts & distribution of all construction drawings
- Responsible for all field drafting

Figure 7-4 Organization chart for major industrial project—professional construction management approach.

111

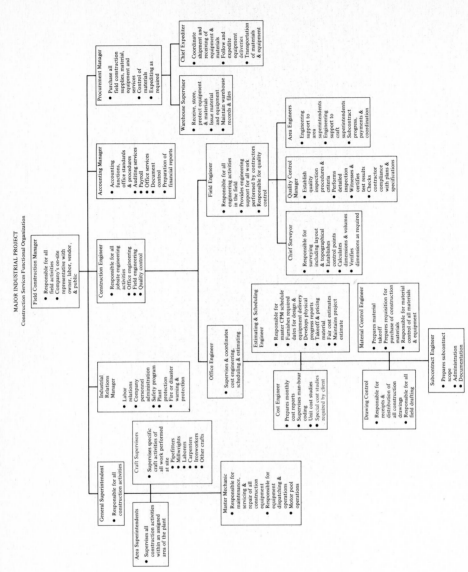

MAJOR INDUSTRIAL PROJECT
Construction Services Functional Organization

Field Construction Manager
- Responsible for all field activities
- Company's on-site representative with owner, labor, vendor, & public

General Superintendent
- Responsible for all construction activities

Area Superintendents
- Supervises all construction activities within an assigned area of the plant

Craft Supervisors
- Supervises specific craft activities of all work performed at site
  - Pipefitters
  - Millwrights
  - Laborers
  - Carpenters
  - Ironworkers
  - Other crafts

Master Mechanic
- Responsible for maintenance, servicing & repair of all construction equipment
- Responsible for equipment dispatching & operations
- Motor pool operations

Industrial Relations Manager
- Labor relations
- Company personnel administration
- Safety program
- Plant protection
- Fire or disaster warning & protection

Construction Engineer
- Responsible for all jobsite engineering activities
- Office engineering
- Field engineering
- Quality control

Office Engineer
- Supervises & coordinates cost engineering, scheduling & estimating

Estimating & Scheduling Engineer
- Responsible for master CPM schedule
- Furnishes required dates for design & equipment delivery
- Develops physical progress reports
- Takeoff & pricing material
- Fair cost estimates
- Maintains project estimate

Cost Engineer
- Prepares monthly cost reports
- Supervises man-hour coding
- Unit cost studies
- Special cost studies required by client

Material Control Engineer
- Prepares material takeoff
- Prepares requisition for purchase of construction materials
- Responsible for material control of all materials & equipment

Drawing Control
- Responsible for receipts & distribution of all construction drawings
- Responsible for all field drafting

Subcontract Engineer
- Prepares subcontract scope
- Administration
- Documentation

Field Engineer
- Responsible for all engineering activities in the field
- Provides engineering support for all work performed by contractors
- Responsible for quality control

Chief Surveyor
- Responsible for surveying including layout & topographical control points
- Establishes dimensions & volumes
- Calculates
- Verifies dimensions as required

Quality Control Manager
- Establish quality inspection procedures & criteria
- Performs detailed inspection
- Witnesses & certifies test results
- Checks contractor compliance with plans & specifications

Area Engineers
- Engineering support to area superintendents
- Engineering support to craft superintendents
- Subcontract payments & coordination

Accounting Manager
- Accounting function
- Office standards & procedures
- Auditing services
- Payroll
- Office services
- Document control
- Preparation of financial reports

Procurement Manager
- Purchase all field construction supplies, material, equipment and services
- Control of materials
- Expediting as required

Warehouse Supervisor
- Receive, store, protect equipment & materials
- Issue material and equipment
- Maintain warehouse records & files

Chief Expediter
- Coordinate shipment and receiving of equipment & materials
- Follow and expedite equipment deliveries
- Transportation of materials & equipment

Figure 7-5 Organization chart for major industrial project—traditional general contract approach.

112

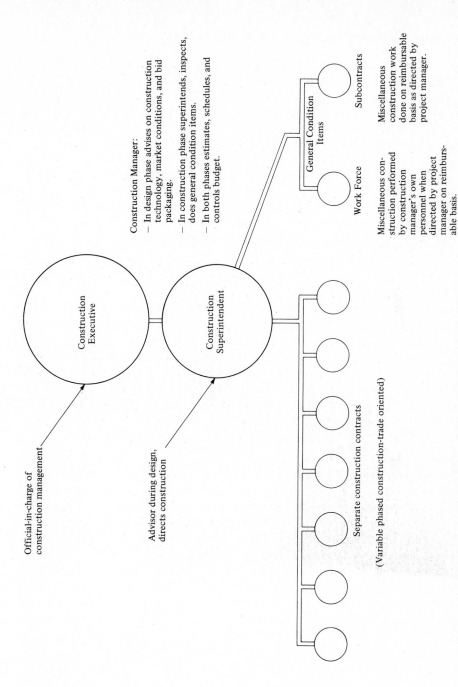

Official-in-charge of construction management

Construction Manager:
- In design phase advises on construction technology, market conditions, and bid packaging.
- In construction phase superintends, inspects, does general condition items.
- In both phases estimates, schedules, and controls budget.

Advisor during design, directs construction

Separate construction contracts

(Variable phased construction-trade oriented)

Construction Executive

Construction Superintendent

General Condition Items

Work Force

Subcontracts

Miscellaneous construction performed by construction manager's own personnel when directed by project manager on reimbursable basis.

Miscellaneous construction work done on reimbursable basis as directed by project manager.

Figure 7-6 Construction management. *(From* The GSA System for Construction Management, *General Services Administration, Public Buildings Service, Washington, D.C., rev. ed. April 1975.)*

113

CONTRACT ADMINISTRATION AND COORDINATION

Contract administration and coordination are basically the application of businesslike common sense and fair play in keeping with the terms and conditions of the contract. Every possible effort should be made to assist each contractor and to establish mutual cooperation among contractors. If each contractor knows where he is expected to be working, who will be working adjacent to him, and when he can expect others to finish their work, a cooperative and mutually helpful job climate will evolve.

Administration of construction contracts requires thorough and timely documentation. Such documentation during the execution phase of a contract will facilitate performance of the work, assist in closeout and acceptance, and help reduce the possibility of claims. Certain reports and records have been found to be helpful; those discussed below outline the documentation requirements for a typical project.

Notice to Proceed

The "Notice to Proceed" should be issued sufficiently in advance of the required starting date to provide the contractor adequate lead time. In cases where contracts are written to provide a fixed number of calendar days for completion, the Notice to Proceed will mark the beginning of the allotted time period. This document is generally a straightforward reference to the provisions of the contract, the type of work to be performed, and the date or dates that the work is to commence. Figure 7-7 shows a sample Notice to Proceed for the example warehouse project.

Change Orders

Change orders document changes from the original scope of the contract, confirm schedule revisions, and set forth other modifications; they are issued, whether or not the amount of compensation to be paid to the contractor will be affected. The change order is generally written on a standard form and includes a complete but concise description of the change and its effect upon the contract schedule and price. Change order requests are normally reviewed by the professional construction manager, who normally compares them with his own fair-cost estimate of the change. After his review, and after negotiation with the contractor if required, the manager may recommend acceptance by the owner, who in turn will formally approve and execute the change order. Figure 7-8 shows a "Request for Change Order" for the example warehouse project.

Progress Payment Reports

"Progress Payment Reports," such as that in Figure 7-9, are normally prepared monthly to authorize and document progress payments to the contractor. The form should be as simple as possible, and is generally divided into three basic parts:

Jensen Excavators   September 25, 198_
155 South First Street
Mountaintown, WestAmerica

                                    Subject: Contract No. M-1
                                             Site Earthwork
                                             Dry Storage Warehouse
Gentlemen:

    Pursuant to the provisions of the subject contract, please consider this letter as your
official "Notice to Proceed" with the site earthwork on:

                                    October 4, 198_

    Please feel free to contact the writer at any time prior to the starting date to discuss any
matters relating to the start-up of your work.

    In accordance with our discussions held during the pre-award conference all field opera-
tions will be conducted in accordance with the provisions of the contract and in general
conformance to the *Contractor Safety Bulletin* presented to your Mr. Snyder at that time.

                                        Very truly yours,

                                        Construction Management & Control

                                        O. Hanson

                                        Field Construction Manager

Figure 7-7 Notice to Proceed.

    1 A heading to identify the contract, project, contract number, progress
payment number, payment period, and other information if required.
    2 The body of the report organized to identify work completed during the
period and to date. Columns are normally provided for recording quantities or
percent complete, and dollar amounts earned for each line item. Provisions for
deducting previous payments and the retainage are normally included so that
the computation of the net amount earned during the period is shown.
    3 Information summarized at the bottom of the form may include total
estimated contract price, signatures of the person who prepared the report and
of the contractor, approvals, and other information.

Final Acceptance

Basic documentation for acceptance of contract work depends somewhat upon
state law and individual preference, but will generally include the following:

    Notice of Completion This form states that all work under the contract is
complete, and that it is being processed for acceptance.

    Completion and Acceptance Certificate This document certifies that all
work is complete in accordance with plans and specifications. Normally signed
by the contractor and the professional construction manager, it serves as
documentation to the owner that the work is complete and ready for accept-

CONTRACTOR:
ADDRESS:

REQUEST FOR CHANGE ORDER

TO:

No._____

Date_____

Project No.
Description:

Below listed are changes in our contract price. Until formal change order has been issued this request for change will be held in suspense status.

Application of increases (or decreases) in price of contract are as follows:

CODE REF.	DESCRIPTION OF WORK	INCREASE	DECREASE
	TOTAL THIS CHANGE REQUEST		
	NET CHANGE		
	CONTRACTOR'S FEE		
	TOTAL CHANGE		

REQUEST CONTRACT TIME EXTENSION (OR DECREASE) OF_____CALENDAR DAYS IF ABOVE ACCEPTED.

CONTRACTOR:

Approved_____ Date_____   By_____ Date_____

Figure 7-8 Request for change order.

ance based upon the contract closeout procedures and requirements. The owner's signature may also be desirable. See Figure 7-10 for an example.

Release and Waiver of Lien An executed release and waiver of lien form,

Job No. _____ Location _____

Contractor: Henri Steel Company

Contract No. _____ M-4
Progress Report No. _____ 3-Final
Period _____ to _____ 3-30

Cost account	Item no.	Description	Unit	Unit prices	Period Quantity or % complete	Period Amount	Cumulative Quantity or % complete	Cumulative Amount
M4.1	1	Fabricate & deliver structural steel	280T	1400.00			280T	392,000
M4.2	2	Fabricate & deliver joists	200T	808.00			200T	161,600
M4.3	3	Erect structural steel	480T	260.00			480T	124,800
M4.4	4	Furnish & erect normal roof deck	165,000SF	1.10	20,000	11,000	165,000SF	181,600
C.O.1	5	Substitute tube columns	L.S.	(5800)			100%	(5,800)

Total estimated contract price	$854,200	
	Totals	11,000	854,200
	Retained 10%	1,100	85,420
	Difference	9,900	768,780
	Less previous payments		758,880
	Net amount this payment		$9,900

Prepared by: _____ Date: _____
Checked by: _____ Date: _____
Approved by: _____ Date: _____
Approved by: _____ Date: _____

Figure 7-9 Contract progress payment report.

117

or other certification from the contractor, is normally required prior to releasing final payment.

Field Transmittal Memorandum

A "Field Transmittal Memorandum" (FTM) is useful in all field contract correspondence, transmittals, instructions, or other communications with the

---

Contract Completion and Acceptance Certificate

This is to advise that the work covered by Contract No. _____ and all Change

Orders numbered _____, was completed as specified

below:

Description of Work   Account No.   Completion Date

Contractor's Certification

This is to certify that the work described by the contract has been fully completed in accordance with the Terms, Conditions, Plans and Specifications set forth in said Contract.

Construction Manager's Certification

This is to certify that the work as covered by this contract has been inspected under our supervision, and to the best of our knowledge and belief it has been completed according to the said contract and Plans and Specifications specified therein and is hereby recommended for acceptance subject to the Terms and Conditions of the Contract.

_____
(Contractor)

By _____

Title _____

Date _____

_____
(Construction Manager)

By _____

Title _____

Date _____

Owner's Acceptance

Based upon the above certification, the work is hereby accepted subject to the Terms and Conditions of the Contract.

_____
(Owner)
By _____

Title _____   Date _____

Figure 7-10   Contract completion and acceptance certificate.

contractor. The FTMs should be consecutively numbered for ease in filing and documentation. Acknowledgment of receipt by the contractor can be required if desired. Figure 7-11 shows one form of FTM that has been successful.

Contract Status Reports

This report, normally issued monthly, can be helpful to show the current status

F.T.M. No. _____ 1 _____

FIELD TRANSMITTAL MEMORANDUM

CONTRACTOR	CONTRACT NO.	Mo.	Day	Yr.
Jensen Excavators	M1	10	1	

Attached for your use as set forth in the Contract are four (4) sets of the Contract Specifications and four (4) sets of the Drawings listed therein. Please review these documents as stipulated under Article 16-A of the Terms and Conditions.

Also attached is one (1) reproducible, Contractor's Performance Schedule form which is to be completed by you in accordance with Article 15 of the Terms and Conditions and submitted for approval not later than October 8, 1976.

SAMPLE

Typical wording for transmitting the drawings and specifications on which the Contract is based. The number of copies of each should not be less than the quantity listed in the specification.

In the event it is desirable to have the Contractor use his own Performance Schedule Form then the last paragraph would be reworded accordingly.

(courtesy of R. C. Wilson who pioneered the adoption of this format)

RECEIVED FOR CONTRACTOR   Construction Manager

BY		BY	
TITLE		TITLE	

Figure 7-11   Field transmittal memorandum.

of each awarded contract. Information contained in the report will include the original contract value, number and amounts of change orders in process, the revised estimated contract value at completion, and estimated completion dates. Figure 7-12 shows a sample "Contract Status Report."

Contract Logs

A separate contract log for each contract documents daily the work performed, conditions affecting progress of the work, delays or interferences, or other items of current interest or possible future significance. The contract log should be in a bound book with consecutively numbered pages, and entries should be made in ink. Particular emphasis should be placed on recording information that might prove helpful in evaluating potential claims and in protecting the owner from unwarranted claims. Figure 7-13 shows a typical entry.

Contract Force Report

If schedules are to be accomplished, sufficient manpower must be provided by the individual contractors. See Figure 7-14 for a sample "Contract Force Report" useful for recording and appraising contractor manpower. It also can serve as an alternate evaluation of progress where a fair-cost estimate, including labor units, has been prepared.

QUALITY CONTROL SERVICES

Each project will require a sound plan for inspection, testing-laboratory services, and basic survey control. On very large projects, all three services can be supplied by the professional construction manager. On smaller ones, the manager may perform some of the services to the extent that his staff will allow, and contract for the balance on a part-time or as-required basis. Normally outside professional service contracts for inspection, testing, and surveying should first be scoped jointly with the designer, and then a joint recommendation for award should be made to the owner.

The manager, owner, and designer should all be aware of the inspection, testing, and surveying responsibilities assumed by each member of the construction management team. The professional construction manager must recognize the professional responsibility of the designer. Conversely, the designer must recognize the responsibilities delegated to the manager by the owner.

On large professional construction management projects, inspection can be fully separated from contract management and administration. On smaller ones, the manager's limited staff can perform both functions.

Testing laboratories can be hired by the owner, architect, or professional construction manager. In any event, a general scope should be developed and one member of the team must be selected to monitor and manage the contract. Reports should be distributed to all members of the team.

Dry Storage Warehouse Contract Status Report

Contract (No. and Description)	Contractor	Original Contract Price	Change Orders		Est. Value of Pending	Revised Estimated Contract Value	% Complete	Completion Date	
			Issued	Value				Contract Completion Date	Estimated Completion Date
1. Site earthwork	Jensen Excavators	206,000	1	3,000	—	209,000	100	12/31	12/22
2. Structural & slab concrete	Hulseman Construction	640,000	2	50,000	—	690,000	100	4/30	4/30
3. Interior special slabs	Palmer Floors	560,000	—	—	—	560,000	100	4/30	4/23
4. Structural steel & deck	Henri Steel	860,000	1	(5,800)	—	854,200	100	2/28	3/24
5. Precast double tees	Gurecki Precast	560,000	—		—	560,000	100	3/31	4/22
6. Plumbing, heating, mechanical	Orne Mechanical	440,000	3	38,000	—	478,000	100	5/31	5/29
7. Fire protection	Morschauser Inc.	350,000	—		—	350,000	100	5/31	5/21
8. Electrical	Jones Electrical	380,000	2	18,000		398,000	100	5/31	5/7
9. Roofing	Rocky Roofing	222,000	1	12,000		234,000	100	4/15	4/22
10. Building finish	Finsand Construction	604,000	4	56,000		660,000	100	5/31	5/31
Total		4,822,000	14	171,200	—	4,993,200			

Prepared by: Betty Willis

Construction Engineer

Figure 7-12 Contract status report.

October 4, 198_

    Jensen excavators moved on the site this date. The following equipment was delivered:

    1 ea CAT No 14 Motor Patrol
    1 ea CAT No D-8 Tractor
    2 ea CAT 613B Scrapers
    1 ea Water Wagon
    1 ea CAT 815 Compactor

Superintendent Snyder advises that work would begin tomorrow with a total of 6 men.

    Typical example of handwritten entry in log for site excavation contract. All important starts, completions, and other significant items which could be of importance in the event of future claims or disagreements should be recorded.

Figure 7-13   Typical log entry.

For survey control, the professional construction manager must at least provide basic line and grade for all contractors. In addition, and depending upon area practice, he may provide detailed construction layout for certain contracts, or he may perform check surveys for critical items. On large projects, a number of survey crews can be fully utilized by the professional construction manager, while on small and medium-sized projects all surveying can be performed on a part-time basis through a professional services contract. The preferable solution will depend upon the job and the area practice as well as on overall economy to the owner.

START-UP AND FINAL CLOSEOUT

System Validation, Testing, and Start-Up

The professional construction manager may be requested to assist the owner in system validation, testing, and start-up. The construction manager is often charged with the responsibility for construction testing of individual pieces of equipment or entire systems as required by applicable codes, drawings, and specifications. The manager often prepares a detail plan for unit and system start-up operation involving contractor, engineer, manufacturer's representative, and owner personnel. Development of a tagging procedure on equipment to ensure safety during initial operation is especially important.

Final Closeout

In addition to final acceptance documentation as previously discussed, the professional construction manager may be responsible for substantial additional duties, either from the job site or from the main office after fieldwork has been completed. Some of these duties will include furnishing or obtaining guarantees, operating information, spare parts, instruction manuals, as-built drawings, bonds, maintenance agreements, inspection certifications, and other documents required under the contracts. Often an inspection is scheduled prior to the expiration of performance guarantees, to ensure that facilities are operating as specified. The submission of a final report showing documented project costs along with schedule performance can be of great value to the owner, designer, and CM firm if sufficient information and explanation are included to form a planning base for other similar projects to be constructed at a future date.

LEGAL CONSIDERATIONS

Claims and Backcharges (Owner's Consideration)

There are potential claims and backcharges in every construction project. In any contractual relationship, situations can develop whereby any or all parties to a contract may believe that they have legitimate claims.

Field personnel must be thoroughly familiar with the contract provisions, rights of the parties, and concepts of contractual relations. In addition, they must be alert to circumstances which may serve as the basis for claims, such as changes in the work, changes in conditions affecting the work, failure of a party to perform contractual obligations, or improper or inadequate performance.

Claims can be much more readily adjudicated when a contract has been thoroughly documented throughout its performance with daily logs indicating events and conditions affecting the work. Proper documentation will include, but not be limited to, the following:

An independent evaluation of the merits of each item outlined in the claim or backcharge, including applicable references to contract provisions; plus an estimate of applicable costs, including overhead and markup as provided by the contract

Minutes of any negotiation meetings, including additional facts or information that may develop

Prompt and timely notification to the other party or parties in accordance with contract provisions

Early notification to the owner and, if indicated, an early request for legal assistance and advice

Written approval of the claim settlement by the owner

Legal Aspects (Manager's Consideration)

Construction, like other businesses, is becoming increasingly legalistic. Architects have replaced the terms "inspection" or "supervision" by "observation" in an attempt to minimize responsibility under the law and thus to minimize insurance rates. Contractors and design firms are facing million-dollar suits for on-the-job accidents and deaths, as well as for design or construction deficiencies.

The position of the professional construction manager is as yet unclear, and each contract will differ in its legal responsibilities. Basically, the usual position of the professional construction manager is that he has hired out his

INTEROFFICE MEMORANDUM

TO   Client Project Manager   DATE November 29, 198_

AT   San Francisco

                 FROM

COPIES TO   Home Office

                 AT   Mountaintown, West America

               JOB NO.

WEEKLY FORCE REPORT FOR PERIOD ENDING: November 28, 198_

SUBJECT

Company	Mon	Tue	Wed	Thu	Fri	Sat	Sun	Week Total	Cum Total	Estimate	%
Jensen excavators		3	3	3	3			12	117	184	64
Hulseman construction	1	2	2	2	4			11	207	966	21
Palmer floors	2	9	9	10	10			40	119	916	13
Orne mechanical	6	6	6	7	7			32	64	531	12
George sprinkler			3	3	3			9	9	403	2
Others										2,688	0
Total man-weeks	9	20	23	25	27			104	516	5,688	9
Total man-hours								832	4,128	45,500	9

Note: At this early stage, all of the contractors have not started work and some contracts have not yet been awarded. For illustration, these have been grouped under others with an estimated man-days. Note that if initial man-hour estimates are accurate, the job is about 9% complete. This figure can be compared to the physical progress calculations (Fig. 9.9 and 9.10). Discrepancies should be further explored.

Figure 7-14 Weekly force report.

expertise as agent to the owner, and the owner should be responsible for business risks incurred by the project that are beyond the manager's control. The manager represents a reasonable degree of professional competence in acting on behalf of the owner, and he should be responsible to the owner for this representation. However, the prudent manager will protect himself against possible litigation and exposure by utilizing competent legal advice in developing the professional construction management services agreement and by maintaining a comprehensive liability insurance program.

SUMMARY

Once the project's contracts have been awarded and committed within budget, work must be completed on schedule and in accordance with plans and specifications if success is to be achieved. The field construction manager and his staff are the ones to ensure that the objectives of the work plan are realized. To do this, they need sufficient authority to carry out these objectives; but these individuals must also be fully accountable to the home office for this delegation.

Should the project control system indicate that primary objectives are not being achieved, replanning is needed. Either initial goals must be modified or changes in contractor programs must be implemented.

Home-office personnel associated with planning generally stop gathering additional information when the "buy-out" phase is completed, and the field construction manager and his staff will have generally surpassed the home-office personnel's knowledge about the job by the time all contracts are awarded. Ideal management delegation for the construction phase will encourage and permit the field construction manager to take action when he is convinced of the right moves. When he is unsure, the home office should respond to his request for help so that a mutually responsible relationship may be provided.

After the contracts are awarded, the emphasis shifts to the field. Home-office personnel who insist upon retaining the authority to make detailed job decisions will find that problems which should be solved at the job level assume major proportions in the home office. On the other hand, home-office managers who fail to exercise overall control may one day discover that the objectives of the job can no longer be met.

Chapter 8

Application of Controls

Previous chapters discussed preparation of the overall plan for the project as well as its implementation. Throughout the project, the control system quantitatively measures actual performance against the plan and acts as an early warning system to diagnose major problems while management action can still be effective in achieving solutions. Development and application of a practical control system to measure progress and costs are among the most important contributions of the professional construction manager.

MANAGEMENT-LEVEL REPORTING

Management-level reporting must provide a straightforward statement of the work accomplished, predict future accomplishment in terms of the project cost and schedule, and measure actual accomplishments against goals set forth in the plan. It should also review current and potential problems and indicate management action underway to overcome the effects of the problems. These requirements are similar on projects ranging in size from $1 million to $100 million and more. They are also relatively independent of the sophistication of the techniques that measure accomplishments; these vary with project size and complexity.

A comprehensive "Monthly Progress Report" can convey this essential information. The contents of a sample report are as follows:

1 Summary of project status
2 Procurement status
3 Construction status
4 Schedule status
5 Cost report summary

Each of these items will be described briefly in the sections below.

Summary of Project Status

This item represents a short, overall summary of project status. It may contain a brief narrative description of the status of each major phase, provide quantitative information such as the physical percentage complete compared with scheduled completion, and forecast "at-completion" costs against budget.

Procurement Status

This item reviews contracts awarded during the period, contracts currently out for bid, and other significant information. A simple bar chart showing actual procurement status and contract awards compared with the original plan is often helpful.

Construction Status

This unit of the Progress Report should provide a description of work accomplished during the period, significant work to be accomplished in the next period, and a discussion of major problems, with solutions or proposed solutions. Quantitative information is more significant than general discussion.

Schedule Status

This item should contain the summary control schedules by contract and by facility, showing actual progress compared to early- and late-start schedules. Where contracts or facilities are behind schedule or are slipping, an explanation of the problems and the indicated solution or measures being adopted to solve the problems should be included.

Cost Report Summary

This summary should show actual recorded costs, committed costs, and estimated costs-to-complete. It should compare "at-completion" costs with project budgets and identify and explain changes from the previous report. An evaluated contingency should be included so that an overall estimate of actual costs at completion is provided. Professional construction management costs should appear in a similar manner. A summary of value-engineering savings to date, and new items added during the period, can be included.

OVERALL COST CONTROLS

Overall cost controls should be integrated with schedule controls. Computer-based systems with common data files facilitate this integration. Overall cost controls, designed to measure project status against budget, include the following:

>   Preliminary estimates
>   Fair-cost estimates
>   Definitive estimate
>   Cost report summary
>   Value-engineering studies
>   Value-engineering status
>   Other significant data

Each of these items will be briefly introduced here with examples from the Mountaintown Warehouse Project, and will be discussed in greater detail in Chapters 10 through 17.

Preliminary Estimates

Preliminary estimates assist the overall cost-control program by serving as the first check against the budget, and by indicating cost overruns early enough for the project team to review the design for possible alternates. Since preliminary estimates are made prior to the completion of detail drawings, the margin for error is usually greater than for fair-cost estimates. Consequently, a larger contingency should be applied; this will vary with the amount of design information available and the extent of cost information obtainable from similar projects.

For a phased construction program, it is especially important to prepare preliminary estimates by contract package. By comparing actual contract awards with the preliminary estimate, a running total of the current status of the project is available. Indicated overruns can stimulate revision of the criteria for later work packages in order to preserve overall budgets.

Fair Cost Estimates

Fair-cost estimates are best prepared from the actual bid documents provided to the bidders. Whenever possible, it is helpful to complete the fair-cost estimate well before receiving bids so that any discrepancies in plans and specifications, duplications in scope, and possible value-engineering alternates suggested by the estimator can be communicated to the bidders via addendums before bids are received. In the event of a major difference from the preliminary estimates, this lead time is always helpful so that an intensive review of possible alternates can be started.

Fair-cost estimates represent the professional construction manager's appraisal of the fair value of the bid package to the owner. Local conditions, such as materials prices, wage rates, labor productivity, and anticipated competition, are important in achieving a reasonable estimate for the area.

Fair-cost estimates in an integrated cost–progress control system will also develop significant additional information for upgrading the usefulness and accuracy of the schedule- and progress-control portion of the overall control system. Some of these items will include the following:

An estimate of total man-hours of field effort required
Estimated quantities for major items
An estimate of reasonable unit costs for various components of the work
Information for allocation of contract costs for owner capitalization and tax considerations

In the event actual bids differ significantly from the fair-cost estimate, the manager can often meet with the low bidder and compare quantities and scope. Many times this comparison can pinpoint the reason for the discrepancy. Decisions regarding award, modification, or rejection of bids will be greatly assisted if the professional construction manager has prepared a careful fair-cost estimate, separately itemizing labor, materials, and equipment costs in a manner similar to that of the bidding contractor. This estimate can be of great value to the field construction manager in scheduling work, in reviewing change order requests, and in determining manpower requirements. Figure 8-1 shows a fair-cost estimate summary for Easyway's Mountaintown warehouse. Details of the estimate are included as Appendix A.

By comparing actual man-hours (or man days) required through computation from the project force report, a measure of local productivity can be developed and compared with the manager's estimate; this has numerous project uses as well as long-range benefits to the manager and to the owner. Table 8-1 shows a manpower summary comparing actual manpower requirements with the estimated man-hours from the fair-cost estimates.

Definitive Estimates

Definitive estimates fix the anticipated cost of the project with little margin for error. As contracts are bid on a phased construction program, the overall estimated cost becomes more certain. When 90 percent of the contracts have been awarded, less contingency is required than at the 50 percent level. When 100 percent of the contracts have been awarded, contingency is generally limited to providing for plan changes due to interference or error, for omissions or conflicts, or for other business risks inherent in the project.

Several numerical and statistical methods have been proposed and applied for forecasting total cost underruns or overruns at various contract award percentages. However, each project is different. On some, a definitive estimate can be prepared with reasonable accuracy when 50 percent of the contracts have been awarded. On others, accurate definitive estimates must wait until almost all contracts have been awarded. The manager's knowledge of the area

Cont. No.	Contracts	Labor Hours	Total Direct Cost	Overhead & Fee	Total
1.	Earthwork—site	1470	197,200	23,600	220,800
2.	Structural & yard concr.	7730	580,800	69,600	650,400
3.	Special slabs	7330	478,600	57,400	536,000
4.	Structural steel	3770	799,000	95,800	894,800
5.	Double tee walls	2640	497,400	59,600	557,000
6.	Mechanical—HVAC	4250	441,200	53,000	494,200
7.	Fire protection	3220	297,600	35,600	333,200
8.	Electrical	3470	354,000	42,000	396,000
9.	Roofing	3150	218,000	26,000	244,000
10.	Building finish	8470	565,600	68,000	633,600
	Total	45,500	4,429,400	530,600	4,960,000
	Contingency @ 5%				240,000

Total estimate $151,600$SF @ 34^{30}/SF = $5,200,000$

Estimate Criteria

1. Labor cost including fringe benifits, payroll taxes, workmen's compensation insurance, public liability & property damage insurance etc. is 30^{00}/HR.

2. Estimates are based upon drawings & specifications.

3. Construction management, survey, testing laboratory, & other owner's costs are not included.

4. Estimates are based upon an 8-month overall construction schedule.

5. Average manpower 34, estimated peak 68.

Figure 8-1 Fair cost estimate summary (Mountaintown Warehouse).

construction and bidding practices, area workload, design considerations, and estimating practices will indicate the point at which a reliable definitive estimate can be prepared.

Cost Report Summaries

Cost report summaries describe the actual and forecast status of the project; they generally commence with the preliminary estimate and end when the project is complete and all claims, if any, have been settled. In a normal program, cost reports showing estimated cost-at-completion can be prepared from the committed cost plus estimated costs-to-complete for the various contracts involved. Some owners prefer that the professional construction manager perform additional accounting for recorded costs when these are paid as progress payments. Others prefer to handle this phase themselves and are interested in the manager's report only to cover total commitments to date and estimated costs-to-complete. Similarly, some owners require continual cash-flow projections to accompany the cost reports, while others prefer to handle this themselves.

Figure 8-2 provides a sample summary cost report for the example project in its early stages, when only a few of the contracts have been awarded. The evaluated contingency reflects this early stage.

Table 8-1 Productivity Summary—Mountaintown Warehouse

Cont. No.	Contract	Man-hrs from fair cost estimate	Man-hrs from change orders	Est. total man-hrs	Actual man-hrs	% Productivity
1	Site Earthwork	1,470	50	1,520	1,288	118
2	Structural & Yard Concrete	7,730	560	8,290	8,272	100
3	Special Slabs	7,330	—	7,330	7,232	101
4	Structural Steel	3,770	—	3,770	4,080	92
5	Double Tee Walls	2,640	—	2,640	2,040	129
6	Mechanical HVAC	4,250	300	4,550	4,136	110
7	Fire Protection	3,220	—	3,220	2,736	118
8	Electrical	3,470	150	3,620	3,952	92
9	Roofing	3,150	100	3,250	2,808	116
10	Building Finish	8,470	600	9,070	8,688	104
	Total	45,500	1,760	47,260	45,232	104

Notes
1. Productivity is defined as estimated man-hours from fair cost estimates plus estimated man-hours for change orders divided by actual man-hours as measured from the force report.
2. Measured man-hours for special slabs has been increased by 1000 to allow for scheduled cement finisher overtime during topping phase.
3. See Figure 11-9 for manpower summary and actual manpower expended, as computed from the project force report, Figure 7-14.

Control account number	Description	Original commitment	Approved changes	Cumulative Total recorded & committed	Estimated Cost To complete	Estimated Cost At completion	Prelim. budget as of estimate	(under) or over budget
1	Site earthwork	206,000		206,000	3,000	209,000	208,000	1,000
2	Foundation & slab concrete	640,000	30,000	670,000	6,000	676,000	616,000	60,000
3	Special floors—interior	560,000		560,000		560,000	548,000	12,000
4	Structured steel	860,000	(5,800)	854,200		854,200	1,048,000	193,800
5	Precast walls	560,000		560,000		560,000	480,000	80,000
6	Plumbing & HVAC				594,200	594,200	380,000	214,200
7	Fire protection				333,200	333,200	300,000	33,200
8	Electrical				330,000	330,000	330,000	
9	Roofing				244,000	244,000	298,000	(54,000)
10	Building finish				590,000	590,000	590,000	
	Total direct cost	2,826,000	24,200	2,850,200	2,100,400	4,950,000	4,798,000	152,600
11	Field general conditions			28,400	143,600	172,000	172,000	
12	Home office fixed fee	200,000		200,000		200,000	200,000	
	Total indirect cost	200,000	28,400	228,400	143,600	372,000	372,000	
	Estimated total cost	3,026,000	52,600	3,078,600	2,244,000	5,322,600	5,170,000	152,600
	Contingency				257,400	257,400	482,000	(224,600)
	Total			3,078,600	2,501,400	5,480,000	5,652,000	72,000

Note: The control budget is based upon the preliminary estimate. At completion estimates are based upon contract awards (5), fair cost estimates (3), and preliminary estimates (2).

Figure 8-2 Summary cost report—early stages (Mountaintown Warehouse).

Control account number	Description	Original commitment	Approved changes	Cumulative Total recorded & committed	Estimated Cost		Prelim. budget as of estimate	(under) or over budget
					To complete	At completion		
1	Site earthwork	206,000	3,000	209,000		209,000	208,000	1,000
2	Foundation & slab concrete	640,000	50,000	690,000		690,000	616,000	74,000
3	Special floors—interior	560,000		560,000		560,000	548,000	12,000
4	Structural steel	860,000	(5,800)	854,200		854,200	1,048,000	193,800
5	Precast walls	560,000		560,000		560,000	480,000	80,000
6	Plumbing & HVAC	440,000	38,000	478,000		478,000	380,000	98,000
7	Fire protection	350,000		350,000		350,000	300,000	50,000
8	Electrical	380,000	18,000	398,000		398,000	330,000	68,000
9	Roofing	222,000	12,000	234,000		234,000	298,000	(64,000)
10	Building finish	604,000	56,000	660,000		660,000	590,000	70,000
	Total direct cost	4,822,000	171,200	4,993,200		4,993,200	4,798,000	195,200
11	Field general conditions			157,000	21,800	178,800	172,000	6,800
12	Home office fixed fee	200,000		200,000		200,000	200,000	
	Total indirect cost			357,000	21,800	378,800	372,000	6,800
	Estimated total cost			5,350,200	21,800	5,372,000	5,170,000	202,000
	Contingency				52,000	52,000	482,000	(430,000)
	Total			5,350,200	73,800	5,424,000	5,652,000	(228,000)

Note: See Figure 7-12 for contract status report and Figure 8-6 for contingency evaluation.

Figure 8-3   Summary cost report—late stages (Mountaintown Warehouse).

Figure 8-3 shows a similar report after nine contracts have been awarded and a fair-cost estimate has been completed for the balance of the work. The evaluated contingency reflects the definitive nature of this state of the project.

Figure 8-4 gives a comparison, at the time of preparation of Figure 8-2's summary cost report, between preliminary estimates, fair-cost estimates, and contract awards to date for the example warehouse project. Note that fair-cost estimates have been prepared for several packages for which bids have not yet been received.

Figure 8-5 shows the detailed evaluation of contingency for the early report. Figure 8-6 shows a similar evaluation after almost all contracts have been awarded.

Contr. no.	Contract package	Contract price	Prelim. estimate Fig. 4.5	Fair cost estimate Fig. 8.1	Over (under) pre. est.	Over (under) F.C. est.
1	Earthwork	206,000	208,000	220,800	(2,000)	(14,800)
2	Concrete	640,000	616,000	650,400	24,000	(10,400)
3	Special slabs	560,000	548,000	536,000	12,000	24,000
4	Struct. steel	860,000	1,048,000	894,800	(188,000)	(34,800)
5	TT walls	560,000	480,000	557,000	80,000	3,000
6	Mechanical		380,000	494,200		
7	Fire protect.		300,000	333,200		
8	Electrical		330,000	—		
9	Roofing		298,000	244,000		
10	Building finish		590,000			
	Estimated		4,798,000			

To Date		Cumul	Cumul	Cumul	Cumul	Cumul
1	Earthwork	206,000	208,000	220,900	(2,000)	(14,800)
2	Concrete	846,000	824,000	871,200	22,000	(25,200)
3	Special slabs	1,406,000	1,372,000	1,407,200	34,000	(1,200)
4	Struct. steel	2,266,000	2,420,000	2,302,000	(154,000)	(36,000)
5	TT walls	2,826,000	2,900,000	2,859,000	(74,000)	(33,000)
6	Mechanical		3,280,000			
7	Fire protect.		3,580,000			
8	Electrical		3,910,000			
9	Roofing		4,208,000			
10	Building finish		4,798,000			

Notes

1. As additional contracts are awarded, the missing blanks are filled in and the final estimated cost becomes more certain.

2. This exhibit compares actual contract price with preliminary and fair cost estimates. See Figure 8-2 summary cost report for estimated cost at completion.

Figure 8-4   Cost comparison before contingency (Mountaintown Warehouse).

Description	Amount	Factor	Evaluation
Open commitments	2,850,200	3.0%	85,600
Definitive estimates	1,071,400	7.5%	80,400
Preliminary estimates	920,000	10.0%	92,000
Estimated total			258,000
			Say 257,400 (Rounding Figure 8-2)

Figure 8-5 Contingency evaluation—early stages (Mountaintown Warehouse).

Value Engineering Studies

Value-engineering studies help in determining the most economical approach prior to detailed design. If best results are to be obtained, value engineering must involve a partnership where the professional construction manager, designer, and owner all work together. Application of construction cost knowledge during design, and consideration of alternates proposed by the team or by the bidders themselves, can be of great benefit to the owner.

Figure 5-2 in Chapter 5 showed a simplified value-engineering study of alternate wall systems for the warehouse. The study was a joint effort by the professional construction manager and the architect, and resulted in the use of double-tees for the project.

Value ·Engineering Status

A report showing value-engineering savings approved to date by the owner can keep the results of the program clearly in focus, and can be of long-term benefit to all parties on future projects. Figure 8-7 shows the approved value-engineering savings achieved on the warehouse project; it features an architect-manager-owner value-engineering program.

Field Cost Controls

Overall cost controls can be developed and administered either at the job site or in the home office, depending upon the particular project. However, evaluation of plan changes, claims, and other change-order requirements can often be done better at the job site.

The professional construction management firm's field construction manager is also the representative of the owner. When drawings are changed, an increase or a decrease in the contract price may be indicated. The adjustment should be fair to both the contractor and the owner.

Description	Amount	Factor	Evaluation
General conditions	1 month	18,000	18,000
Building finish claim	44,000	50.0%	22,000
Electrical claim	24,000	50.0%	12,000
Estimated total			52,000

Figure 8-6 Contingency evaluation—late stages (Mountaintown Warehouse).

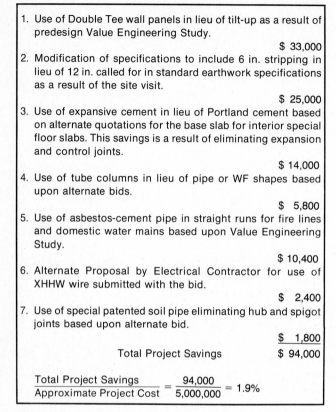

1. Use of Double Tee wall panels in lieu of tilt-up as a result of predesign Value Engineering Study.

$ 33,000

2. Modification of specifications to include 6 in. stripping in lieu of 12 in. called for in standard earthwork specifications as a result of the site visit.

$ 25,000

3. Use of expansive cement in lieu of Portland cement based on alternate quotations for the base slab for interior special floor slabs. This savings is a result of eliminating expansion and control joints.

$ 14,000

4. Use of tube columns in lieu of pipe or WF shapes based upon alternate bids.

$ 5,800

5. Use of asbestos-cement pipe in straight runs for fire lines and domestic water mains based upon Value Engineering Study.

$ 10,400

6. Alternate Proposal by Electrical Contractor for use of XHHW wire submitted with the bid.

$ 2,400

7. Use of special patented soil pipe eliminating hub and spigot joints based upon alternate bid.

$ 1,800

Total Project Savings $ 94,000

$$\frac{\text{Total Project Savings}}{\text{Approximate Project Cost}} = \frac{94,000}{5,000,000} = 1.9\%$$

Figure 8-7 Value engineering savings (Mountaintown Warehouse Project).

In one helpful technique, the contract terms require an itemized breakdown by labor and materials to be supplied by the contractor for all changes, including applicable quantities. Preparation of an independent fair-cost estimate based upon an independent quantity takeoff by the field construction manager can often pinpoint differences, lead to reasonable agreements, and prevent later disputes.

Whenever possible, the price for a change should be settled before the work is performed. However, in many cases the schedule demands immediate performance. Here, the contractor can be directed to proceed on a time-and-materials (force-account) basis, and a lump-sum change can be requested and negotiated soon thereafter. If agreement cannot be reached, the work can continue on force account in accord with contract compensation terms.

Probably the most troublesome changes to adjudicate involve work modifications that eliminate certain items and replace them with other more or less complicated items. Here, performance of the work on a time-and-materials basis is not possible unless a credit is negotiated for work not performed.

An important item of field cost control is scheduling contractors to avoid interference, delays, and other detrimental effects of one contractor's operations upon another's. In a professional construction management program, the owner through his manager is largely responsible for the coordination involved among site contractors.

SCHEDULE AND PROGRESS CONTROLS

Control schedules are developed and refined through preparation and revision of the overall plan. As project construction proceeds, it is evident that actual accomplishments must be compared with the overall plan if effective control is to be achieved.

Many items discussed in cost control are equally applicable to progress control. Cost–schedule–progress control systems integrated via a common computerized data base have been successful on very large projects. On smaller projects, the same integrated approach can be followed with little or no use of the computer.

CPM Control Schedule

The Critical Path Method, or CPM, is the foundation of the progress control system. A simplified CPM precedence diagram giving the construction schedule for the example project is shown in Appendix A. Figure 8-8 shows a bar-chart schedule, fully consistent with the CPM, upon which superimposed S curves show "cumulative percent completes" at the end of each month for both early- and late-start schedules. The double-S curves form an envelope. If actual performance is within the envelope, project goals have a good chance of being accomplished. If actual performance falls below the late-start schedule, the project will normally not be completed on schedule without a revised program.

Field effort in man-hours is the criterion for weighing the various components in the chart. This information is obtained from the fair-cost estimate. Basing progress upon estimated man-hours has numerous advantages in an integrated cost–schedule–progress control system. Manpower forecasts can be developed and compared with actual man-hours expended to accomplish key sections of the work. Contractor productivity can be calculated monthly.

Physical Progress Measurement

Figure 8-9 shows a worksheet for calculating the physical percentage complete for a single contract; it is based upon actual quantities completed during the period. The productivity of the construction forces compared with the manager's estimate can be calculated by comparing actual hours with calculated hours.

Figure 8-10 shows the summary of all contract data entered and plotted upon Figure 8-8. For a multifeature project, work can be grouped and tabulated

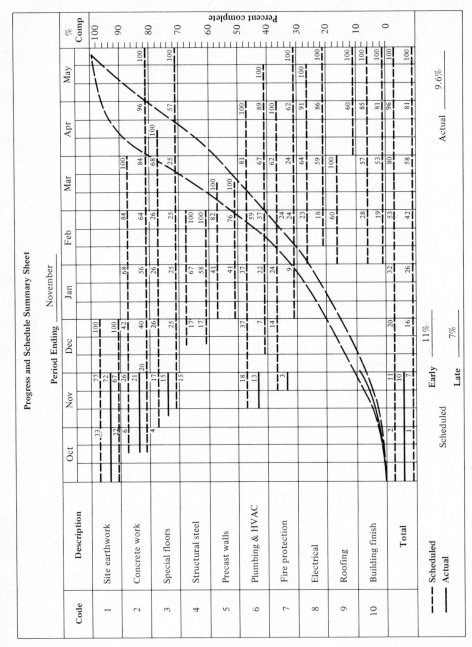

Figure 8-8 Construction schedule summary.

Contract	Unit 1	Budget 2	Quantity To Date 3	At Compl 4	5 % Complete 3/4	Weighted Value 6	7 Earned Value 3/4 × 6	Actual Man-hours 8	Productivity % 7/8	Comments
1.0 Site earthwork										
1.1 Site grading	CY	15,000	15,000	15,000	100.0	490	490			Start
1.2 Compacted building fill	CY	25,000	14,000	28,000	50.0	810	405			10-4-8_
1.3 Fencing	LF	4,680	4,800	4,800	100.0	170	170			
Subtotal earthwork					72.4	1,470	1,065	936	114	
2.0 Concrete										
2.1 Excavation & backfill	CY	5,250	3,000	6,000	50.0	1,600	800			Start
2.2 Yard paving-3000#	CY	3,850				1,970				10-13-8_
2.3 Building foundations	CY	440	200	440	45.0	1,630	734			
2.4 Misc. concrete	CY	60				330				
2.5 Paving joints	LF	13,180				420				
2.6 Paving—slab finish	SF	159,000				1,590				
2.7 Misc. metal, bolts, etc	%	100	40	100	40.0	190	76			
Subtotal concrete					20.8	7,730	1,610	1,656	97	

Figure 8-9 Mountaintown Warehouse physical progress worksheet.

139

Contract	Unit 1	Budget 2	Quantity To Date 3	At Compl 4	5 % Complete 3/4	Weighted Value 6	7 Earned Value 3/4 × 6	Actual Man hours 8	Productivity % 7/8	Comments
3.0 Interior special slabs										
3.1 Base slab—place 5¼"	CY	2,500	1,000	2,500	40.0	1,670	668			Start
3.2 Reinforcing steel	#	140,000	60,000	140,000	43.0	930	397			11-8-8_
3.3 Screed & cure base slab	SF	144,500				770				
3.4 Topping incl finish ¾"	SF	144,500				2,890				
3.5 Curbs, misc concr., emb.	%	100				1,070				
Subtotal special slabs					14.5	7,330	1,065	952	112	
6.0 Mechanical—HVAC										
6.1 Storm sewers	LF	2,240	1,030	2,100	49.0	790	387			Start
6.2 Sanitary sewers	LF	450	460	460	100.0	120	120			11-15-8_
6.3 Domestic water	LF	200	100	200	50.0	80	40			
6.4 Plumbing	%	100				1,130				
6.5 Sheet metal	%	100				1,000				
6.6 Heating	%	100				1,130				
Subtotal mechanical					12.9	4,250	547	512	107	
7.0 Fire protection										
7.1 Fire loop	LF	1,800	200	1,800	11.1	720	80			Start
7.2 Interior sprinklers	SF	150,000				2,500				11-24-8_
Subtotal fire protection					2.5	3,220	80	72	111	
Total to date							4,367	4,128	106	

Figure 8-9 Mountaintown Warehouse physical progress worksheet (continued)

Acct no.		% Complete 1	Weighted value 2	Earned value 3	Start	Finish
1.0	Site earthwork	72.4	1,470	1,065	10-4-8_	
2.0	Concrete	20.8	7,730	1,610	10-13-8_	
3.0	Special slabs	14.5	7,330	1,065	11-8-8_	
4.0	Structural steel		3,770			
5.0	Double tee walls		2,640			
6.0	Mechanical	12.9	4,250	547	11-15-8_	
7.0	Fire protection	2.5	3,220	80	11-24-8_	
8.0	Electrical		3,470			
9.0	Roofing		3,150			
10.0	Building finish		8,470			
	Total	9.6	45,500	4,367		

$$\text{Productivity} = \frac{\text{Earned Value (Man-Hrs)}}{\text{Cumulative Actual Man-Hrs}} = \frac{4367}{(516)(8)} = 106\%$$

Notes

1. Shows computation of physical % complete for overall project based upon earned value compared to weighted value (man-hours) as determined from fair cost estimates.

2. Results are shown in Figure 8-8, construction schedule summary, expressed as overall % complete.

3. If original schedules are to be maintained the weighted value is not adjusted for actual overruns or underruns in quantities. Actual productivity computations must take these variations into account.

4. See Figure 8-9 for individual computations of % complete & earned value.

5. This report can be easily adapted to an integrated overall computer-assisted, management-control system with a common data base in man-hours. See Figure 7-14 for cumulative actual man-hours used in productivity calculation above.

Figure 8-10 Physical progress contract summary (Mountaintown Warehouse Project).

by facility as well as by contract in order to determine the status of its various components.

The examples in Figures 8-8, 8-9, and 8-10 were chosen to illustrate a manual approach, but the system is the same whether or not it is computerized. The choice is one of project complexity; at some point it becomes cheaper to use the computer than to make the computations manually.

Field Schedules and Progress Controls

The preceding examples represent control schedules. If actual progress stays within the S-curve envelope, the project appears to be heading on a course that will achieve project goals.

However, field scheduling must provide much more detail than can ever be shown on a precedence diagram prepared during the planning stages. The key milestones are set forth in the plan, but the field construction manager, his staff, and the contractors must develop more detailed schedules to accomplish short-term goals.

Weekly meetings with all contractor representatives are a must; they provide the opportunity to review the current status of the program and to develop key dates for "move in," "move out," and completion of critical items affecting several contractors. The minutes of the meetings should be promptly distributed to all participants.

Preparation and job-site posting of a detailed bar-chart schedule, listing key requirements for each contractor, can be helpful. It may be revised frequently; but, if geared to detailed plans for accomplishing project objectives, it will assist all contractors and eliminate bottlenecks and interference.

Reporting by the field construction manager of actual quantities completed each month forms the heart of the overall progress control previously discussed. When an integrated system is being used, the computer can economically take much of the clerical and computational effort out of this task even on relatively small projects.

SUMMARY

This chapter reviewed the application of controls. However, the control system is only a tool which can assist the manager in shaping the completed product. In itself it cannot manage; it cannot tell what must be done to improve unsatisfactory performances; if it receives faulty or incomplete information, its final printed output nonetheless appears as authoritative as similar reports based upon sound input data.

The control system will never replace the judgment of competent home-office and job-site managers. Managers must be knowledgeable enough to use the control system as a valuable tool; but they must also have sufficient experience and skill to know when the tool has become dull.

Chapter 9

Selecting a Professional Construction Manager

Selecting a professional construction manager is in many ways similar to selecting an architect or a consulting engineer. Criteria may include overall experience, understanding of the project, preliminary plans submitted for completing the project, and price. These factors may be weighed differently by different owners, but all are important in selecting the right professional construction manager for a new project. By outlining a proven approach to selection, this chapter will tie together many of the concepts that have been introduced earlier in this book.

BASIC QUALIFICATIONS

Certain basic qualifications should almost always be investigated. Among the most important are the following:

Overall experience
General contracting
Professional construction management
Project planning and control
Inspection

Value engineering
Scheduling methods
Estimating methods
Design knowledge
Other applicable experience

Financing status
Adequacy for project under consideration
Overall financial strength

Depth of organization
Present workload
Available personnel
Key personnel
Recruiting requirements

Specialized experience
Area familiarity
Special knowledge
Industry experience

References
Current clients
Prior clients

Understanding project requirements
Anticipation of problems
Understanding of special features
Understanding owner objectives
Understanding project features
Understanding area practices
Understanding site conditions

Preliminary plans for implementation
Overall approach
Preliminary schedules
Preliminary costs
Proposed organization
Services to be provided
Services not to be provided

Price and compensation
Reimbursable costs
Nonreimbursable costs
Fee basis
Other basis

TYPICAL METHODS

Various owners have developed different methods for selecting a professional
construction manager. Some are very formal, such as those based upon a

numerical grading system; others are very informal, leaving the presentation to be largely determined by the proposer. The following sections will illustrate some common approaches.

General Services Administration (GSA)

A 1975 booklet, *The GSA System for Construction Management*,[1] contains a suggested "Construction Management Project Notice" which generally outlines this agency's method of selecting a construction manager. This section is quoted below:

CONSTRUCTION MANAGEMENT PROJECT NOTICE
FOR ISSUANCE IN THE COMMERCE BUSINESS DAILY

Y—Construction Management Services

The General Services Administration seeks construction management services for the proposed (insert building name and location) to provide approximately (insert) gross square feet within an estimated cost range between $(insert) and $(insert) million. Design and construction will be concurrently phased with separate construction contracts awarded as segments of the design are completed by the architect-engineer.

Consideration will be given to firms or joint ventures generally meeting the following requirements:
(1) Experience as a Construction Manager or potential competence to perform construction management services; (2) Financial ability to provide the services required by the Government; (3) Competence in civil, mechanical, electrical and structural engineering; construction estimating, cost accounting and control; tenant coordination; project management; contract negotiation and administration; construction superintendence and inspection; and other related fields; (4) Experience in constructing buildings in the general geographic area of this project, or good recent knowledge of local conditions in the project area, or ability to retain others with such knowledge; (5) Proven competence in the implementation and maintenance of network-based construction management systems and in the application of systematic cost control throughout the design and construction process; (6) Good professional and business reputation, and an on-time and within-budget performance record; and (7) Ability to provide professionally qualified key personnel with a minimum of 12 years' satisfactory experience in the design and construction industry. Satisfactory experience should include:
a Eight years in work related specifically to the duties to be performed in the designated position for this project; and
b Four years in positions with requirements equal to those for the designated position of this project.

Prospective construction management firms or joint ventures who are interested in the project are invited to ask for Request for Qualifications Submission which will

[1] General Services Administration, Public Buildings Service, Washington, D.C., April 1975, rev. ed.

be issued by the office below on or by (insert date). Qualifications will be received until (insert date) at the office below, and then evaluated on the basis of the requirements and criteria contained in the Request for Qualifications Submission. Request for Priced Proposal will be subsequently issued to only those firms or joint ventures whose Qualifications have been determined by GSA as being within a competitive range. Only Priced Proposals specifically requested by the Government will be considered.

Associated General Contractors of America (AGC)

An AGC report titled *Construction Management Guidelines for Use by AGC Members*[2] includes the following section illustrating the AGC selection recommendations:

HOW IS THE CONSTRUCTION MANAGER MEMBER
OF THE CONSTRUCTION TEAM SELECTED?

The Construction Manager will be selected on the basis of an objective analysis of his professional and general contracting qualifications. In this selection, major considerations will be given to:

a His success in performing the normal general contractor's function on projects of comparable type, scope, and complexity.

b His financial strength, bonding capacity, insurability, and ability to assume a financial risk if the owner requires it.

c His in-house staff capability and the qualifications of the person who will manage the project.

d His record for completing projects on time and within the budget.

e His demonstrated ability to work cooperatively with the Owner and the Architect-Engineer throughout the project, and to display leadership and initiative in performing his tasks as a member of the Construction Team.

Airport Expansion Program

A western city requested construction management proposals for a $40-million terminal addition as a part of an overall master plan. Here the city initially screened firms and selected four to submit proposals. The general scope of the facilities to be constructed was spelled out, and relationships and criteria for operation under the city engineer and airports director were set forth. The notice was general, and included the statement, "What we will want to learn from you is what service you can provide to the City, how would you organize to perform the work, and on what basis would we expect to pay for such Construction Management Services." A copy of the master plan and development program was attached. Arrangements were also made to interview firms submitting proposals, and a $1^{1}/_{2}$-hour period was tentatively selected. Within this framework, selected firms were free to develop their own programs for consideration.

[2]The Associated General Contractors of America, 1957 E Street, N.W., Washington, D.C., Feb. 15, 1972, p. 3.

Management Contracting

A novel approach, called "Management Contracting," was developed at the University of California. Other universities in Alaska and Colorado have followed this approach. In summary, the method provides the opportunity for the university to achieve shortest overall design-construction time under a negotiated contract while complying with competitive bid requirements imposed by the state. Bidders are rated both on experience through a complicated points evaluation to ensure prequalification, and on certain items of cost, including profit, which are bid on a lump-sum or unit-price basis. All other costs are reimbursable up to a "Guaranteed Outside Price" (GOP) which is negotiated near the close of design work. Any savings below the GOP are split between the contractor and the university, based upon the percentages set forth in the contractor's bid.

Other Examples

Private construction owners commonly adopt portions of all the above approaches. "Requests for Proposals for Construction Management" can range from an individually designed prequalification requirement, coupled with specific information including pricing, to a simple verbal or written request leaving the content of the proposal largely up to the ingenuity of the bidder.

RECOMMENDED METHODS

What is the best method for the owner to use when selecting a professional construction manager? The ideal selection process would first develop a list of qualified firms based upon prior accomplishment. Next, each of these firms would be given an opportunity to show its ingenuity, planning ability, and estimating and scheduling abilities by submitting a preliminary program or work plan for the new project. Finally, questions of costs to the owner, such as fees and services to be included and not included, would be taken into consideration.

Were the authors to be requested by a construction owner to develop criteria for the selection of a professional construction manager, the program would evolve along the following lines:

Prequalification

Initially, interested firms would be requested to submit *overall experience* qualifications as previously set forth. A standard form can readily be developed so that the required information can be inserted or attached by the prospective professional construction manager. Upon receiving all forms, the owner should check references, especially present and past clients, and make an overall judgment of the manager's qualifications. Firms designated as qualified would proceed to the next step in the selection process, and those designated as not qualified would be so notified. No statistical or numerical order would be developed on the basis of past experience. Once the owner determines which firms are qualified, the selection process continues in order to identify the one that appears to be best suited for the particular project under consideration.

Owners should be primarily interested in what a professional construction manager can do for them. One hundred successful past jobs for others will be of no benefit to the owner if the new job is not completed on schedule and within budget. The next stage of the selection process is thus the most important; it is designed to obtain a project work plan from each of qualified candidates so that the best and most practical plan can be selected by the owner for implementation.

Request for Proposals

The request for proposals should be carefully designed to give all candidates a basic amount of information so that all proposed plans are founded on common criteria. The more information about the project that can be given the candidates, the better the plan that can be expected.

A request for a proposal for professional construction management services might be outlined as follows:

1 Owner's Basic Criteria   The owner assembles and includes all pertinent, current information about the proposed project as developed from his feasibility study or other preplanning information. While some of the information will not be available or desirable to include, such criteria may include the following:

Feasibility studies
General layout or preliminary drawings
Preliminary specifications or design criteria
Owner's operating requirements
Owner's contracting requirements
Design schedules
Completion requirements
Location of job site
Designer, if selected
Appropriation estimate
Other owner requirements

2 Proposed Work Plan   Within these parameters, considerable leeway should be given to each candidate in developing his implementation plan. The purpose of this request is to determine the candidate's understanding of the project requirements and his ingenuity and skill in developing a preliminary work plan for implementing those requirements. Some of the items which the owner can request candidates to include in their work plans are:

Description of overall approach
Services to be provided in field office
Services to be provided in home office

Proposed contract package, scope, and general contracting program
Preliminary procurement schedule
Proposed value-engineering program
Preliminary construction schedule
Cost-and-progress control system
Additional construction cost estimates (if sufficient information available in criteria)
Estimates of professional construction management costs and fixed fee (or other compensation requirements)
Definitions of reimbursable and nonreimbursable costs if applicable
Proposed project organization, and résumés of key personnel .

3 Technical Evaluation of Proposals   Proposals can now be evaluated on the basis of the candidates' demonstrated knowledge and ingenuity in developing a program to implement the basic criteria available. While evaluation criteria will be different for all projects, some key questions important in determining the interest, understanding, ingenuity, practicality, and skill of the candidate will include:

Are the schedules and programs outlined in the proposal based upon the particular project criteria, and do they reflect an effort to avoid problems and to present a practical plan tailored to fit the proposed project conditions?

Has the plan been individually developed by practical construction professionals, or is it a modification of standard documents adapted by sales personnel and featuring "buzz words" and other impressive but undefined techniques?

Is the method for control of costs clearly identified and explained?

Is the method for control of schedules and progress clearly identified and explained?

On the basis of the owner's interviews with the proposed home-office project manager, the field construction manager, and other key personnel, what does he believe was their part in preparing the proposals, what does he think of their background, and does he believe them to be individually suitable for this project?

What part will people who developed the proposal play in the project implementation?

Is the value-engineering program described specifically enough for it to be evaluated under anticipated project conditions?

Is the overall tone of the proposal aimed at presenting a well thought-out plan to achieve a successful program for the project under consideration, or is it generally aimed at listing past accomplishments, past solutions of problems, and broad overall skills?

4 Final Selection   After the technical evaluation has been completed, an overall evaluation of costs and fees is needed. Fees should be reasonably related to the services to be provided. In the real world, price is certainly a factor, but in view of the construction manager's level of influence on costs, the potential savings associated with the choice of the best-qualified professional would appear to be greater than a small difference in fee.

COMPENSATION AND FEES

The subject of fees for professional construction management has been one of considerable misunderstanding. Since each job is different, comparison is difficult. In some cases, fees are defined to include all costs of professional construction management, including home-office costs, field costs, and profit. In other cases, fees are defined to be profit only and do not include home-office or field-office costs.

Current Practices

Field and home-office responsibilities can vary widely for different projects. Field costs are largely determined by the extent of the field organization coupled with the extent of general conditions services that the manager is expected to provide.

Surveying, inspection, testing laboratory, utility bills, sanitary facilities, security services, and other items broadly set forth as general conditions can be included or omitted depending upon the particular project. Therefore, it probably is not feasible to develop a meaningful comparison of overall charges for different projects.

Many negotiated general construction, as well as professional construction management, contracts provide for a fee to cover home-office cost and profit. The fee can be expressed as a lump sum, as a percentage of total estimated construction cost, or as a percentage of actual cost. Other contracts provide for full reimbursement of field and home-office costs plus a fixed fee for profit.

Representative Fees

Figure 9-1 gives two curves which show the low and high ranges of home-office costs plus profit for approximately 50 actual or proposed jobs performed in the United States and Canada, many of which were professional construction management projects. In order to obtain sufficient data to draw the curves, a number of negotiated contracts for general contractor services, where the preponderance of work has been subcontracted, have also been included. The project data were obtained from publicly reported projects and from reported data obtained from sources considered to be reliable; they cover projects constructed for different owners by different managers and contractors.

The curves are not intended to be fee curves for any proposed projects. Rather, they are intended simply to indicate the range of fees for profit and home-office services that have actually been charged for a representative number of projects. Reasonable fees expressed in this manner may range from the high curve to the low curve depending upon project duration, the nature of the project, the extent of the services, and other factors.

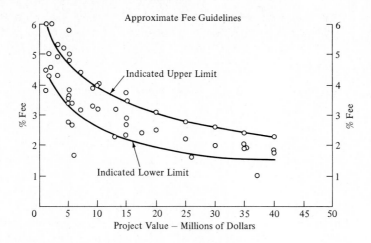

Figure 9-1   Approximate fee guidelines.

Notes
1. Fee includes all home office costs including profit & overhead.
2. All field expenses are reimbursable.
3. Based upon 52 construction management and negotiated general contract projects throughout the U.S. & Canada.
4. Includes 4 projects for USGS & DOE; balance are for public & private owners.
5. Fees can vary widely dependent upon profit & amount of work done in the home office.

OWNER RESPONSIBILITIES

If professional construction management is to prosper, not only does the manager have responsibilities to both the designer and the owner, but the owner has definite responsibilities to the designer and the manager. Some of these responsibilities are the following:

Define Responsibilities

The owner must clearly develop or agree to a delineation of the responsibilities borne by all three members of the professional construction management team. Each must understand his own responsibilities as well as the extent of responsibilities delegated to the others. The owner must clearly spell out to the professional construction manager the extent of his procurement and cost authorities. The manager must be fully accountable to the owner to the extent of such delegations.

Maintain Professional Relationships

The designer and the professional construction manager must respect the professional relationships of each other, and the owner must also respect the professional integrity of each. The owner should place particular emphasis upon respecting the manager's position in dealing with all project contractors. Although the owner may normally retain the final approval, he should refrain from entering into negotiations separately except in unusual circumstances. Nothing can destroy the professional relationship faster than an owner who will deal directly with project contractors and conclude agreements or modifications directly in the absence of the manager.

Make Timely Decisions

Where owner decisions are required, the owner has a right to expect alternative evaluations and recommendations from the manager. In turn, if the manager is to be held accountable for the project schedules and costs, the owner must make decisions he has reserved for himself in a manner that is timely and that will not prejudice the program.

For professional construction management to work, the three-party team of owner, designer, and professional construction manager must truly function as a team with all parties working for the overall benefit of both the owner's project and the industry. This fact must be kept clearly in mind when selecting a designer as well as a professional construction manager.

MARKETING CM SERVICES

Marketing of CM services varies according to both the potential client and the individual CM firm.

Public Clients

Public potential clients generally have a list of qualifications and requirements similar to the GSA requirement previously discussed. Firms are usually asked to submit qualification proposals, and through a system of ranking and scoring individual firms, the top three or so firms are "short-listed" to proceed with the final selection process, which may involve further qualification requests, development of a proposed organization, and nomination of the proposed project personnel, as well as a proposed plant for implementing the program.

Fees are often quoted in this selection process, and the final choice is sometimes dependent upon the fee as well as qualification.

Other agencies have relatively standard methods of negotiating fees, and the selection process is restricted to the determination of the best qualified firm. A contract is then negotiated with the chosen firm.

Marketing success for public clients depends highly upon the proposal response, the quality and believability of the proposed project personnel, and the impression given during a personal interview with proposed team members and top management as a part of the selection process.

Private Clients

Considerable ingenuity can be developed in marketing CM services to private clients. Personal contact with potential clients well in advance of a particular project inception can often turn up opportunities for negotiating a project with minimum or no competition. Offering to provide preliminary work plans, schedules, and even conceptual cost estimates is often very helpful to the owner preparing funding requests. Many times such "free services" can result in a negotiated project where the construction manager has the opportunity to carry out his proposed program. One of the best marketing tools is to perform an outstanding job on the first project, thus obtaining repeat business with minimal or no competition.

In the private sector, price is always a consideration. However, ingenuity by the construction manager in preparing programs that may save substantial sums in contruction costs is a very effective basis of marketing and can lead to substantial future work if such savings are in fact achieved.

Marketing CM is similar to marketing other professional services. It helps to understand the owner objectives, to be able to effectively propose programs to acheive these objectives, and to present to the potential client the firms' qualifications in the best possible light.

SUMMARY

In outlining an approach to the selection of a professional construction manager, this chapter in effect has reviewed several of the major advantages of the professional construction management approach. Important qualifications for the manager include overall experience, financial status, depth of organization, experience in the project locality and type of work, an understanding of the owner's requirements, references, the preliminary plan for implementation, and the reimbursement and fee structure. The selection process should involve, in the order given, prequalification, request for proposals, evaluation of proposals, and final selection including fee considerations. Fees themselves will vary depending on the type and scope of the project, the services to be provided by the professional construction manager, and the allocation of costs to the reimbursable and nonreimbursable categories.

This chapter has concluded with guidelines regarding the owner's responsibilities. To make professional construction management work beneficially, it is important that all three parties, owner, designer, and professional construction manager, are indeed united in a nonadversary team best to serve the needs of the project.

Part Three

Methods in Professional Construction Management

Chapter 10

Concepts of Project Planning and Control

This chapter first describes interrelationships between engineering, design, construction, and operation costs for a facility and shows how the level of control over these costs decreases as a project evolves. An analogy and a model then introduce basic concepts of the information feedback-control process used on well-managed projects. The objective here is to provide a broad perspective against which to reference specific subsystems discussed in the subsequent nine chapters of Part 3; these will include estimating, project planning and scheduling, cost engineering, materials procurement and tracking, quality assurance, value engineering, and safety. Key components of the feedback control process to be examined in greater detail include: means for measuring and controlling progress; methods for information processing; requirements for effective reporting; and guidelines for taking corrective action to keep a project on target.

DESIGNING TO REDUCE CONSTRUCTION COSTS[1]

The concept to be explained in this section lies at the heart of professional construction management. The basic idea is not new. Variously described as

---

[1]This section is based on Boyd C. Paulson, Jr., "Designing to Reduce Construction Costs," *Journal of the Construction Division*, ASCE, vol. 102, no. CO4, December 1976, pp. 587–592.

"level of influence," "percent of effective control," "possible cost savings," "ability to control" and "degree of effectiveness," it has been well understood in some sectors of industry for many years, particularly in manufacturing, in heavy-industrial design-construct work, and more recently by general contractors interested in professional construction management. This chapter will adopt the term "level of influence" and will explore some of its implications in more detail.

Level of Influence on Project Costs

Figure 10-1 illustrates essential features of the level-of-influence concept. The lower portion simplifies the life of a project to a three-activity bar chart consisting of (1) engineering and design, (2) procurement and construction, and (3) utilization or operation. The upper portion plots two main curves. The curve

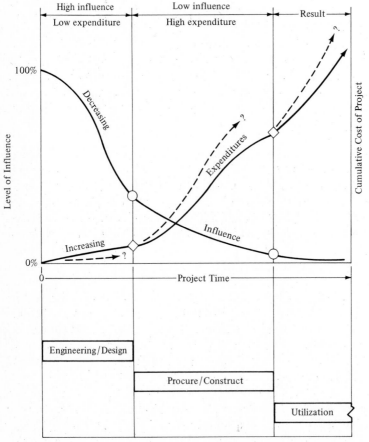

Figure 10-1   Level of influence on project costs. *(From Boyd C. Paulson, Jr., "Designing to Reduce Construction Costs," Journal of the Construction Division, ASCE, vol. 102, no. CO4, December 1976, p. 588.)*

ascending to the right-hand ordinate tracks cumulative project expenditures. The curve descending from the left-hand ordinate shows the decreasing level of influence. The bar chart and both curves are plotted against the same horizontal abscissa: project time.

The parts of the figure interrelate as follows: In the early phases of a project, that is, during feasibility studies, preliminary design, and even detail design, the relative expenditures are small compared with those of the project as a whole. Typically, engineering and design fees amount to well under 10 percent of total construction costs. Similarly, capital costs invested by the time that construction is completed often are but a small fraction of the operation and maintenance costs associated with a project's complete life cycle. However, although actual expenditures during the early phases of a project are comparatively small, decisions and commitments made during that period have far greater influence on what later expenditures will in fact be.

On the first day, management has a 100 percent level of influence in determining future expenditures. Paraphrased simply, the question is: To build or not to build? A decision of not to build requires no expenditure at all for the project. A decision to build requires more decision making, but initially at a very broad level. For example, shall a new power plant use fossil or nuclear fuel? If nuclear, how many units and how big? Shall the basic technology be pressure water reactor (3-cycle PWR) or boiling water reactor (2-cycle BWR)? (Those familiar with the industry know that this decision alone narrows down the potential choice of vendors for the nuclear steam supply system.) As engineering and design continue, decisions become more detailed, but the implications are no less significant. Shall we use a thicket of number 11 (3.5 cm) bars or more widely spaced number 18's (5.7 cm) in reinforcing this part of the containment? And so on until the final drawing change is stamped, signed, and approved.

As these decisions evolve and commitments are made, the remaining level of influence on what the project costs will ultimately become precipitous drops. For example, a rough but educated guess would put the remaining level of influence at about 25 percent of the original by the time field construction commences on a grass-roots petroleum refinery. This 25 percent represents the control that construction contractors have through productive use of labor, innovative uses of equipment and methods, and wise materials procurement practices. But it is the designer who has more radically influenced construction costs. It is the designer who may or may not have packed the reinforcing steel so densely that concrete cannot be placed by economical procedures. It is the designer who may or may not have specified nonstandard sizes, impossible formwork configurations, techniques requiring incompatible mixtures of labor crafts, bronze fittings where galvanized were more than adequate, etc. All too often such decisions are made without the slightest notion as to their impact on construction costs, but they influence the costs nonetheless. "Value-engineering" clauses in construction contracts are at best after-the-fact remedies for such fundamental oversights.

In like manner, decisions made during construction, even within the 25 percent or so remaining level of influence, can greatly impact the costs of operating and maintaining a facility. Skimping on quality in workmanship or substituting inferior materials may save a few dollars in construction costs, and in contracts with a "profit-sharing" clause even the owner may be pleased in the short run, but costs resulting from excessive maintenance, downtime, and inefficient operations can consume those "savings" many times over. By the time construction is completed, however, the die is cast. What little influence remains after project start-up often takes the form of shutting the facility down for expensive rework, modifications, or retrofitting.

Costs to Whom?

Many problems associated with the level-of-influence concept result from cost suboptimization inherent in the contractual structure for a project. As a hypothetical example, assume that an owner desiring a new ore-processing facility has obtained a fixed-fee contract with an engineering firm and plans to let a competitively bid construction contract once designs are complete. Assume also that the engineer has designed several similar plants in the past, and has thus negotiated his fee, say $400,000 including 20 percent ($80,000) profit and general overhead, on the assumption that much of the design can be adapted from earlier drawings.

Two of the required drawings describe the electrical instrumentation and controls for a crushing and grinding circuit. Since it is similar to one done before, the engineering budget provided for it as follows:

80 design-hours × $30/design-hour = $2400

However, assume that these drawings represent $320,000 worth of equipment, materials, and field construction labor.

When the electrical engineer was about 60 percent complete on these drawings, he got into a discussion with a vendor who described a new system for this application that, through the use of solid-state technology, could save approximately 20 percent of the costs of purchasing and installing a conventional facility, or $64,000 in this case. The vendor had the facts to back up his numbers.

After this discussion, the electrical engineer went to his supervisor to suggest that this change be incorporated. His supervisor denied the request with the following reasoning:

Costs to date for adapting conventional design:
60% of $2400	$1440

Estimate for revised design using new technology:
200 design-hours × $30/design-hour	6000
Subtotal	$7440
Initial estimate for drawings E-247 and I-186	(2400)
Design cost overrun:	$5,040

The fact that this potential 210 percent overrun on these two drawings represented over 6 percent of the profit and overhead for the whole job was but one problem. It might have been negotiated as a change with the owner. However, the design as a whole was already two months behind schedule, and the client was thought to be in no mood to even hear of, let alone approve, such a change at this time, or so rationalized the supervisor to the electrical engineer. Also, he argued, "This new technology is not well proven yet. Stick with conventional designs that we know will work."

Similar decisions are made every day in practice. The one just described suboptimized costs at the level of the engineering and design firm at the expense of potentially much greater savings ($64,000 versus $5,040) at the capital-cost level. Analogously, capital costs are too often suboptimized at the expense of life-cycle costs. For example:

> Unit A costs $250,000 and operates at $1.20/ton.
> Unit B costs $300,000 and operates at $1.15/ton.
> Annual production is 800,000 tons.

The $0.05 per ton saved by unit B times 800,000 tons per year represents annual savings in operation costs of $40,000. This should quickly recoup the extra $50,000 capital cost, but again, if a design-construct contract puts too strong an incentive on reduced capital costs, a bad economic decision for the owner may result.

Even at the owner's level, costs can be suboptimized at the expense of industry as a whole or of society. An owner sometimes moves into an area to construct a large project where "time is of the essence" and construction cost is secondary. Perhaps the objective is a factory to produce a new small car to stem the tide of foreign competition, or a pipeline of high national priority to deal with the energy crisis. Too often, however, the indirect costs resulting from the distortion of the labor market, the economic and social impact on nearby communities, and the disruption to other firms competing for the same scarce labor and material resources far exceed the savings to the individual owner.

The point here is that contractual structures can be adjusted to minimize the consequences of suboptimization of the type described above. The first prerequisite, however, is an understanding of some of the economic forces involved. The level-of-influence concept as shown in Figure 10-1 may help toward this end.

Contractual Implications

Two important conclusions can be drawn from the level-of-influence concept. First, owing to the tremendous impact that design decisions have on construction and operation costs, contractual arrangements should be drawn to assure that construction and, where appropriate, operations thinking is strongly injected in the conceptual, preliminary, and detail design processes. Second, efforts to suboptimize design costs alone, for example by requiring competitive bidding for professional engineering and architectural services, can have disastrous consequences for the owner's budget when construction and utilization costs are considered.

Injecting Construction Knowledge In the first case, several current contractual arrangements, if properly applied, can at least inject construction thinking into the design phase. Major examples include professional construction management and also design-construct or turnkey contracts. The name alone, however, does not guarantee results. For example, an architect may offer "professional construction management" services. If by this he means that, acting as agent for the owner, he will let and administer separate construction contracts, possibly on a phased construction basis, one has to assume that he has a wealth of contractor-type construction knowledge if there are to be any savings at all. Knowing how to package separate construction contracts along recognized trade and jurisdictional boundaries, as well as accurate knowledge for estimating time and costs for the different operations, are essential. Few design consultants really have these capabilities.

Design-construct has its pitfalls also. First, third-party objectivity and interaction at the design-construct interface are lost. Even in a fully professional and highly ethical firm, organizational inertia can perpetuate obsolete practices to the exclusion of innovative thinking. Where separate design and professional construction management firms are teamed in different combinations, innovations are more likely to be transferred. Another problem is that even in design-construct firms, one too often finds people on the drawing boards who rarely if ever get to the field to see the physical results of their decisions, for better or worse.

It is also important to reemphasize that no one contractual arrangement is best for all situations. For example, one large private university increasingly uses professional construction management only in the design phase, and it sees considerable benefits from injecting construction thinking there. However, the university discerns much less benefit for professional construction management during construction, where it has gone back to letting conventional competitively bid general contracts instead. Some professional construction management enthusiasts would object that the latter forgoes the time savings resulting from phased construction. Where there are revenue-generating time pressures for beneficial occupancy, phased construction's uncertainty and the possible increase in direct costs are often a risk worth taking. In the university's case, however, risk of overrun when the later contracts are let is unacceptable because fund limitations are often absolute. Also, time pressures for beneficial occupancy are much lower, and potential short-run economic returns are more difficult to quantify, since the size of the student body, faculty, and staff is held constant anyway. New facilities serve mainly for replacement or enhancement rather than for generating new revenue.

Competitive Bidding The second case, that of competitive bidding and related procurement techniques for professional services, is more insidious.

Volumes of material have been written on this subject in recent years, and much of it has been read into the *Congressional Record*. It is nevertheless important to view the subject again in light of the level-of-influence concept.

The assumption that one can save money by choosing an architect/engineer solely on the basis of lowest design fee is false economy of the worst sort. On the other hand, this need not imply that there is a direct linear correlation between the amount spent on design and the quality or utility of the structure. But knowledgeable owners and agencies need the authority to evaluate alternative professional firms through selection procedures that will engage the firm that can most competently produce a structure of maximum utility for the lowest overall costs, including social and environmental costs as well as design, construction, and operation costs. Selection solely on the basis of lowest fee is likely to perpetuate obsolete designs based upon drawings long since filed away and to force the use of other short-cuts for cost shaving.

PROJECT PLANNING AND CONTROL[2]

Once the professional construction manager has been chosen, and even when fair and equitable contractual agreements have united all members of the project team and oriented them toward the owner's goals, the team will still face the most challenging part of project management: planning and control to bring the project to completion on schedule, within budget, and in accordance with the owner's functional objectives. For this they will need the fullest understanding of the planning and control process and all the practical tools that can be put at their disposal.

How will they cope? To begin, consider an analogy.

Planning and Control: An Analogy

In many ways, planning and control principles applied on a complex engineering and construction project resemble those needed in planning and taking a trip in a car. Assume, for example, that a family intended to travel from Chicago to Los Angeles for a two-week Disneyland vacation. At one extreme, they could start with no plans; they would simply set out without maps, without a planned budget, and with only the general notion that Disneyland is near Los Angeles, which, in turn, is somewhere west or southwest of Chicago. After ending up lost, broke, out of gas, tired, and distraught on a lonely highway somewhere between Riddle, Idaho, and Wild Horse, Nevada, the trip—their "project"—would most likely be declared an unmitigated disaster, or perhaps, more charitably, a "unique experience."

Now consider the other extreme. Assume that several months before starting, the wife engaged a licensed highway engineer to study the most feasible alternative routes, select the best one, then literally survey that route

---

[2]This section is based on Boyd C. Paulson, Jr., "Concepts of Project Planning and Control," *Journal of the Construction Division*, ASCE, vol. 102, no. CO1, March 1976, pp. 67–80.

and prepare a log documenting, at 20-foot intervals, all stop signs, intersections, potholes, curves in the road, speed limits, gas stations, motels, and other details. The engineer would then prepare a detailed list of instructions telling the speeds to maintain, when to apply the brakes, when to turn, where to stop for the night, and so forth. Once underway at 55 miles per hour, this detailed information would come so fast and in such great volumes that the whole family would constantly have to be reading the plan to figure out what was happening. They would be so engrossed in the documentation of what had gone past that they might miss unexpected opportunities en route, or, worse yet, the driver would not be prepared to deal with unexpected emergencies, such as a child running into the street, a detour ahead, or a truck overturned. Clearly, this approach to planning and control is another formula for disaster. Not only would the "information system" be inordinately expensive, but it would also prove so distracting that it not only would fail in its basic purpose but would inhibit human judgment and reasoning as well.

Both approaches have been and continue to be used in construction, and both cause analogous results. What is needed is something between these two extremes. One should have good basic planning before commencing a project as well as a journey, but the approach taken must also allow management the flexibility to respond to, and even turn to advantage, the unexpected changes and events that will inevitably occur. A project should have a budget; its designs should be on paper; it should have a schedule which in turn forecasts the requirements for resources of labor, equipment, and materials; but it also needs a dynamic and responsive feedback-control system to cope with the operations underway.

Consider again the analogy from a moment ago. A car with its driver is, in effect, such a dynamic feedback control system. The car in motion is the project. The driver looks down the road, that is, into the future, and receives information: the road curves to the right; there is a stop sign; the car ahead brakes suddenly to miss a deer. The driver takes this information, analyzes it, and through her body and the mechanism of the car, takes responsive action to keep the vehicle safely on the road; that is, she controls her project.

Now take this analogy of the car and do a rather odd thing. Paint out the windshield so that the driver can only look to the sides to see where she is, and to the rear to see where she has been. This may not be as absurd as it sounds. If the driver has driven the road hundreds of times, say from the family farm to town, with caution she might well be able to start the engine and proceed slowly to her destination. The information from the sides is better than none at all, and it at least keeps her on the road. This is analogous to the type of information system in construction that does a good job of documenting how the project has progressed to date, but has little or no provision for forecasting where it is going or what its needs will be in the future. If a foreman arrives at work and finds that he is out of bricks, he will order more at that time. If delivery takes 3 weeks, the project is delayed but will nonetheless be completed, slowly and inefficiently, but eventually. Many contractors have managed to operate this way for years.

Now successively paint out the side windows and the rear window of the car, until there is no outside vision at all. Perhaps by the feel of an old familiar road, the woman from the farm may still find her way to town, but the hazards will be great. Clearly, if she finds herself in this situation at 55 miles per hour on a crowded urban freeway, that is, on a larger, unfamiliar project, she is really in trouble. This, again, is analogous to construction planning and control systems with successively slower and slower feedback of less and less information, until finally either the bank or the Internal Revenue Service informs the contractor (the driver's counterpart) that she was bankrupt some time ago.

Although the extremes in the analogy of the automobile may seem a little absurd to any reasonable construction contractor, it is nonetheless astonishing how many of these same contractors continue to run their projects at the analogous extremes. If this book brings slightly more order to this chaos, it will have served its purpose.

Objectives

General objectives for an information system designed to aid management in the planning and control of engineering and construction projects may be stated as follows:

1 To provide an organized and efficient means of measuring, collecting, verifying, and quantifying data reflecting the progress and status of operations on the project with respect to schedule, cost, resources, procurement, and quality.

2 To provide standards against which to measure or compare progress and status. Examples of standards include CPM schedules, control budgets, procurement schedules, quality control specifications, and construction working drawings.

3 To provide an organized, accurate, and efficient means of converting the data from the operations into information. The information system should be realistic and should recognize (*a*) the means of processing the information (e.g., manual versus computer), (*b*) the skills available, and (*c*) the value of the information compared with the cost of obtaining it.

4 To report the correct and necessary information in a form which can best be interpreted by management, and at a level of detail most appropriate for the individual managers or supervisors who will be using it.

In keeping with the principles of management by exception, the following two objectives should be added:

5 To identify and isolate the most important and critical information for a given situation, and to get it to the correct managers and supervisors, that is, those in a position to make best use of it.

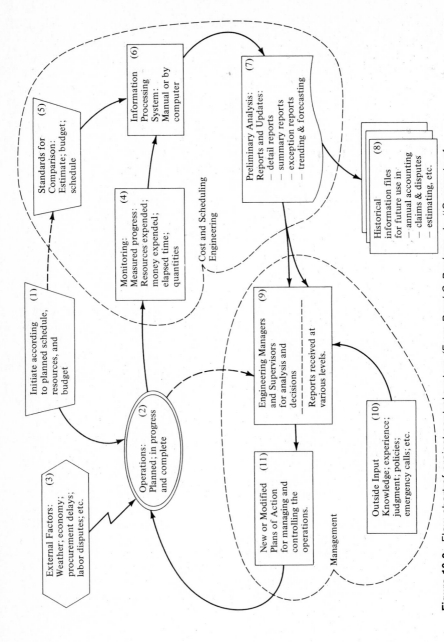

Figure 10-2 Flow chart of project control system *(From Boyd C. Paulson, Jr., "Concepts of Project Planning and Control," Journal of the Construction Division, ASCE, vol. 102, no. CO1, March 1976, p. 71.)*

6 To deliver the information to them in time for consideration and decision making so that, if necessary, corrective action may be taken on those operations that generated the data in the first place.

Project Planning and Control: A Model

The flowchart in Figure 10-2 models the operations, flow of information, and decision-making processes characteristic of a feedback control system appropriate for a medium to large sized engineering construction project. It has been designed to reflect the objectives stated in the preceding section.

Note that although this flowchart applies equally well in the conventional design and construction process where the two phases are largely separated, a control system of this type can have its greatest impact in the professional construction management approach where there is a strong interplay between all aspects of the system: concept; design; procurement; and construction. This approach is especially prevalent in the large heavy-industrial projects, such as refineries, mining developments and nuclear power plants, and in the commercial building field, with projects such as the New York World Trade Center and the Chicago Sears Tower. In structures of this type, engineers involved in design and those in construction interact continuously to optimize the facilities from both points of view.

Components In the flowchart, the project is initiated according to a predefined plan (box 1) and operations get underway (box 2). The plans also become reference standards for control purposes (box 5). As operations continue, external factors (box 3) such as recently imposed standards or newly available materials in design, or bad weather, strikes, procurement delays, foundation excavation problems, or even unexpectedly good conditions on the site, may cause the course of operations to differ from the plan, or may provide opportunities for improving on the plan. The operations underway generate indicators or progress (quantities in place, elapsed time, money expended, or resources consumed) which may be measured (box 4) and fed as data into a system (box 6) to produce information for decision makers. This information processing system refers to planned standards (box 5), such as schedules and budgets, to show deviations, variances, and trends. The information is analyzed and made available through reports (box 7), which may be stored for future reference (box 8), or given to engineering managers and supervisors for their further analysis and decision making (box 9), or both. They combine and compare this information with their own knowledge, experience, policies, and other qualitative and quantitative information and judgment (box 10) in order to produce new or modified plans for continuing and controlling the project operations (box 11).

Feedback This is a feedback control system, and it operates continuously throughout the life of a project. Associated with it is a feedback time. Ideally, the time through parts 4, 6, and 7 should be as short as possible so that engineering managers and supervisors can receive accurate and up-to-date information in time to make decisions and formulate plans of action so as to have maximum impact in controlling those operations which are generating the information in the first place.

On a small project, it is possible to short-circuit the path from box 2 to box 9 and provide direct feedback. A master builder who works with his own tools in constructing custom suburban homes is a common example of this. If something is wrong, he knows about it immediately.

On a large project, such as the design and construction of a rapid transit system or a nuclear power plant, direct feedback to the decision makers of all information on all activities is no longer possible. One needs a staff and an organized system to measure, process, analyze, and report the most important information to the decision makers. In engineering design and construction, this staff consists largely of scheduling engineers and cost engineers. Nevertheless, the goal remains to provide feedback to decision makers in minimum time for maximum impact in controlling operations. Needless to say, however, it is here that the industry experiences some of its greatest difficulties.

A major need in project planning and control is significantly to improve and expedite the operations represented by boxes 4, 5, 6, and 7 on the flowchart in order to help resolve these difficulties and improve the quality of information available to decision makers. On larger projects, some improvements are being made through computer applications. Indeed, like a neighborhood power outage on a cold winter's night, it almost takes a computer failure these days to dramatize the extent to which such projects are coming to take their computers for granted.

The following sections will focus on some of the key components of the system that has been described and will amplify some of the concepts presented in the model.

Status and Progress

Numerous measures can be taken to determine the progress or status of operations on a project. Quantities of work units in place can be physically surveyed and compared with those shown on the drawings. Elapsed *time* can be compared with the estimated activity or project durations. *Money* committed or expended can be compared with the estimated budget. *Resource usage* can be plotted versus expected requirements for labor, materials, and equipment. Finally, an experienced professional construction manager can simply apply his *judgment* to estimate the percentage completed on individual activities or on the project as a whole.

Each of these measures has its advantages and disadvantages. For example, field measurements may be more accurate than judgment estimates of percentage complete, but it is expensive to use a surveying crew to obtain these data. Judgment, in turn, can reflect qualitative factors, not evident in the quantities themselves. Just as pulse, temperature, blood tests, and x-rays give several different readings on the condition of one's body, each of the aforementioned measures tells something different about the project. All of them are necessary to gain a full understanding of the status and progress of the operations.

Nonlinear Relationships In applying such measures, it is important to recognize nonlinear relationships among them. For example, there may be a nonlinear relationship between quantities in place and elapsed time. To illustrate, if the bulk of the work is scheduled to be completed earlier in the activity's scheduled duration, then when the time is 50 percent elapsed, the work might actually and correctly be 60 percent complete. Similar nonlinear relationships apply among the other measures. The time at which money is expended on materials, for example, might be only loosely related to the actual time those materials are used.

When comparing the expenditure of labor resources over time, one can also often recognize nonlinear "learning-curve" effects. Learning curves relate time, resources consumed, and quantities produced. Their basic principle is that skill and productivity in performing tasks improve with experience and practice. The nonlinear implications of learning curves are different for planning, or estimating, than they are for control. Chapter 11 will discuss these concepts in greater detail.

Source of Data Data reflecting status and progress come from numerous sources. In the formal information system, sources include labor and equipment time cards, purchase orders, invoices, field quantity reports, quality control reports, and so forth. In all cases, accuracy, timeliness, and completeness are important. Human considerations are particularly essential at this point if good management information is to be produced.

In addition to the formal sources, there are numerous other inputs to management, some of which short-circuit most of the regular steps. If there is a serious accident on the job, the superintendent or project manager is told about it almost immediately. Similarly, a manager simply cannot wait for a computer printout to tell him the cofferdam is about to be overtopped. However, if the more routine aspects of planning and control are organized into an accurate and effective information system, management is in an even better position to cope with the unexpected events that inevitably occur.

Information Processing

Later chapters will go into the methods and techniques that are applied in analyzing data and converting them into useful information. Broad categories include activity and resource scheduling tools such as bar charts and critical path networks, cost engineering budgets and cash flows, materials procurement and tracking systems, and statistical quality control.

In concept, information processing systems take progress and status data, compare them against reference standards such as budgets or schedules, and convert the results to information needed by the managers and supervisors on the project. As stated in the objectives, the level of detail, the variety, and the frequency of reports to be produced should be appropriate to the people who will use them, should be feasible for the means of processing the information (manual or computer), should recognize the skills available, and should realistically assess the value of the information compared with the cost of obtaining it. Finally, the system should be fast, efficient, and accurate.

In practice, several related subsystems are needed fully to plan and control projects. Examples include activity and resource scheduling and control, cost engineering, materials procurement and tracking, and quality control. Each of these systems is important, but if fully integrated into one system, the sheer volume of data would dominate and obscure the vital information that is needed from any one of them. An interrelated modular system is thus essential. That is, each subsystem should be largely self-sufficient, but it should be logically coordinated and compatible with the others.

Consider the whole process from the point of view of a network-based subsystem for activity and resource scheduling and control. Costs, materials, and quality functions can also be identified with activities, so it is possible to use the activities as a means to tie into other systems. In summary, an information processing system for project planning and control should recognize that there are many subsystems involved in the process, and it should further recognize the interrelationships among those subsystems.

Reporting

Reporting can take many forms, ranging from conversations and telephone calls through tabular presentations of cost information and graphical presentations on bar charts, cumulative progress ("S") curves and CPM diagrams, to up-to-the-minute reports from computers transmitted via microwave or satellite telecommunication links to sophisticated terminals in the field. Certain basic principles should guide each of these, however, if the reporting is to be effective for control purposes.

Content   Regardless of the form, in order to be effective for control purposes, a complete report should have five main components:

1   *Estimates*: either total, to-date, or this period, that provide a reference standard against which to compare actual or forecast results
2   *Actuals*: what has already happened, either this period or to-date
3   *Forecasts*: based on the best knowledge at hand, what is expected to happen to the project and its elements in the future
4   *Variances*: how far actual and forecast results differ from those which were planned or estimated
5   *Reasons*: anticipated or unexpected circumstances that account for the actual and forecast behavior of the project and its operations, and especially that explain significant variances from the plans

The following paragraphs will discuss some related reporting principles in more detail.

Selectivity and Subreporting   One of the objectives stated previously was to report the correct and necessary information in a form which can best be interpreted by management and at a level of detail most appropriate for the individual managers who will be using the information. Selectivity and subreporting are important here. Since time is among their scarcest resources, construction managers and supervisors simply cannot afford to wade through piles of extraneous data to obtain the information they need. The concrete superintendent should have reports focusing on concrete operations. The project manager should have summary reports as well as logically coordinated detail reports to back them up.

Variances   Reports for control purposes should calculate variances to show which operations are relatively more in need of attention than others. "Variance" is used here to mean a deviation from a planned or budgeted item. The variances, in turn, should be expressible in both relative (percentage) and absolute (quantities, dollars, etc.) terms. For example, is it more important for a manager to focus attention on a $100,000 operation with an absolute variance of plus $2,000 (overrun) and a relative variance of plus 2 percent, or on a $10,000 operation with a relative variance of plus 15 percent and an absolute variance of $1,500? With both types of variance information, the manager can apply his judgment as he thinks best.

Management by Exception   By showing only those operations with variances or other parameters exceeding certain predefined limits, exception reports focus management attention directly upon those operations most in need of control. The principle here is to identify and isolate the most important and critical information for a given situation, and to give it to the right person as quickly as possible for his consideration, decisions, and action. To be truly effective, however, it is particularly important that exceptions be related to standards that are indeed accurate.

Forecasting and Trending   If management is to have clear vision ahead and be able to anticipate problems before they arise, reports must look to the future as well as document the past. Forecasting and trending are two means by which this is done. In network-based schedule and resource control, the network logic itself provides a vehicle for determining what effect a change in one operation will have on the project as a whole. Procurement and tracking systems should be similarly designed so that a superintendent does not arrive at work one morning to find that a critical 6-month lead-time item of equipment to be installed that day has not even been ordered yet. Related principles apply to other systems.

Feedback Time   In all the aforementioned cases, the information reported must be received in time so that, if necessary, corrective action may be taken on those operations that generated the information in the first place.

Example   Figure 10-3 shows an example report that illustrates many of the ideas mentioned here. First of all, note that the report is selective in showing only those operations that are of interest to the concrete superintendent. Second, it is an exception report showing only those items with variances exceeding 10 percent. The actual cutoff used here is variable. A great deal of information is shown for each operation, including estimated, actual, and projected schedule times, costs, quantities, and unit costs, as well as variances and trends. To some users, this may prove confusing and would therefore need to be simplified. However, if the format were standardized and applied not only for exception reports, but also for detail reports, subreports, summary reports, and so forth, users would quickly become accustomed to it and would learn to benefit from all the information shown. The complete status for an operation is all conveniently in one place.

The report uses multiple lines for each operation rather than having one long line with some 30 or 40 columns, as is typical of many manually prepared job progress reports. An obvious reason for this use of multiple lines is that the printers used by computers are generally limited to 120- or 132-character widths. However, certain advantages are inherent in this approach that may not be readily apparent. First of all, if additional information were to be added, such as work-hours by craft or equipment usage hours, or a breakdown of cost into labor, materials, equipment, and subcontracts, it could easily be inserted as additional lines where desired, yet still preserve the same basic and familiar appearance. Second, the close grouping of information in this way assists in a pattern-recognition process that will analyze reasons for apparent inconsistencies. For example, on a given item, the cost may show a 12 percent overrun and the quantity may show a 28 percent overrun, both high and possibly bad, yet the unit cost will be under the estimate, which ought to be good. If this is a unit-price item, all is well. If it is a lump-sum item, there apparently are problems. The format helps a manager to apply this type of reasoning quickly and take the appropriate action.

This report is presented only as an example and not as a recommended standard. It illustrates the type of information that might be provided to a manager for control purposes. The next section considers what a manager might do upon receiving this information.

Corrective Action

When a control report indicates that something is "wrong" with an operation, that is, that its measures are deviating significantly from the plan, management should first investigate to find and understand the reasons behind the symptoms reported. Assuming that the source of the problem can be identified, one alternative course of action, and often the best one, is basically to do nothing

EXCEPTION REPORT BASED ON COST VARIANCES

ACTIVITIES SHOWN HAVE VARIANCES GREATER THAN 10%

ACTIVITIES ARE SORTED AS FOLLOWS:

ES PRIMARY SORT

DUR SECONDARY SORT

PROJECT NUMBER: 198301
PROJECT TITLE: EXAMPLE CONCRETE BRIDGE
PROJECT LOCATION: STANFORD, CALIFORNIA

START DATE: 04/21/83
DATA DATE: 07/11/83
REPORT DATE: 07/14/83

LAB. CODE	ACTIVITY DESCRIPTION	UNIT	ESTI-MATED	ACTUAL TO DATE	EST. TO COMPL.	EST. TTL @ COMPL.	PERCENT COMPL.	FORECAST VARIANCE	PERCENT VARIANCE	TREND
CFF. 0310	**CONCRETE FORMWORK FOR FOUNDATION**	SF								
EST START: 06/02/83	DURATION:		34	29	9	38	76%	4	11.8%	HIGH
ACT START: 06/02/83	COSTS:		$49800	$47600	$14900	$62500	76%	$12700	25.5%	HIGH
EST FINISH: 07/18/83	QUANTITIES:		15860	13600	4150	17750	77%	1890	11.9%	HIGH
ACT FINISH: / /	UNIT COSTS:		$3.14	$3.50	$3.59	$3.52		$0.38	12.1%	HIGH
CRF. 0320	**CONCRETE RE-STEEL FOR FOUNDATION**	LB								
EST START: 06/09/83	DURATION:		29	21	9	30	70%	1	3.5%	HIGH
ACT START: 06/12/83	COSTS:		$39400	$31700	$13610	$45310	70%	$5910	15.0%	HIGH
EST FINISH: 07/18/83	QUANTITIES:		82400	74410	31890	106300	70%	23900	29.0%	HIGH
ACT FINISH: / /	UNIT COSTS:		$0.48	$0.43	$0.43	$0.43		-$0.05	-10.4%	LOW
CPF. 0330	**CONCRETE PLACING FOR FOUNDATION**	CT								
EST START: 06/16/83	DURATION:		34	16	21	37	43%	3	8.8%	HIGH
ACT START: 06/19/83	COSTS:		$73400	$35540	$46660	$82200	43%	$8800	12.0%	HIGH
EST FINISH: 08/01/83	QUANTITIES		1200	690	850	1540	45%	340	28.0%	HIGH
ACT FINISH: / /	UNIT COSTS:		$61.17	$51.51	$54.89	$53.38		-$7.79	-12.7%	LOW
CRW. 0320	**CONCRETE RE-STEEL FOR WALLS**	LB								
EST START: 06/30/83	DURATION:		34	9	26	35	26%	1	2.9%	LOW
ACT START: 06/30/83	COSTS:		$37800	$8320	$24940	$33260	25%	-$4540	-12.0%	LOW
EST FINISH: 08/15/83	QUANTITIES:		78750	19730	59170	78900	25%	150	0.2%	
ACT FINISH: / /	UNIT COSTS:		$0.48	$0.42	$0.42	$0.42		-$0.06	-12.2%	LOW

- - - END OF REPORT - - -

Figure 10-3 Example control report. (Adapted From Boyd C. Paulson, Jr., "Concepts of Project Planning and Control," *Journal of the Construction Division*, ASCE, vol. 102, no. CO1, March 1976, p. 77.)

except update the reporting system to reflect the reality on the job. Because of the dynamics of the operations on the project, the situation as it exists may actually be better in some ways than that which was planned. From day 1 onward, project management has more information than the planner had originally. The point here is that one should not take corrective action merely for the sake of making the job conform to the original plans. That is, budgets, schedules, and related standards are tools to be used by management. Returning to the earlier analogy, the driver, not the steering wheel, should control a car. Managers should use their control system as a guide, but they need flexibility and should be prepared to take advantage of and adapt to new conditions as they arise. Chapter 12 will have more to say on this subject.

SUMMARY

This chapter began by showing how the level of influence in determining and controlling costs drops rapidly as a project evolves from preliminary and detail design, through procurement and construction, to beneficial operation or utilization. The level of influence is by far the greatest during engineering and design, while actual expenditures at that stage are relatively small.

Understanding the level-of-influence concept can be helpful in forming contractual arrangements that minimize the suboptimization of costs for one party at the expense of overall project costs and benefits. Contractual arrangements should be drawn so as to be sure that current construction and even operations knowledge will be injected in the design process. Professional construction management and design-construct are two forms that, if appropriately tailored to the needs of the particular situation, can be useful for this purpose.

A second important conclusion is that efforts to suboptimize design costs by requiring competitive bidding for professional services are likely to produce much higher project costs in the long run. Owners need much more flexibility than this approach allows in selecting those professionals who can design structures producing maximum benefits for the lowest overall costs.

Both improved methods and the better application of existing principles are needed in the planning and control of engineering and construction projects. Using an analogy and a model, this chapter went on to explain basic concepts of the information feedback-control process used on well-managed projects. The objective was to provide a broad perspective against which to reference specific subsystems such as project planning and scheduling, cost engineering, materials procurement and tracking, and quality control. The chapter then amplified several key components of the feedback-control model, including means for measuring and controlling progress, information processing, requirements for effective reporting, and guidelines for taking corrective action.

The remaining nine chapters of Part 3 will explain in more detail each of the major methods and procedures available to the professional construction manager for planning and controlling projects. These include estimating project costs (Chapter 11), schedule and resource planning and control (Chapter 12), cost engineering (Chapter 13), procurement (Chapter 14), value engineering (Chapter 15), quality assurance (Chapter 16), computer applications (Chapter 17), safety and health (Chapter 18), industrial relations (Chapter 19), and a review of the current state of the art of professional construction management (Chapter 20). Although these subjects are developed in separate chapters, the reader should recognize by now that they are each highly interrelated and interdependent parts, each focusing on different aspects of the same overall project planning and control system.

Chapter 11

Estimating Project Costs

Chapter 10 showed how the costs of projects can be evaluated at several levels. These range from the construction contractor's costs for the time and resources consumed in building the structure itself, through the owner's overall costs not only for design and construction but for long-term operation and maintenance, and more broadly to the socioeconomic costs to society as a whole. This chapter will focus on costs associated with the capital facility; these primarily consist of design, procurement, and construction costs.

INTRODUCTION AND OVERVIEW

There are numerous methods and levels of accuracy for preparing capital cost estimates for a construction project. Each method has its appropriate applications and limitations, but it is important to recognize and emphasize that all estimates are approximations based upon judgment and experience. Even the final reported cost figures on completed projects will differ in detail from what the true costs really were, because considerable judgment is required in recording and allocating cost figures while operations are in progress.

Estimates range in scope and detail from "educated guesses" to contractor bid estimates. The latter are based on a relatively complete set of plans and specifications, and they involve much more than simply applying historical unit costs to computed quantities. Indeed, a thorough, accurate, and detailed estimate, especially in heavy and industrial construction, is much broader in concept than merely determining costs. To get the costs, the estimator must practically build the project on paper. He must assess quantities not only of the contract materials reflected in the drawings, but also of the temporary materials, such as formwork for concrete and temporary plant. The latter estimates, in turn, require that the estimator hypothesize alternative methods that could be used to build the different components of the project, determine the resources of labor, equipment, and materials that would be required by each method, evaluate the productivity and costs, and select those methods which, taken together, will complete the project on schedule and at the lowest overall cost.

It is also important to note that several different types of estimates are required as a project evolves. Clearly, a detailed estimate based on computed quantities cannot be made at the concept, feasibility study, or preliminary design stage, because the project itself is not yet defined in terms of the plans and specifications upon which computations of quantities are based. Furthermore, the estimating process itself becomes increasingly expensive as more detailed and accurate techniques are applied. Estimates for large projects sometimes cost hundreds of thousands of dollars. When the detail and accuracy are not required, simpler forms of estimating can suffice. Figure 11-1 shows a tabulation of estimate types and the level of information required for each.

This chapter will discuss the types of estimates that can be used during the evolution of a project under the professional construction management approach. In general, we will proceed from the less detailed to the more accurate estimates in the following categories:

1 Conceptual and preliminary estimates
2 Detailed estimates
3 Definitive estimates

The chapter will next present a more detailed discussion about estimating and controlling labor costs. We shall then introduce a new European approach to estimating that has promise for increasing the accuracy and reducing the time required for detailed estimates.

Estimates, in turn, become the reference standard for cost control when the project is executed, but for many good reasons they are not always used directly. The last portion of this chapter will therefore address considerations for converting an estimate into a control budget for a project.

CONCEPTUAL AND PRELIMINARY ESTIMATES[1]

Conceptual and preliminary estimates, as the name implies, are generally made

---

[1]The background for parts of this section, particularly the cost-capacity factor and component ratios, came from O. T. Zimmerman, "Capital Investment Cost Estimation," in chap. 15 in F. C. Jelen (ed.), *Cost and Optimization Engineering,* McGraw-Hill Book Company, New York, 1970.

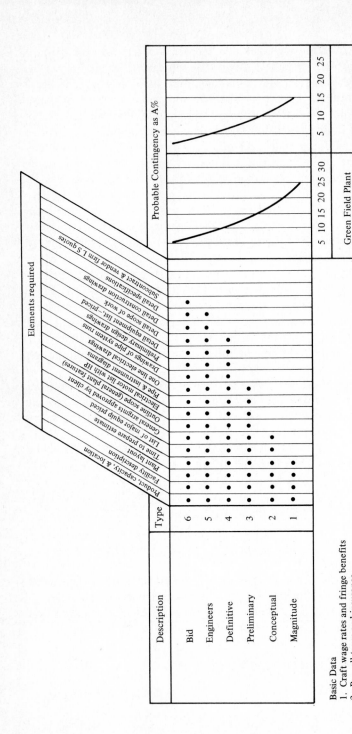

Figure 11-1 Estimate types. *(From Building Construction Handbook, 2d ed., 1975, McGraw-Hill Book Company.)*

178

in the early phases of a project. Initially they tell an owner whether a project of the scope he has in mind is anywhere near to being economically feasible. Once underway, say in the preliminary and detailed engineering phases, successively refined estimating techniques incorporate new information and thus keep a continuously updated estimate or budget available for control purposes. This in turn provides feedback to design to keep the overall project within budget.

Conceptual and preliminary estimating methods vary considerably from one type of construction to another. Generally the most sophisticated and accurate procedures have been developed for large projects in the industrial construction sector, but high levels of sophistication are also found in individual design firms, construction contractors, professional construction managers, and other sectors of construction as well.

Most of the existing conceptual and preliminary estimating methods fall into one or more of the following categories:

1 Time-referenced cost indices
2 Cost-capacity factors
3 Component ratios
4 Parameter costs

They are listed generally in ascending order of accuracy, and correspondingly in ascending order of cost and complexity to produce. The sections that follow will introduce each of these categories in turn.

Cost Indices

Cost indices show changes in cost over time. Some types also reflect changes in technology, methods, and productivity as well as inflationary trends. Generally they are applied to the construction phase of projects, though they can account for the total design-construction package as well. Many of these indices are published periodically in the technical press. The "Quarterly Cost Roundup," published by the *Engineering News-Record*, lists over a dozen of these, including its own well-known "Construction Cost Index" and "Building Cost Index."

Types of Cost Indices   The cost indices themselves are derived from two quite different approaches. The first periodically reprices and totals a constant package of resources that serve as *input* to a typical construction project. The index is computed by dividing this cost by the cost of the resources in a base reference period.

For example, the *Engineering News-Record*'s "Construction Cost Index" is computed as follows:

Components: 1088 board feet of lumber (2x4, S4S, 20-city average)
2500 pounds of structural-steel shapes, base mill price
2256 pounds of portland cement (bulk, 20-city average)
  200 man-hours of common labor (20-city average)

We can convert from one base period to another as demonstrated below:

"Current cost" = 3800 (assumed)
Base cost (1967) = 672

$$\text{Index on 1967 base} = \frac{\text{index to be converted}}{\begin{array}{c}\text{index of 1967 base}\\\text{relative to original}\\(1913 = 100)\text{ base}\end{array}} \qquad (11\text{-}1)$$

$$= \frac{3800}{672} \times 100\% = 565\%$$

The second approach is based on the cost of a completed construction project, such as a particular building, or else on a survey of completed unit costs of selected components of projects, such as concrete pavement for highways. In both cases, the index is based on the *output* of the construction process. From there on, however, the process of computing the index is similar to that of the index based on input components. That is, the cost of the project or unit under current conditions is divided by the cost in a base reference period. Both types of indices can be computed as national averages, or they can be computed for particular geographic areas. Examples of published output-type cost indices include those of the American Appraisal Company, the Austin Company, the George A. Fuller Company, and the Port Authority of New York and New Jersey. These and others are reported by the *Engineering News-Record.*

Limitations   Before applying cost indices, it is important to understand how they are derived, their limitations, and the differences in the basic methods. For example, there are obvious problems if the proportions of the input components in an input-type cost index do not reflect the resources used on the project in question. To illustrate, about 40 percent of the costs in a petrochemical project are in piping, yet neither pipe nor pipe fitters are included in the most widely used general cost indices. Similarly, where the index is based on the final (output) costs of a particular building, the project under consideration may have very little in common with that structure. One must also know whether factors such as land, interest on financing, and contractor's profit are included.

Other limitations become evident when one compares advantages and disadvantages of the two types of indices. For example, indices based on input components do not consider factors such as productivity, changes in technology, and competitiveness of contractors. These factors are reflected to some extent in indices based on project outputs, or completed structures. On the other hand, the output type of indices are usually much more narrow in scope, and it is difficult to interpret one based on, say, commercial office buildings, to apply it to another type of work, such as a concrete dam. The input type of indices is much more general and can thus be applied to a broader range of construction projects. In both indices, it is important to recognize their geographic and demographic bases. Both prices and productivity can vary radically around the country and around the world; competitive market conditions for suppliers and contractors can be strong in one type of construction, such as industrial, at the same time that they are weak in another, say, building.

For these and many other reasons, owners, designers, contractors and professional construction managers must use careful judgment and draw upon well-documented personal experience before applying any type of index for purposes of conceptual estimating. Wise firms maintain their own records and do their own studies as well as use published sources. Properly applied, however, such indices can yield accuracies within 20 to 30 percent of actual costs and can provide this information with almost negligible time and effort. Such information can be valuable for policy and planning decisions early in the life of a project.

Example   To illustrate the use of a cost index, let us apply *Engineering News-Record*'s "Building Cost Index" to a warehouse. Assume that we have an estimate on file for a similar structure that we completed in 1978 for a cost of $4,200,000. We were planning to build the new warehouse in 1982.

The ENR index for 1978, relative to a base date of 1967, was 1674/672 =2.49, or 249 percent. The projected index for 1982 was 2220/672 = 3.30, or 330 percent. Therefore, the estimated cost for a project of similar size will be

$$\frac{330\%}{249\%} \times \$4,200,000 = \$5,566,000$$

Recognizing the level of accuracy, we might round this to $5,600,000.

Cost-Capacity Factor

Whereas cost indices focus on cost changes over time, cost-capacity factors apply to changes in size, scope, or capacity of projects of similar types. They reflect the nonlinear increase in cost with size, as a result of economies of scale. In simple analytical terms, the cost-capacity factor is expressed by the following exponential equation:

$$C_2 = C_1 \left(\frac{Q_2}{Q_1}\right)^x \tag{11-2}$$

where C_2 = estimated cost of new facility of capacity Q_2
 C_1 = known cost of facility of capacity Q_1
and the exponent X = the cost-capacity factor for this type of work.

The exponents represented by X are empirically derived factors based on well-documented historical records for different kinds of projects. The capacities, represented by Q, are some parameter that reasonably reflects the size of the facility, such as maximum barrels per day produced by a refinery or tons of steel per day produced by a steel mill operating at capacity. In a structure such as a warehouse, gross floor area or enclosed volume might be a reasonable measure of capacity.

Table 11-1 Example Cost-Capacity Factors*

Process	Capacity	Unit	Cost-Capacity factor	Capacity range
Acetylene	10	Tons/day	0.73	3.5 - 250
Aluminum (from alumina)	100M	Metric Tons/yr	0.76	20M - 200M
Ammonia (by steam-methane reforming)	100	Tons/day	0.72	100 - 3M
Butadiene	10M	Tons/yr	0.65	5M - 300M
Butyl alcohol	100MM	Lb/yr	0.55	8.5MM - 700MM
Carbon black	1	Tons/day	0.53	1 - 150
Chlorine	100	Tons/day	0.62	10 - 800
Ethanol, synthetic	10MM	Gal/yr	0.60	3MM - 200MM
Ethylene	100M	Tons/yr	0.72	20M - 800M
Hydrogen (from refinery gases)	10MM	Cu ft/day	0.64	500M - 10MM
Methanol	10MM	Gal/yr	0.83	5MM - 100MM
Nitric acid (50-60%)	100	Tons/day	0.66	100 - 1M
Oxygen	100	Tons/day	0.72	1 - 1.5M
Power plants, coal	100	Mw(elec)	0.88	100 - 1M
Nuclear	100	Mw(elec)	0.68	100 - 4M
Styrene	10M	Tons/yr	0.68	4M - 200M
Sulfuric acid (100%)	100	Tons/day	0.67	100 - 1M
Urea	250	Tons/day	0.67	100 - 250
Urea	250	Tons/day	0.20	250 - 500

*Adapted from O.T. Zimmerman and I. Lavine, *Cost Eng.*, vol. 6, July 1961, pp. 16-18; O.T. Zimmerman, *Cost Eng.*, vol. 12, October 1967, pp. 12-19; and F.C. Jelen (ed), *Cost and Optimization Engineering*, McGraw-Hill Book Company, New York, 1970, p. 312.

Cost-capacity factors have been most widely used in the petrochemical sector of the industrial construction industry. The "six-tenths factor rule" ($X = 0.6$) is typical, and applies fairly accurately to some types of plants. Table 11-1 lists some other typical factors.

For our warehouse, cost varies fairly closely with floor area, so, for example purposes, assume first that a cost-capacity factor of $X = 0.8$ is representative of this type of work. Second, assume that we have a current estimate for a similar warehouse, located nearby, with a usable area of 120,000 square feet. Let us further assume that the prospective owner for the new warehouse wants a structure with a usable area of 150,000 square feet. Our estimate of the cost-capacity factor for the new warehouse can then be computed as follows:

$$C_2 = \$4,200,000 \left(\frac{150,000}{120,000} \right)^{0.8}$$

$$= \$5,020,000$$

$$\cong \$5,000,000$$

This is a very approximate and very preliminary estimate, but it would at least give the client an idea of the order of magnitude of what the cost of the new warehouse might be. Properly applied, and assuming well-documented empirical records, such estimates of the cost-capacity factor can be accurate to within 15 to 20 percent of actual costs.

It should be obvious at this stage that both cost indices and cost-capacity factors can be combined to take into account changes in both time and capacity. Our analytical formula can then be modified as follows:

$$C_2 = C_1 \times \left(\frac{I_2}{I_1}\right) \times \left(\frac{Q_2}{Q_1}\right)^x \tag{11-3}$$

where I_1 and I_2 are the relative cost indices for the times associated with the known and proposed facilities, respectively.

Assuming that $I_1 = 1.60$ and $I_2 = 2.15$ for the warehouse in question, thus putting off construction of the warehouse to some time in the future, the estimated cost will become

$$C_2 = \$4,200,000 \times \left(\frac{2.15}{1.60}\right) \times \left(\frac{150,000}{120,000}\right)^{0.8}$$

$$= \$6,746,000$$

$$\cong \$6,800,000$$

As with either approach taken alone, both extreme caution and judgment should be exercised in applying and interpreting estimates based on a combination of the two.

Component Ratios

As engineering and design progress, more information can be obtained about a project and its elements. Once the size and type of major items of installed equipment are identified, the designer or professional construction manager is in a position to solicit price quotations from the manufacturers of these components. Examples of equipment or plant components include compressors, pumps, furnaces, refrigeration units, belt conveyors, and turbine generators. Given good price quotations, designers and constructors in many sectors of industry, again especially in industrial construction, have good historical documentation and analytical techniques that enable them to improve the accuracy of their earlier conceptual estimates. To do this, they use techniques such as "equipment-installation-cost-ratios" or "plant-cost-ratios." We shall refer to both of these as "component ratios."

The first approach, equipment cost ratios, multiplies the purchase cost of the equipment by an empirically documented factor to estimate the installation cost of that equipment, including shipping, erection labor, and ancillary fittings and supplies. Table 11-2 lists some example equipment installation factors.

Table 11-2   Typical Equipment Installation Factors*

Item	Installation cost, %
Belt conveyors	20-25
Bucket elevators	25-40
Centrifugals, disk or bowl	5-6
Top suspended	30-40
Continuous	10-25
Crystallizers	30-50
Dryers, continuous drum	100[†]
Vacuum rotary	150-200[†]
Rotary	50-100[†]
Dust collectors, wet	220-450[†]
Dry	10-200[†]
Electrostatic precipitators	33-100[†]
Electric motors plus controls	60
Filters	25-45
Gas producers	45-250
Instruments	6-300
Ion exchangers	30-275[†]
Towers	25-50
Turbine generators	10-30

*Adapted from F.C. Jelen (ed.), *Cost and Optimization Engineering,* McGraw-Hill Book Company, New York, 1970, p. 316.
[†]Includes accessories.

These factors average around 50 percent of f.o.b. cost, but they range widely. With good records to base them on, this type of estimate can be accurate to within 10 to 20 percent of final costs.

Plant cost ratios, examples of which are given in Table 11-3, use equipment-vendor-price-quotations as a basis for determining the cost of the whole constructed facility. Two approaches can be used. In the first, the estimator adds the costs of all major items of equipment, and then multiplies this sum by a single ratio found to be appropriate for the type of project being constructed. For example, if the f.o.b. cost for all the equipment for a fluid process plant adds to $4,000,000, and a good historically valid plant cost ratio for this type of project is 4.5, then the estimated total cost will be

$$\$4,000,000 \times 4.5 = \$18,000,000$$

Clearly, the degree to which shop fabrication is used on the equipment items, the cost and productivity of field labor, and numerous other factors can seriously affect the accuracy of such estimates if the estimator lacks the judgment and experience to take them into account.

A variation on the plant cost ratio takes the cost of each major item of

Table 11-3 Process-Plant Cost Ratio from Individual Equipment*

Equipment	Factor†
Blender	2.0
Blowers and fans (including motor)	2.5
Centrifuges (process)	2.0
Compressors:	
Centrifugals, motor-driven (less motor)	2.0
Steam turbine (including turbine)	2.0
Reciprocating, steam and gas	2.3
Motor-driven (less motor)	2.3
Ejectors (vacuum units)	2.5
Furnaces (package units)	2.0
Heat exchangers	4.8
Instruments	4.1
Motors, electric	8.5
Pumps:	
Centrifugal, motor-driven (less motor)	7.0
Steam turbine (including turbine)	6.5
Positive displacement (less motor)	5.0
Reactors—factor as approximate equivalent type of equipment	
Refrigeration (package unit)	2.5
Tanks:	
Process	4.1
Storage	3.5
Fabricated and field-erected (50,000 + gal)	2.0
Towers (columns)	4.0

*From W. F. Wroth, "Factors in Cost Estimation," *Chem. Eng.*, vol. 67, October, 1960, p. 204; and F. C. Jelen (ed.), *Cost and Optimization Engineering*, McGraw-Hill Book Company, New York, 1970, p. 317.

†Multiply purchase cost by factor to obtain installed cost, including cost of site development, buildings, electrical installations, carpentry, painting, contractor's fee and rentals, foundations, structures, piping, installation, engineering, overhead, and supervision.

equipment separately, multiplies each by its own ratio, then takes the sum of the factored components. An example follows:[2]

Item	Cost	Factor	Plant cost
Blowers and fans	$ 10,000	× 2.5	$ 25,000
Compressors	50,000	× 2.3	115,000
Furnaces	100,000	× 2.0	200,000
Heat exchangers	80,000	× 4.8	384,000
Instruments	50,000	× 4.1	205,000
Motors, electric	60,000	× 8.5	510,000
Pumps	20,000	× 7.0	140,000
Tanks	125,000	× 2.4	260,000
Towers	200,000	× 4.0	800,000
Total	$685,000		$2,639,000

This approach allows the estimator to apply at a more detailed level judgment

[2]Adapted from Zimmerman, op. cit., pp. 317–318.

regarding such things as the degree of shop fabrication, and it can thus produce greater accuracy. This assumes, of course, that good historical data are available for developing the individual factors for each item of equipment.

Parameter Costs

Estimates based on parameter costs are most commonly used in building construction. *Engineering News-Record* usually publishes about five examples in each of its "Quarterly Cost Roundup" issues.

The parameter cost approach relates all costs of a project to just a few physical measures, or "parameters," that reflect the size or scope of that project. For example, the "gross enclosed floor area" would be a typical parameter for a structure such as a warehouse. General and specialty materials and labor costs, such as interior masonry, foundations, structural steel, roofing and flashing, heating and ventilating, and painting, would then be expressed in terms of unit prices related to the gross enclosed floor area, such as $0.12 per square foot for interior masonry. Note that this cost is not expressed as square feet of the masonry itself, but in relation to the building as a whole. A price related to the masonry itself would be a simple unit price and should not be confused with parameter costing. Nevertheless, with good historical records on comparable structures, parameter costing can give reasonable levels of accuracy for preliminary estimates.

To illustrate, Figure 11-2 provides parameter cost data for two buildings that are typical of those reported by *Engineering News-Record*. The first is an office complex; the second is a warehouse similar to our example project. Note that all costs associated with these buildings, including all the different trade items in the lower portion of the table, relate back to no more than 14 basic parameter measures, such as floor area, curtain wall area, heating, ventilating, and air conditioning (HVAC), etc. The warehouse, being a simpler structure, actually uses only 2 of the 14 possible measures: (1) gross enclosed floor area [which equals the gross area supported (2) and the roof area (4)], and (10) the area of curtain wall. The column headed "Code," under "Parameter cost," shows only codes 1 and 10 for all the trade items computed. The office complex, being a more complicated structure, uses parameters 1, 2, 4, 5, 10, 12, and 14 for computing costs, even though more are used to characterize the structure.

Note that this type of estimate requires at least schematic drawings sufficient for computing these few parameters. However, a parameter cost estimate can be prepared long before detailed drawings are complete. With this approach, an experienced estimator with access to well-documented records can quickly prepare an estimate and budget that will help influence the design and control costs in the early phases of a project.

DETAILED ESTIMATES

After conceptual design has been approved and after most or all of the detail design work is complete, approximate estimates are generally supplemented by detailed estimates. These normally require a careful tabulation of all the quantities for a project or portion of a project; this is called a "quantity takeoff." These quantities are then multiplied by selected or developed unit costs, and the resulting sum represents the estimated direct cost of the facility. The addition of indirect costs, plant and equipment, home-office overhead, profit, escalation, and contingency will develop the total estimated project cost. Since a careful takeoff can minimize or eliminate the unknowns regarding the amount of work to be performed, the margin for error is considerably reduced. Contingency requirements decrease since the cost of the work is the major variable left to the estimator's judgment.

Two types of detailed estimates will be explored in this section: the fair-cost estimate and the contractor's-bid estimate. Referring again to Figure 11-1, the fair-cost estimate is equivalent to the Type 5 engineer's estimate, and the contractor-bid estimate is equivalent to the Type 6 bid estimate.

Proper evaluation of labor productivity, effects of local practices, market competitiveness, weather conditions, and completeness of plans and specifications are extremely important in the preparation of detailed estimates. Significantly different appraisals of these factors can result in sizable differences in finished estimates based upon exactly the same quantity takeoff.

Fair-Cost Estimates

As mentioned in Chapter 8, fair-cost estimates for construction projects are best prepared from the actual bid documents provided to the bidders (before award) or used by the constructors (for changes). It is helpful to complete the fair-cost estimate well before receiving bids or before performance of change work. For an example of a fair-cost estimate for the Mountaintown Warehouse Project, please refer back to Figure 8-1.

The major differences between a professional construction manager's fair-cost estimate and a contractor's-bid estimate are (1) the absence of lump-sum subcontract quotations, and (2) a somewhat simplified number of line items. For example, in Figure 8-1, the markup included indirect costs, corporate overhead, profit, and contingency. A contractor estimate for the work would probably estimate the field indirect costs, might estimate or allocate office costs, and could establish separate profit and contingency (or risk) figures. The contractor estimate would also make separate provisions for material and subcontractor quotations, and for outside and company-owned equipment rentals.

However, a knowledgeable professional construction manager will prepare an equally accurate quantity takeoff and will choose the number of line items to be estimated on the basis of the objectives of the particular project and the level of detail required to achieve these objectives. On a professional construction management project, the fair-cost estimate is one of the primary tools in establishing a basis for measuring job progress and for the schedule and cost control discussed in Chapters 12 and 13. When properly applied, it can also result in productivity evaluation, permit comparison with contractor estimates,

	Office complex (d)	Health care facility	Hospital
Type of Building	Office complex (d)	Health care facility	Hospital
Location	Atlanta, Ga.	West Seneca, N.Y.	Cambridge, Minn.
Construction start/complete	May '74/Jun. '75	Feb. '74/Oct. '74	Jul. '75/Sept. '76
Type of owner	Private	Private	Public
Frame	Rein. concrete	Structural steel	Reinf. conc.: Precast
Exterior walls	Glass	Masonry	Glass: metal curtain wall
Special site work	None	None	None
Fire rating	NA	2 hr. part. & doors	NA

PARAMETER MEASURES:

	Office complex (d)	Health care facility	Hospital
1. Gross enclosed floor area	233,300 sf	59,500 sf	96,000 sf
2. Gross area supported (excl. slab on grade)	233,300 sf	59,500 sf	96,000
3. Total basement floor area	—	—	—
4. Roof area	77,800 sf	59,500 sf	50,000 sf
5. Net finished area	87,300 sf	259,000	81,000 sf
6. No. of floors including basements	3(f)	1	4
7. No. of floors excluding basements	3(f)		
8. Area of face brick	—	—	—
9. Area of other exterior wall	1,600 sf	5,800 sf	30,000 sf
10. Area of curtain wall incl. glass	85,800 sf	4,700 sf	5,000 sf
11. Store front perimeter	48 lf	105 lf	230 lf
12. Interior partitions	4,600 lf	—	—
13. HVAC	172 tons(f)	—	300 tons
14. Parking area	278,388 sf	10,500 sf	14,400 sf

OTHER MEASURES:

	Office complex (d)	Health care facility	Hospital
Area of typical floor	19,440 sf	59,500 sf	15,000 sf
Story height, typical floor	144 in	112 in	144 in
Lobby area	4,720 sf	600 sf	—
No. of plumbing fixtures	188	—	—
No. of elevators	8	—	4

DESIGN RATIOS:

	Office complex (d)	Health care facility	Hospital
A/C ton per building sq ft	.0007	—	.0031
Parking sq ft per building sq ft	1.1933	0.1765	.1500

Figure 11-2 Parameter cost estimates for five projects

TRADE	P1 Code	P1 Unit	P1 Cost	P1 Amount	P1 %	P2 Code	P2 Unit	P2 Cost	P2 Amount	P2 %	P3 Code	P3 Unit	P3 Cost	P3 Amount	P3 %
General conditions and fee	1	sf	1.13	263,957	6.09	1	sf	1.43	85,123	5.27	1	sf	1.89	181,600	4.87
Sitework (clearing and grubbing)	1	sf	0.21	49,729	1.15	1	sf	0.40	23,600	1.46	1	sf	0.21	20,000	0.54
Utilities	—	—	—	—	—	—	—	—	34,500	2.14	—	—	—	54,000	1.45
Roads and walks	—	—	—	3,071	0.07	—	—	—	14,600	0.90	—	—	—	—	—
Landscaping	1	sf	0.04	10,322	0.24	—	—	—	8,500	0.53	1	sf	0.53	50,500	1.35
Excavation	1	sf	0.04	9,816	0.23	1	sf	0.14	65,900	4.08	2	sf	0.94	90,000	2.41
Foundation	2	sf	0.41	94,896	2.19	2	sf	1.11	81,684	5.06	2	sf	0.31	30,000	0.80
Caissons and pilings	2	sf	4.48	1,045,682	21.12	—	—	—	—	—	—	—	—	—	—
Formed concrete	—	—	—	—	—	2	sf	1.37	85,000	5.27	2	sf	3.44	330,000	8.84
Exterior concrete	—	—	—	—	—	8	sf	14.66	850	0.05	8	sf	4.33	130,000	8.84
Interior masonry	12	sf	17.38	79,935	1.84	1	sf	0.01	—	—	2	sf	0.42	40,000	1.07
Stone, granite, marble	—	—	—	—	—	—	—	—	—	—	2	sf	1.20	115,000 (a)	3.08
Structural steel	2	sf	0.22	51,086	1.18	2	sf	1.69	100,794	6.25	—	—	—	—	—
Misc. metal, incl. stairs	2	sf	0.03	5,989	0.14	2	sf	0.13	7,750	0.48	2	sf	0.48	46,000	1.23
Ornamental metal	5	sf	0.48	41,651	0.96	—	—	—	—	—	—	—	—	—	—
Carpentry	—	—	—	1,122	0.03	5	sf	0.21	12,624	0.78	5	sf	0.27	22,000	0.59
A/C enclosures	—	—	—	—	—	4	sf	0.06	3,600	0.22	—	—	—	—	—
Waterproofing and dampproofing	4	sf	1.22	94,569	2.18	5	sf	1.03	61,000	3.78	4	sf	1.56	78,000	2.09
Roofing and flashing	5	sf	0.24	20,674	0.48	5	sf	0.27	70,485	4.37	5	sf	0.40	32,000	0.86
Metal doors and frames	—	—	—	—	—	5	sf	0.12	30,537	1.89	5	sf	0.33	27,000	0.72
Metal windows	—	—	—	—	—	—	—	—	—	—	5	sf	0.43	35,000	0.94
Wood doors, windows, and trim	5	sf	0.07	6,316	0.15	5	sf	0.09	23,100	1.43	5	sf	0.54	44,000	1.18
Hardware	5	sf	0.15	13,198	0.30	5	sf	0.02	4,875	0.30	5	sf	0.53	43,000	1.15
Glass and glazing	—	—	—	—	—	—	—	—	—	—	11	sf	217.39	50,000 (b)	1.34
Store front and lobby	—	—	—	—	—	—	—	—	—	—	—	—	—	—	—
Curtain wall	10	sf	6.38	547,099	12.62	—	—	—	—	—	5	sf	0.49	40,000	1.07
Lath & plaster	12	lf	41.85	192,490	4.44	5	sf	0.66	172,000	10.66	5	sf	2.72	220,000	5.90
Dry wall	5	sf	0.48	41,757	0.96	5	sf	0.05	12,800	0.79	11	lf	0.30	24,000	0.64
Tile work	—	—	—	—	—	—	—	—	—	—	—	—	—	—	—
Terrazzo	—	—	—	—	—	5	sf	0.10	24,970	1.55	5	sf	0.59	48,000	1.29
Acoustical ceiling	5	sf	1.01	88,211	2.03	5	sf	0.15	38,821	2.41	5	sf	0.52	42,000	1.13
Resilient flooring	5	sf	0.02	1,454	0.03	5	sf	0.10	24,625	1.53	—	—	—	15,000	0.40
Carpet	—	—	—	—	—	—	—	—	—	—	1	sf	0.42	40,000	1.07
Painting	1	sf	0.16	36,801	0.85	1	sf	0.07	1,111	0.07	5	sf	0.01	600	0.02
Toilet partitions	5	sf	0.23	19,744	0.46	—	—	—	—	—	—	—	—	—	—
Special waste treatment	—	—	—	—	—	—	—	—	—	—	—	—	—	—	—
Venetian blinds	—	—	—	—	—	—	—	—	—	—	—	—	—	—	—
Special equipment	—	—	—	—	—	—	—	—	—	—	—	—	—	78,258	2.10
Elevators	om,1	ea	22,566.63	180,533	4.16	1	sf	4.20	250,184	15.50	om,1	ea	30,000.00	120,000	3.22
Plumbing	1	sf	3.71	865,280	19.96	1	sf	1.33	79,136	4.90	1	sf	3.95	379,379	10.17
Sprinklers	—	—	—	—	—	—	—	—	—	—	—	—	—	—	—
HVAC	1	sf	1.68	392,700 (e)	9.06	1	sf	3.83	228,000	14.13	13	tons	2,366.33	709,900	19.03
Electrical: Contracts	—	—	—	—	—	—	—	—	—	—	5	sf	5.53	531,000	14.23
Fixtures	—	—	—	—	—	—	—	—	—	—	—	—	—	—	—
Miscellaneous trades	—	—	—	—	—	1	sf	1.14	67,541	4.19	1	sf	0.80	65,000 (c)	1.74
Parking: outside, encl.	—	—	—	—	—	—	—	—	—	—	—	—	—	—	—
Parking: open, paved	14	sf	0.64	176,916	4.08	—	—	—	—	—	—	—	—	—	—
TOTAL	1	sf	18.58	4,334,998	100.00	1	sf	27.12	1,613,710	100.00	1	sf	38.87	3,731,237	100.00

● (a) Precast concrete tees ● (b) store front only ● (c) store front only ● (d) four buildings ● (e) includes millwork, rails & special doors ● (f) each building

● (a) Precast concrete tees ● (b) store front only ● (c) includes millwork, rails & special doors ● (d) four buildings ● (e) included in plumbing ● (f) each building

Figure 11-2 Parameter cost estimates. (*From* "Parameter Costs Computed for Five Projects," Engineering News-Record, *vol. 196, no. 12, Mar. 18, 1976, pp. 83–84.*)

	Hospital	Warehouse
Type of Building	Hospital	Warehouse
Location	Dayton, Ohio	Southeast
Construction start/complete	Mar. '74/Sept. '75	Aug. '73/Sept. '74
Type of owner	Private	Private
Frame	Structural steel	Structural steel
Exterior walls	Veneer masonry	Precast
Special site work	None	None
Fire rating	Non combustible	NA

PARAMETER MEASURES:

	Hospital	Warehouse
1. Gross enclosed floor area	30,000 sf	256,900 sf
2. Gross area supported (excl. slab on grade)	30,000 sf	256,900 sf
3. Total basement floor area	2,000 sf	
4. Roof area	10,000 sf	256,900 sf
5. Net finished area	90,000 sf	
6. No. of floors including basements	4	
7. No. of floors excluding basements	3	
8. Area of face brick	25,000 sf	
9. Area of other exterior wall		
10. Area of curtain wall incl. glass		
11. Store front perimeter	18 lf	81,229 sf
12. Interior partitions	2,500 lf	
13. HVAC		
14. Parking area		

OTHER MEASURES:

	Hospital	Warehouse
Area of typical floor	144 ln	282 ln
Story height, typical floor	400 sf	
Lobby area		
No. of plumbing fixtures	1	
No. of elevators		

DESIGN RATIOS:

	Hospital	Warehouse
A/C ton per building sq ft		
Parking sq ft per building sq ft		
Plumbing fixtures as per building sq ft		

TRADE:	Parameter Cost: Code	Unit	Cost	Total Cost: Amount	%	Parameter Cost: Code	Unit	Cost	Total Cost: Amount	%
General conditions and fee	1	sf	$5.27	158.102	13.29	1	sf	$0.94	240.326	9.81
Roads and walks	—	—	—	20.185	1.70	—	—	—	*—	—
Excavation	3	sf	17.96	35.929	3.02	—	—	—	—	—
Foundation	2	sf	1.35	40.494	3.40	1	sf	1.39	357.997	14.62
Caissons and pilings	2	sf	1.55	46.551	3.91	1	sf	0.11	28.515	1.16
Formed concrete	2	sf	2.35	70.507	5.93	1	sf	0.06	15.988	0.65
Exterior masonry	8	sf	7.24	181.069	15.22	—	—	—	—	—
Interior masonry	—	—	—	—	—	—	—	—	—	—
Structural steel	2	sf	5.20	156.087	13.12	1	sf	1.13	289.853	11.83
Misc. metal, incl. stairs	2	sf	1.11	33.253	2.80	1	sf	0.15	38.361	1.57
Ornamental metal	5	sf	0.14	12.855	1.08	—	—	—	—	—
Carpentry	5	sf	0.12	10.521	0.88	—	—	—	—	—
Waterproofing and dampproofing	1	sf	0.25	7.358	0.62	—	—	—	—	—
Roofing and flashing	4	sf	2.11	21.147	1.78	1	sf	1.97	505.978	20.66
Metal doors and frames	5	sf	0.16	13.992	1.18	1	sf	0.06	15.136	0.62
Metal windows	5	sf	0.12	10.936	0.92	—	—	—	—	—
Wood doors, windows, and trim	5	sf	0.13	11.507	0.97	—	—	—	—	—
Hardware	5	sf	0.29	25.906	2.18	—	—	—	—	—
Glass and glazing (total)	5	sf	0.16	14.500	1.22	1	sf	0.02	4.672	0.19
Store front and lobby	11	lf	61.11	1.100	0.09	10	sf	3.13	253.889	10.37
Curtain wall	—	—	—	—	—	—	—	—	—	—
Lath and plaster	12	lf	50.29	125.729	10.57	1	sf	0.01	3.249	0.13
Drywall	—	—	—	—	—	1	sf	0.10	26.585	1.09
Tile work	5	sf	0.09	8.300	0.70	—	—	—	—	—
Terrazzo	5	sf	0.24	21.925	1.84	1	sf	0.01	3.083	0.13
Acoustical ceiling	5	sf	0.12	11.210	0.94	—	—	—	—	—
Resilient flooring	5	sf	0.05	4.252	0.36	—	—	—	—	—
Carpet	—	—	—	—	—	1	sf	0.13	32.580	1.33
Painting	5	sf	0.19	17.462	1.47	—	—	—	—	—
Toilet partitions	5	sf	0.04	3.155	0.27	1	sf	0.01	2.148	0.09
Special equipment	—	—	—	59.165	4.97	1	sf	0.17	44.747	1.83
Plumbing	—	—	—	(a)		1	sf	0.39	99.692	4.07
Sprinklers	—	—	—	(a)		1	sf	0.61	156.805	6.40
HVAC	—	—	—	(a)		1	tons	0.42	107.890	4.40
Electrical: Contracts	—	—	—	(a)		1	sf	0.30	76.282	3.11
Electrical: Fixtures	—	—	—	(a)		1	sf	0.34	86.789	3.54
Miscellaneous trades	1	sf	—	66.534(b)	5.59	1	sf	—	58.743	2.40
TOTAL	1	sf	39.66	1.189.731	100.00	1	sf	9.53	2.449.308	100.00

● (a) not included in contract ● (b) includes demolition, $15.730, skylights, $4.807, millwork $4.439, vibration isolation, $15.238, fireproofing, $26.320

Figure 11-2 (continued)

and assist in continually updating the professional construction manager's estimating knowledge and skills.

Contractor's Bid Estimate

The contractor's-bid estimate is his foundation for a successful project. He must bid low enough to obtain the work, yet high enough to make a profit.

Many people in the construction industry think of estimating as a more or less structured undertaking like engineering design. But a look at bids received for a typical project in a competitive area will sometimes show more than a 50 percent difference between the low and high bidders. When large amounts of subbids are involved, the spread tends to be smaller because most bidders will use the most competitive subcontractors.

For many years, numerous successful smaller contractors were able to compete effectively using the unit-cost system in which overall unit costs, including costs of labor, material, equipment, and overhead, were applied directly to actual quantity takeoffs. However, with the sharp price changes for all components in recent years, this method is becoming increasingly rare in successful companies. Almost all successful contractors now estimate new projects with separate categories and evaluations for labor, materials, equipment usage, and subcontractors.

In one way, bid estimates are sometimes less detailed than fair-cost estimates. Subcontractors often account for some 30 to 80 percent of the project. The general or prime contractor does not usually prepare a detailed cost estimate for this work, but rather, merely incorporates the low bidders' quotations in his own proposal. General contractors acting as professional construction managers, however, must develop in-house estimating capability for electrical, plumbing, piping, roofing, and other specific work which is not normally estimated by the traditional general contractor.

Figure 11-3 (pp. 194 and 195) shows the low bidder's competitive contractor estimate for the structural steel work on the Mountaintown Warehouse, and can be compared with the construction manager's fair-cost estimate shown in Appendix A.

DEFINITIVE ESTIMATES

As a project evolves, initial approximate estimates become more refined and more accurate as additional information is developed. Finally, there comes a time when a definitive estimate can be prepared that will forecast the final project cost with little margin for error. This error can be minimized through the proper addition of an evaluated contingency.

Projects can be separated into four broad categories for purposes of reviewing definitive estimates:

1   Unit-price projects
2   Traditional
3   Design-construct

4 Professional construction management

Each of these classifications will be discussed below.

Unit-Price Projects

These projects usually encompass heavy construction jobs such as dams, tunnels, highways, and airports. Here the prices have been set constant, while quantities vary within limits inherent in the nature of the work. Quantities may overrun or underrun owing to a number of potential causes, such as additional foundation excavation to solid rock, poor ground conditions, excessive water in tunnels, or other factors usually associated with the anticipated accuracy of geological and geophysical interpretation.

In the event of favorable readings on market conditions, project location, history of similar projects, project duration, duration of collective bargaining agreements, and numerous other factors, a true definitive estimate can be developed before going out for bids and prior to completion of the detailed design. On the other hand, in the absence of firm collective bargaining agreements, with sketchy geological data and an unsettled price structure, a truly definitive estimate may not be possible until the project is well underway.

For heavy construction work featuring reasonably accurate geological exploration accompanied by accurate interpretations, the estimate may be considered to be definitive at the time bids are received. Even here, however, the estimate should be accompanied by an evaluated contingency to allow for potential quantity increases. On the other hand, if geological work was either inadequate or was subject to faulty interpretations, and if this factor can cause significant differences in the cost and time involved in performing the work, a reasonably accurate definitive estimate from the owner's standpoint may not be obtainable until after the contractor's costs are known and agreement to a price change is achieved.

In the extreme, where there is lack of agreement on whether or not the character of the work has changed, the final costs may not be estimated accurately until the results of lengthy and costly litigation are known.

Traditional Projects

Projects in this category include lump-sum, guaranteed maximum-price, and cost-plus-a-fee negotiated contracts.

On lump-sum projects, the definitive estimate can be developed, in the absence of changed conditions, using the low bidder's quotation plus an evaluated contingency to cover anticipated changes.

On negotiated projects featuring a guaranteed maximum price, this price is often fixed at a point somewhere between the requirements of a Type 4 or Type 5 estimate, in the terminology of Figure 11-1. Most, but not all, of the detailed drawings are usually complete; firm subcontracts have been obtained for a sizable portion of the work; and an evaluated contingency is added to allow for the remaining unknowns.

On negotiated cost-plus-a-fixed-fee construction projects, a definitive

Title **Mountaintown Warehouse**

Client **Easyway Grocery Co.**   Location **M'taintown, WA**

Subject **Structural Steel Estimate Summary**

			Units			
Code	Description	Quantity	Man-hours	Labor	Material	Equipment
	Fabricate in Shop			@ 24.00/Hr		
	Beams & columns	280 Ton	10 Hrs/Ton	240	620	100
	Roof joists-purch.	200 Ton	—	—	780	
	Detailing, etc.	300 Hr		20.00		
	Subtotal directs	480 Ton				
	Shop overhead	80% Labor		1.60		
	Estimated cost					
	Profit & overhead	12.5%				
	Estimated shop price					
	Erection & Field					
	Steel Erection Crew					
	1 Foreman	1 @ 35.00		35.00		
	4 Ironworkers	4 @ 31.50		126.00		
	1 Operator	1 @ 35.00		35.00		
	1 Oiler	1 @ 29.50		29.50		
	2 Ironworkers	2 @ 31.50		63.00		
	9 Total Crew		9 Hr @ 32.06 = 288.50			
	Furnish Fab Steel	480 T			L.S.	
	Erect struct. Steel	280 T	7 Hrs/Ton	224.00		
	Erect joists Steel	200 T	5 Hrs/Ton	160.00		
	Equipment Usage	2.0 Mos.				12000
	Misc. supp. & tools	10% Labor				
	Deck—subcontract	L.S.				
	Estimated cost					
	Profit & overhead			20%	3%	—
	Estimated price					
	Final bid price					

Figure 11-3 Structural steel-bid estimate summary.

estimate can generally be prepared at approximately the same period as was possible for the guaranteed maximum price.

Design-Construct Projects

Design-construct projects can be generally divided into lump-sum, guaranteed maximum-price, and cost-plus-a-fixed-fee categories similar to the traditional approach.

Lump-sum contracts on design-construct projects can be extremely misleading to an unknowledgeable owner. Basing his decisions on performance criteria, a designated amount of floor space, or other parameters, the design-constructor (or engineer-contractor) agrees to provide a facility for a fixed price. Unless the details of the components of the facility are fully described

Job No. _____

Date _____   By _____

Sheet _____   Of _____

Man-hours	Labor	Material & subs	Equipment	Total
2,800	67,200	173,600	28,000	268,800
		156,000		156,000
300	6,000			6,000
3,100	73,200	329,600	28,000	430,800
	58,600			58,600
	131,800	329,600	28,000	489,400
				30,600
				550,600
			Say	550,000

Schedule Computations

$$\frac{2960 \text{ Hrs}}{72 \text{ Hrs/crew day}} = 41 \text{ days}$$

$$= 8.2 \text{ weeks}$$

$$\text{duration} = 2.0 \text{ months}$$

Man-hours	Labor	Material & subs	Equipment	Total
		550,000		550,000
1,960	62,800			62,800
1,000	32,000			32,000
			24,000	24,000
		9,400		9,400
		142,000		142,000
2,900	94,800	701,400	24,000	820,200
	19.000	21,000		40,000
				860,200
			Use	860,000

Figure 11-3 (continued).

and specified in the contract, the owner may find that he has purchased a facility which, while meeting the contract conditions, is much less than he thought he was getting. On the other hand, if the lump sum is fixed after substantial design work is complete, much of this objection disappears and the situation becomes quite similar to the guaranteed maximum-price condition.

On negotiated projects featuring a guaranteed maximum price, the definitive estimate can generally be prepared at about the same time as on a negotiated project. Because one entity is performing both design and construction, it may be able to develop such an estimate with less detail design than in the traditional approach.

On heavy industrial projects where the process equipment forms a major share of the cost, a definitive estimate can often be prepared with reasonable accuracy after a detailed scope of work has been developed and after all major equipment has been purchased. This situation is illustrated in Figure 11-1 as a Type 4 estimate.

On negotiated projects featuring a cost-plus-a-fixed-fee contract, the definitive estimate can generally be prepared at about the same time as in the guaranteed maximum-price situation.

Professional Construction Management Projects

Definitive estimates for professional construction management projects can be accurately prepared about the same time as the guaranteed-maximum or cost-plus-a-fixed-fee option under the traditional or the design-construct approach. Because of the interrelationships among progress measurement, schedule, and cost control, it is very helpful to have fair-cost estimates for a majority of the contracts prior to completing the definitive estimate so that the base for the control system will be as accurate as possible.

The definitive estimate for the Mountaintown warehouse project whose Summary Cost Report was shown in Figure 8-3 was issued when physical progress on the project was 9.6 percent complete. At this time eight fair-cost estimates had been prepared and eight contracts had been awarded. Detailed design was about 95 percent complete.

The application of a proper contingency is an important part of any definitive estimate. Figure 11-4 shows the development of an evaluated contingency for an industrial project. Figure 11-5 shows a definitive budget estimate and cost summary for a major project.

ESTIMATING AND CONTROLLING CONSTRUCTION LABOR COSTS[3]

One of the most difficult aspects of preparing a fair-cost estimate, a detailed definitive estimate, or a control budget based on the estimate is the labor component. This section therefore outlines basic principles and concepts for estimating and controlling field labor costs on construction projects. The basic approach is to divide labor costs into two main components and develop them separately. These components are (1) prices in money terms and (2) productivity. Both are essential to determining labor costs. For purposes of comparison, the concepts of "estimating" and "control" will be developed in parallel. Chapters 12 and 13 will deal more extensively with the control phase itself.

Components of Labor Costs

Two major factors determine labor costs in construction work. The first is the money or prices associated with hourly wages, fringe benefits, payroll insurance and taxes, and wage premiums. Though calculations of the money components can be complex, most of the parameters can at least be readily and accurately quantified. The second factor is productivity, the amount of work that a worker or crew can accomplish in a defined period of time. Of the two

---

[3]From B. C. Paulson, Jr., "Estimating and Controlling Construction Labor Costs," *Journal of the Construction Division*, ASCE, vol. 101, no. CO3, September 1975, pp. 623–633.

Description	Amount	Factor	Evaluation
Open commitments	$7,259,128	3	$ 216,000
Estimate to complete:			
Direct accounts			
Earthwork	706,000	20	141,200
Concrete	878,000	20	175,600
Architectural	604,000	20	120,800
Mechanical	1,160,000	10	116,000
Piping	732,000	10	73,200
Electrical	715,600	10	71,600
Equipment purchase	366,000	10	36,600
Contractors field overhead	701,200	10	70,000
Construction plant	21,000	10	2,000
Engineering, Supervision, and procurement		Allow	30,000
Escalation	170,000	10	16,000
Start		Allow	400,000
Special exposures			
Contractor ABC claim		Allow	95,000
Total			$1,564,000

Contingency Evaluation
Format for evaluating the cost exposures (unknown) not covered or anticipated in the current estimate to complete. Evaluation is based on applying "experience factors" to the remaining work and estimated cost.

Figure 11-4 Typical contingency evaluation (as of October).

main factors, productivity is by far the harder to determine. While wages and other money components may stay essentially constant over the duration of an operation, productivity can fluctuate wildly. To estimate and control productivity, one not only needs accurate, consistent, and up-to-date records, but a great deal of experience and judgment as well.

The basic mathematics for labor costs is quite simple. For example, assume the following:

Price of all money elements $= P$ ($/hour)
Productivity of labor $= q$ (units/hour)
Combining these and dividing gives:

$$\text{Unit labor cost} = \frac{P \text{ \$/hour}}{q \text{ units/hour}}$$

$$= P/q \text{ (\$/unit)} \tag{11-4}$$

Control account number	Description	Recorded costs		Open commitments	Cumulative total recorded & committed	Estimated Cost		Budget	Under or over budget
		Current period	Cumulative to date			To complete	At completion		
	Direct Cost								
1000.0000	Site development and improvements	$ 64,430	$ 2,558,396	$ 264,332	$ 2,822,728	$ 202,994	$ 3,025,722	$ 3,075,600	$(49,878)
2000.0000	Buildings and structures	1,204,598	12,551,752	495,366	13,047,118	1,254,954	14,302,072	14,470,000	(167,928)
3000.0000	Process equipment and systems	457,672	3,462,266	3,401,458	6,863,724	1,676,758	8,540,482	8,720,000	(179,518)
4000.0000	Utilities distribution	221,120	3,650,100	2,505,204	6,155,304	1,506,696	7,662,000	7,631,800	30,200
6000.0000	Distributable directs	82,456	613,378	592,768	1,206,146	690,244	1,896,390	2,000,600	(104,210)
	Total direct cost	$2,030,276	$22,835,892	$7,259,128	$30,095,020	$5,331,646	$35,426,666	$35,898,000	$(471,334)
	Indirect Cost								
7100.0000	Contractors field services	$ 51,578	$ 677,790	$ 21,000	$ 698,790	$ 701,210	$ 1,400,000	$ 1,446,000	$(46,000)
7200.0000	Construction plant	22,914	128,546	6,334	134,880	21,120	156,000	156,000	0
7300.0000	Construction equipment	19,228	95,498	2,502	98,000	0	98,000	100,000	(2,000)
	Total indirect cost	$ 93,720	$ 901,834	$ 29,836	$ 931,670	$ 722,330	$ 1,654,000	$ 1,702,000	$(48,000)
	Total construction cost	$2,123,996	$23,737,726	$7,288,964	$31,026,690	$6,053,976	$37,080,666	$37,600,000	$(519,334)
8100.0000	Engineering, supervision and procurement	$ 34,674	$ 1,898,790	0	$ 1,898,790	$ 201,210	$ 2,100,000	$ 2,200,000	$(100,000)
8900.0000	Contingency	0	0	0	0	1,564,000	1,564,000	3,600,000	$(2,036,000)
9000.0000	Clearings	$ (2,608)	$ 7,142	4,060	$ 11,202	$ (11,202)	$ 0	$ 0	0
	Total project	$2,156,062	$25,643,658	$7,293,024	$32,936,682	$7,807,984	$40,744,666	$43,400,000	$(2,655,334)

This report is a monthly summary (highest level) of cost, estimates, and comparisons to budget prepared for distribution

Figure 11-5 Project cost summary.

Productivity can also be expressed in terms of worker-hours per unit of output (W hours/unit, where $W = 1$), in which case one would multiply the two elements to obtain unit cost:

$$\text{Unit labor cost} = P \; \frac{\$}{\text{hour}} \times W \; \frac{\text{hours}}{\text{unit}}$$

$$= P \times W \; (\$/\text{unit}) \tag{11-5}$$

By multiplying the unit cost times the total quantity (Q) of work associated with the operation, one obtains the total labor cost for the operation:

$$\text{Total labor cost} = Q \times P/q \; (\$) \tag{11-6}$$

or

$$= Q \times P \times W \; (\$) \tag{11-7}$$

The mathematics at this stage is trivial and thus belies the complexity of estimating and controlling labor costs. The difficulty, of course, is in finding and calculating the correct prices of the money elements (P), and in determining the productivity (q or W) of labor. The following sections will discuss these subjects in much greater detail.

Estimating and Controlling the Money Component

Estimating the money component of labor costs is more difficult in construction than in any other United States industry. Reasons for this situation include the scope and variety of the work involved, the craft structure of labor unions, and the regional and local autonomy of labor and employer collective bargaining units. There are literally thousands of different wage rates, fringe benefits, insurance rates, and work rules, and there are exceptions to almost all of them. Superimposed upon this are federal, state, and local laws, taxes, and special programs such as wage-and-price control.

Even if given identical money elements for labor, contractors vary widely in the way they analyze, combine, and distribute them for estimating and control purposes. Some prefer to put all elements into a direct hourly rate. Others prefer to split off various elements into the "indirect" or "overhead" category. Some estimate by craft and some by crew. Some combine scheduled overtime with straight time to produce an "average" hourly rate, and some keep them separate. There is not one, but several, correct methods, and there are generally good reasons why a particular contractor uses a specific method in his own type of work. Therefore, rather than present a single method, this section will outline the major money elements which should be recognized in any approach. They include basic wages, fringe benefits, payroll insurance and taxes, and wage premiums. We will also point out some of the more subtle factors which are often overlooked in calculating these elements.

This material will be presented mostly in terms of conventional union-labor construction work. Many of the principles will apply equally well to "open-shop" construction.

Basic Wages   Basic wages vary by location, by craft, and, in many cases, by type of work within each craft. They also vary with time, both from increases scheduled within existing labor agreements and through increases to be negotiated in future contracts. For purposes of estimating, the contractor must determine the applicable location and labor agreement(s), the type of craft(s) to perform the desired work (this is often difficult in borderline jurisdictional cases), the appropriate classifications within the craft(s), and the wage rate(s) applicable at the time the work is to be done. This last item may itself have to be estimated if an agreement is not yet available for the time planned.

For purposes of control, the contractor cannot have much direct effect on the basic wage, except to be sure that he has the proper craftsmen and classifications for the work being done. That is, if all other things are equal, he should not use a higher-paid worker where a lower-paid worker is permitted. The contractor can have some indirect effect by working through and supporting his collective bargaining association when new labor agreements are being negotiated.

Fringe Benefits   Fringe benefits paid to workers variously include contributions to funds for health insurance, vacations, pensions, dental plans, apprenticeship training, industry advancement, and numerous others. They vary widely by region and by craft. As with basic wages, for estimating the contractor must determine the applicable location and agreement(s), crafts and classifications, and timing of the work. Similarly, for control he cannot have much direct effect on the fringes and must be sure that he complies with, but does not unwittingly exceed, the agreement.

Insurance Based on Payroll   Several kinds of insurance and related programs are based directly on payroll. These include workmen's compensation, public liability, property damage (WC, PL, and PD), social security benefits (FICA, employer's contribution), and state disability and unemployment insurance (SDI, employer's contributions).

WC, PL, and PD premiums are quoted on the basis of rate per $100 of direct (straight-time equivalent) payroll. Standard manual rates vary from about $2 to over $40 per $100.

For estimating and controlling WC, PL, and PD premiums, two important facts should be recognized. First, the premiums charged to a particular contractor vary significantly with the frequency, severity, and size of risk characterized in his accident record. His actual rates can vary from less than half to more than double the manual rate. Therefore, efforts made to minimize accidents can yield direct financial returns in lower insurance premiums and accident costs. Indirect benefits have been estimated to be 4 to 7 times this amount.[4,5]

The second important factor regarding WC, PL, and PD rates is that they vary widely with the classification (and hazardousness) of work. Records which accurately document the type of work being done by individual employees can be used to significantly reduce costs. For example, the rate for the general classification "high-rise concrete building construction" might be $18 per $100 base payroll. However, a carpenter building prefabricated forms in an on-site, grade-level shop on the same job might qualify for a much lower rate—say $4 per $100. If the contractor's cost system could document this fact, he could save $14 per $100 on this person's WC, PL, and PD insurance premium.

FICA and most SDI contributions are calculated as a percentage (6.70 percent for FICA in early 1982) of gross wages, including premium time. This amount is both subtracted from the employee's pay and added to the employer's payroll burden, so the net contribution is double the percentage shown. The important thing to recognize here about the FICA and SDI contributions is that there is an upper cutoff value above which payments no longer must be made. For example, the FICA ceiling in early 1982 was $32,400. If a construction craftsman moves from one employer to another, he may wind up paying more than required. However, like any other taxpayer, he can reclaim any excess on his income tax return. His employer, unfortunately, lacks the documentation to reclaim his excess payment. However, had the employer been able to offer continuous employment, he may have been able to reduce or avoid excess payments.

Taxes Based on Payroll Taxes based on payroll include federal income tax, state income tax, and sometimes local taxes. For the most part, these are deductions withheld from the employee's earnings and, unlike FICA, there is no matching employer's contribution. Therefore, such taxes are more a matter for payroll accounting than they are for estimating and control.

Wage Premiums Wage premiums include extra money paid for overtime work, shift-work differentials, and premiums for hazardous or unusually arduous work. Overtime work in construction is paid at a minimum of time and a half (150 percent of base), is increasingly paid at double time (200 percent), and in some cases, especially on holidays, at triple time (300 percent). Ordinarily, overtime is paid for work in excess of a 40-hour, 5-day week, but the base period may be less. For example, in some areas electricians have been paid overtime for work in excess of a 25-hour week.

[4]H. Knox, "Construction Safety as It Relates to Insurance Costs," *AACE Bulletin*, vol. 16, no. 3, June 1974, pp. 71–73.

[5]Michael R. Robinson, *Accident Cost Accounting as a Means of Improving Construction Safety,* Technical Report No. 242, Stanford University, Dept. of Civil Engineering, The Construction Institute, Stanford, Calif., August 1979.

There are several ways of paying a premium for multishift work. One way is to pay an extra percentage of the base wage for afternoon shift (swing) and night shift (graveyard) work. A common method encountered in the western states, as an example, is to give 8-hours' pay for the first 7 or 7$^{1}/_{2}$ hours work, and overtime thereafter.

Premiums for hazardous or unusually arduous work are commonly paid as a fixed increase over the base wage rate. For example, cement masons working on a swinging scaffold more than 25 feet above grade might receive an extra $0.70 per hour. Electricians might get an extra $1.20 per hour when working underground. A crane operator might get an extra $0.80 per hour if the boom is over 185 feet long. These rates would in turn be multiplied along with the base wage for overtime and multishift work.

In estimating premium costs, the most important thing is to thoroughly understand all the implications of the relevant labor agreements and government legislation. When it comes to control, there is a great deal that can be done by the contractor. Discussion of most of this area will be deferred to the section on productivity. However, to illustrate briefly the money side for overtime and shift differentials, the alternatives are shown on Figure 11-6. Curve *A* shows the average hourly wages for working 8 hours straight time at $10 per hour. Curve *B* shows the increasing average hourly wages for working 9, 10, up to 16 hours, with double time paid for overtime in excess of 8 hours. Curve *C* shows the average hourly cost for working two 8-hour shifts under the premium clause: "pay 8 hours for the first 7 hours' work, and double time thereafter." Curve *D* shows the average hourly cost for working two 10-hour shifts under the conditions defined for curve *C*. These simplified examples use base wages and premiums only. They ignore fringes, insurance, etc. Most important, they ignore the reduced productivity which is encountered with premium work. Nevertheless, they do illustrate several important concepts. Readers may be interested to calculate the percentage increases incurred and the break-even points encountered under various conditions when using the terms of their own local labor contracts.

Estimating and Controlling Labor Productivity

In contrast with the money component of labor costs, productivity is much more difficult to estimate. Many of the factors influencing labor productivity are highly qualitative in nature, and a great deal of experience and judgment is needed to develop the type of quantitative information that is required. However, the productivity component also offers the contractor by far the greatest opportunity to control his labor costs, assuming that he has some basic understanding for the factors that influence this variable in the equation.

This section will discuss some of these factors and the principles and concepts related to them. It includes the effect of location and regional variations, the learning curve, work schedule (overtime and multishift), work rules, weather and other environmental effects, experience of the craftsmen employed, and management factors such as job morale, safety, and motivation.

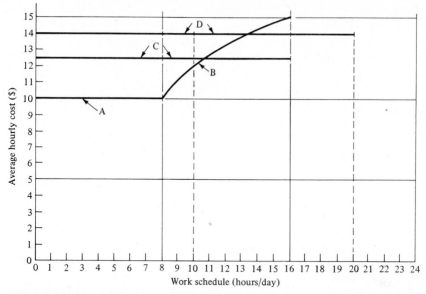

Figure 11-6 Impact of wage premiums on average labor costs. *From Boyd C. Paulson, Jr., "Estimation and Control of Construction Labor Costs," Journal of the Construction Division, ASCE, vol. 101, no. CO3, September 1975, p. 627.)*

Regional Variations Apart from environmental and other effects discussed below, two factors related more directly to labor cause considerable regional variation in productivity. These include (1) the training, experience, and skill of the local labor force in the various crafts and (2) the work rules which are negotiated between employers and unions. These factors can cause productivity in some parts of the country to be more than double that in others. When working overseas they can be even more significant. Other things being equal, labor costs will vary accordingly.

Clearly, for both estimating and control a contractor working in more than one area must take regional variations into account. This is generally done by establishing base productivity levels for various crafts or activities in one region, and then applying index multipliers to ratio the base to other areas. If properly documented, a contractor's records will be his best source for developing such multipliers. Otherwise, he will be obliged to rely upon the experience of others as reflected in published sources. Precautions for this situation are mentioned briefly later in this chapter.

The amount of training and experience certainly varies from worker to worker even within a single craft in a local area. Formal distinctions are drawn between "apprentice" and "journeyman," but of course there are wide ranges within these. Although the estimator usually cannot forecast which craftsmen will work on which tasks, this is a factor that is very much subject to control by project management. Within the prescribed work rules, good superintendents can apply selective hiring, firing, and assignment of craftsmen in order to improve productivity. On a grander scale, contractors can actually set up their own training programs to enhance the skills of their employees. This has happened on many large overseas projects and is now being done in several "open-shop" areas in the United States.

Environmental Effects   The environment affects productivity on many levels. The weather, terrain, topography, and similar natural phenomena have obvious implications which need not be belabored here. The physical locations and working conditions of individual craftsmen can be equally significant. These include height above grade, heat, noise, light, constrictions, stability of work station, dust, and several others. Clearly, the productivity of an ironworker laboring outdoors during the Illinois winter would be different from one working in the Southern California sunshine. A carpenter erecting small form panels for an outside wall on the tenth story of a building would most likely produce less than if he were working in an on-site shop assembling the same panels into large ganged forms which would then be hoisted into place by crane.

Estimators generally take environmental conditions into account in preparing their estimates. Thorough preplanning can minimize the impact of many of these. Careful scheduling of outdoor operations with respect to seasons can help reduce weather effects, as can the appropriate use of enclosures. Thoughtful layout of construction facilities can offset the effects of difficult topography. A good comparative analysis of alternative methods of accomplishing specific operations can provide on-site working conditions conducive to higher productivity.

For controlling labor costs, management can also have considerable influence on the environmental effects on labor productivity. A monograph by Russo[5] shows how contractors can use readily available weather information services to improve their operations markedly. Parker and Oglesby[6] offer numerous hints for analyzing and improving work methods in order to significantly increase labor productivity. The construction trade and professional literature provide many other sources of information in this area.

Learning Curves   The basic principle of the "learning curve" is that skill and productivity in performing tasks improve with experience and practice. For example, the tenth of ten identical concrete footing pours should take less time and be done more skillfully than the first.

It is not the purpose here to set forth the theory and mathematics of learning curves. These are adequately explained in construction textbooks such as that by Parker and Oglesby.[7] What will be done here is to show how these concepts apply to estimating and controlling labor costs.

Consider the example learning curve shown in Figure 11-7a. For estimating purposes, the curve should be integrated through the number of units to be constructed, here defined as n, to obtain the total number of worker-hours

---

[5]J. A. Russo, Jr., *The Complete Money-Saving Guide to Weather for Contractors*, Environmental Information Services Associates, Newington, Conn., September 1971.

[6]H. W. Parker and C. H. Oglesby, *Methods Improvement for Construction Managers*, McGraw-Hill Book Company, New York, 1972.

[7]Ibid.

required. Graphically, this may be expressed as the shaded area under the curve. Dividing the total number of worker-hours by the number of units gives the *average* worker-hours required per unit as shown by *w* on Figure 11-7*b*. This is the number that should be used for estimating. Note that if the number of units is greater, as shown by *n'*, the average worker-hours per unit should be less, as shown by *w'*. It is therefore not sufficient simply to take average figures from one project and apply them directly to similar operations on a project being estimated. This fact also should be recognized by the estimator.

For control purposes, management should recognize that the worker-hours required for the first few of a number of repetitive operations should be expected to be higher than the average given by the estimator. However, as the operations continue, the worker-hours per unit required should drop below the estimated average so that the actual completed average is less than, or equal to, the estimated average. This concept is illustrated on Figure 11-7*c*. Another important feature of the learning curve that should be recognized for control is that if repetitive operations are interrupted or otherwise interfered with, an "unlearning curve" effect takes place which can cause the estimate to be exceeded. This is shown in Figure 11-7*d*. Therefore, for controlling labor costs

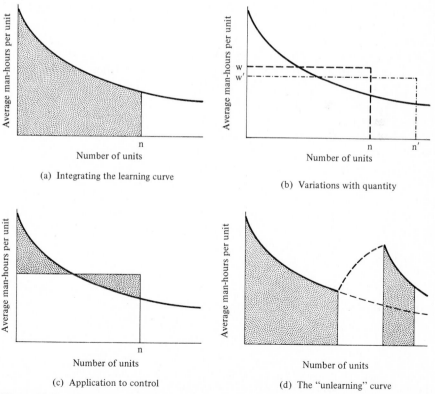

Figure 11-7 Learning curve relationships in estimating and control. *(From Boyd C. Paulson, Jr.,* "Estimation and Control of Construction Labor Costs," *Journal of the Construction Division, ASCE, vol. 101, no. CO3, September 1975, p. 627.)*

it is generally good practice to provide continuity of work on repetitive operations.

At least one large engineering and construction firm builds a reference to learning curves into the cost codes for project control reports. Several learning curves have been defined and the one most appropriate to the operation concerned is chosen. Therefore, rather than make inaccurate linear projections of expected productivity based on work completed to date (which may be at the higher end of the learning curve), the learning curve is included in the calculations (done by computer) to make a more accurate forecast for control purposes. When combined with computerized exception reporting, this becomes a powerful management tool.

Work Schedule "Work schedule" here refers to using variations on straight time only, scheduled overtime, or multishift work for accomplishing project objectives. Note that scheduled overtime refers to the situation where operations are regularly scheduled to exceed the normal 8-hour day, 40-hour week. It does not refer to the occasional use of overtime to finish operations that could not be completed in a normal workday, such as finishing concrete pour that took longer to set up than expected.

The section on the money component dealt with the strictly financial aspects of work schedules. This section will focus mainly on the productivity side, but will also show how the two are combined for the total labor-cost impact.

The self-defeating effect of scheduled overtime has been documented in a recent study by the Task Force of the Construction Users Anti-Inflation Roundtable under the chairmanship of Weldon McGlaun.[8,9] Findings of this study are summarized in Figure 11-8. Note that as the cumulative effects of scheduled overtime begin to set in, the actual total output for a 50- or 60-hour week drops below that for a 40-hour week. Specific consequences include reduced effectiveness due to fatigue, increased absenteeism, attraction of less-qualified workers, disruption of daily operations, reduced work pace and increased accident rates. The study further concluded that:

> Placing field construction operations of a project on a *scheduled* overtime basis is disruptive to the economy of the affected area, magnifies any apparent labor shortages, reduces labor productivity, and creates excessive inflation of construction labor cost with no material benefit in schedule.[10]

This, combined with the 50 to 100 percent increase in labor costs reflected in Figure 11-8*b*, should provide sobering second thoughts to owners and contractors hoping to save time and money by putting projects on scheduled overtime.

Scheduling projects on a multishift basis can avoid some but not all of the

[8]Construction Users Anti-Inflation Roundtable, "Effect of Scheduled Overtime on Construction Projects," *AACE Bulletin*, vol. 15, no. 5, October 1973, pp. 155–160.
[9]Weldon McGlaun, "Overtime in Construction," *AACE Bulletin*, vol. 15, no. 5, October 1973, pp. 141–143.
[10]Construction Users Anti-Inflation Roundtable, op. cit.

ill effects of scheduled overtime. This assumes, of course, that the shifts themselves do not run on a scheduled overtime basis. Nevertheless, as seen earlier, multishift work does incur a significant financial premium, and it can introduce productivity problems as well.

Parker and Oglesby point out that when shifts are regularly rotated (say on a weekly or biweekly basis), the natural bodily rhythms of the workers are continuously disrupted and the workers are therefore kept well below their peak efficiency.[11] The effect is not unlike that caused by the frequent changes

[11]Parker and Oglesby, op. cit.

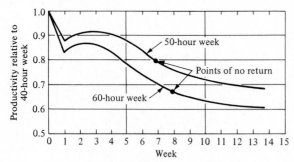

(a) Cumulative effect of overtime on productivity

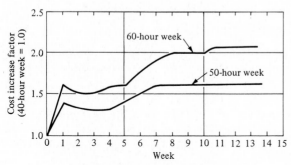

(b) Cumulative cost of overtime (including
    productivity & premium losses)

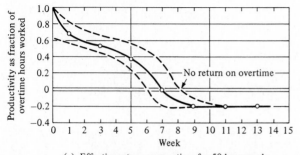

(c) Effective return on overtime for 50-hour weeks

Figure 11-8 Scheduled overtime versus productivity. *(From "Effect of Scheduled Overtime on Construction Projects," AACE Bulletin, vol. 15, no. 5, October 1973, pp. 155–160.)*

of time zones encountered by international travelers. Body functions affected include temperature, kidney activity, hormone level, and corticosteroid production. Some adjustments can effectively take place within 1 or 2 days, but others may take several months.

Another factor pointed out by Parker and Oglesby is the research finding that some people are indeed "day" people and others are "night" people. They actually perform much better when their work fits their physiological schedule.

From these two findings it would appear that multishift work could be made more productive if (1) shifts were not regularly rotated, and (2) an effort were made to match employees to the shift on which they would be likely to perform the best.

Management

Possibly the most difficult of all the components to analyze is the interrelationship of labor and management. This alone can produce orders of magnitude variations in labor productivity. Factors involved include such things as management philosophy; motivation and morale; safety policies; employee participation in planning, incentives, and rewards; relationships with union locals; and many others. Entire books have been written on the subject and have barely scratched the surface. Little can be added here. For a quick introduction to the subject, the reader is referred to two earlier ASCE articles by Charles Schrader[12] and to the aforementioned text by Parker and Oglesby.[13] They in turn will lead to a whole body of theoretical and practical literature.

Using Published Cost Information

There are numerous published sources of information pertaining to construction labor costs and man-hour productivity norms. The most basic of these are the local and national labor agreements negotiated by labor organizations and contractor representatives. Others include cost indices and labor statistics published by the U.S. Department of Labor, state and local governments, and numerous construction magazines and professional organizations. Annual reference works with unit-price and productivity information are published by a number of business firms.

No attempt is made here to catalog all these various reference sources. Rather, the important thing to recognize at this stage is that before using any published information, be it a cost index, unit price or whatever, for estimating and controlling construction work, one must thoroughly understand exactly what the information does and does not include. For example, consider a unit-labor price for laying brick. Which of the various money components does it include? Is it just the base wage, or does it comprise fringes, insurance, and premiums? What does it assume for productivity? Does it consider regional

---

[12]C. R. Schrader, "Motivation of Construction Craftsmen," *Journal of the Construction Division*, ASCE, vol. 98, no. CO2, September 1972, pp. 257–273; and C. R. Schrader, "Boosting Construction-Worker Productivity," *Civil Engineering*, vol. 42, no. 10, October 1972, pp. 61–63.
[13]Parker and Oglesby, op. cit.

differences, learning-curve variations with quantity, environmental effects, work schedule, or management approach?

When tempered with a contractor's own experience and judgment on his own company's operations, such published sources can be a valuable source of supplementary information. Ultimately, however, the contractor's personal experiences as documented accurately, consistently, and in a well-organized and readily accessible manner by his labor-cost control system should be the primary source for estimating and controlling construction work.

The Importance of Man-Hours

Hourly wages and fringe benefits continue to increase in the construction industry. Different sections of the country have vastly different basic hourly rates and varying fringe benefits. An electrician or other skilled craftsman may make 50 percent more in high-cost areas than he does in low-cost areas, and overtime premiums distort unit-labor costs. It has become almost a hopeless task to compare unit-labor costs from one section of the country to another, and it is equally difficult to compare today's costs with those of a few years ago.

By keeping productivity records in man-hours, however, one neutralizes the money component. For example, a contractor may determine that unit productivity for foundation forms is anticipated to be 0.10 man-hours per square foot (s.f.). If labor costs are $15.00/hr including fringes, the unit-labor cost is $1.50/s.f. If labor costs are $20.00/hr, the unit cost becomes $2.00/s.f. If the contractor has kept his cost-accounting records in man-hours as well as in unit costs, he can review performance in all projects and can compare actual productivity with estimated productivity in a straightforward manner.

When a truly integrated management control system is utilized, actual man-hours can be compared to estimated man-hours, and actual productivity for components and for the entire project can be easily measured. Manpower forecasts by craft will automatically be available from an integrated system based upon estimated man-hours, and these forecasts can be continually modified on the basis of actual productivity compared with the estimate.

Even today some contractors keep unit-labor cost or unit-cost records in dollars rather than man-hours. These contractors are therefore finding it increasingly difficult to prepare accurate labor-cost estimates in an ever-changing construction-cost climate. To illustrate, Figure 11-9 shows the actual manpower compared with the professional construction manager's fair-cost estimate for each contract in the actual Mountaintown warehouse project. Table 8-1 shows productivity calculated from this information.

SUCCESSIVE ESTIMATING[14]

In this chapter it is worth introducing one additional approach to estimating that is being increasingly used in Northern Europe. Known there as "succes-

[14]For additional information, see Steen Lichtenberg, "Project Management Systems— Monsters or Assistants to the Manager," in *Proceedings of the 8th Annual Seminar/Symposium of the Project Management Institute*, Montreal, October 1976, pp. 152–158.

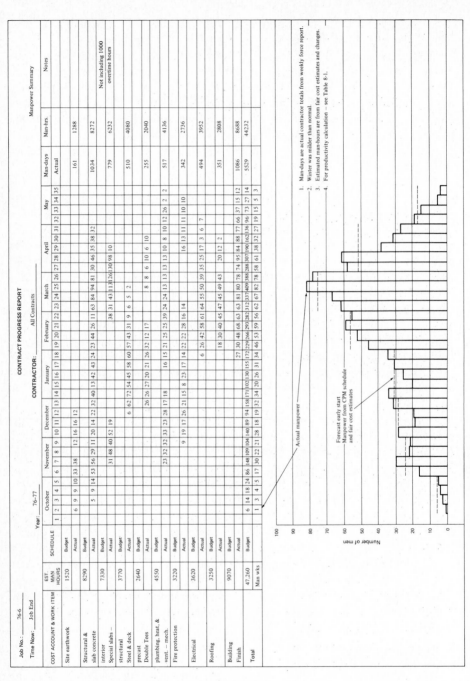

Figure 11-9 Example project manpower summary.

sive estimating" or "successive planning," it was developed by Prof. Steen Lichtenberg of the Technical University of Denmark for network-based planning and scheduling as well as for estimating.

Successive estimating uses statistical principles both to improve the accuracy and greatly to reduce the amount of effort required for estimating the cost of a project. The reduction in time and effort can also permit estimators to explore and refine many more alternative approaches to project execution than would normally be possible.

In essence, the successive approach requires that an estimator not only estimate the cost for each of the elements of a project, but also assess the uncertainty associated with the estimate for each element. By expressing the elemental uncertainties as standard deviations, squaring these to get variances, then taking the square root of the sum of the variances, one can quantify the uncertainty for the estimate as a whole. The estimator then focuses on the element that most adversely affected the uncertainty for the project as a whole: he subdivides and analyzes that element in greater detail to reduce the uncertainty associated with it, then recomputes the variances, or uncertainty, for the project as a whole. This process is repeated until either the estimator is satisfied with the level of accuracy of the whole estimate, or the estimate reaches an irreducible level of uncertainty about which the estimator can do nothing. For example, there is no point in computing the exact cost of bolting connections if one does not even yet know for sure whether the designer will specify welding instead of high-strength bolting.

To illustrate, consider a hypothetical project subdivided initially into the six elements shown in Figure 11-10. Each box lists the estimated cost of the element, such as $100 for element A, a range of accuracy of the cost, in this case ± $20, and the variance (400) which is the square of the range. The "inevitable uncertainty" might be due to factors beyond the control of the project, such as contingencies associated with inflation or changes in environmental regulations. In this case, they are quantified as $100 ± $70, with a variance of 4900. The total cost for the project is

$$\$100 + \$500 + \$80 + \$150 + \$100 + \$50 + \$100 = \$1,080$$

The variance is

$$(20)^2 + (80)^2 + (15)^2 + (30)^2 + (30)^2 + (10)^2 + (70)^2 = 13,825$$

The standard deviation for the project as a whole is

$$\sqrt{13,825} = \pm 118$$

The cost estimate at this stage is thus:

$$\$1,080 \pm 118$$

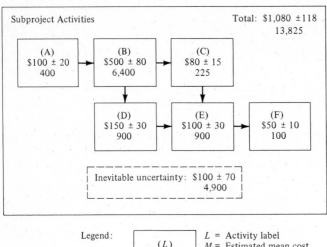

Legend:

(L)	L = Activity label
$M \pm S$	M = Estimated mean cost
$V = S^2$	S = Standard deviation
	V = Statistical variance

Figure 11-10 Subproject activities. *(From Steen Lichtenberg, "Successive Planning," Technical University of Denmark, June 1971.)*

Clearly, the estimate at this point is most adversely affected by the ± $80 uncertainty in element B. It will thus be further subdivided for analysis in greater detail. Assume it can be broken down as shown in Figure 11-11. In this way, element B's estimate is refined from $500 to $440, and its uncertainty is reduced to ± $44, which alters the uncertainty for the whole project as follows:

$$(20)^2 + (44)^2 + (15)^2 + (30)^2 + (30)^2 + (10)^2 + (70)^2 = 9361$$
$$\sqrt{9361} = \pm \$97$$

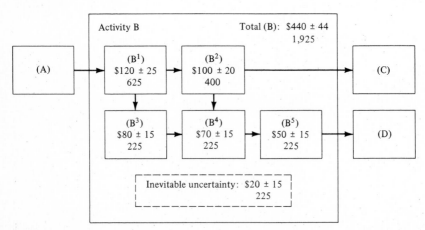

Figure 11-11 Activity "B" subdivision..

giving a new estimate of 1020 ± 97. This moves much closer than ± 118 to the irreducible uncertainty of ± 70.

Note that in this case element B as a subunit was analyzed as if it were a project in its own right, so that its summary statistics (440 ± 44) can still be treated at the higher level. Further to refine the estimate, attention would now focus on elements D and E, which now have the largest deviations, $\pm \$30$. Figure 11-12 gives example calculations for element D. Assuming element E also produced subelements with uncertainties less than ± 25, attention would then focus back to subelement B1 of element B, which has an uncertainty of $\pm$ $25. This might be further subdivided as shown in Figure 11-13.

As this process continues, one approaches but never quite reaches the irreducible uncertainty of $\pm \$70$, but one does reach a point where successive refinements are no longer worthwhile in comparison with the irreducible uncertainty. European designers and constructors report that reaching this point takes only about 20 percent of the effort of conventional approaches, where all elements are subdivided into uniform levels of detail whether they need it or not. In the successive approach, estimators are also much more aware of where the uncertainties in a project really are. The time saved in this approach can then be invested in exploring alternative ways of mitigating the irreducible uncertainties, such as shifting to a design using materials not subject to such large price uncertainties. Alternatively, the estimators might more productively be preparing estimates for other projects. Either alternative is far preferable to grinding out numbers fruitlessly without regard to their impact on the accuracy of the estimate.

CONVERTING ESTIMATE TO CONTROL BUDGET

Chapter 13, which deals with cost engineering, will discuss control budgets in greater detail after it has introduced the subject of cost codes. At this stage,

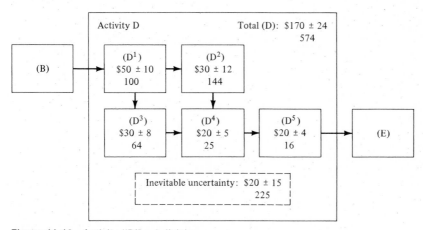

Figure 11-12 Activity "D" subdivision.

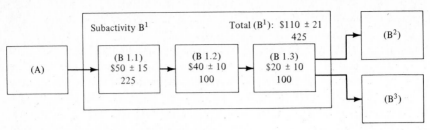

Figure 11-13　Subactivity "B1" subdivision.

however, it is worth pointing out some differences in philosophy and content that should be recognized in converting an estimate to a control budget.

Estimates often organize costs in different categories and in different levels of detail from those most appropriate for cost-control purposes. For example, for a unit-price bid, the estimate would most probably be prepared against the schedule of quantities in the owner's bidding documents. This organization might be convenient for the owner, but quite likely would not be the way the contractor's historical costs and job costs are kept. Thus, once the job is awarded, the contractor might reorganize the costs into a form suitable for his cost control system.

An important philosophical difference is that estimates should be based on averages, whereas budget standards for control purposes should be somewhat tighter. The reasons for this are: (1) If estimates are consistently more optimistic than the contractor's historically average performance, there is a greater than 50 percent chance that the project will lose money, ignoring for the moment profit and contingency factors. Presumably, a firm would want at least a 50 percent chance of making its costs. (2) On the other hand, if one uses averages for control purposes, one can expect average results. There is little built-in incentive for improvement.

The distinction is illustrated in the frequency distribution curve in Figure 11-14. This shows the historical pattern of costs, or worker-hours, for a

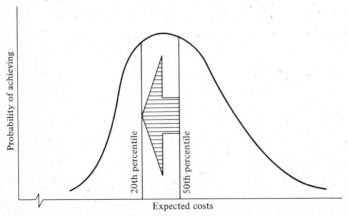

Figure 11-14　Estimating standards versus control standards.

particular type of activity, such as finishing concrete slabs. The distribution is typically skewed because the potential overruns on most operations can far exceed the potential underruns. The average, however, is the point where there is a 50 percent chance of overrunning or underrunning, and equally divides the area under the curve.

For control purposes, however, one could set a realistically achievable but somewhat tighter standard, such as controlling against the 20th percentile of costs, as shown in the figure. There is 1 chance in 5 that one will "beat" the estimate, and this will happen often enough that supervisors and workers will know it can be done. It thus becomes a goal worth striving for. With a proper managerial approach, a competitive spirit can be built up on the job that will try to pull the average closer to the control standard. Setting the standard too tight, however, such as the 1st percentile, would be self-defeating, because the budget numbers would appear fictitious, unrealistic, and unachievable, and would therefore become a source of frustration rather than of motivation.

Anyone familiar with the managerial abuses of time studies and piecework in the late nineteenth and early twentieth centuries will recognize that the approach to control described here can also be abused. To be successful, it requires a positive, enlightened approach to managerial leadership. It will quickly defeat itself if simply used as another tool under an authoritarian approach.

Assuming that the approach is to be used, however, it will be necessary to convert the estimate, which may have been based on averages, to a control budget based on something tighter than the 50th percentile. Needless to say, this conversion requires documentation of historical cost ranges as well as averages, and good, practical judgment based on the field experience of the person doing the conversion.

The technique itself is most appropriate to the productivity-oriented components, like labor for form fabrication, rather than to capital-intensive components, such as materials. Therefore, owing to inflation and like factors, it is best if the historical records are kept in terms of production, such as worker-hours per unit of output, rather than in terms of monetary unit costs.

SUMMARY

This chapter has examined several approaches to estimating the costs of a construction project. They included conceptual estimating techniques that require little data and effort to give approximate estimates that can provide budget and planning guidance in the early phases of a project, and fair-cost estimates and definitive estimates to provide more accuracy and control as the project evolves further. Owing to its complexity and importance, labor-cost estimating was examined in even greater detail. "Successive estimating," a technique now used in Europe, was introduced as an approach that can improve accuracy and reduce the corresponding level of effort in preparing estimates. Finally, considerations for converting estimates to control budgets were briefly described.

Techniques examined for conceptual and preliminary estimates were (1) cost indices, (2) cost-capacity factors, (3) component ratios, and (4) parameter-cost estimates. Cost indices mainly reflect time-dependent changes in costs resulting from inflation, changes in technology, market competition, the state of the economy, etc. Cost indices can also reflect regional variations in costs. Cost-capacity factors account for nonlinear "economies of scale" when comparing projects of similar types but of differing magnitudes. Component ratios proceed from vendor price quotations on major items of equipment, and factor these quotations to reflect either installed equipment costs or completed project costs. Parameter costs relate all cost elements of a project to just a few basic parameters that characterize its type and scope. All these techniques depend on good historical documentation and on the estimator's experience-based judgment.

Fair-cost estimates are best prepared from completed plans and specifications. They are based upon actual quantity takeoffs which are multiplied by unit prices developed by the estimator.

Contractor's-bid estimates are based upon similar information, but may be developed in considerably more detail depending upon the contractor's own procedures. Bid estimates typically include lump-sum or unit-price material and subcontract quotations.

A professional construction manager must develop sufficient in-house estimating ability in mechanical, electrical, and other specialty items so that he can effectively forecast the cost of the work as well as be able to determine the fair cost of changes and modifications.

The concept of a definitive estimate as developed in this chapter represents the stage at which the final project cost can be forecast with little margin for error. This error can be minimized through the addition of an evaluated contingency. The determination of the proper time to classify an estimate as "definitive" will vary according to the nature of the project, the anticipated accuracy of the underlying information, and the degree of risk the owner is prepared to accept.

The labor-cost section outlined basic principles for estimating and controlling field labor costs on construction projects. It divided labor costs into two main categories. The first dealt with the strictly financial aspects. These included basic wages, fringe benefits, insurance, taxes, and wage premiums. Most of these are readily quantifiable. The second category introduced factors related to productivity. These included regional variations in skill and work rules; environmental effects ranging from weather and topography to the immediate working conditions of individual craftsmen; learning-curve relationships; project work schedule; and interrelationships of labor and management. Productivity factors are difficult to quantify and require much experience and judgment to do so. However, they offer the contractor the greatest opportunity for control. In both the financial and productivity categories, several of the more subtle cost implications of the various factors were explained. Brief precautionary reference was also made to the many published sources of labor-cost data.

The "successive estimating" approach developed by Steen Lichtenberg of Denmark provides an efficient and desirable alternative to traditional estimating methods. By incorporating assessments of uncertainty with the cost estimates for the various elements of a project, it uses proven statistical concepts to allow selective detailing to refine the accuracy of the estimate. Rather than prepare the whole estimate at an arbitrarily uniform level of detail, this approach produces equal or better levels of accuracy with about 20 percent of the normal time and effort. This time saving enables estimators to explore more alternatives within a project, or to prepare estimates for more projects.

In converting an estimate to a control budget, two important differences should be considered. First, the organization and categorization of costs suitable for preparing an estimate are often not compatible with a company's cost-control system. Second, estimates necessarily must deal in averages, whereas tighter standards, such as striving for the 20th percentile, are desirable for control purposes where better-than-average results are wanted. For these and other reasons, careful thought should go into converting estimates to control budgets. Chapter 13 will explore this subject further.

This chapter has by no means been exhaustive in either content or scope. However, it has set forth some basic concepts for estimating and controlling costs of projects. There are many legitimate approaches for estimating project costs, and each has its appropriate applications and limitations. Of importance for any method, however, is that (1) it correctly accounts for all the various cost and productivity factors in designing and constructing a project, and (2) it is applied uniformly and consistently from one project to another.

By no means is this chapter intended as a substitute for a textbook or work manual devoted entirely to the subject. Some of the references at the end of this book provide access to further reading and study. Most important for developing good estimators, however, is experience in construction, and thorough, well-organized documentation of work that has been done.

Chapter 12

Planning and Control of Operations and Resources

Planning, scheduling, and control of the functions, operations, and resources of a project are among the most challenging tasks faced by a professional construction manager. Normally, this responsibility involves coordinating design with construction to produce the necessary plans and specifications, to package them along recognized trade and subcontractor boundaries, and to contract with the construction organizations best qualified to carry out their work efficiently and economically in conjunction with other contractors on the site. In the construction phase, the professional construction manager normally provides the overall planning, scheduling, and control needed to sequence operations properly and to allocate efficiently the resources involved.

This chapter deals with the methods and procedures available to the professional construction manager for accomplishing these objectives and offers practical guidelines for their effective application. Although network-based critical path methods (PERT and CPM) are among the tools available, no attempt will be made in this chapter to explain these techniques and their methods of computation. Appendix E and several references in the bibliography are given at the end of this book for the reader who is unfamiliar with network-based methods. Rather, CPM will be presented in this chapter as but one of many possible control tools that may best suit the needs of a particular project or a particular management situation; owing to the importance of the network methods, however, some additional emphasis will be placed on their application in the control phase.

In addition to discussing methods and procedures for planning, scheduling, and control, this chapter will introduce some concepts and guidelines for the contractual implications, including documentation and analysis of change orders, changed conditions, delays, claims, and disputes. Although it may not be obvious at this stage, the many impact costs associated with these contractual problems will enable their discussion to build quite logically upon the earlier parts of this chapter.

PLANNING AND CONTROL TOOLS

There are many different analytical tools and graphical techniques for the planning, scheduling, and control of operations and resources. A few that will be introduced here include bar charts, progress curves, matrix schedules, linear balance charts, and critical path networks. It is important to emphasize at the outset, however, that none of these is in and of itself the *plan* for the project. The complete plan, if it exists at all, exists only in the minds of the planners. All the tools that have been mentioned are merely abstract means to aid the planners in *organizing* and *documenting* their thinking and assumptions and in *communicating* that thinking to those persons responsible for putting the plan into action. These tools succeed only to the extent that they at least accurately document the major parameters of the plan and effectively communicate the planners' intentions to others.

The situation here is somewhat analogous to the process of composing, documenting, and playing music.[1] The composer, be he Beethoven, John Lennon, or whoever, is the planner, and initially the plan exists only in his head. Our standard form of musical notation enables him to document his thoughts as he goes so that (1) he does not have to keep everything in mind at once, and (2) he can refer to what he has documented for modifications and revisions while the composition as a whole takes shape. Once the composer is satisfied with his plan, possibly having tested it as he went, the final plan, or sheet music, can be neatly rendered and possibly published. Eventually a musician gets hold of this plan, reads and comprehends it, and, analogous to the execution of a project, carries out the planner-composer's intentions in a concert or for his own enjoyment.

In contrast with all existing "notations" for documenting the planners' intentions for the execution of a construction project, musical notation is remarkably clear and comprehensive. It transcends language barriers to communicate effectively with musicians in Europe, Asia, the Americas, Africa, Australia—wherever people have acquired knowledge of its basic principles. It also communicates effectively through time. A Bach concerto can be rendered today precisely as the maestro intended, and deviations from the plan are intentional.

[1]This analogy is from Prof. D. W. Halpin of the Georgia Institute of Technology.

No existing tool for documenting and communicating plans for engineering and construction even approaches the capabilities of musical notation. Even network-based methods capture only the barest outlines of the planner's thinking, and all the tools discussed in this chapter should be viewed in the context of these limitations. Expecting too much from existing techniques accounts for many of their so-called failures in practical applications.

Each tool should be evaluated with respect to its suitability for documenting the characteristics of the planned project, the knowledge and level of sophistication of those who are expected to use it, the desired level of detail, and the means available for updating and revision. One should not immediately discard simpler tools when a more powerful one seems appealing. It is often the very simplicity of such tools as bar charts and progress curves that makes them more effective as a means of communication. Similarly, even the more powerful techniques can be mismatched to the physical and managerial characteristics of certain projects. For example, CPM is often a poor choice for linear or repetitive operations, such as a pipeline or tunnel, and sometimes even for major earthmoving operations, where artificially strict logic constraints can critically impair the better judgment of a good superintendent. As another example, for both documentation and communication, matrix schedules and linear balance charts can be more effective than other techniques for coordinating the subcontractors on a high-rise building. Several of these applications and limitations will be explored in the context of the techniques introduced here.

Bar Charts

Bar charts date back at least to the Gantt Charts developed by Henry L. Gantt in the early part of this century. Technically speaking, there are a number of differences between the two, but in this chapter all forms of these diagrams will be called "bar charts."

A bar chart graphically describes a project consisting of a well-defined collection of tasks or activities, the completion of which marks its end. An *activity* is a task or closely related group of tasks whose performance contributes to completion of the overall project. A typical activity noted in a bar chart for a building project could be "Excavate foundation."

A bar chart is generally organized so that all activities are listed in a column at the left side of the diagram. A horizontal time scale extends to the right of the list, with a line corresponding to each activity in the list. A bar representing the progress of each activity is drawn between its corresponding scheduled start and finish times along its horizontal line. A simple bar chart for a small concrete gravity-arch dam is shown on Figure 12-1.

Bar charts differ in the way they show *planned* progress on the horizontal scale, in the way they *report* progress, and in numerous details of diagrammatic style. Although these differences may at first seem trivial, they have important but subtle implications that can create serious misunderstandings for people who are unfamiliar with them. Three of the more common types of bar charts

Item No.	Description	First Year												Second Year											
		J	F	M	A	M	J	J	A	S	O	N	D	J	F	M	A	M	J	J	A	S	O	N	D
M-10	Mobilization																								
E-10	Foundation excavation																								
D-10	Diversion stage – 1																								
D-20	Diversion stage – 2																								
G-40	Foundation grouting																								
C-10	Dam concrete																								
I-20	Install outlet gates																								
I-30	Install trash racks																								
P-10	Prestress																								
R-80	Radial gates																								
S-50	Spillway bridge																								
G-60	Curtain grout																								
L-90	Dismantle plant, clean up																								

Figure 12-1 Bar chart for concrete gravity-arch dam.

are therefore discussed in some detail below. Since they have no known standard names, they are arbitrarily called Type I, Type II, and Type III bar charts in this chapter.

Type I: Linear Time-scaled for Planning; Linear Progress-scaled for Reporting Type I, a common form of bar chart, assumes that progress on an activity is a direct linear function of elapsed time. Therefore, in *planning*, no attempt is made to show the physical percentage completion at any point on the bar representing an activity. The basic form is the open bar shown on Figure 12-2*a*.

In order to report progress, a parallel bar is sometimes placed immediately below the plan bar, and is initially open also. Then, as the job progresses, it is shaded in direct proportion to *physical work* (not necessarily elapsed time) completed on the activity. This is shown on Figure 12-2*b*. Alternatively, a narrow, shaded reporting bar could be superimposed on an open plan bar, as shown on Figure 12-2*c*. Other variations are also used. Note that the current physical progress, a work function, does not necessarily coincide with the current reporting date, a time function. By comparing the shaded reporting bar with the open plan bar and with the current date, one obtains only a rough indication of whether the activity is behind or ahead of schedule.

The example in Figure 12-2 shows that 5 months were originally scheduled for the activity (shown by the open plan bar) and that 60 percent of the time (3 months out of 5) has elapsed by the reporting period. However, the shaded bar reports that only 50 percent of the physical work in the activity has been completed. On first appearance, it may seem that the activity is about one-half month, or 10 percent, behind schedule. This may or may not be true. It is quite possible that the bulk of the resource hours and dollars was scheduled to be expended during the latter half of the activity's duration, as shown in Figure 12-3*a*. In this case, the activity may actually be on or ahead of schedule. On the other hand, if the bulk of the effort has been planned as in Figure 12-3*b*, the

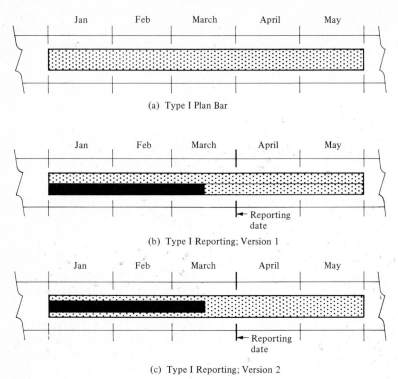

(a) Type I Plan Bar

(b) Type I Reporting; Version 1

(c) Type I Reporting; Version 2

Figure 12-2 Type I bar charts.

activity may be much more than 10 percent behind schedule. The point is, the Type I bar chart accurately reflects activity status only when cumulative progress is indeed a direct linear function of time. This knowledge is important in avoiding serious misinterpretations of the diagram.

Type II: Time-scaled for Planning; Time-scaled for Reporting Type II bar charts start by scheduling an activity with the same kind of open plan bar that was shown in Figure 12-2*a* for Type I charts. However, an important difference is that *planned* cumulative progress percentages (in terms of physical work completed, man-hours expended, dollar value in place, etc.) are written at the end of each *basic time interval* (day, month, week, etc.—one month is used here). A convention must be established so that they are consistently written either above or below the bar. For example purposes, planned percentages are written above the bar, as shown on Figure 12-4*a*. This progress need not be uniformly linear; it can be distributed as shown in Figure 12-3.

Progress may be reported on Type II bar charts by using either of the graphical conventions explained for Type I, using Figure 12-2*b* and *c*. Figures 12-4*b* and *c* use the superimposed shaded-bar convention. Note, however, that there are important differences in what the reporting bar says in Type II. It is shaded to show the actual *time* worked on the activity up to the current date or

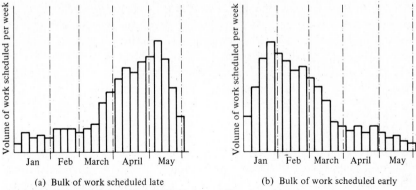

(a) Bulk of work scheduled late   (b) Bulk of work scheduled early

Figure 12-3   Activities scheduled with nonuniform workloads.

to completion, whichever is earlier. Figures giving the *actual* percentage cumulative progress are written on the opposite side of the bar (lower side, here) from the planned progress.

As with the Type I bar chart, it is important that subtleties and limitations of the Type II chart be clearly understood. Because the reporting bar is shaded to the current date or to completion, the reporting bar in itself gives no indication of whether a current activity is ahead of or behind schedule. This progress is shown only by writing the *actual* cumulative percentages by the bar

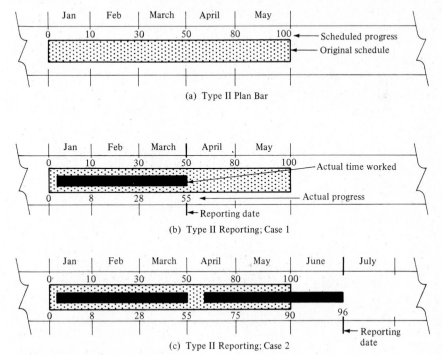

(a) Type II Plan Bar

(b) Type II Reporting; Case 1

(c) Type II Reporting; Case 2

Figure 12-4   Type II bar charts.

on the opposite side of the planned percentages. Comparison of actual and planned percentages is the only way to evaluate the status of a current activity, so it is essential that these figures be written on the diagram. This convention has some graphical disadvantages, but it does show more vividly what happened on activities which are already complete. This, of course, has little relevance for project control purposes.

Type III: Time-scaled for Planning; Variable Progress-scaled for Reporting Type III bar charts start by representing an activity with a horizontally divided open bar such as that shown in Figure 12-5a. Planned percentage progress figures are written at the end of each basic time interval (month used here) above the bar. The example shows that 50 percent of the work is planned to be performed in the last 2 of the 5 months (in 40 percent of the time) scheduled for the activity.

When the activity gets underway, work completed is reported by shading in alternating areas in the lower and upper portions of the bar, one for each basic time interval worked. The segments are shaded in proportion to the physical work actually performed during the basic time interval compared with the scale for the basic time interval in the range being shaded. The reporting date is marked with an arrow or heavy line on the calendar scale for the bar chart. It is important to recognize that the scale of progress generally changes during each basic time interval considered unless progress is indeed a direct linear function of time. Figure 12-5b shows an example.

The major advantage of the Type III graphical representation is that it shows much more information than Types I and II and can more accurately portray actual job conditions. A possible disadvantage is that some of its implications are more difficult to understand at first and may require considerable explanation. A person who is unfamiliar with it might draw some improper

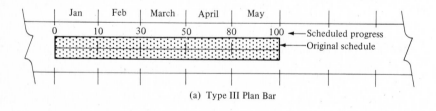

(a) Type III Plan Bar

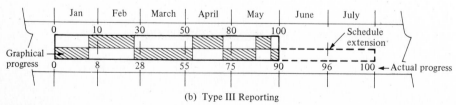

(b) Type III Reporting

Figure 12-5 Type III bar charts.

conclusions. It is therefore especially important to explain it to the owner if it is to be included in his reports. Interpretation, of course, is a problem with all three forms of the bar chart.

Advantages and Limitations of Bar Charts Bar charts have a number of advantages over other scheduling systems. Their simple graphical form results in relatively easy general comprehension. This, in turn, has led to their common acceptance and widespread use as a good form of communication in industry, with a basic understanding usually found at all levels of management. Also, they are fairly broad planning and scheduling tools, so they require less revision and updating than more sophisticated systems. This feature is especially helpful in the turbulent early stages of an engineering and construction project when frequent changes and revisions are a fact of life.

In addition to the specific problems of interpretation and misunderstanding mentioned with each of the three specific formats discussed in this chapter, the use of bar charts has a number of general limitations. First, because of their broad planning nature, they become very cumbersome as the number of line activities, or bars, increases. If several sheets are required, logical interconnections are difficult to comprehend. Second, although the planner who prepared the bar chart undoubtedly considers the logical interconnections and constraints of the various activities in the project, this logic is not expressed in the diagram. It therefore becomes very difficult for another individual to reconstruct the logic and to recognize sequence constraints unless a substantial amount of documentation is included with the chart. Third, although the bar chart is a good planning and reporting tool, it is difficult to use it for forecasting the effects that changes in a particular activity will have on the overall schedule, or even to project the progress of an individual activity. It is therefore limited as a control tool. With due regard to these and other limitations, bar charts will nevertheless continue to be valuable assets in project management. An understanding of their limitations, however, is important to their effective and appropriate application.

Progress Curves

General Principles Progress curves, also called S curves, graphically plot some measure of cumulative progress on the vertical axis against time on the horizontal axis. Progress can be measured in terms of money expended, quantity surveys of work in place, man-hours expended, or any other measure which makes sense. Any of these can be expressed either in terms of actual units (dollars, cubic meters, etc.) or as a percentage of the estimated total quantity to be measured.

The shape of a typical S curve results from integrating progress per unit of time (day, week, month, etc.) in order to obtain cumulative progress. On most projects, expenditures of resources per unit time tend to start slowly, build up to a peak, then taper off near the end. This causes the slope of the cumulative curve to start low, increase during the middle, then flatten near the top.

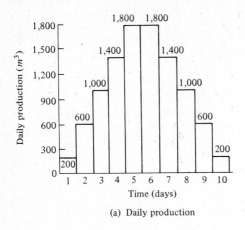

(a) Daily production

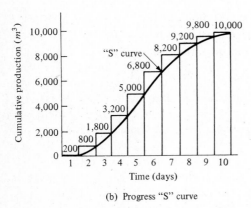

(b) Progress "S" curve

Figure 12-6 Development of a progress curve.

These principles will be illustrated by using cubic meters excavated to measure progress on a 10,000 cubic meter, 10-day earth-moving activity. Assume that daily excavation quantities are as shown on Figure 12-6*a*. Summing all the daily excavation quantities through any particular day gives the cumulative quantity by that day. For example, by the end of day 4, the cumulative quantity is the sum of excavation on days 1, 2, 3, and 4. That is,

$$3200 = 200 + 600 + 1000 + 1400$$

The shape of the S curve can be seen by connecting the points at the end of each day's cumulative production, as shown on Figure 12-6*b*.

Planning and Reporting Progress Like bar charts, progress curves can express some aspects of project plans. Once the project is underway, actual progress can be plotted and compared with that which was planned. It is then possible to make projections based on the slope of the actual progress curve. Such projections, however, should neither be made nor interpreted without a good understanding of the reasons for deviations, if any, from planned progress, and of the current and future plans of project management. Basic concepts of planning, reporting, comparing, and projecting progress are shown on Figure 12-7.

Early, Late, and Actual Progress This section requires some understanding of the critical path network concepts discussed later in this chapter.

Free float and total float on noncritical activities gives managers considerable flexibility in rescheduling activities without delaying the overall project. The scheduling of an activity has a close correlation to the timing of its resource expenditures (money, labor, materials, etc.) and, of course, to its accomplishment. It follows that if all activities in a project are scheduled as early as possible (an early-start schedule), the progress will take place and be reported earlier. Conversely, if all activities are scheduled at their late starts, progress takes place and is reported later. These ideas are illustrated in Figure 12-8.

Figure 12-8a shows total progress measured during each basic time interval of the project with activities scheduled at their early starts. Curve *ES* on Figure 12-8c is the corresponding cumulative progress curve. Figure 12-8b shows total progress in each period for the late-start schedule. Curve *LS* on Figure 12-8c is the cumulative late-start progress curve. Note that the two curves start and end at the same point, but that at any other point the *LS* curve falls below or to the right of the *ES* curve. Actual planned and reported progress should most likely fall between these two extremes, as shown by curves *P* and *R* respectively on Figure 12-8c.

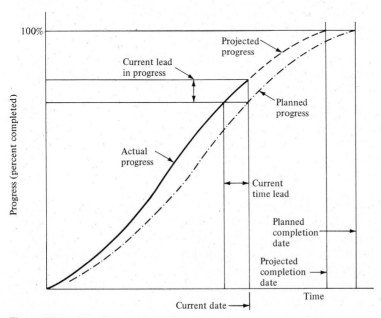

Figure 12-7 Planning and reporting progress.

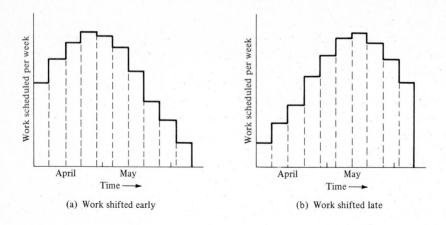

(a) Work shifted early   (b) Work shifted late

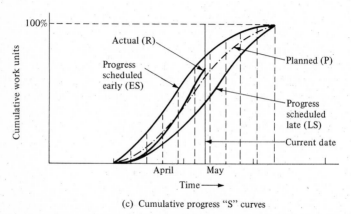

(c) Cumulative progress "S" curves

Figure 12-8 Early, late, and actual progress. *(Adapted from Boyd C. Paulson, Jr., "Concepts of Project Planning and Control," Journal of the Construction Division, ASCE, vol. 102, no. CO1, March 1976, p. 74.)*

Cash Flows Cash flows may be shown graphically by plotting one progress curve for expenditures on the same graph with a second curve for income. A third curve representing the financing required or cash surplus at any time may then be plotted by subtracting the expenditures ordinate from the income ordinate at each point in time. This idea is shown on Figure 12-9.

Superimposing Progress Curves on Bar Charts Planned and actual progress curves can be superimposed on a bar chart to make a useful hybrid report. An example report of this kind was shown on Figure 8-8. Note that although the bar chart and the progress curves share a common horizontal time scale, there is generally no correlation between the vertical scale of the progress curves, usually shown on the right, and the vertical list of activities on the left. In this kind of report, any type of bar chart can be combined with any type of progress chart.

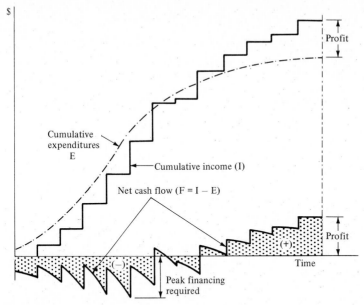

Figure 12-9 Cash flows.

Matrix Schedules

Matrix schedules are a tool that has evolved and become fairly common on high-rise buildings with successive floors repeating essentially the same plan. The technique is fairly narrow in its application, but it does serve to illustrate how, in the right context, a simple idea can be quite effective for documenting and communicating a plan.

A typical schedule, partially rendered, is shown in Figure 12-10. It is no coincidence that at first glance the schedule looks like a cross section or elevation of the building itself. The horizontal rows on the schedule do indeed correspond to floors within the building, starting with one or more basement levels at the bottom and working up to the top floor. The vertical columns, however, are not structural features, but rather, they correspond to the operations to be performed on each floor. They read from left to right, and list the operations on each floor roughly in chronological order. The descriptions are given at the top of the columns. In a sense, the building's schedule then proceeds from the lower left-hand corner of the matrix to the upper right-hand corner. A typical sequence of operations on a floor might include such items as:

Erect columns and girders for structural frame
Place decking
Place floor inserts
Place lightweight concrete
Intermediate operations
Paint and carpet

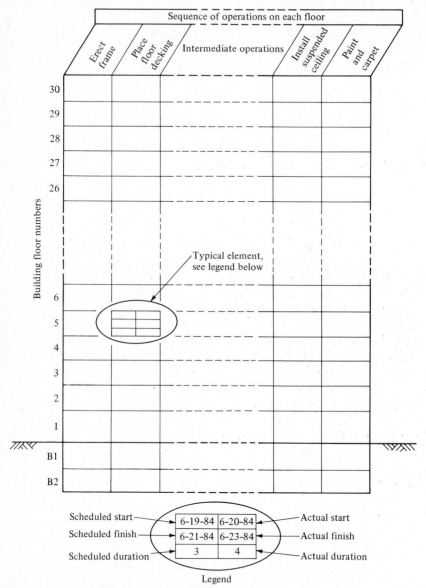

Figure 12-10 Matrix schedule for high-rise building.

Each operation is scheduled by a box like the typical example shown in the insert in Figure 12-10. The box is subdivided to show the scheduled start and finish dates and the expected duration, and it provides space for the actual dates to be entered in the field. Additional graphics can be provided by coloring the boxes as they are completed, so that just a quick look shows the status of the building.

This type of schedule has numerous advantages when it comes to communication on a project of this type. First, the vertical correlation of floors to rows is immediately obvious to anyone and requires no explanation. Contrast this with the debates between "arrows" and "circle" notation in CPM. Second, the chronological, left-to-right flow of each floor's operations is easy to see. The logical interrelationships among operations are also more obvious than in a bar chart. And, very important, with some forethought the vertical columns can be made to correspond to the specialty subcontractors; thus, there is built-in selectivity in reporting. When a subcontractor walks into the office to discuss his work, all his operations are shown in one or a few adjacent columns, so he does not have to sort his activities from a maze of others. Also, the relationships to the other subcontractors that most affect him or are affected by his work are readily apparent. All this information is right there in one compact, easily understood, one-page schedule.

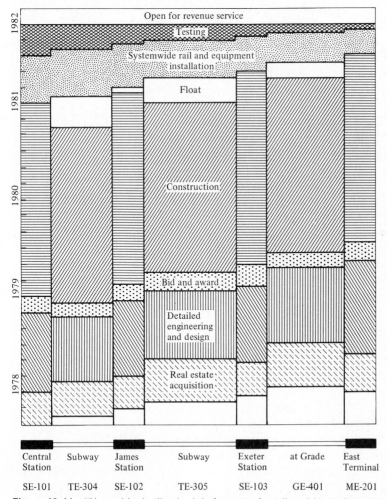

Figure 12-11 "Horse blanket" schedule for part of a rail rapid transit system. *(Adapted from schedules used on Washington, D.C., and Atlanta, Ga., rapid transit projects.)*

The "Horse Blanket"

A variation on the matrix schedule used in high-rise buildings has been gaining acceptance on some major rail–rapid transit systems. An example is shown on Figure 12-11. Essentially, what it shows is a section of the system intended to go "on-line" as a unit, at the same date, for revenue service. The section may consist of several stations and connecting sections of grade, subway, or aerial rail line, and will normally be contracted for design and construction in several different segments. The horizontal axis corresponds to the line itself and its several contractual subdivisions. The vertical axis, working chronologically from the bottom upward, shows the major phases for each contractual section, including planning, real estate acquisition, preliminary design, detail engineering, key reviews and approvals, bidding, construction of the main structures, and construction of systemwide components (track, train controls, etc.). The amount of leeway left at the top of various sections gives management a good idea of which parts are most critical to the project's scheduled start-up.

The name "horse blanket" was given to this schedule because the schedules that have been produced use brilliant colors for the various phases of each contractual section, and the overall matrix therefore has a patchwork pattern reminiscent of the brightly colored horse blankets used by many Indian tribes in the Western United States. The schedule itself is at the milestone level, and is thus best for policy-level planning at higher levels of management. Nonetheless, when copies are displayed at many offices around the system, designers, contractors, and others can also readily see where their own projects fit into the "grand scheme of things."

Linear Balance Charts

Linear balance charts, called the "Vertical Production Method" or "VPM" by one author,[2] are similar in concept to the line of balance charts used by industrial engineers for optimizing output on manufacturing production lines. They apply best to linear and repetitive operations, such as tunnels, pipelines, highways, and even to the type of building projects appropriate to matrix schedules. An example is shown in Figure 12-12.

The vertical axis typically plots cumulative progress or percentage completed for different systems of a project, such as the structural, electrical, mechanical, and other trade subcontractors on a high-rise building. The horizontal axis plots time. The sloping lines can each represent trade subcontractors moving up from one floor to another on a high-rise building, or perhaps the clearing, excavation, stringing, welding, pipe-laying, and backfill operations on a pipeline. As long as the slopes are either equal or decreasing as one moves to the right, the project should proceed satisfactorily. However, if early scheduling shows one operation proceeding too rapidly, with a high slope compared with those preceding it, the time and location of the first conflicts become rapidly apparent. To illustrate this, Figure 12-12 shows the eighth

---

[2]James J. O'Brien, "VPM Scheduling for High-Rise Buildings," *Journal of the Construction Division*, ASCE, vol. 101, no. CO4, December 1975, pp. 895–905.

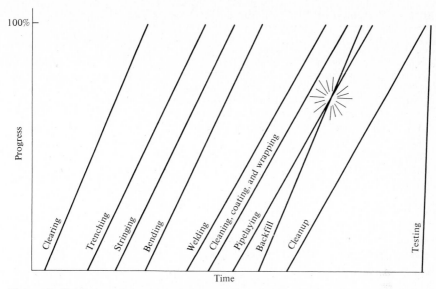

Figure 12-12   Example linear balance chart for pipeline.

operation starting to conflict with the seventh when each is about 70 percent complete.

Concepts of Network-Based Schedules

Having introduced four alternative methods, it is still worth noting that for general applications in construction, critical path networks and their related techniques for schedule, resource, and cost analysis are still by far the most powerful analytical tools that we have for project planning and control. This section will briefly review their basic concepts and compare them with other methods. The remaining sections will focus on networks for demonstrating more general ideas in project control, and also for the analysis and documentation of claims and disputes.

Network Concepts   Essential elements in almost all project networks are *activities*, their *durations*, and the *logical interrelationships* among them. Given these, one can compute each activity's early start, late start, early finish, late finish, total float (slack), and free float. These computations also yield the total expected duration for the project, and, of great importance, they focus attention upon the most *critical activities* and hence the *critical path* for the project. This is a powerful concept that greatly aids management in setting its priorities for allocating resources to operations.

As stated earlier, it is not our purpose here to explain the intricacies of CPM computation. Rather, for quick reference purposes, we will make do with the concise algorithmic summary in Table 12-1. The reader who is uncomfortable with these computations is strongly encouraged to consult Appendix E or one of the CPM references listed in the bibliography at the end of this book.

Table 12-1   Summary of CPM Notation and Equations

Notation

$D(x)$ = Estimate of *d*uration for activity x
$ES(x)$ = *E*arliest (expected) *s*tart time for activity x
$EF(x)$ = *E*arliest (expected) *f*inish time for activity x
$LS(x)$ = *L*atest allowable *s*tart time for activity x
$LF(x)$ = *L*atest allowable *f*inish time for activity x
$TF(x)$ = *T*otal *f*loat for activity x
$FF(x)$ = *F*ree *f*loat for activity x
S = Project *s*tart time
T = *T*arget project completion time

Equations for calculating the CPM parameters

Forward Pass

$ES(x)$ = S for beginning activities, or
$ES(x)$ = Max (EF (all predecessors of activity x))
$EF(x)$ = ES(x) + D(x)

Backward Pass

$LF(x)$ = T for ending activities, or
$LF(x)$ = Min (LS (all followers of activity x))
$LS(x)$ = LF(x) − D(x)

Floats

$TF(x)$ = LS(x) − ES(x)
       = LF(x) − EF(x)
$FF(x)$ = Min (ES (all immediate followers of activity x)) − EF(x)

Critical Path

A critical path is a continuous chain of activities with the minimum total float value. By summing activity durations, it is the longest duration path through the network. There may be more than one critical path in various parts of the network.

There are two basic types of graphical representations for CPM: "Arrow notation" and "Precedence notation." Figures 12-13 and 12-14 illustrate the differences between the two. Also see Figure 4-8 for an example diagram.

Arrow notation uses the lines or vectors in the diagram to represent activities and shows the logical relationships among activities by the nodes which connect them. It is also necessary at times to use "dummy" arrows to correctly show the logic. Precedence diagrams, also called "activity-on-node" or "circle" diagrams, reverse the convention. The nodes represent the activities and the lines or vectors show the logic. We shall make no attempt to enter into the long-standing and inconclusive debate regarding the relative merits of these two techniques. Briefly stated, precedence notation is generally easier to learn and is less prone to errors in logic, while arrow notation was introduced earlier and has thus gained wider acceptance. Most important, commercially available computer programs will accept either notation; readers are advised to have a working knowledge of both approaches—as the computer does.

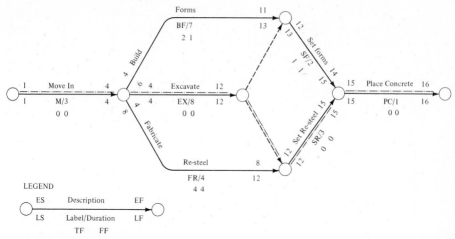

Figure 12-13 CPM arrow diagram.

There have been numerous useful extensions to the basic elements of activities, time, and logic in networks. The strict logic requirements of basic CPM have been relaxed somewhat with techniques permitting activities to be overlapped or to have delays inserted between them. The methods of probability and statistics have also been applied to both time and logic. Other enhancements include addition of costs and resources. Cost enhancements include analytical procedures for time-cost trade-off analysis, network-based cash flows, and network-based cost control. By identifying resources of labor, materials, and equipment with activities, planners and managers can take advantage of powerful analytical techniques for resource allocation to assure that the project can be completed within finite resource limits, and of resource leveling to ensure the efficient and continuous utilization of resources.

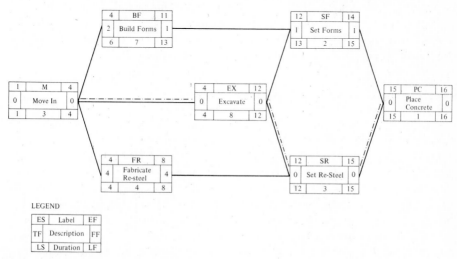

Figure 12-14 CPM precedence diagram.

Some of these concepts will be briefly explained, as needed, in later parts of this chapter and in Appendix E, but their full development is beyond the scope of this book. Again, several of the books devoted solely to critical path methods deal with at least some of these subjects, and the reader is encouraged to consult the bibliography for further information.

Advantages of Networks   It is most common to illustrate the advantages of networks by comparing them with bar charts. First, networks can much more concisely represent large numbers of activities. More important, one of the major aspects of a planner's thinking, that is, the logical interrelationships and dependencies among activities, is not really shown on bar charts, but is inherent in networks. This in turn means that networks are much more useful for forecasting and control. For example, the impact on the whole project of a delay in an activity, a change in an activity's scope, or the addition or deletion of activities is readily transmitted, by network logic and computations, through the whole schedule.

Networks are also said to encourage a higher level of logical discipline in the planning, scheduling, and control functions, and to stimulate more attention to both long-range and detailed planning. Assuming that a standard notation and diagramming convention can be established at least within an organization and that there are willing and knowledgeable users, networks provide a more powerful means for documenting and communicating project plans, schedules, and performance. Finally, it is worth reemphasizing that, in contrast to other techniques, they identify the most critical elements in the project schedule and thus allow management to set priorities and focus attention on them.

Most of the advantages of networks over bar charts also hold in comparing them with the other techniques we have described. Even in matrix schedules, the logic is only imprecisely implied, and there really is no assessment of criticality. Nevertheless, returning to the importance of documentation and communication, all the various techniques do have their appropriate and best applications, and none should be discarded—at least not until something with the power analogous to musical notation comes along.

APPLYING NETWORK-BASED PROJECT CONTROL

From day 1 onward, those responsible for the management and control of a project have more information than did the planners who prepared the schedule for the project's guidance. Management should recognize this fact and should not be intimidated by the network, nor should they ignore it. The network is basically a graphical expression of the experience, judgment, intuition, decisions, and assumptions of the planner. If the planner is worth listening to, then his network deserves careful attention. But, since each day brings new information about the project, one must continuously be prepared to justify or question the thinking that went into the plan. If the network is indeed to be a viable control tool on the project, it must be subject to revision, change, and improvement. Planners can aid this process if, in defining activities and preparing the original network, they think ahead to the people who will be expected to use it. We shall therefore suggest a few practical guidelines for this purpose.

Defining Activities

In defining the content and level of detail of a network, consider who will use it: Project management? Staff scheduling engineers? Foremen? What will they use it for, and how? What is the size of the project, and what is the scope of work under the intended users' control? Especially on larger projects, a hierarchy of schedules is necessary, with selectivity and subreporting. For example, a CPM network might serve for general and detailed project control by superintendents and the engineering staff. But it might be reduced to a summary network or even a bar chart or progress curve for higher management. At the other extreme, individual activities might be expanded to narrative work plans for foremen.

Who will maintain and update the schedule? Managers and supervisors on an intermittent basis? Or a trained staff of scheduling engineers? How will they do this? Manually or by computer? On site or in the home office? If the work is manual, does the network conveniently allow for selectively detailing portions of it, say activities on the critical path? Will the accuracy of logic and time estimates be affected by the level of detail? How?

If the planner considered alternatives and exceptions that are not shown on the network, or if there are assumptions that were made for diagrammatic or computational convenience rather than necessity, are these facts clearly cross-referenced from the diagram to a supporting set of notes? For example, with basic CPM networks it is difficult to distinguish in logic between technological constraints and resource constraints. To illustrate, Figure 12-5a shows two concrete pours that might be done in either order. However, the planner has assumed that only one crew will be available, and so, to make the project duration come out right, he has arbitrarily sequenced the activities as shown in Figure 12-15b. When the superintendent goes to do pour 1, he finds the subgrade is too wet, so he shifts the crew to pour 2 instead. When this was reported to the computer, it blew a fuse, and the network had to be revised and submitted again. This is but one example of where computational details peculiar to the technique can have little to do with practical field operations.

Will the feedback time of the information system (recall Figure 10-2) be compatible with the scope and duration of activities? In general, activity durations should be long enough so that management can take corrective action if schedule reports indicate this is necessary.

These are just a few ideas for the definition of activities. These decisions should be made with the overriding criteria being the needs, skills, and cooperation of the users.

Preparing a Network

Although the technical details of network preparation are beyond the scope of this book, it is worth reviewing the general procedure to further indicate where a good planner will include the needs of users. The steps listed here should also show that the actual mechanics of the process are fairly simple; they apply to large as well as small networks. Also, note that there are strong parallels between estimating and network planning; they are interdependent functions.

    1 Begin by learning all you can about the project itself. Study the plans and specifications, include a site reconnaissance if possible, and above all, seek input from all key parties known to be involved in the planning or execution of the project. These can be the owner's representatives, the designer, subcontractors, major suppliers, labor organizations, regulators, and, of course, the professional construction manager's own staff designated for the project.

    2 Make a preliminary listing of some key activities, keeping in mind the guidelines for defining activities.

    3 Put a key activity on the diagram—first, last, or in between—but make a start. If one is intimidated by the prospect of constructing a large network, this first activity is often the hardest step. Steps 4, 5, and 6 follow fairly easily, and will produce an initial diagram.

    4 Ask yourself the following questions:

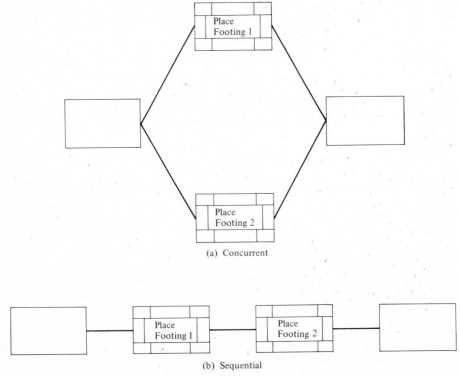

(a) Concurrent

(b) Sequential

Figure 12-15 Arbitrary use of network logic for resource constraint.

    a What must be completed immediately before this activity can begin?

    b What activities can follow once this activity is complete?

5 Put these new activities on the diagram.

6 Repeat steps 4 and 5 until you have a reasonably comprehensive diagram of the project. Its organization at this stage will inevitably be chaotic, but tidiness can wait.

7 Reexamine the plans, specifications, and other sources of information to be sure that all parts of the project are covered and none is duplicated.

8 Check and double-check the logic and content for factors such as improper "dummies" (a common source of error only in arrow networks), possible recursive "loops," and for assurance that each activity has an intentionally defined start and finish point.

9 At this stage you have a rough diagram. Before drafting the final version, recheck it with those parties who were consulted for input in step 1 to be sure it does indeed represent their thinking. This step is particularly important: it is futile to impose an unworkable schedule on the people responsible for the execution of the project.

10 Repeat the earlier steps as needed to produce a satisfactory network. Only at this stage should one proceed to an elegant presentation. The next section will offer some guidelines for this purpose.

Organizing the Network

The physical organization of activities on a network should proceed according to some rational pattern representing the needs and characteristics of the project. Some possible areas of organization that may be used alone or in combination include the following:

1 By responsibility: trades, type of work, supervisors, etc.

2 By geographic area and facility within the project, so there is some locational correlation between activities on the diagram and, perhaps, the plot plan of the site

3 By time scale

4 By project cost code (see Chapter 13)

Reporting

Sources of information for schedule control are in part the same as those for cost engineering. They include labor and equipment time sheets, field quantity reports, and various kinds of trend reports. Also included are informal oral reports from field to office and conscientiously updated field diaries.

    Particularly useful, however, are preprinted forms requesting actual and estimated time and resource information associated with specific activities. One good type of information form, and one that minimizes the amount of writing requested, will provide space for overwriting information on one of the duplicate copies of subreports sent to specific supervisors in the field. Used in this way, the subreport becomes a "turnaround" document. Figure 12-16 gives an example of a subreport concerning concrete activities that are either in progress or scheduled to start in the near future. The superintendent apparently believes that the report is accurate except for activity CPF, which is expected to start 2 days later than planned, and activity CFF, which is only 30 percent complete instead of the 60 percent scheduled. This document is then returned to the office where it is used as input for the next schedule update. Though normally used mainly in computer-based systems, this technique can also be applied in manual reporting systems.

Once data come in to be processed, numerous different reporting techniques may be employed to disseminate the updated information to the managers and supervisors who need it. The most notorious method is to use the computer as a sorting and printing device and to issue the same complete detail reports on the whole project to all parties, regardless of needs and interests. This approach has almost invariably failed. In keeping with the principles discussed in Chapter 10, computerized tabular reporting is most effective only when it has the capacity of selective subreporting, exception reporting, and summary reporting in order to get the right information to the right people at the right level of detail and in time for decisions and corrective action.

Other useful means of reporting include different kinds of graphical reports. Many projects make very effective use of color coding to update prominently located network diagrams to keep key people informed of project status. There are also commercially available mechanical equivalents of this centrally located graphic presentation, such as the "Planalog" system described in the next subsection. Computer-based plotters can be effectively employed to redraft updated schedules periodically. Some firms then use a Xerox-reduction process to issue these schedules, folded accordion-style, in a form that a supervisor can carry in his pocket. These graphical reports are particularly useful to field people.

Mechanical Aids As with other graphical means of communications used in engineering and construction, bar charts require considerable time and expense on behalf of planners, engineers, and draftsmen for both initial preparation and updating. In order to help reduce this time and expense, especially for updating, mechanized alternatives to conventional drafting and reproduction have been developed. They include boards which allow the repositioning of preprinted cards, charts mounted on continuous rollers which can be modified with grease pencils, boards that accept magnetic strips on which activity information is written, and others. Patented systems include the "Board Master" (Graphics Systems, Yanceville, North Carolina), "Roll-a-Chart" (W. A. Steward Company, Somerset, California), "Magnetic Visual Control Systems" (Methods Research Corporation, Staten Island, New York), "Sched-U-Graph" (Remington Rand), and "Planalog" (Planalog Company, Gladwyne, Pennsylvania).

The last-named system, "Planalog," developed by S. Mendell in 1962, has been favorably accepted and applied on a number of projects. It is actually much more than a bar chart since it actually represents and updates CPM schedules in bar-chart form. Activity bars are represented by scaled sliders,

SUNNYSTATE CONSTRUCTION COMPANY, INC.

Copy 2

Subreport Code: 03 Concrete
Report Date: 19 June 1978

Project: Mountaintown Warehouse
Location: Mountaintown, Westamerica

Note changes to schedule in the blank spaces provided.

Return Copy 2 to Home Office Scheduling Department.

Act. Label	Description	Planned Duration	Planned Start	Planned Finish	Early Start	Early Finish	Total Float	Percent Complete	Critical
CFR	Concrete Fabricate Resteel	8	2JUN78	14JUN78	2JUN78	14JUN78	0	100%	**
CFF	*Concrete Fabricate Forms	6	13JUN78	21JUN78	2JUN78	12JUN78	8	30% 60%	
CPR	Concrete Place Resteel	10	14JUN78	28JUN78	14JUN78	28JUN78	0	20%	**
CPF	Concrete Place Forms	3 4	21JUN78 23	27JUN78 28	12JUN78	16JUN78	8	0%	
CPC	Place and Finish Concrete	2	28JUN78	30JUN78	28JUN78	28JUN78	0	0%	**

END SUBREPORT 03

Figure 12-16 Example schedule subreport "turnaround" document.

called gauges, which run on horizontal tracks. The logical interconnections between activities are made by vertical components called fences. These basic components are shown on Figure 12-17.

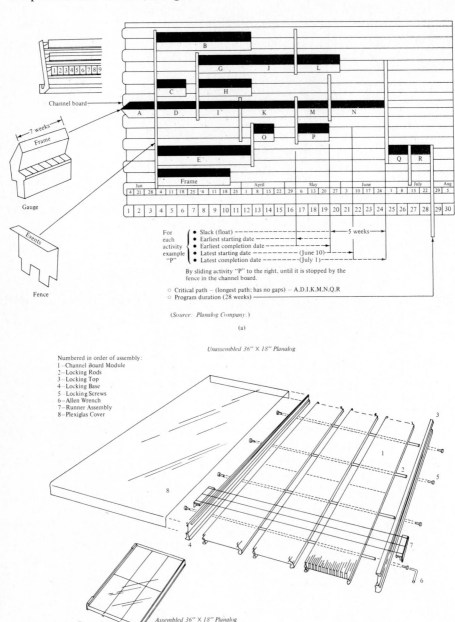

For each activity example "P"
- Slack (float) --------------------------- 5 weeks ----
- Earliest starting date ----------------
- Earliest completion date ----------------
- Latest starting date --------- (June 10)-
- Latest completion date --------- (July 1)-

By sliding activity "P" to the right, until it is stopped by the fence in the channel board.

○ Critical path — (longest path; has no gaps) — A,D,I,K,M,N,Q,R
○ Program duration (28 weeks) —

(Source: Planalog Company.)

(a)

Unassembled 36" × 18" Planalog

Numbered in order of assembly:
1—Channel Board Module
2—Locking Rods
3—Locking Top
4—Locking Base
5—Locking Screws
6—Allen Wrench
7—Runner Assembly
8—Plexiglas Cover

Assembled 36" × 18" Planalog

(Source: Planalog Company.)

(b)

Figure 12-17 Planalog scheduling device. *(Courtesy Planalog, Inc., Gladwyne, Pa.)*

Updating Considerations

There are several procedures for updating network-based schedules. With low-cost computer processing, it is feasible to carry out complete activity-by-activity computations on a periodic or demand basis. When larger networks are to be updated by hand, techniques such as those developed by John Fondahl enable schedulers to focus only on the parts of the network that are currently of interest, and thus greatly to reduce their computation burden.[3]

Regardless of the approach, in updating we wish to compare planned with actual progress and to calculate variances to highlight problem areas. Parameters of interest include the following:

1   Floats, especially in critical and near-critical activities
2   Changes in the critical path
3   Logic changes, including new and deleted activities
4   Resource usage, especially to predict constraints and reduce idleness
5   Changes in durations
6   Activities which were completed, and percentage complete on those in progress

One often hears debates among scheduling people about the best frequency with which to update schedules: daily? weekly? monthly? The debates, however, miss the point. If we have gone 6 months and the project has essentially progressed as planned, fine! Apart from checking off completed activities and verifying this progress, no real updating is necessary. On the other hand, if we worked until late last night doing this month's revision, and then this morning we get word that a change order is brewing to add a whole new wing to our building project, we are back to base 1 already. The important thing is not how often a schedule is updated, but how accurately the schedule reflects the actual conduct of the work.

Corrective Action

Assuming that exception reports from our last schedule update show that some activities are deviating significantly from the plan, what do we do? Think before acting! Recall again that from day 1 onward we have more information than did the original planner who developed the schedule. It is quite possible that unforeseen favorable developments are simply causing the work to go better than expected. Certainly we should verify these trends and analyze the reasons behind them, but it will quite likely be the plan that needs corrective action, not the project.

In some cases, however, activities may be slipping well behind their scheduled start times, possibly because of a delayed material delivery. Here is

[3]John W. Fondahl, *A Non-Computer Approach to the Critical Path Method for the Construction Industry*, Technical Report No. 9, Stanford University, Dept. of Civil Engineering, The Construction Institute, Stanford, Calif., November 1961. Also, John W. Fondahl, *Methods for Extending the Range of Non-Computer Critical Path Applications*, Technical Report No. 47, ibid., 1964.

where the "float" properties of the critical path method become a real asset. If the activities in question have sufficient free float, and if we can verify that the delayed deliveries will be made within this range, again it may be possible that no corrective action is necessary. This assumes, of course, that the resource allocation is not adversely affected.

But what if delays or resource overruns on critical activities appear to be seriously jeopardizing the completion date of the project? In the past, the response was too frequently to accelerate the whole job, without knowledge of which operations most affected duration. Here again, the critical path in CPM focuses management's attention on the activities that really count. Using the principles from CPM's "time-cost trade-off" extensions, a rational plan can be developed for most economically accelerating the project. Where feasible, new information and constraints might even make it economical to alter the logic of the schedule.

As mentioned in Chapter 10, one should not take corrective action merely for the sake of keeping to the original plan. That is, the schedule alone does not run the job. Rather, use it as a guide, but be prepared to take advantage of, and adapt to, new conditions as they arise. Where corrective action is warranted, the schedule can also help to focus thinking and set priorities for efficient solutions.

DOCUMENTATION FOR CHANGES, CLAIMS, AND DISPUTES

Changed conditions, change orders, delays, claims, and disputes occur in some measure on almost all projects of significant size. Occasionally there will be malicious intent or even dishonesty on behalf of one or more parties to a contract; the subject of this section, which deals with the documentation of facts, will be of no help to their cause, though it may help the other parties to defend themselves. But even when all parties to a contract are doing their level best to interpret its terms and conditions honestly and objectively, there are bound to be differences of opinion simply because of the specific interests of those involved in trying to get the job done as economically, quickly, and skillfully as possible. Thus, there has evolved a body of law and accepted practices which help to achieve just, equitable, and fair resolution of disputes. In contracts, these often take the form of clauses pertaining to changed conditions, change orders, delays, contract time, liquidated damages, disputes, and claims. But the process only starts here.

This section is by no means intended as an introduction to contracts, specifications, and their legal implications. Rather, we assume some reader background in this area, and will illustrate a few cases where the planning, scheduling, and control tools discussed in this chapter can have a constructive impact. Briefly stated, five of the most important guidelines regarding matters of changes, delays, disputes, and claims in contract administration are as follows:

1 Documentation
2 Knowledge of contracts and the law
3 DOCUMENTATION
4 Good working relationships between all parties to the contract
5 D-O-C-U-M-E-N-T-A-T-I-O-N

Changed Conditions and Change Orders

Changed conditions occur when the nature of the work encountered on a project is significantly different from that described in the contract documents. Change orders, which are directives from the owner or his agent, and which usually result from negotiations with the contractor, can alter the terms and conditions of the contract, say, to add extra work, delete work, change the standards of the work, etc. Change orders can thus provide an equitable means of dealing with changed conditions arising from unforeseen events, such as an unexpectedly bad foundation problem. Change orders can also be used, however, when an owner simply wishes to alter some part of the facility—say, add a wing to a building—after the contract has started.

The impact of changes differs depending on the nature of the contract. For example, if there is a quantity variation within the range of a unit-price contract, the nature of the price schedule automatically handles the changes. In a lump-sum contract, however, an overrun is likely to generate a claim. In a negotiated contract, a change in scope might be agreed upon, with adjustments in direct reimbursable costs and possibly an adjustment in the fee. In any of these types of contracts, however, one needs to be able to evaluate both the direct costs and the impact costs of the change and to determine how these are allocated among the parties to the contract.

The direct and impact costs of delays and time extensions will provide a simple illustration. Four situations will be considered and common settlements will be indicated.

Extra Work Requiring More Time   The document for this situation is a change order, and it normally justifies both a time extension and extra reimbursement for the contract. Either the time and cost are settled at the time of the request, or, to avoid default, the contractor can give written notice and proceed under protest.

Delay Caused by Owner or His Agent   If the owner or his agent causes a delay, say by late delivery of working drawings or tardiness in approving shop drawings, the contractor will normally be entitled to a time extension, and may also have a legitimate claim for extra compensation.

Excusable Third-Party Delays   Often there are delays caused by forces beyond either the owner's or the contractor's control. Examples that are normally unquestioned include fire, floods, earthquakes and other so-called "acts of God." Others that are sometimes subject to dispute include strikes, embargoes on freight, accidents, and reasonable delays in materials delivery. Excluded are conditions that existed at the time of bidding, and normal bad weather. Where agreed upon, these types of delays usually result in extensions of time but no additional compensation.

Contractor-caused Delays Such delays usually result in no extensions of time and no additional compensation. Indeed, in the extreme they can lead to breach of contract.

All these situations, even the fourth, if needed for the owner's defense, require accurate and equitable means of determining extensions to time and changes in compensation. We shall start by dissecting the direct and impact costs in more detail.

The Effects of Changes[4]

The effects of changes can be subdivided into three main categories:

1 Direct costs
2 Time extension
3 Impact costs

Even the first two can be difficult to assess, and impact costs are almost certain to provoke disagreement. It is worth exploring each in turn.

Direct Costs All labor and all its overhead burdens, contractual and temporary materials, construction equipment, and even supervisory and staff time that can be clearly attributed to work associated with a change or delay constitute direct costs. *If* these costs are well documented, it is normally not too difficult to justify them in a claim. The main caution is to avoid settling the whole claim at this level without thoroughly analyzing the next two categories.

Time Extension If a change can be shown to delay the completion date of a project, all parties to the contract will most probably incur additional expenses for the overhead associated with keeping the support staff and facilities for this extra time. Increasingly, this delay can also seriously increase the financing and escalation costs in a project. The problem is to verify the degree to which a delay in one or a few activities affects the project as a whole. In concept, the delay in an activity in a CPM network could be propagated through its successors to assess the effect. If there is ample float, there is no delay in the project. If not, then the amount of project delay can be directly computed. But this is often far too simple. For example, what if we had to

---

[4]This section is based on an outstanding paper by Carroll J. Collins, "Impact—The Real Effect of Change Orders," *Transactions of the American Association of Cost Engineers*, San Francisco, June 21–24, 1970, pp. 188–191. His paper is strongly recommended reading for anyone involved in the construction process.

complete the activity called "Divert river" before the spring runoff started? If successful, the project could continue as shown on the schedule. But a 1-month delay in this activity might result in overtopping a partially completed cofferdam and the loss of a full year's work. Nevertheless, networks and other types of scheduling tools can be useful in determining the effects of even these kinds of time extensions.

Impact Costs   The last example leads us indirectly to the area of impact costs. These costs are among the most difficult to define, let alone quantify, but they are very real and they can far exceed all others. Let us proceed with four increasingly accepted categories:

1   Acceleration
2   Job rhythm
3   Morale
4   Learning curve

Acceleration, or speeding up the project, is often a deliberate response when a delay in project completion cannot be tolerated. Methods here include (*a*) shift work, (*b*) overtime, and (*c*) increased crew sizes. None of these is as economical as the original plan, for reasons discussed in Chapters 10 and 11.

The impact on job rhythm is particularly severe on projects with a repetitive production cycle. For example, consider a high-rise reinforced-concrete building where flying forms are jumped on a 1-week cycle, and weekends are needed to satisfy the specified curing time. One day's loss can cause a week's delay, during which "morale" and the "learning curve" can also suffer. Similar situations occur on drill-and-blast tunnel jobs, where meal times and shift changes allow no-loss time to shoot and ventilate the fumes. Numerous other examples could be cited.

The relationship of morale to production is well understood in the armed services, but seems to make little headway as a factor in justifying claims in construction. But the fact is that construction workers and their supervisors sense pride in accomplishment just like anyone else—both in quantity of work in place and in the professional skill and efficiency that go into it. Changes requiring that existing work be extensively modified or torn out breed frustration, cynicism, and resentment. Doubts about the usefulness or permanence of one's work, whether conscious or unconscious, will most certainly reduce motivation, slow production, and drive up costs.

Learning curves were introduced in Chapter 10. The point here is that they do not happen automatically, but are a result of supervisors and workers who are determined to stay with a repetitive task and who strive to do it better. Recall from Figure 11-7*d* that there is an "unlearning curve" as well as a learning curve; interruptions in production also can only increase costs.

Assessing the Costs   This book is not really the proper forum for debating the relative merits of these various types of costs. There are volumes of legal precedents particularly in the areas of direct costs and time extension, and modern court decisions are increasingly recognizing some categories of impact costs. The problem is, however, that too frequently only the lawyers win in court; owners, engineers, and contractors—though they more and more frequently resort to litigation—are the losers. Ideally, as more commonly happened in the not too distant past, disputes should be settled among the parties to the contract. A reasonable, experienced resident engineer or a professional construction manager, trusted with sufficient authority by the owner, should be able to resolve most problems with a professional, experienced and reasonable contractor's project manager. But specific considerations for the new areas of cost, especially in the impact area, and the dissolution of authority have made this solution increasingly difficult. More and more emphasis is put on the importance of thorough documentation to arm the attorneys when they go to court. The fact is, however, that good documentation and analysis can short-circuit many such claims before they become a real issue. The following section describes a method that is valuable in either situation; its wider application could help bring back the times when the parties to the contract could "reason together" at the project level.

Factual Networks

Factual networks or their equivalent have been used for nearly two decades for the documentation of projects, but too often they have been prepared long after the fact—with the "facts" themselves muddled from poor memory and adversary objectives—for use in court. Ideally, they should be prepared as the project evolves, serving a purpose analogous to the "as-built" drawings. That is, they should document how things happen when they happen. Furthermore, they should be supplemented with good narrative documentation, and they should be cross-referenced to pertinent correspondence on file.

There are numerous special techniques for constructing such networks. Figure 12-18 shows a sample of the approach taken by Antill and Woodhead.[5] The networks can also be supplemented by other useful graphical methods. As an expert witness in litigation for a large underground powerhouse, John Fondahl of Stanford University developed a method for plotting accumulated delays versus time in a manner that clearly pinpointed causes and responsibilities for the delays. An example is shown in Figure 12-19.

SUMMARY

This chapter introduced several important methods and concepts for the planning, scheduling, and control of operations and resources on engineering

---

[5]James M. Antill, "Critical Path Evaluations of Construction Work Changes and Delays," *The Institution of Engineers, Australia Civil Engineering Transactions*, vol. 77, no. 1, April 1969, pp. 31–39. This paper also serves as the basis for chap. 11 in J. M. Antill and R. W. Woodhead, *Critical Path Methods in Construction Practice*, 2d ed., John Wiley & Sons, Inc., New York, 1970.

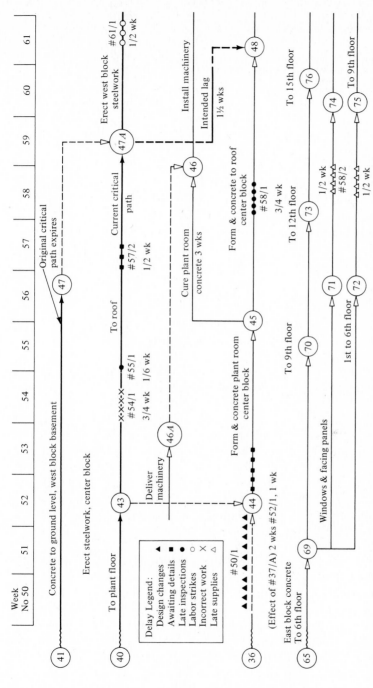

Figure 12-18 Portion of time-scaled factual network for building project. *(From James M. Antill and Ronald W. Woodhead, Critical Path Methods in Construction Practice. John Wiley & Sons, Inc., New York, 1970, p. 282.)*

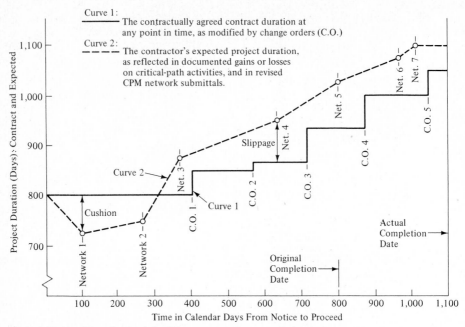

Figure 12-19   Plot of schedule delays versus time recognized.

and construction projects. The ideas discussed here are another major part of the overall system for the management of projects.

Five basic scheduling tools include bar charts, progress curves, matrix schedules, linear balance charts, and critical path networks. Depending on the nature of the project and the needs and capabilities of its staff, each of these has advantages and disadvantages. Regardless of focus, any analytical tool for planning and control should be evaluated with respect to two main criteria: First, how well does it document the thinking of the planner; does it capture his intentions and the main constraints that influenced him? Second, how well does it communicate the planner's thinking to the people charged with the execution of the project? No matter how accurate and meticulously prepared, a plan is of no value if its language is foreign to its users.

Because of its generality and its power as an analytical tool, we focused in some depth on network-based project control. The success of critical path methods begins with clear, unambiguous definition of activities, involvement of users in preparation of the schedule, and the physical organization of the network itself. Once a good schedule-control standard has been developed, the main criterion for updating it should be how well it represents the actual operations on the project. When deviations from the schedule are detected, one should consider all main alternatives before applying corrective action. Where corrective action is warranted, the critical path concept can aid in its most effective application.

In contract administration, changes, delays, claims, and disputes frequently arise as a natural consequence of the differences in the interests of the parties to the contract. Factors affecting time and cost include the direct costs, time extension, and impact costs, the last-named including acceleration, job rhythm, morale, and the learning curve. Good documentation is essential here. As a means of documentation, network-based methods can aid in the just, equitable, and fair resolution of differences.

Chapter 13

Cost Engineering

Cost engineering, which is one of the key responsibilities of a professional construction manager, provides the analytical methods and procedures for monitoring, analyzing, forecasting, and, most important, controlling the costs on a construction project. Like estimating and schedule and resource control, it is but one of several highly interdependent parts of what is basically the same project planning and control system. In scope, its concepts can be applied from conceptual planning, through engineering and design, to construction and start-up. In its effective application, all the principles of the feedback control system that were introduced in Chapter 10 are fundamental. These include consideration of nonlinearity in monitoring and measuring cost status, converting raw data to accurate information for analysis and reporting, the application and limitations of variances for exception reporting, forecasting and trending procedures, and the appropriate application or abstention from corrective action.

A good, definitive *control budget* is the basic document against which the cost engineer measures and compares actual progress. He also uses and thus must understand the project schedule and procurement documents. His reports to management must be accurate, current, and measured against a standard for them to have much value. In order to have effective cost control, the trends of the cost must be established as soon as possible, no matter how tenuous the indications, and be compared against both the planned and the actual progress so that management can take remedial action if required.

This chapter can only introduce some of the basic concepts of this large and diverse field. Recommendations for further study are given in the bibliography. The reader who expects to be more deeply involved in this field should also seriously consider joining the American Association of Cost Engineers, and thus gain access to the publications, experience, and professional contacts available through that organization.

The topics to be introduced here include the development and application of standard cost codes and project cost codes, conversion of a cost estimate to a control budget, guidelines for obtaining good input cost data, and the application of engineering economy in cost engineering.

COST CONTROL AND COST ENGINEERING

It is important that "cost engineering" not be confused with the financial accounting functions on a project. Certainly they are closely related, especially where cost engineering provides information for the general ledger and for payroll purposes, but there are major differences.

First, the word "engineering" in cost engineering is not mere window dressing. The reason for this is that in order to monitor and report costs properly, and especially to forecast trends, one must be able to read plans and specifications intelligently and must have a solid technical understanding for the work going on in the field.

A second major distinction is the emphasis on forecasting and trending in cost engineering. The accountant deals mainly in historical, documentable facts so that he can correctly pay the bills, make out invoices, prepare tax returns, compute the payroll, etc. Even the pennies count here. On the other hand, the cost engineer must often deal with and interpret some of the most tenuous information, including rumors and third-party knowledge to the effect that an item of materials might be late, or that there might be a jurisdictional dispute between crafts, in order to keep his forecasts as up to date as possible.

The cost engineer plays an important role in providing information and control systems that help toward the timely and profitable completion of a project. In this role, he is often at the interface between all the other key figures in the project, including management, line supervisors, scheduling, procurement, accounting, and field engineers.

COST CODES

Cost codes provide the basic framework upon which a cost-engineering system is built. In a sense, they provide a structural discipline analogous to what CPM networking methods give to schedule and resource planning and control. Like networks, a good cost code can facilitate the cost-engineering process and hence aid project management; a poorly developed code can cause nothing but trouble. It is therefore vital that management as well as cost engineers understand the proper development and application of cost codes, and that they have insight into some of the details that determine a code's success or failure.

Types of Cost Codes

Cost codes in most organizations fall into two major categories:

1. Standard cost code
2. Project cost code

The first provides for uniformity, transfer, and comparison of information among projects. The second serves as the framework for the control budget on a specific project. Both are also often used to interface with the numbering of drawings and specifications, materials procurement documents, activity labels on schedules, quality assurance reports, etc. In many cases the codes form the focal point for all these elements in the project control system. It is therefore important to understand the purpose, content, and differences of these two types of codes and to know how to convert from one to the other.

Standard Cost Code A standard cost code is a systematic classification and categorization of all items of work or cost pertaining to a particular *type of work*. There may be different standard codes for different types of work, even within the same organization. In fact, one of the major problems in development of a cost code for a project results from forcing a standard cost code for one type of work to be used in another.

Some examples of different types of work that might each have its own standard cost code are the following:

General building construction (offices, schools, warehouses, etc.)
Thermal power plants (both nuclear and fossil-fueled)
Heavy engineering projects (dams, levees, hydroelectric schemes, etc.)
Process plants (oil refineries, petrochemical plants, etc.)

In some sectors of construction, there are more or less widely accepted industry standard cost codes. The best-known example is the Cost Analysis Format in the Uniform Construction Index,[1] reproduced in Appendix D, which was developed as a joint effort of eight industry and professional associations.[2] It is primarily designed for building construction.

[1] *Uniform Construction Index*, The Construction Specifications Institute, 1150 17th Street, N.W., Washington, D.C. 20036, 1972.
[2] The American Institute of Architects, the Associated General Contractors of America, Inc., The Construction Specifications Institute, the Consulting Engineers Council of the United States, the Council of Mechanical Specialty Contracting Industries, Inc., The Professional Engineers in Private Practice/National Society of Professional Engineers, The Producers Council, Inc., and the Specification Writers Association of Canada.

The Uniform Construction Index (UCI) is actually much more than a cost code. It also provides a standard for numbering and classifying sections of plans and specifications, a standard system for manufacturers to catalog literature about construction materials and equipment, and an office filing system for a contractor's own documents and correspondence on projects. It is thus possible to organize an estimate by the same numbering system that can be used for the control budget, easily to look up technical data on materials for estimating or procurement, quickly to locate sections of the plans and specifications needed by various specialty subcontractors, and to keep all correspondence with the architect, vendors, and subcontractors filed the same way. It is not a perfect system, but it is a good one and has thus been widely adopted. Unfortunately, there is little to compare with it in other sectors of the construction industry. The Nuclear Regulatory Commission imposes one system on the nuclear power industry, and there have been attempts at other industry standards, but none has been nearly as comprehensive or widely adopted as the Uniform Construction Index.

In developing a standard cost code, it is appropriate to create a relatively exhaustive checklist of all the items that might be found in its generic type of construction. For example, the Uniform Construction Index lists items as diverse as "Boat Facilities," "Poured Gypsum Deck," "Ceramic Veneer," "Clay Roofing Tiles," "Hangar Doors," "Hospital Cubicles," "Flagpoles," "Baptismal Equipment," "Radiology Equipment," "Mortuary Equipment," "Prison Equipment," "Zoo Structures," "Chilled Water System," and "Outdoor Lighting Fixtures." No one building would require more than a few items even from this subset, but in constructing many buildings over a period of several years, a diversified contractor might encounter most of them. If they should crop up, the standard cost code provides a good checklist to help prevent such items from being overlooked in the estimate, budget, and materials procurement schedule.

Project Cost Code A project cost code is a systematic classification and categorization of all items of work or cost pertaining to a particular *project.* There is normally a different project cost code for each project, but each should be derived from the standard cost code so that different projects can be compared, and especially so that meaningful information can be maintained for estimating purposes. It is also important that the project code be prepared as soon as possible after the project is authorized so that costs from the very beginning can be accurately distributed.

A project code, however, is adapted to incorporate the particular features and characteristics of the specific project. It thus contains some components not found in the standard code, and it deletes anything not required for the job at hand. In contrast with the exhaustive checklist desirable for the standard code, the project cost code is a day-by-day working document; for practical purposes it must be kept as concise and simple as possible, in keeping with the objectives for planning, documentation, and control. A good rule of thumb in selecting items for the project code is, "If in doubt, delete it."

Once developed, the project cost code may be used for referencing and documenting items such as the following:

Expenditures and commitments for:
   Labor
   Materials
   Equipment
   Subcontracts
   Indirect costs
Procurement documents, such as:
   Requisitions
   Purchase orders
   Receiving slips
   Invoices

The project cost code serves as an interface among all parties involved in the administration and supervision of the project, as indicated in Figure 13-1.

Additional features of the project code will become more clear if we first show how it is derived from the standard cost code.

Deriving a Project Cost Code

The item code taken from the standard cost code becomes just one part of the code for a typical project code item. This part we will refer to as the "work-type code." In addition to this, it is common to add a "project number,"

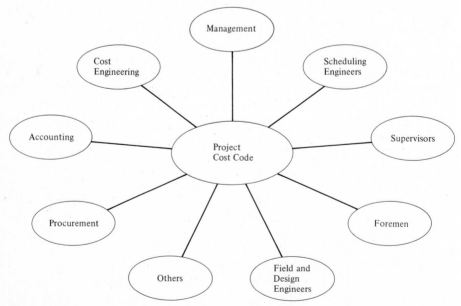

Figure 13-1 Project cost code: A means for communication.

an "area-facility code," and a "distribution code" to form the complete code for a particular item in the project code. An organization will normally have standards specifying how these additional elements are formed, but the actual codes, at least for the project number and area facilities, will be unique to the project at hand. Figure 13-2 illustrates how the conversion from standard code to project code takes place.

The section below will discuss how each of the four elements is derived.

Project Number The project number is chosen to identify the costs collected for this code specifically with the particular project from which they came. The number will often be a shorthand notation in itself that indicates such things as the type of project (e.g., H = heavy construction), the type of contract (e.g., L = lump sum), the year it was started, its sequence with other projects started that year, and possibly its location. In this way, if the home-office estimator is trying to figure out why one set of costs for, say, concrete footings differs so much from another set, the project numbers, which may show that one set was from an arctic project and the other from Southern California, help give the reason for the discrepancy.

The project number is normally implicit rather than explicit in the day-to-day project reports that use the cost code. For example, rather than include the extra digits for the project number on each line item reported, it is normally printed just in the heading for the report. Similarly, in computer files

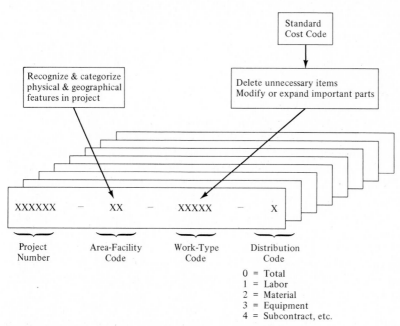

Figure 13-2 Developing project code from standard code.

using magnetic media, the project number will normally appear only at the beginning of the file, and not in each cost record.

Area-Facility Code   Often in a project, there are certain distinct geographic and physical features that logically separate one part of a project from another. Often the management of a project is also structured according to these physical or technological features. For example, a hydroelectric project might logically be separated into "dam," "tunnel," "shaft," "penstock," "powerhouse," "transmission lines," and "support facilities." These major breakdowns we shall refer to as "areas." Within each area, there are normally logical subdivisions which we shall refer to as "facilities." For example, the powerhouse might have four separate turbine-generator units, each of which might be considered a "facility." Further breakdown into intake valves, scrollcase, turbine, drive shaft, generator, transformer, controls, etc., would normally be handled in the work-type code, which is based on the standard code, rather than in the area-facility code. These are characteristics common to almost all hydroelectric turbines, whereas the fact that there are four such units is unique to this project. It is important not to confuse the application of the area-facility code with the work-type code.

Once derived, the area-facility code helps keep track of costs in the different areas, and it can isolate the costs attributable to the different managers and supervisors on the project. The work-type code, especially where, like the Uniform Construction Index, it is categorized along recognized trade and subcontractor specialties, also helps in identifying costs with the parties responsible for them.

Work-Type Code   The work-type code is the part that is based on the standard cost code. However, as indicated in Figure 13-2, considerable thought should go into the conversion. Clearly, one should start by deleting all items that have no relationship to the project at hand. For example, all mortuary and ecclesiastical equipment would normally be deleted from a code for a public school building. But the process should go deeper than this. For example, is the level of *detail* in the standard code appropriate to all items in the project? To illustrate, if the only UCI code 5 metalwork on a precast concrete[3] building is a stair railing, one might simply collect this cost at the level of the major breakdown. On the other hand, the standard cost code may not have enough detail for the other parts of the project. For example, if this is a four-story precast-prestressed-concrete parking garage, code 03430 may need to be subdivided into more components to record accurately the costs of the elements involved. With these considerations, the work-type components of the project cost codes are developed.

Distribution Code   The Uniform Construction Index, like many standard

[3]Note that UCI reinforcing steel is in code 03.

codes, does not separately break out the resource components of the various types of work, such as separating out the labor, materials, equipment, and subcontract costs. In practice, however, such a breakdown is often important, and it is normally handled with a "distribution code" such as that shown on Figure 13-2. In this way the costs associated with labor can interface with the payroll system, the materials costs can tie into the procurement schedule and the accounts payable, equipment costs can be internally accounted or paid to rental agencies, subcontractor costs can go into accounts payable, and all components can aid in the development of more accurate cash-flow forecasts. Normally there will be a company standard for the distribution codes, so that, for example, "1" is always labor, "2" is material, "3" is equipment, "4" is subcontracts, etc.

Example Figure 13-3 gives an example of a code for a particular item in a project cost code. Here the project code 78NB04 means that this is the fourth (04) negotiated (N) building construction (B) job started in 1978 (78). The area-facility breakdown, assuming this is a typical high-rise building, is chosen to give a separate "area" to each floor, with no further breakdown to "facilities" on the floor. The code "11" here refers to work on the eleventh floor. The work-type code, "03320," indicates that the costs are for placing lightweight-aggregate concrete. Distribution code "2" means that in this code we are collecting the material cost.

Account Hierarchy

Normally the desired level of detail in a cost code is reflected in the account hierarchy. This concept can apply in a standard cost code and in each of the four elements that make up a typical project cost code. Terminology commonly encountered here includes "prime account" and "subaccount."

Prime Account The "prime account" is the highest level of enumeration in a cost code. For example, in the Uniform Construction Index, the first two digits of each code form the prime account. "Concrete," "Carpentry," and "Electrical" are represented by prime accounts "03," "06," and "16" respectively.

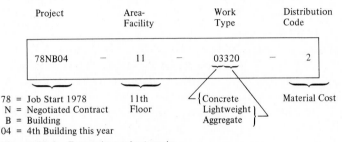

Figure 13-3 Example project code.

Subaccounts Subdivisions for greater detail within prime accounts are referred to as "subaccounts" and these in turn can have their own subhierarchies. For example, at the next level down within "03 Concrete," we have "030—Alternates," "031—Concrete Formwork," "032—Concrete Reinforcement," "033—Cast-in-place Concrete," "034—Precast Concrete," etc. These in turn can be subdivided to the desired level of detail.

Applications The account hierarchy has several important applications. First, as mentioned above, the level of detail of the code can be set at the level appropriate to the scope of work that is represented. For example, if concrete is a relatively minor part of a structure, consisting say, of a few miscellaneous footings for a large but temporary asphalt batch plant, one might appropriately collect all costs at the prime-account level, rather than go to the trouble and expense of breaking out the cement, aggregates, mixing, placing, labor, materials, etc.; it might be sufficient for future estimates to know that it cost $92 per cubic meter to construct the footings for this type of batch plant at this location in this year.

The account hierarchy is also useful for tuning the level of detail of reporting to the appropriate levels of management. For example, the concrete superintendent might want the full detail for the concrete accounts only. On the other hand, the project manager might as a routine matter look only to the major areas, the prime accounts, and the first level of subaccounts, but for all the prime-account divisions. If a particular item at that level of detail appeared to be deviating significantly from the planned budget, he or she could then request additional detail on that item.

These capabilities for summary reporting, exception reporting, and other techniques for getting the right information at the appropriate level of detail to the right person for decisions in time for corrective action, are made possible by a well-designed account hierarchy and structure.

Direct versus Indirect Costs

In general terms, *direct costs* are those which can be immediately associated in the field with work directly contributing to the physical completion of the permanent facility contracted for by the owner. Examples include (1) finishing labor for a concrete floor slab, (2) materials for a structural steel frame, (3) equipment for a foundation excavation, and (4) a subcontractor's charges for installing the air-conditioning system.

Conversely, *indirect costs* are those which necessarily contribute to the support of a project as a whole, but cannot be identified directly with specific work items in the permanent facility. Examples commonly include (1) job and office personnel salaries; (2) materials, supplies, and utilities for the temporary warehouse; (3) staff vehicles; (4) safety and first-aid expenses; and (5) the portion of home-office support required for the project. The Uniform Construction Index puts most of these in prime accounts 00 and 01.

Although these are commonly accepted meanings of "direct" and "indirect" costs, the meanings are by no means uniformly interpreted. For example, in many negotiated contracts, including those involving the professional construction management approach, "direct" costs include those which are specifically billed to the owner, and those often comprise, for example, the salaries and benefits paid to the project manager and the field staff. "Indirects" in this context are those which can be recovered only in the negotiated general "overhead" figure, or in the profit for the contract.

Similarly, even in the traditional meanings as they were first introduced, there is no real uniformity in identifying exactly what is "direct" and what is "indirect." For example, although the wages of given trades might be specifically identified with items in the field, what about the "payroll burdens" such as union fringe benefits, payroll insurance, and social security payments? Similarly, if it would take excessive and meaningless effort to state specifically what an item of support equipment was doing at any given time, such as a hoist for a high-rise building that serves many different trades and subcontractors, should that item be directly charged? Or should it be in the indirect costs?

Actual practice varies widely from one company to another in questions of this type. Only two general guidelines can thus be offered here. First, such decisions should be thoroughly studied and deliberated, rather than be made haphazardly, and should recognize the special needs of the organization and its projects. Second, once these decisions are made, they should be documented and incorporated as standard policy, and they should be applied uniformly from one project to another. Exceptions should be thoroughly justified and should be approved by higher management. Otherwise, comparisons of costs from one project to another will be meaningless.

Practical Considerations

There are numerous practical considerations, such as those that were just mentioned, that can make all the difference in the success or failure of a cost code and the cost-engineering system that builds upon it. This section will further discuss these and add several more examples to illustrate the in-depth thinking that should go into the development of a cost code. This is by no means intended to be an exhaustive or balanced set of guidelines, but merely a set of representative examples. Some of the examples are fairly subtle, and to the novice reader some may at first even seem trivial. But in the authors' experience, each of these examples, at one time or another, has been an item of controversy that had potential adverse effects on one or more major projects. The experienced reader will no doubt appreciate this, and the novice will understand in time. Codes which arbitrarily ignore such considerations will be difficult if not impossible to live with in the field.

Tracking Bulk Materials   From the time they are identified in design or in the plans and specifications, through formal requisition, solicitation, purchase orders, shop-drawing or sample approval, vendor fabrication, shipping, delivery, inspection, storage, and installation in the permanent structure, it is necessary to keep track of all major and minor items of materials and equipment required on a project. Failure in this procurement process is one of the most common causes of delays and cost overruns in construction. The process can be greatly improved through a well thought-out and intelligently applied project cost code.

In some items it is indeed appropriate to account for costs at the level of the specific area-facility and detailed work-type codes in each of the above steps. For example, a large diesel-driven pump for an oil pipeline might have its final cost code attached to it when it is first requisitioned. This code will then be cross-referenced to equipment serial numbers in the factory and be tracked at this level until it is installed and tested on site. Similar guidelines will generally apply to items such as prefabricated structural steel and bent-and-tagged reinforcing steel.

In terms of bulk materials, however, such as raw stocks of lumber, unfabricated reinforcing steel, and small pipe, this level of detail is seldom desirable and generally is not even feasible until specific quantities are actually fabricated and installed in the structure in the final step. How, then, should one account for these items?

To illustrate, consider an extreme but too frequently attempted case. Globe valves for pipe are going to be required in 10 areas, in 4 work-type codes, and in 6 different sizes. Simple multiplication shows that the total number of detail accounts may potentially number 240. This would mean at least 240 arithmetic extensions and a minimum of 240 lines to check on purchase orders, invoices, receiving reports, etc. If this concept were carried through to all bulk items, the cost code would have created a bureaucratic nightmare requiring an army of clerks to handle the detail—or more probably, the system would be ignored altogether, with most items being classified as "miscellaneous."

These same concepts for materials procurement apply to the field labor associated with the materials until they are actually used. For example, it would be unrealistic to use area and detail accounts for labor required in unloading and warehousing materials when they are delivered to the site.

How, then, does one avoid this unnecessary detail? The usual procedure is to create a *suspense account*, also called a *holding account* or *clearing account*, to keep track of all costs associated with the materials up to the point where they are drawn for use in the project. In the example of the globe valves, there might only be one suspense account for them, or possibly one for each of the six sizes. All costs incurred during procurement, receiving, and storage on site would be accumulated at this level. Then, when a valve is actually drawn for installation in a particular area for a particular work type, the suspense account could be *relieved*, that is, decreased, to charge the area and detail account for the cost of the valve, and possibly for a pro rata share of the accumulated procurement and handling expenses incurred to that point. If all valves were used on the project, suspense accounts could feasibly be reduced to $0.

Control Costs Where Incurred   Problems sometimes arise when a cost code attempts to account for costs at some point where they are not really incurred. Consider, for example, prefabricated wooden forms. If all costs for prefabrication are charged directly to the area and detail accounts where the forms are actually used, but not made, one may be holding the concrete foreman responsible for costs over which he has no real control. The costs of fabrication were incurred in the carpentry shop, not at the point where the forms were erected for the pour.

The same idea applies to ready-mix concrete, on-site batch plants, and shops for fabrication of reinforcing steel, ventilation pipe, and like items. It is desirable to neutralize the impact that cost variances in these shops will have on the operations where their products are actually used. To do this, it is common to charge a constant rate per unit for the fabricated item at all points where such items are used, and not try to pass on daily, weekly, or monthly fluctuations in actual prefabrication costs to the point of use. If required, any net cost overruns or underruns can later be prorated to the points of use, once all related operations have been completed.

Alternatively, all costs of fabrication could be retained in the shop accounts, with no materials costs allocated to the point of use. This, however, would not put the responsibility for waste and damage where it belongs. In any case, attempts to pass on variations in prefabrication costs will not only create an unnecessarily complex documentation burden; it will also cause considerable frustration in line supervisory personnel if they are held accountable for costs over which they have no real control.

Code for Cost Impact, not Design Purpose   One common mistake is to confuse engineering design requirements with factors that actually affect construction costs. For example, consider piping. Factors that do have a real impact on construction costs include size ($1^{1}/_{2}''$ and below, $2''$ to $4''$, etc.), whether the piping is on-site or off-site, materials (carbon steel, alloy, etc.), and height of installation (below $15'$, $15'$ to $25'$, etc.). It serves no real purpose from the construction point of view[4] to segregate piping costs into "project," "process," "service," and "utility," for example. These are flowsheet and process definitions, not construction *cost* factors. As one experienced hand put it, "It doesn't matter whether the 4-inch carbon steel pipe carries steam or green cheese; it is the installation cost that one seeks to accumulate from a project cost code!"

Coding Direct Labor   As a general rule, direct labor costs should be identified, as we stated above, to the extent possible with the items where they

---

[4]Though it might to the owner. More on this later.

are incurred. One can create real problems, however, when one tries to use the actual monetary costs associated with direct labor for control purposes.

Typically, and especially on longer projects, estimates and budgets are prepared without exact knowledge as to what wages, fringe benefits, payroll-based insurance, and other related burdens will actually be when the item in question is eventually built. Wage rates often take several hikes during the course of a project. Social security and state disability insurance premiums can reach a cutoff point during each calendar year for a given worker who stays on the job long enough, and the next week's cost report can show reduced unit costs for no other reason than this. Workmen's compensation insurance premiums are subject to readjustment and rebates a year or more after the time they were actually incurred.

Most of these payroll details have little or nothing to do with controlling productivity on operations in progress. To impose them on a supervisor responsible for maintaining and improving production unnecessarily adds confusion to an already tough situation; yet many "cost-control" systems continue to operate this way.

Two means are commonly used to put the focus on production control. One is to budget, monitor, and control in terms of worker-hours, not monetary units. Another is to use a monetary figure that approximates the average cost of the workers, but hold that figure constant throughout the life of the project. If actual wage-and-burden rates do climb higher than expected during the life of the project, this is a problem for higher levels of management and is not subject to control by first-line supervision. These escalation costs can be recognized separately in the indirect-cost portion of the cost code.

Construction Equipment Costs As with labor, costs of construction equipment should theoretically be identified directly with operations on which they are incurred. In large, ongoing earthmoving operations this is often quite feasible, assuming that one actually can compute all the costs of the equipment. Problems arise, however, especially when trying to charge off the ownership costs (depreciation, interest, taxes, insurance, etc.), and when equipment concurrently serves many different area and detail accounts.

Ownership costs are largely a function of annual utilization of equipment, its expected life, and the time value of money. Where the equipment can be identified with specific operations over long periods of time, or where the equipment is rented or leased, these ownership costs can be determined fairly accurately. Difficulties arise, however, when equipment is frequently moved from operation to operation and project to project. This is a large and complex field that can only be mentioned here. The interested reader should refer to a whole book on this subject by James Douglas.[5]

The second problem area, equipment that simultaneously serves several operations, occurs with machines, such as cranes and hoists, and central

[5]*Construction Equipment Policy*, McGraw-Hill Book Company, Inc., New York, 1975.

compressor and generating stations. For example, on a high-rise building, a crane might set a column on the top floor, deliver decking two floors down, assist in a concrete pour below that, help install some mechanical equipment still further down, etc. It would almost take one full timekeeper simply to account for the crane's daily activities. The same is often true of cranes on industrial construction projects. These situations are normally best handled by putting such equipment and its related costs as separate cost centers in the indirect-cost category.

Avoid Imprecision and Ambiguity   Imprecision and ambiguity in the written descriptions for the codes are two of the most common sources of confusion and error in cost engineering. Paperwork as a rule is anathema to most field construction people, and they have little patience to figure out what was meant by a vague code description. Given a choice between two or more codes where an item might be classified, they are more likely to choose at random than to call for clarification. Along this line, many knowledgeable cost engineers strongly recommend against using codes for "miscellaneous" or "other." Experience has taught them that if field line supervisors are left to code their work, somewhere on the order of half the costs in the project is "miscellaneous," and the bulk of the remainder becomes "other"; something is lacking here for control or for future estimating!

Human Considerations   Several of the suggestions that have been made thus far relate to the needs and limitations of the human beings involved in the cost-engineering process. Two other little examples, both from one of the largest heavy industrial engineering and construction companies, will further illustrate this need.

This company's cost-engineering department decided that one way to help their field superintendents accurately code the time sheets for work accomplished each day would be to print the code, plus a small plot plan showing the major areas and facilities, in a pocket-sized notebook. Unfortunately, the first edition failed in its purpose. The reason? The notebooks sent by the printer were approximately 1/4 inch wider than the standard size pocket, and were therefore kept in the office.

Once the new, correctly sized notebooks arrived, the concept began to work as planned, and the accuracy of coding improved markedly. But, over time, another problem developed. On large projects of long duration, there is considerable turnover even of supervisory personnel. Also, as with drawings, specifications, and other works of engineers, there were successive revisions and new editions of the cost-code notebooks. The problem that arose was that in time, possession of older editions of the notebooks began to be associated with seniority and its related stature on the project. Consequently, several versions of the cost codes were being reported.

Each of these little examples may seem inconsequential in and of themselves. But in practice they are exactly the sorts of things that determine whether or not a system will be a success. In spite of twentieth-century computer automation, we must still make allowances for human idiosyncrasies, and we are better off for it.

Concluding Guidelines

Briefly stated, project cost codes must be simple, clean, concise, and easy to interpret. Use the standard cost code as a guide only. Do not incorporate its exhaustive detail. Ask only for essential and readily identifiable units of work. Area-facility breakdown should be logical and practical, and should never be changed in the middle of a project. Such a change destroys all chance of consistency in cost records, even though a new breakdown might later seem to suit the project better. Rarely is a project cost code made too simple. But far too often they are bogged down with responses to individual requests of, "Wouldn't it be nice if we had the costs of . . .," or, "Although this isn't really needed on this project, someday it might be useful to have the costs of . . .," etc. Like the travel itinerary planned to 20-foot intervals in Chapter 10, this type of code only gets in the way and causes problems once the project is underway. As a rule, if it doesn't add, it detracts. If an item cannot be coded easily and accurately by hard-pressed field personnel, forget it! Bad information is worse than none at all.

CONTROL BUDGETS

The control budget is the basic reference standard for monitoring and controlling cost status on a project. The structure for the control budget is the project cost code. Its standards for reference are derived from the cost estimate and include the quantities associated with each item of work in the code. In addition, the control budget usually makes provision for recording and reporting the following:

> Actual performance, to-date and this period
> Projections or forecasts to completion
> Variances in absolute and/or relative terms
> Reasons or conditions associated with excessive variances

A typical control budget report format was shown in Figure 10-3. Figure 13-4 shows a simple format based on the example warehouse project. In creating such reports, there is always a trade-off between the amount of information to supply and the danger of confusing or inundating the user. Again, simplicity and consistency are the best guidelines here.

For tight project control, it is not enough simply to take figures from the estimate and plug them into the cost codes. Some of the reasons for this were given in Chapter 11 in the section on converting an estimate to a control budget. First of all, for any number of good reasons, the estimate might not even have

Division: __WestAmerica__ Date: __8-1-8–__ Project No. __7625__

Facility __Dry Storage Warehouse__ Prepared by __R.A.G.__

Location __Mountaintown, WestAmerica__ Approved by __G.L.R.__

Description of project (attach separate schedules and drawings as required).

__150,000 square foot Dry Storage Warehouse. Pallet and flow racks__

__required. See attached drawings Nos. G-1, G-2, and G-3__

	Allocation	Amount Requested	Total
1.	Architect/engineer		$ 260,000
2.	Site work	$ 798,000	
3.	Buildings and utilities	4,000,000	
4.	Repair and maintenance		
5.	Other owner's cost (CM)	372,000	
6.	Subtotal (items 2–5)	5,170,000	
7.	Contingency	430,000	
8.	Total building cost		5,600,000
9.	Operating and process equip.	360,000	
10.	Repair and maintenance		
11.	Other owner's cost	140,000	
12.	Subtotal equipment	500,000	
13.	Contingency	40,000	
14.	Total equipment cost		540,000
15.	Total land cost		100,000
16.	Total estimated cost		$6,500,000

Figure 13-4 Example project budget.

been done against the standard-cost-code categories. For example, where the contract bid documents specify a unit-cost proposal with a schedule of quantities, these may serve as the dominant breakdown, and will certainly have to be accommodated for payment purposes in the course of a project. There must then at least be a conversion and redistribution process to get the costs into their appropriate project code categories. Similarly, owners, for purposes of capital depreciation and taxation, will often impose a code on a contractor that is of little value for construction cost control. Some government agencies, such as the Nuclear Regulatory Commission, also can impose a separate code on the contractor. This often requires the contractor to maintain project costs in two or three entirely different code classifications. With good computer programming, this is not as bad as it sounds, since the second and third distributions can be largely automated. Needless to say, however, without such automation it can be a huge paperwork burden.

Another important concept was implied in the discussion of learning curves in Chapter 10, and was amplified in Chapter 11. Estimates necessarily must be based on averages. However, if one controls only against averages, one might expect average results. Figure 11-14 gave a graphical expression of this idea. It may therefore be desirable to control against tighter standards, say the 20th percentile, assuming the concept is appropriately and intelligently applied, with an open and positive, rather than a punitive, managerial approach.

SOURCES OF DATA FOR COST CONTROL

No control system, whether computerized or not, and regardless of the skill of its developers, is of any value without accurate, timely input data. In field cost control, this especially requires good data for materials, equipment, and labor. The last two are particularly important, since these are the resources whose productivity and costs can change most rapidly and are thus the ones over which a contractor has most control. As discussed in Chapter 10, regarding the "level of influence" concept, the die is largely cast for materials costs by the time construction starts, and the feedback time is not nearly so critical.

The main sources of data for field cost control are (1) labor and equipment time sheets; (2) field surveys of quantities of work in place; (3) any other fragments of information that will assist in forecasting cost trends; and (4) data obtained from other parts of the project control system, including scheduling, procurement, and quality assurance. Each of these is important, and comparisons between these various measures are essential to evaluate project status satisfactorily.

The first two sources of data, time sheets and field quantity surveys, are the most basic sources of data for routine cost reports and will be discussed in more detail here. They are also important, of course, as sources of data for scheduling, procurement, and payroll accounting, but often they are the primary responsibility of the cost engineer.

Time Sheets

Labor and equipment time sheets are usually filled out and submitted either daily or weekly by foremen, operators, superintendents, or timekeepers, depending on company policy. They normally contain the following information:

Labor Time Sheets	*Equipment Time Sheets*
Employee name(s) and/or number(s)	Machine description(s) and/or number(s)
Date(s) worked	Date(s) worked
Craft or classification(s)	Type of work done
Hours worked (straight time (ST) and overtime (OT)	Hours worked (ST & OT)
Classification by cost code	Classification by cost code
Hourly rates (ST & OT)	Hourly rates
Total hours and dollars, by day and by code	Total hours and dollars, by day and by code
Special conditions (weather, etc.)	Special conditions (breakdowns, etc.)

The time sheets are generally preprinted on standard forms, and are organized so that they are partially self-checking through "crossfooting" (adding and extending both horizontally by rows and vertically by columns). An example of a daily time sheet for labor is shown in Figure 13-5. A weekly time sheet for a front-end loader is shown in Figure 13-6. Note that, on daily sheets, it is common to list several employees or machines on the same sheet, since the two-dimensional matrix allows for both these and the cost codes in which they worked. Weekly sheets need one dimension for days of the week, and hence only one employee or machine is listed per card.

As a rule, to capture more accurate information it is desirable to use daily time sheets. Week-long memories can quickly fade in the last 15 minutes on Friday afternoon if one expects supervisors to recall everything at this time, even with the aid of their diaries. Also, several companies with computer systems and daily time-data input actually process their time-data information

WESTAMERICA CONSTRUCTION COMPANY, INC.														
DAILY LABOR TIME CARD														

PROJECT: Mountaintown Warehouse   WEATHER: Clear, 90 F, light wind
DATE: August 23, 1980   PROJECT NO.: 83WH04   PREPARED BY: B. C. Paulson

Employee Number	Name	Craft	Str. Time Over Time	ST Wage Rate	Cost Code: Area & Work-Type								Total Hours	Gross Amount
					F12-03120	A27-06181								
622	J. Douglas	C	ST	29.28	8								8	$234.24
			OT											
714	J. Fondahl	C	ST	29.28		8							8	234.24
			OT	44.72		2							2	89.44
582	H. Parker	C	ST	29.28	4	4							8	234.24
			OT	44.72		2							2	89.44
529	M. Philips	C	ST	29.28		8							8	234.24
			OT	44.72		2							2	89.44
453	G. Roberts	L	ST	21.64	8								8	173.12
			OT											
642	G. Sears	L	ST	21.64		8							8	173.12
			OT	32.94		2							2	65.88
			ST											
			OT											
			ST											
			OT											
			ST											
			OT											
Total Hours			ST		20	28								
			OT			8								
Total Cost					$524.48	$1,092.92								$1,617.48 1,617.48

Figure 13-5 Daily labor time card. (*Adapted from Richard Clough,* Construction Contracting, *3rd ed., John Wiley & Sons, Inc., New York, 1975, p. 244*)

WESTAMERICA CONSTRUCTION COMPANY, INC.

WEEKLY EQUIPMENT TIME CARD

PROJECT: Mountaintown Warehouse   MACHINE: Cat 977

WEEK ENDING: Aug. 23, 198_ PROJECT NO.: 83WH04   MACHINE NO.: L-5   RATE ST: 84.80 /hr.   Idle/Repair: 32.40 /hr. OT: 69.20 /hr.

Day	Str. Time / Over Time	Cost Code: Area & Work-Type F10-02220	S01-02222				Total Hours Str. Time	Over Time	Repair	Idle	Total Cost	Weather & Comments
Monday	ST	8					8				678.40	Clear, 85
	OT											
Tuesday	ST	6					6		2		573.60	Clear, 80 / Hydraulic hose burst
	OT											
Wednesday	ST	8					8				678.40	Cloudy, 70
	OT											
Thursday	ST		8				8				678.40	75, light wind
	OT											
Friday	ST		8				8				816.80	80, clear
	OT		2							2		
Saturday Sunday	OT											
Total Hours		22	18				38	2	2			PREPARED BY:
Total Cost		1,865.60	1,495.20						64.80		3,425.60 / 3,425.60	B. C. Paulson

Figure 13-6 Weekly equipment time card.

the night it is received and have critical cost reports available on site the next morning. Some argue, however, that daily time cards are too time-consuming for field people. However, if you actually study the two examples, you will see that the total number of entries would be the same.

Both approaches can be greatly facilitated if a computer preprints all information on the cards except for the time entries and special condition notes. That is, a supervisor receives a sheet that already lists the names and numbers of his crew and equipment, plus the cost codes in which they are likely to work. There may be a few extra spaces each way for writing in additional names or codes if needed. Anything that can be done to minimize the time field people need to write will generally improve the accuracy and completeness of reporting.

Some also claim that field supervisors cannot be expected to code their work accurately. Their failure to do so usually results first of all from unnecessarily complex and ambiguous cost codes and, second, from lack of training in the use and importance of the cost system. Where problems are still experienced in obtaining accurate distributions from field supervisors, it may be necessary to have them submit their reports in narrative form and to let the timekeeper or cost engineer do the actual coding. However, the fact that many organizations do get good cost data coded directly by field supervisors is proof that this can be done, and it is the most desirable alternative where possible. Careful attention to the human factors in management can usually make for successful reporting.

Measuring and Reporting Work Quantities

In order to associate labor and equipment costs with physical work achieved, it is necessary, on the same reporting time cycle (daily, weekly), to estimate or measure the quantities of each elementary work item that have been accomplished during that period. The same estimates will serve not only for cost reports on labor, materials, and equipment, but also for scheduling, procurement, and other parts of the control system.

Normally such quantity reports are a mixture of actual measurements and judgment estimates. For example, on major earthworks items where daily or weekly reports are desired, the actual surveying of cross sections and quantities will most likely be done only for monthly or semimonthly progress payments. In between, it will normally suffice to use projections based on past production rates, to count truck loads, or to use some similar approximation. These can then be readjusted if necessary when the results of the next physical survey are obtained. The point is that in all quantity reporting there is a trade-off between the cost of obtaining additional accuracy in information (field survey crews are expensive) and the value of that precision in reporting.

Once the quantity data are combined with the expenditure of labor, equipment, and material resources, one can compute unit costs, study learning-curve improvements, make projections of costs at completion, and apply corrective action to operations that are in trouble. Figure 13-7 gives an example summary report that brings two of these factors together to compare relative labor productivity against physical progress.

ENGINEERING ECONOMY IN COST ENGINEERING

Especially in the planning and design stages but also in construction, cost engineers are often called upon for studies requiring a thorough understanding of the principles and methods of engineering economy. This section will not attempt to explain these methods, but it will mention some of the main concepts and give examples of where they apply. The bibliography lists a few basic texts that will provide the needed theory and procedures. It is worth emphasizing, however, that all engineers, whether involved in design, construction, or operations, should have a working knowledge of this vital subject.

Comparative Economic Studies

Cost engineers are often called upon for studies and recommendations requiring the comparative economic evaluation of alternatives in technology and procedures. The design of a building, for example, might require a comparison between two different systems for heating and air conditioning. The first, which incorporates some relatively unproven solar collectors, has a comparatively high first cost but, on the basis of expected energy costs, would have a lower annual operating cost than the alternative. The alternative has a lower first cost, uses reliable and proven technology, but relies on natural gas or

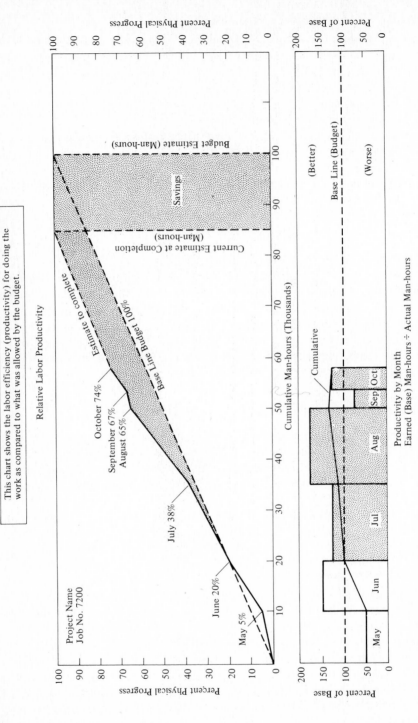

This chart shows the labor efficiency (productivity) for doing the work as compared to what was allowed by the budget.

Relative Labor Productivity

Project Name
Job No. 7200

Percent Physical Progress

Cumulative Man-hours (Thousands)

May 5%
June 20%
July 38%
August 65%
September 67%
October 74%

Base Line Budget 100%
Estimate to complete
Current Estimate at Completion (Man-hours)
Budget Estimate (Man-hours)
Savings

Percent of Base

(Better)
Base Line (Budget)
(Worse)

Cumulative

May Jun Jul Aug Sep Oct

Productivity by Month
Earned (Base) Man-hours ÷ Actual Man-hours

Figure 13-7 Relative labor productivity.

electricity as its energy source and hence can expect increasing annual operating costs.

Typical examples in the construction stage require comparative studies between alternative systems of equipment and their associated crews for accomplishing a construction objective. For example, contractors evaluating systems for excavating and transporting fill for an earth-rock dam might look at alternatives between shovels, front-end loaders, or bucket-wheel excavators for loading, and trucks, rail cars, or conveyor belts for the main haul, or combinations of these.

The ability objectively and rationally to make studies of this kind requires a thorough understanding of the time value of money so that capital costs, operating costs, replacement costs, and other costs can somehow be reduced to a common basis for comparison. Techniques and concepts involved include present-worth analyses, equivalent annualized costs, benefit/cost analyses, break-even or payout time, rate of return on investment, and cash-flow analyses. These days it is also important to be able to allow for general inflation and equipment cost escalation in these analyses. Readers who are uncomfortable with any of these terms owe it to themselves to acquire this knowledge or risk being handicapped in today's economically constrained environment.

Project Finance

In addition to studies of the type described, cost engineers must often also work closely with managers, accountants, financial analysts, and scheduling engineers to forecast the cash or borrowing needs of the project. Such analyses can be done from the point of view of the owner, the contractor, the lenders, or all of these. Cash-flow problems, even on seemingly profitable projects, have too often caused failures.

The main tool for these studies is the discounted cash flow and its associated rate of return on invested capital. The concept was illustrated in Figure 12-9. Development of the curves shown there requires knowledge of the amounts and timings of the cash flows and also of the interest on borrowed funds. Determining the amounts and timings of cash flows, in turn, requires an intimate knowledge of the planned schedule, resources, methods, and technology to be incorporated on the project, and the contractual terms and conditions that relate the owner, designer, contractor, subcontractors, suppliers, and labor forces on the project. This is why the input of cost engineers is particularly important.

SUMMARY

This chapter has introduced some of the major concepts needed in cost engineering. This is one of the most vital control functions on any project, and it is important that the reader who will be working in this field seek more in-depth knowledge of the subject. This chapter is only the beginning.

Cost codes provide the basic framework upon which a cost-engineering system is built. Two types were introduced. A standard cost code contains and systematically categorizes a relatively complete enumeration of all the types of work in a generic type of construction, such as general building construction. The Uniform Construction Index is one of the best-known examples. A project cost code, while derived from the standard code, is developed for a specific project and hence contains additional elements for the project number, major areas and facilities within it, and a means of distributing costs for resources, such as labor, materials, and equipment.

In contrast with the exhaustive checklist sought in a standard cost code, a workable project cost code must be kept simple, clean, concise, and easy to interpret. Guidelines suggested for doing this include: (1) Use suspense accounts for procurement of bulk materials; (2) control costs at the point where they are incurred; (3) code for cost, not design function; (4) do not attempt to use detailed payroll costs for control of labor productivity; (5) avoid unrealistically detailed equipment cost distribution; (6) avoid imprecision and ambiguity in code description; and (7) consider the human factors in cost engineering.

Control budgets are derived from estimates of costs and quantities, and usually provide for recording actual performance, making forecasts, showing variances, and documenting reasons for unexpected problems. There is often need to recategorize the costs from the estimate to serve the needs of cost control or for owner or agency requirements. Also, it is desirable to set control standards tighter than the averages used for estimating, to provide a realistic goal for achieving better-than-average results.

Field construction cost control concentrates mainly on labor and equipment. The main sources of data here are labor, equipment time sheets, and estimates or surveys of quantities of work in place. Data from other parts of the control system, including scheduling, accounting, procurement, and quality assurance, are also important for consistency, comparisons, and interrelated factors.

Engineering economy supplies cost engineers with some of their most useful and powerful analytical tools. The cost engineer is often called upon to apply a thorough working knowledge of the theory and principles of engineering economy in making comparative economic evaluations of alternatives in design or construction and in developing cash flows for project finance.

As a key figure in project control, the cost engineer is often at the interface between management, line supervisors, scheduling, procurement, accounting, field engineers, and others. It is an interesting and challenging job that takes the economic pulse of the whole project.

Chapter 14

Procurement

In the broadest sense, procurement and procurement-related activities occur during all phases of a construction project. Periodically recurring scarcities of both manufactured goods and raw materials, both on a domestic and on a worldwide basis, will continue to offer a challenge to experienced industry professionals. Major procurement for a project may be handled almost entirely by one organization, as happens in a design-construct project, or it may be split between the owner, designer, general contractor, and subcontractors. On a professional construction management project, the manager often handles procurement of long-lead items in order to advance overall completion dates.

Methods and practices, of course, differ with individual firms and projects. A general contractor may receive bids from subcontractors, material suppliers, and equipment manufacturers who can refer to completed plans and specifications before bidding. On a traditional project he will have procurement practices that significantly differ from those of a design-constructor or turnkey firm normally engaged in a phased construction program. Nevertheless, certain basic principles are common to each general approach to construction procurement. This chapter will explain general industry practices and will show how procurement and procurement-related activities interface with other project activities and controls throughout the life cycle.

CONCEPTS OF PROCUREMENT

Procurement includes purchasing of equipment, materials, supplies, labor, and services required for construction and implementation of a project. It also includes related activities of tracking and expediting, routing and shipment, materials and equipment handling, accountability and warehousing, final acceptance documentation, and ultimate disposal of surplus items at job end.

Procurement is normally performed at several levels. Major equipment, such as a boiler on a coal-fired power plant, may be purchased by the owner long before the ground-breaking ceremony. A general contractor's home office may arrange for procurement of subcontractors and major materials and equipment to be installed by the contractor's own forces. The job-site field office will normally procure supplies, incidental rentals, and other requirements. On a professional construction management project, certain long-lead items may be procured by the owner, others by the manager, and less critical items by each of the contractors involved in the program.

Ethical standards of behavior in procurement-related activities are difficult to define. What is generally accepted practice in some industries, countries, and locations may be considered borderline or unethical in others. The conduct of owners, designers, general contractors, subcontractors, and professional construction managers is subject to varying degrees of economic risk that will also have an effect upon generally accepted standards. Therefore, a professional construction manager, general contractor, and subcontractor must have sufficient overall industry knowledge, as well as knowledge of practices in the area or country where they are doing business, to maintain an ethical and reasonable approach.

THE PROCUREMENT CYCLE

Procurement of materials ranges from simple purchases of supplies at the time they are needed, such as running down to the hardware store for a few more boards and a box of nails, to major design, manufacturing, and shipment procedures, such as those required for the fabricated structural steel for a 500-meter cantilever bridge. In general, however, the cycle involves all or some of the following steps:

1 Identification or recognition of the need during design or estimating
2 Determination of the design characteristics required to perform the desired function
3 Quantification of the elements needed, and preparation of procurement specifications
4 Issuance and processing of internal requisition
5 Solicitation of bids or price quotations
6 Receipt and evaluation of proposals
7 Issuance of purchase order, subcontract or lease
8 Vendor's or subcontractor's preparation and submission of shop drawings or samples

    9 Review and approval of shop drawings by contractor and owner's architect/engineer

    10 Fabrication by vendor or subcontractor

    11 Tracking and expediting

    12 Shipping and traffic

    13 Delivery and inspection

    14 Storage and handling on site prior to use

    15 On-site fabrication operations

    16 Installation and testing in constructed facility

    17 Owner acceptance/rejection, warranties, corrections, and other follow-up

Not all these steps are required for all types of materials. For example, a contractor might already have an open purchase order with a ready-mix concrete supplier. The concrete superintendent simply phones in the specifications, quantity, and delivery requirements the afternoon before a day's pour, and the next morning the concrete is batched, trucked, and delivered and slump tests and cylinders are made, but there is no further on-site fabrication. The process is condensed to less than a day. On the other hand, for some procurement operations the above list is grossly oversimplified. Consider the procurement of bridge steel from Japan for erection in Australia, or the process of getting a nuclear steam supply system made in the United States delivered to a power plant in the Middle East. The preparation of shop drawings and fabrication are full-scale projects in themselves, months or years in duration, with hundreds or thousands of activities to be closely interfaced to the operations in the project for which the materials or equipment are intended. Shipping, especially of large or bulky items and particularly if multimode (truck, rail, barge, ship) carriers and international passage are needed, is a highly complex, time-consuming process that often baffles even the most knowledgeable and experienced professionals. In other words, procurement can involve far more than merely requesting the stereotyped "green-eye-shade" purchasing agent to phone around town for the lowest price on thin-wall conduit.

    In today's projects, where design-construct and professional construction management contracts and performance specifications leave much to the judgment of the constructor or construction manager, procurement also requires up-to-date knowledge of the types of materials and equipment that can best meet the desired performance standards for the lowest capital and operating costs (life-cycle costs). If one material becomes unavailable or too costly, procurement specialists must know where they can get a substitute that will meet or exceed the original requirements.

DEFINITIONS OF PRINCIPAL DOCUMENTS

The following definitions will be helpful in understanding the principal documents needed in the purchasing process.

Prime Contract

A prime contract is one let by the owner to a contractor who is in turn responsible for performing the work according to the contract specifications. Under the single-contract traditional method, only one prime contract was generally awarded by the owner to a prime contractor. With multiple-contract and professional construction management approaches, the owner may award a number of prime contracts. Appendix C contains a sample prime contract.

Purchase Order

A purchase order, such as that shown in Figure 14-1, is a short form of contract normally issued for procurement of materials, permanent equipment, and supplies. It may also be used for certain professional services such as surveying, or soils and concrete testing, but is not normally employed where on-site labor is involved.

Subcontract

A subcontract is a form of lower-tier contract for procurement of work and services to be performed by other than a prime contractor at a construction site. Traditionally, the subcontractor is responsible to the general or prime contractor for some or all of the provisions of the prime contract. Under professional construction management, the manager may, as the owner's agent, award subcontracts for performance of on-site work. See Appendix C for a sample subcontract for award by a general contractor to a subcontractor.

Agreements and Leases

Agreements and leases are forms of contracts often used for procurement of technical services and for rental or lease of automobiles, construction or office equipment, or other temporary items that are not consumed or do not become part of the finished work.

PURCHASING AND CONTRACTING PRACTICE

Normal purchasing and contracting practices and procedures are outlined below. Each individual firm will develop its own methods and documents; but each must be sufficiently flexible to cope with an ever changing construction climate, to meet special client directions, or to comply with other outside requirements.

Requisitions

Where a formal purchasing department is maintained, construction managers or supervisors usually initiate purchasing and subcontracting by issuing standard-form requisitions asking the purchasing department to obtain bids for equipment, materials, work, or services as described in the requisition and the applicable plans and specifications attached or referenced. Figure 14-2 gives an example of a requisition form.

ADDRESS ALL CORRESPONDENCE TO

**PURCHASE
ORDER NO.** _____

SHEET _____ OF _____ SHEETS

DATE	TO BE SHIPPED

PURCHASE ORDER

**THIS ORDER NUMBER MUST
APPEAR ON ALL INVOICES,
PACKAGES, PACKING SLIPS,
BILLS OF LADING, ETC.**

NO CHARGES ALLOWED FOR PACKING, BOXING OR
CRATING. DO NOT SUBSTITUTE OR BACK ORDER.
EXCEPT WHEN PERMISSION IS GIVEN BY US.

PLEASE ENTER OUR ORDER BASED ON YOUR QUOTATION AND OFFER HERETOFORE SUBMITTED AND SUBJECT TO TERMS, CONDITIONS AND
INSTRUCTIONS ON THE FACE OF THIS ORDER AND ATTACHED HERETO AS EXHIBIT "B" AND SCHEDULE 1 AND BY THIS REFERENCE MADE A
PART HEREOF.

SHIP TO: TERMS:

                                                 F.O.B. POINT:

                                                 INFORM US PROMPTLY IF UNABLE TO SUPPLY GOODS AS ORDERED.

*VIA: * DO NOT CHANGE ROUTING WITHOUT AUTHORITY.

ITEM NO.	QUANTITY	UNIT	DESCRIPTION	UNIT PRICE	TOTAL	ACCOUNT NO.
				TOTAL OF ORDER		

REQ'N
NO. _____

BY _____

BY _____

Figure 14-1 Purchase order.

Prequalification and Bid List Preparation

All purchasing departments develop and maintain lists of material suppliers, specialty contractors, equipment suppliers, and other vendors. Prequalification of potential suppliers, manufacturers, contractors, and subcontractors is often

REQUISITION

Date _____

For Purchase of: _____

End use: _____

In Accordance with Drawings and/or Specification _____

Rev. No. _____

Req. No. _____

Job No. _____

ITEM	QUANTITY	UNIT	DESCRIPTION	COST CODE & BUDGET EST.

Engineering Review Required.   Yes _____   No _____

Date Required at Destination _____

Destination: _____

F. O. B. Point: Vendors _____   Destination _____

For Required Information Data and Conditions, See back of sheet.

_____   _____
Prepared By   Date

_____   _____
Approved-Project Engineer   Date

Figure 14-2a   Requisition (page 1).

PROCUREMENT CONDITIONS
(Please Check Items Required)

A. Information Required with Quotation
   1.___Specifications of proposed materials and workmanship.
   2.___General Dimension and Outline Drawings
   3.___General description of equipment operation.
   4.___Performance curves and data.
   5.___Vendor's recommended lists of spare parts. _____with prices.

B. Data Required After Purchase. In Sets, as follows:
   1.___General Arrangement Drawings.   8.___Wiring Diagrams.
   2.___Detail Drawings.   9.___Elementary Drawings.
   3.___Certified Dimension Prints.   10.___Spare Parts Lists.
   4.___Reproduced Tracings.   11.___Installation Instructions
   5.___Show Drawings.   12.___Operating Instructions.
   6.___Performance Curves.   13.___Maintenance Manuals.
   7.___Erection Drawings   14._____

   _____Sets of No._____ above for approval.
   _____Sets of No._____ above after approval.
   Above data to be directed to:

                        Attn:_____Project Engineer

C. Conditions and Services Required After Purchase
   15.___Inspection to be the responsibility of Vendor.
   16.___Inspection to be the responsibility of Purchaser.
   17.___Installation by Purchaser.
   18.___Installation supervision to be furnished by Vendor.
   19.___Guarantee to be Vendor's standard against defective workmanship and materials for a minimum
         period of one year from date of acceptance of material or equipment, with liability limited to
         replacement of parts.
   20.___Vendor to hold and save Purchaser harmless from patent liability of any nature or kind arising
         out of this equipment, its application, or its use.

Comments: _____
_____

Figure 14-2b   Requisition (page 2).

appropriate on certain work, but may be less desirable in other situations. Where possible, prequalification to ensure that the award can always be made to the low responsive bidder can often improve job-site performance, particularly in the professional construction management method. On government and other selected work, use of minority contractors or subcontractors may be specified, and prequalification takes on a different aspect from the usual performance and financial requirements. On certain work, requiring a payment and performance bond results in prequalification of bidders by their ability to obtain a bond from a bonding company.

Preparation of bid lists varies with the different contractual methods. General contractors on competitively bid projects often advertise in trade papers that they will accept sub-bids up to a stated deadline. Other general contractors will make telephone calls or send out postcards to a predetermined list. When potential subcontractors cannot be prequalified, last-minute decisions regarding the qualifications of a low bidder can often become difficult just before bid time.

Design-constructors often keep card files and qualification data on a large number of potential vendors and subcontractors in different areas of the country. An area investigation will also normally turn up additional firms that may be more qualified in the local area than larger regional or nationwide suppliers and contractors. On the other hand, large international projects may include procurement of major engineered equipment from a prequalified list of firms from several different countries. On one major hydroelectric project, turbines were purchased from Germany, generators were purchased from Japan, and all the coordination required to ensure compatibility was handled from the California job site where the equipment was ultimately erected.

Prequalification and bid list preparation on professional construction management projects were discussed in Part 2, Professional Construction Management in Practice. Prequalification to ensure that only qualified firms are invited to bid, and restriction of the bid list to a reasonable number of firms so that all will be seriously interested, are extremely important in a professional construction management program.

Requests for Quotation

Requests for quotation can range from a simple advertisement in a local trade journal requesting sub-bids to an elaborate bid package with plans, specifications, and other contract documents fully delineating all aspects of the proposed purchase. Bid packages should be kept simple and consistent with individual requirements, but they might include some or all of the following documents:

- Specifications
- Drawings
- Scope of Work
- Bills of Materials
- Commercial Documents
- Notice to Bidders
- Proposal Form
- Contract Form
- Terms and Conditions

- Shipping Instructions
- Schedules
- Insurance Requirements
- Special Requirements
- Payment and Performance Bond Form

Bid Receipt and Evaluation

As in other procurement actions, good practice will vary with the nature of the project. Acceptance of last-minute telephone quotations on materials and sub-bids is common practice in many areas on competitively bid, single general contracts. Such a practice, however, would not be considered normal for an engineer-constructor who has sufficient time to accept written quotations on preprepared forms.

Government agencies generally hold public bid openings, whereas many private owners open all bids privately and never divulge the comparative figures to the bidders. In the professional construction management method, bids are often opened at a semiprivate bid opening to which all persons submitting a bid are invited. Other owners open bids in private but furnish all responsive bidders with a tabulation of actual evaluated results. Such a tabulation may show the component parts of each bid compared with the estimate (if available) and also note any omissions, inaccuracies, or other discrepancies. An evaluation to cover such discrepancies is often made so that the evaluated bid price may be higher than the actual bid.

If negotiations are required, they should normally be conducted with the low bidder or others equally in contention. It is in this sensitive area that ill will and misunderstandings often develop. The professional construction manager should endeavor to conduct himself like Caesar's wife, above even the hint of suspicion.

Recommendation for Purchase

Most medium-sized and large firms formalize recommendations for purchase with a document approved up through various levels of management; the level of approval required normally depends on the dollar value or potential risk associated with the transaction. In the case of complicated items of engineered equipment, an engineering review is usually also required as part of the preparation of the "Recommendation for Purchase." With reasonable care in preparation of bidding documents and in the selection of bidders, awards can almost always be made to the evaluated low bidder. See Figure 14-3 for a form combining the requisition and the recommendation for purchase.

Award and Preparation of Documents

Award of a purchase order, contract, or subcontract can be made verbally with completed documents to follow, or can be formalized by a "Notice of Award" advising the successful bidder that his quotation has been accepted. Figure 14-4 gives an example of such a notice. Purchase orders may be issued confirming a

REQUISITION & RECOMMENDATION TO PURCHASE

Required Delivery _____
Type of Quotation: Verbal ☐ Written ☐
Engineering Review Required ☐

Page _____ of _____
Req. No. _____
Date _____
Material _____

To be used for _____

Coded by _____

Attention

Quantity	Description Give Complete Data-Drawing Number, Etc.	Account Number	Unit	Bid No.			Bid No.			Bid No.		
				Unit Price	Amount		Unit Price	Amount		Unit Price	Amount	
										Total		

Originator _____   Approved _____

Item No.	Purchase Order or Sub Contract Recommended To Be Placed With	P. O. No.

F. O. B.
Terms
Shipping
Shipping Point
Price Policy

REASON SUPPLIER SELECTED

☐ Lowest Price   ☐ Only Source
                        Known
☐ Required Design   ☐ Early Delivery

Remarks: _____

Prepared By _____ Distribution
Purchasing Agent _____
APPROVED:
Field Engr. _____
General Supt. _____
Resident Mgr. _____
Owner _____

Figure 14-3 Requisition and recommendation to purchase.

284

DOMESTIC TELEGRAM		INTERNATIONAL CABLE
☐ Full Rate ☐ Day Letter ☐ Night Letter	**WIRE MESSAGE** ☐ PREPAID ☐ COLLECT	☐ Full Rate ☐ Night Letter

Job No._____ Authorized by _____ Sender's Extension No._____ Dept._____

Date ___9/24/76___

JENSEN EXCAVATORS
210 FIRST STREET
MOUNTAINTOWN, WEST AMERICA

RE: NOTICE OF AWARD
     CONTRACT M1, EASYWAY WAREHOUSE,
     MOUNTAINTOWN, WEST AMERICA

CONTRACT NO. M1, SITE EARTHWORK IN THE LUMP SUM AMOUNT OF TWO HUNDRED SIX
THOUSAND DOLLARS ($206,000) HAS BEEN AWARDED TO YOU THIS DATE. CONSIDER THIS
TELEGRAM AS NOTICE TO PROCEED WITH ALL WORK EXCEPT FIELD WORK. NOTICE TO PRO-
CEED WITH FIELD WORK WILL BE ISSUED BY O. HANSON, FIELD CONSTRUCTION MANAGER.

EASYWAY FOOD COMPANY

BY_____L. JAMES_____
                 PROJECT MANAGER

Figure 14-4 Notice of award.

bidder's offer, and may not always require the vendor's signature. On the other hand, contracts and subcontracts are almost always formally signed by both parties. Bid bonds are often used by some owners, especially in the public sector, to ensure that the low bidder will in fact execute the contract.

Procurement Schedule and Status Report   **JOB NO.**
    REPORT: MASTER LIST BY COST-CODE

FAC. CMP. SHP EQ. ITEM	COST-CODE SPEC/REQ NO	P.O. CO AMOUNT	DESCRIPTION & QUANTITY VENDOR & ORIGIN	SCH CLA
46-0960-00-00-00	1501-5700	46001-00	STEAM METER #2	
46-1010-00-00-00	1501-5700		HEATEXC FOR HOT WATER SYSTEM	
46-1020-00-00-00	1501-5700		HEATEXC FOR HOT WATER SYSTEM	
46-1030-00-00-00	1501-5700		HEATEXC FOR HOT WATER SYSTEM	
46-1040-00-00-00	1501-5700		HEATEXC FOR HOT WATER SYSTEM	
46-1060-00-00-00	1501-5700		DOMESTIC WATER HEATER	
46-1080-00-00-00	1501-5700		DOMESTIC HOT WATER CIRCULAT-	
46-1110-00-00-00	1501-5700		HOT WATER CIRCULATING PUMP	
46-1120-00-00-00	1501-5700		HOT WATER CIRCULATING PUMP	
46-1130-00-00-00	1501-5700		HOT WATER CIRCULATING PUMP	
46-1300-00-00-00	1501-5700		SUMP PUMP FLOOR AREA 100 GPM	
46-1310-00-00-00	1501-5700		SUMP PUMP FLOOR AREA 100 GPM	
46-1350-00-00-00	1501-5700		BRINE PUMP	
46-1360-00-00-00	1501-5700		BRINE PUMP	
20-0001-00-01-00	2101-3100	101-00	PRIMARY CRUSHING PLANT	
20-0001-00-02-00	2101-3200	101-00	PRIMARY CRUSHING PLANT	
20-0001-00-03-00	2101-3200	101-00	PRIMARY CRUSHING PLANT	
20-1100-00-00-00	2101-4400		VERTICAL LIFT DOORS MOTORIZED	
20-1110-00-00-00	2101-4400		VERTICAL LIFT DOORS MOTORIZED	
20-1140-00-00-00	2101-4400		VERTICAL LIFT DOORS MOTORIZED	
20-1150-00-00-00	2101-4400		DUST SEAL SWING DOOR 44' W x	
30-0550-00-00-00	2102-4800		MCC PRESSURIZING UNIT 6000	
30-0600-00-00-00	2102-4800		VERTICAL LIFT DOORS MOTORIZED	
30-0360-00-00-00	2102-5800		MONORAIL HOIST 3 T 10L 20'RUN	

Figure 14-5 Procurement schedule and status report.

Changes in Contract Documents

Changes in purchase orders, contracts, and subcontracts should conform where possible to general principles outlined in the original procurement action. Above all, one should avoid verbal instructions, authorizations, or agreements; these may expedite initiation of the work, but can cause substantial honest disputes among the contracting parties when the bill is submitted. Figure 7-8 gave a sample change-order request form.

RELATION TO OTHER CONTROL SYSTEMS

Procurement is but one of many interdependent planning and control systems on a project, and as such it must fit in with the others. It must relate especially closely to the project schedule for operations and resources.

One approach would be simply to merge the procurement activities with the operations activities, say on a CPM diagram. If this were done, however, the detailed procurement activities would clearly dominate the overall sched-

PROJECT

REQ-DTE BID-REC	KE-RECM CLNT-OK	AWARDED	ENGNRNG RELEASE	SHIP EX PLANT	ARRIVE AT JOB	EARLY START	DIFF CPM
A08FEB2		A30MAR2	02MAY2	31JUL2	15AUG2	01SEP2	17
A30MAR2	13MAY2	28MAY2	07JUL2	24NOV2	09DEC2	15SEP2	85-
A30MAR2	13MAY2	28MAY2	07JUL2	24NOV2	09DEC2	15SEP2	85-
A30MAR2	13MAY2	28MAY2	07JUL2	24NOV2	09DEC2	15SEP2	85-
A30MAR2	13MAY2	28MAY2	07JUL2	24NOV2	09DEC2	15SEP2	85-
F05JUL2	19AUG2	03SEP2	13OCT2	02MAR3	17MAR3	30APR3	44
F21JUN2	26JUL2	10AUG2	09SEP2	08NOV2	23NOV2	30NOV2	7
F21JUN2	26JUL2	10AUG2	09SEP2	08NOV2	23NOV2	30NOV2	7
A18JAN2		A01MAR2	F10FEB3	F01APR3	F15APR3	01MAY3	16
A18JAN2		A01MAR2	F10FEB3	F01APR3	F15APR3	01MAY3	16
A18JAN2		A01MAR2	F10FEB3	F01APR3	F15APR3	01MAY3	16
A 0MAR2	17MAY2	01JUN2	11JUL2	11NOV2	25NOV2	02NOV2	23-
A 0MAR2	17MAY2	01JUN2	11JUL2	11NOV2	25NOV2	02NOV2	23-
A 0MAR2	17MAY2	01JUN2	11JUL2	11NOV2	25NOV2	02NOV2	23-
F18SEP2	02NOV2	17NOV2	27DEC2	16MAY3	31MAY3	31MAY3	
F19MAY2	03JUL2	18JUL2	27AUG2	14JAN3	29JAN3	31MAR3	61
A30MAR2	17MAY2	01JUN2	11JUL2	28NOV2	13DEC2	31MAY3	169
F26MAY2	25JUN2	10JUL2	30JUL2	08SEP2	23SEP2	31JUL3	311

PROCUREMENT SCHEDULE AND STATUS REPORT

The PSSR reflects the status of engineered equipment/material items for a project. The reports show the following:

Facility no., equipment no., component no., item no., shipment no., cost account no., spec./req. no., description, schedule class, requisition date, bid received date, recommendation to award date, award date, engineers release date, date due to ship, arrival date, CPM early start date, difference between arrival date and early start date.

Figure 14-5 (continued)

ule. Each of the operations activities could conceivably be preceded by a dozen or more steps from the list given early in this chapter.

The preferred approach, whether manually or by computer, is to develop modular, interrelated subsystems. For example, a field operation from the main schedule can define the desired latest availability date for one or more items of materials that will be needed in that operation. At most, that activity on the main schedule will be preceded by only one overall activity, such as "Procure steel doors," that will define the total time needed for all the steps in procuring those doors. Alternatively, if procurement is the time constraint, the cumulative times from the procurement steps will define the earliest time that the field operation will begin, or alert management to the need for expediting.

The details will be filled in on a detailed procurement schedule—possibly a network or bar chart, but more probably a two-dimensional matrix in paper or electronic form—which will list the item, details of its suppliers, its cost, and the start and end dates for each of the applicable procurement steps. The final column in the matrix will be the interface point to the project schedule, each referring, for example, to "Install doors in building 4." Figure 14-5 gives an example of such a procurement schedule and status report.

Reporting

Either through manual clerical attention, semimanual Cardex files, or full computer automation, the procurement schedule serves as a reference to assure that each item on the project is tracking through its required steps on time. Where items start falling behind, exception reports alert management that either field operations will be delayed from their scheduled start dates or, if the operations are critical, that procurement expediting will be necessary to bring them back on schedule. The principles of reporting and management by exception are basically the same as those described in Chapters 10 and 12, and will not be detailed again here. The concept of expediting, however, does deserve some explanation.

Expediting

.The popular image of expediting is that it is a frantic, last-ditch effort to speed up the movement of materials that were not delivered when they were needed. In organizations that terminate the procurement function with the issuance of a purchase order, this is too often the case. With good project control, however, expediting involves monitoring all steps in the procurement cycle, with special focus on those involving the vendor or subcontractor, to assure reliable, economical, on-schedule delivery. The essence of professional expediting is in anticipating problems before they arise and in offering solutions before delays are encountered.

Expediting for major or critical items often requires periodic visits to vendors' shops and factories on a routine, not emergency, basis, plus frequent telephone follow-ups to check vendor progress, raw materials supplied, workload, completed product inventory, shop drawings, manuals, fabrication procedures, quality control, code certifications, and delivery status. An important underlying purpose in this is to be sure that the contractor retains high priority among other firms for whom the vendor may simultaneously be working.

Even with the best procedures, however, problems will arise that require corrective action. Sometimes, the contractor's own schedule changes require that procurement of critical items be accelerated ahead of dates originally agreed with suppliers or subcontractors. Other delays might arise from design, purchasing, vendor fabrication, shipping, etc. Figure 14-6 shows a typical form for reporting and seeking action when trouble arises. Table 14-1 provides a checklist for things to analyze in seeking both the sources of problems and solutions to them. It is largely the role of experienced and professional expediters to find the most effective means to keep procurement on schedule with the minimum adverse effect on cost. Alternatives may include seeking backup or secondary suppliers, switching to faster means of shipment, or merely identifying snarls in red tape. All too often, delays result simply because a procurement document—say a requisition, purchase order, or shipping request—gets lost in some clerk's "In" file.

Table 14-1 Expediting Checklist. *(Courtesy Holmes & Narver, Inc., Anaheim, Calif.)*

HOLMES & NARVER, INC. ENGINEERS · CONSTRUCTORS A RESOURCE SCIENCES COMPANY

EXPEDITING CHECK LIST

Engineering Status	Material Status	Production Status	Analysis of Delays	Shipping Status
Is engineering required by the manufacturer? By purchaser?	Has the bill of material been issued?	When will the order be in production?	How many shifts working and number hours per shift.	Are the shipping instructions available and understood?
Obtain the engineering schedule. Is it being done on schedule?	Is the material in stock? Check inventory! Obtain a restricted allotment for H&N order where possible.	What is the estimated fabrication time? How does this compare with the time allowed in the shipping promise?	Will overtime improve delivery? How much? At what cost?	When will the invoice and packing lists be forwarded? Copies of all packing slips are to be issued to Expediting.
Do the drawings need approval?	Obtain the sub-order numbers and schedules of the materials ordered.	What is the production and shipping schedule of the main unit and all auxiliary equipment?	Is there any other order interference? Give details.	On export orders report invoice number and date. Name of carrier and export agent.
When were drawings forwarded to whom?	Indicate those orders needing special expediting assistance. Give full details.	Are any production problems anticipated?	Can substitution be made? Obtain full details.	Is packing and crating material available?
Have the drawings been released to the shop?	Has advance placement of critical material been made?	If there are material shortages, take steps to get production started.	Press manufacturer to expedite critical sub-orders.	When will shipment go forward? What is the method and routing?
Can the order be released for fabrication?	If castings are required, what is the status of the patterns? Check the status of all accessories to be shipped with unit.	Are the inspection requirements understood on both the main unit and all auxiliary equipment?	Contact top management when necessary.	When shipment is extremely urgent, have manufacturer report full details. Pieces and weight. Name of carrier and Pro No. Rust Traffic will follow.

HOLMES & NARVER INC. _____ Date _____ *(Internal)* EXPEDITING REPORT-TROUBLE _____

H&N P.O. No. _____   Seller _____

Plant Location _____   Contact _____   Phone _____

Job No. _____   Client _____   Equipment _____

P.O. Item No.	1	2	3	4	5	6	7
Tag No.							
Shop Order No.							
Delivery Required							
Original Promise							
New Promise							

—PROBLEM—

—ACTION REQUIRED—

Signature of Expeditor

Distribution	—RESPONSE— (Optional)

Form 1540/18-175-1   Signature   Date

Figure 14-6 Expediting trouble report. *(Courtesy Holmes & Narver, Inc., Anaheim, Calif.)*

CONTROL OF MATERIALS PROCUREMENT

The control of materials procurement costs is somewhat different from the control of field labor and construction equipment costs. In the latter case, productivity is the main criterion, and it requires continuous attention by management. Daily time sheets and overnight exception reporting can have an important impact.

In the case of materials, the main sources of information are requisitions, bids and quotations, purchase orders and subcontracts, shipping documents, receiving documents, and invoices. In most cases, these provide enough feedback for control. The actual costs of the materials themselves are largely predetermined by the designer. Certainly the constructor can and should attempt to shop for the best price/performance characteristics he can obtain within the specifications.

Other important opportunities for control of materials costs on large projects are in:

1 Requisition procedures (specs for shipping, packaging, delivery, etc.)
2 Minimization of rehandling and shortages
3 Inventory procedures and policies

These are closely related to, and to a large extent reduce to, the problem of controlling the *timing* of the various steps in the procurement process. As long as everything runs smoothly and materials arrive on time and in good condition, their actual purchase costs are not of dominant concern in on-the-job project control. It is in its indirect impacts that the procurement process can cause the most concern at the working level.

There is an old saying, "For the want of a shoe, the horse was lost." Analogously, the late arrival of a small embedded instrument can stop a large concrete pour. Similarly, materials arriving too soon, or in the wrong order, can also wreak havoc, particularly in a crowded work site, such as a downtown high-rise building or a nuclear power plant.

Comparison of actual receipts with invoiced quantities is also an important matter in project control. Figure 14-7 gives an example of a materials receiving report, which is a key document for this purpose.

INVENTORY THEORY

Regardless of the potential for their practical application in construction, the manufacturing and marketing industries' operations research techniques, collectively called "inventory theory," can provide a good understanding of the basic economics of materials procurement for construction projects. Their concepts will therefore be briefly introduced in this chapter and will be expressed in terms more applicable to construction.

Components of Costs

The general objective of quantitative inventory methods is to optimize trade-offs among the following four categories of costs in order to minimize total costs:

| MATERIAL RECEIVED REPORT | M.R. No.:_____ |

THIS ORDER IS:
  COMPLETE ☐
  NOT COMPLETE ☐
  REC. DAMAGED ☐

PAGE_____OF_____

P. O. NO.:_____

REQ. NO.:_____

DATE RECEIVED:_____

ORDERED FROM: _____

SHIPPED BY: _____

SHIPPED TO:_____ PACKING SLIP NO.:_____

VIA:_____ F.O.B. POINT:_____

		NO.
CARRIER		
FREIGHT BILL		NO.
EXPRESS BILL		WGT.
PARCEL POST		DATE
	PREPAID	AMT. $
	COLLECT	AMT. $
	RAIL LINE	
	CAR NO.	
	DOCK NO.	

P.O. ITEM NO.	QUANTITY	UNIT	DESCRIPTION	LOCATION	ACCOUNT NO.

DWG. NO._____

B M NO._____

REQ. ORIGINATOR_____

DELIVERED TO

CHECKED BY

WAREHOUSE SUPT.

Figure 14-7 Material received report.

1 Purchase costs
2 Shipping costs
3 Holding costs
4 Shortage costs

Purchase Costs Purchase costs are those associated with (1) the actual overhead incurred in requisitioning, soliciting, and evaluating quotations, and in issuing purchase orders; (2) the actual materials prices obtained through effective negotiation, variations in unit costs with quantities, the amount of time allowed for fulfilling the order, etc.; and (3) costs associated with shipping materials to the site, which in turn are related to quantity, distance, and mode of transport.

On the administrative side, it is best to have policy guidelines for different procedures to use for different magnitudes of orders. Obviously, one should not spend $50 of administrative effort to order $10 worth of miscellaneous office supplies. On the other hand, one would not rely on a general foreman to place an order for elevators in a 20-story building. There should be clearly documented policies and procedures for these different procurement situations and for others in between.

Unit prices of materials vary not only with bargaining leverage, quantities, and delivery time, but also with design characteristics. Designers often unknowingly and unnecessarily increase prices by specifying odd sizes, say of windows or structural steel shapes, where a similar standard size could perform the same function equally well or better. Bargaining leverage often favors larger organizations whose long-term buying volume may cause vendors to give them lower prices on smaller orders also. Unit prices often vary inversely with quantity, much as they do in retail stores, but large quantities can often adversely affect holding costs, which are discussed below, and cause problems in cash flow. Sometimes it is possible to gain the best of both worlds, however, by placing a single large order with a low unit price and requesting incremental delivery dates. This is the usual approach for the bulk cement on a large concrete dam. Delivery time can adversely affect prices if the purchaser requests delivery sooner than the vendor's normal production schedule will allow. Some portion of the vendor's overtime and rescheduling costs will be passed on to the buyer.

Shipping Costs The shipping component of purchase costs can be reduced on a unit basis as quantities become larger. For example, rail shipment by the carload, say of lumber, is much cheaper than less-than-carload (LCL) rates. Chartering an ocean freighter is usually cheaper and assures quicker delivery than shipping as just part of a cargo that is delivered to several different ports. The same applies to truck and air freight. Regarding variations in price with mode, water, rail, truck, and air shipping generally increase in price in that order, assuming convenient ports and terminals and ignoring transshipment; but shipping costs alone can sometimes be misleading. Clearly, on delicate, high value per weight items, such as computers and electronic controls, the better and quicker handling of air freight can often more than justify itself. In remote locations, also, costs can be deceptive. One of the authors once bid an arctic soil-cement runway project where the price of shipping bulk cement was about equal for ocean barge and air freight. Once the uncertainty of getting barges through the arctic ice was considered, air freight became the obvious choice.

Holding Costs   Holding costs include storage space and warehouse overhead, deterioration and obsolescence, theft, misplacement, insurance and taxes, rehandling, and interest on funds invested in inventory.

Even outdoor storage space can be at a premium on crowded work sites. Renting a city block of prime commercial real estate near a building project can be absurdly expensive. Warehouse space even on remote, wide-open sites involves the capital and operations costs for construction, staff, security, and utilities. These costs can often exceed the "savings" obtained through purchasing large quantities of materials before they are needed.

Several types of construction materials are perishable and therefore cannot be delivered very far in advance of need. Portland cement is a common example. Similarly, changes in building codes and government health and safety regulations can make some items obsolete before they are installed. as can the fact that new products can sometimes perform the jobs of their predecessors better and at less cost.

Theft is a real problem in some areas. Whole reels of copper cable, innumerable small tools and supplies, and even major items of equipment have been known to disappear from projects, sometimes at a cost of several million dollars on just one large job. Too often these losses have been attributable to well-organized criminal operations.

Even misplacement is a problem, especially where warehouses and storage yards are poorly organized. Materials cannot be found at the time they are needed on site, their purchases are duplicated, and they are found to be in surplus when the job is completed—or sometimes they have quite literally disappeared forever beneath the mud in the storage yard.

Insurance costs are higher when larger quantities of materials are on hand, and property tax assessors delight in finding surpluses for their coffers. At today's interest rates, the cost of the money prematurely invested in inventory can also add an often unnecessary expense, either for the contractor or for the owner if the contract permits these costs to be passed on.

Perhaps the most important of all are the costs of rehandling resulting from premature deliveries. Ideally, there should be a perfectly coordinated flow of materials where trucks arrive on site and their burdens are hoisted directly to the point where they are needed. Even in the best-run operations, however, most materials are rehandled at least once. If management is in good control, the materials arrive, are unloaded, and are stored in logically preplanned and documented locations, either in the warehouse or in the yard, so that they can be readily and directly retrieved when they are needed. Too frequently, however, deliveries are unplanned, materials are stored at random locations, and when an item is finally needed in construction, there is first a frantic search to find it, and, once found, a whole load of reinforcing steel, two large pumps, and several other items must first be moved before workers can get to it. In this chaotic, unmanaged siutation, materials are moved about like the pea in a shell game, are often rehandled a half-dozen or more times, and often are seriously damaged before their time comes for installation in the structure. This rehandling is done not for free, but by today's high-priced labor and equipment, and generally with poor supervision and inefficiency.

All these factors contribute to the holding costs resulting from materials being delivered too soon, in the wrong order, and in unpredictably large quantities.

Shortage Costs   The corollary of holding costs, of course, is the impact of shortages on project operations costs. It is often the fear of shortage costs that leads to the conservative delivery schedules that adversely affect holding costs.

In classic inventory theory, shortage costs are the "loss of sales," in the retail sense, from not having in stock the item that the customer wants—a toaster. TV, or whatever. The customer then walks down the street and buys from someone else, and the sale is lost. This accounts for the perennial inventory policy battle between the marketing side and the supply side of such organizations.

Shortage costs, however, can also result from interrupted production for lack of input materials. In construction, shortage costs are the direct and indirect costs of delayed and interrupted work (recall the interrupted learning curve in Figure 11-7), and they are especially catastrophic if the operations affected are critical to the completion schedule for the project.

These impact costs in turn motivate the incurrence of other types of shortage costs, those of expediting and special handling. To get things moving, management may be willing to pay more to get the materials from a different vendor, ship by air freight instead of rail, and complete some shop-fabrication operations at higher cost in the field.

Trade-offs   It should be clear by this stage that purchase costs, holding costs, and shortage costs are highly interrelated, especially where risk and uncertainty are concerned, and in large measure they are in conflict with one another. A great deal of research has been done to show how their interrelationships can be modeled, and how, at least in theory, the expected sum of their costs can be optimized. Details of these techniques, however, are beyond the scope of this book. Some of the references in the bibliography will enable the interested reader to pursue this subject as deeply as desired.

SUMMARY

In an era combining global shortages of resources with a proliferation of new types of materials, procurement demands the increasing attention of professionals experienced in this phase of project planning and control. First of all, they must be knowledgeable of procedures and options in all parts of the procurement cycle, from recognition of need through requisition, prequalification of bidders, evaluation, selection, vendor fabrication, expediting, shipping, delivery, and inspection, to on-site storage and handling. The process is far more complex than just shopping around for the cheapest purchase price.

Purchase orders are a short form of contract generally used for the procurement of materials, equipment, and supplies. Contracts and subcontracts are normally used for the procurement of construction work involving on-site labor. Agreements and leases are often used for the rental of construction equipment and other items not incorporated into the finished work. Purchasing documents and steps will include requisitions, prequalification and bid list preparation, requests for quotation, bid receipt and evaluation, recommendation for purchase and award, and later finalization of change orders.

Materials control is different from the control of labor and equipment in several important ways. The importance of operations productivity, in particular, gives way to the importance of scheduling and timing and the indirect consequences that poor materials management can have on the whole project. It is particularly important that materials procurement systems be closely coordinated with the systems for the planning, scheduling, and control of operations and resources on the project. Reporting for materials control, in turn, emphasizes detailed tracking through all steps of the procurement cycle, and exception reporting can in turn lead to application of professional expediting procedures.

Quantitative analytical techniques, collectively known as "inventory theory," can provide real insight into the basic economics of materials management and can also find practical application in construction. In concept, these methods seek the optimum trade-off between procurement costs, holding costs, and shortage costs that will produce the lowest overall materials costs for a project.

Chapter 15

Value Engineering

Value engineering emerged during World War II when shortages of critical resources necessitated changes in methods, materials, and traditional designs; many of these changes resulted in superior performance at a lower cost. After the war, the General Electric Company pioneered in the development and implementation of an organized value analysis program for industry, and this technique was soon adopted by several other companies and government agencies. In 1962, value engineering became a mandatory requirement in the Armed Services Procurement Regulations (ASPR). This change in ASPR introduced value engineering to two of the largest construction agencies in the country, the U.S. Army Corps of Engineers and the U.S. Navy Bureau of Yards and Docks. During the 1960s and the 1970s, several other government agencies and jurisdictions adopted value engineering, including the Bureau of Reclamation, the National Aeronautics and Space Administration (NASA), the Department of Transportation, and the Public Buildings Service of the General Services Administration (GSA).

Growth of construction applications of value engineering in the public sector has thus been fostered by legislation and regulation. However, there is little sign of an equally impressive growth in the private sector. As noted by

[1] *Value Analysis in Design and Construction*, McGraw-Hill Book Company, New York, 1976.

James J. O'Brien in the preface to his book on the subject,[1] at present only about half the construction industry's designers and contractors are even aware of value engineering, and perhaps only about 1 percent are actively and successfully applying its techniques. If the approach is indeed useful, one wonders why its adoption is taking so long.

To help answer this question, this chapter will (1) summarize the state of the art in governmental and traditional applications; (2) briefly describe life-cycle costing and its specialized tools; (3) inquire into reasons slowing acceptance of value-engineering principles in the private sector; (4) suggest ways of overcoming this reluctance; and (5) present documented results of a program that has received enthusiastic acceptance on professional construction management projects.

POTENTIAL SAVINGS

L. D. Miles's book[2] on value analysis and engineering includes the following definition: "Value analysis/engineering is an organized, creative approach which has for its purpose the effective identification of unnecessary costs, i.e., costs which provide neither quality nor use nor life nor appearance nor customer features." But to whom do these savings accrue, and what are they really worth?

In 1974 the Army Corps of Engineers estimated that the total cumulative savings through value engineering was almost $234 million. The Public Buildings Service indicated that its value-engineering program had generated savings of $4.53 for every dollar spent, for total savings to GSA of $1.8 million in fiscal 1973. During fiscal year 1970, the Department of Defense estimated a saving of about $4.40 from contractor-sharing incentives for each $1 spent on the program. It further estimated an additional return of four times this amount resulting from in-house programs during the design phase and prior to contract award.

Alphonse Dell'Isola's book on value engineering[3] established potential savings guidelines as follows:

On total budget	1 to 3%
On large facilities	5 to 10%
Incentive contracting	0.5 to 1%

Realizing these potential savings requires a systematic and innovative approach. Generally accepted techniques include a job plan for value engineering which will have a number of phases:

---

[2] *Techniques of Value Analysis and Engineering*, 2d ed., McGraw-Hill Book Company, New York, 1972.
[3] *Value Engineering in the Construction Industry*, Construction Publishing Corp., Inc., New York, 1974. (With permission of Van Nostrand Reinhold Company.)

Develop information and requirements.
Speculate on alternatives.
Analyze and evaluate alternatives.
Develop the program.
Proceed with proposal, presentation, and selling.

This plan can be implemented over the life cycle of a construction project, and will have potential savings related to time and cost in varying degrees, depending upon which of the following phases of development the project is in:

Conception
Development
Detail design
Construction
Start-up and use

The following section will discuss this approach in greater detail.

VALUE-ENGINEERING JOB PLAN

In his book, Dell'Isola designed a value-engineering job plan accomplished in four phases:[4]

1 *Information*: Get facts
2 *Speculative*: Brainstorm
3 *Analytical*: Investigate, evaluate
4 *Proposal*: Sell

These phases can be expanded and explained as follows:

Informative Phase

This phase includes these purposes:

1 To gather and tabulate data concerning the item as presently designed
2 To determine the item's function(s)
3 To evaluate the basic function(s)

During information gathering, certain questions must be answered:

1 What is the item?
2 What does it do?
3 What is the worth of the function?
4 What does it cost?
5 What are the needed requirements?
6 What is the cost/worth ratio?
7 What high-cost or poor-value areas are indicated?

[4]Ibid., pp. 17–51.

O'Brien says the question, "What does it do?" should be answered by two words (a verb and a noun) for each function; for example, a water pipe *transports water*.[5] Such definitions may require careful analysis. To illustrate, a door may provide access, limit access (as in a prison), provide security, exclude or contain fire, control traffic, provide visibility, or express prestige.

Considerable effort, ingenuity, and investigation are required to answer these questions. The value-engineering group must determine what criteria and constraints existed at the time of the original design and whether they still apply at the present time.

Other important questions may be:

1 How long has this design been used?
2 What alternative systems, materials, or methods were considered during the original concept?
3 What special problems were or are unique to this system?
4 What is the total use or repetitive use of this design each year?

Brainstorming

The purpose of this phase is to generate numerous alternatives for providing the item's *basic* function(s). By definition, a brainstorming session is a problem-solving conference wherein each participant's thinking is stimulated by others in the group. A team may consist of four to six people of different disciplines, sitting around a table and spontaneously generating ideas. Production of the maximum number of ideas is encouraged, and no idea is criticized.

The Gordon technique[6] has also been successful. With this technique only the group leader knows the exact nature of the problem, and he asks questions to generate ideas. This approach can stimulate freer thinking than brainstorming.

Analytical Phase

The purposes in this phase are:

1 To evaluate, criticize, and test the alternatives generated during the speculation phase
2 To estimate the dollar value of each alternative
3 To determine the alternatives which offer the greatest potential for cost savings

During this phase, also known as the evaluation and investigation phase, the group examines alternatives generated during the brainstorming and tries to develop lower-cost solutions.

The principal tasks are:

1 To evaluate

---

[5]O'Brien, *Value Analysis in Design and Construction*, pp. 12–14.
[6]William J. J. Gordon, *Synetics, The Development of Creative Capacity*, Harper & Row, New York, 1961.

2 To refine
3 To cost-analyze
4 To form a possible list of alternatives in order of descending savings potential

Aristotle said that worth can have economic, moral, aesthetic, social, political, religious, and judicial value. This is a valuable precept for value-engineering team members as well as for philosophers.

James J. O'Brien believes a value index such as "worth divided by cost" or "utility divided by cost" can be very beneficial during this phase.

The route of ideas is the following:

1 Eliminate ideas which do not meet environmental and operating conditions.
2 Set aside, for future discussion, ideas with potential but which are beyond present capability or technology.
3 Cost-analyze remaining ideas.
4 List ideas with useful savings, including their potential advantages and disadvantages.
5 Select ideas where advantages outweigh disadvantages and offer the greatest cost savings. (Often dollar values are not readily assignable and must be considered using statistical approaches.)
6 Finally, consider weighted constraints, such as aesthetics, durability, and salability, in order to produce a completed list.

Proposal Phase

Also called the program planning and reporting phase, this is the final portion of Alphonse Dell'Isola's plan. This phase must accomplish three things:

1 A thorough review of all alternate solutions must be prepared to assure that the highest value and significant savings are really being offered.
2 A sound proposal must be made to management.
3 The group must present a plan for implementing the proposal. If the proposal will not convince management to act, no savings will result.

U.S. GOVERNMENT VALUE-ENGINEERING JOB PLANS

A different perspective on this process can be achieved by considering other job plans. For example, the U.S. Army Corps of Engineers' job plan[7] involves five phases:

Information
Speculation
Analysis
Development
Presentation

[7]U.S. Dept. of Defense, *Handbook*, 5010.8–4 (1963).

This list differs from Dell'Isola's list in that it splits the proposal into two phases:

Development
Presentation

Development Phase

The purposes are:

1 To assess the technical feasibility of each surviving alternative
2 To obtain firm information concerning each surviving alternative
3 To develop written recommendations

Presentation Phase

The purposes are:

1 To present a value-engineering study report
2 To present the report to the decision maker(s)
3 To ensure that the report recommendations are implemented

In 1968 the Department of Defense (DOD) made two changes in this list. First, a new phase identified as "Orientation" was added at the top of the list. The orientation phase has three basic purposes:

1 Selection of appropriate areas to be studied
2 Selection of the appropriate team to accomplish the study
3 Determination of the policies needed to assist in the accomplishment of these determinations

Second, the last phase, "Presentation," was expanded to include follow-up. By 1972, the DOD job plan had again been expanded, this time by splitting the last phase, "Presentation and Follow-up," into separate phases and by adding the phase "Implementation" in between them. Figure 15-1 summarizes the job plan at this stage of development.

A composite list of value-engineering and job-plan categories is shown in Table 15-1. Though these plans emphasize various aspects of the process, they are basically similar in approach and sequencing. With a sound knowledge of both the purposes for each phase and the route of ideas, one can either select the job plan best suited to the project's needs or create a new one.

LIFE-CYCLE COSTING

Accurate cost measurement is one of the most important requirements of a successful value-engineering program. Most cost estimates and cost records

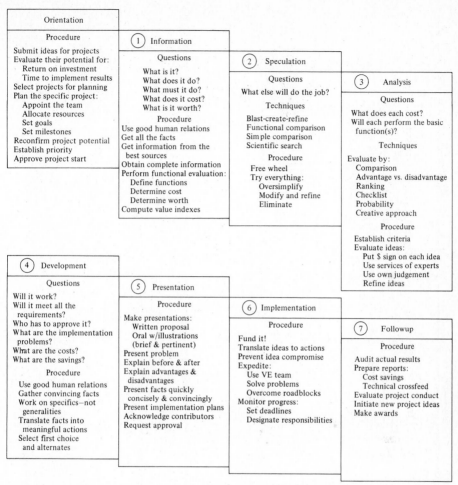

Figure 15-1 Major phases of a job plan. *(Adapted from General Services Administration, Public Building Service, Manual No. P8000.1, Value Engineering, Washington, D.C.)*

used in the construction industry deal with capital costs from the viewpoint of the contractor or the ultimate user of the facilities. Yet the life of the building or facility will extend over 20 to 50 or more years. During this period the cost of maintaining and servicing the facility, including the cost of utilities such as fuel oil, electric power, or natural gas, will equal or exceed the capital cost. Value analysis from the viewpoint of the owner must therefore take into account both capital and future operation and maintenance costs if maximum value is to be achieved for minimum overall investment. In the final analysis, we are trying to find out how much additional capital expenditure is warranted today to achieve future cost benefits over the life of the facility.

However, as we endeavor to estimate the cost of future events, our cost estimates for the life cycle become less reliable when compared with capital or

Table 15-1 Job Plan Category Comparison

Dell'Isola*	GSA-PBS P 8000.1 1972	L. D. Miles† 1961	L. D. Miles‡ 1972	E. D. Heller§ 1971	A. E. Mudge¶ 1971	PBS VM Workbook 1974
Information	Orientation	Orientation	Information	Information	Project selection	Information
Speculation	Information	Information	Analysis	Creation	Information	Function
Analysis	Speculation	Speculation	Creation	Evaluation	Function	Creative
Proposal	Analysis	Analysis	Judgment	Investigation	Creation	Judicial
	Development	Program planning	Development	Reporting	Evaluation	Development
	Presentation	Program execution		Implementation	Investigation	Presentation
	Implementation	Summary and conclusion			Recommendation	Implementation
	Follow-up					Follow-up

*A. J. Dell'Isola, *Value Engineering in the Construction Industry*, Construction Publishing Corp., Inc., N.Y., 1974.
†L. D. Miles, *Techniques of Value Analysis and Engineering*, 1st ed., McGraw-Hill, New York, 1961.
‡L. D. Miles, *Techniques of Value Analysis and Engineering*, 2d ed., McGraw-Hill, New York, 1972.
§E. D. Heller, *Value Management: Value Engineering and Cost Reduction:* Addison-Wesley, Reading, Mass., 1971.
¶Arthur E. Mudge, *Value Engineering.* McGraw-Hill, New York, 1971.

construction cost estimates. To illustrate, consider some of the items that are important in analyzing future life-cycle costs for a project:

Maintenance and operating costs
Energy and utility costs
Value of money
Cost of insurance
Anticipated future income growth
Ease and timing of expansions
Fringe benefits difficult to analyze, including aesthetics, durability, and overall future image
Effect of the facilities on the productivity of operating, administrative, and maintenance personnel
Present and future trends in real estate and property taxes, income taxes, and investment credits
Location and operational costs based upon community growth, competitive patterns, and other factors

Each of the items includes choices among multiple alternatives, uncertain forecasts of future costs, and uncertain effects of future events. To help solve these general problems, a number of specialized tools is available; of these, the following are among the most important:

Present worth analysis
Sensitivity analysis
Break-even analysis
Discounted cash-flow and rate-of-return analysis

All these are useful economic tools for value engineering. However, it is beyond the scope of this book to examine them in detail. The reader who lacks knowledge in this area is strongly encouraged to consult the classic text on engineering economy by Grant, Ireson, and Leavenworth[8] or to read other related books listed in the bibliography.

VALUE ENGINEERING IN THE PRIVATE SECTOR

We have reviewed several accepted job plans that illustrate the state of the art of value analysis or value engineering and have emphasized the importance of life-cycle costing. Now consider some of the pitfalls of the traditional approaches in nongovernmental design and construction programs.

Major design-construct companies involved in large industrial projects have accounted for the greatest dollar value of construction work per individual firm in recent years. One might therefore expect that these firms would be the leaders in promoting and using value engineering since, in addition to offering

[8]Eugene L. Grant, W. Grant Ireson, and Richard S. Leavenworth, *Principles of Engineering Economy*, 6th ed., The Ronald Press Company, New York, 1976.

considerable potential savings benefits to the clients, they control both design and construction operations. Yet value engineering has in general not been consistently adopted in any organized form by these firms or by many others in the private sector. In a magazine article, Dell'Isola appears to have identified some of the reasons for this.[9]

In this article, Al Dell, the value engineer, has convinced a reluctant Joe Weakley, design director, to try a value-engineering analysis. After the value-engineering team completed its study, a 15 percent overall savings developed. Even Joe Weakley was impressed by the action of the team. Later Dell inquired about the two engineers who had been responsible for the original design. "Those two?" replied Weakley. "I had them transferred. I won't tolerate people who can't design economical facilities." Note Joe Weakley's basic lack of understanding of value engineering: that it is a team effort and no one person can have all the answers.

In today's rapidly changing economy, the old traditional rules of thumb that designers relied on to produce economic designs and to choose between alternative solutions simply are not cost-effective. No designer can hope to master the current knowledge of the cost of individual items of labor and materials in the locality of the project. In fact, studies performed in a given locality often become out of date very quickly as certain materials and labor costs increase more rapidly than others or even become unattainable in reasonable delivery periods.

The theoretical value-engineering job-plan approach is technically sound and has been shown to be successful when given an opportunity, but it still has generally failed when it has been tried in the industrial and commercial areas where the greatest incentive for its use should be present. We shall further explore reasons for this in the context of the three main contractual approaches introduced in Chapter 2: those of the traditional general contractors, design-construct, and the professional construction manager.

Traditional Single General Contractor

The traditional method usually employs an architect or engineer who is often compensated on a fixed price, a percentage of construction cost, and/or a guaranteed maximum. If a multidiscipline value-engineering team reviews the design and comes up with suggested savings, a redesign is almost always involved. When confronted with major changes for which he is expected to pay additional design fees, the unsophisticated owner will generally feel that the designer should have done the work right the first time, even though estimates show that an overall saving may be achieved.

The designer responsible for the original design will generally resent any criticism of it, and the principals of the design firm will be concerned about the additional design hours for which they may not be compensated. This was

[9]Alphonse J. Dell'Isola, "A Value Engineering Case Study," *Heating, Piping and Air Conditioning*, June 1970, pp. 50–54.

illustrated in Chapter 10's discussion of the "level of influence." Other design principals or supervisors will criticize the original designer for not producing the right design the first time. Furthermore, when the fee is the traditional percentage of construction cost, the more money spent on engineering to lower the construction cost, the lower the profit the design firm will realize.

An additional difficulty is the accuracy of estimates. On competitive bids not involving a large percentage of subcontracts, bid spreads often range from 25 to 50 percent or more above the low bidder. Cost to the owner is influenced by how much the low bidder desires the work as well as his individual evaluation of the anticipated cost. This evaluation may be quite different from that of an estimator working for the value-engineering team, since he is not under such competitive pressures.

Design-Construct or Turnkey

Design-constructors have in-house all the disciplines associated with a value-engineering team. Why haven't they generally adopted value-engineering programs?

Again the method of compensation often creates the situation where spending more money on engineering may reduce the overall cost but may also reduce the amount of profit to the design-constructor. In other cases, the result may be an overrun of the predetermined design budget.

Design-constructors also generally have highly structured design organizations. Internal design reviews are normally performed by discipline supervisors; outside review is generally interpreted as criticism, and it stimulates a natural reaction to justify the original design.

Estimating may generally be geared to the conceptual level rather than to the detailed level of the trade contractors. This approximate estimating may work well with broad trade-off studies and development of general concepts. However, it may prove to be misleading in the later verdict of the competitive marketplace.

Joe Weakley and his "we should have done it right the first time" philosophy continue to inhibit the use of value engineering by the only organizations that have all the internal skills to make it work under a single management.

Professional Construction Management

The emergence of professional construction management and the early involvement of the constructor in the design process have fostered the use of value engineering. The professional construction managers who have understood the attitude of Dell'Isola's Joe Weakley and who have appreciated the financial considerations of the design firms have generally had more success with value engineering in the private sector than have those firms that have tried the more traditional methods with modification. When a way can be found in which the three-party professional construction management team manages value engineering without outside independent design critique, and where each team member can be credited equally, in the eyes of the owner, for any savings, a healthy climate for implementation of suggestions exists.

One of the advantages of successful professional construction management is the absence of the adversary relationships often present between the architect/engineer and the general contractor. The architect who criticizes the professional construction manager to the owner quickly finds that he is equally vulnerable to criticism by the manager. Everyone benefits when discrepancies are discussed internally and straightened out before finalizing construction contracts. This same concept applies to the value-engineering effort.

A PRACTICAL VALUE-ENGINEERING PROGRAM THAT WORKS

A practical value-engineering program has been developed within the past decade as a part of the senior author's professional construction management program. This program was created in an effort to eliminate the prejudices that have kept value engineering from realizing its potential in the private industrial and commercial sectors. Although the program is relatively unsophisticated, it has achieved significant cost savings for owners when compared with projects constructed along older, more traditional methods.

Program Criteria

In an effort to eliminate the objections of a Joe Weakley, the following criteria were developed for the program, and all parties—owner, architect/engineer, and professional construction manager—were enlisted in carrying it out:

1 The professional construction manager, owner, and designer will educate all their personnel to be on the lookout for alternate methods and concepts at any stage of the project. Suggestions are actively encouraged, and they are to be submitted to the manager.

2 The professional construction manager is given the responsibility for documenting and investigating initial feasibility and for preparing estimates and working out a presentation for all suggestions deemed feasible.

3 The designer is given the responsibility for ruling on the engineering suitability of the suggestions and for making the determination as to whether the proposed suggestion is equal, superior, or inferior to the original concept.

4 Together with an analysis of effects on the schedule or other like factors, all suggestions which are deemed technically feasible by the designer and which result in cost savings are submitted to the owner for final approval. In the event that significant redesign is required, the owner will compensate the designer accordingly, and the design costs will be subtracted from the indicated savings.

5 If possible, each bid package should contain several alternates that are equally acceptable to the owner and designer. Thus the bidders themselves will participate in the program, and the owner will receive the benefit of bidder preference and current cost estimates.

6 Potential bidders should be encouraged to develop alternates, which, if

technically equal to the base bid, will receive consideration in evaluating bids. Thus by his ingenuity a bidder who is not low under the base bid may become the low bidder. The owner receives a cost saving, and the ingenious bidder receives the contract.

7   The criterion for determining whether a suggestion should be classified as a value-engineering saving is whether or not the saving is a result of the three-party team concept. (Suggestions may be made by any party—owner, manager, designer, or even the construction contractors themselves.) If, in the final judgment of the owner, it is a product of the three-party team, it is classified as a value-engineering saving and is documented by the professional construction manager.

It is worth noting that the program, summarized in Table 15-2, was successful with five different owners and six different architects involved in these ten projects. Each enthusiastically accepted the program and lived up to his individual responsibilities. The key to this enthusiastic acceptance has been the team concept where all members receive credit for an implemented suggestion. Many of the suggestions were relatively simple, but would not have been incorporated on a project using the traditional methods.

Simplified Example

Savings on one of the projects will be outlined in more detail to show the types of things achieved. The following savings were achieved for a distribution center expansion with the joint cooperation of the owner, architect, and construction manager.

Value Engineering, Item 1   Metal roof deck for the produce warehouse in lieu of double-tee decking as initially called for.   **Savings: $ 62,000**

Value Engineering, Item 2   Systems procurement package for the frozen foods warehouse which specified results rather than individual proprietary details and resulted in competition among all major manufacturers. Savings are based upon an evaluated life cycle of 20 years since maintenance, insurance, financing, and other costs varied depending upon the particular manufacturer's system.   **Savings: $113,000**

Value Engineering, Item 3   Glu-laminated beams, wooden-metal span joists and plywood decking in lieu of an all-steel roof support system for the freezer room and canopy of the frozen foods warehouse additions.

Savings: $ 33,783

Value Engineering, Item 4   Acceptance of general contractor's alternate bid for steel erection of the meat warehouse rather than of fabricator's price.

Savings: $ 6,130

Value Engineering, Item 5 Acceptance of an alternate proposal to use a local painter for a specialty product rather than an out-of-town manufacturer's installer, while preserving original guarantees. **Savings: $ 12,500**

Value Engineering, Item 6 Proprietary cement product to increase joint spacing for the grocery warehouse's special floors, rather than the specified portland cement. **Savings: $ 10,800**

Value Engineering, Item 7 Forty-five concrete placings for special floors in the frozen foods warehouse in lieu of the ninety specified.
Savings: $ 1,389

Value Engineering, Item 8 Insulated structural-styrofoam panel walls along column line 2 of the meat warehouse in lieu of specified product.
Savings: $ 17,167

Value Engineering, Item 9 Glassboard facing over built-up insulation for meat warehouse columns rather than the prefabricated insulated panels as specified. **Savings: $ 6,300**

Value Engineering, Item 10 Sloped concrete retaining walls in lieu of conventional walls around fuel-oil storage tanks. **Savings: $ 6,105**

Value Engineering, Item 11 Call for alternate refrigeration–support-steel quotations incorporating modified design after initial bids appeared high.
Savings: $ 6,619

Value Engineering, Item 12 Credit allowance as a result of good working conditions and smooth job coordination during caisson installation in frozen foods section, which was performed on a negotiated guaranteed maximum-price, share-of-savings concept. **Savings: $ 3,250**

Total value engineering savings: **$279,043**

Demonstrated Results

Table 15-2 tabulates value-engineering results for 10 projects constructed over a 5-year period with the professional construction management approach. These projects were completed with the active innovation, cooperation, and participation of a number of leading owner and architectural and engineering firms.

Some of the savings may be considered to be borderline if measured against the above criteria. However, it is believed that the overall saving of 3.5 percent of the applicable building cost would not have been realized by the owner under traditional contracting programs; it is clearly a direct result of the value-engineering partnership program utilized on a professional construction management project.

Table 15-2   Value Engineering Savings Achieved on Projects

Description	No. of savings	Value of savings	Applicable building cost	% Savings
Distribution center	17	343,379	8,030,000	4.3
Meat fabrication plant	7	125,419	3,040,000	4.2
Bakery	7	63,240	4,020,000	1.6
Distribution center	10	215,979	3,600,000	6.0
Meat processing plant	11	164,219	8,000,000	2.0
Distribution center	12	279,043	8,000,000	3.5
Light manufacturing plant	16	484,950	6,600,000	7.3
Plating & reclaim facility	6	8,315	1,100,000	.8
Meat fabrication plant	18	196,525	6,000,000	3.3
Water treatment plant	7	56,047	4,400,000	1.3
Totals	111	1,937,116	52,790,000	3.7

SUMMARY

This chapter reviewed value analysis methods utilized by a number of government agencies and summarized the job-plan concept. Several public agencies have reported significant savings achieved through their formalized programs, but the approach has had less widespread acceptance in private work.

An important feature of value engineering is life-cycle costing; this allows for the effect of future operational, overhead, carrying, and maintenance costs as well as initial capital or construction costs. Such future operational phase costs may be equally important to the owner in determining the nature and cost of the initial investment.

The less-than-enthusiastic acceptance that value engineering has received in the private sector is due in a large measure to the nature of the marketplace, the inherent fear of criticism on the part of the designers, and the adversary relationships which are often present among designers, contractors, and owners. The professional construction management approach, however, offers a greater application of the potential benefits of value engineering because it minimizes adversary relationships and involves the original engineer in analyzing the technical acceptability of proposed modifications.

As our economy becomes more mature, value-engineering techniques that reduce costs while preserving basic value will become even more important than they were during the decades of heavy growth following World War II.

Chapter 16

Quality Assurance

Planning and controlling standards for quality are fundamental in both the design and construction phases of a project. This aspect of a project, while closely interrelated with costs, schedule, procurement, and value engineering, deserves its own amplification.

Quality assurance involves economic studies to select the types of materials and methods to be included in design, making certain that the design is in accordance with all applicable building codes and other regulations, and controlling the construction on the project to be sure that the work is performed according to the standards specified in the contract documents. Methodology here ranges from computerized documentation of accepted governmental, technical and professional criteria for design, to sampling and testing concrete, earthwork, welding, bolting, and structural dimensions in the field.

This chapter will begin with some basic definitions pertaining to different phases of quality on a project. It will then discuss important organizational factors on a project. Basic economic concepts related to quality in both the design and construction phases will be presented next, followed by a brief introduction of statistical methods for quality control in construction.

BASIC CONCEPTS AND DEFINITIONS

Quality criteria affect all phases of a project. This section will briefly introduce some basic concepts and define some common terms used in the industry.

Definitions

Three key aspects of quality relate to engineering, control, and assurance. Each will be briefly defined below.

Quality Engineering This term often describes procedures used to ensure that the engineering and design for a structure proceed according to recommended and mandatory criteria set by related professional and trade associations, building code authorities, and federal, state, and local organizations such as the Environmental Protection Agency, the Nuclear Regulatory Commission, the Occupational Safety and Health Administration, and others. Many of these standards are required by law and several are revised frequently, so it is important for the architects and engineers to be both knowledgeable and up to date on all applicable standards. It is very expensive to correct mistakes once construction has begun.

Quality Control This process includes (1) setting specific standards for construction performance, usually through the plans and specifications; (2) measuring variances from the standards; (3) taking action to correct or minimize adverse variances; and (4) planning for improvements in the standards themselves and in conformance with the standards. In other words, once the architects and engineers have set the criteria for construction, quality control ensures that the physical work conforms to those standards.

Quality Assurance Although its definition is not well standardized, quality assurance is generally a broader, more nearly all-encompassing term for the application of standards and procedures to ensure that a product or a facility meets or exceeds desired performance criteria. It also usually includes the documentation necessary to verify that all steps in the procedures have been satisfactorily completed. The term transcends both quality engineering and quality control, where in the first phase it includes the design of a product whose quality is economical in terms of its end use, and in the second it includes the development and application of procedures which will, at economical levels, assure attainment of the designed quality.

Elements of Quality

Basic elements of quality include (1) quality *characteristics*, (2) quality of *design*, and (3) quality of *conformance*. Each will be explained in the following paragraphs.

Quality Characteristics As with the East Indian legend of the blind men and the elephant, there are many ways we could evaluate and describe any given product. We use the term "quality characteristic" for the one or more properties that define the nature of a product for quality-control purposes. Quality characteristics include dimension, color, strength, temperature, etc.

To illustrate, consider concrete, a material common to all types of construction. Quality characteristics that commonly specify and control concrete quality include compressive strength after a fixed curing time (usually measured indirectly by failure-testing cylinders cast at the time concrete is placed), slump, size of aggregate, the ratio of water to cement, surface finish, and sometimes color. Clearly, these are not the only characteristics of concrete—one might judge its taste and smell, for example—but they are the characteristics considered relevant to quality for structural purposes.

Quality of Design   Designers generally recognize that no human undertaking produces absolutely perfect results. Therefore they often specify not only the desired standard for the characteristics that define a product, such as a dimension or strength, but also tolerances or ranges for acceptable variations from the standard. For example, reinforcing-bar spacing might be specified as 12 cm $\pm$ 0.5 cm, or a concrete specification requesting a compressive strength of 200 kg/cm^2 might further state that no more than 20 percent of the compressive-strength sample cylinder breaks can fall below this value. To specify a spacing tolerance of $\pm$ 0.2 cm or an understrength limit of 10 percent would be setting a higher quality of design. In each case we are recognizing the statistical nature of work processes.

In design, we should further recognize the impact that higher standards of quality and tighter tolerance limits have on costs. One of the easiest ways to drive up the costs of a project unnecessarily is to design in standards of quality that are inappropriate to the intended function; this applies whether the standards are too high or too low. For example, to specify architectural concrete finish standards on buried footings or other unexposed surfaces is setting standards too high. The designer of one large sewage treatment plant specified almost unachievable tolerances of 1/32 of an inch on submerged concrete surfaces; this specification required unnecessary and costly grinding on most of the concrete! On the other hand, specifying cheap and failure-prone materials may provide lower initial costs, but it will also drive up overall costs in the long run. It is the designer's responsibility, with input from the professional construction manager, to specify a quality of design that is most economical and functional for the overall project.

Quality of Conformance   Once the quality of design has been specified, the quality of conformance is the degree to which the physical work produced conforms to this standard. For example, a journeyman welder producing pipe welds with a reject rate of only 3 per 100 has a much higher quality of conformance than an apprentice with a reject rate of 17 per 100.

As with quality of design, there is a close correlation between standards for conformance and the cost of achieving those standards. There are trade-offs to be considered between costs of the work methods and quality-control procedures and the costs of rejects. These economic considerations will be discussed further below.

The Quality System

All the elements of quality that have been described thus far combine to determine the quality of the final product. The relationship between these elements is shown in Figure 16-1. The *owner's needs* are expressed in the *design criteria* that guide the *engineering and design process* that produces the *technical specifications* for the project. This in effect sets the quality of design.

The quality of conformance is influenced by (1) the actual *field construction methods*, including the skill of the workers, the capabilities of their tools and equipment, and the quality of their raw materials; (2) the *supervision* they receive and the managerial *controls* that are applied to direct the workers in accordance with the plans and specifications; and (3) the *inspection* and quality-control procedures that are applied, including the knowledge and skill of the inspectors and the reliability of their methods and tools for measuring the quality characteristics specified by the designers. The last-mentioned is particularly important, because too often the problems are with factors such as poor statistical analysis or miscalibrated or inaccurate tools used for quality control. The combination of these three produces the *degree of conformance* to the design specifications.

Quality of design and quality of conformance, in turn, determine the *quality of the constructed facility*. In considerable measure, they also affect the cost. The economics of this process will be discussed in the next section.

ECONOMICS OF QUALITY

The economics of quality assurance must be considered in both design and construction. Economic concepts applicable to each will be introduced here.

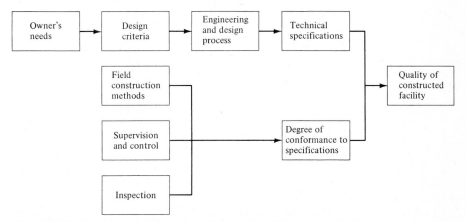

Figure 16-1   The elements of quality. *(Adapted from Elwood G. Kirkpatrick,* Quality Control for Managers and Engineers, *John Wiley & Sons, Inc., New York, 1970, p. 5.)*

Quality Economics in Design

In the simplest form, Figure 16-2 illustrates the relationship between the cost and value of quality. The horizontal axis relates to the quality of design as reflected by the quality characteristics chosen for the item concerned. As quality increases, the vertical axis shows that both the cost and the value of the quality increase as well, but in a different manner. The value curve is concave downward. As quality increases, the value increases, but at a decreasing rate. In other words, as quality increases, the marginal value, or the value of one additional unit of quality, becomes less.

On the other hand, the cost curve shows that as the quality of design increases, the marginal cost of each additional unit of quality increases more with each step. The last increment of quality costs far more than the first, until eventually it becomes too costly to specify higher standards.

In concept, the optimum level of quality occurs at the level where the marginal cost of one additional unit equals the marginal value. In Figure 16-2, this occurs where the slopes of the two curves are equal. Below this, an additional dollar of cost buys more than a dollar's worth of quality. Beyond it, the additional quality costs more than it is really worth for the functional objectives of the project.

The concept, of course, is simple compared with the reality of quantifying quality, cost and value, and determining the optimum point for design. Also, numerous other parameters affect the actual performance criteria. For example, as the quantity increases, it becomes more economical to specify higher levels of quality, since fixed costs can be written off over more units of production. To illustrate, one might justify high-quality steel forms for 100

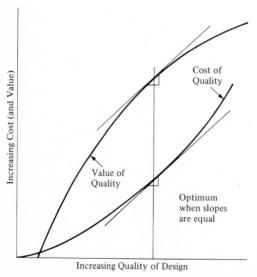

Figure 16-2 Economics of quality of design. *(Adapted from Elwood G. Kirkpatrick,* Quality Control for Managers and Engineers, *John Wiley & Sons, Inc., New York, 1970, p. 8.)*

precast concrete units, but these could not be justified for a half-dozen units. Nevertheless, by focusing on the trade-offs between cost and value, the concepts in Figure 16-2 are worth bearing in mind as design progresses.

Economics of Quality of Conformance

Simply stated, quality control costs money. There are two main ingredients to this cost: (1) the cost of the skilled labor, equipment, materials, methods, and supervision to produce quality output; and (2) the costs of monitoring and verifying the quality of output and of correcting or replacing defective work. Figure 16-3 illustrates the trade-offs between these two categories of costs.

Note that to achieve increasing quality of conformance directly from the resources and methods, one must invest more money in them, and hence the direct construction cost goes up. On the other hand, as the reliability of the methods and resources improves, less investment is required for monitoring their performance and for correcting and replacing defective work, so the costs of quality control go down. To optimize conformance costs for a given quality of design, one seeks to minimize the sum of the direct construction costs and the quality-control costs, as shown in the upper curve in Figure 16-3.

For example, a contractor might be faced with the need to prepaint metal components for a building. If the quantity is large, he might invest in a semiautomated, on-site paint shop that will assure a quality paint job with few rejects. If the quantity is small, the production cost might more than offset the quality cost, so a more manual approach, with due allowance for touch-ups and rejects, might be better.

By considering quantity, this example has also illustrated that in reality

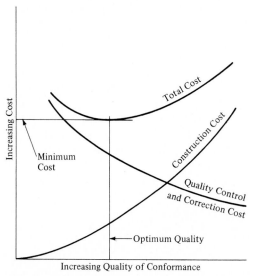

Figure 16-3 Economics of quality of conformance. *(Adapted from Elwood G. Kirkpatrick, Quality Control for Managers and Engineers, John Wiley & Sons, Inc., New York, 1970, p. 10.)*

there are more parameters than appear on the simplified model in Figure 16-3. Again, however, by focusing on just a few variables, the figure does emphasize the most important economic concepts in quality of conformance.

ORGANIZATION FOR QUALITY ASSURANCE

The quality assurance objectives of the various parties associated with a construction project differ and often conflict. The owner wants to maximize the quality of characteristics associated with the intended function of a project, yet do so without undue costs. These functional characteristics might be aesthetic, production-oriented, or whatever. The designer wants a level of quality that will assure satisfactory performance of the structure and be a credit to his professional reputation, but again without undue cost overruns. A constructor on a fixed-price contract will be interested mainly in satisfying the specifications at minimum direct cost. And increasingly, external regulatory agencies are setting quality standards for characteristics that may not even be directly related to the primary function of the project, and often with little consideration for cost. Controls on emissions to the environment are among the best-known examples, and often are a primary area of conflict. One of the most important functions of a professional construction manager is to provide third-party objectivity in setting standards of quality that, first, satisfy all mandatory regulations, and second, provide the most economical quality-cost performance in keeping with the objectives of the project.

Typical Organizations

Resolving the conflicts in objectives between the various parties generally makes the organization and responsibilities of quality assurance somewhat different from those for other parts of the project planning and control system. Especially for conformance-oriented quality control, more attention is given to separating the responsibility for judging quality from those charged with carrying out the work. For example, in traditional competitively bid public works, quality control is one of the primary responsibilities of the resident engineer and his inspectors. The relationship is shown in Figure 16-4. Incentives for cost-and-time control are normally built into the contract so that the major responsibility remains with the constructors. In private works, also, the architect and his inspectors focus mainly on quality during the construction phase.

Even in design-construct work, owner or governmental requirements often mandate that quality assurance be separated from production operations. For example, Figure 16-5 shows a setup typical of a nuclear power plant. Although the quality assurance people are employed by the same company, they are organizationally separated not only from the project manager, but from the whole operations organization as well. The idea is to set up an autonomous, independent, and, it is hoped, objective group that is free to apply controls without fear of censure from higher levels in the operations organization. By and large, this approach has been adopted by the nuclear power industry, where

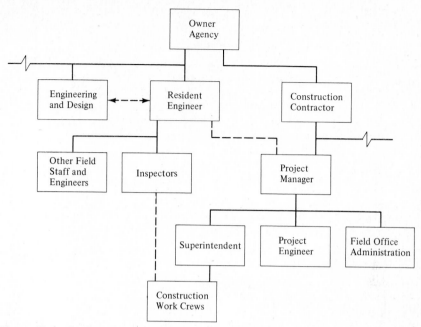

Figure 16-4 Quality control organization in a competitively bid public works project.

the quality assurance organization does indeed put quality above cost considerations at the project level.

In professional construction management, the professional construction manager provides objective third-party input into determining the quality of design, as well as inspection services to control quality of conformance. In each case this objectivity provides a new dimension and a level of effectiveness not found in most alternative forms of contracts. Where design organizations are left to set their own quality of design, they commonly tend toward conservative overdesign, often out of ignorance of the implications for construction costs. Where the design organization also inspects the work of contractors, there are legitimate questions of fairness to the contractor in the resolution of disputes regarding conflicts between quality of design and quality of conformance. An experienced and knowledgeable professional construction manager can provide the necessary objectivity.

Tasks, Responsibilities, and Procedures[1]

Early in a project, tasks and functions must be identified and the methods of accomplishing them must be determined. Figure 16-6 uses a convenient matrix form to show the important relationships for quality assurance, and in effect

[1]The figures and concepts in this section are based on the paper titled "System for Control of Construction Quality," by Roland M. Parsons, *Journal of the Construction Division*, ASCE, vol. 98, no. CO1, March 1972, pp. 21–36. The paper contains a detailed narrative discussion of all four figures (16-6 through 16-9), and is strongly recommended to the reader for further study.

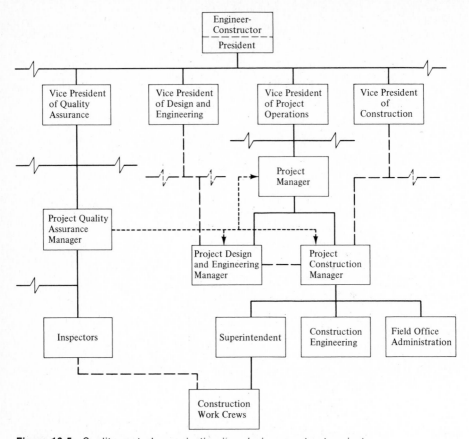

Figure 16-5 Quality control organization in a design-construct project.

summarizes the whole program. As with the detailed thinking required by CPM scheduling, the preparation of such a chart can spotlight areas of conflict and omission at the planning stage.

The left-hand column of the chart lists methods in five categories: documentation, tracking, inspection, testing, and administration. Along the top of the chart is a list of functions and tasks for a typical project. The reader is encouraged to study this figure for a moment to gain an appreciation for what is involved here and to see how quality assurance procedures differ for the different kinds of tasks. Note that critical or complex tasks are subject to more control procedures than are the simpler or less important ones. In preparing such a diagram, one tries to achieve a balanced program that will provide the most economical approach to quality assurance.

Delegating Responsibility and Authority   Once the necessary tasks and methods have been identified, it is necessary to delegate responsibility and authority for accomplishing them to persons in the project organization. In addition to organization charts such as those given in Figures 16-4 and 16-5, a

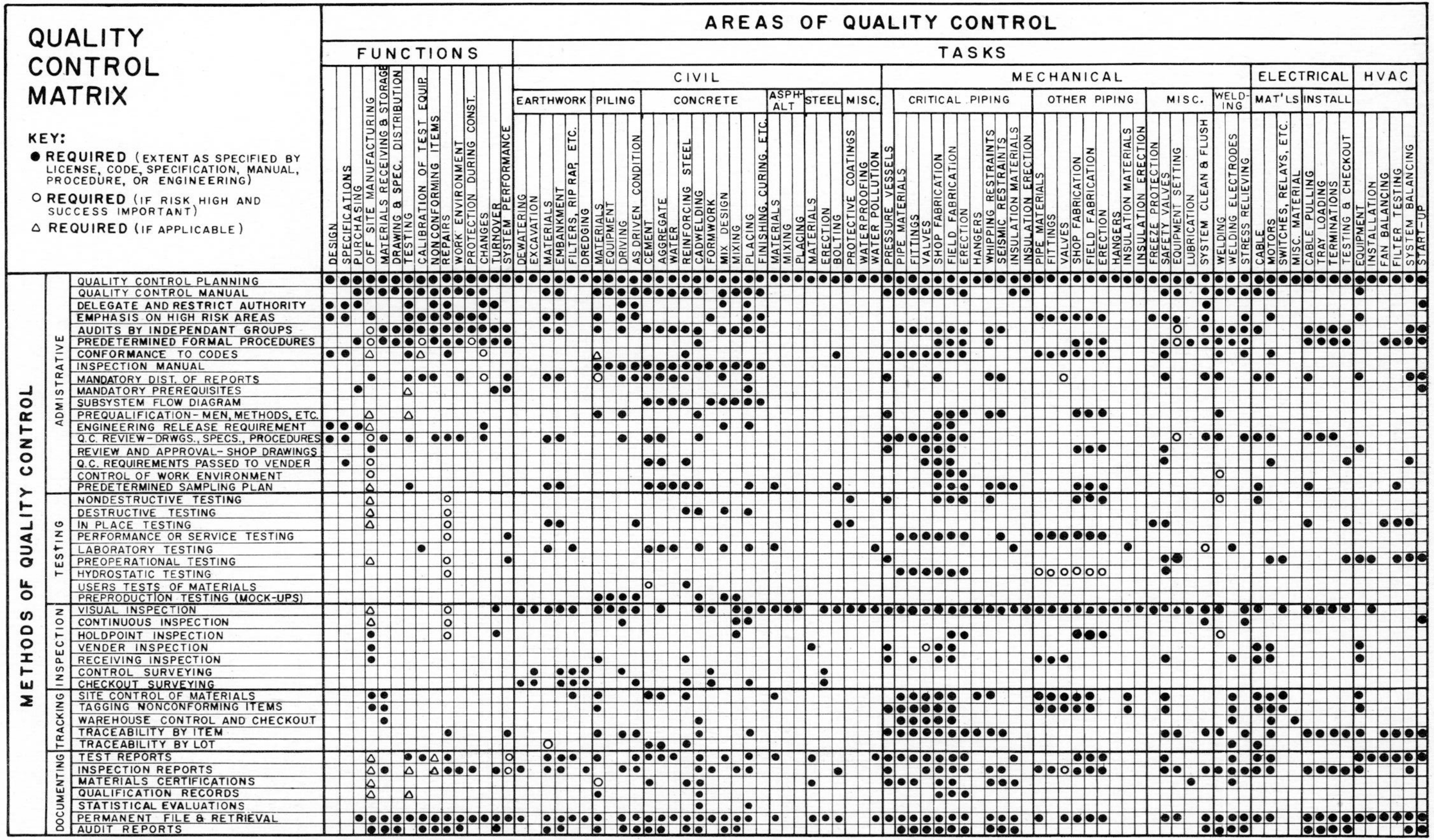

Figure 16-6 Quality control matrix. *(From "System for Control of Construction Quality," Journal of the Construction Division, ASCE, vol. 98, no. CO1, March 1972, pp. 28–29.)*

linear responsibility chart, such as that presented in Figure 16-7, clearly shows the responsibilities and relationships among the key parties. Tasks are listed in the left-hand column, positions are listed across the top, and symbols define responsibilities. Note that a single vertical column also provides the quality assurance portion of the listed individual's job description. Preparation of such a chart requires a thorough understanding of the project and the contractual relationships of the parties; it also clarifies ambiguities and identifies omissions and conflicts.

LINEAR RESPONSIBILITY CHART

• KEY •

●	PRIMARY RESPONSIBILITY
▲	JOINT RESPONSIBILITY
■	APPROVAL RESPONSIBILITY
○	MUST BE CONSULTED
△	MAY BE CONSULTED
□	AUDITS OR REVIEWS

Task	Mgr. of New Constr.	Chief Engineer	Board of Review	Site Representative	Project Manager	Project Engineer	Responsible Design Engineer	Materials Engineer	Project Superintendent	Construction Superintendent	Site Q.C. Supervisor	Site Q.A. Supervisor	Home Office Q.A. Chief	Purchasing Agent	Startup Engineer	Regulating Agency
	OWNER				**ENGINEER**				**CONSTRUCTOR**							
Select quality objectives	▲				▲				▲							▲
Define activities affecting quality	■	△	□		●	△	△	△	○							□
Specify quality standards	■	△	□		■	●	△	△	○							□
Prepare quality control manual	■	△	□		■	○		△	○				●			□
Prepare quality control procedures		□			■					○	●		■			□
Prepare construction method procedures				□		□			■	●	○	□				□
Prepare welding and NDT procedures			□	□	■			●								□
Establish design criteria	■	●	□													□
Perform design	■	■	□		■	■	●									□
Define vendor quality control requirements		■			■	●	○	○							△	□
Prepare procurement documents	■	△	□		○									□	●	
Evaluate vendor quality capability	■	△	□		■	○			○						●	□
Inspect off site manufacturing		□	□			□	△						●		○	□
Control distribution of plans and specifications				□		○			○	●						□
Specify sampling plans		□	□			□	△		○				●			□
Train and qualify craftsmen				□						○	●	○	□			□
Train and qualify inspection personnel			□	□								●	□			□
Direct construction operations									○	●						
Inspect work in progress			□	□		□	△			△	●	□				□
Accept work in progress			□	□	□	△	□	△			●	□				□
Stop work in progress		△		□	□	○		△		○	●					□
Inspect materials upon receipt				□			△	△			●	□				□
Monitor and evaluate quality trends			□	□	□								●			□
Maintain file of quality control documents			□	□									●			□
Determine disposition of nonconforming items	■	△	□	△	●	△	△	△	○		○	○				□
Investigate failures		○	□	□	○	○	△	△	△	△	●	△	△			□
Release systems and components to operations			□						□	●					■	□
Conduct flushing and cleaning operations				■											●	□
Conduct preoperational testing			□	■											●	□
Accept completed plant as to quality	●	○	△													■

Figure 16-7 Linear responsibility chart (LRC) for quality control organization. (From "System for Control of Construction Quality," Journal of the Construction Division, *ASCE, vol. 98, no. CO1, March 1972, p. 31.*)

Implementation The two charts in Figures 16-6 and 16-7 fit into the overall system for quality assurance as shown in Figure 16-8. Note again that this follows the pattern of the feedback control system introduced in Chapter 10, Figure 10-2.

Figure 16-9 gives a detailed example of how the procedures operate in the case of quality control on concrete construction. Although there is more detail here than might be required on some simpler projects, a thorough study of the figure will deepen the reader's understanding of the quality assurance process.

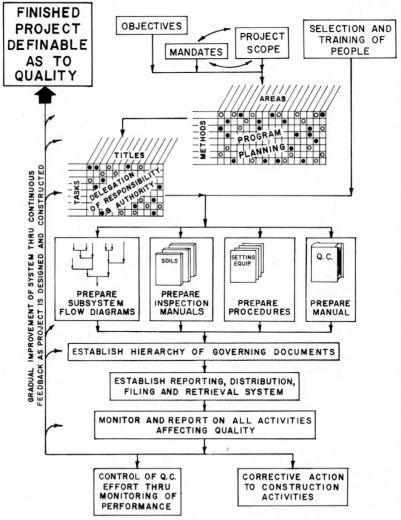

Figure 16-8 System for control of construction quality. *(From "System for Control of Construction Quality," Journal of the Construction Division, ASCE, vol. 98, no. CO1, March 1972, p. 22.)*

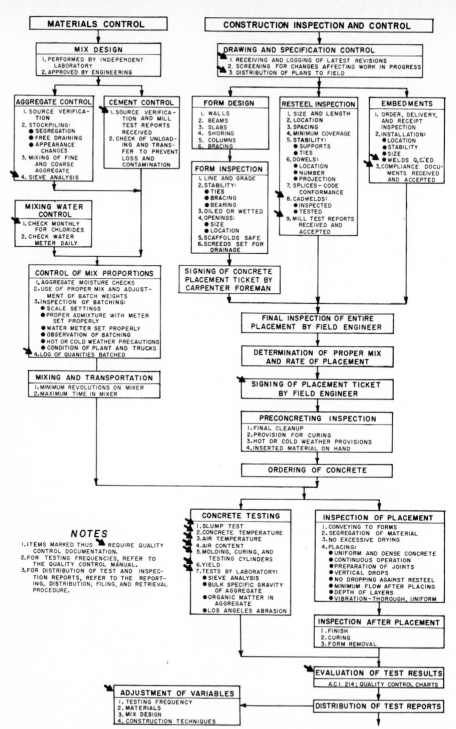

Figure 16-9 Flow diagram, quality control of concrete construction. *(From "System for Control of Construction Quality," Journal of the Construction Division, ASCE, vol. 98, no. CO1, March 1972, p. 33.)*

METHODOLOGY

Most modern approaches to quality assurance, and more specifically to quality control, require an understanding of probability and statistics. It is beyond the scope of this text to do more than mention a few basic concepts and methods. Two good introductory books listed in the bibliography include *Fundamentals of Statistical Quality Control*, by Samson, Hart, and Rubin, and *Quality Control by Statistical Methods*, a self-teaching manual by Knowler and others. A good management-oriented book is *Quality Control for Managers and Engineers*, by Kirkpatrick. Grant and Leavenworth's *Statistical Quality Control* is one of the most widely used in-depth texts in the field. The reader requiring a knowledge of this field—and this includes almost anyone with a responsible position in engineering and construction—is strongly encouraged to pursue this subject further through these and other books.

Basic Statistical Concepts

Two main categories of statistical quality control are (1) that which deals with quality characteristics that can be *measured*; and (2) that which deals with qualitative observations or *attributes*. Examples of the first type include spacing of columns, compaction density of earth, shear and compressive strength for structural lumber, and spacing of reinforcing bars. Examples in the second category include light bulbs that do or do not illuminate, welds which do or do not pass inspection, electronic control elements that do or do not work, etc.

Control Charts In the case of measurements, important statistical properties include measurements of central tendencies (mean, median, mode) and measures of dispersion (range and standard deviation). Both are important for quality control.

Control charts documenting the central tendency and dispersion most commonly record (1) average and range of samples and (2) average and standard deviation. Figure 16-10 shows a control chart for the average and standard deviation of concrete compressive strengths, and it will serve to illustrate several concepts for statistical quality control.

Figure 16-10*a* records the average or mean of successive batches of cylinder breaks. The successive tests proceed left to right on the horizontal axis, and the mean is on the vertical axis. For comparison, we shall assume that the tests in range A are typical of normal performance, with a good quality of design and a good quality of conformance. Figure 16-10*b* shows the corresponding standard deviation for each batch of tests, and Figure 16-10*c* uses a graphical distribution to illustrate the pattern of the individual strengths within each batch.

By contrast, range B shows that the mean has shifted higher, probably through overdesigning the concrete mix, while the quality of conformance to the higher standard, indicated by the standard deviations about the mean, remains about the same. Range C is similar in concept, except that the average has been shifted below the desired strength.

In range D, on the other hand, although on the average the results are oscillating around the mean, the wide scatter of the averages and the correspondingly larger standard deviations indicate that the construction procedures, and consequently the quality of conformance, appear to have become badly out of control.

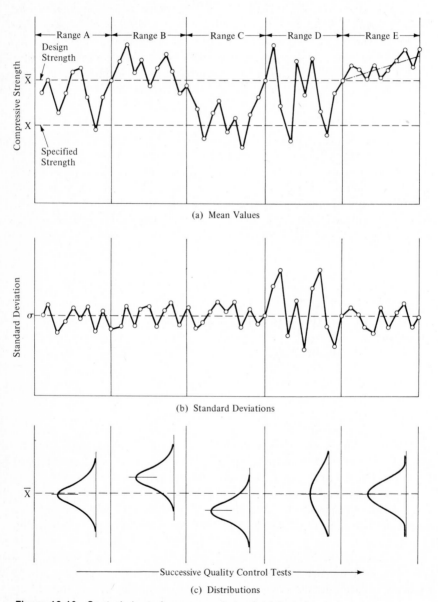

(a) Mean Values

(b) Standard Deviations

(c) Distributions

Figure 16-10 Control charts for mean and standard deviation.

Range E is included to show one of many other types of situations that can be revealed through control charts. The gradual uptrending pattern might indicate continuous wear on a key component in the process—possibly the mechanism that closes the gate that lets the cement into the concrete batch. These and other problems can be spotted by an experienced user of this type of quality-control tool.

Sampling Attributes   The second category of statistical quality control, sampling by attributes, provides an opportunity to introduce concepts associated with the sampling process itself. Random sampling is used either as an economic measure to reduce the expense of testing every unit produced, or in situations involving destructive testing where the element tested is intentionally tested to failure. The assumption is that one can select a sample from a lot that will be statistically representative of the whole. For example, Figure 16-11 shows a sample of size 5 selected from a lot of size 25 that has 10 defective units. If the sample has 2 defective and 3 good units, it is indeed representative. But what if 5 of the 15 good units are selected? Or what if 3 or more defective units are selected? The sample would then give misleading information that could lead to a bad decision.

There is a trade-off here. Increasing the size of a sample increases the reliability of inspection, but it also increases the cost. Reducing the size reduces reliability and might result in acceptance of lots that will require expensive rework later in the project, or rejection of satisfactory lots.

Figure 16-12 illustrates some of the probabilities associated with the process. It assumes that a large lot will be randomly sampled, and that the tolerable limit of defectives is normally 4 percent. The horizontal axis plots the actual percentage that is defective in a given lot, and the vertical axis indicates the probability that a random sample from a lot will show less than 4 percent to be defective. For example, if the lot is 8 percent defective, there is a

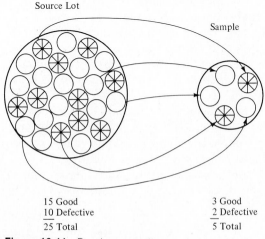

15 Good	3 Good
10 Defective	2 Defective
25 Total	5 Total

Figure 16-11   Random sampling.

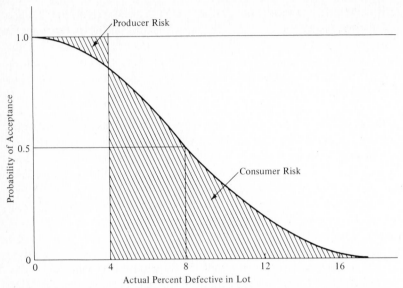

Figure 16-12 Risk and uncertainty in sampling. *(Adapted from Charles Samson, Philip Hart, and Charles Rubin,* Fundamentals of Statistical Sampling, *Addison-Wesley Publishing Company, Reading, Mass., 1970, p. 87.)*

50 percent chance that the sample would contain only 4 percent defectives, and thus allow the whole lot to be accepted. The shaded area to the left of the 4 percent line is called the "producer risk," that is, it is the chance that a random sample would reject a lot that is actually satisfactory. The shaded area to the right is called the "consumer risk," which would have to be handled through repair or replacement warranties, or simply have to be absorbed by the consumer.

Practical Considerations   At all times one must be on the lookout for extraneous factors affecting the quality assurance process. A real case history will illustrate this point. A supplier of ready-mix concrete for highway construction in the state of Oregon has reported that every summer the state laboratory reports on the quality of his concrete start to go very bad about 28 days after the state university closes for the summer. His own testing indicates that his concrete really does not change at all in quality. Rather, what happens is that in the summer the state highway department temporarily hires college engineering students for the prime construction season. In their first few days on the job, the students are inexperienced in making the cylinders for concrete testing. The results are reflected in the tests after 28 days of curing. There are innumerable other examples of aberrations introduced by human factors, mechanical defects in test equipment, or environmental factors beyond the control of both constructors and testers.

Example: Concrete Quality Control

The design and control of concrete quality illustrate much of what we have discussed in this chapter. The designer, in quality engineering, prepares specifications on strength, size of aggregate, dimensional tolerances, slump, finish, etc. Assuming the designer has done so, the constructor still has considerable latitude in trading off quality control against methods to produce the required quality of conformance.

For the materials costs, cement is normally by far the most expensive component. The water/cement ratio is in turn a key factor in determining the strength of concrete. For a given design strength, one can reduce cement and hence materials costs in at least three ways: (1) Use larger aggregate, thus reducing the surface area. This is common in mass concrete. (2) Maintain the water/cement ratio while reducing both water and cement. This, of course, reduces the slump and makes the concrete harder to place. (3) With better quality control, bring the mix design strength closer to the specified strength for the concrete.

The first two alternatives are generally constrained by the specifications and by the methods and conditions of placement. The statistical implications of the third are most important for our purposes here.

A typical concrete specification may recognize the statistical nature of quality control in one of the following ways:

1 No more than 10 percent of samples tested may fall more than 10 percent below the specified strength.
2 No more than 20 percent of samples tested may fall below the specified strength.

To achieve this quality, one must design the concrete mix for a higher average strength than that specified, unless the specification allows 50 percent or more of the tests to fall below the specified strength. This concept is illustrated in Figure 16-13, where X is the specified strength, and $\overline{X}$ is the mix design strength.

Knowing X, $\overline{X}$ can be derived as follows:

Assume X_i = observed strength for test i

σ = standard deviation

$$= \sqrt{\frac{\sum_{i=1}^{n}(X_i - X)^2}{n}} \tag{16-1}$$

where n = number of cylinders tested

V = known coefficient of variation determined for the batch plant being used

$$= \frac{\sigma}{X} \times 100\% \tag{16-2}$$

t = standard variable, the number of standard deviations from the mean (design) to the specified strength

$$= \frac{X - \overline{X}}{\sigma} \tag{16-3}$$

Now, by substitution of

$$\sigma = V\overline{X} \text{ for } \sigma$$

$$\therefore t = \frac{X - \overline{X}}{V\overline{X}} \tag{16-4}$$

which gives

$$\overline{X} = \frac{X}{1 + Vt} \tag{16-5}$$

This is the design strength that should satisfy the specification for the specified strength. The specifications define X. The standard variable t is from statistical tables for the normal distribution and corresponds to the owner's specification for the fraction of samples permitted to be substandard. V is developed from

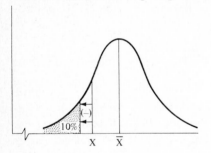

(a) No more than 1 in 10 less than 0.9X

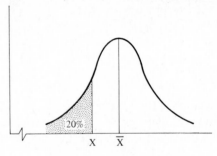

(b) No more than 1 in 5 less than X

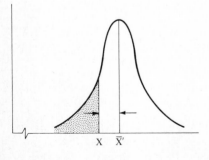

(c) Tighter Control

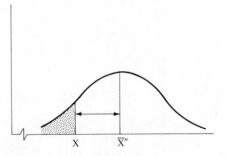

(d) Looser Control

Figure 16-13 Various levels of concrete quality control.

the contractor's or the ready-mix supplier's concrete quality control. If V can be kept low, one can design closer to the specified strength and thus keep the concrete material costs down. The trade-off is in the better equipment and supervision required to keep V under tight control.

Example 1   Determine the design strength required to satisfy the specified strength of 300 kg/cm² (4,270 psi) under the terms of the first specification above. Assume $V = 20$ percent.

$X - 10\% = 300 - 30 = 270$ kg/cm²

$10\% \Rightarrow t = -1.383$ (assuming 10 tests; $t = -1.282$ for ∞ tests)

$$\therefore \overline{X} = \frac{270}{1 + 0.2\,(-1.383)}$$

$= 373$ kg/cm² (5,300 psi)

Example 2   As above, but use the second statistical specification.

$20\% \Rightarrow t = -0.383$ (for 10-test average)

$$\overline{X} = \frac{300}{1 + 0.2\,(-0.883)}$$

$= 364$ kg/cm² (5,180 psi)

Example 3   To illustrate the effect of better quality control, assume the data from example 2, but change V to 10 percent.

$$\overline{X} = \frac{300}{1 + 0.1\,(-0.883)}$$

$= 329$ kg/cm² (4,680 psi)

Example 4   To illustrate the effect of a specification that ignores statistical variations and in effect demands perfection by requiring that *no* cylinders fall below the specified strength, consider the following:

First, to have numbers to work with, approximate "no" cylinders to "no more than 3 standard deviations below" (i.e., 1 in 741). This gives a t of -3.000 standard deviations. Otherwise, assume X and V from example 2.

$$\overline{X} = \frac{300}{1 + 0.2\,(-3.0)}$$

$= 750$ kg/cm² (10,670 psi)

This is a very high design that would require extraordinarily expensive procedures. For this reason, almost all modern specifications do recognize the statistical implications of quality control.

SUMMARY

Quality assurance, which encompasses both quality engineering and quality control, involves (1) the application of standards and procedures to ensure that a product or facility meets or exceeds desired performance criteria, and (2) documentation to verify the results obtained. Quality engineering involves the application of procedures to ensure that design proceeds according to recommended and mandatory criteria set by professional associations, building code authorities, and the environment, while it produces a facility that most economically serves the owner's needs. Quality control includes the development and application of procedures that will, at economical levels, assure attainment of the designed quality when the project is constructed.

The elements of quality include quality characteristics, quality of design, and quality of conformance. Quality characteristics are those properties chosen to define the nature of a product for design and control purposes. The quality of design relates to the design tolerances set for the chosen characteristics that will enable a product to function at the desired level of reliability and economy. Quality of conformance is the degree to which the physical work produced conforms to the specified design. All these factors have cost implications on the project.

Quality economics in design involves trade-offs between the value of quality and the cost of obtaining it. In theory, the optimum design is at a level where the marginal value of an additional unit of quality equals its marginal cost. Economics of quality of conformance involves a minimum-cost balance between the costs of better but more costly construction methods to improve conformance and the costs of rejects and a greater control effort resulting from poor conformance. In reality, numerous other parameters, such as quantity, affect both the design and the conformance trade-offs, but the basic concepts must first be understood.

Organization for quality assurance differs from other phases of a project control system, and reflects the varying and often conflicting interests of the parties to the contract as well as the interests of society as imposed through governmental regulation. Briefly stated, there is often considerable emphasis on keeping the quality assurance function separate from project operations in order to ensure that third-party objectivity will prevail in decision-making. This chapter included four figures which detail the tasks and methods involved in quality assurance and show how responsibility and authority for these tasks can be delegated.

Methodology for most modern approaches to quality assurance requires at least some understanding of probability and statistics. There are two major categories of statistical quality control: one deals with quality characteristics that can be measured, and the other deals with qualitative observations or attributes. In both categories, there are various types of control charts and sampling procedures that can assure good quality control at economical levels.

Chapter 17

Computer Applications in Construction

INTRODUCTION—INFLUENCES OF TECHNOLOGY

In electronic technologies, the last few years have been like a time warp. Technical terms that once shielded the computer elite from mere mortals have become household words. Whimsically named companies founded by child prodigies with capital from hocked momentos of the counterculture have grown by megabucks to become producers of mass consumer goods. Little machines more powerful than prestigious blue-chip business processors of two decades ago are mistaken for—indeed, used as—toys.

The "toy" that plays "Startrek," "Spacewar," and "Adventure" in thousands of homes is also keeping business records for the national association of the nation's largest constructors. Hard-headed contractors who would not have touched a keyboard 5 years ago are now overheard comparing notes with others on PRINT USING statements and DOS files, though still somewhat clandestinely lest the unconverted think they have substituted electronics for judgment and experience. Their colleagues do indeed whisper about them, but the whisperers are becoming more wistful and will continue to do so until they too figure out how the little machines can be used to cut through office drudgery.

The motor car was a toy of the elite, a rich man's luxury, until the Model T made it accessible to every person and also made a driver's license a socio-economic necessity. The microprocessor has become the Model T of computers, and proficiency in its application in individual professional activities will be essential to the productivity and success of future construction managers. Those equipped with skills in word processing for job-site correspondence (yes, they must type!), electronic communications, and tools like Visicalc for estimates and payment requests will leave the unprepared drowning in paper.

Low-cost computers have arrived none too soon if construction professionals are to cope with the growing administrative burdens imposed by internal and external demands. Already, many major construction companies have software far more sophisticated than that available a decade ago, especially in cost control, procurement, estimating, and scheduling. Until recently, however, computer hardware acquisitions in smaller and medium-sized firms did not keep pace with the level of technology available in industry. It is catch-up ball, but microcomputers at least enable smaller firms to stay in the game. Central computer centers become increasingly obsolete, and $100,000 minicomputers are out of the question for most small companies, but many do seem to be able to break loose $2000 to $5000 from tight-fisted controllers, so the micros are cropping up all over.

What does the money buy? Mostly hardware. Typical acquisitions involve one or more Apples or TRS-80s or IBM PCs, with 48,000 to 256,000 characters of memory, one or two floppy disk drives, a small printer, a TV/CRT, the disk operating system (DOS), one or more languages (BASIC, PASCAL, FORTRAN, COBOL), and perhaps a few games. But what do you do when you get tired of playing "Space Invaders?" It is surprising how many people will willingly spend several thousand dollars for hardware but not invest a few hundred more for useful software such as a word processor and a spread-sheet program like Visicalc. It took only money to leave the Model T parked in the driveway for the neighbors to admire, but learning how to drive the car required an investment of time and effort. It also takes time and effort to learn how to use software—and develop it—but that is the key to productive use of computing machines. Whether acquired or developed, software must be the focus of computer efforts in construction management and engineering.

This chapter will first provide a brief overview of computer hardware and software technology. It will then review present and potential construction application areas. For those contemplating in-house development, criteria for software development and documentation are outlined. The last main section illustrates several examples of commercially available systems designed for construction management.

For the reader who would like to stay up to date in this area, a new information source is worth mentioning: WPL/CCM Publications, which publishes the monthly *Construction Computer Applications Newsletter (CCAN)* and the *Construction Software Applications Directory*. Although there are numerous technical and business computer publications in the computer industry, these are believed to be the only ones that specifically focus upon construction.

---

[1]1105-F Spring St., Silver Spring MD 20910.

OVERVIEW OF AVAILABLE TECHNOLOGY

It is well beyond the scope of this chapter to explain computer technology, but it is worth outlining the subjects that must be studied to become knowledgeable in this area. Two major categories to be considered are the software or programs that make it possible to use the computer in various applications and the computer hardware itself. Two subjects that fall somewhere between these two categories are the storage of information in files or in a data base, and telecommunications. Each subject is reviewed briefly in the following subsections.

Computer Hardware

The hardware is the part of computer systems most familiar to the general public because it is the easiest to display in photographs and movies. The hardware itself can be broadly divided into two main categories: (1) the central processing unit (CPU) and its high-speed electronic memory and (2) peripheral devices ranging from disk and tape drives for mass storage of information to input devices such as terminals and card readers and output devices like CRTs and printers.

The processors are generally classified into three main ranges, primarily on the basis of size, cost, and capability. The largest systems are called "mainframes," and these historically have been found in the central computing facilities of major universities, government agencies, and large companies. An example is shown in Figure 17-1, the IBM 3081. The next category is generally called "minicomputers," and these range from small single-user systems on up to "superminis," whose capabilities exceed those of the mainframes of only a few years ago. Figure 17-2 shows the Digital Equipment Corporation PDP-11/44 minicomputer, which contains a 16-bit processor and 1 million characters of main memory. Figure 17-3 shows a widely used supermini, the Digitial Equipment Corporation VAX 11/782, which has been gaining wide acceptance in engineering design companies and university computer science and engineering departments. The smallest category of processors includes what are currently called "microcomputers," whose main distinctions are that the processor is normally contained on a single small silicon chip and the whole machine is often configured in the size of a typewriter or desk-top calculator. Microcomputers include small dedicated microcomputers used as controllers for home appliances and automobile engines on up to 16 and 32-bit machines whose capabilities exceed those of the minicomputers of but a few years ago. A widely used Apple II microcomputer is shown in Figure 17-4. Given the rapid changes in technology, the distinctions between these categories of machines are disappearing, and improved capabilities are largely a function of time. Today's more advanced microcomputers are far more powerful than all but the largest mainframes of two decades ago.

The memory in the processors is measured in units called "bytes"; a byte is approximately equal to one alphabetic or numeric character of storage. Al-

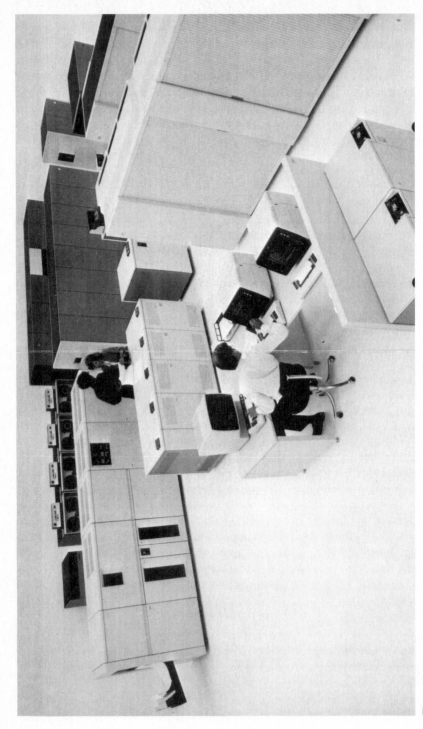

Figure 17-1: IBM 3081 Mainframe Computer System (Courtesy of IBM)

Figure 17-2: Digital Equipment Corporation PDP-11/44 Minicomputer

though for historical reasons the memory is commonly called "core," today's memories are almost all based upon semiconductor technology. Two general categories are random access memory (RAM), which means that information can both be stored in and retrieved from memory, and read only memory (ROM), where information is permanently encoded in the memory and can only be retrieved by the processor but not written or replaced. ROM is generally used to store parts of the computer system software rather than for applications.

Figure 17-3: Digital Equipment Corporation VAX11/782 Computer (Courtesy of Digital Equipment Corporation)

(a)

(b)

Figure 17-4:   Apple II and IBM PC Microcomputers

Figure 17-5: High-Speed 9-Track Magnetic Tape Drive (Courtesy of Stanford Center for Information Processing)

The most important peripherals are the disk and tape devices that store information on magnetic media. Tape drives are similar in concept to the audio tape decks found in most homes. The computer types range from small tape drives that quite literally are the same as those used for audio storage on up to large dedicated units that store information on half-inch magnetic tape at densities of up to 65,000 characters per inch. An example of a high-capacity tape drive connected to an automated tape library is shown in Figure 17-5. Since the length of a tape is typically 2400, ft, over 1 billion characters of information can be stored in a relatively small space. This is equivalent to about 1 million pages of normal manuscript typing. As with audio tape drives, access to the information is sequential, so tape drives are normally more appropriate for what is called "batch processing."

Disk drives have a storage medium that looks somewhat like a 33-rpm record in an audio hi-fi system. However, the method of encoding and retrieving information is magnetic, like that for tape drives, and rather than the information being along spiral grooves, the tracks or circles storing the information on disks are concentric. Because the read heads can move from point to point relatively directly, somewhat like the tone arm on a record player moves, disk drives are especially appropriate where information is to be accessed in a nonsequential or, as it is sometimes loosely called, "random" manner. Storage in the form of disk technology ranges from small $5\frac{1}{4}$-in. diameter floppy diskettes (Figure 17-6) with capacities of 100,000 to 500,000 characters, through removable-pack cartridge disks with capacities ranging from 10 million to 300 million

Figure 17-6: Drive for "Floppy" Diskettes

characters (Figure 17-7), on up to fixed-pack "winchester" disks with capacities of up to 1 billion characters. The cost of comparable drives for tape or disk media is similar, but regarding the storage media itself (disk cartridges or magnetic tape), it is much cheaper to store tape than disks, based upon cost per character. Disk or tape drives are normally connected to the computer's processor via an interface device called a "controller."

Other important categories of peripherals are input and output devices. Broadly speaking, disk and tape drives fall into this category, but they are classified separately because information stored in them is not directly accessible by human beings. On the other hand, human beings normally do help prepare the data via input devices such as card punches and card readers, and hard copy and CRT terminals. Similarly, output devices such as printers and plotters exist mainly for converting computer data into a form for human consumption. Figure 17-8 shows a typical CRT terminal, Figure 17-9 shows a hard-copy terminal, and Figure 17-10 shows card-punch equipment, A small dot matrix printer is shown in Figure 17-11, and a high-speed laser printer is shown in Figure 17-12. The matrix printer works at approximately 3 lines per second; the laser printer goes through paper at the rate of about 17,000 lines per minute. Figure17-13 shows a small pen plotter, and Figure 17-14 shows a large electrostatic plotter.

Figure 17-7: Removable-Pack Catridge Disk Drive

Telecommunications

Although it involves a mixture of hardware and software, telecommunications is described here because this subject is particularly important to construction companies since their production centers, or projects, tend to be decentralized from the principal place of business. In its most common form, telecommunications technology is that which interfaces between computer systems and the common carriers such as the telephone company to enable information to be transmitted from one computer system or device to another, or to enable users with terminals to remotely access a distant computer.

The most frequently encountered device for telecommunicaitons is a modem (short for "modular-demodulator"), which converts the computer's digital electronic signal into the type of analog voice-grade signal that can be transmitted over a telephone. At the other end of the line is another modem that translates the analog signal back into the digital signal the receiving device wants to hear. Common modems have transmission speeds ranging from 30 characters per second (cps) to about 240 cps, with corresponding costs ranging from about $200 to about $1000 per connection.

With the digital networks being established by special-purpose public and private carriers, the speed and reliability of transmission are increasing rapidly, and costs per unit of capacity are decreasing. The more advanced technologies include devices such as "statistical multiplexers," microwave and satellite transmission, and various kinds of encryption schemes to preserve the confidentiality of data.

Closely related to this subject is that of office automation and electronic

Figure 17-8: C. Itoh CIT-101 CRT Terminal

mail. This is as much a software subject as one of hardware, and it involves local networking within office buildings as well as long-distance communications. Electronic mail in particular removes the requirement for both ends of the

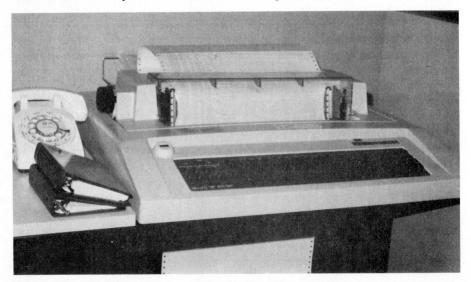

Figure 17-9: Digital Equipment Corporation LA-36 Hard Copy Terminal

Figure 17-10:   IBM Card Punch(Courtesy of Stanford Center for Information Processing)

converation to be connected at the same time, which is a major advantage given that the average business telephone call takes approximately three iterations of "telephone tag" to complete. This whole field is developing rapidly, and it is important for today's construction managers who wish to remain competitive to stay up with the technology.

Computer Software

Computer software can be classified into that used for running the system itself and that used for applications. The former category is discussed in this section. The system software consists of a program or group of programs called the

Figure 17-11:   Epson MX-80 Dot Matrix Printer

Figure 17-12: IBM Model 3800 Laser Printer (Courtesy of Satnford Center for Information Processing)

"operating system," program-development tools such as editors, compilers and linkers, and utilities for creating, maintaining, deleting, backing up and moving files, and for other miscellaneous system tasks.

The operating system supervises the utilization of the computer's resources.

Figure 17-13: Hewlett Packard 4-Color Pen Plotter

Figure 17-14: Electrostatic Plotter (Courtesy of Versatec)

It is responsible for loading programs from storage devices such as disks and tapes into memory at the time when the programs are to be executed, and in general for handling the traffic between peripherals and the processor. The operating system also divides and allocates the computer's resources among various competing programs and users and protects the users from mistakes that might be made by others. The operating system also might handle the accounting for the utilization and billing of system resources, the security to restrict access to the system to authorized users, and so on.

The program-development software consists of text editors that enable a programmer to type a program or data into the computer for initial development and modification and programs called compilers and linkers that translate the source program from its alphabetic and numeric form into the binary form that is understandable and executable by the computer. Useful program-development tools also include libraries of common subroutines for operations such as input, output, and mathematical functions and programs that assist in the debugging of new programs under development.

Although it is not essential that a construction manager understands this kind of software, it is important to appreciate that the success or failure of a computer installation in a construction company is, if anything, even more dependent upon the system's software than upon the hardware itself. Construction managers must therefore be certain that experts are involved in the selection of computer hardware and software that best suits the needs of the organization.

Files and Data Bases

An area that relates to both hardware and software is the method of storing information for later use. Physical locations of the files of information can be "online," meaning that the device containing the information is continuously attached to the computer and ready for access, and "offline," meaning that the information might be contained on tapes or disk packs stored away from the drives on which they can be mounted. Online storage is used for information needed on a continuous basis, such as the files for an airline reservation system, whereas offline storage serves for archiving annual records, backing up online files, and so forth.

Within conventional file systems, the data can be organized " sequentially" or for "direct access." "Sequential" means that to get to a particular item of information, it is first necessary to search and check the information that precedes it in the file. Data stored on tape is inherently sequential, but disk files can also be organized this way. "Direct access" means that the computer programs can instruct the computer to go directly to the location on a device such as a disk that contains the item of information desired. Applications that need quick reference to items of information in an unpredictable order need direct access. For example, an airline reservation system needs to be able to respond promptly to any caller making an inquiry. Sequential systems are more suitable to well-organized files of information that are processed on a periodical basis, such as a weekly payroll.

The term "data base" is loosely used to mean the collection of files contained at a particular computer installation. However, in the data processing profession today, data base refers to a complex system of software and hardware that integrates the various files for a number of different applications into one commonly accessible pool of information. This integration makes it possible to reduce the duplication of items, such as the names of people that might be needed by both personnel and payroll applications, and also provides for direct ties between different applications, such as a materials procurement and tracking system with an accounts payable system. Data base technologies in turn can be subdivided into three main types: network, hierarchical, and relational; however, it is beyond the scope of this book to go into that level of detail.

THE RANGE OF POSSIBLE APPLICATIONS

Cumputers can be of assistance in all aspects of project planning and control. Topics corresponding to major sections of this book include estimating, cost control, scheduling, quality assurance, procurement, and the general subjects of administation and productivity analysis. Each topic is addressed briefly in the following sections.

Estimating

Computers can help estimators in most phases of their work. For example, a good application of smaller computers is to help with the partial automation of a quantity takeoff. In this case, an estimator can use a stylus or cursor on a drawing laid over a digitizer board to directly input measurements and item counts. An electronic image of the project's geometry can be built up and even displayed on graphical CRTs. Simultaneously, the computer can be building a file containing the bill of materials.

In developing crews and evaluating the productivity of labor and equipment, computers can first provide data from files of past projects and second assist with specialized engineering programs for calculations such as cableway cycles, earth-moving fleet simulation, formwork calculations, and so on. In the costing phase, a computer can maintain files of current cost information, and with remote access it is now becoming possible to tie into various data bases maintained by traditional estimating firms. As the estimate nears completion, a computer can be particularly valuable for developing spread sheets and in bid-sheet preparation. This is especially important in the final hectic hours of competitive bidding, when newly arrived subcontractor bids and materials quotations can make frequent recalculations of the estimate necessary. With the calculations accurately and reliably under control, management can also indulge in sensitivity analysis to determine which aspects of the bid contain the greatest risk and thus more intelligently determine the best markup. Computer programs providing a rough cash flow can also enable the markup to be based upon desired rate of return rather than simply a percentage of gross profit.

Cost Control

In larger construction companies, computers were often first installed under the control of the accounting department. Therefore, it was not surprising that cost control systems were generally extensions of the payroll and accounting and finance people. Over the years, however, job costing and cost-engineering systems have evolved that, although perhaps connected to the company's accounting system through a data base, are deliberately oriented toward the needs of company and project management. Some of the more sophisticated systems apply the principles of engineering economy to include the time value of money in project decision making. Other advanced systems integrate with the schedule, again possibly through a data base, for cash-flow forecasting. An important aspect of any cost control system is to make the data available to management in a timely manner, so there is an increasing trend to interactive applications using terminals or microcomputers directly in the hands of managers and supervisors.

Scheduling

Critical path scheduling was one of the earliest applications of computers in construction, but it has taken time for it to gain wide acceptance. Like cost control, this is an application that should be directly in the hands of management, so the slow acceptance may be a result of the fact that earlier computers were not easily used by non-dataprocessing people. Powerful scheduling tools are now becoming available even on personal microcomputers, however, so the trend toward wider acceptance of quantitative scheduling methods can only be expected to accelerate in the future.

Scheduling programs on computers typically at least have basic CPM computations, and most will at least produce a bar chart on a line printer. As the level of sophistication increases, the programs will include resource loading and aggregation (where resources can be assigned to activities and their total usage by period can be accumulated); resource allocation and leveling, where the computer program attempts to do some rescheduling to balance the utilization of resources; network-based cost control, which can either be intregrated with the job-costing system or used for time-cost trade-off applications; and there is an increasing trend toward utilization of graphic output on interactive CRTs and on plotters.

Quality Assurance

Quality assurance applications can begin with the online retrieval of specifications, codes, and standards. Quality assurance systems also assist in the documentation of procedures and testing requirements and in the reporting of test results and completion of administrative steps to various interested agencies and parties. Some of the most advanced applications involve not only administrative procedures but direct production control. For example, modern automated concrete-batch plants enable the operator to call up any of several predefined mixes; the computer then operates the plant until the correct mix is discharged into a waiting concrete truck; batch information is printed out and copies are given to the truck driver to take to the point of delivery for an inspector's confirmation and approval before the concrete goes into the pour. Copies are also attached to samples made at the pour site, and the loop is closed following testing, when sample results are logged and sent back to the quality assurance department. Similar applications are gaining acceptance in welding, asphalt paving, and so forth.

Procurement

Simpler procurement systems are just extensions of the accounting department's accounts payable program. However, in larger organizations, there are separate programs for procurement scheduling and expediting to be sure that steps such as requisitions and shop drawings are not overlooked or to bring problems and delays to management's attention before they become too acute. Materials and procurement systems can also include simple or sophisticated inventory control systems for job materials, tools, and supplies. When linked to a data base, the procurement applications can interface to the quality assurance application for testing and documentation, to the acounts payable system for multiproject vendor correlations, and to the scheduling system to assess the impact of procurement delays on overall project status.

Administration

Even the simpler personal microcomputers can almost immediately pay for themselves in various kinds of administrative applications. For example, numerous lists must be maintained on projects for drawing logs, tool inventories, safety equipment, and so on. Any number of microcomputer file systems can handle such applications. Word processing software on small or large computers can assist with letters and the documentation of transmittals, claims, and so forth. Tools such as Visicalc can be of immense benefit for financial planning and budgeting as the project evolves. In effect, most of the administrative drudgery that is typically assigned to junior engineers and office clerks can be greatly mitigated through the intelligent applicaion of microcomputers on the job site.

Productivity

Deliberate and systematic efforts to improve productivity on construction projects are becoming increasingly common. Computers can assist with the statistical analysis of questionnaires distributed to workers and supervisors, with the simulation of operations before they are implemented, and so on. This is a new area, but with the improved availability of computers on job sites, it is expected to become increasingly common in the future.

CRITERIA FOR SOFTWARE DEVELOPMENT AND DOCUMENTATION

Software development requires a great deal of careful preparation. It is not possible to directly write a complex program, hurriedly throw together the documentation, and hope for successful implementation. From the original design steps until final testing and write-up, the program must conform to good programming and documentation guidelines.

Software Development[1]

Important considerations in software development include choice of programming languages, structured programming techniques, user-friendly design, and thorough debugging. Each subject is now discussed.

[1]This section was originally written by S. A. Douglas for a paper presented with B. C. Paulson at the June 1981 conference of the American Society for Engineering Education and published in the Spring 1982 issue of *Civil Engineering Education*.

Choice of Programming Language   Choice of progamming language is a part of the system analysis and design. Because transferability is of major importance, we recommend that only high-level standard languages be used. The most common and well-standardized scientific language is FORTRAN, although it lacks the control statements of structured programming. It also requires more memory and a disk operating system since it is a compiler.

Traditionally, most business programs on larger computers have been written in COBOL. It has advantages of being somewhat self-documenting by permitting a descriptive coding style and has strengths in input, reporting, and structured file handling. It is also the language most commonly interfaced to large-scale data base management systems.

Another highly recommended compiler is PASCAL. Its control structures encourage the preparation of well-designed, easily transferred programs. The problem with PASCAL is that it is a relatively new language and does not have standardized file and string operations.

BASIC is the fourth recommendation for programming. Because it is an interpreter in most implementations, it is very popular and available on more computer systems than any other language. BASIC requires little memory in the computer. Its simple statements and interactive editing (in the interpreter version) make it suitable for many beginning programmers. BASIC would be the language of choice except that it is not standardized and lacks many structured programming features, thus becoming especially unwieldy when programs become large. Still, it is possible to write programs with very simple BASIC statements that will transfer to most implementations of the language.

We stress standardized languages because of the enormous amount of time it takes to translate from one language into another or even from one dialect into another. Most implementations of even a standardized language have extensions made by the particular manufacturer, and these must be avoided if the program is to be implemented on other machines. If machine-dependent features are necessary, they should be isolated in the program and well-documented.

Structured Programming Techniques   How the program is written is as important as the language in which it is written. In the last decade, programming technology has been concerned with techniques for structured programming. Ideally, a program should be designed to optimize simplicity, linearity of logic flow, and modularity in organization. As mentioned, FORTRAN and BASIC were created before these concepts evolved and do not lend themselves easily to good structured programming techniques. However, even FORTRAN and BASIC can benefit from a conscious design and coding effort to implement these features.

The program should be organized into sections or modules that perform a particular task. These modules are typically called from a main control section. Each module should be restricted to a page or less of code. The separation of a program into modules enhances its readability and provides reusable code for other programs. Libraries of general modules can often significantly reduce programming effort. Another benefit of modularity is that it eases the implementation of large programs on small computers through the use of overlays of segments of code as the program executes.

Linear logic flow is critical to the readability of a program by someone who did not write it (and sometimes even to the one who did!). Recommended control structures are sequential execution of statements, forward skipping upon the results of a stipulated test, and iteration. The infamous GOTO statement of FORTRAN and BASIC should be avoided where feasible and used only for transfer of control forward. Some versions of BASIC and FORTRAN implement structured control with statements such as IF. . .THEN. . .ELSE and DO. . .WHILE, but these are not standard features of the original languages. This suggests that in languages such as FORTRAN or BASIC there may be a conflict between the goals of improving programming for transfer by using structured programming techniques and improving transfer by standardizing the language.

User-Friendly Design   Since many programs execute interactively as opposed to batch, the interaction with the user at the terminal is of prime importance. A software designer must be very aware of the psychological impact of an interactive program. One of the most important factors is the difference between users who are learning the program and experienced users.

Learners require much explanation and dialogue to help them choose appropriate responses. Prolific instructions on how to use the program should be embedded in an introduction, to be followed upon program initiation. An emergency or help option should be available at all times to give further information. Errors need to be anticipated and processed smoothly. All interaction must be in clear English, with the vocabulary of the user's application, not computerese! All possible choices to a response should be illustrated, or a typical response should be shown. Dialogue methods particularly helpful to learners are menus of choices, form-filling, question-answer formats, and mnemonic command languages. The designer should be very attentive to the aesthetics of the final screens and the context they create, to help the users remember where they are (in which phase of the program).

On the other hand, the experienced user wants efficiency and speed. The redundancy of verbose explanations becomes very tedious to the expert. Command languages are the most usable dialogue method for the expert since they give the user maximum control.

If programs are to be used frequently after an initial introduction, perhaps they should be designed to have both learner and expert modes. This can easily be done by querying the user in the introduction and then suppressing verbose explanations.

Debugging   The importance of thoroughly debugging a program before serving it up before a group of demanding users need not be emphasized for those who have done it. It is equally important for a program that will be sent to other organizations or divisions. Minimum and maximum ranges of input variables should be tested for their effect upon the program. In general, all input responses should be read from the terminal in alphanumeric format to avoid the abrupt and very confusing halt of a program reading an alphabetic character in a numeric-only field. We recommend that organizations not implement programs that have not been tested before a live audience, at least not without a clearly specified caution. Good programming practice always suggest that programs receive extensive pilot tests with real users before they are released.

Documentation

Documentation for a transferable, enduring program must be especially thorough. It may be divided into these three sections:

1. Technical documentation within the program
2. Technical documentation external to the program
3. Educational documentation

Technical Documentation Within the Program Documentation should begin with the first lines of code. Every program should have an introductory section that describes the program in an abstract form, the programmer, the institution, the target computer, and the date. Modules of the program and even individual lines of code should have commentary explaining the function of the module, the variables, the specifications and sources of formulas or algorithms, and any tricky or nonobvious coding. The readability of the program will be improved with indentation that shows the various levels of logic flow. Variables should be mnemonically chosen to represent the real entities of formulas or objects. Any machine-dependent code should be clearly marked.

Technical Documentation External to the Program The following documents should be included with all programs:

Abstract of the program: what it does, who wrote it, where it comes from, when it was written, and for what computer it was written
Program listing
Flowchart or other graphical illustration of program modules
Description of all input variables
Description of all output variables
Description of all files created and/or used
Description of all mathematical formulas, algorithms, or tables of values used
Transcript of a sample run with both interaction of the user and a report listing

Documentation can often be incorporated into the program so that the user can retrieve it online with a help command. In any case, it should be written with the aim of explaining the program to someone who knows nothing about it.

User Documentation In addition to the technical documentation both internal and external to the program, application software must have a user guide and preferably a tutorial manual. The user guide should include a description of the theories, principles, and methodologies that are used by the program. It is very important to make explicit any assumptions about the required background knowledge of the user. If the program deviates from standard content (e.g., simplification of concepts), it is important to point this out. Further reading and reference materials should be listed.

After presenting the explanation of the program content, the user guide should lead the user through a sample interaction. This sample should be chosen to illustrate typical but fairly simple use of the program. Finally, the user guide could contain supplemental examples and possibly exercises to solve, additional areas of application, and related topics.

EXAMPLES OF APPLICATIONS IN CONSTRUCTION

Numerous examples of computer reports are included throughout this book: cost control, scheduling, procurement, and so on. This section therefore focuses on some of the commercially available computer systems and software for applications in project planning and control. Applications today range from small microcomputer systems with packaged hardware and software offering reasonable capabilities for smaller and medium-sized projects up to multimillion dollar timesharing systems with individual software modules costing as much as $100,000 or more.

Factors to be considered when determining whether to develop systems in-house, with the criteria discussed earlier in this chapter, or acquire commercial packages include the following:

Size of company
Availability of software suitable for company needs
Adaptability of available programs to specific needs
Extent to which company is committed to its current systems, and quality and effectiveness of current systems
Interest and capability of employees

Generally, given the time and resources required for in-house development, it is wise to examine all possible alternatives before embarking on an in-house development effort; this is especially true for small to medium-sized companies and companies lacking current in-house capabilities.

Available applications software and systems have different strengths and weaknesses, depending upon the needs of the particular company under consideration. For example, the company's organizational structure should be considered in view of the available technologies. A centralized system might be quite suitable for a regional builder with project managers operating from the home office. However, a national heavy civil firm with district offices and autonomous projects might be better served with decentralized on-site micro-computer or minicomputer hardware and modular software applications. Tech-nological considerations also include telecommunications networking and its cost trade-offs and the costs of maintaining a centralized computer versus that of a decentralized network of smaller computers. Other considerations include online versus offline file storage, separate files versus an integrated data base, whether the user interface should be indirect via technicians and media such as cards or direct versus terminals, and facilities planning if major computer installations are to be brought in-house. When considering more complicated applications packages, availability and quality of vendor training and support are also very important.

With this background in mind, a few examples of a variety of different approaches to computer systems for project planning and control are presented. The systems chosen include Construct, a minicomputer-based interactive system that implements the standard business finance and accounting modules as well as some moderately sophisticated project control tools; Project/2, a project cost and schedule planning and control application that is normally accessed via timesharing on a company mainframe computer or at a remote timesharing service; a small microcomputer-based package called PMS80; and two advanced minicomputer-based systems, VISION and ARTEMIS, which seem to be leading a trend to dedicated and powerful interactive and graphics-based systems for project management. These systems illustrate a range of possibili-ties, and each system is suitable and appropriate in different circumstances. The systems considered here are representative rather than comprehensive, and their inclusion is not an endorsement of the individual vendors or their software and hardware systems. Any system or software acquisition effort should begin first with a comprehensive review of the market, and there are dozens if not hundreds of alternatives available, depending upon specific needs and applica-tions.

Construct

Construct is an integrated system of modules offered by the Construction Information Systems Company[2]. Its most widely marketed form operates on a minicomputer system that has its own integrated data base. Figure 17-15 shows the links between the various modules that can operate in this system. This vendor provides a wide range of applications, and the level of cost and technology is about in the range of a home-office system for a medium-sized company or a job-site system for a very large project.

Construct operates interactively through a series of screens and menus and is designed for easy direct user interaction. The system uses an industry-standard operating system and data base software environment, which makes it transport-able to machines manufactured by several vendors, including Microdata, Prime, and Honeywell. Of the five systems described here, it is the only one that offers

[2]Box 484, Mill Valley CA 94941.

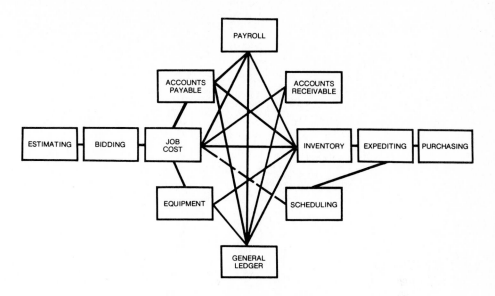

CONSTRUCT'S Modular Plan

Modules which can be purchased individually include:

- Payroll
- Accounts Payable
- Job Cost
- Accounts Receivable
- General Ledger
- Network Scheduling

- Equipment Management
- Inventory Control
- Estimating
- Expediting
- Purchasing
- Bidding

Figure 17-15: Linkages between Construct Software Modules (Courtesy Construction Information Systems Co.)

the standard business accounting and payroll modules as well as a moderate to advanced level of capability in various project control functions.

Project/2

Project/2 is an example of a system that focuses principally upon schedule control, with some facility for cost control. It is offered by Project Software and Development, Inc. (PSDI)[3]. The software is primarily suitable for larger construction companies and projects and runs on computers ranging from the DEC VAX11/780 to larger UNIVAC 1100 series and IBM 30 series processors. It is primarily a batch-oriented system and includes eight processors: basic network and CPM schedule, target processor, resource allocation, cost control, resource-constrained scheduling, network graphics, and multiproject processor. Some interactive facility is being included with the new module called Quiknet. Schedule portions of the package can handle up to 32,750 activities. The software is available for lease on a company's in-house computer, or it can be accessed via commercial timesharing services. Figure 17-16 summarizes the components of the Project/2 package.

[3]14 Storey Street, Cambridge MA 02138.

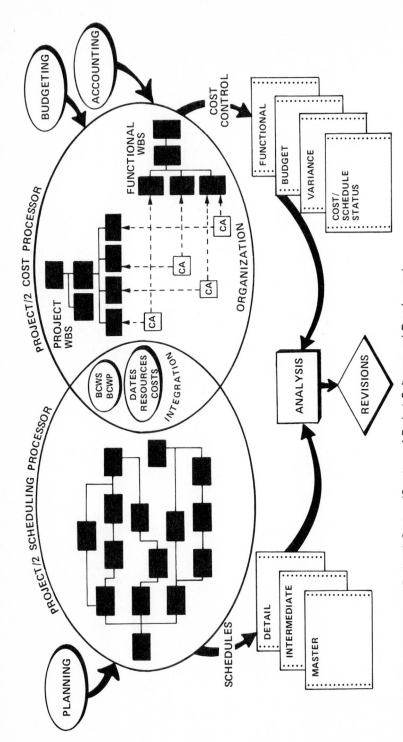

Figure 17-16: Summary of Project/2 System (Courtesy of Project Software and Development, Inc.)

Pinnell Engineering PMS80

At the other end of the size spectrum, a number of microcomputer-based systems are evolving, such as PMS80 by Pinnell Engineering[4]. Capabilities of the system include:

Basic CPM critical path scheduling (CPSR2)
Contractors progress payment request (CPSR3)
Resource forecast (CPSR4 with RESE)
Resource use and cost—cost estimating and accounting (CPSR5)
Financial report (CPSR7)
Bar chart—daily (CPSR8)
Bar chart—weekly summary (CPSR9)

Figure 17-17 shows a user at a PMS80 microcomputer system console. Note the integrated CRT, keyboard, and printer. Figure 17-18 shows a flow diagram for use of the PMS80 software modules.

Systonetics[5] VISION System

VISION has evolved from the EZ-PERT schedule plotting package developed in the late 1960s to an integrated superminicomputer-based system focusing more broadly upon network-based cost, schedule, and resource planning and analysis. A photograph of a typical installation is shown in Figure 17-19. Within its scope VISION covers almost all the available options and techniques, including arrow, PERT, and precedence diagrams, work-breakdown structures (see Figure 17-20) and earned-value reporting, and so forth. The system is particularly known, however, for its graphic output, such as that shown in Figure 17-21. It also uses an interactive relational data base supplied by the computer hardware vendor, and similarly, it can implement telecommunications software for decentralized processing and interaction with their computers. The system runs interactively, and the user has a series of menus displayed on a CRT screen (see Figure 17-22), which serve as reminders of available options and indicate the type of input required. The system is thus of a type where the end user is expected to interact with it directly rather than go through technical staff to get information and reports.

ARTEMIS by Metier Management Systems[6]

ARTEMIS is a dedicated minicomputer-based project management system with capabilities similar to Systonetics' VISION. It is implemented on Hewlett-Packard HP-1000 series equipment and uses Hewlett-Packard's standard RTE-Plus multiuser operating system. An example system in shown in Figure 17-23.

[4]5331 Southwest Macadam Avenue, Suite 270, Portland OR 97201.
[5]P.O.Box 4395, 801 East Chapman Avenue, Fullerton CA 92631.
[6]10175 Harwin Drive, Suite 100, Houston TX 77036

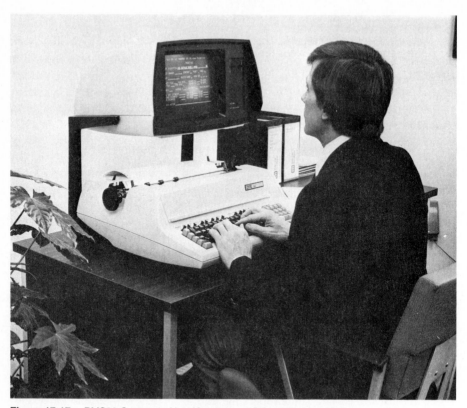

Figure 17-17: PMS80 System in Use (Courtesy of Pinnell Engineering)

Like VISION, the principal components supplied by Metier are network-based schedule, resource and cost analysis, with an extensive series of color-graphics reports (the example in Figure 17-25 is reproduced in black and white but used four colors), and has a powerful general-purpose relational data base software system.

Metier emphasizes the flexibility of a relational data base in enabling users to implement company- and project-tailored applications for cost estimating, cost engineering, materials management, and records management. The situation for such applications here is somewhat like that of the excellent spreadsheet program called Visicalc [7] for microcomputers, in that the user still must set up the specific structures that operate within the general framework. Note that in a relational data base, however, the applications can draw data from system files, and links can be made between data elements in many different applications. Figure 17-24 is a conceptual illustration of such links. The efficient initial structuring of such applications, however, would probably require that the

[7]Trademark of Visicorp, Sunnyvale CA.

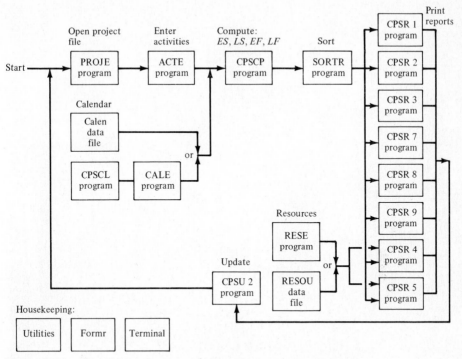

Figure 17-18: Flow Diagram for Use of PMS80 (Courtesy of Pinnell Engineerig)

company or project have a staff member knowledgeable or trainable in some of the technical and systems aspects of ARTEMIS. Once models are established, the online interactive nature of the system should make the information directly accessible by managers, engineers, supervisors, and staff personnel.

Implementation Comments

Systonetics' VISION and Metier's ARTEMIS are representative of a number of systems that reflect a trend to dedicated or stand-alone computers for project management applications. Although such systems are currently implemented on minicomputers in the $100,000 to $500,000 range, it is likely that the capabilities of some will be implemented on the more powerful microcomputers that are now becoming available, enabling smaller firms to use this level of capability. As such, it is worth outling here the capabilities of such a system: The following categories are from VISION brochures, but if listed for ARTEMIS, the capabilities would be similar.

Standard Configurations
   PRIME 50 series systems
      Virtual operating system
      Maximum size of application programs: 32M bytes

Figure 17-19: Typical VISION Prime Computer Installation (Courtesy of Systonetics)

Memory size: 1M bytes
Bit architecture: 32 Bits
Cache memory
Field upgradable
Terminals supported: 1-123
Data Storage Capacity
96 MB standard
Upgradable to 2.4 billion bytes
Terminals
    Standard: Two 15-in. CRT terminals with 132-column displays with printer ports
    Optional: Tektronix 4010 compatible graphics display 200 cps printer with graphics-printing capability
Printers and Plotters
    Standard: One 300 1pm printer/plotter
    Optional: 200 cps or 300 1pm printer for remote locations
    Optional: CalComp and Versatec plotters
VISION Software Components
ADM or PDM
32,000 activities/project

COST PERFORMANCE REPORT - BY WBS

PAGE

CONTRACTOR: SYSTONETICS INC	CONTRACT TYPE/NO.:	PROGRAM NAME/NUMBER:	REPORT PERIOD:	SIGNATURE, TITLE & DATE:
LOCATION ANAHEIM CA	CPFF AF19552035	PROJECT X RON3	FROM: 5/ 1/1980 TO: 8/30/1980	
RDT&E _____ PRODUCTION _____				

QUANTITY	NEGOTIATED COST	EST COST AUTH. UNPRICED WORK	TOT PROFIT/FEE%	TOT PRICE	EST PRICE	SHARE RATIO	CONT CEILING	EST CONT CEILING
0	$325.K	$0	15	325.K	350.K	80/20	$350.K	$350.K

WBS	CURRENT PERIOD — BUDGETED COST WORK SCHED	WORK PERF	ACTUAL COST WORK PERF	VARIANCE SCHED	VARIANCE COST	CUMULATIVE TO DATE — BUDGETED COST WORK SCHED	WORK PERF	ACTUAL COST WORK PERF	VARIANCE SCHED	VARIANCE COST	REPROGRAMMING ADJUSTMENTS COST VAR	BUDGET	AT COMPLETION BUDG	LATEST REVISED EST	VARIANCE
2111ADM	23.9	23.9	23.8	0.0	0.1	23.9	23.9	23.8	0.0	0.1			23.9	23.8	0.1
2112ADM	2.6	2.6	2.2	0.0	0.4	2.6	2.6	2.2	0.0	0.4			12.3	11.9	0.4
2112MFG	7.4	7.4	8.2	0.0	-0.8	7.4	7.4	8.2	0.0	-0.8			7.41	8.2	-0.8
2113ENG	0.0	0.0	0.0	0.0	0.0	0.0	0.0	0.0	0.0	0.0			23.5	23.5	0.0
3111ENG	13.8	13.8	13.1	0.0	0.7	13.8	13.8	13.1	0.0	0.7			13.8	13.1	0.7
3112DRF	7.5	7.5	8.5	0.0	-1.0	7.5	7.5	8.5	0.0	-1.0			7.5	8.5	-1.0
4111MFG	3.7	3.7	3.8	0.0	-0.1	3.7	3.7	3.8	0.0	-0.1			127.1	127.2	-0.1
4121MFG	3.8	1.4	4.6	-2.4	-3.2	3.8	1.4	4.6	-2.4	-3.2			7.2	7.3	-0.1
4211PRO	5.1	5.1	5.6	0.0	-0.5	5.1	5.1	5.6	0.0	-0.5			5.1	5.6	-0.5
4211PRO1	12.9	12.9	12.9	0.0	0.0	12.9	12.9	12.9	0.0	0.0			12.9	12.9	0.0
4211PROC	2.5	2.5	2.8	0.0	-0.3	2.5	2.5	2.8	0.0	-0.3			2.5	2.8	-0.3
5111ENG	0.0	0.0	0.0	0.0	0.0	0.0	0.0	0.0	0.0	0.0			8.1	8.1	0.0
5111TST	0.0	0.0	0.0	0.0	0.0	0.0	0.0	0.0	0.0	0.0			5.9	5.9	0.0
6111ADM	1.8	1.8	2.1	0.0	-0.3	1.8	1.8	2.1	0.0	-0.3			1.8	2.1	-0.3
6112ADM	1.6	1.6	1.9	0.0	-0.3	1.6	1.6	1.9	0.0	-0.3			1.6	1.9	-0.3
6211ADM	13.9	13.9	14.5	0.0	-0.6	13.9	13.9	14.5	0.0	-0.6			13.9	14.5	-0.6
COST OF MONEY															
GEN & ADMIN	12.6	12.3	13.0	-0.3	-0.7	12.6	12.3	13.0	-0.3	-0.7			34.3	34.7	-0.3
UNDIST BUDGET	XXXXXXX	XXXXXXX	XXXXXXX	XXXXXXX	XXXXXXX	XXXXXXX	XXXXXXX	XXXXXXX	XXXXXXX	XXXXXXX	XXXXXXX	XXXXXXX	XXXXXXX	XXXXXXX	XXXXXXX
SUBTOTAL	113.1	110.4	117.0	-2.7	-6.6	113.1	110.4	117.0	-2.7	-6.6			308.8	312.0	-3.1
MGMT RESERVE	XXXXXXX	XXXXXXX	XXXXXXX	XXXXXXX	XXXXXXX	XXXXXXX	XXXXXXX	XXXXXXX	XXXXXXX	XXXXXXX	XXXXXXX				
TOTAL	113.1	110.4	117.0	-2.7	-6.6	113.1	110.4	117.0	-2.7	-6.6	-6.6		308.8	312.0	-3.1

Figure 17-20: Cost Performance Report by Work Breakdown Structure (Courtesy of Systonetics)

361

VIS1ON

Example — BASELINE TARGET BARCHART

SYSTONETICS, INC.			PLANNED BY	DATE
PUTTING PROJECT MANAGEMENT				
AT YOUR FINGERTIPS				
NETWORK RON3	RCF NAME BATA			
PROJECT X			APPROVED BY	DATE
FABRICATION OF FIRST ARTICLE PRODUCT				
RUN DATE 12MAR82	DATA DATE 22SEP83			
BASELINE TARGET BARCHART				
DRAWN BY EZPERT. PATENT 3684871. SYSTONETICS INC.				

I NODE	J NODE	DESCRIPTION	BASELINE EARLY START	BASELINE LATE FINISH	BASE ORIG	BASE REM	EARLY START	EARLY FINISH	LATE START	LATE FINISH	CURR ORIG	CURR REM	TTL FLT	PCT CMP
S	1	START PLANNING	06MAY83	21MAY83	10	10	ACS05MAY83	ACF17MAY83	05MAY83	17MAY83	10	0		100
S	11	ADM HAMMOCK					HMK05MAY83	28NOV83	05MAY83	28NOV83	149	49	0	68
1	2	DEFINE SPECIFICATION	20MAY83	30MAY83	7	7	ACS20MAY83	ACF24MAY83	20MAY83	24MAY83	5	0		100
2	3	PREPARE WORK STATEMENT	29MAY83	13JUN83	10	10	ACS28MAY83	ACF19JUN83	28MAY83	19JUN83	10	0		100
3	4	AUTHORIZE WORK	12JUN83	27JUN83	10	10	ACS21JUN83	ACF24JUN83	21JUN83	24JUN83	10	0		100
3	5	ADM CONF HAMMOCK					HMK21JUN83	23SEP83	21JUN83	18NOV83	67	1	40	99
4	5	PREPARE COST ACCOUNTS	26JUN83	11JUL83	10	10	ACS24JUN83	ACF06JUL83	24JUN83	06JUL83	10	0		100
5	6	CONFIGURATION MANAGEMENT	10JUL83	06AUG83	4	4	ACS08JUL83	24SEP83	08JUL83	24SEP83	4	1	0	75
5	18	ENGINEERING DESIGN	10JUL83	19JUL83	6	6	ACS08JUL83	ACF15JUL83	08JUL83	15JUL83	6	0		100
5	21	ENGR HAMMOCK					HMK08JUL83	ACF19AUG83	08JUL83	19AUG83	31	0		100
6	7	DATA MANAGEMENT	16JUL83	13AUG83	5	5	ACS12JUL83	ACF18JUL83	12JUL83	18JUL83	5	0		100
18	12	DEFINE LONG LEAD HARDWARE	18JUL83	06AUG83	12	12	ACS16JUL83	ACF31JUL83	16JUL83	31JUL83	12	0		100
18	16	PROC HAMMOCK					HMK16JUL83	07OCT83	16JUL83	07OCT83	60	10	0	84
18	19	ENGINEERING DRAFTING SPECIFICATION	18JUL83	01AUG83	2	2	ACS17JUL83	ACF18JUL83	17JUL83	18JUL83	2	0		100
7	21	CUSTOMER DATA APPROVAL	23JUL83	20AUG83	5	5	ACS19JUL83	ACF25JUL83	19JUL83	25JUL83	5	0		100
19	20	ENGINEERING DRAFTING	22JUL83	15AUG83	10	10	ACS01AUG83	ACF14AUG83	01AUG83	14AUG83	10	0		100
13	14	PLACE PURCHASE ORDERS	09AUG83	19AUG83	5	5	ACS07AUG83	ACF13AUG83	07AUG83	13AUG83	5	0		100
20	21	RELEASE DRAWINGS TO FABRICATION	05AUG83	20AUG83	3	3	ACS15AUG83	ACF19AUG83	15AUG83	19AUG83	3	0		100
12	13	WRITE PURCHASE ORDERS	05AUG83	12AUG83	4	4	ACS16AUG83	ACF26AUG83	16AUG83	26AUG83	4	0		100
15	16	FABRICATE ELECTRICAL COMPONENTS	22AUG83	13SEP83	15	15	ACS22AUG83	07OCT83	22AUG83	07OCT83	15	8	0	35
15	10	HAMMOCK ACTIVITY / FABRICATION					HMK22AUG83	19NOV83	22AUG83	19NOV83	64	39	0	40
15	8	COMPLETE FABRICATION SPECIFICATION	22AUG83	07NOV83	4	4	ACS23AUG83	ACF28AUG83	23AUG83	28AUG83	4	0		100
8	17A	DEFINE LONG LEAD HARDWARE	28AUG83	08NOV83	1	1								
8	9	APPROVE FABRICATION SPECIFICATION					ACS30AUG83	ACF31AUG83	30AUG83	31AUG83	1	0		100
16	17	FABRICATE MECHANICAL COMPONENTS	12SEP83	11OCT83	20	20	ACS31AUG83	21OCT83	31AUG83	21OCT83	20	10	0	50
14	15	RECEIVE MATERIAL	16AUG83	23AUG83	4	4	ACS16SEP83	ACF21SEP83	16SEP83	21SEP83	4	0		100
21	15	WRITE SHOP ORDERS	08AUG83	23AUG83	3	3	ACS16SEP83	ACF19SEP83	16SEP83	19SEP83	3	0		100
21	17A	MFG HAMMOCK					HMK16SEP83	16SEP83	16SEP83	18NOV83	46	39	0	16
17	17A	ASSEMBLY FABRICATION	10OCT83	08NOV83	20	20	22OCT83	18NOV83	22OCT83	18NOV83	20	20	0	0
17	22	DEVELOP TEST PROCEDURES	10OCT83	30OCT83	4	4	22OCT83	25OCT83	29OCT83	01NOV83	4	4	5	0
22	23	PREPARE TEST PROCEDURES	16OCT83	06NOV83	5	5	28OCT83	01NOV83	04NOV83	08NOV83	5	5	5	0
23	11	COMPLETE CONFIGURATION REPORT	23NOV83	22NOV83	5	5	04NOV83	08NOV83	22NOV83	28NOV83	5	5	14	0
23	10	COMPONENT TESTING	23OCT83	15NOV83	7	7	04NOV83	12NOV83	11NOV83	19NOV83	7	7	5	0
17A	10	DUMMY	07NOV83	15NOV83	5	5	19NOV83	19NOV83	19NOV83	19NOV83	4	4	5	0
10	11	TEST UNIT	14NOV83	24NOV83	9	9	20NOV83	28NOV83	20NOV83	28NOV83	9	9	0	0
10	E	HAMMOCK ACTIVITY / TESTING					HMK20NOV83	29NOV83	20NOV83	29NOV83	8	8	0	0

Figure 17-21: Example Graphics Report (Courtesy of Systonetics)

Multiple calendars
User-defined activity coding
Milestones and Hammocks
Target schedules and comparison
Graphical plotting capability
    Networks—Arrow or precedence
    Bar charts—Gantt, milestone, and baseline/target
    XY graphs—includes tabular data
Resource Allocation
    Unlimited size of resource library
    Unlimited assignment of resources to activities
    Complex availability profiles
    Resource Leveling
Multiple resources

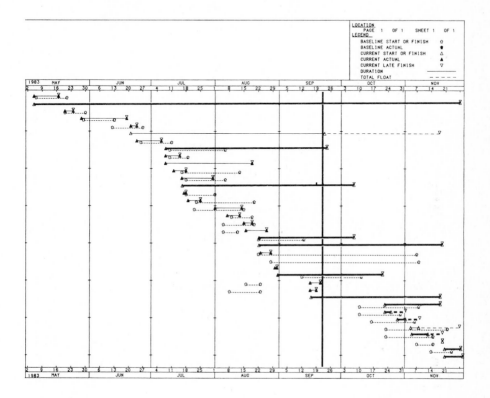

Multiple projects
Elastic activities
   Resource Costing
Conversion from quantity to dollars
Multiple escalation values per resource
Resource cost values maintained
   Budget
   EAC (estimate at completion)
   ETC (estimate to completion)
   Actual
Resource quantity values maintained
   Budget
   EAC (estimate at completion)
   ETC (estimate to completion)

```
VISION                                                      PROJECT TRGI
                    PROJECT DIRECTORY DATA DISPLAY


    PROJECT NAME   TRGI                    TYPE of SCHEDULING( PDM,I-J ) I-J
    MODIFICATION #   1  SCHEDULING #   1    REPORT #    0    PLOT #    0
    NUMBER of ACTIVITIES    16  Resource Library: NAME <PASSWORD>    <    >

    DEFAULT: REPORT TITLE    TRAINING WORKBOOK PROJECT
       PROJECT DESCRIPTION    CONSTRUCTION OF A NEW HOME

    CALENDAR:  (Work Days/Week, Start Day, Work Periods/Day, Start Period)
       #1: 5  MO   1   1        #2: 7  MO   1   1        #3: 7  MO   1   1
       PROJECT PERIODS per DAY:  1  Date Type( MIlitary, INteger, MEtric ) MI
                                           DDMMMYY   DDMMYY   YYMMDD
       Accounting Calendar:  Start 31JAN82   Five-Week Months MAR JUN SEP DEC

    PROJECT DATES:  Start   08APR82  Schedule          Finish

    ACTIVITY CODE FIELD DEFINITION:  ( 16 Characters Available )
       Field Name       RESP  DEPT  CODE
       Starting Position   1    3    5    0    0    0    0    0
       Length of Field     2    2    2    0    0    0    0    0
                                                              enter
```

Figure 17-22: Example CRT Screen from Interactive User Session (Courtesy of Systonetics)

   Actual
      Reporting
   Standard report formats
   User-oriented free format report writer
      Data Base Management System
   Interface to VISION data
   Relational capability
   Online inquiry/updating
   Data manipulation
   Accounting interface
   User-designed applications
      Other Software Available
   Business
   Scientific/engineering
   Languages
   FORTRAN
   BASIC
   COBOL
   PL/1
      Optional Communications to Other Computers
   IBM RJE-HASP/3780/2780

Figure 17-23:　Hewlett-Packard Computer Installation for ARTEMIS System (Courtesy of Metier Management Systems, Inc.)

IBM Interactive 3270
X.25 International Protocol
CDC RJE—200 UT
UNIVAC RJE—1004 RBT
Honeywell RJE—GRTS

Since most of the dedicated systems implement only a subset of the management and business functions that might be needed on a project, it is important to check the computer hardware and operating system environment on which the package runs and be sure that it is compatible with other software. For example, VISION and ARTEMIS focus mainly upon cost, schedule, and resource analysis. Although their relational data bases could ease the implementation of other functions, such as estimating, materials control, and quality assurance, these are not standard. However, VISION and ARTEMIS use the PRIME and Hewlett-Packard computer companies' standard PRIMOS and RTE-Plus operating systems, respectively, and because both are fairly widely

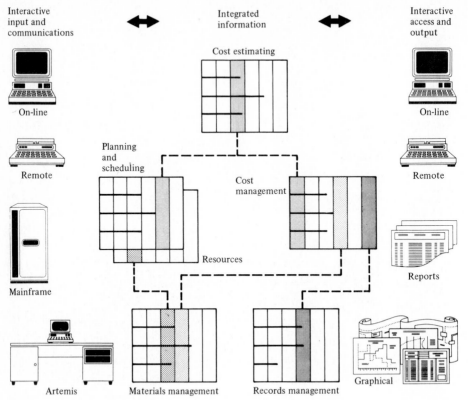

Figure 17-24: Linkages Between Various Modules in a Relational Data Base (Courtesy of Metier Management Systems, Inc.)

used computers, probably general business functions (accounting and payroll) and possibly some of the missing project management functions could be obtained from other vendors. Had Systonetics or Metier modified the standard operating systems or used a nonstandard or dedicated operating system, as has been done by other vendors, adding third-party software packages to fill the gaps would have been difficult and expensive, if not impossible. These packages keep the options open.

SUMMARY

This chapter covered a variety of topics related to computer applications in construction. The related computer technology is moving so rapidly that the number and variety of applications in construction will have increased markedly even by the time this book is published. A promising trend at present is that through microcomputers and user-oriented software, the computer tools are finally getting directly into the hands of the project managers and supervisors

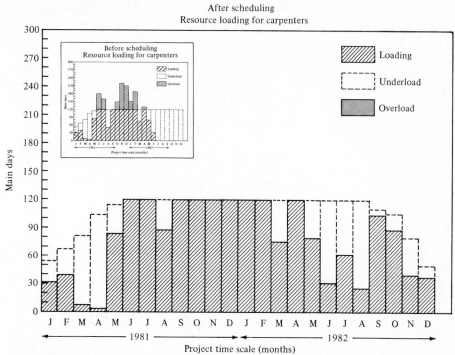

Figure 17-25: Graphic Resource Allocation Report from ARTEMIS System (Courtesy of Metier Management Systems, Inc.)

who need them. With this occurrence, however, is the need for such people to become more knowledgeable about the capabilities and limitations of computers and their related software for construction planning and control. This chapter was therefore an overview of the available technology, including computer hardware, systems software, telecommunications, and files and data bases. Some understanding of each topic is becoming part of the basic knowledge required by today's managers.

The range of possible applications includes estimating, cost control, scheduling, quality assurance, procurement, administration, and productivity. No one contractor, large or small, has the best in all these areas, but sophisticated applications can be found in both large and small firms for many of them. If intelligently used, all applications can improve the efficiency and effectiveness of project management and reduce the drudgery that has become an increasing burden in administrative applications.

Although most managers will not be directly involved in programming, it is nevertheless important to understand some basic criteria for software development and documentation so that they might better influence and guide the selection or development of such software for their companies and projects. Software development involves the choice of appropriate programming languages, the use of structured programming techniques, user-friendly design, and thorough debugging. Managers should insist on high standards for documentation, including not only the technical documentation within the program, but especially the documentation for the users of the program.

The final section of this chapter provided examples of commercial software that is available for construction planning and control. There are numerous approaches, including package microcomputer systems with all the software for on-site planning and control, speciality programs for applications such as estimating in the home office and for scheduling and resource allocation, and access to timesharing systems for advanced programs that are only occasionally needed in the company. Since the needs of construction companies vary so widely, no one vendor can best suit them all. Rather, for a particular company or application, a study should be made of several alternative vendors, and careful selection criteria should be developed to choose the one best suited to the needs. Given the time and cost involved in developing quality software, one should consider all available vendor alternatives before embarking on an in-house development effort for any major application.

All that can be certain in computer applications at present is that there will be rapid and continuing change. Today's managers and supervisors must be sensitive to these changes and alert for applications that will improve their effectiveness and efficiency.

Chapter 18

Safety and Health in Construction

The state of safety and health in construction is reflected by the fact that of all the chapters in this book, this is the one that many readers will be most inclined to skip—or, with a slight nag from conscience, skim. Like "motherhood, the flag, and apple pie," safety is a subject to which most people are quite willing to pay lip service, but which too few are willing really to do something about. To put to rest any illusions of self-righteousness, the authors must admit to having been as remiss as many of their colleagues in this respect. For this very reason, however, the words in this chapter are more deeply felt than any others.

The facts show that construction is indeed a dangerous industry; U. S. Department of Labor and National Safety Council statistics indicate that although construction employees account for only about 6 percent of the total labor force, they incur 12 percent of all occupational injuries and illnesses (about 250,000 to 300,000 lost-time injuries per year in construction), and 19 percent of all work-related fatalities (about 3000 per year by National Safety Council estimates, and about 1000 according to the Occupational Safety and Health Administration). Related costs to the industry are estimated to run between $5 *billion* and $10 *billion* per year.[1] Research findings also show that

---

[1]Raymond E. Levitt, *The Effect of Top Management on Safety in Construction*, Technical Report No. 196, Stanford University, Dept. of Civil Engineering, The Construction Institute, Stanford, Calif., July 1975, pp. 8–9.

these losses are far higher than they need to be. Many of the industry's most successful and profitable firms also have the best records in safety and health, as do many of the best and most productive workers, foremen, superintendents, and top managers. These findings are no coincidence, and they serve as a goal for the rest of the industry.

Safety and health are as much a part of effective project planning and control as are costs, schedules, procurement, and quality. Indeed, they are all closely interrelated. Many of the same principles of management and engineering that have been described in earlier chapters also apply equally well here. In this chapter we shall describe the problem, then focus on constructive steps an organization can take to improve its occupational safety and health performance.

MOTIVATORS FOR IMPROVED PERFORMANCE

Safety and health are of concern to today's organizations on several levels. These include humanitarian concern, economic costs and benefits, legal and regulatory constraints, liability consequences, and organizational image. All are important, though changes in constraints and attitudes both within and imposed from outside the industry cause some factors to receive more emphasis than others.

Humanitarian Concern

On a purely humanitarian level, the purpose of improved occupational safety and health is to reduce the human pain and suffering, to workers' families as well as to themselves, that result from accidents and work-induced illnesses. It is difficult to quantify in economic terms, though the statistics quoted in the opening paragraphs tell at least part of the story. Three thousand deaths mean at least that many bereaved families: widows, children without fathers, lost sons and brothers. Further suffering is inevitable for the 300,000 and their families who each year incur lost-time injuries. Even the strongest human beings are frail creatures when subjected to the forces of nature and the industrial hazards associated with the moving machinery, dust, explosives, heat, electricity, noise, potential for falling, and toxic substances that form the everyday environment of construction. The resulting injuries are often cruelly disfiguring and result in lifetime handicaps and disabilities. But because it is so difficult to quantify the humanitarian factors in preparing estimates and making operating decisions on projects, we must move beyond these into the economic costs of safety and health programs and their economic benefits.

Economics

Like national statistics on injuries, illnesses, and deaths in construction, on a personal or organizational level it is also difficult to relate to costs in the range of "$5 billion to $10 billion per year." More relevant, perhaps, is the fact that a high experience-modification factor on the workers' compensation insurance rate can put a contractor out of business in competitively bid construction work.

Standard manual rates for insurance depend on the performance of the whole industry; typical averages are about 6 percent of field labor costs in commercial building work, and 12 percent in heavy construction. But a contractor's individual premiums are adjusted up or down to reflect his performance relative to the industry, so a particular company may actually pay from less than 50 percent of the manual rate to over 150 percent. Furthermore, contractors with good safety records can also earn significant end-of-year "dividends" over and above the reduction in premiums reflected in the modification factor. Assuming labor to be 50 percent of project costs on a heavy construction job, the insurance premium will range from about 4 to 9 percent of the total direct costs, with the 5 percent difference being enough either to lose the bid or to wipe out the profit.

The impact of these differences is not limited to competitively bid work. In negotiating cost-plus-fee contracts, knowledgeable owners are increasingly taking a hard look at prospective contractors' insurance costs and safety records.

When the indirect as well as the direct costs of accidents and illnesses are considered, costs associated with insurance premiums, claims settlements, and the like are only a small portion of the whole. Even at the project level, it is often estimated that the indirect and impact costs resulting from interrupted production, reduced morale, lower productivity, and ripple effects on the schedule can be several times the direct costs associated with hospitalization, disability pay, spoiled materials, damaged equipment, and reconstruction. The indirect impact costs must normally be absorbed directly by the project.

Much the same analysis applies at the worker's level. Although today's headlines frequently report multimillion-dollar liability settlements, more typical settlements under workers' compensation are limited mainly to workers' medical expenses and a fraction of lost salaries. Furthermore, the indirect impact of the psychological and emotional disruption to the families is very real, but not easy to quantify. Where long-term or permanent disability results, there is an unknown lost potential for both earnings and future growth and development.

The industry as a whole also suffers from the loss of each worker. The cold fact is that skilled workers are a scarce and valuable resource; considerable time, money, and effort are invested in their training. A career interrupted at age 25 means that 40 additional years of skilled production have been lost. With today's shortages, it is a foolish, let alone callous, misjudgment to say there will be someone else to take the accident victim's place.

For these and other reasons, the more enlightened organizations in the engineering and construction industry—owners, constructors, designers, and agencies alike—have recognized that effective programs to improve performance in safety and health are not expenses, but investments. Some have estimated that each $1 invested in safety and health pays $4 to $8 in return. We need not be concerned so much, then, in justifying these investments as in optimizing them. Few other investment opportunities have such outstanding potential.

Legal and Regulatory Constraints

Like almost all laws, the increasing burden of legislation and regulation in occupational safety and health has developed in response to those individuals and organizations who have demonstrated irresponsible behavior when left to their own devices. Also like almost all other laws, the unfortunate side effect is further to curb the freedoms and even hamper the positive efforts of the responsible segments of the industry. The problem in construction is compounded by the intensely competitive nature of the industry, where short-run expediency in cost-cutting areas such as safety and health often seems attractive and even necessary for business survival. This not only runs counter to the productivity of long-term investments in safety described above, but this general attitude of expediency also accounts in large measure for the high rate of business failure in construction.

Regardless of the origins, the consequences of the irresponsible safety and health performance of some individuals and firms have brought on laws and regulations as a leveler for all. If these laws or their enforcers at times appear misguided and impractical, our recourse now is not to repeal the laws, but to redirect their application so that they do focus on real problem areas for the overall benefit of workers, the industry, and the economy. It is not our objective here to defend the current state of governmental regulation, but to recognize the reasons for it and to emphasize the importance of improving its effectiveness where it is really needed.

In construction, the main federal agency for regulation is the Occupational Safety and Health Administration, generally known as OSHA. The enabling legislation also authorizes state agencies to assume the functions of the federal OSHA, provided that the state agencies enforce standards at least as strict as those at the federal level. Some projects, however, will operate under different regulations. At the time of this writing, some construction projects on mine properties come under the Mining Enforcement and Safety Administration, known as MESA, which is within the Department of Interior's Bureau of Mines. Contracting agencies, such as the Army Corps of Engineers and the Bureau of Reclamation, will also sometimes prescribe regulations that go beyond those of OSHA.

For most construction, however, OSHA is the key agency. Established under the Occupational Safety and Health Act of 1970, it generally applies to all sectors of the private economy. In construction this includes designers, owners, and workers, as well as contractors. The law itself is a relatively concise document of 31 pages, but that is only the beginning. Hundreds of pages of regulations have subsequently been published in the *Federal Register* (starting with the issues of April 27 and May 29, 1971). These in turn incorporate by reference whole bookshelves full of published industry and government safety manuals in every conceivable field of endeavor. Employers have been made responsible for understanding and interpreting a seemingly impenetrable maze of material, a task which many agencies and committees are now striving to simplify. It is well beyond the scope of this chapter even to outline, let alone describe, those that apply just to construction.

In philosophy, however, the intent of the Act is quite straightforward. The essence is captured in Section 5, quoted here:

DUTIES

Sec. 5. (a) Each employer—
    (1) shall furnish to each of his employees employment and a place of employment which are free from recognized hazards that are causing or are likely to cause death or serious physical harm to his employees;
    (2) shall comply with occupational safety and health standards promulgated under this Act.
    (b) Each employee shall comply with occupational safety and health standards and all rules, regulations, and orders issued pursuant to this Act which are applicable to his own action and conduct.

Like any other major piece of social or economic legislation, this law has been controversial, to say the least. First of all, to mandate that employers provide "employment and a place of employment which are free from recognized hazards" is a significant change in legal philosophy. Workers' compensation laws were considered a major step forward in the late nineteenth and early twentieth centuries when they relieved an employee's individual burden by denying employers the three old common law defenses of (1) the worker's assumption of risk in taking employment, (2) contributory negligence by the employee, and (3) negligence of fellow employees. But the underlying assumption remained that injury and death were inevitable expenses of production; what changed was that their burden shifted from individual workers to the industry as a whole. With OSHA, however, the assumption is that the "employment and place of employment" should be such that injury and death do not happen in the first place. This certainly is a noble goal, but the economy has only begun to comprehend the full implications of this shift in social and economic philosophy. Disputes over the details of its application and implementation will likely continue well into the twenty-first century. Suffice it to say that the law exists, it has "teeth," it is being enforced; all engineering and construction organizations must understand it and learn to operate within its constraints.

Liability Problems

A general trend in the courts to increasing frequency of lawsuits and increasingly large jury awards has also been causing problems for projects. The tentacles of liability have been reaching out to ensnarl parties with only loose connections to the administration of a project, such as a bank that provides a mortgage loan. Therefore it is important that managers of engineering and construction organizations stay abreast of trends in liability suits, including those that at present appear frivolous, and take steps to minimize liability expense on projects.

In construction safety and health, this only begins with being sure that, to the extent humanly possible, all operations are carried out within recognized standards and regulations. Numerous other factors are also coming into play. For example, loss of hearing is now recognized as justification for a worker's compensation claim, but hearing loss is cumulative. Nevertheless, unless an employer can show that the claimant's hearing was poor before starting work on the project in question and that it suffered no further deterioration, the employer might be stuck with the full claim. To compound matters, medical testing has shown that the hearing of many young people these days is damaged by listening to overamplified music long before they seek their first job in construction. Some such music is played in the range of 120 to 130 decibels, which is roughly the unmuffled range of some of the noisiest construction operations, such as percussion drilling in a hard-rock tunnel. It appears that if liability claims for hearing loss become prevalent, it will be only prudent for employers to test employees' hearing when hired, retest when terminated, and document the results. The documentation should not backfire as long as the project is being run within current noise regulations. Already, however, union and legal restrictions are being imposed to prevent such testing.

Similar problems can be cited in other categories of occupational illness and disability. For example, spinal disorders appear to be a real consequence of operating some types of equipment, such as undampened scrapers with two-wheel tractors. Verified disabilities of this type can indeed be cause for legitimate claims, and manufacturers are working hard to correct the source of the problem. But as a generic problem, the so-called "backache" or "back trouble" also appears to some industry observers to have become a means for malingerers to collect unemployment and disability benefits. Their problem may actually be minor, or psychosomatic, or even pure fabrication, but when they go to a physician, who faces his own dire malpractice consequences if he is sceptical and ignores the "problem," it is not hard to get medical certification that the "problem" exists and that the employee should not work. This is a complex area, and a test-in–test-out procedure like the hearing test would be much more difficult to apply. The best present remedy is to include real or imagined backache complaints in past employee records, and to monitor such employees carefully. As in other liability and claims problems, good documentation is generally the best defense.

Organizational Image

Some companies and government agencies pride themselves on their good safety "image," both among their employees and among the public at large. Levitt cited this as one of three key motivators stated by top managers as justification for a safety program (the others being humanitarian concern, and workers' compensation and other accident costs).[2]

Especially in negotiated work, this image can be decisive in the award of contracts. Some owners, priding themselves on their own image, do not want a contractor coming onto their job who will do anything to tarnish that reputation. Others, simply looking at the balance sheet, want to minimize payment of excess insurance costs on the project and to avoid publicity-grabbing liability suits. In any case, the constructor with a proven good accident record and an effective no-nonsense safety program can also have a real competitive edge in negotiating contracts.

To other companies, a good safety image is both a matter of pride among industry peers and solid evidence of responsiveness to employee needs that can in turn engender higher morale and productivity and stronger employee loyalty. It is no coincidence that such companies can often better attract and keep skilled professionals in their ranks.

PROBLEMS IN SAFETY AND HEALTH

In the area of safety, it has long been recognized that many types of construction operations present serious hazards. Only recently, however, have occupational health problems in construction received much attention. This section will discuss each in turn.

Safety

Safety hazards are those that pose imminent danger of causing injury or death to workers or damage to materials, equipment, or structures. They result not only from obvious physical dangers, but also from human factors such as lack of training, poor supervision, attitudes, poor planning, or even from workers who are so familiar with the work that they become oblivious to it.

Many of the physical aspects of construction safety result from the sheer scale of the work when compared with the frailty of the people performing it. In this environment workers are exposed to falls of hundreds of feet, yet are often injured or killed when falling off a stepladder. Even a hard hat is but an eggshell to a rock popping off the roof of a tunnel, a pipe wrench falling from the fortieth floor, or a 20-ton beam swinging out of control at the end of a cable. Fires in some types of building materials move quickly and generate intense heat. Lay people are generally astonished at the size of the 100-ton trucks, 20-yard shovels, and other large machines on an earthmoving job, but the operators and those working nearby too often become complacent about the amount of energy they are dealing with. Similarly, electricians who admonish their children to be careful with 110-volt, 15-amp household wiring often need to heed their own warnings when taking shortcuts in making repairs to live 4000-volt circuits.

[2]Raymond E. Levitt, op. cit., p. 5.

These forces are present on most large jobs, but they are not the real safety hazards. In most accidents, people are the problem. We shall examine this subject later in this chapter.

Health Problems in Construction

Until recently it was popularly assumed that construction provides rugged, out-in-the-fresh-air work and ideal summer training for athletes, and is healthy for anyone who can stand its pace. Although hard hats had gained some legitimacy as a safety device, health protectors such as earplugs, respirators, and shock absorbers were for "sissies"; no "real man" would be caught dead using them. Too many, unfortunately, are dead for lack of them, and others are handicapped for life.

Health hazards in construction include, among others, heat, radiation, noise, dust, shocks and vibrations, and toxic chemicals. Perhaps the main hazard here, however, is human optimism. Since the effects are not immediately felt, we say: "I can work in this dust from rock drilling for a few more hours. A hot, steamy shower will clear it out!" "I can go into the tunnel heading without ear plugs. The pain stops when I come out!" "I'll just ride these backbreaking scrapers until I'm 40, then I'll retire to a D-8!" "It sure is hot out, and I'm feeling dizzy and have a real headache coming on, but it's only an hour until quitting time. There's no point in stopping this truck for a drink of water now!" And, "I've been working with asbestos installation for 20 years and I'm not sick. What's this business about its causing cancer?"

Increasingly, it is being recognized that occupational diseases have indeed been a serious problem in construction. There are substantial direct costs for medical treatment and disability claims, and indirect costs through the premature loss of skilled workers. Many of the hazards are being not only identified but eliminated. Asbestos is but one of many recent examples. It is vitally important that all organizations involved in construction stay up to date with developments in occupational health and implement methods proven to reduce health hazards. If humanitarian concerns are insufficient, the liability implications should be more than enough reason. Two good starting points for information are *Methods Improvement for Construction Managers*, a book by Parker and Oglesby,[3] and *Occupational Health in the Construction Industry*, a report by Lance W. deStwolinski.[4]

IMPLEMENTATION GUIDELINES

An effective construction safety and health program has many parallel functions. Parker and Oglesby[5] broadly categorize these as follows:

[3]Henry W. Parker and Clarkson H. Oglesby, *Methods Improvement for Construction Managers*, McGraw-Hill Book Company, New York, 1972.
[4]Lance W. deStwolinski, *Occupational Health in the Construction Industry*, Technical Report No. 105, Stanford University, Dept. of Civil Engineering, The Construction Institute, Stanford, Calif., May 1969.
[5]Parker and Oglesby, op. cit.

Personal or behavioral factors
- Worker: his training, habits, beliefs, impressions, educational and cultural background, social attitudes, and physical characteristics
- Job environment: attitudes and policies of the employers and the managers, supervisors, foremen, and coworkers on the project

Physical factors
- Job conditions: dictated by hazards inherent in the work being performed, as well as by health hazards arising from methods and materials and the location of the job
- Mechanical hazard elimination: use of barriers, devices, and procedures to shield workers physically from hazardous areas or situations (trench shields, chain guards, etc.)
- Protection: use of such variables as hard hats, safety glasses, respirators, earplugs, seat belts, roll bars, and other devices to protect the individual's health and safety

All these factors are essential to a well-rounded safety program. Traditionally, major company safety expenditures as well as government regulatory programs have been aimed mainly at the physical factors. One senses this strong emphasis in most of the OSHA publications as well as in others, and OSHA inspections and fines also reflect this. Studies have shown, however, that roughly 80 percent of all industrial accidents result from unsafe acts in the accident chain, and not just from unsafe conditions. This finding implies that there should be much heavier emphasis on the personal and behavioral side rather than solely on the physical aspects. The disproportionate emphasis on the physical side partially accounts for the disappointing results of many safety programs, including those of OSHA.

Why the heavy emphasis on physical approaches to health and safety? For one thing, only recently have studies indicated the importance of the human side. For another, physical programs are much easier to visualize and implement, especially for people in technical or production-oriented industries. Finally, it is much more difficult to know how to approach the human side of safety and health, especially in a high-turnover and fast-changing industry like construction. Recent construction research studies, however, have been producing some clear and workable guidelines for the behavioral approach, and there is hope that in the near future we may see constructive changes and improved results in safety and health in construction.

Again, however, it is important to emphasize that both the behavioral and the physical sides must be developed simultaneously in an effective safety and health program. This chapter will thus present each in turn. The following section will summarize the findings of four research studies giving policy guidelines at levels from worker to top management. A subsequent section will present the physical aspects of construction safety. The reader is strongly encouraged to consult references cited in this chapter and in the bibliography to obtain detailed information in each area.

Behavioral Approaches to Safety and Health

Essentially all the findings and recommendations published in this section are the products of nearly a decade of research in Stanford University's Graduate Program in Construction Engineering and Management. This research was conducted by engineering faculty with years of experience in construction, a research social psychologist with some 30 years' experience in her field, and numerous graduate students. At the time of this writing, the research is still in progress, but the findings published to date have already gained wide recognition.

In essence, the studies have been based on extensive survey work conducted in the field with the aid of construction companies, labor organizations, insurance companies, and their employees at all levels. Four separate but interrelated studies have focused on (1) top management, (2) superintendents and project management, (3) foremen, and (4) workers. The guidelines summarized below give only a glimpse of the depth of the research and the reported findings, but they at least will give the reader a point of departure. In effect, the source reports themselves contain a practical and workable program to enable an organization to increase its emphasis on the behavioral side of occupational safety and health in construction.

Guidelines for Top Managers   The results below are quoted from the study of top managers by Dr. Raymond E. Levitt.[6] The study provided strong evidence that top managers can reduce accident costs significantly by:

1   Knowing the safety records of all field managers and using this knowledge in evaluating them for promotion or salary increases.
2   Communicating about safety on job visits, in the same way that they communicate about costs and schedules.
3   Using the cost accounting system to encourage safety by:
    •allocating safety costs to a company account.
    •allocating accident costs to projects.
4   Requiring detailed work planning to ensure that equipment or materials needed to perform work safely are at hand when required.
5   Insisting that newly hired employees receive training in safe work methods.
6   Discriminating in the use of safety awards. The data suggest that:
    •Safety awards for workers, if used, should be incentives (awards of nominal monetary value), based on first-aid injuries rather than on lost-time accidents.
    •If correctly applied, safety awards for field managers should be bonuses (awards of substantial monetary value, made in private) based on lost-time accidents or insurance claims costs.
7   Making effective use of the expertise of safety departments, where these exist.

[6]Levitt, op. cit., p. 6.

Guidelines for Superintendents and Project Managers The middle-management study was conducted by Dr. Jimmie Hinze.[7] His findings, the summary of which is paraphrased here, showed that middle managers can reduce injuries significantly by:

    1 Showing concern for and establishing rapport with foremen and workers. They can do so by making sure to:
        a Orient new workers to the job and acquaint them with other job personnel. Particular attention should be given to the new workers in their first few days of employment.
        b Be involved in worker-foremen conflicts, and in so doing, to recognize the worker's viewpoint. This is not to undermine the foreman's authority, but rather, to assure that the workers are fairly treated.
        c Show respect for the ability of foremen, but also to accept the fact that foremen are not immune to error. This can be done by permitting foremen to select their own crew members (but not granting them the sole authority to terminate employees).
    2 Keeping unnecessary pressures off the workers and foremen. Pressures to be avoided include:
        a Stressing strict adherence to detailed cost estimates.
        b Stressing adherence to detailed time estimates.
        c Condoning or encouraging competition between crews on the job.
    3 Actively supporting job safety policies, for example, by:
        a Including safety as a part of job planning.
        b Giving positive support to "toolbox" meetings.
    4 Accepting responsibility for eliminating unsafe conditions and unsafe activities from the job.

Furthermore, Hinze found that top management can help supervisors reduce job accidents by:

    1 Personally stressing the importance of job safety through their informal and formal contacts with field supervisors.
    2 Stressing safety in meetings held at the company level.

Because some of these findings indicate that pressures on cost, schedule, and competition should be reduced, it is worth pointing out that these studies also showed that safe supervisors, foremen, and workers can also be among the most productive. They in effect put to rest the myth that schedules and budgets must necessarily be traded off against safety and health. Indeed, by relaxing tensions, employees are in a better position for getting on with the job and

[7]Jimmie Hinze, *The Effect of Middle Management on Safety in Construction*, Technical Report No. 209, Stanford University, Dept. of Civil Engineering, The Construction Institute, Stanford, Calif., June 1976, pp. 4–6.

doing it well. Again, the reader is encouraged to consult the source reports for the documentation that supports these summary conclusions.

Guidelines for Foremen   The foremen study was the primary focus of research social psychologist Dr. Nancy Morse Samelson.[8] In a preliminary outline, she sought answers to the question: How do highly effective (both safe and productive) construction foremen manage their crews? The answers form a set of probing guidelines in themselves:

1   *They handle the new worker differently:*
   • They ask him more questions and less threatening ones.
   • They are watchful and keep a connection with the new worker rather than putting him right to work or putting him with an older worker and leaving it at that.
2   *They keep stresses off their crews:*
   • They show high ability to "keep their cool" rather than show anger toward crew members.
   • Their reaction to lack of crew accomplishment is to analyze the problem rather than focus on changing the workers by telling them to work harder.
3   *Their approach to safety is different:*
   • They integrate safety into the job with personal work rules rather than having a set of safety admonitions.
   • They are neither safety "nit-pickers" nor are they unaware of safety violations—they are in between.

Guidelines for Workers   The study of construction workers was conducted by Lance deStwolinski.[9] His objective was more to identify characteristics of safe and unsafe workers than to prescribe a set of guidelines. These characteristics can then be used by management in selection and in tailoring supervision and assignments to recognize the needs and limitations of individuals. Parker and Oglesby[10] summarized deStwolinski's findings as follows:

Mere recognition of these relationships is not sufficient to solve the job-accident problem, however. A patterned program of evaluation is necessary. The following simple procedure offers one approach. The implication here is that the enlightened supervisor can work the odds to his benefit in safety if he takes the trouble to analyze his crews (especially those working under hazardous conditions) and gives extra attention to those individuals and situations that fit the following known critical characteristics that may lead to accident involvement:

[8]Nancy M. Samelson, *The Effect of Foremen on Safety in Construction,* Technical Report No. 219, Stanford University, Dept. of Civil Engineering, The Construction Institute, Stanford, Calif., June 1977.
   [9]Lance W. deStwolinski, *A Survey of the Safety Environment of the Construction Industry,* Technical Report No. 114, Stanford University, Dept. of Civil Engineering, The Construction Institute, Stanford, Calif., October 1969.
   [10]Parker and Oglesby, op. cit., pp. 173–174.

    1 The man with abnormal time loss (absenteeism)

    2 The man whose time losses pattern into Mondays or days after payday as the days lost most frequently

    3 The individual who requires the most supervision to produce normally

    4 The man working in isolated areas

    5 The man with problems from home, skirmishes with the law, and the like

    6 The individual who acts abnormally to attract attention (e.g., dress, hair style, hot rodders)

    7 The man whose attitude changes with the time of day and the day of the week

    8 New men with less than one year of service or men with more than 10 years' service

    9 Any individual whose name "crops up" frequently in any unfavorable light (e.g., absent, sick, frequently leaves job site)

    10 The man whose personal appearance changes noticeably (watch for sudden change in gait, color, or actions)

When a new man is hired, he should be assessed as to his possible susceptibility to accidents. The safety questionnaire (used by deStwolinski) indicated that answers to the questions listed below showed a high correlation to a man's accident record, indicating that attitudinal factors toward himself, his foreman, and job management may be significant in accident statistics.[11] Although these questions were designed for a study of a specific union in a specific section of the country, it is probable that other groups might have similar findings; however, such a correlation needs to be tested. Reevaluations of continuing employees is also necessary from time to time to determine those whose attitudes, home environment, or habits may have changed.

    The significant questions as reported by deStwolinski have been reworded into statements and are listed here in the order of significance. "Yes" answers to these or similar questions indicate that the worker is in the accident-susceptible class.

    1 My job management does not know its job well.

    2 I have worked a relatively short time in my present job classification.

    3 I would like to have an opportunity for a good family life.

    4 My foreman is stubborn.

    5 My coworkers are boring.

    6 My job management does not praise good work.

    7 My coworkers are not safety minded.

    8 Risk taking is a part of the job.

It should be noted that most of these questions reflect worker-coworker-supervisor interactions rather than worker attitudes alone. In fact, recent studies which have attempted to isolate worker characteristics associated with accidents separately from other influences have been unsuccessful.

[11]deStwolinski, *A Survey of the Safety Environment,* op. cit., pp. 53–66.

Other Behavioral Factors   Several other results from deStwolinski's study are worth summarizing here. These relate to safety instruction, job safety meetings, and safety equipment.

Policies on Safety Instruction   When new employees are hired, the introduction to the job and its surrounding conditions plays an important role. Safety instruction is an important aspect of this introduction. Thus, the response from 40 percent of the nonsupervisory operating engineers that instructions were not given at all, or if they were given, they were not to the workers' satisfaction, indicated that the situation is not good. Dissatisfaction with instruction probably results from poor-quality instruction, unsatisfactory instructional materials, or a lack of understanding on the part of the individual employee. The future trend may well be toward greater dissatisfaction with the quality of instruction. This results because of the rising education level of the younger operating engineers, an increasing number of whom have high school and some college education.

The most significant finding, related to safety instruction, is that there is a direct relationship between minor and lost-time accidents and the presence or absence of effective safety instruction at the time of initial employment. Those receiving instructions to their satisfaction have significantly better records than those who were not given, or did not understand, instruction, or who were not given effective instructions.

Job Safety Meetings   Job (toolbox) safety meetings have been used for some time to provide safety education on the job. In a number of states they are required by law. For example, in California it is required that job safety meetings be held at least every 10 working days.

A disturbing finding was that having or not having safety meetings seemed to have no effect on the lost-time or minor-accident rate. This is not to imply that all job safety meetings are ineffective. But it does say that the presence or absence of safety meetings had no marked effect on accident experience. A possible explanation was brought out through the survey. It was that, although those conducting the safety meetings were considered as knowledgeable, the meetings were often so dull and for the most part the "same old stuff" that they had no effect on worker attitude or behavior.

It seems that to make job safety meetings more effective, there is a need for more practical and current subject material given by a variety of qualified speakers. They might come from outside, from either the union or the company itself. Smaller meetings for specific crafts also may be appropriate, with more discussion dealing with immediate problems. For crews which have a variety of work assignments, discussion of the safety aspects of each new assignment might be held before the task is begun. The real point is that changes must be made if job safety meetings are to be effective and productive to the employee and employer.

Safety Equipment   Responses on this subject showed that, except for the requirement for hard hats (stipulated by 60 percent of the respondents), little else in the line of safety equipment was required by contractors. A good percentage used gloves (41 percent) and safety glasses or goggles (27 percent) on a voluntary basis. However, very few employers required that the workers wear earplugs or muffs, special clothing, steel-toed boots, gloves, or safety glasses. In light of the problems of accident potential and increased health hazards from dust, noise, and noxious agents, such items as these should be required on all jobs.

Physical Approaches to Safety and Health

The physical side of construction safety requires:

1 Education and training in correct methods and procedures.
2 Provision and proper utilization and application of good-quality, well-maintained tools and equipment, both for construction operations and for mechanical elimination of hazards. Examples of items currently being emphasized include roll-over protection on earthmoving equipment, and noise-level controls.
3 Enforced use of approved equipment for personal protection: hard hats, seat belts, earplugs, etc., as required by specific operations.
4 Good housekeeping on the job site.
5 Frequent and thorough job-site inspections by knowledgeable and objective professionals.
6 Incorporation of a safety review as a routine part of thorough preplanning for the actual methods and procedures to be carried out in field operations.

There are numerous excellent safety manuals that provide detailed elaboration on items 1, 2, 3, and 4 above. Many large construction companies have developed outstanding in-house manuals tailored to their own type of work. Good examples that are available to the public include the following:

Manual of Accident Prevention in Construction, 6th ed., The Associated General Contractors of America, Washington, D.C., 1971.
California Construction Safety Orders, Dept. of Industrial Relations, Division of Industrial Safety, San Francisco. Also, *Tunnel Safety Orders*, from the same agency.
General Safety Requirements, Manual EM385-1-1, and Supplements 1 and 2, U.S. Army Corps of Engineers, Washington, D.C.
Safety Requirements for Construction by Contract, Dept. of the Interior, U. S. Bureau of Reclamation, Washington, D.C.
OSHA publications:
Compliance Operations Manual, OSHA 2006, U.S. Dept. of Labor, Occupational Safety and Health Administration, Washington, D.C., January 1972.
"Construction Safety and Health Regulations," U.S. Dept. of Labor, Occupational Safety and Health Administration; *Federal Register*, vol. 39, no. 122, June 24, 1974, Washington, D.C.
Construction Industry: OSHA Safety & Health Standards Digest,

OSHA 2202, Superintendent of Documents, U.S. Government Printing Office, Washington, D.C., June, 1975.

Clearly, it is beyond the scope of this chapter to attempt the type of detailed elaboration contained in those manuals. Suffice it to say that detailed knowledge of this type is fundamental to an effective program in construction safety and health. We shall take a moment here, however, to comment on the fifth and sixth elements mentioned in discussing the physical factors: inspection and preplanning.

Inspection　Good in-house inspection by personnel authorized to implement changes is becoming increasingly common these days, in part as a matter of self-defense against OSHA fines. Other companies are making good use of experienced inspectors provided by insurance companies. In some cases this approach either directly or indirectly affects insurance premiums. Regardless of the motivation, the trend toward objective and qualified inspection of work sites is a good one, and it has been a long time in coming. Inspection has always been an essential part of an effective safety and health program.

It is essential that the inspectors themselves be experienced in construction operations, and that they be objective, fair, and practical in their recommendations and directives to project managers and supervisors. Nothing can destroy a safety program more quickly than conspicuously ignorant and inexperienced inspectors who compensate with missionary zeal for what they lack in knowledge. However, given that we can have intelligent and objective inspectors, it is also important that they have the authority, either directly or through recommendations backed by higher management, to see that safety and health standards are maintained on job sites. Many companies are providing the necessary clout by making the inspector an independent entity on the job site, reporting directly to the project manager, or to the home office rather than to project management. There are advantages and disadvantages to this approach, but the organizational relationship is much like that for the quality control function shown in Figure 16-5.

The inspector's task is eased somewhat if he has a set of standards to use in his work. Figure 18-1 reproduces one of a complete series of checklists published by *Construction Methods and Equipment* magazine for this purpose; these are practical forms that have found wide acceptance in the construction industry. The example form, describing personal protective equipment, also illustrates typical factors that would be considered in items 1 through 4 of the list of physical factors at the beginning of this subsection.

Preplanning　Thorough and conscientious preplanning is essential to economy, efficiency, and high productivity in almost all construction operations; safety and health considerations should be an integral part of this process. Safety professionals should participate in the development of stan-

Safety and Health On Worksites

CM&E's series of SHOW checklists are designed to make sure you're in full compliance with every aspect of the Construction Safety Act (Federal Register: April 17, 1971, Part II; May 29, 1971, Part II) and all the subsequent revisions, corrections, and amendments.....before things happen, not after.

No. 4

Project _____

Inspection area _____ Area supervisor _____

Inspected by _____ Date _____

Subject / Personal protective equipment	Yes	No	Action / comments
Head protection **1.** Do your employees wear protective helmets whenever they work in areas where there is the possible danger of a head injury from impact and penetration of falling and flying objects, or from electrical shock and burns? **2.** Do the helmets worn by your employees for the protection against impact and penetration of falling and flying objects meet the specifications in ANSI Z89.1-1969–Safety Requirements for Industrial Head Protection? **3.** Do the helmets worn by those of your employees exposed to high voltage electrical shock and burns meet the specifications in ANSI Z89.2-1970?			
Hearing protection **1.** Do you provide ear protective devices for your employees whenever it is not feasible to reduce noise levels or duration of exposure as specified?			

Hr duration per day	dBA level slow response	
8	90	
6	92	a. Variations in noise level including maxima at intervals of 1
4	95	sec or less are considered as continuous.
3	97	b. Daily noise exposure composed of two or more periods of noise
2	100	exposure should be considered in combination, rather than indi-
1½	102	vidually.
1	105	c. Exposure to impulsive or impact noise should not exceed 140
½	110	
¼ or less	115	dBA peak sound pressure level.

Subject / Personal protective equipment	Yes	No	Action / comments
2. Do you make sure that your employees use the ear protective devices you provide for them? **3.** If these ear protective devices are inserted in the ear, are they fitted or determined individually for each employee by competent persons? *Important: Plain cotton is not an acceptable protective device.*			

Eye and face protection
1. Do you provide your employees with eye and face protection equipment when machines or operators present potential eye or face injury from physical, chemical, or radiation agents?
2. Does the eye and face protection that you provide your employees meet the requirements specified in ANSI Z87.1-1968–Practice for Occupational and Educational Eye and Face Protection?
3. If any of your employees, whose vision requires the use of corrective lenses in spectacles, are required to wear eye protection, are the goggles or spectacles that you provide for their protection one of the approved types?
  a. Spectacles whose protective lenses provide optical correction.
  b. Goggles that can be worn over corrective spectacles without disturbing the adjustments of the spectacles.
  c. Goggles that incorporate corrective lenses mounted behind the protective lenses.
4. Do you keep face and eye protection equipment clean and in good repair?
5. Do you forbid the use of any of this type of equipment having structural or optical defects?
<div align="right">*continued on next page*</div>			

Figure 18-1 Example safety checklist. *(From* Construction Methods and Equipment, *vol. 54, no. 8, August 1972, pp. 23–24.)*

CM&E SHOW Checklist

Safety and Health On Worksites

No. 4

Project _____

Inspection area _____ Area supervisor _____

Inspected by _____ Date _____

Subject / Personal protective equipment	Yes	No	Action / comments

continued

6. Does the equipment that you provide your employees for face and eye protection conform to the standards for such protection from the hazards and operations as listed below?

Operation	Hazards	Recommended Protection
Acetylene–burning	Sparks, harmful rays	7,8,9
Acetylene–cutting	Molten metal	7,8,9
Acetylene–welding	Flying particles	7,8,9
Chemical handling	Splash, acid burns, and fumes	2,10 (for severe exposure add 10 over 2)
Chipping	Flying particles	1,3,4,5,6, 7A, 8A
Electric (arc) welding	Sparks, intense rays, and molten metal	9,11 (11 in combination with 4,5,6 in tinted lenses)
Furnace operations	Glare, heat, and molten metal	7,8,9 (for severe exposure add 10)
Grinding–light	Flying particles	1,3,4,5,6,10
Grinding–heavy	Flying particles	1,3,7A, 8A (for severe exposure add 10)
Laboratory	Chemical splash, and glass breakup	2 (10 when in combination with 4,5,6)
Machining	Flying particles	1,3,4,5,6,10
Molten Metals	Heat, glare, sparks, and splash	7,8 (10 in combination with 4,5,6 in tinted lenses)
Spot welding	Flying particles, sparks	1,3,4,5,6,10

Eye and face protector selection guide:
1. Goggles–Flexible fitting, regular ventilation
2. Goggles–Flexible fitting, hooded ventilation
3. Goggles–Cushioned fitting, rigid body
*4. Spectacles–Metal frame, with sideshields
*5. Spectacles–Plastic frame, with sideshields
*6. Spectacles–Metal-plastic frame, with sideshields
**7. Welding goggles–Eyecup type, tinted lenses
7A. Chipping goggles–Eyecup type, clear safety lenses
**8. Welding goggles–Coverspec type, tinted lenses
8A. Chipping goggles–Coverspec type, clear safety lenses
**9. Welding goggles–Coverspec type, tinted plate lens
10. Face shield–Plastic or mesh window
**11. Welding helmet

*–Non-side shield spectacles are available for limited hazard use requiring only frontal protection.
**–See following table for filter lens shade numbers.

Selection of shade numbers for welding filter

1. Do you provide your employees the proper filter lense or plate for protection against radiant energy in welding, as specified in the following table?

Welding operation	Shade number
Shielded metal-arc welding 1/16, 3/32, 1/8, 5/32-in.-dia electrodes	10
Gas-shielded arc welding (nonferrous 1/16, 3/32, 1/8, 5/32-in.-dia electrodes	11
Gas-shielded arc welding (ferrous) 1/16, 3/32, 1/8, 5/32-in.-dia electrodes	12
Shielded metal-arc welding 3/16, 7/32, 1/4-in.-dia electrodes	12
5/16, 3/8-in.-dia electrodes	14
Atomic hydrogen welding	10-14
Carbon-arc welding	14
Soldering	2
Torch brazing	3 or 4
Light cutting, up to 1 in.	3 or 4
Medium cutting, 1 to 6 in.	4 or 5
Heavy cutting, over 6 in.	5 or 6
Gas welding (light) up to 1/8 in.	4 or 5
Gas welding (medium) 1/8 to 1/2 in.	5 or 6
Gas welding (heavy) over 1/2 in.	6 or 8

Laser protection

1. Do you furnish employees, whose occupation or assignment requires exposure to laser beams, suitable laser safety goggles which will protect them for the specific wavelength of the laser and be of optical density adequate for the energy involved as specified in the following table?

Intensity		Attenuation
CW max power density	Attenuation density	Optical factor
(w/cm²)	(O.D.)	
10^{-2}	5	10^5
10^{-1}	6	10^6
1.0	7	10^7
10.0	8	10^8

(Output levels falling between lines in this table shall require the higher optical density.)

2. Do all your protective goggles bear a label identifying:
a. Laser wavelength for which use is intended?
b. Optical density of those wavelengths?
c. Visible light transmission?

Figure 18-1 (continued).

dard procedures and should review job-operation plans for considerations such as the following:

  1 To verify that the method selected does indeed adhere to recommended and required standards and regulations for safety and health
  2 To be certain that the correct tools and equipment will be available for the work, including the necessary personal protection gear
  3 To express reservations about supervisors or workers who lack the skills that will be needed, and to suggest remedial training procedures where appropriate
  4 To anticipate hazards inherent in the work and recommend precautionary steps for dealing with them

Preplanning of this type, with good supervision to see that the plan is indeed executed, is one of the best methods to assure not only high levels of safety and health, but high production as well. Parker and Oglesby's *Methods Improvement for Construction Managers* focuses on this subject in detail.[12]

SUMMARY

Statistics show that safety and health are critical problems in construction. In the United States alone, construction deaths and lost-time injuries run up to 3000 and 300,000 per year respectively; annual direct and impact costs are estimated at $5 billion to $10 billion. Some companies, however, are bucking the trends; their outstanding safety and health records show that the industry as a whole can do much better. Basically, these industry leaders have discovered that safety and health are as much a part of effective project planning and control as are costs, schedules, procurement, and quality.

    Motivations for improved performance include humanitarian concern, economic costs and benefits, legal and regulatory mandates, liability consequences, and organizational image. Humanitarian objectives boil down to reducing the human pain and suffering resulting from accidents and illnesses. Economic incentives include not only reducing insurance premiums, but minimizing the staggering indirect costs as well. Regulatory constraints have been imposed mainly by government agencies, and they serve as a lever in attempting to bring inept and irresponsible organizations into compliance with industry standards. Increasing liability problems, including high accident claims settlements for injuries and illnesses often taken for granted in the past, have led prudent employers to test and document key health factors of their employees. Finally, the positive image generated by good safety and health performance helps both in employee relations and in contract negotiations.

    Safety hazards are those that pose imminent danger of causing injury or death to workers. They include falling from heights, fire, moving machinery

---

[12]Parker and Oglesby, op. cit.

and vehicles, explosives, electricity, and falling objects. Health hazards may or may not produce immediate symptoms, but they have been gaining wider recognition in construction. Among these dangers are heat, radiation, noise, dust, shocks and vibrations, and toxic chemicals.

Effective implementation programs should focus on both the physical and the behavioral sides of safety and health. Traditional approaches have concentrated on the physical or "hardware" aspects, yet roughly 80 percent of all industrial accidents involve unsafe acts and not just unsafe conditions. A balance between the different components of safety and health is therefore essential.

On the behavioral side, recent research has produced practical and workable guidelines aimed at the attitudes and actions of top management, project managers and superintendents, foremen, and workers. The intent is to identify the characteristics of managers and workers who are both safe and productive so that selection, assignments, supervision, and efforts for improvement can take these factors into account.

The physical side of safety involves: (1) education and training; (2) proper utilization and maintenance of correct tools and equipment; (3) equipment for personal protection; (4) good housekeeping; (5) frequent inspections by knowledgeable and objective professionals; and (6) integrating safety and health into thorough preplanning for field operations.

Chapter 19

Industrial Relations

This chapter on industrial relations in the construction industry includes a discussion of organized labor, summarizing the organization and control of the building trades unions affiliated with the AFL-CIO, and the advantages and disadvantages of union membership for both the contractor and the worker. The section on open shop similarly reviews the nonunion and coexistant postions. A comparison of the union and nonunion approaches sets forth the current situation in the industry. Increasingly, ethnic minorities and women are becoming a major factor in the construction work force, and compliance with the law and recognized affirmative action programs is becoming increasingly important in contractor operations. Also included is a description of contractor and owner organizations, designed to further the interests of each individual group. Finally, a description of the duties of an industrial relations department of a large contractor helps illustrate how contractors try to develop harmonious relationships at all levels.

ORGANIZED LABOR[1]

The major force in organized labor within the construction industry is the American Federation of Labor (AFL), which began in 1886 under the leadership of Samuel Gompers. Gompers developed two policies that contributed to the

---

[1]This section is based partly upon a chapter from *Directions in Managing Construction,* Donald S. Barrie (ed.), prepared by Dr. John Borcherding, John Wiley & Sons, Inc., New York, 1981.

successful growth of this building trades union: (1) national unions were guaranteed trade autonomy, and (2) each union was granted exclusive jurisdiction. At the present time, continuing demands include higher wages, shorter hours, improved working conditions, job security, and the right to represent the work force.

Table 19-1 lists the building trades unions affiliated with the AFL-CIO. The Teamsters Union is not now affiliated but normally cooperates fully with the building trades at the local level.

Organization and Control

Organized labor is split into three levels, the federation, the national unions, and the local unions. The federation is the AFL and the Congress of International Organizations (CIO), which merged into the AFL-CIO in 1955 after a split of 17 years. Table 19-2 shows the organizations chart. The federation is a coalition of 106 national and international (both United States and Canada) unions. The principal role of the AFL-CIO is political since it does not take part in local collective bargaining. The state-level organization is open to membership on a voluntary basis. Its structure and functions are similar to the national organization except that it is oriented to local and state activities.

The building trades national and international unions are the basis of American union activities in the construction industry. The national union has its own exclusive jurisdiction, and although collective bargaining is performed at the local level, that power is delegated from the national union. Unions have their own officers and manage their own affairs. Usually a national union

Table 19–1 AFL-CIO Construction Unions

1. Bricklayers, Masons and Plasterers' International Union
2. Brotherhood of Painters, Decorators, and Paperhangers of America
3. Granite Cutters' International Association of America
4. International Association of Bridge, Structural and Ornamental Iron Workers
5. International Association of Heat and Frost Insulators and Asbestos Workers
6. International Association of Marble, Slate and Stone Polishers, Rubbers and Sawyers, Tile and Marble Setters Helpers and Terrazzo Helpers
7. International Brotherhood of Boiler Makers, Iron ship Builders and Helpers of America
8. International Brotherhood of Electrical Workers
9. International Union of Elevator Constructors
10. International Union of Operating Engineers
11. Laborers International Union of North America
12. Operative Plasterers and Cement Masons' International Association
13. Sheet Metal Workers' International Association
14. United Association of Journeymen and Apprentices of the Plumbing and Pipe Fitting Industry of the United States and Canada
15. United Brotherhood of Carpenters and Joiners of America
16. United Slate, Tile, and Composition Roofers, Damp and Waterproof Workers' Association
17. Wood, Wire, and Metal Lathers' International Union

Table 19–2 Structural Organization of the AFL-CIO

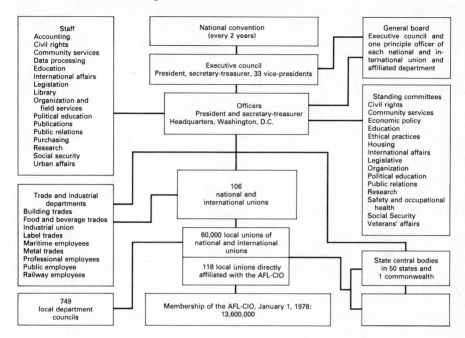

Staff Accounting Civil rights Community services Data processing Education International affairs Legislation Library Organization and field services Political education Publications Public relations Purchasing Research Social security Urban affairs	National convention (every 2 years)	General board Executive council and one principle officer of each national and in- ternational union and affiliated department
	Executive council President, secretary-treasurer, 33 vice-presidents	
	Officers President and secretary-treasurer Headquarters, Washington, D.C.	Standing committees Civil rights Community services Economic policy Education Ethical practices Housing International affairs Legislative Organization Political education Public relations Research Safety and occupational health Social Security Veterans' affairs
Trade and industrial departments Building trades Food and beverage trades Industrial union Label trades Maritime employees Metal trades Professional employees Public employee Railway employees	106 national and international unions	
	60,000 local unions of national and international unions	
	118 local unions directly affiliated with the AFL-CIO	State central bodies in 50 states and 1 commonwealth
749 local department councils	Membership of the AFL-CIO, January 1, 1978: 13,600,000	

vice-president is given authority over local unions, districts, or other collective groups throughout the United States.

The third level in the union hierarchy is the local union. Locals are chartered by the national body and derive their power from the constitution of the national union. Local building trades unions are fairly autonomous and responsible for collective bargaining and jurisdictional preservation for a specific area. The local union is responsible for all activities pertaining to the craft within its boundaries. Affiliated local unions often join together to form district councils to make rules or understandings for the district. Building trades councils are made up of local unions from different construction trades and are instrumental in setting the political and collective bargaining pattern within their area.

Advantages and Disadvantages of Union Membership

Advantages of union membership are cited for both workers and construction company management.

Worker Advantages　Most workers are concerned with such economic and other issues as:

1. Hiring hall for job referral
2. Apprenticeship training
3. Right to strike, wages, job conditions, benefits, and job security

4. Power to act collectively as a group to enforce demands
5. Camaraderie through belonging to an organization

Management Advantages   Management can achieve a number of advantages through a healthy relationship with organized labor, including:

1. Source of a pool of skilled labor.
2. Fixed wages and uniform conditions through negotiations that can have a stabilizing influence in the area and preclude unfair competition.
3. Progressive unions may exercise a stabilizing influence among their own members and may help control the entry and actions of irresponsible or marginal contractors.

Worker Disadvantages   Workers may also suffer disadvantages through union membership, including

1. Payment of initiation fees, dues, or assessments
2. No choice of employer, lack of merit promotions, equal pay regardless of performance, and general subordination of gain from outstanding individual performance
3. Restriction on utilizing certain methods, elimination of incentive programs, less flexibility in work assignments, and loss of work during jurisdictional disputes
4. Less number of hours of work during the year and less flexibility to make up for bad weather or other factors causing temporary layoff

Management Disadvantages   Management criticizes unions for

1. Restrictive work rules that decrease productivity, such as supervisor ratios, nonworking supervisors, guaranteed work week, prohibition against operating several pieces of equipment, and other featherbedding examples
2. No incentive upon the part of the individual worker to be innovative or especially productive since everyone gets the same pay
3. Little loyalty to the employer, which results in less management opportunities for innovation and development of a team spirit to improve both production and work-life quality
4. Jurisdictional disputes that can result in economic hardship through no fault of the contractor

THE OPEN SHOP[2]

Under United States labor law, construction firms have the right to decide whether they will operate an open or a union shop. The line between union and

[2]This section is prepared partly from a chapter in *Directions in Managing Construction*, prepared by Dr. Raymond L. Levitt and Donald S. Barrie (ed.), John Wiley & Sons, Inc., New York, 1981.

nonunion firms is not always clear. Many nonunion firms may sign formal project agreements or informal agreements that effectively make them union firms on a particular project. Nonunion firms often hire unemployed union members who "put their card in their shoe."

Open shop has been steadily growing, both in its share of the overall construction market and in geographic penetration throughout the United States in more traditional union locations. Based upon the results of a study prepared for the Department of Housing and Urban Development by the Massachusetts Institute of Technology, a number of comparisons were developed between unions and nonunion firms that help clarify their interrelationship.

Organization and Control

To try to achieve some of the advantages that progressive labor unions can bring to both employees and employers, groups of open shop contractors have bonded together to form the associations discussed in the "Employer Organizations" section. Open shop continues to grow and has now achieved a preponderence of work in the broadly defined construction industry. See Figure 19-1 for the growth of the open shop market share during the past decade.

Comparison of Union and Nonunion Construction

The Department of Housing and Urban Development (HUD) sponsored a major survey of the construction industry to compare many aspects of union and nonunion construction. Eight large metropolitan areas were chosen for the

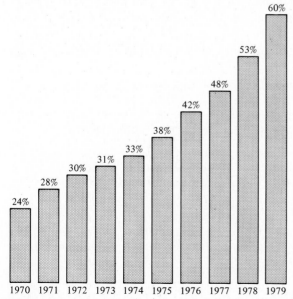

Figure 19-1 Open shop market share. *(From Associated Builders and Contractors, Inc., Washington, D.C.)*

study, which was developed by a number of questionnaires and interviews. Findings are summarized as follows:

Markets and Individual Firm Size.   In all eight areas, most of the union firms identified themselves as performing the majority of their work in commercial/industrial or heavy and highway construction. The open shop firms were engaged primarily in residential or commercial/industrial work or both. Table 19-3 compares employment by product market. In all areas, the open shop firms were smaller than their union counterparts. However, it was evident that there are now a number of very large open shop firms, both general and specialty contractors. Based upon the substantial continued growth of open shop, it is expected that this size differential will become less pronounced.

Occupational Structure and Overall Size   Open shop firms were found to be developing and utilizing important innovations in both occupational and skill structure. Open shop firms often find it economical to use lead persons as working supervisors, helpers for unskilled work crossing trades lines, and new classifications relating pay to skill levels rather than to traditional craft lines. Figure 19-2 is a map of the industry, with a rough assessment of the predominant classifications by size and type of construction.

Impact of Prevailing Wage Laws   There is considerable controversy about whether the Davis-Bacon Act and other prevailing wage laws significantly raise the cost of construction. The HUD study showed that there really is no prevailing wage in nonunion labor markets. The dispersion of nonunion wages for any trade in any given area automatically tends to favor the union rate, which is generally some 30 to 50 percent higher than the average nonunion rate. Whether increased productivity is achieved through higher wages was not addressed by the study and remains a controversial issue in many states with heavy union representation.

Table 19–3   Percentage of Union and Open shop Employment by Product Market for Study Sample

	Union, As a Percentage			Open shop, As a Percentage		
SMSA (1)	Residential (2)	Commercial/ Industrial (3)	Heavy and Highway (4)	Residential (5)	Commercial/ Industrial (6)	Heavy and Highway (7)
Boston	11	72	17	55	41	4
Baltimore	2	63	35	49	46	5
Atlanta	0.6	91	8.4	26	65	9
New Orleans	0.5	92	7.5	16	82	2
Grand Rapids	1	48	51	48	49	3
Kansas City	7	61	32	68	32	0
Denver	6	73	21	68	29	3
Portland	11	72	17	67	24	9

Sector	Size	Small $2 m	Medium $2-$10 m	Large +$10 m
Residential	Single family	◇	○	○
Residential	Garden apartment	◇	○	□
Residential	High rise	○	○	□
Commercial/Industrial	Stores and shopping center	◇	○	□
Commercial/Industrial	Offices	◇	○	□
Commercial/Industrial	Manufacturing	○	□	○
Commercial/Industrial	Educational	○	□	□
Commercial/Industrial	Medical	□	□	□
Heavy	Utilities	○	□	□
Heavy	Transportation	○	□	□
Heavy	Water and sewage	○	○	□

□ Union   ◇ Nonunion   ○ Mixed

Figure 19-2 "Map of" the industry, with a rough assessment of open shop activity.

ETHNIC MINORITIES AND WOMEN[3]

Few subjects in construction can generate more controversy than the principal of affirmative action to increase participation of ethnic minorities and women in the construction work force. The Public Works Employment Act of 1977 made available $4 billion in federal subsidies for construction projects, provided that 10 percent or more of the work be awarded to ethnic minority companies, subcontractors, craftspeople, or suppliers.

Ethnic Minorities

A serious effort to resolve discrimination problems in the construction industry has been underway in the United States for some time. The Constitution has been interpreted to forbid discrimination in government and private employment. The Equal Employment Opportunity Commission was created in 1964 to investigate allegations of discrimination. Other acts forbid discrimination on the basis of age, sex, and national origin.

In many sections of the country, it was considered normal for blacks and other groups to occupy positions of leadership in local unions for laborers, cement finishers, and teamsters. In years gone by, there were often separate

[3]This section is based partly upon portions of a chapter from *Directions in Managing Construction,* Donald S. Barrie (ed.), prepared by Gerald Challenger and Audrey Barrie, John Wiley & Sons, Inc., New York, 1981.

local unions for blacks in the southern states., The most significant areas of exclusion for blacks, hispanics, and sometimes others are in the metal trades. Until recently, black electricians, pipefitters, ironworkers, and other metal trades personnel were largely nonexistant. The current accomplishments of black minorities have been largely tied to government-funded training or government-mandated affirmative action. In the final analysis, future affirmative action programs must be designed to increase productivity as well as to redress past wrongs through large-scale training and other incentives in a way that will benefit society, the individual, and the industry.

Minority firms play a new role in the overall development of minority participation in the construction industry. Ideally, the government-mandated set-aside program requiring that a designated percentage of work be performed by minority firms can be followed to both upgrade the utilization of minorities in the industry and maintain or improve present productivity standards.

Women

The Civil Rights Act enacted in 1964 and amended in 1972 prohibits discrimination because of race, sex, or creed. Employment doors previously closed to women were suddenly open. The Department of Labor mandated that certain quotas of women be hired on construction projects. However, in spite of supportive legislation and an excellent pay scale, the women are clearly not yet beating a path to the crafts. Except for Rosie the Riveter, active in the shipyards in World War II, it is rare to find a woman who was in the building trades before the enactment of civil rights legislation. Society continues to perceive women as a protected, more delicate species, incapable of doing "mans' work." Because of this perception, many women continue to limit themselves to employment deemed more traditional for their sex.

Professional and white collar women are making substantially better progress in the construction industry. Women are appearing in essentially all the salaried functional tasks required in the construction industry, including accounting, purchasing, labor relations, scheduling, estimating, design engineering, construction engineering, supervisions, and project management. Of all the minority engineers being graduated in the United States, women are the fastest growing group.

Several support organizations have evolved to assist the upwardly mobile female construction professional. Women in Construction embraces all women in construction administrative, managerial, and other white collar positions. The National Association of Women in Construction (NAWIC) awards scholarships for outstanding achievement, sponsors a four-year home-study course leading to a Certified Construction Associate degree, and serves as a clearinghouse for job openings. Local NAWIC chapters hold periodic meetings and sponsor workshops and other educational events. NAWIC conducts similar undertakings on a national scale.

The Society of Women Engineers (SWE) is a professional, nonprofit, educational service organization of graduate engineers and others of equivalent engineering experience. Specific objectives of the society are to:

- Inform young women and other interested parties of qualifications, achievements, and opportunities open to women engineers
- Assist women engineers in readying themselves for a return to active work after temporary retirement or a leave of absence
- Serve as an information center for women in engineering
- Encourage women engineers to obtain higher levels of education and professional achievement

SWE administers several award, certificate, and scholarship programs. Sections are located in 40 states and in Puerto Rico. Student sections have been chartered in 92 colleges and universities. The Society has an international membership of over 5000 and about 60 corporate members, including many of the largest employers of engineers in the United States.

CONTRACTOR AND OWNER ORGANIZATIONS

Most contractors in the United States belong to one or more contractor or industry associations. Some of the organizations are purely national in scope; others are active at both the local and the national level; and others represent contractors only in a particular area. Table 19-4 lists a number of the major

Table 19–4   List of Several Major National Construction Associations, 1979

Associated General Contractors of America 1957 E Street, N.W. Washington D.C. 20006	National Constructors Association 1001 Fifteenth Street, N.W. Suite 1000 Washington, D.C. 20005
The Business Roundtable (owner association) 405 Lexington Avenue New York, New York 10014	National Electrical Contractors Association 7351 Wisconsin Avenue Washington, D.C. 20014
Mason Contractors Association of America 601 Fourteenth Street, #17W Oakbrook Terrace, Illinois 60181	National Insulation Contractors Association 1001 Connecticut Avenue, N.W. Suite 800 Washington, D.C. 20036
Mechanical Contractors Association of America 5530 Wisconsin Avenue, N.W. Washington, D.C. 20015	National Utility Contractors Association 815 Fifteenth Street, N.W. Washington, D.C. 20005
National Association of Plumbing-Heating-Cooling Contractors 1016 Twentieth Street, N.W. Washington, D.C. 20036	Painting and Decorating Contractors of America 7223 Lee Highway Falls Church, Virginia 22046
National Construction Employers Council 2033 K Street, N.W. Suite 200 Washington, D.C. 20006	Sheet Metal and Air Conditioning Contractors National Associations, Inc. 8224 Courthouse Road-Tysons Corner Vienna, Virginia 22180

national construction contractor associations. In addition, the Business Round-table, made up of a large number of major construction owners, has been very active in the construction area.

Union Contractor Organizations

Major associations of unionized contractors include the Associated General Contractors of America (open shop also), the National Constructors Association, the Mechanical Contractors Association of America, the National Electrical Contractors Association, and a number of associations for specialty trades.

National Constructors Association   The National Constructors Association (NCA) was formed in 1947 to represent large national contractors engaged primarily in industrial construction and who generally also have engineering capability to perform design-build or design-manage projects. Engineer-contractor or contractor members of the NCA hold national or international agreements with the national building trades unions that have been negotiated by the national office. The national agreements generally adopt the wage scale and fringe benefits that are negotiated by the local union in the job-site area. However, the national agreement provides for the adjudication of disputes first with the local union and then with the national union, bypassing the provisions of the local agreements. National agreements also often provide for the elimination of certain local practices that may conflict with the national agreement.

The NCA has negotiated several other agreements that provide more favorable terms to member union contractors competing against open shop in designated areas and in maintenance or "turnaround" work in operating plants. Project agreements are often specially negotiated for large projects by NCA members, which generally follow local wage rates but which may provide for different working conditions or other provisions. The NCA is generally the representative of the larger engineer-contractor who offers turnkey services to industrial owners on heavy industrial projects throughout the United States.

The Associated General Contractors of America   The Associated General Contractors of America (AGC) was formed in Chicago in 1918 and was the first major association of general contractors. The AGC has historically handled wages and contract negotiations with the local building trades throughout the United States. Members are usually signatory to local agreements through their membership in the AGC and can operate in other jurisdictions simply by joining the local group and becoming signatory to the agreements and grievance procedures. In contrast to the NCA, grievance procedures are generally set forth in the local agreement and are binding upon both the union and the contractor. The AGC generally negotiates for the five or six basic trades usually employed by a general contractor. Other specialty contractors are often negotiated by the National Electrical Contractors Association (NECA), the Mechanical Contractors Association of America (MCA), or other specialty or independent groups.

With the rise in open shop, a number of AGC chapters now include both unions and nonunion contractors who cooperate in an effort to improve productivity and help mitigate unreasonable wage and work-condition demands by the unions. The AGC generally represents the local contractors and certain national contractors who are generally without the engineering capability to perform turnkey work. Most of the contracts are competitively bid, in contrast to the negotiated contract favored by members of the NCA. It is not surprising that relationships between the AGC and the NCA, while coexisting at the national level, have never been closely aligned at the local levels or mutually supportive nationally.

Specialty Contractor Associations   Other specialty groups, including the NECA, MCA, Painting and Decorating Contractors of America, and Mason Contractors Association of America, have historically performed services for their members similar to those provided by the AGC, including the negotiation of local contracts covering wages and working conditions. These associations, like the AGC, operate both nationally and locally, but the major effort is in the local area, in contrast to the NCA, which negotiates agreements at the national level.

Open Shop Organizations

The Associated Builders and Contractors (ABC) is a national organization formed in 1950 by a group of Baltimore contractors who became disillusioned with accepting union control of the industry. They established what is called merit shop: open shop, but not necessarily antiunion. By concentrating in the suburban and outlying areas, ABC members and other open shop groups began building up strength, until today they are clearly in the majority in their strong areas and are making solid gains in almost all areas of the United States.

In mid-1979 there were about 80 actual ABC chapters in 42 states. The association has a national office in Washington D.C. and publishes a monthly magazine, *Merit Shop Contractor,* which in format and content is not unlike the AGC's magazine, *Constructor.*

Advantages in ABC membership for open shop contractors include the availability of insurance, employee benefit plans, referral agencies, craft training programs, and other programs that can be more economically obtained as a part of an organized group of employers.

A tribute to the success of the ABC is the emergence of the dual role of the AGC, which is increasingly being made up of both union and nonunion contractors. The AGC continues to negotiate wages and working conditions with local building trades unions in areas with substantial open shop strength. The substantial pressure from the open shop membership of the AGC has helped mitigate construction-wage increases in the unionized sector and is contributing to increased productivity in many areas through open competition in right-to-work states and elsewhere, where both union and nonunion contractors coexist peacefully on individual projects.

In other areas, local groups of open shop or nonunion contractors have formed a local "builder's exchange" or other association that often supplies a central plan room, arranges for group insurance and other fringe benefits, and in general endeavors to promote the welfare of the building industry in their particular locale.

Owner Associations

Owner associations include such groups as the Electric Power Research Association, American Public Works Association, American Association of State Highway Officials, American Water Works Association, and a number of others. These associations have largely been concerned with technical and engineering-oriented objectives rather than with those usually associated with work force or union relationships.

Certainly the major effort by owners to influence the industrial relations elements in construction has been through an association of many of the largest buyers of construction in the United States: the Business Roundtable. The Roundtable grew from the National Conference on Construction Problems sponsored by the U.S. Chamber of Commerce in 1968 to review the rapid rise in industrial construction costs. The conference called for the formation of an organization of major purchasers of construction to establish mutual cooperation between purchaser and contractors, particularly in construction industry labor relations. The construction User Anti-Inflation Roundtable was then established, with Roger Blough, Chief Executive Officer, U.S. Steel, as the first chairman.

The main thrust of "Rogers' Roundtable" was to educate users about the detrimental effect of certain decisions, such as working through strikes or requiring excessive overtime, upon both the overall industry and their own jobs. The Roundtable also promoted the establishment of local user groups to help educate local member companies as well as other local businesspeople. The organization has now completed phase II of a massive four-phase project titled the Business Roundtable Construction Industry Cost Effectiveness (CICE) study, which explores a comprehensive list of areas in addition to labor relations that could increase productivity in the future. Initial results of the phase II study along with recommendations to be placed in effect in phase III were outlined in 1982; publication of the complete study was completed in early 1983.

INDUSTRIAL RELATIONS DEPARTMENT

The industrial relations department of a major construction firm might include a number of functions, each headed by a separate manager in the case of a large company or shared in the case of a smaller firm. Functions are briefly described as follows.

Department Manager

The department manager is often responsible to the general manager for the integration of the personnel, safety, and security functions and the labor relations in the home office setting broad policies for the company. Field projects may be delegated some of all of the on-site responsibility for the various functions through one or more on-site representation. See Figure 19-3 for a simplified organizations chart for an industrial relations division home-office organization.

Personnel

The personnel manager may be given overall responsibility for the development of policies and procedures applicable to the salaried work force. This will include development and administration of programs for employee benefits, such as vacations, holidays, medical insurance, life insurance, retirement plans, profit sharing plans, and others. Duties will also normally include responsibility for development of a uniform, competitive, and workable wage and salary program for the company, including position descriptions and pay grades. Recruiting, hiring, and development of employment policies round out the assignment.

Safety and Security

A manager for safety and security will often develop internal procedures for safety, security, and fire protection. Follow-up with periodic field visits and close liason with the company's insurance carrier are equally important. Favorable workers' compensation rates and accident experience can give the farsighted contractor a substantial edge in today's competitive climate. Safety requirements are spelled out in considerable detail in Chapter 18, *"Safety and Health in Construction."*

Labor Relations

The labor relations manager may be responsible for negotiating project labor agreements, may be a member of the AGC committee that negotiates craft agreements with the local building trades, and may be responsible for adjudicating grievances and developing a uniform and fair labor relations policy. In nonunion companies, the duties are similar but without the formal agreements and grievance procedures spelled out in the local contract. Legal representation, either through an in-house representative or through use of an outside law firm, is becoming increasingly important in today's complex environment. Ensuring equal employment opportunity and developing and administrating affirmative action plans in accordance with the law, the contract, or company policies and

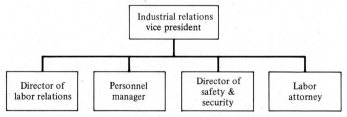

Figure 19-3 Simplified organization chart for home-office industrial relations division.

training individual employees continue to be increasingly important to the progressive firm.

In union construction companies, particularly those engaged in industrial construction, the handling of jurisdictional work assignments with the various trades is especially important. Often a prejob conference is held prior to starting work, to delineate proposed jurisdictional assignments for work to be performed by the contractor's own forces sufficiently in advance to avoid work stoppages or other nonproductive attempts at solutions. The development of a complete file of area practice and a history of work assignments for similar work is an especially important task.

SUMMARY

Industrial relations is important to the progressive contractor in the union, nonunion, and open shop areas of operation. This chapter briefly discussed the hierarchy of organized labor as represented by the building trades affiliated with the AFL-CIO. Open shop, and its leading proponent merit shop, continues to grow, and increasingly, both union and nonunion contractors are engaging in direct competition, to the overall competitive benefit of the industry. Affirmative action programs and equal employment opportunities for ethnic minorities and women have been mandated on federally funded projects and are offering significantly greater opportunities on private projects.

The industry has developed a number of contractor organizations that have proved very successful in certain areas. However, the local contractor operating through the AGC, the large engineer-contractor associated with the NCA, and the merit shop contractor associated with the ABC continue to go their separate ways, with little cooperation at the national level.

The responsibility for developing harmonious and beneficial relationships between the manual, salaried, and clerical work force in the construction industry is generally described as industrial relations. Its challenges in the future will be even more demanding than they are today.

Chapter 20

Current State of the Art
of Professional
Construction Management

Professional construction management is maturing and has now been generally accepted as a distinct method of construction. This chapter will review its evolution over the past decade and its blending with the emerging program management concept. The chapter will also discuss the elimination of adversary relationships among team members and suggest guidelines for some of the more controversial areas where substantial differences of opinion still remain.

A DECADE OF CONSTRUCTION MANAGEMENT

Construction management has been recognized as a distinct method of construction projects for more than a decade. In an Apr. 16, 1981 editorial, the ENR stated: "For more than a dozen years, contracts increasingly have been for construction management (CM). And in recent years, with the emergence of super projects, program management has arrived as a construction service that might include no design, no direct construction responsibility—only overall management of a program of projects. . . .CM's definition is hardly more agreed upon now than when ENR first attempted to pin it down in a May 4, 1972 cover story." Yet principles are generally agreed upon sufficiently to permit the ENR to tabulate a list of the largest CM firms and include a list of 20 of the largest annually beginning in its Apr. 16, 1981 issue.

The AGC and the AIA continue to differ slightly in their approach to construction management. In general, the differences are generally what we would expect, considering that the AGC has approached construction management from the viewpoint of the general contractor, who is often willing to accept some risk, compared to the evolution from the viewpoint of the architect, who was reluctant to accept responsibility or risk in the on-site construction activity. The AGC's handbook *CM for the General Contractor* sets both that organization's guidelines for CM and includes a comparison of the AGC and AIA standard forms of agreement. The definition of professional construction management (PCM), first presented at an ASCE convention in Denver, Colorado, in 1975, followed both the AGC definition and the *Study Committee Report on Construction Management* published by the Consulting Engineer Council in January 1972. The architects' viewpoint was spelled out in *Professional Construction Management and Project Administration* in 1972. An excellent Article summarizing the overall concept entitled *How to Avoid Construction Headaches,* was published in the *Harvard Business Review* in 1973. Other organizations and books have developed similar definitions; a number are in the Bibliography.

These organizations and definitions generally reflect the three-party team concept of owner, architect-engineer, and construction manager. Increasingly, the principles of construction management are being applied by design-constructors using the design-manage form of contractual approach as a part of a turnkey project. Many architects as well as engineer-contractors have broadened their approach to perform both the design and the construction management for an individual project. Consulting engineers are similarly entering the field. The definition of professional construction management and professional construction manager in this book remains middle-of-the-road, generally applicable to include somewhat more narrow definitions published by other, more specialized organizations. If the definition of professional construction management is interpreted to include design and construction departments of a design-constructor or knowledgeable architectural firm, the definition and methods are equally applicable to the design-manage form of construction management, with one organization supplying both the design and construction expertise in a professional association with the owner.

All the above forms, including the new program management concept, are generally included in the broad understanding of the term construction management as used in the industry today.

GUIDELINES FOR SUCCESSFUL PROFESSIONAL CONSTRUCTION MANAGEMENT[1]

Professional construction management involves a three-party team of owner, designer, and construction manager. Its success depends upon elimination of

[1]This section is adapted from D. S. Barrie, "Guidelines for Successful Construction Management," *Journal of the Construction Division,* ASCE, vol. 106 no. C03, September 1980, pp. 237–245.

adversary relationships among team members. Should one or more of the team members introduce concepts or policies detrimental to mutually satisfactory relationships, the concept deteriorates into an adversary situation, with inevitable negative effects upon both the project and individual participants. This section reviews some of the still somewhat controversial and undefined areas of construction management and suggests guidelines to consider if the partnership atmosphere necessary for successful project performance is to be achieved.

Liability and Risk Implications

Many owners, designers, and even some who profess to be construction managers do not fully appreciate the differences in liability and risk implications between PCM and the traditional fixed-price general-contractor method. With certain exceptions, CM is much closer to the traditional negotiated cost-plus-a-fixed-fee general contractor who has settled for a smaller guaranteed profit as a trade-off to potential higher profits through the assumption of risks. For a fixed fee, the construction manager agrees to perform certain professional services for the client. Under this concept, the construction manager should certainly have some liability for actions under his control. However, under the PCM concept, he should not be assigned liability or risk for actions that are clearly outside his control.

It is not feasible to categorically define liabilities and risks that should or should not be assumed by the construction manager. Owners and CM firms are of varying degrees of size and financial strength, have varying degrees of insurance protection, and are willing to assume varying degrees of risk in any venture. Each project is unique, and each agreement for services must contain a meeting of the minds regarding liabilities and risks of each party under the contract.

Generally, the following guidelines are suggested for PCM projects:

1. The construction manager should be responsible for the actions of his key personnel, including reasonable and prudent skill and judgment. Many firms place a limit upon the amount of this liability in the contract.

2. The construction manager should be responsible for his own liability covering specific acts of his employees, including automobile accidents and other public liability and property damage exposure, which normally can be fully insured.

3. CM firms normally try to eliminate any responsibility for consequential damages from the agreement with the owner since current fee sturctures do not permit assumption of risks that could have catastrophic consequences.

4. CM firms have a responsibility under the law regarding the Occupational Safety and Health Act. Whenever a number of contracts are let, there are bound to be overlapping safety requirements that must be handled by the construction manager. On the other hand, the project contractors must also be required to fully assume all their responsibilities.

5. By far the most difficult area of risk associated with the concept involves interfaces between the project contractors and the interfaces with the designer.

In the traditional single-contract fixed-price approach, the general contractor took on the burden of adjudicating subcontractors' conflicting claims and other conflicts resulting from overlapping responsibilities, unclear specifications, or errors or misinterpretation in the bidding documents. Most owners were unaware of these conflicts since their single contract effectively insulated them from these internal squabbles. Architects and engineers were usually called in to adjudicate or interpret conflicting provisions, but in the absence of litigation, they were unaware of the underlying conflicts, many of which were a result of ambiguities or overlapping specifications. A professional construction manager has a higher duty than the general contractor. The professional construction manager, if the concept is to survive, must impartially adjudicate contractor claims regarding both interpretation of the design documents and the area of scope of the bidding documents for which the manager may have primary responsibility. The surviving firms will find a way to accomplish this without alienating the owners who employ them or the designers with whom they have an equally professional relationship.

6. Owners have a similar responsibility. If the concepts are successful, the owner will achieve the overall benefits. Minor errors or omissions by the designer or construction manager are sometimes inevitable in a fast-track program. A contingency of some 3 to 5 percent of the contract award values should take care of minor additions, minor omissions, or ambiguities in the drawings, specifications, or bid packages. This should be pointed out to the owner by both the designer and the construction manager and should be included in project budgets. If in the judgment of the owner, managers or designers do not live up to these standards, the project is a failure and the owner will probably have the ultimate responsibility of accepting the consequences in the absence of litigation. On the other hand, if owners insist upon making an example of minor errors or omissions by team members, the professional concept will obviously not survive.

Labor Relations Considerations

The construction manager is not a general contractor. He must insulate himself from direct agreements with the labor unions, but it is extremely helpful for him to maintain a businesslike and cordial relationship with the local building trades and employer associations. On very large jobs, the owner and/or the construction manager may consider negotiation of a project agreement covering a specific project with the labor unions.

In right-to-work states and open shop areas, there is often a mixture of union and open shop contractors. Local contractors have developed certain practices that tend to minimize or eliminate open conflicts or disruptive practices.

Labor relations considerations from the standpoint of the professional construction manager generally consist of making a careful study of the fundamental relationships between local contractors and the labor unions. Talking with both contractor and labor representatives is essential if an unbiased assessment of the facts is to be developed. The results of this type of investigation can be used in the development of bid packages that follow the normal pattern for the area.

The construction manager can help achieve harmonious labor relations by carefully studying the way business is normally done in the area and then taking this information into account when developing and choosing the contract-bid packages.

Compensation and Fee Structures

Fees for the construction manager are the result of negotiation between the parties and subject to considerable misunderstanding. Professional construction managers apply the skills of workwise general and specialty contractors to a three-party partnership program. Compensation should be comparable to that for the architect, engineer, or other professional.

Professional construction management programs have been successfully performed under a variety of fee structures:

1. Cost reimbursement for home-office and field costs plus a fixed fee (sometimes award fee based upon performance)
2. Fixed fee for home-office services, including profit plus cost reimbursement for all job-site costs
3. Guaranteed maximum cost for CM services under a cost-reimbursement-plus-fixed-fee-type contract
4. Lump sum

Under professional construction management definitions, the construction manager does not guarantee the overall cost of the project or quote a lump sum for the entire project. His profits are therefore minus the risk component that must be included in the traditional lump-sum contract.

Forms of Contract

In the private sector, the professional construction management contract is the subject of negotiation between the owner and the construction manager. In the public sector, several agencies have developed a relatively standard form of contract.

Normal forms of contract for PCM services parallel the compensation and fee structure previously described:

- Cost reimbursement for home-office and field costs plus a fixed fee
- Fixed fee for profit and home-office costs plus cost reimbursement for field costs
- Guaranteed maximum cost for professional services
- Lump sum

Both the AGC and AIA have developed standard forms for CM services. A joint committee, with representation from the Consulting Engineers Council and the Project Management Institute, once explored the feasibility of a joint agreement; to date, such an all-encompassing document has not emerged.

Many private owners and CM firms have developed their own standard contracts that are used with appropriate modifications to fit the objectives and negotiating skills of the parties.

Organizational Concepts

Organization of a particular project will depend upon many variables. Planning, estimating, procurement, contract award, and other services may be performed in the home office. On the other hand, some or all of these services may be better performed at the job site, depending upon individual project considerations. Obviously, the choice of the field project manager and the staff may depend upon the organizational concepts involved.

The emerging PCM concept is an extension of the old functional organization for traditional projects. The concept substitutes a CM firm for the general contractor under a nonadversary position. Thus the professional concept of a three-party team of owner-designer-construction manager has now been recognized as competition not only to the traditional single-contract concept but to the concept of design-construction, engineer-contractor, or turnkey.

Licensing Considerations

The question of licensing is being reviewed in almost every state. Should we have a separate licensing system for construction managers? Should licenses be required for architects, engineers, or general contractors? Most states license architects, engineers, and general and specialty contractors. Professional construction managers require some of the skills of each of the building team professionals. How could CM firms be licensed? Who would take the examination? Who would define CM in the face of industry inability to agree upon other than overall conceptual standards?

Since CM contracts are flexible, it is difficult to determine which licenses, if any, may be required. The prudent construction manager will obtain a general contractor's license when appropriate or unclear. He may also be wise to obtain an engineering license, depending upon his duties under the contract and the individual laws of the state.

In the absence of a universally accepted definition of construction management, separate licensing of construction managers is neither feasible nor desirable at present.

Owner Responsibilities

Some owners are never wrong. They hire an architect or an engineer, and a construction manager, and then place a number of constraints upon the authority of both parties. When things go wrong, either the construction manager or the designer must suffer the consequences.

Other owners are more tolerant and perceptive. They recognize that the PCM concept involves a three-party team in which the owner as well as the construction manager and designer have definite responsibilities. Even the owner can occasionally make a mistake. When the owner reserves certain functions for himself, he should be accountable to the team for performance.

No concept can prosper and grow when inefficiency is tolerated or excused. Designers and construction managers who cannot put together successful projects under the professional concept will not survive in the competitive environment. One of the strongest recommendations for a CM approach is repeat business from clients.

Designer Responsibilities

Association under a three-party team concept is a new experience for many architects and engineers. The professional construction manager has taken over some of the traditional duties previously carried out by the designer. On the other hand, the concept has released the designer from some of the responsibilities over which he had little or no control.

Many traditional designers (architects and engineers) are somewhat like general contractors. Some are so wrapped up in the traditional adversary position that they cannot see that the emerging professional concepts offer an opportunity for both to compete with the turnkey or design-construction approach which has gained stature in the past several decades. However, the partnership program requires a mutually cooperative environment.

The construction manager must play fair with the designer. The designer must reciprocate and develop the ability to be cooperative and communicate with the construction manager in a manner that does not prejudice their individual responsibilities to the owner.

Designers who try to participate with construction managers in a three-party-team concept but who look upon the construction manager as an adversary will find that the concepts do not work. Construction managers who do not recognize the inherent professional design responsibilities of the architect or engineer or who criticize the designer to the owner will also find difficulty in achieving successful projects.

Construction Manager Qualifications and Responsibilities

The CM firm must live up to its responsibilities. First it must have the proper qualifications:

- An understanding of the workings of a design office, fundamental engineering principles, and appreciation of the role of the designer
- Skills of a successful general contractor, including the ability to estimate the cost of work and handle bid-package preparation, prequalification of contractors, bid evaluation, contract award and administration, and overall management of the construction program
- Skills and estimating ability for electrical and mechanical work items and specialties that old-line general contractors traditionally subcontracted
- Most importantly, the ability to visualize the overall objectives of the program and act as the leader of the three-party team in all matters relating to construction, in an effort to achieve these objectives

The construction manager must carry out his responsibility to the other team members. In addition, he has a responsibility to the labor unions, to the overall industry, and to the general and specialty contractors operating in the area. He must faithfully try to achieve the owner's objectives while preserving a fair and businesslike relationship with project contractors, public agencies, and others.

Some general contractors continue to deprecate the CM firms, identifying them with "brokers" who have traditionally subcontracted all the work while engaging in "bid shopping" or other questionable practices. The professional construction manager understands this criticism and continues to conduct himself above even the appearance of suspicion.

SUMMARY

The construction management concept has had both successes and failures in the past decade. It is maturing and is generally accepted as another distinct option for completing construction projects. Detail definitions differ among individual groups, but an overall consensus regarding the general principles is beginning to emerge. The established construction manager and the emerging program manager must be prepared to offer a sizable list of services. Such services must be framed to take into account normal industry operating methods and practices in the area. Adversary relationships must be avoided if a successful professional program is to be achieved. Suggested guidelines for handling some of the still undefined and somewhat controversial aspects of construction management have been set forth, to encourage the partnership atmosphere necessary for successful project performance.

Description of the
Example Project

The example project warehouse represents a simplified version of an actual project designed by Leo Rosenthal, A.I.A., a practicing Denver architect, and constructed using the professional construction management concept. Figure 4-2 in Chapter 4 shows photographs from a similar project which was featured in the *Kaiser Builder*, August 1972. The following descriptive information is included in this section:

1. Specification Summary

An outline of the specifications which are required for each bid package has been developed in summary format to illustrate the general nature of the technical specifications required for each bid package.

2. Fair-Cost Estimates

Fair-cost estimates for each of the 10 bid packages have been prepared from the drawings and specifications.

3. Engineering Drawings

The following drawings were required for the project:

Drawing SI-1   Plot Plan and Utility Plan
Drawing A-1   Foundation and Floor Plans, and Finish Schedule
Drawing A-2   Roof Framing, Plan and Details
Drawing A-3   Elevation and Roof Plan
Drawing PH-1 Plumbing and Heating Plan
Drawing E-1   Electrical Plan

The architect has generously consented to make available full-size reproducible tracings or full-size prints to readers or educational institutions at prevailing reproduction and shipping prices. Inquiries should be addressed directly to the architect:

> Leo Rosenthal, A.I.A.
> 620 Sherman
> Denver, Colorado 80203

SPECIFICATION SUMMARY
CONSTRUCTION MANAGEMENT PROGRAM
MOUNTAINTOWN WAREHOUSE

1. Site Earthwork and Fencing

1.01 General
1.02 Scope
1.03 Related Work Not Included
1.04 Drawings and Site Examination
1.05 Removal of Vegetation and Top Soil
1.06 General Cut
1.07 Rejected Material
1.08 Scarifying and Recompaction
1.09 Fill
1.10 Grading at Railroad Tracks
1.11 Maintenance of Finish Grades
1.12 Dust Control
1.13 Inspection and Tests
1.14 Fencing and Gates

2. Structural and Yard Concrete

2.01 General
2.02 Scope
2.03 Related Work Not Included
2.04 Structural Excavation
2.05 Backfill and Fine Grading
2.06 Materials
2.07 Forms and Appurtenances
2.08 Metal Reinforcement
2.09 Embedded Items
2.10 Concrete Proportions and Consistency
2.11 Mixing and Placing of Concrete
2.12 Yard Concrete Paving
2.13 Placing and Finishing Yard Concrete
2.14 Expansion and Contraction Joints
2.15 Grouting and Dry Pack
2.16 Miscellaneous Work
2.17 Inspection and Tests

3. Interior Special Slabs

3.01 General

FAIR-COST ESTIMATE SUMMARY
MOUNTAINTOWN WAREHOUSE

Contract Package	Labor	Material	Markup	Total
1. Site earthwork	44,000	153,200	23,600	220,800
2. Structural & yard concrete	231,800	349,000	69,600	650,400
3. Special floors	219,800	258,800	57,400	536,000
4. Structural steel	113,000	686,000	95,800	894,800
5. Precast walls	79,200	418,200	59,600	457,000
6. Plumbing & HVAC	127,600	313,600	53,000	494,200
7. Fire protection	96,600	201,000	35,600	333,200
8. Electrical	104,000	250,000	42,000	396,000
9. Roofing	94,400	123,600	26,000	244,000
10. Building finish	255,000	310,600	68,000	633,600
Total	1,365,400	3,064,000	530,600	4,960,000

	Labor hours	Hours, sq.ft.	Cost, sq.ft.
1. Site earthwork	1,470	.0097	1.46
2. Structural & yard concrete	7,730	.0510	4.30
3. Special floors	7,330	.0484	3.54
4. Structural steel	3,770	.0249	5.90
5. Precast walls	2,640	.0174	3.68
6. Plumbing & HVAC	4,250	.0280	3.26
7. Fire protection	3,220	.0212	2.20
8. Electrical	3,470	.0229	2.62
9. Roofing	3,150	.0208	1.60
10. Building finish	8,470	.0559	4.18
Total	45,500	.3002	32.74

Job duration	8 months
Total manpower	45,500 hours
Total manpower	5,688 man-days
Total manpower	268 man-months
Average manpower	34 men
Estimated peak	68 men
Average labor cost	$30.00/hour (including taxes, ins., and fringes)

Title <u>Mountaintown Warehouse</u>

Client <u>Easyway</u>   Location <u>M'tntown WA</u>   Date <u>12-23-76</u>

Subject <u>Fair Cost Estimate Summary</u>   By <u>E.P.M.</u>

Description	Quantity	Unit cost Labor	Unit cost Mat'l	Labor	Material	Total
Site Earthwork						
Site Grading	15000 CY	1.00	2.40	15000	36000	
Compacted Building Fill	25000 CY	.60	3.00	15000	75000	
Fencing	4680 LF	3.00	9.00	14000	42200	
Direct Cost	1470 HR			44000	153.200	197200
Overhead & Fee @ 12%						23.600
Total Construction Cost						220800
Structural & Yard Concrete						
Structural Excav & Backfill	5000 CY	8.00	6.00	40000	30000	
Hand Excavation	250 CY	20.00		5000	–	
Fine Grade for Yard Paving	159000 SF	.02	.04	3180	6360	
Concrete 3000–Yard Paving	3850 CY	14.00	52.00	53900	200200	
–Bldg Fdns	440 CY	20.00	52.00	8800	22880	
–Misc	60 CY	50.00	52.00	3000	3120	
Forms–Edge for Paving	1000 SF	2.00	.80	2000	800	
–Bldg Fdns	11300 SF	3.00	1.00	33900	11300	
–Misc	1700 SF	4.00	1.00	6800	1700	
Reinforcing Steel-Bldg	30000 LBS	.20	.40	6000	12000	
Grout at Base of Wall Panels	500 CF	4.00	4.00	2000	2000	
Set Anchor Bolts	432 EA	8.00	2.00	3460	860	
Grout Base Plates	108 EA	20.00	6.00	2160	660	
Paving–Expansion Joint "A"	2500 LF	2.00	3.20	5000	8000	
–Construction Jt. "B"	3440 LF	.40	.60	1380	2060	
–Contraction Jt. "C"	5960 LF	1.00	.40	5960	2380	
–Edge Type "D"	1280 LF	.40	.56	520	720	
Paving Slab Finish	159000 SF	.30	.04	47700	6360	
6" ϕ Pipe Guards @ Islands	10 EA	80.00	120.00	800	1200	
Embedded Rail in R.R. Bumper	30 LF	8.00	16.00	240	480	
Equipment Usage–Concrete	4350 CY	–	8.00		34800	
–Forms	14000 SF	–	.08		1120	
Direct Cost	7730 HR			231800	349000	580800
Overhead & Fee @ 12%						69600
Total Construction Cost						650400

Description	Quantity	Unit cost Labor	Unit cost Mat'l	Labor	Material	Total
Interior Special Slabs						
Base Slab 5¼" 3000#	2500 CY	20.00	52.00	50000	130000	
Fill Blockouts at Columns	20 CY	30.00	52.00	600	1040	
Ramp Slab	8 CY	30.00	52.00	240	420	
12" Curbs at O.H. Doors	12 CY	60.00	52.00	720	620	
Forms for Blockouts	730 SF	4.00	1.00	2920	720	
Reinforcing Steel	140000 LBS	.20	.40	28000	56000	
Screed & Cure Base Slab	144500 SF	.16	.04	23120	5780	
Float & Cure Ramp Slab	300 SF	.30	.04	100	20	
Topping on Base Slab ¾"	144500 SF	.60	.20	86700	28900	
Const. & Contraction Joints	13600 LF	.80	.20	10880	2720	
Greased Dowels #5	4700 EA	.40	.50	1880	2360	
Premoulded Expansion Jt. ½" × 6"	2000 LF	.40	.40	800	800	
Curbs–4" × 18"	1000 LF	6.00	8.00	6000	8000	
–12" × 12"	60 LF	6.00	10.00	360	600	
R.R. Dock Angle 3 × 3 × $\frac{5}{16}$	2500 LF	.90	.50	2240	1260	
Channel at Dock Doors 10[15.3	4000 LBS	.80	.50	3200	2000	
Steel Plate Curb Enclosures	2900 LBS	.70	.80	2040	2320	
Equipment Usage	2540 CY	–	6.00	–	15240	
Direct Cost	7330 HR			219800	258800	478600
Overhead & Fee @ 12%						57400
Total Construction Cost						536000
Structural Steel & Deck						
Structural Steel	280 Ton	20000	135000	56000	378000	
Roof Joists & Bridging	200 Ton	12000	38000	24000	176000	
Metal Deck 1½; 22 Ga.	165000 SF	.20	.80	33000	132000	
Direct Cost	3770 HR			113000	686000	799000
Overhead & Fee @ 12%						95800
Total Construction Cost						894800
Precast Double Tees						
Prestressed ᴨ's 22" + 4"	44300 SF	1.20	6.50	53160	288000	
Prestressed ᴨ's 16" + 5"	21700 SF	1.20	6.00	26040	130200	
Direct Cost	2640 HR			79200	418200	497400
Overhead & Fee @ 12%						59600
Total Construction Cost						557000

Description	Quantity	Unit cost Labor	Unit cost Mat'l	Labor	Material	Total
Plumbing, Heating, Mechanical						
Plumbing						
Roof & Floor Drainage	165000 SF	.12	.32	19800	52800	
Fixtures	30 EA	500.00	1500.00	15000	45000	
Direct Cost	1160 HR			34800	97800	132600
Sheet Metal						
Cap Flashing	2200 LF	2.00	3.00	4400	6600	
Surface Flashing & Reglet	600 LF	6.00	5.00	3600	3000	
Roof Expansion Joint	350 LF	20.00	20.00	7000	7000	
Roof Hatches	49 EA	200.00	1000.00	9800	49000	
Misc. Flashing	Allow	–		5000	10000	
Direct Cost	990 HR			29800	75600	105400
Heating						
Piping Av. Size = $2\frac{1}{2}''$	2200 LF	12.00	20.00	26400	44000	
Unit Heaters-Gas	33 EA	100.00	920.00	3300	30360	
Unit Heater Supports	33 SFS	40.00	100.00	1320	3300	
Thermostats	33 EA	40.00	80.00	1320	2640	
Gas Meter Pit	1 EA	–	–	720	1100	
Roof Vents	Allow	–	–	940	6000	
Direct Cost	1130 HR			34000	87400	121400
Yard Underground						
Storm Sewers– 6"	500 LF	5.00	8.00	2500	4000	
8"	320 LF	6.00	9.00	1920	2880	
10"	780 LF	8.00	12.00	6240	9360	
12"	140 LF	9.00	14.00	1260	1960	
15"	200 LF	10.00	18.00	2000	3600	
18"	170 LF	12.00	24.00	2040	4080	
21"	130 LF	14.00	30.00	1820	3900	
Sanitary Sewers–4"	80 LF	8.00	8.00	640	640	
6"	370 LF	8.00	10.00	2960	3700	
Domestic Water–$\frac{3}{4}''$	160 LF	8.00	8.00	1280	1280	
2"	40 LF	12.00	12.00	480	480	
Manholes & Catch Basins	9 EA	650.00	1880.00	5860	16920	
Direct Cost	970 HR			29000	52800	81800
Total Direct Cost	4250 HR			127600	313600	441200
Overhead & Fee @ 12%						53000
Total Construction Cost						494200
Fire Protection						
Sprinkler System	150000 SF	.50	1.10	75000	165000	
Fire Loop–10" ϕ	1800 LF	12.00	20.00	21600	36000	
Direct Cost	3220 HR			96600	201000	297600
Overhead & Fee @ 12%						35600
Total Construction Cost						333200

		Unit cost				
Description	**Quantity**	**Labor**	**Mat'l**	**Labor**	**Material**	**Total**
Electrical						
Site Work	Allow	–	–	7000	9000	
Distribution	Allow	–	–	17000	50000	
Lighting & Misc Power	Allow	–	–	66000	166000	
Motors & Controls	Allow	–	–	8400	14200	
Misc Systems	Allow	–	–	5600	10800	
Direct Cost	3470 HR			104000	250000	354000
Overhead & Fee @ 12%						42000
Total Construction Cost						396000
Roofing						
Built-up Roofing	165000 SF	.36	.44	59400	72600	
1″ Rigid Insulation	165000 SF	.20	.30	33000	49500	
4″ Fibre Csnt.	4000 LF	.50	.38	2000	1500	
Direct Cost	3150 HR			94400	123600	218000
Overhead & Fee @ 12%						26000
Total Construction Cost						244000
Building Finish						
Miscellaneous Metals						
Furnish only Angles	9600	–	1.00	–	9600	
Anchors	500	–	1.20	–	600	
Exp. Shields	50	–	4.00	–	200	
Tube Steel	500	–	2.40	–	1200	
Pipe Rail	20 LF	–	30.00	–	600	
Nosings	100 LF	–	10.00	–	1000	
Furn. & Install Angles	8400	.80	1.00	6720	8400	
Pipe Guards	4500	.80	1.00	3600	4500	
Plates	12000	1.20	1.00	14400	12000	
Railing	16 LF	18.00	44.00	280	700	
Direct Cost	830 HR			25000	38800	63800
Carpentry & Millwork						
Interior Structures Roof Fmg.	3200 bm	1.00	1.00	3200	3200	
Plywood ¾″	2000 SF	.40	1.20	800	2400	
Roof Curbs, Nailers	10000 bm	1.80	1.20	18000	12000	
Redwood Facia	600 bm	1.20	1.40	720	840	
Benches	200 bm	1.00	2.00	200	400	
Service Counters	2 EA	600.00	2000.00	1200	4000	
Rough Hardware	Allow			80	760	
Direct Cost	810 HR			24200	23600	47800
Doors & Windows						
Ind. Steel Doors, Fmes. Hdwe.						
Sing.	17 EA	200.00	500.00	3400	8500	
Dble.	1 PR	400.00	800.00	400	800	
Vert. Lift Steel Drs. 7′-0 × 7′-6	34 EA	200.00	1400.00	6800	47600	
Rolling Stl. "B" Lab. N.O.						
17′-0 × 22′-6	1 EA	–	–	2000	12100	
Window Sash	500 SF	4.00	6.00	2000	3000	
Direct Cost	490 HR			14600	72000	86600

Description	Quantity	Unit cost		Labor	Material	Total
		Labor	Mat'l			
Building Finish, cont'd						
Masonry						
Concrete Block–8″	5500 EA	3.00	.80	16500	4400	
–6″	400 EA	2.80	.70	1120	280	
–4″	1100 EA	2.60	.60	2860	660	
Scaffolding	4200 SF	.60	.60	2520	2520	
Clean Down	8100 SF	.24	.10	1940	800	
Mortar	10 CY	–	60.00	–	600	
Durawal	2000 LF	.20	.20	400	400	
Reinforcing Steel	4200 LB	.30	.40	1260	1680	
Set Door Frames	13 EA	100.00	20.00	1300	260	
Set Tubes	500 EA	1.20	–	600	–	
Supplies, Misc.	Allow	–	–	100	800	
Direct Cost	950 HR			28600	12400	41000
Painting						
Structural Steel	480 Tons	100.00	40.00	48000	19200	
Doors	5000 SF	.80	.60	4000	3000	
Office & Toilet Areas	3700 SF	1.00	.60	3700	2220	
Pipe Coding	Allow	–	–	10000	4000	
Exterior Mechanical Units	Allow	–	–	12000	4100	
Misc. Iron not Galvanized	Allow	–	–	6500	2080	
Direct Cost	2810 HR			84200	34600	118800
Metal Partitions & Screens						
Toilet Partitions	13 EA	100.00	500.00	1300	6500	
Urinal Screens	7 EA	100.00	190.00	700	1300	
Direct Cost	70 HR			2000	7800	9800
Glass & Glazing						
Windows & Doors	600 SF	3.00	2.00	1800	1200	
Mirrors W/St./Stl. Fmes.	30 SF	6.60	20.00	200	600	
Pass Window Incl. Track Ass'y	1 EA	–	–	400	1000	
Misc. Glazing Cleaning	Allow			1400	1000	
	130 HR			3800	3800	7600
Building Finish, cont'd.						
Acoustical Treatment						
Gypsum Board ½″	3200 SF	.40	.60	1280	1920	
Ac. Tile on Gyp. Bd.	1500 SF	.60	1.40	900	2100	
Trim at Ceiling	400 LF	–	–	420	580	
Direct Cost	90 HR			2600	4600	7200
Caulking						
Double II Panels–Both Sides	15000 LF	2.00	1.40	30000	21000	
Doors & Windows in Ext. Walls	700 LF	2.00	2.00	1400	1400	
Direct Cost	1050 HR			31400	22400	53800

Description	Quantity	Unit cost Labor	Unit cost Mat'l	Labor	Material	Total
Building Finish, cont'd.						
Furnishings & Equipment						
Adjustable Dock Ramps	3 EA	1000.00	4400.00	3000	13200	
Permanent Dock Boards	31 EA	200.00	400.00	6200	12400	
Door Seals	34 EA	600.00	1200.00	20400	40800	
Jib Crane	1 EA	–	–	1000	10000	
Double Post Lift	1 EA	–	–	600	3000	
Direct Cost	1040 HR			31200	79400	110600
Bituminous Paving						
Base Course 4″ Gravel	80 CY	10.00	12.60	800	1000	
Paving 2″	60 Ton	10.00	30.00	600	1800	
Direct Cost	50 HR			1400	2800	4200
Guard House	200 HR	–	–	6000	8400	14400
Total Building Finish	8470 HR			255000	310600	565600
Overhead & Fill @ 12%						68000
Total Construction Cost–Building Finish						633600

Mountaintown Warehouse Milestone CPM

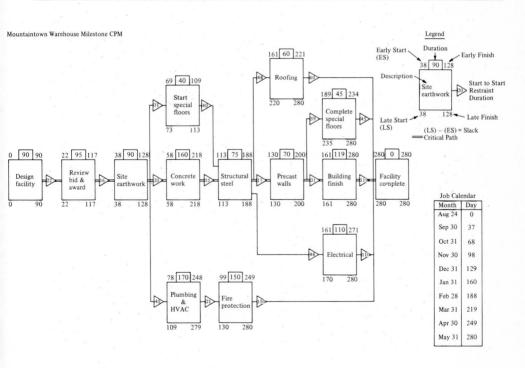

Appendix B

Example Bid Package

The example site earthwork bid package has been prepared, incorporating plans and specifications developed by the architect. The preparation of bid packages for a professional construction management program must be a joint effort involving all team members, owner, architect, and construction manager. One of the parties must be delegated the responsibility for preparation of the basic package. A careful review should be performed by the other parties. The example bid package contains the following information:

SITE EARTHWORK AND FENCING

I   Invitation to Bid
II   Bid Form (including Bid Breakdown)
III   Construction Contract (Courtesy of The American Institute of Architects)
IV   General Conditions (Courtesy of The American Institute of Architects)
V   Special Conditions (including Supplemental Provisions)
VI   Simplified Specifications, Addendums, and Drawings
VII   Owner-furnished Items
VIII   Construction Schedule

I INVITATION TO BID

September 10, 198_

EASYWAY FOOD COMPANY
DESIGN AND CONSTRUCTION DEPARTMENT
200 MADISON STREET
MOUNTAINTOWN, WESTAMERICA 99999

Gentlemen:

Re: INVITATION TO BID
NO. 16

We are pleased to enclose one set of plans and specifications covering Site Earthwork and Fencing for the Dry Storage Warehouse to be constructed in Mountaintown, West America.

Bids will be received until 2:00 P.M., September 22, 1976, at our main office at the above address. All bids shall be binding for 30 days thereafter. Bidders are invited to send one representative to a bid opening which will be conducted at the above specified time.

While we are asking all bidders to base their bids in accordance with the Owner's schedule, alternate completion dates will be given consideration based upon our evaluation of the advantages or disadvantages of the proposed schedule.

Attached hereto is the following information:
1. Three copies each of our Bid Form.
2. Two copies of the Construction Contract including Exhibit A and attachments listed therein.

Two copies of the executed Bid Form are to be submitted with your bid. All bids are requested to be itemized as noted on the Bid Form.

If you are the successful bidder, it will be necessary for you to furnish a 100% Payment and Performance Bond in accordance with "The Standard Form of Bond" latest edition, copyrighted by the American Institute of Architects and issued by a Surety Company satisfactory to Owner. You will also be expected to execute a contract in the form included with the attached documents.

Owner reserves the right to reject any and all proposals or to waive irregularities therein. Owner reserves the right to evaluate each and every proposal in his absolute discretion and to accept any particular proposal even though the price or completion date, or both, may not be as favorable as some other proposal.

Bidders requesting additional information are advised to address their inquiries to Construction Management and Control, Inc., Attention: Mr. O. Hanson, telephone number (000) 123-4567.

EASYWAY FOOD COMPANY

By Peter J. Cleaveland
Manager, Design and Construction
Department

II Bid Form (including Bid Breakdown)

BID FORM

DATE _____ September 10 _____
INVITATION TO BID: 16
SITE EARTHWORK AND FENCING
DRY STORAGE WAREHOUSE
MOUNTAINTOWN, WESTAMERICA

TO: EASYWAY FOOD COMPANY
    Design and Construction Department
    200 Madison Street
    Mountaintown, West America   99999

Gentlemen:
Having examined the plans and specifications including addendas Nos. _____
_____ and having familiarized ourselves with the job and site
conditions, the undersigned does hereby tender the following bids for construction work at the Mountain Distribution Center, Mountaintown, West America, in
accordance with invitation to Bid No. 16 and all attachments thereto.

Our firm price bid is in the amount of _____
_____ Dollars ($_____) which price includes the cost of the Perform-
ance Bond. The undersigned further agrees to complete the work in _____
calendar days after date specified in the Notice to Proceed with the work.

Attached hereto is a list of subcontractors whom we propose to use for those
branches of work exceeding $1,000 in contract cost.

We submit the following proposals for alternates and/or substitutions:

Alternate Bid A $ Add_____   Deduct_____

    Describe _____

    _____

Alternate Bid B $ Add_____   Deduct_____

    Describe _____

    _____

Our total firm price bid is itemized in component parts as follows:

    Site Grading   _____

    Imported Borrow   _____

    Fencing   _____

    Performance Bond   _____

        Total Firm Price Bid $_____

The undersigned agrees to execute the Construction Contract Form provided with
the Invitation to Bid. The undersigned certifies that he is:

1. A Corporation incorporated in the State of _____.-

2. A Partnership consisting of the following partners _____

_____

_____.-

3. An individual whose name is _____.

The foregoing offer shall be binding upon the undersigned until_____

_____.

_____

                                                      Contractor

_____   _____

Signed by   Date

_____

Title

_____

Address

_____

_____

Telephone Number

_____

Contractors License No.   State

EXHIBIT A

Attached to and a part of Agreement No. 16 are contract documents referred to in Article 6 the Contract.

In general the work consists of all site earthwork and fencing as described in the attached plans and specifications for the Dry Storage Warehouse located in Mountaintown, WestAmerica.

Drawings and specifications as set forth in Article 6 Contract Documents are enumerated and included as follows:

A. Invitation to Bid
B. Bid Form
C. General Conditions
D. Special Conditions
E. Technical Specifications
   1. Section E-1, Site Grading and Compaction
   2. Section E-2, Fencing and Gates
F. Drawings

Number	Rev. No.	Date
SI-1	0	9-1-8_
A-1	0	9-1-8_

G. Owner-Furnished Items
H. Owner's Construction Schedule

THE AMERICAN INSTITUTE OF ARCHITECTS

AIA DOCUMENT
SEPT. 1963 ED.   A107

THE STANDARD FORM OF AGREEMENT
BETWEEN OWNER AND CONTRACTOR

THE AIA SHORT FORM CONTRACT FOR

SMALL CONSTRUCTION CONTRACTS

WHERE THE BASIS OF PAYMENT IS A

STIPULATED SUM

FOR OTHER CONTRACTS THE AIA ISSUES THE STANDARD FORMS OF OWNER-CONTRACTOR AGREEMENTS AND THE STANDARD GENERAL CONDITIONS FOR THE CONSTRUCTION OF BUILDINGS FOR USE IN CONNECTION THEREWITH

THIS AGREEMENT

made the   day of   in the year Nineteen Hundred and

BY AND BETWEEN

hereinafter called the Owner, and

hereinafter called the Contractor.

WITNESSETH,

That the Owner and the Contractor, for the considerations hereinafter named agree as follows:

ARTICLE 1. SCOPE OF THE WORK—
The Contractor shall furnish all of the material and perform all of the work for

as shown on the Drawings and described in the Specifications entitled

prepared by   Architect
all in accordance with the terms of the Contract Documents.

ARTICLE 2. TIME OF COMPLETION—The work shall be commenced and completed as follows:

ARTICLE 3. CONTRACT SUM—The Owner shall pay the Contractor for the performance of the Contract subject to the additions and deductions provided therein in current funds, the sum of

dollars. ($)

ARTICLE 4. PROGRESS PAYMENTS—The Owner shall make payments on account of the contract, upon requisition by the Contractor, as follows:

ARTICLE 5. ACCEPTANCE AND FINAL PAYMENT—Final payment shall be due   days after completion of the work, provided the contract be then fully performed, subject to the provisions of Article 16 of the General Conditions.

ARTICLE 6. CONTRACT DOCUMENTS—Contract Documents are as noted in Article 1 of the General Conditions. The following is an enumeration of the drawings and specifications:

GENERAL CONDITIONS

ARTICLE 1. CONTRACT DOCUMENTS

The contract includes the AGREEMENT and its GENERAL CONDITIONS, the DRAWINGS, and the SPECIFICATIONS. Two or more copies of each, as required, shall be signed by both parties and one signed copy of each retained by each party.

The intent of these documents is to include all labor, materials, appliances and services of every kind necessary for the proper execution of the work, and the terms and conditions of payment therefor.

The documents are to be considered as one, and whatever is called for by any one of the documents shall be as binding as if called for by all.

ARTICLE 2. SAMPLES

The Contractor shall furnish for approval all samples as directed. The work shall be in accordance with approved samples.

ARTICLE 3. MATERIALS, APPLIANCES, EMPLOYEES

Except as otherwise noted, the Contractor shall provide and pay for all materials, labor, tools, water, power and other items necessary to complete the work.

Unless otherwise specified, all materials shall be new, and both workmanship and materials shall be of good quality.

All workmen and sub-contractors shall be skilled in their trades.

ARTICLE 4. ROYALTIES AND PATENTS

The Contractor shall pay all royalties and license fees. He shall defend all suits or claims for infringement of any patent rights and shall save the Owner harmless from loss on account thereof.

ARTICLE 5. SURVEYS, PERMITS, AND REGULATIONS

The Owner shall furnish all surveys unless otherwise specified. Permits and licenses necessary for the prosecution of the work shall be secured and paid for by the Contractor. Easements for permanent structures or permanent changes in existing facilities shall be secured and paid for by the Owner, unless otherwise specified. The Contractor shall comply with all laws and regulations bearing on the conduct of the work and shall notify the Owner if the drawings and specifications are at variance therewith.

ARTICLE 6. PROTECTION OF WORK, PROPERTY, AND PERSONS

The Contractor shall adequately protect the work, adjacent property and the public and shall be responsible for any damage or injury due to his act or neglect.

ARTICLE 7. ACCESS TO WORK

The Contractor shall permit and facilitate observation of the work by the Owner and his agents and public authorities at all times.

ARTICLE 8. CHANGES IN THE WORK

The Owner may order changes in the work, the Contract Sum being adjusted accordingly. All such orders and adjustments shall be in writing. Claims by the Contractor for extra cost must be made in writing before executing the work involved.

ARTICLE 9. CORRECTION OF WORK

The Contractor shall re-execute any work that fails to conform to the requirements of the contract and that appears during the progress of the work, and shall remedy any defects due to faulty materials or workmanship which appear within a period of one year from the date of completion of the contract. The provisions of this article apply to work done by subcontractors as well as to work done by direct employees of the Contractor.

ARTICLE 10. OWNER'S RIGHT TO TERMINATE THE CONTRACT

Should the Contractor neglect to prosecute the work properly, or fail to perform any provision of the contract, the Owner, after seven days' written notice to the Contractor, and his surety if any may, without prejudice to any other remedy he may have, make good the deficiencies and may deduct the cost thereof from the payment then or thereafter due the contractor or, at his option, may terminate the contract and take possession of all materials, tools, and appliances and finish the work by such means as he sees fit, and if the unpaid balance of the contract price exceeds the expense of finishing the work, such excess shall be paid to the Contractor, but if such expense exceeds such unpaid balance, the Contractor shall pay the difference to the Owner.

ARTICLE 11. CONTRACTOR'S RIGHT TO TERMINATE CONTRACT

Should the work be stopped by any public authority for a period of thirty days or more, through no fault of the Contractor, or should the work be stopped through act or neglect of the Owner for a period of seven days, or should the Owner fail to pay the Contractor any payment within seven days after it is due, then the Contractor upon seven days' written notice to the Owner, may stop work or terminate the contract and recover from the Owner payment for all work executed and any loss sustained and reasonable profit and damages.

ARTICLE 12. PAYMENTS

Payments shall be made as provided in the Agreement. The making and acceptance of the final payment shall constitute a waiver of all claims by the Owner, other than those arising from unsettled liens or from faulty work appearing thereafter, as provided for in Article 9, and of all claims by the Contractor except any previously made and still unsettled. Payments otherwise due may be withheld on account of defective work not remedied, liens filed, damage by the Contractor to others not adjusted, or failure to make payments properly to subcontractors or for material or labor.

ARTICLE 13. CONTRACTOR'S LIABILITY INSURANCE

The Contractor shall maintain such insurance as will protect him from claims under workmen's compensation acts and other employee benefits acts, from claims for damages because of bodily injury, including death, and from claims for damages to property which may arise both out of and during operations under this contract, whether such operations be by himself or by any subcontractor or anyone directly or indirectly employed by either of them. This insurance shall be written for not less than any limits of liability specified as part of this contract. Certificates of such insurance shall be filed with the Owner and architect.

ARTICLE 14. OWNER'S LIABILITY INSURANCE

The Owner shall be responsible for and at his option may maintain such insurance as will protect him from his contingent liability to others for damages because of bodily injury, including death, which may arise from operations under this contract, and any other liability for damages which the Contractor is required to insure under any provision of this contract.

ARTICLE 15. FIRE-INSURANCE WITH EXTENDED COVERAGE

The Owner shall effect and maintain fire insurance with extended coverage upon the entire structure on which the work of this contract is to be done to one hundred per cent of the insurable value thereof, including items of labor and materials connected therewith whether in or adjacent to the structure insured, materials in place or to be used as part of the permanent construction including surplus materials, shanties, protective fences, bridges, temporary structures, miscellaneous materials and supplies incident to the work, and such scaffoldings, stagings, towers, forms, and equip-

OWNER-CONTRACTOR AGREEMENT   FOUR PAGES

ment as are not owned or rented by the contractor, the cost of which is included in the cost of the work. EXCLUSIONS: The insurance does not cover any tools owned by mechanics, any tools, equipment, scaffolding, staging, towers, and forms owned or rented by the Contractor, the capital value of which is not included in the cost of the work, or any cook shanties, bunk houses or other structures erected for housing the workmen. The loss, if any, is to be made adjustable with and payable to the Owner as Trustee for the insureds and contractors and subcontractors as their interests may appear, except in such cases as may require payment of all or a proportion of said insurance to be made to a mortgagee as his interests may appear.

Certificates of such insurance shall be filed with the Contractor if he so requires. If the Owner fails to effect or maintain insurance as above and so notifies the Contractor, the Contractor may insure his own interests and that of the subcontractors and charge the cost thereof to the Owner. If the Contractor is damaged by failure of the Owner to maintain such insurance or to so notify the Contractor, he may recover as stipulated in the contract for recovery of damages. If other special insurance not herein provided for is required by the Contractor, the Owner shall effect such insurance at the Contractor's expense by appropriate riders to his fire insurance policy. The Owner, Contractor, and all subcontractors waive all rights, each against the others, for damages caused by fire or other perils covered by insurance provided for under the terms of this article except such rights as they may have to the proceeds of insurance held by the Owner as Trustee.

The Owner shall be responsible for and at his option may insure against loss of use of his existing property, due to fire or otherwise, however caused.

If required in writing by any party in interest, the Owner as Trustee shall, upon the occurrence of loss, give bond for the proper performance of his duties. He shall deposit any money received from insurance in an account separate from all his other funds and he shall distribute it in accordance with such agreement as the parties in interest may reach or under an award of arbitrators appointed, one by the Owner, another by joint action of the other parties in interest, all other procedure being as provided elsewhere in the contract for arbitration. If after loss no special agreement is made, replacement of injured work shall be ordered and executed as provided for changes in the work.

The Trustee shall have power to adjust and settle any loss with the insurers unless one of the Contractors interested shall object in writing within three working days of the occurrence of loss, and thereupon arbitrators shall be chosen as above. The Trustee shall in that case make settlement with the insurers in accordance with the directions of such arbitrators, who shall also, if distribution by arbitration is required, direct such distribution.

ARTICLE 16. LIENS

The final payment shall not be due until the Contractor has delivered to the Owner a complete release of all liens arising out of this contract, or receipts in full covering all labor and materials for which a lien could be filed, or a bond satisfactory to the Owner indemnifying him against any lien.

ARTICLE 17. SEPARATE CONTRACTS

The Owner has the right to let other contracts in connection with the work and the Contractor shall properly cooperate with any such other contractors.

ARTICLE 18. THE ARCHITECT'S STATUS

The Architect shall be the Owner's representative during the construction period. He has authority to stop the work if necessary to insure its proper execution. He shall certify to the Owner when payments under the contract are due and the amounts to be paid. He shall make decisions on all claims of the Owner or Contractor. All his decisions are subject to arbitration.

ARTICLE 19. ARBITRATION

Any disagreement arising out of this contract or from the breach thereof shall be submitted to arbitration, and judgment upon the award rendered may be entered in the court of the forum, state or federal, having jurisdiction. It is mutually agreed that the decision of the arbitrators shall be a condition precedent to any right of legal action that either party may have against the other. The arbitration shall be held under the Standard Form of Arbitration Procedure of The American Institute of Architects or under the Rules of the American Arbitration Association.

ARTICLE 20. CLEANING UP

The Contractor shall keep the premises free from accumulation of waste material and rubbish and at the completion of the work he shall remove from the premises all rubbish, implements and surplus materials and leave the building broom-clean.

IN WITNESS WHEREOF the parties hereto executed this Agreement, the day and year first above written.

Owner _____

Contractor _____

OWNER-CONTRACTOR AGREEMENT   FOUR PAGES

AIA DOC. A107   SEPT. 1963 ED.   PAGE 4

V SPECIAL CONDITIONS

Article 1   Conflict with General Conditions

In case of conflict between these SPECIAL CONDITIONS and the GENER-AL CONDITIONS, the Special Conditions shall govern.

Article 2   Superintendence and Supervision

The Contractor shall keep on the premises, during the progress of the work, a competent Supervisor, satisfactory to the Owner. The Supervisor shall not be changed except with the consent of the Owner unless the Supervisor proves to be unsatisfactory to the Contractor or Owner or ceases to be in the Contractor's employ. The Supervisor shall represent the Contractor in his absence and all instructions given to him shall be as binding as if given to the Contractor. The Contractor shall at all times enforce strict discipline and good order among his employees, and shall not employ on the work any unfit person or anyone not skilled in the work assigned to him.

Article 3   Compliance with Executive Order

Contractor agrees to be bound by, and to implement, all of the non-discrimination requirements of Executive Order 11246 and any amendments thereof.

Article 4   Safety

Contractor shall comply with and shall require all subcontractors to comply with all applicable health and safety laws, rules and regulations, including without limitations, the Occupational Safety and Health Act of 1970 and the rules and regulations issued pursuant thereto.

Article 5   Surveys

Surveys furnished by the Owner as set forth in ARTICLE 5, GENERAL CONDITIONS, SURVEYS, PERMITS, & REGULATIONS shall include basic survey controls only consisting of two permanent benchmarks, monuments designating property corners, and basic horizontal control points for building corners. All construction layout shall be performed by Contractor who shall be responsible for the accuracy thereof.

Article 6   Construction Manager

The Owner has engaged Construction Management and Control, Inc., hereinafter referred to as Construction Manager, to act as Owner's designated representative in the administration of this Construction Contract and in the management and coordination of work performed on the project. The word "Architect" as set forth in Article 18 of the General Conditions shall be replaced by Construction Manager. The Architect, however, shall continue to exercise surveillance and observation over the work and will be responsible for interpretation of plans and specifications prepared under his direction.

VI SIMPLIFIED SPECIFICATIONS, ADDENDUMS, AND DRAWINGS

SECTION E-1 SITE GRADING AND COMPACTION

E-1:01 General
1. All this work shall be subject to the General Conditions, Special Conditions, and other Contract Documents.

E-1:02 Scope
The Contractor shall furnish all labor, material, tools and equipment required to complete all site grading as shown on the plans and herein specified. The principal items of work are the following:
1. Removal of vegetation and topsoil on the project area.
2. General cut, where called for on the plans, and as hereafter specified.
3. Scarifying of existing and cut surfaces and recompaction.
4. Furnishing and installation of compacted fill over areas of yards, and at building area and spur track.
5. Finish grading, swales, and slopes to swales.

E-1:03 Related work not included
1. Excavation and backfilling for footings and foundation walls of buildings.
2. All excavation and backfilling in connection with storm and sanitary sewer systems, utility lines, sprinkler mains and electrical service.
3. Topsoil for planting areas.
4. Aggregate base course under paving.

E-1:04 Drawings and site examination
1. The Contractor is referred to the site drawings, which show existing ground elevations as well as finish grades for building floors, paved yards, and unpaved areas. Where floors (concrete) or paving (concrete or asphaltic concrete) are indicated, the finish grades shown on the plans indicate the surface of such floors or paving. Where unpaved areas are indicated, the finish grades are finished ground surface.
   a *In Concrete Paved Areas*, grading work shall be to the elevation of the bottom of the aggregate base, or 18 in. below top of slab.
   b *In Asphaltic Concrete Paved Areas*, grading work shall be to elevation of bottom of the aggregate base, or 12 in. below top of slab.
2. It shall be the duty of the Contractor to visit the site and ascertain all existing conditions before submitting his bid. No allowance will subsequently be made on account of Contractor's neglect of this requirement.

E-1:05 Removal of vegetation, and topsoil
1. Over that portion of the site where project work is called for, areas where there is vegetation, loose earth, or trash, shall be cut sufficiently to remove such material. Remove brush and roots. Such cut material shall be removed from the site.
2. Filling work, as specified hereinafter, shall include allowance for this material removed, as part of the contract.

E-1:06 General cut
Contractor shall make general cut as required by existing ground surfaces to meet requirements outlined in Article E-1:04, paragraph 1, including allowance for compacted fill or rock where called for.

E-1:07 Rejected material

After excavation, and prior to scarifying and recompaction, the Soils Engineer shall inspect the exposed cut surface. Those areas of original in-place soil rejected by the Soils Engineer as being unsuitable as a base for construction of engineered fill, shall be excavated and removed from the site. This work shall be done only on written order from the Owner, and will be compensated for in accordance with an agreed price. Note that this does not include removal of vegetation, loose earth, and trash as specified above, or does not include correction of faulty work by the Contractor which has been rejected by the Soils Engineer as not meeting the specifications, or work under the contract which has become damaged due to rain, construction traffic, or failure to maintain proper drainage and dewatering, etc.

a   Installation of fill to replace such rejected original material shall be done only on written order from the Owner, and will be compensated for in accordance with an agreed price. Use imported compacted fill, as hereafter specified.

E-1:08 Scarifying and recompaction

Before placing any fill or base course thereon, existing and cut surfaces shall be scarified to a minimum depth of 6″, brought to, or just above, optimum moisture content and recompacted to a minimum relative compaction of 95%.

E-1:09 Fill

1. *Fill* for this project shall be as outlined below:
    a   General fill material shall be on-site material, excavated from grading work, or imported fill. On-site material shall be placed first when both are required.
    b   Imported granular earth, free of vegetation, debris, and other objectionable material, shall meet the following requirements:
    Maximum particle size   3 inches
    Passing #4 sieve   30–90%
    Passing #200 sieve   0–20%
    Maximum Plasticity Index   15
2. Organic soils, topsoils, and other material with sod or humus shall not be used for Compacted Fill. No frozen material, stumps, roots, all or parts of trees, brush, or other perishable material shall be placed. Clean sand shall not be used.
3. *Installation of Fill*
    a   The Compacted Fill shall be constructed to provide adequate drainage at all times, and the surface kept uniformly graded and compacted. Each lift shall extend longitudinally or transversely over the entire area and be kept smooth. The Contractor shall route his equipment at all times, by equal distribution of travel, to prevent rutting. The equipment shall be operated so as to break up into small particles any cemented gravel or other soil particles so that they may be incorporated into the material of each lift or layer. Contractor shall be responsible for the stability of the fill, until the work is complete and accepted by the Owner, and shall replace any portion of which, in the opinion of the Soils Engineer, has become displaced, unstable, or damaged.
    b   Compacted fill shall be placed in 6″ maximum layers of loose depth for the full width of fill, except that thick layers may be used providing the Contractor can satisfy the Engineer that requirement densities can be

obtained. All earthfill shall be compacted to at least 95% of maximum density at the optimum moisture content as determined by the A.S.T.M. D-1577-66T method of testing. If the material is too wet or too dry, compaction work on all portions of the compacted fill affected shall be delayed until the material has been either dried or sprinkled, whichever is necessary, to provide compacted densities and moisture contents as specified. Compaction of fill shall be performed by Sheeps Foot rollers or Rubber Tired rollers. All equipment shall be approved by the Soils Engineer.

4. Toe of slope of building fill shall be as shown on Plot Plan Drawing SI-1 and slope shall extend on a 1:1 slope to underside of finish floor at elevation 99′6″.

E-1:10 Grading at railroad tracks

Strip, scarify, and recompact as specified above, and furnish and install compacted imported fill as required for installation of railroad tracks at the location shown. Grading work shall be to the elevation of the bottom of ballast, shall meet fill requirements specified in E-1:09 above, and shall be to lines and grades approved by the Railroad Company.

E-1:11 Maintenance of finish grades

Finish grades, unless otherwise indicated, shall be uniform levels or slopes between points where elevations are indicated or between such points and existing grades at vicinity of boundary lines. The Contractor shall maintain and protect all grading, filling and excavation work, and drainage ditches, to the required elevations and slopes during the construction period. At completion of the work, finish surface of unpaved areas shall meet the above requirements to the satisfaction of the Owner.

a The site of the work shall be left in a clean, orderly condition, free of all debris, trash, etc., resulting from said work.

E-1:12 Dust control

Contractor shall prevent the blowing of dust and dirt, generated by the project work or vehicular traffic, over onto adjacent or nearby developed areas.

E-1:13 Inspection and tests

Selection of fill material, placing, method of compaction, scarifying and recompaction of existing and cut surfaces, shall be performed under the supervision and control of a qualified Soils Engineer, appointed by and acting under the direction of the Architect. All costs in connection with this supervision and testing will be paid for by the Owner. The Soils Engineer will make "in-place" density and moisture tests, the Engineer may require the Contractor to make changes in his operations necessary to obtain the specified values for these items.

SECTION E-2   FENCING AND GATES

E-2:01 General

This work shall be subject to the General Conditions, Special Conditions, and other Contract Documents.

E-2:02 Scope

Furnish all labor, materials, and equipment to install complete all work required under this section, including, but not limited to, the following:

1. Demolition (paving, curbs, etc) at site entrances.

2. Fencing and gates.

E-2:03 Fencing and gates

1. Around site and parking, furnish and install chain link fence and gates, as detailed. Fencing shall be chain link type as manufactured by Manufacturer A, B, or C. All materials shall be hot dip galvanized. Furnish shop drawings covering all fencing and gates to the Architect for approval.

    a *Fabric* shall be "galvanized after weaving" chain link, No. 9 wire, woven in a 2″ mesh. Top and bottom selvages to have a twisted, barbed finish; barbing to be done by cutting wire on a bias, creating sharp points. Wire pickets of which fabric is made shall stand a tensile strength test of 90,000 psi, based on the cross-sectional area of the galvanized wire.

    b *Line Posts* H-column (2″ × 2¼″), weight 4.1 lbs. per lineal foot, or 2-3/8″ round, 3.65 lbs. No used, re-rolled or open seam material will be permitted in posts or rails.

    c *Terminal & Gate Posts* End, corner, and pull posts, small gate posts, 3″ O.D., 5.79 lbs. per lineal foot. Large Gate posts, 6″ O.D. Gate posts to have ball top.

    d *Top and Bottom Rail* 1-5/9″ O.D., or H-section, weight 2.27 lbs. per lineal foot. Top rail to pass through base of line post tops and form a continuous brace from end to end of each stretch of fence. Rails shall be securely fastened to terminal posts by pressed steel connections.

    e *Braces* Same material as top rail. To be spaced midway between top rail and bottom rail and to extend from terminal post to first adjacent line post. Fasten braces securely to posts by means of suitable pressed steel connection, and truss from line post back to terminal post with a 3/8″ round rod.

    f *Gates* Gate frames to be made of 2″ O.D. pipe, weight 2.72 lbs. per lineal foot. Corner fittings heavy pressed steel or malleable castings. Fabric to be same as fence fabric. Gates to be complete with malleable iron ball and socket hinges and center rest. Where so detailed, hinges shall permit gates to swing back against fence, 180° if required. Small gates to have catch stops, large gates hook posts and hooks. Provide sliding gates (manual) where shown.

2. *Erection* Install fencing and gates in locations shown on plans. Space posts in line of fence not farther apart than 10′ on centers. Posts in concrete paving and curbs shall be set in 2′ long pipe sleeves and grouted in place. Install gates, and turnstiles, and adjust for proper operation. Extend fence fabric across top of turnstiles. Fasten fabric to line posts with fabric bands spaced approximately 14″ apart, and to top and bottom rails with tie wires spaced approximately 24″ apart. Furnish sleeves and locations for setting in concrete (by others).

VII OWNER-FURNISHED ITEMS

    1 Temporary electrical supply at point designated by Owner.

    2 Water in limited amounts for domestic and miscellaneous construction uses.

    3   Areas for contractors' facilities, materials and equipment storage at locations determined by Owner.

    4   Sanitary services (portable toilets) at locations determined by Owner.

    5   Basic Survey Controls as set forth in the SPECIAL CONDITIONS.

VIII CONSTRUCTION SCHEDULE

The attached Owner's Construction Schedule (Figure 4-4 in Chapter 4) is to be used as a guide for overall performance of the project. Actual dates to begin work will be transmitted by the NOTICE TO PROCEED. Actual completion time will be as set forth in the AGREEMENT.

Portions of the Example Bid Package have been adapted from bidding documents developed by E. A. Bonelli & Associates, San Francisco, California, and Leo Rosenthal, A.I.A., Denver, Colorado.

Appendix C

Contract Forms

This appendix contains the following example contract forms:

1 Construction Manager—AGC version
(Reproduced with the permission of The Associated General Contractors of America)
2 Construction Manager—AIA version
(This document has been reproduced with the permission of The American Institute of Architects under application number 77025. Further reproduction, in part or in whole, is not authorized)
3 Lump-Sum General Contract—AGC/ASCE version
(Reproduced with the permission of The Associated General Contractors of America and the American Society of Civil Engineers)
4 Subcontract
(Reproduced with the permission of the Associated General Contractors of America and the Associated Specialty Contractors, Inc.)

THE ASSOCIATED GENERAL CONTRACTORS

STANDARD FORM OF AGREEMENT BETWEEN OWNER AND CONSTRUCTION MANAGER

(GUARANTEED MAXIMUM PRICE OPTION)

(See AGC Document No. 8a for Establishing the
Guaranteed Maximum Price)

This Document has important legal and insurance consequences; consultation with an attorney is encouraged with respect to its completion or modification.

AGREEMENT

Made this   day of   in the year of Nineteen Hundred and

BETWEEN   the Owner, and

the Construction Manager.

For services in connection with the following described Project: (Include complete Project location and scope)

The Architect/Engineer for the Project is

The Owner and the Construction Manager agree as set forth below:

Certain provisions of this document have been derived, with modifications, from the following documents published by The American Institute of Architects: AIA Document A111, Owner Contractor Agreement, © 1974, AIA Document A201, General Conditions, © 1976, AIA Document B801, Owner Construction Manager Agreement, © 1973, by The American Institute of Architects. Usage made of AIA language, with the permission of AIA, does not apply AIA endorsement or approval of this document. Further reproduction of copyrighted AIA materials without separate written permission from AIA is prohibited.

TABLE OF CONTENTS

ARTICLE 1

The Construction Team and Extent of Agreement

The CONSTRUCTION MANAGER accepts the relationship of trust and confidence established between him and the Owner by this Agreement. He covenants with the Owner to furnish his best skill and judgment and to cooperate with the Architect/Engineer in furthering the interests of the Owner. He agrees to furnish efficient business administration and superintendence and to use his best efforts to complete the Project in an expeditious and economical manner consistent with the interest of the Owner.

1.1 *The Construction Team:* The Construction Manager, the Owner, and the Architect/Engineer called the "Construction Team" shall work from the beginning of design through construction completion. The Construction Manager shall provide leadership to the Construction Team on all matters relating to construction.

1.2 *Extent of Agreement:* This Agreement represents the entire agreement between the Owner and the Construction Manager and supersedes all prior negotiations, representations or agreements. When Drawings and Specifications are complete, they shall be identified by amendment to this Agreement. This Agreement shall not be superseded by any provisions of the documents for construction and may be amended only by written instrument signed by both the Owner and the Construction Manager.

1.3 *Definitions:* The Project is the total construction to be performed under this Agreement. The Work is that part of the construction that the Construction Manager is to perform with his own forces or that part of the construction that a particular Trade Contractor is to perform. The term day shall mean calendar day unless otherwise specifically designated.

ARTICLE 2

Construction Manager's Services

The Construction Manager will perform the following services under this Agreement in each of the two phases described below.

2.1 Design Phase

2.1.1 *Consultation During Project Development:* Schedule and attend regular meetings with the Architect/Engineer during the development of conceptual and preliminary design to advise on site use and improvements, selection of materials, building systems and equipment. Provide recommendations on construction feasibility, availability of materials and labor, time requirements for installation and construction, and factors related to cost including costs of alternative designs or materials, preliminary budgets, and possible economies.

2.1.2 *Scheduling:* Develop a Project Time Schedule that coordinates and integrates the Architect/Engineer's design efforts with construction schedules. Update the Project Time Schedule incorporating a detailed schedule for the construction operations of the Project, including realistic activity sequences and durations, allocation of labor and materials, processing of shop drawings and samples, and delivery of products requiring long lead-time procurement. Include the Owner's occupancy requirements showing portions of the Project having occupancy priority.

2.1.3 *Project Construction Budget:* Prepare a Project budget as soon as major Project requirements have been identified, and update periodically for the Owner's approval. Prepare an estimate based on a quantity survey of Drawings and Specifications at the end of the schematic design phase for approval by the Owner as the Project Construction Budget. Update and refine this estimate for the Owner's approval as the development of the Drawings and Specifications proceeds, and advise the Owner and the Architect/Engineer if it appears that the Project Construction Budget will not be met and make recommendations for corrective action.

2.1.4 *Coordination of Contract Documents:* Review the Drawings and Specifications as they are being prepared, recommending alternative solutions whenever design details affect construction feasibility or schedules without, however, assuming any of the Architect/Engineer's responsibilities for design.

2.1.5 *Construction Planning:* Recommend for purchase and expedite the procurement of long-lead items to ensure their delivery by the required dates.

2.1.5.1 Make recommendations to the Owner and the Architect/Engineer regarding the division of Work in the Drawings and Specifications to facilitate the bidding and awarding of Trade Contracts, allowing for phased construction taking into consideration such factors as time of performance, availability of labor, overlapping trade jurisdictions, and provisions for temporary facilities.

2.1.5.2 Review the Drawings and Specifications with the Architect/Engineer to eliminate areas of conflict and overlapping in the Work to be performed by the various Trade Contractors and prepare prequalification criteria for bidders.

2.1.5.3 Develop Trade Contractor interest in the Project and as working Drawings and Specifications are completed, take competitive bids on the Work of the various Trade Contractors. After analyzing the bids, either award contracts or recommend to the Owner that such contracts be awarded.

2.1.6 *Equal Employment Opportunity:* Determine applicable requirements for equal emloyment opportunity programs for inclusion in Project bidding documents.

2.2 Construction Phase

2.2.1 *Project Control:* Monitor the Work of the Trade Contractors and coordinate the Work with the activities and responsibilities of the Owner, Architect/Engineer and Construction Manager to complete the Project in accordance with the Owner's objectives of cost, time and quality.

2.2.1.1 Maintain a competent full-time staff at the Project site to coordinate and provide general direction of the Work and progress of the Trade Contractors on the Project.

2.2.1.2 Establish on-site organization and lines of authority in order to carry out the overall plans of the Construction Team.

2.2.1.3 Establish procedures for coordination among the Owner, Architect/Engineer, Trade Contractors and Construction Manager with respect to all aspects of the Project and implement such procedures.

2.2.1.4 Schedule and conduct progress meetings at which Trade Contractors, Owner, Architect/Engineer and Construction Manager can discuss jointly such matters as procedures, progress, problems and scheduling.

2.2.1.5 Provide regular monitoring of the schedule as construction progresses. Identify potential variances between scheduled and probable completion dates. Review schedule for Work not started or incomplete and recommend to the Owner and Trade Contractors adjustments in the schedule to meet the probable completion date. Provide summary reports of each monitoring and document all changes in schedule.

2.2.1.6 Determine the adequacy of the Trade Contractors' personnel and equipment and the availability of materials and supplies to meet the schedule. Recommend courses of action to the Owner when requirements of a Trade Contract are not being met.

2.2.2 *Physical Construction:* Provide all supervision, labor, materials, construction equipment, tools and subcontract items which are necessary for the completion of the Project which are not provided by either the Trade Contractors or the Owner. To the extent that the Construction Manager performs any Work with his own forces, he shall, with respect to such Work, perform in accordance with the Plans and Specifications and in accordance with the procedure applicable to the Project.

2.2.3 *Cost Control:* Develop and monitor an effective system of Project cost control. Revise and refine the initially approved Project Construction Budget, incorporate approved changes as they occur, and develop cash flow reports and forecasts as needed. Identify variances between actual and budgeted or estimated costs and advise Owner and Architect/Engineer whenever projected cost exceeds budgets or estimates.

2.2.3.1 Maintain cost accounting records on authorized Work performed under unit costs, actual costs for labor and material, or other bases requiring accounting records. Afford the Owner access to these records and preserve them for a period of three (3) years after final payment.

2.2.4 *Change Orders:* Develop and implement a system for the preparation, review and processing of Change Orders. Recommend necessary or desirable change to the Owner and the Architect/Engineer, review requests for changes, submit recommendations to the Owner and the Architect/Engineer, and assist in negotiating Change Orders.

2.2.5 *Payments to Trade Contractors:* Develop and implement a procedure for the review, processing and payment of applications by Trade Contractors for progress and final payments.

2.2.6 *Permits and Fees:* Assist the Owner and Architect/Engineer in obtaining all building permits and special permits for permanent improvements, excluding permits for inspection or temporary facilities required to be obtained directly by the various Trade Contractors. Assist in obtaining approvals from all the authorities having jurisdiction.

2.2.7 *Owner's Consultants:* If required, assist the Owner in selecting and retaining professional services of a surveyor, testing laboratories and special consultants, and coordinate these services, without assuming any responsibility or liability of or for these consultants.

2.2.8 *Inspection:* Inspect the Work of Trade Contractors for defects and deficiencies in the Work without assuming any of the Architect/Engineer's responsibilities for inspection.

2.2.8.1 Review the safety programs of each of the Trade Contractors and make appropriate recommendations. In making such recommendations and carrying out such reviews, he shall not be required to make exhaustive or continuous inspections to check safety precautions and programs in connection with the Project. The performance of such services by the Construction Manager shall not relieve the Trade Contractors of their responsibilities for the safety of persons and property, and for compliance with all federal, state and local statutes, rules, regulations and orders applicable to the conduct of the Work.

2.2.9 *Document Interpretation:* Refer all questions for interpretation of the documents prepared by the Architect/Engineer to the Architect/Engineer.

2.2.10 *Shop Drawings and Samples:* In collaboration with the Architect/Engineer, establish and implement procedures for expediting the processing and approval of shop drawings and samples.

2.2.11 *Reports and Project Site Documents:* Record the progress of the Project. Submit written progress reports to the Owner and the Architect/Engineer including information on the Trade Contractors' Work, and the percentage of completion. Keep a daily log available to the Owner and the Architect/Engineer.

2.2.11.1 Maintain at the Project site, on a current basis: records of all necessary Contracts, Drawings, samples, purchases, materials, equipment, maintenance and operating manuals and instructions, and other construction related documents, including all revisions. Obtain data from Trade Contractors and maintain a current set of record Drawings, Specifications and operating manuals. At the completion of the Project, deliver all such records to the Owner.

2.2.12 *Substantial Completion:* Determine Substantial Completion of the Work or designated portions thereof and prepare for the Architect/Engineer a list of incomplete or unsatisfactory items and a schedule for their completion.

2.2.13 *Start-Up:* With the Owner's maintenance personnel, direct the checkout of utilities, operations systems and equipment for readiness and assist in their initial start-up and testing by the Trade Contractors.

2.2.14 *Final Completion:* Determine final completion and provide written notice to the Owner and Architect/Engineer that the Work is ready for final inspection. Secure and transmit to the Architect/Engineer required guarantees, affidavits, releases, bonds and waivers. Turn over to the Owner all keys, manuals, record drawings and maintenance stocks.

2.2.15 *Warranty:* Where any Work is performed by the Construction Manager's own forces or by Trade Contractors under contract with the Construction Manager, the Construction Manager shall warrant that all materials and equipment included in such Work will be new, unless otherwise specified, and that such Work will be of good quality, free from improper workmanship and defective materials and in conformance with the Drawings and Specifications. With respect to the same Work, the

Construction Manager further agrees to correct all Work defective in material and workmanship for a period of one year from the Date of Substantial Completion or for such longer periods of time as may be set forth with respect to specific warranties contained in the trade sections of the Specifications. The Construction Manager shall collect and deliver to the Owner any specific written warranties given by others.

2.3 Additional Services

2.3.1 At the request of the Owner the Construction Manager will provide the following additional services upon written agreement between the Owner and Construction Manager defining the extent of such additional services and the amount and manner in which the Construction Manager will be compensated for such additional services.

2.3.2 Services related to investigation, appraisals or valuations of existing conditions, facilities or equipment, or verifying the accuracy of existing drawings or other Owner-furnished information.

2.3.3 Services related to Owner-furnished equipment, furniture and furnishings which are not a part of this Agreement.

2.3.4 Services for tenant or rental spaces not a part of this Agreement.

2.3.5 Obtaining or training maintenance personnel or negotiating maintenance service contracts.

ARTICLE 3

Owner's Responsibilities

3.1 The Owner shall provide full information regarding his requirements for the Project.

3.2 The Owner shall designate a representative who shall be fully acquainted with the Project and has authority to issue and approve Project Construction Budgets, issue Change Orders, render decisions promptly and furnish information expeditiously.

3.3 The Owner shall retain an Architect/Engineer for design and to prepare construction documents for the Project. The Architect/Engineer's services, duties and responsibilities are described in the Agreement between the Owner and the Architect/Engineer, a copy of which will be furnished to the Construction Manager. The Agreement between the Owner and the Architect/Engineer shall not be modified without written notification to the Construction Manager.

3.4 The Owner shall furnish for the site of the Project all necessary surveys describing the physical characteristics, soil reports and subsurface investigations, legal limitations, utility locations, and a legal description.

3.5 The Owner shall secure and pay for necessary approvals, easements, assessments and charges required for the construction, use or occupancy of permanent structures or for permanent changes in existing facilities.

3.6 The Owner shall furnish such legal services as may be necessary for providing the items set forth in Paragraph 3.5, and such auditing services as he may require.

3.7 The Construction Manager will be furnished without charge all copies of Drawings and Specifications reasonably necessary for the execution of the Work.

3.8 The Owner shall provide the insurance for the Project as provided in Paragraph 12.4, and shall bear the cost of any bonds required.

3.9 The services, information, surveys and reports required by the above paragraphs or otherwise to be furnished by other consultants employed by the Owner, shall be furnished with reasonable promptness at the Owner's expense and the Construction Manager shall be entitled to rely upon the accuracy and completeness thereof.

3.10 If the Owner becomes aware of any fault or defect in the Project or non-conformance with the Drawings and Specifications, he shall give prompt written notice thereof to the Construction Manager.

3.11   The Owner shall furnish, prior to commencing work and at such future times as may be requested, reasonable evidence satisfactory to the Construction Manager that sufficient funds are available and committed for the entire cost of the Project. Unless such reasonable evidence is furnished, the Construction Manager is not required to commence or continue any Work, or may, if such evidence is not presented within a reasonable time, stop the Project upon 15 days notice to the Owner. The failure of the Construction Manager to insist upon the providing of this evidence at any one time shall not be a waiver of the Owner's obligation to make payments pursuant to this Agreement nor shall it be a waiver of the Construction Manager's right to request or insist that such evidence be provided at a later date.

3.12   The Owner shall communicate with the Trade Contractors only through the Construction Manager.

ARTICLE 4

Trade Contracts

4.1   All portions of the Project that the Construction Manager does not perform with his own forces shall be performed under Trade Contracts. The Construction Manager shall request and receive proposals from Trade Contractors and Trade Contracts will be awarded after the proposals are reviewed by the Architect/Engineer, Construction Manager and Owner.

4.2   If the Owner refuses to accept a Trade Contractor recommended by the Construction Manager, the Construction Manager shall recommend an acceptable substitute and the Guaranteed Maximum Price if applicable shall be increased or decreased by the difference in cost occasioned by such substitution and an appropriate Change Order shall be issued.

4.3   Unless otherwise directed by the Owner, Trade Contracts will be between the Construction Manager and the Trade Contractors. Whether the Trade Contracts are with the Construction Manager or the Owner, the form of the Trade Contracts including the General and Supplementary Conditions shall be satisfactory to the Construction Manager.

4.4   The Construction Manager shall be responsible to the Owner for the acts and omissions of his agents and employees, Trade Contractors performing Work under a contract with the Construction Manager, and such Trade Contractors' agents and employees.

ARTICLE 5

Schedule

5.1   The services to be provided under this Contract shall be in general accordance with the following schedule:

5.2   At the time a Guaranteed Maximum Price is established, as provided for in Article 6, a Date of Substantial Completion of the project shall also be established.

5.3   The Date of Substantial Completion of the Project or a designated portion thereof is the date when construction is sufficiently complete in accordance with the Drawings and Specifications so the Owner can occupy or utilize the Project or designated portion thereof for the use for which it is intended. Warranties called for by this Agreement or by the Drawings and Specifications shall commence on the Date of Substantial Completion of the Project or designated portion thereof.

5.4   If the Construction Manager is delayed at any time in the progress of the Project by any act or neglect of the Owner or the Architect/Engineer or by any employee of either, or by any separate contractor employed by the Owner, or by changes ordered in the Project, or by labor disputes, fire, unusual delay in transportation, adverse weather conditions not reasonably anticipatable, unavoidable casualties or any causes beyond the Construction Manager's control, or by delay authorized by the Owner pending arbitration, the Construction Completion Date shall be extended by Change Order for a reasonable length of time.

ARTICLE 6

Guaranteed Maximum Price

6.1 When the design, Drawings and Specifications are sufficiently complete, the Construction Manager will, if desired by the Owner, establish a Guaranteed Maximum Price, guaranteeing the maximum price to the Owner for the Cost of the Project and the Construction Manager's Fee. Such Guaranteed Maximum Price will be subject to modification for Changes in the Project as provided in Article 9, and for additional costs arising from delays caused by the Owner or the Architect/Engineer.

6.2 When the Construction Manager provides a Guaranteed Maximum Price, the Trade Contracts will either be with the Construction Manager or will contain the necessary provisions to allow the Construction Manager to control the performance of the Work. The Owner will also authorize the Construction Manager to take all steps necessary in the name of the Owner, including arbitration or litigation, to assure that the Trade Contractors perform their contracts in accordance with their terms.

6.3 The Guaranteed Maximum Price will only include those taxes in the Cost of the Project which are legally enacted at the time the Guaranteed Maximum Price is established.

ARTICLE 7

Construction Manager's Fee

7.1 In consideration of the performance of the Contract, the Owner agrees to pay the Construction Manager in current funds as compensation for his services a Construction Manager's Fee as set forth in Subparagraphs 7.1.1 and 7.1.2.

7.1.1 For the performance of the Design Phase services, a fee of
which shall be paid monthly, in equal proportions, based on the scheduled Design Phase time.

7.1.2 For work or services performed during the Construction Phase, a fee of
which shall be paid proportionately to the ratio the monthly payment for the Cost of the Project bears to the estimated cost. Any balance of this fee shall be paid at the time of final payment.

7.2 Adjustments in Fee shall be made as follows:

7.2.1 For Changes in the Project as provided in Article 9, the Construction Manager's Fee shall be adjusted as follows:

7.2.2 For delays in the Project not the responsibility of the Construction Manager, there will be an equitable adjustment in the fee to compensate the Constructon Manager for his increased expenses.

7.2.3 The Construction Manager shall be paid an additional fee in the same proportion as set forth in 7.2.1 if the Construction Manager is placed in charge of the reconstruction of any insured or uninsured loss.

7.3 Included in the Construction Manager's Fee are the following:

7.3.1 Salaries or other compensation of the Construction Manager's employees at the principal office and branch offices, except employees listed in Subparagraph 8.2.2.

7.3.2   General operating expenses of the Construction Manager's principal and branch offices other than the field office.

7.3.3   Any part of the Construction Manager's capital expenses, including interest on the Construction Manager's capital employed for the project.

7.3.4   Overhead or general expenses of any kind, except as may be expressly included in Article 8.

7.3.5   Costs in excess of the Guaranteed Maximum Price.

ARTICLE 8

Cost of the Project

8.1   The term Cost of the Project shall mean costs necessarily incurred in the Project during either the Design or Construction Phase, and paid by the Construction Manager, or by the Owner if the Owner is directly paying Trade Contractors upon the Construction Manager's approval and direction. Such costs shall include the items set forth below in this Article.

8.1.1   The Owner agrees to pay the Construction Manager for the Cost of the Project as defined in Article 8. Such payment shall be in addition to the Construction Manager's Fee stipulated in Article 7.

8.2   Cost Items

8.2.1   Wages paid for labor in the direct employ of the Construction Manager in the performance of his Work under applicable collective bargaining agreements, or under a salary or wage schedule agreed upon by the Owner and Construction Manager, and including such welfare or other benefits, if any, as may be payable with respect thereto.

8.2.2   Salaries of the Construction Manager's employees when stationed at the field office, in whatever capacity employed, employees engaged on the road in expediting the production or transportation of materials and equipment, and employees in the main or branch office performing the functions listed below:

8.2.3   Cost of all employee benefits and taxes for such items as unemployment compensation and social security, insofar as such cost is based on wages, salaries, or other remuneration paid to employees of the Construction Manager and included in the Cost of the Project under Subparagraphs 8.2.1 and 8.2.2.

8.2.4   Reasonable transportation, traveling, moving, and hotel expenses of the Construction Manager or of his officers or employees incurred in discharge of duties connected with the Project.

8.2.5   Cost of all materials, supplies and equipment incorporated in the Project, including costs of transportation and storage thereof.

8.2.6   Payments made by the Construction Manager or Owner to Trade Contractors for their Work performed pursuant to contract under this Agreement.

8.2.7   Cost, including transportation and maintenance, of all materials, supplies, equipment, temporary facilities and hand tools not owned by the workmen, which are employed or consumed in the performance of the Work, and cost less salvage value on such items used but not consumed which remain the property of the Construciton Manager.

8.2.8   Rental charges of all necessary machinery and equipment, exclusive of hand tools, used at the site of the Project, whether rented from the Construction Manager or other, including installation, repairs and replacements, dismantling, removal, costs of lubrication, transportation and delivery costs thereof, at rental charges consistent with those prevailing in the area.

8.2.9   Cost of the premiums for all insurance which the Construction Manager is required to procure by this Agreement or is deemed necessary by the Construction Manager.

8.2.10   Sales, use, gross receipts or similar taxes related to the Project imposed by any governmental authority, and for which the Construction Manager is liable.

8.2.11   Permit fees, licenses, tests, royalties, damages for infringement of patents and costs of defending suits therefor, and deposits lost for causes other than the Construction Manager's negligence. If royalties or losses and damages, including costs of defense, are incurred which arise from a particular design, process, or the product of a particular manufacturer or manufacturers specified by the Owner or Architect/Engineer, and the Construction Manager has no reason to believe there will be infringement of patent rights, such royalties, losses and damages shall be paid by the Owner and not considered as within the Guaranteed Maximum Price.

8.2.12   Losses, expenses or damages to the extent not compensated by insurance or otherwise (including settlement made with the written approval of the Owner).

8.2.13   The cost of corrective work subject, however, to the Guaranteed Maximum Price.

8.2.14   Minor expenses such as telegrams, long-distance telephone calls, telephone service at the site, expressage, and similar petty cash items in connection with the Project.

8.2.15   Cost of removal of all debris.

8.2.16   Cost incurred due to an emergency affecting the safety of persons and property.

8.2.17   Cost of data processing services required in the performance of the services outlined in Article 2.

8.2.18   Legal costs reasonably and properly resulting from prosecution of the Project for the Owner.

8.2.19   All costs directly incurred in the performance of the Project and not included in the Construction Manager's Fee as set forth in Paragraph 7.3.

ARTICLE 9

Changes in the Project

9.1   The Owner, without invalidating this Agreement, may order Changes in the Project within the general scope of this Agreement consisting of additions, deletions or other revisions, the Guaranteed Maximum Price, if established, the Construction Manager's Fee and the Construction Completion Date being adjusted accordingly. All such Changes in the Project shall be authorized by Change Order.

9.1.1   A Change Order is a written order to the Construction Manager signed by the Owner or his authorized agent issued after the execution of this Agreement, authorizing a Change in the Project or the method or manner of performance and/or an adjustment in the Guaranteed Maximum Price, the Construction Manager's Fee, or the Construction Completion Date. Each adjustment in the Guaranteed Maximum Price resulting from a Change Order shall clearly separate the amount attributable to the Cost of the Project and the Construction Manager's Fee.

9.1.2   The increase or decrease in the Guaranteed Maximum Price resulting from a Change in the Project shall be determined in one or more of the following ways:

.1   by mutual acceptance of a lump sum properly itemized and supported by sufficient substantiating data to permit evaluation;

.2   by unit prices stated in the Agreement or subsequently agreed upon;

.3   by cost as defined in Article 8 and a mutually acceptable fixed or percentage fee; or

.4   by the method provided in Subparagraph 9.1.3.

9.1.3 If none of the methods set forth in Clauses 9.1.2.1 through 9.1.2.3 is agreed upon, the Construction Manager, provided he receives a written order signed by the Owner, shall promptly proceed with the Work involved. The cost of such Work shall then be determined on the basis of the reasonable expenditures and savings of those performing the Work attributed to the change, including, in the case of an increase in the Guaranteed Maximum Price, a reasonable increase in the Construction Manager's Fee. In such case, and also under Clauses 9.1.2.3 and 9.1.2.4 above, the Construction·Manager shall keep and present, in such form as the Owner may prescribe, an itemized accounting together with appropriate supporting data of the increase in the Cost of the Project as outlined in Article 8. The amount of decrease in the Guaranteed Maximum Price to be allowed by the Construction Manager to the Owner for any deletion or change which results in a net decrease in cost will be the amount of the actual net decrease. When both additions and credits are involved in any one change, the increase in Fee shall be figured on the basis of net increase, if any.

9.1.4 If unit prices are stated in the Agreement or subsequently agreed upon, and if the quantities originally contemplated are so changed in a proposed Change Order or as a result of several Change Orders that application of the agreed unit prices to the quantities of Work proposed will cause substantial inequity to the Owner or the Construction Manager, the applicable unit prices and Guaranteed Maximum Price shall be equitably adjusted.

9.1.5 Should concealed conditions encountered in the performance of the Work below the surface of the ground or should concealed or unknown conditions in an existing structure be at variance with the conditions indicated by the Drawings, Specifications, or Owner-furnished information or should unknown physical conditions below the surface of the ground or should concealed or unknown conditions in an existing structure of an unusual nature, differing materially from those ordinarily encountered and generally recognized as inherent in work of the character provided for in this Agreement, be encountered, the Guaranteed Maximum Price and the Construction Completion Date shall be equitably adjusted by Change Order upon claim by either party made within a reasonable time after the first observance of the conditions.

9.2 Claims for Additional Cost or Time

9.2.1 If the Construction Manager wishes to make a claim for an increase in the Guaranteed Maximum Price, an increase in his fee, or an extension in the Construction Completion Date, he shall give the Owner written notice thereof within a reasonable time after the occurrence of the event giving rise to such claim. This notice shall be given by the Construction Manager before proceeding to execute any Work, except in an emergency endangering life or property in which case the Construction Manager shall act, at his discretion, to prevent threatened damage, injury or loss. Claims arising from delay shall be made within a reasonable time after the delay. No such claim shall be valid unless so made. If the Owner and the Construction Manager cannot agree on the amount of the adjustment in the Guaranteed Maximum Price, Construction Manager's Fee or Construction Completion Date, it shall be determined pursuant to the provisions of Article 16. Any change in the Guaranteed Maximum Price, Construction Manager's Fee or Construction Completion Date resulting from such claim shall be authorized by Change Order.

9.3. Minor Changes in the Project

9.3.1 The Architect/Engineer will have authority to order minor Changes in the Project not involving an adjustment in the Guaranteed Maximum Price or an extension of the Construction Completion Date and not inconsistent with the intent of the Drawings and Specifications. Such Changes may be effected by written order and shall be binding on the Owner and the Construction Manager.

9.4 Emergencies

9.4.1 In any emergency affecting the safety of persons or property, the Construction Manager shall act, at his discretion, to prevent threatened damage, injury or loss. Any increase in the Guaranteed Maximum Price or extension of time claimed by the Construction Manager on account of emergency work shall be determined as provided in this Article.

ARTICLE 10

Discounts

All discounts for prompt payment shall accrue to the Owner to the extent the Cost of the Project is paid directly by the

Owner or from a fund made available by the Owner to the Construction Manager for such payments. To the extent the Cost of the Project is paid with funds of the Construction Manager, all cash discounts shall accrue to the Construction Manager. All trade discounts, rebates and refunds, and all returns from sale of surplus materials and equipment, shall be credited to the Cost of the Project.

ARTICLE 11

Payments to the Construction Manager

11.1   The Construction Manager shall submit monthly to the Owner a statement, sworn to if required, showing in detail all moneys paid out, costs accumulated or costs incurred on account of the Cost of the Project during the previous month and the amount of the Construction Manager's Fee due as provided in Article 7. Payment by the Owner to the Construction Manager of the statement amount shall be made within ten (10) days after it is submitted.

11.2   Final payment constituting the unpaid balance of the Cost of the Project and the Construction Manager's Fee shall be due and payable when the Project is delivered to the Owner, ready for beneficial occupancy, or when the Owner occupies the Project, whichever event first occurs, provided that the Project be then substantially completed and this Agreement substantially performed. If there should remain minor items to be completed, the Construction Manager and Architect/Engineer shall list such items and the Construction Manager shall deliver, in writing, his unconditional promise to complete said items within a reasonable time thereafter. The Owner may retain a sum equal to 150% of the estimated cost of completing any unfinished items, provided that said unfinished items are listed separately and the estimated cost of completing any unfinished items likewise listed separately. Thereafter, Owner shall pay to Construction Manager, monthly, the amount retained for incomplete items as each of said items is completed.

11.3   The Construction Manager shall promptly pay all the amounts due Trade Contractors or other persons with whom he has a contract upon receipt of any payment from the Owner, the application for which includes amounts due such Trade Contractor or other persons. Before issuance of final payment, the Construction Manager shall submit satisfactory evidence that all payrolls, materials bills and other indebtedness connected with the Project have been paid or otherwise satisfied.

11.4   If the Owner should fail to pay the Construction Manager within seven (7) days after the time the payment of any amount becomes due, then the Construction Manager may, upon seven (7) additional days' written notice to the Owner and the Architect/Engineer, stop the Project until payment of the amount owing has been received.

11.5   Payments due but unpaid shall bear interest at the rate the Owner is paying on his construction loan or at the legal rate, whichever is higher.

ARTICLE 12

Insurance, Indemnity and Waiver of Subrogation

12.1   Indemnity

12.1.1   The Construction Manager agrees to indemnify and hold the Owner harmless from all claims for bodily injury and property damage (other than the Work itself and other property insured under Paragraph 12.4) that may arise from the Construction Manager's operations under this Agreement.

12.1.2   The Owner shall cause any other contractor who may have a contract with the Owner to perform construction or installation work in the areas where Work will be performed under this Agreement, to agree to indemnify the Owner and the Construction Manager and hold them harmless from all claims for bodily injury and property damage (other than property insured under Paragraph 12.4) that may arise from that contractor's operations. Such provisions shall be in a form satisfactory to the Construction Manager.

12.2 Construction Manager's Liability Insurance

12.2.1   The Construction Manager shall purchase and maintain such insurance as will protect him from the claims set forth below which may arise out of or result from the Construction Manager's operations under this Agreement whether such operations be by himself or by any Trade Contractor or by anyone directly or indirectly employed by any of them, or by anyone for whose acts any of them may be liable:

12.2.1.1   Claims under workers' compensation, disability benefit and other similar employee benefit acts which are applicable to the Work to be performed.

12.2.1.2   Claims for damages because of bodily injury, occupational sickness or disease, or death of his employees under any applicable employer's liability law.

12.2.1.3   Claims for damages because of bodily injury, death of any person other than his employees.

12.2.1.4   Claims for damages insured by usual personal injury liability coverage which are sustained (1) by any person as a result of an offense directly or indirectly related to the employment of such person by the Construction Manager or (2) by any other person.

12.2.1.5   Claims for damages, other than to the Work itself, because of injury to or destruction of tangible property, including loss of use therefrom.

12.2.1.6   Claims for damages because of bodily injury or death of any person or property damage arising out of the ownership, maintenance or use of any motor vehicle.

12.2.2   The Construction Manager's Comprehensive General Liability Insurance shall include premises — operations (including explosion, collapse and underground coverage) elevators, independent contractors, completed operations, and blanket contractual liability on all written contracts, all including broad form property damage coverage.

12.2.3   The Construction Manager's Comprehensive General and Automobile Liability Insurance, as required by Subparagraphs 12.2.1 and 12.2.2 shall be written for not less than limits of liability as follows:

a. Comprehensive General Liability
    1. Personal Injury $_____Each Occurrence

                                $_____Aggregate
                                (Completed Operations)

    2. Property Damage $_____Each Occurrence

                                $_____Aggregate

b. Comprehensive Automobile Liability
    1. Bodily Injury $_____Each Person

                                $_____Each Occurrence

    2. Property Damage $_____Each Occurrence

12.2.4   Comprehensive General Liability Insurance may be arranged under a single policy for the full limits required or by a combination of underlying policies with the balance provided by an Excess or Umbrella Liability policy.

12.2.5   The foregoing policies shall contain a provision that coverages afforded under the policies will not be cancelled or not renewed until at least sixty (60) days' prior written notice has been given to the Owner. Certificates of Insurance showing such coverages to be in Force shall be filed with the Owner prior to commencement of the Work.

12.3 Owner's Liability Insurance

12.3.1   The Owner shall be responsible for purchasing and maintaining his own liability insurance and, at his option, may purchase and maintain such insurance as will protect him against claims which may arise from operations under this Agreement.

12.4 Insurance to Protect Project

12.4.1   The Owner shall purchase and maintain property insurance in a form acceptable to the Construction Manager upon the entire Project for the full cost of replacement as of the time of any loss. This insurance shall include as named insureds the Owner, the Construction Manager, Trade Contractors and their Trade Subcontractors and shall insure against loss from the perils of Fire, Extended Coverage, and shall include "All Risk" insurance for physical loss or damage including, without duplication of coverage, at least theft, vandalism, malicious mischief, transit, collapse, flood, earthquake, testing, and damage resulting from defective design, workmanship or material. The Owner will increase limits of coverage, if necessary, to reflect estimated replacement cost. The Owner will be responsible for any co-insurance penalties or deductibles. If the Project covers an addition to or is adjacent to an existing building, the Construction Manager, Trade Contractors and their Trade Subcontractors shall be named as additional insureds under the Owner's Property Insurance covering such building and its contents.

12.4.1.1   If the Owner finds it necessary to occupy or use a portion or portions of the Project prior to Substantial Completion thereof, such occupancy shall not commence prior to a time mutually agreed to by the Owner and Construction Manager and to which the insurance company or companies providing the property insurance have consented by endorsement to the policy or policies. This insurance shall not be cancelled or lapsed on account of such partial occupancy. Consent of the Construction Manager and of the insurance company or companies to such occupancy or use shall not be unreasonably withheld.

12.4.2   The Owner shall purchase and maintain such boiler and machinery insurance as may be required or necessary. This insurance shall include the interests of the Owner, the Construction Manager, Trade Contractors and their Trade Subcontractors in the Work.

12.4.3   The Owner shall purchase and maintain such insurance as will protect the Owner and Construction Manager against loss of use of Owner's property due to those perils insured pursuant to Subparagraph 12.4.1. Such policy will provide coverage for expediting expenses of materials, continuing overhead of the Owner and Construction Manager, necessary labor expense including overtime, loss of income by the Owner and other determined exposures. Exposures of the Owner and the Construction Manager shall be determined by mutual agreement and separate limits of coverage fixed for each item.

12.4.4   The Owner shall file a copy of all policies with the Construction Manager before an exposure to loss may occur. Copies of any subsequent endorsements will be furnished to the Construction Manager. The Construction Manager will be given sixty (60) days notice of cancellation, non-renewal, or any endorsements restricting or reducing coverage. If the Owner does not intend to purchase such insurance, he shall inform the Construction Manager in writing prior to the commencement of the Work. The Construction Manager may then effect insurance which will protect the interest of himself, the Trade Contractors and their Trade Subcontractors in the Project, the cost of which shall be a Cost of the Project pursuant to Article 8, and the Guaranteed Maximum Price shall be increased by Change Order. If the Construction Manager is damaged by failure of the Owner to purchase or maintain such insurance or to so notify the Construction Manager, the Owner shall bear all reasonable costs properly attributable thereto.

12.5 Property Insurance Loss Adjustment

12.5.1   Any insured loss shall be adjusted with the Owner and the Construction Manager and made payable to the Owner and Construction Manager as trustees for the insureds, as their interests may appear, subject to any applicable mortgagee clause.

12.5.2   Upon the occurrence of an insured loss, monies received will be deposited in a separate account and the trustees shall make distribution in accordance with the agreement of the parties in interest, or in the absence of such agreement, in accordance with an arbitration award pursuant to Article 16. If the trustees are unable to agree on the settlement of the loss, such dispute shall also be submitted to arbitration pursuant to Article 16.

12.6 Waiver of Subrogation

12.6.1   The Owner and Construction Manager waive all rights against each other, the Architect/Engineer, Trade Contractors, and their Trade Subcontractors for damages caused by perils covered by insurance provided under Paragraph 12.4, except such rights as they may have to the proceeds of such insurance held by the Owner and Construction Manager as trustees. The Construction Manager shall require similar waivers from all Trade Contractors and their Trade Subcontractors.

12.6.2 The Owner and Construction Manager waive all rights against each other and the Architect/Engineer, Trade Contractors and their Trade Subcontractors for loss or damage to any equipment used in connection with the Project and covered by any property insurance. The Construction Manager shall require similar waivers from all Trade Contractors and their Trade Subcontractors.

12.6.3 The Owner waives subrogation against the Construction Manager, Architect/Engineer, Trade Contractors, and their Trade Subcontractors on all property and consequential loss policies carried by the Owner on adjacent properties and under property and consequential loss policies purchased for the Project after its completion.

12.6.4 If the policies of insurance referred to in this Paragraph require an endorsement to provide for continued coverage where there is a waiver of subrogation, the owners of such policies will cause them to be so endorsed.

<h3 style="text-align:center">ARTICLE 13</h3>

<h4 style="text-align:center">Termination of the Agreement and Owner's
Right to Perform Construction Manager's Obligations</h4>

13.1 Termination by the Construction Manager

13.1.1 If the Project, in whole or substantial part, is stopped for a period of thirty days under an order of any court or other public authority having jurisdiction, or as a result of an act of government, such as a declaration of a national emergency making materials unavailable, through no act or fault of the Construction Manager, or if the Project should be stopped for a period of thirty days by the Construction Manager for the Owner's failure to make payment thereon, then the Construction Manager may, upon seven days' written notice to the Owner and the Architect/Engineer, terminate this Agreement and recover from the Owner payment for all work executed, the Construction Manager's Fee earned to date, and for any proven loss sustained upon any materials, equipment, tools, construction equipment and machinery, cancellation charges on existing obligations of the Construction Manager, and a reasonable profit.

13.2 Owner's Right to Perform Construction Manager's Obligations and Termination by the Owner for Cause

13.2.1 If the Construction Manager fails to perform any of his obligations under this Agreement including any obligation he assumes to perform Work with his own forces, the Owner may, after seven days' written notice during which period the Construction Manager fails to perform such obligation, make good such deficiencies. The Guaranteed Maximum Price, if any, shall be reduced by the cost to the Owner of making good such deficiencies.

13.2.2 If the Construction Manager is adjudged a bankrupt, or if he makes a general assignment for the benefit of his creditors, or if a receiver is appointed on account of his insolvency, or if he persistently or repeatedly refuses or fails, except in cases for which extension of time is provided, to supply enough properly skilled workmen or proper materials, or if he fails to make proper payment to Trade Contractors or for materials or labor, or persistently disregards laws, ordinances, rules, regulations or orders of any public authority having jurisdiction, or otherwise is guilty of a substantial violation of a provision of the Agreement, then the Owner may, without prejudice to any right or remedy and after giving the Construction Manager and his surety, if any, seven days' written notice, during which period the Construction Manager fails to cure the violation, terminate the employment of the Construction Manager and take possession of the site and of all materials, equipment, tools, construction equipment and machinery thereon owned by the Construction Manager and may finish the Project by whatever reasonable method he may deem expedient. In such case, the Construction Manager shall not be entitled to receive any further payment until the Project is finished nor shall he be relieved from his obligations assumed under Article 6.

13.3 Termination by Owner Without Cause

13.3.1 If the Owner terminates this Agreement other than pursuant to Subparagraph 13.2.2 or Subparagraph 13.3.2, he shall reimburse the Construction Manager for any unpaid Cost of the Project due him under Article 8, plus (1) the unpaid balance of the Fee computed upon the Cost of the Project to the date of termination at the rate of the percentage named in Subparagraph 7.2.1 or if the Construction Manager's Fee be stated as a fixed sum, such an amount as will increase the payment on account of his fee to a sum which bears the same ratio to the said fixed sum as the Cost of the Project at the time of termination bears to the adjusted Guaranteed Maximum Price, if any, otherwise to a reasonable estimated Cost of the Project when completed. The Owner shall also pay to the Construction Manager fair compensation, either by purchase or rental at the election of the Owner, for any equipment retained. In case of such termination of the Agreement the Owner shall further assume and become liable for obligations, commitments and unsettled claims that the Construction Manager has previously undertaken or incurred in good faith in connection with said Project. The Construction Manager shall, as a condition of receiving the payments referred to in this Article 13, execute and deliver all such papers and take all such steps, including the legal assignment of his contractual rights, as the Owner may require for the purpose of fully vesting in him the rights and benefits of the Construction Manager under such obligations or commitments.

13.3.2   After the completion of the Design Phase, if the final cost estimates make the Project no longer feasible from the standpoint of the Owner, the Owner may terminate this Agreement and pay the Construction Manager his Fee in accordance with Subparagraph 7.1.1 plus any costs incurred pursuant to Article 9.

ARTICLE 14

Assignment and Governing Law

14.1   Neither the Owner nor the Construction Manager shall assign his interest in this Agreement without the written consent of the other except as to the assignment of proceeds.

14.2   This Agreement shall be governed by the law of the place where the Project is located.

ARTICLE 15

Miscellaneous Provisions

15.1   It is expressly understood that the Owner shall be directly retaining the services of an Architect/Engineer.

ARTICLE 16

Arbitration

16.1   All claims, disputes and other matters in questions arising out of, or relating to, this Agreement or the breach thereof, except with respect to the Architect/Engineer's decision on matters relating to artistic effect, and except for claims which have been waived by the making or acceptance of final payment shall be decided by arbitration in accordance with the Construction Industry Arbitration Rules of the American Arbitration Association then obtaining unless the parties mutually agree otherwise. This Agreement to arbitrate shall be specifically enforceable under the prevailing arbitration law.

16.2   Notice of the demand for arbitration shall be filed in writing with the other party to this Agreement and with the American Arbitration Association. The demand for arbitration shall be made within a reasonable time after the claim, dispute or other matter in question has arisen, and in no event shall it be made after the date when institution of legal or equitable proceedings based on such claim, dispute or other matter in question would be barred by the applicable statute of limitations.

16.3   The award rendered by the arbitrators shall be final and judgment may be entered upon it in accordance with applicable law in any court having jurisdiction thereof.

16.4   Unless otherwise agreed in writing, the Construction Manager shall carry on the Work and maintain the Contract Completion Date during any arbitration proceedings, and the Owner shall continue to make payments in accordance with this Agreement.

16.5   All claims which are related to or dependent upon each other, shall be heard by the same arbitrator or arbitrators even though the parties are not the same unless a specific contract prohibits such consolidation.

AGC DOCUMENT NO. 8 • OWNER-CONSTRUCTION MANAGER AGREEMENT   JULY 1980

This Agreement executed the day and year first written above.

ATTEST: OWNER:

ATTEST: CONSTRUCTION MANAGER:

THE ASSOCIATED GENERAL CONTRACTORS

AMENDMENT TO OWNER-CONSTRUCTION MANAGER CONTRACT

Pursuant to Article 6 of the original Agreement, AGC Form No. 8, dated _____

between _____ (Owner)

and _____ (the Construction Manager),

for _____ (the Project),

the Owner desires to fix a Guaranteed Maximum Price for the Project and the Construction Manager agrees that the design, plans and specifications are sufficiently complete for such purpose. Therefore, the Owner and Construction Manager agree as set forth below.

ARTICLE I

Guaranteed Maximum Price

The Construction Manager's Guaranteed Maximum Price for the Project, including the Cost of the Work as defined in Article 8 and the Construction Manager's Fee as defined in Article 7 is _____ Dollars ($ _____). This price is for the performance of the Work in accordance with the documents listed and attached to this Amendment and marked Amendment Exhibit A.

(*OPTIONAL SAVINGS CLAUSE*) It is further agreed that if, upon completion of the work, the actual cost of the work plus the Construction Manager's Fee is less than the Guaranteed Maximum Price as set forth herein and as adjusted by approved change orders that the Owner agrees to pay to the Construction Manager an amount equal to _____% of such savings, as additional compensation.

AGC DOCUMENT NO. 8A • AMENDMENT TO OWNER-CONSTRUCTION MANAGER CONTRACT • JUNE 1977
© ASSOCIATED GENERAL CONTRACTORS OF AMERICA 1977

ARTICLE II

Time Schedule

The Construction Completion date established by this Amendment is:

OWNER:

ATTEST:

By: _____

Date: _____

_____

CONSTRUCTION MANAGER:

_____

By: _____

ATTEST:

Date: _____

_____

THE AMERICAN INSTITUTE OF ARCHITECTS

AIA copyrighted material has been reproduced with the permission of The American Institute of Architects under permission number 82067. Further reproduction is prohibited.

Because AIA Documents are revised from time to time, users should ascertain from the AIA the current editions of the Document reproduced herein.

Copies of this AIA Document may be purchased from The American Institute of Architects or its local distributors.

AIA Document B801

Standard Form of Agreement Between
Owner and Construction Manager

1980 EDITION

THIS DOCUMENT HAS IMPORTANT LEGAL CONSEQUENCES; CONSULTATION WITH AN ATTORNEY IS ENCOURAGED.

This document is intended to be used in conjunction with
AIA Documents A101/CM, 1980; B141/CM, 1980; and A201/CM, 1980.

AGREEMENT

made as of the   day of   in the year of Nineteen
Hundred and

BETWEEN the Owner:

and the Construction Manager:

For the following Project:
(Include detailed description of Project location and scope.)

the Architect:

The Owner and the Construction Manager agree as set forth below.

Copyright 1973, © 1980, by The American Institute of Architects, 1735 New York Avenue, N.W., Washington, D.C. 20006. Reproduction of the material herein or substantial quotation of its provisions without written permission of the AIA violates the copyright laws of the United States and will be subject to legal prosecution.

AIA DOCUMENT B801 • OWNER-CONSTRUCTION MANAGER AGREEMENT • JUNE 1980 EDITION • AIA®
©1980 • THE AMERICAN INSTITUTE OF ARCHITECTS, 1735 NEW YORK AVE., N.W., WASHINGTON, D.C. 20006

TERMS AND CONDITIONS OF AGREEMENT BETWEEN OWNER AND CONSTRUCTION MANAGER

ARTICLE 1
CONSTRUCTION MANAGER'S SERVICES AND RESPONSIBILITIES

The Construction Manager covenants with the Owner to further the interests of the Owner by furnishing the Construction Manager's skill and judgment in cooperation with, and in reliance upon, the services of an architect. The Construction Manager agrees to furnish business administration and management services and to perform in an expeditious and economical manner consistent with the interests of the Owner.

BASIC SERVICES

The Construction Manager's Basic Services consist of the two Phases described below and any other services included in Article 16 as Basic Services.

1.1 PRECONSTRUCTION PHASE

1.1.1 Provide preliminary evaluation of the program and Project budget requirements, each in terms of the other. With the Architect's assistance, prepare preliminary estimates of Construction Cost for early schematic designs based on area, volume or other standards. Assist the Owner and the Architect in achieving mutually agreed upon program and Project budget requirements and other design parameters. Provide cost evaluations of alternative materials and systems.

1.1.2 Review designs during their development. Advise on site use and improvements, selection of materials, building systems and equipment and methods of Project delivery. Provide recommendations on relative feasibility of construction methods, availability of materials and labor, time requirements for procurement, installation and construction, and factors related to cost including, but not limited to, costs of alternative designs or materials, preliminary budgets and possible economies.

1.1.3 Provide for the Architect's and the Owner's review and acceptance, and periodically update, a Project Schedule that coordinates and integrates the Construction Manager's services, the Architect's services and the Owner's responsibilities with anticipated construction schedules.

1.1.4 Prepare for the Owner's approval a more detailed estimate of Construction Cost, as defined in Article 3, developed by using estimating techniques which anticipate the various elements of the Project, and based on Schematic Design Documents prepared by the Architect. Update and refine this estimate periodically as the Architect prepares Design Development and Construction Documents. Advise the Owner and the Architect if it appears that the Construction Cost may exceed the Project budget. Make recommendations for corrective action.

1.1.5 Coordinate Contract Documents by consulting with the Owner and the Architect regarding Drawings and Specifications as they are being prepared, and recommending alternative solutions whenever design details affect construction feasibility, cost or schedules.

1.1.5.1 Provide recommendations and information to the Owner and the Architect regarding the assignment of responsibilities for safety precautions and programs; temporary Project facilities and equipment, materials and services for common use of Contractors. Verify that the requirements and assignment of responsibilities are included in the proposed Contract Documents.

1.1.5.2 Advise on the separation of the Project into Contracts for various categories of Work. Advise on the method to be used for selecting Contractors and awarding Contracts. If separate Contracts are to be awarded, review the Drawings and Specifications and make recommendations as required to provide that (1) the Work of the separate Contractors is coordinated, (2) all requirements for the Project have been assigned to the appropriate separate Contract, (3) the likelihood of jurisdictional disputes has been minimized, and (4) proper coordination has been provided for phased construction.

1.1.5.3 Develop a Project Construction Schedule providing for all major elements such as phasing of construction and times of commencement and completion required of each separate Contractor. Provide the Project Construction Schedule for each set of Bidding Documents.

1.1.5.4 Investigate and recommend a schedule for the Owner's purchase of materials and equipment requiring long lead time procurement, and coordinate the schedule with the early preparation of portions of the Contract Documents by the Architect. Expedite and coordinate delivery of these purchases.

1.1.6 Provide an analysis of the types and quantities of labor required for the Project and review the availability of appropriate categories of labor required for critical Phases. Make recommendations for actions designed to minimize adverse effects of labor shortages.

1.1.6.1 Identify or verify applicable requirements for equal employment opportunity programs for inclusion in the proposed Contract Documents.

1.1.7 Make recommendations for pre-qualification criteria for Bidders and develop Bidders' interest in the Project. Establish bidding schedules. Assist the Architect in issuing Bidding Documents to Bidders. Conduct pre-bid conferences to familiarize Bidders with the Bidding Documents and management techniques and with any special systems, materials or methods. Assist the Architect with the receipt of questions from Bidders, and with the issuance of Addenda.

1.1.7.1 With the Architect's assistance, receive Bids, prepare bid analyses and make recommendations to the Owner for award of Contracts or rejection of Bids.

1.1.8 With the Architect's assistance, conduct pre-award conferences with successful Bidders. Assist the Owner in preparing Construction Contracts and advise the Owner on the acceptability of Subcontractors and material suppliers proposed by Contractors.

1.2 CONSTRUCTION PHASE

The Construction Phase will commence with the award of the initial Construction Contract or purchase order and, together with the Construction Manager's obligation to provide Basic Services un-

AIA DOCUMENT B801 • OWNER-CONSTRUCTION MANAGER AGREEMENT • JUNE 1980 EDITION • AIA®
©1980 • THE AMERICAN INSTITUTE OF ARCHITECTS, 1735 NEW YORK AVE., N.W., WASHINGTON, D.C. 20006

B801 — 1980 2

der this Agreement, will end 30 days after final payment to all Contractors is due.

1.2.1 Unless otherwise provided in this Agreement and incorporated in the Contract Documents, the Construction Manager, in cooperation with the Architect, shall provide administration of the Contracts for Construction as set forth below and in the 1980 Edition of AIA Document A201/CM, General Conditions of the Contract for Construction, Construction Management Edition.

1.2.2 Provide administrative, management and related services as required to coordinate Work of the Contractors with each other and with the activities and responsibilities of the Construction Manager, the Owner and the Architect to complete the Project in accordance with the Owner's objectives for cost, time and quality. Provide sufficient organization, personnel and management to carry out the requirements of this Agreement.

1.2.2.1 Schedule and conduct pre-construction, construction and progress meetings to discuss such matters as procedures, progress, problems and scheduling. Prepare and promptly distribute minutes.

1.2.2.2 Consistent with the Project Construction Schedule issued for the Bidding Documents, and utilizing the Contractors' Construction Schedules provided by the separate Contractors, update the Project Construction Schedule incorporating the activities of Contractors on the Project, including activity sequences and durations, allocation of labor and materials, processing of Shop Drawings, Product Data and Samples, and delivery of products requiring long lead time procurement. Include the Owner's occupancy requirements showing portions of the Project having occupancy priority. Update and reissue the Project Construction Schedule as required to show current conditions and revisions required by actual experience.

1.2.2.3 Endeavor to achieve satisfactory performance from each of the Contractors. Recommend courses of action to the Owner when requirements of a Contract are not being fulfilled, and the nonperforming party will not take satisfactory corrective action.

1.2.3 Revise and refine the approved estimate of Construction Cost, incorporate approved changes as they occur, and develop cash flow reports and forecasts as needed.

1.2.3.1 Provide regular monitoring of the approved estimate of Construction Cost, showing actual costs for activities in progress and estimates for uncompleted tasks. Identify variances between actual and budgeted or estimated costs, and advise the Owner and the Architect whenever projected costs exceed budgets or estimates.

1.2.3.2 Maintain cost accounting records on authorized Work performed under unit costs, additional Work performed on the basis of actual costs of labor and materials, or other Work requiring accounting records.

1.2.3.3 Recommend necessary or desirable changes to the Architect and the Owner, review requests for changes, assist in negotiating Contractors' proposals, submit recommendations to the Architect and the Owner, and if they are accepted, prepare and sign Change Orders for the Architect's signature and the Owner's authorization.

1.2.3.4 Develop and implement procedures for the review and processing of Applications by Contractors for progress and final payments. Make recommendations to the Architect for certification to the Owner for payment.

1.2.4 Review the safety programs developed by each of the Contractors as required by their Contract Documents and coordinate the safety programs for the Project.

1.2.5 Assist in obtaining building permits and special permits for permanent improvements, excluding permits required to be obtained directly by the various Contractors. Verify that the Owner has paid applicable fees and assessments. Assist in obtaining approvals from authorities having jurisdiction over the Project.

1.2.6 If required, assist the Owner in selecting and retaining the professional services of surveyors, special consultants and testing laboratories. Coordinate their services.

1.2.7 Determine in general that the Work of each Contractor is being performed in accordance with the requirements of the Contract Documents. Endeavor to guard the Owner against defects and deficiencies in the Work. As appropriate, require special inspection or testing, or make recommendations to the Architect regarding special inspection or testing, of Work not in accordance with the provisions of the Contract Documents whether or not such Work be then fabricated, installed or completed. Subject to review by the Architect, reject Work which does not conform to the requirements of the Contract Documents.

1.2.7.1 The Construction Manager shall not be responsible for construction means, methods, techniques, sequences and procedures employed by Contractors in the performance of their Contracts, and shall not be responsible for the failure of any Contractor to carry out Work in accordance with the Contract Documents.

1.2.8 Consult with the Architect and the Owner if any Contractor requests interpretations of the meaning and intent of the Drawings and Specifications, and assist in the resolution of questions which may arise.

1.2.9 Receive Certificates of Insurance from the Contractors, and forward them to the Owner with a copy to the Architect.

1.2.10 Receive from the Contractors and review all Shop Drawings, Product Data, Samples and other submittals. Coordinate them with information contained in related documents and transmit to the Architect those recommended for approval. In collaboration with the Architect, establish and implement procedures for expediting the processing and approval of Shop Drawings, Product Data, Samples and other submittals.

1.2.11 Record the progress of the Project. Submit written progress reports to the Owner and the Architect including information on each Contractor and each Contractor's Work, as well as the entire Project, showing percentages of completion and the number and amounts of Change Orders. Keep a daily log containing a record of weather, Contractors' Work on the site, number of workers, Work accomplished, problems encountered, and other similar relevant data as the Owner may require. Make the log available to the Owner and the Architect.

1.2.11.1 Maintain at the Project site, on a current basis: a record copy of all Contracts, Drawings, Specifications, Addenda, Change Orders and other Modifications, in good order and marked to record all changes made during construction; Shop Drawings; Product Data; Samples; submittals; purchases; materials; equipment; applicable handbooks; maintenance and operating manuals and instruc-

AIA DOCUMENT B801 • OWNER-CONSTRUCTION MANAGER AGREEMENT • JUNE 1980 EDITION • AIA®
©1980 • THE AMERICAN INSTITUTE OF ARCHITECTS, 1735 NEW YORK AVE., N.W., WASHINGTON, D.C. 20006

SAMPLE

tions; other related documents and revisions which arise out of the Contracts or Work. Maintain records, in duplicate, of principal building layout lines, elevations of the bottom of footings, floor levels and key site elevations certified by a qualified surveyor or professional engineer. Make all records available to the Owner and the Architect. At the completion of the Project, deliver all such records to the Architect for the Owner.

1.2.12 Arrange for delivery and storage, protection and security for Owner-purchased materials, systems and equipment which are a part of the Project, until such items are incorporated into the Project.

1.2.13 With the Architect and the Owner's maintenance personnel, observe the Contractors' checkout of utilities, operational systems and equipment for readiness and assist in their initial start-up and testing.

1.2.14 When the Construction Manager considers each Contractor's Work or a designated portion thereof substantially complete, the Construction Manager shall prepare for the Architect a list of incomplete or unsatisfactory items and a schedule for their completion. The Construction Manager shall assist the Architect in conducting inspections. After the Architect certifies the Date of Substantial Completion of the Work, the Construction Manager shall coordinate the correction and completion of the Work.

1.2.15 Assist the Architect in determining when the Project or a designated portion thereof is substantially complete. Prepare for the Architect a summary of the status of the Work of each Contractor, listing changes in the previously issued Certificates of Substantial Completion of the Work and recommending the times within which Contractors shall complete uncompleted items on their Certificate of Substantial Completion of the Work.

1.2.16 Following the Architect's issuance of a Certificate of Substantial Completion of the Project or designated portion thereof, evaluate the completion of the Work of the Contractors and make recommendations to the Architect when Work is ready for final inspection. Assist the Architect in conducting final inspections. Secure and transmit to the Owner required guarantees, affidavits, releases, bonds and waivers. Deliver all keys, manuals, record drawings and maintenance stocks to the Owner.

1.2.17 The extent of the duties, responsibilities and limitations of authority of the Construction Manager as a representative of the Owner during construction shall not be modified or extended without the written consent of the Owner, the Contractors, the Architect and the Construction Manager, which consent shall not be unreasonably withheld.

1.3 ADDITIONAL SERVICES

The following Additional Services shall be performed upon authorization in writing from the Owner and shall be paid for as provided in this Agreement.

1.3.1 Services related to investigations, appraisals or evaluations of existing conditions, facilities or equipment, or verification of the accuracy of existing drawings or other information furnished by the Owner.

1.3.2 Services related to Owner-furnished furniture, furnishings and equipment which are not a part of the Project.

1.3.3 Services for tenant or rental spaces.

1.3.4 Consultation on replacement of Work damaged by fire or other cause during construction and furnishing services in conjunction with the replacement of such Work.

1.3.5 Services made necessary by the default of a Contractor.

1.3.6 Preparing to serve or serving as a witness in connection with any public hearing, arbitration proceeding or legal proceeding.

1.3.7 Recruiting or training maintenance personnel.

1.3.8 Inspections of, and services related to, the Project after the end of the Construction Phase.

1.3.9 Providing any other services not otherwise included in this Agreement.

1.4 TIME

1.4.1 The Construction Manager shall perform Basic and Additional Services as expeditiously as is consistent with reasonable skill and care and the orderly progress of the Project.

ARTICLE 2
THE OWNER'S RESPONSIBILITIES

2.1 The Owner shall provide full information regarding the requirements of the Project, including a program, which shall set forth the Owner's objectives, constraints and criteria, including space requirements and relationships, flexibility and expandability requirements, special equipment and systems and site requirements.

2.2 The Owner shall provide a budget for the Project, based on consultation with the Construction Manager and the Architect, which shall include contingencies for bidding, changes during construction and other costs which are the responsibility of the Owner. The Owner shall, at the request of the Construction Manager, provide a statement of funds available for the Project and their source.

2.3 The Owner shall designate a representative authorized to act in the Owner's behalf with respect to the Project. The Owner, or such authorized representative, shall examine documents submitted by the Construction Manager and shall render decisions pertaining thereto promptly to avoid unreasonable delay in the progress of the Construction Manager's services.

2.4 The Owner shall retain an architect whose services, duties and responsibilities are described in the agreement between the Owner and the Architect, AIA Document B141/CM, 1980 Edition. The Terms and Conditions of the Owner-Architect Agreement will be furnished to the Construction Manager, and will not be modified without written consent of the Construction Manager, which consent shall not be unreasonably withheld. Actions taken by the Architect as agent of the Owner shall be the acts of the Owner and the Construction Manager shall not be responsible for them.

2.5 The Owner shall furnish structural, mechanical, chemical and other laboratory tests, inspections and reports as required by law or the Contract Documents.

2.6 The Owner shall furnish such legal, accounting and insurance counseling services as may be necessary for the Project, including such auditing services as the Owner may require to verify the Project Applications for Payment or to ascertain how or for what purposes the Contractors have used the monies paid by or on behalf of the Owner.

2.7 The Owner shall furnish the Construction Manager a sufficient quantity of construction documents.

2.8 The services, information and reports required by Paragraphs 2.1 through 2.7, inclusive, shall be furnished at the Owner's expense, and the Construction Manager shall be entitled to rely upon their accuracy and completeness.

2.9 If the Owner observes or otherwise becomes aware of any fault or defect in the Project, or nonconformance with the Contract Documents, prompt written notice thereof shall be given by the Owner to the Construction Manager and the Architect.

2.10 The Owner reserves the right to perform work related to the Project with the Owner's own forces, and to award contracts in connection with the Project which are not part of the Construction Manager's responsibilities under this Agreement. The Construction Manager shall notify the Owner if any such independent action will in any way compromise the Construction Manager's ability to meet the Construction Manager's responsibilities under this Agreement.

2.11 The Owner shall furnish the required information and services and shall render approvals and decisions as expeditiously as necessary for the orderly progress of the Construction Manager's services and the Work of the Contractors.

ARTICLE 3
CONSTRUCTION COST

3.1 Construction Cost shall be the total of the final Contract Sums of all of the separate Contracts, actual Reimbursable Costs relating to the Construction Phase as defined in Article 6, and the Construction Manager's compensation.

3.2 Construction Cost does not include the compensation of the Architect and the Architect's consultants, the cost of the land, rights-of-way or other costs which are the responsibility of the Owner as provided in Paragraphs 2.3 through 2.7, inclusive.

3.3 Evaluations of the Owner's Project budget and cost estimates prepared by the Construction Manager represent the Construction Manager's best judgment as a professional familiar with the construction industry. It is recognized, however, that neither the Construction Manager nor the Architect has control over the cost of labor, materials or equipment, over Contractors' methods of determining Bid prices or other competitive bidding or negotiating conditions. Accordingly, the Construction Manager cannot and does not warrant or represent that Bids or negotiated prices will not vary from the Project budget proposed, established or approved by the Owner, or from any cost estimate or evaluation prepared by the Construction Manager.

3.4 No fixed limit of Construction Cost shall be established as a condition of this Agreement by the furnishing, proposal or establishment of a Project budget under Subparagraph 1.1.1 or Paragraph 2.2, or otherwise, unless such fixed limit has been agreed upon in writing and signed by the parties to this Agreement. If such a fixed limit has been established, the Construction Manager shall include contingencies for design, bidding and price escalation, and

shall consult with the Architect to determine what materials, equipment, component systems and types of construction are to be included in the Contract Documents, to suggest reasonable adjustments in the scope of the Project, and to suggest a revised Bids to the Construction Documents to adjust the Construction Cost to the fixed limit. Any such fixed limit shall be increased in the amount of any increase in the Contract Sums occurring after the execution of the Contracts for Construction.

3.4.1 If Bids are not received within the time scheduled at the time the fixed limit of Construction Cost was established, due to causes beyond the Construction Manager's control, any fixed limit of Construction Cost established as a condition of this Agreement shall be adjusted to reflect any change in the general level of prices in the construction industry occurring between the originally scheduled date and the date on which Bids are received.

3.4.2 If a fixed limit of Construction Cost (adjusted as provided in Subparagraph 3.4.1) is exceeded by the sum of the lowest figures from bona fide Bids or negotiated proposals plus the Construction Manager's estimate of other elements of Construction Cost for the Project, the Owner shall (1) give written approval of an increase in such fixed limit, (2) authorize rebidding or renegotiation of the Project or portions of the Project within a reasonable time, (3) if the Project is abandoned, terminate in accordance with Paragraph 10.2, or (4) cooperate in revising the scope and quality of the Work as required to reduce the Construction Cost. In the case of item (4), the Construction Manager, without additional compensation, shall cooperate with the Architect as necessary to bring the Construction Cost within the fixed limit.

ARTICLE 4
CONSTRUCTION SUPPORT ACTIVITIES

4.1 Construction support activities, if provided by the Construction Manager, shall be governed by separate contractual arrangements unless otherwise provided in Article 16.

ARTICLE 5
DIRECT PERSONNEL EXPENSE

5.1 Direct Personnel Expense is defined as the direct salaries of all of the Construction Manager's personnel engaged on the Project, excluding those whose compensation is included in the fee, and the portion of the cost of their mandatory and customary contributions and benefits related thereto such as employment taxes and other statutory employee benefits, insurance, sick leave, holidays, vacations, pensions, and similar contributions and benefits.

ARTICLE 6
REIMBURSABLE COSTS

6.1 The term Reimbursable Costs shall mean costs necessarily incurred in the proper performance of services and paid by the Construction Manager. Such costs shall be at rates not higher than the standard paid in the locality of the Project, except with prior consent of the Owner. Reimbursable Costs and costs not to be reimbursed shall be listed in Article 16.

SAMPLE

AIA DOCUMENT B801 • OWNER-CONSTRUCTION MANAGER AGREEMENT • JUNE 1980 EDITION • AIA®
©1980 • THE AMERICAN INSTITUTE OF ARCHITECTS, 1735 NEW YORK AVE., N.W., WASHINGTON, D.C. 20006

6.2 Trade discounts, rebates and refunds, and returns from sale of surplus materials and equipment shall accrue to the Owner, and the Construction Manager shall make provisions so that they can be secured.

ARTICLE 7
PAYMENTS TO THE CONSTRUCTION MANAGER

7.1   PAYMENTS ON ACCOUNT OF BASIC SERVICES

7.1.1 An initial payment as set forth in Paragraph 15.1 is the minimum payment under this Agreement.

7.1.2 Subsequent payments for Basic Services shall be made monthly and shall be in proportion to services performed within each Phase of Services, on the basis set forth in Article 15.

7.1.3 If and to the extent that the time initially established for the Construction Phase of the Project is exceeded or extended through no fault of the Construction Manager, compensation for such Basic Services required for such extended period of Administration of the Construction Contract shall be computed as set forth in Paragraph 15.3 for Additional Services.

7.1.4 When compensation is based on a percentage of the total of the Contract Sums of all the separate Contracts, and any portions of the Project are deleted or otherwise not constructed, compensation for such portions of the Project shall be payable to the extent services are performed on such portions, in accordance with the schedule set forth in Subparagraph 15.2.1, based on (1) the lowest figures from bona fide Bids or negotiated proposals, or (2) if no such Bids or proposals are received, the most recent estimate of the total of the Contract Sums of all the separate Contracts for such portions of the Project.

7.2   PAYMENTS ON ACCOUNT OF ADDITIONAL SERVICES AND REIMBURSABLE COSTS

7.2.1 Payments on account of the Construction Manager's Additional Services, as defined in Paragraph 1.3, and for Reimbursable Costs, as defined in Article 16, shall be made monthly upon presentation of the Construction Manager's statement of services rendered or costs incurred.

7.3   PAYMENTS WITHHELD

7.3.1 No deductions shall be made from the Construction Manager's compensation on account of penalty, liquidated damages or other sums withheld from payments to Contractors, or on account of the cost of changes in Work other than those for which the Construction Manager is held legally liable.

7.4   PROJECT SUSPENSION OR ABANDONMENT

7.4.1 If the Project is suspended or abandoned in whole or in part for more than three months, the Construction Manager shall be compensated for all services performed prior to receipt of written notice from the Owner of such suspension or abandonment, together with Reimbursable Costs then due and all Termination Expenses as defined in Paragraph 10.4. If the Project is resumed after being suspended for more than three months, the Construction Manager's compensation shall be equitably adjusted.

7.4.2 If construction of the Project has started and is stopped by reason of circumstances not the fault of the Construction Manager, the Owner shall reimburse the Construction Manager for the costs of the Construction

Manager's Project-site staff as provided for by this Agreement. The Construction Manager shall reduce the size of the Project-site staff after 90 days delay or sooner if feasible, for the remainder of the delay period as directed by the Owner and, during that period, the Owner shall reimburse the Construction Manager for the costs of such staff prior to reduction and any relocation or employment termination costs. Upon the termination of the stoppage, the Construction Manager shall provide the necessary Project-site staff as soon as practicable.

ARTICLE 8
CONSTRUCTION MANAGER'S ACCOUNTING RECORDS

8.1 Records of Reimbursable Costs and costs pertaining to services performed on the basis of a Multiple of Direct Personnel Expense shall be kept on the basis of generally accepted accounting principles and shall be available to the Owner or the Owner's authorized representative at mutually convenient times.

ARTICLE 9
ARBITRATION

9.1 All claims, disputes and other matters in question between the parties to this Agreement arising out of or relating to this Agreement or the breach thereof, shall be decided by arbitration in accordance with the Construction Industry Arbitration Rules of the American Arbitration Association then obtaining unless the parties mutually agree otherwise. No arbitration arising out of or relating to this Agreement shall include, by consolidation, joinder or in any other manner, any additional person not a party to this Agreement except by written consent containing a specific reference to this Agreement and signed by the Construction Manager, the Owner, and any other person sought to be joined. Any consent to arbitration involving an additional person or persons shall not constitute consent to arbitration of any dispute not described therein or with any person not named or described therein. This agreement to arbitrate and any agreement to arbitrate with an additional person or persons duly consented to by the parties to this Agreement shall be specifically enforceable under the prevailing arbitration law.

9.2 Notice of demand for arbitration shall be filed in writing with the other party to this Agreement and with the American Arbitration Association, and a copy shall also be filed with the Architect. The demand shall be made within a reasonable time after the claim, dispute or other matter in question has arisen. In no event shall the demand for arbitration be made after the date when institution of legal or equitable proceedings based on such claim, dispute or other matter in question would be barred by the applicable statute of limitations.

9.3 The award rendered by the arbitrators shall be final, and judgment may be entered upon it in accordance with applicable law in any court having jurisdiction thereof.

ARTICLE 10
TERMINATION OF AGREEMENT

10.1 This Agreement may be terminated by either party upon seven days' written notice should the other party fail substantially to perform in accordance with its terms through no fault of the party initiating the termination.

10.2 This Agreement may be terminated by the Owner upon at least fourteen days' written notice to the Construction Manager in the event that the Project is permanently abandoned.

10.3 In the event of termination not the fault of the Construction Manager, the Construction Manager shall be compensated for all services performed to the termination date together with Reimbursable Costs then due and all Termination Expenses.

10.4 Termination Expenses are defined as Reimbursable Costs directly attributable to termination for which the Construction Manager is not otherwise compensated.

ARTICLE 11
MISCELLANEOUS PROVISIONS

11.1 Unless otherwise specified, this Agreement shall be governed by the law in effect at the location of the Project.

11.2 Terms in this Agreement shall have the same meaning as those in the 1980 Edition of AIA Document A201/CM, General Conditions of the Contract for Construction, Construction Management Edition.

11.3 As between the parties to this Agreement: as to all acts or failures to act by either party to this Agreement, any applicable statute of limitations shall commence to run, and any alleged cause of action shall be deemed to have accrued, in any and all events not later than the relevant Date of Substantial Completion of the Project, and as to any acts or failures to act occurring after the relevant Date of Substantial Completion of the Project, not later than the date of issuance of the final Project Certificate for Payment.

11.4 The Owner and the Construction Manager waive all rights against each other, and against the contractors, consultants, agents and employees of the other, for damages covered by any property insurance during construction, as set forth in the 1980 Edition of AIA Document A201/CM, General Conditions of the Contract for Construction, Construction Management Edition. The Owner and the Construction Manager shall each require appropriate similar waivers from their contractors, consultants and agents.

ARTICLE 12
SUCCESSORS AND ASSIGNS

12.1 The Owner and the Construction Manager, respectively, bind themselves, their partners, successors, assigns and legal representatives to the other party to this Agreement, and to the partners, successors, assigns and legal representatives of such other party with respect to all covenants of this Agreement. Neither the Owner nor the Construction Manager shall assign, sublet or transfer any interest in this Agreement without the written consent of the other.

ARTICLE 13
EXTENT OF AGREEMENT

13.1 This Agreement represents the entire and integrated agreement between the Owner and the Construction Manager and supersedes all prior negotiations, representations or agreements, either written or oral. This Agreement may be amended only by written instrument signed by both the Owner and the Construction Manager.

13.2 Nothing contained herein shall be deemed to create any contractual relationship between the Construction Manager and the Architect or any of the Contractors, Subcontractors or material suppliers on the Project; nor shall anything contained in this Agreement be deemed to give any third party any claim or right of action against the Owner or the Construction Manager which does not otherwise exist without regard to this Agreement.

ARTICLE 14
INSURANCE

14.1 The Construction Manager shall purchase and maintain insurance for protection from claims under workers' or workmen's compensation acts; claims for damages because of bodily injury, including personal injury, sickness, disease or death of any of the Construction Manager's employees or of any person; from claims for damages because of injury to or destruction of tangible property including loss of use resulting therefrom; and from claims arising out of the performance of this Agreement and caused by negligent acts for which the Construction Manager is legally liable.

SAMPLE

AIA DOCUMENT B801 • OWNER-CONSTRUCTION MANAGER AGREEMENT • JUNE 1980 EDITION • AIA®
©1980 • THE AMERICAN INSTITUTE OF ARCHITECTS, 1735 NEW YORK AVE., N.W., WASHINGTON, D.C. 20006

ARTICLE 15
BASIS OF COMPENSATION

The Owner shall compensate the Construction Manager for the Scope of Services provided, in accordance with Article 7, Payments to the Construction Manager, and the other Terms and Conditions of this Agreement, as follows:

15.1 AN INITIAL PAYMENT of   dollars ($) shall be made upon execution of this Agreement and credited to the Owner's account as follows:

15.2 BASIC COMPENSATION

15.2.1 FOR BASIC SERVICES, as described in Paragraphs 1.1 and 1.2, and any other services included in Article 16 as part of Basic Services, Basic Compensation shall be computed as follows:

For Preconstruction Phase Services, compensation shall be:
(Here insert basis of compensation, including fixed amounts, multiples or percentages.)

For Construction Phase Services, compensation shall be:
(Here insert basis of compensation, including fixed amounts, multiples or percentages.)

15.3 COMPENSATION FOR ADDITIONAL SERVICES

15.3.1 FOR ADDITIONAL SERVICES OF THE CONSTRUCTION MANAGER, as described in Paragraph 1.3, and any other services included in Article 16 as Additional Services, compensation shall be computed as follows:
(Here insert basis of compensation, including fixed amounts, multiples or percentages.)

15.4 FOR REIMBURSABLE COSTS, as described in Article 6 and Article 16, the actual costs incurred by the Construction Manager in the interest of the Project.

15.5 Payments due the Construction Manager and unpaid under this Agreement shall bear interest from the date payment is due at the rate entered below, or in the absence thereof, at the legal rate prevailing at the principal place of business of the Construction Manager.
(Here insert any rate of interest agreed upon.)

(Usury laws and requirements under the Federal Truth in Lending Act, similar state and local consumer credit laws, and other regulations at the Owner's and Construction Manager's principal places of business, the location of the Project and elsewhere may affect the validity of this provision. Specific legal advice should be obtained with respect to deletion, modification or other requirements such as written disclosures or waivers.)

15.6 The Owner and the Construction Manager agree in accordance with the Terms and Conditions of this Agreement that:

15.6.1 IF THE SCOPE of the Project or the Construction Manager's Services is changed materially, the amounts of compensation shall be equitably adjusted.

15.6.2 IF THE SERVICES covered by this Agreement have not been completed within
(   ) months of the date hereof, through no fault of the Construction Manager, the amounts of compensation, rates and multiples set forth herein shall be equitably adjusted.

ARTICLE 16
OTHER CONDITIONS OR SERVICES

(List Reimbursable Costs and costs not to be reimbursed.)

SAMPLE

This Agreement entered into as of the day and year first written above.

OWNER   CONSTRUCTION MANAGER

_____   _____

_____   _____

_____   _____

AIA DOCUMENT B801 • OWNER-CONSTRUCTION MANAGER AGREEMENT • JUNE 1980 EDITION • AIA®
©1980 • THE AMERICAN INSTITUTE OF ARCHITECTS, 1735 NEW YORK AVE., N.W., WASHINGTON, D.C. 20006   **B801 — 1980 9**

A.G.C. STANDARD FORM 3
ASCE FORM JCC-1

FORM OF CONTRACT

for

Engineering Construction

Projects

1966 EDITION

Prepared Jointly by the

AMERICAN SOCIETY OF CIVIL ENGINEERS, AND
THE ASSOCIATED GENERAL CONTRACTORS OF AMERICA

FORM OF AGREEMENT FOR ENGINEERING CONSTRUCTION
LUMP SUM BASIS

THIS AGREEMENT, made on the_____day of_____, 19_____,

by and between _____

party of the first part, hereinafter called the OWNER, and _____

_____

_____

party of the second part, hereinafter called the CONTRACTOR.

It is understood ENGINEER representing Owner shall be _____

_____

_____

WITNESSETH, That the Contractor and the Owner, for the considerations hereinafter named, agree as follows:

ARTICLE I — Scope of the Work

The Contractor hereby agrees to furnish all of the materials and all of the equipment and labor necessary, and to perform all of the work shown on the Drawings and described in the specifications for the project entitled _____

_____

all in accordance with the requirements and provisions of the following Documents which are hereby made a part of this Agreement:

(*a*) Drawings prepared for same by _____

numbered _____

and dated _____, 19_____.

(*b*) Specifications consisting of:

1. "Standard General Specifications" issued by _____

_____, _____ Edition.

Lump Sum—10

2. "Special Conditions" as prepared by_____

_____ dated _____

3. The "General Conditions of Contract for Engineering Construction"—1966 Edition.

4. Addendum

No. _____ Date _____

ARTICLE II — Time of Completion

(a) The work to be completed under this Contract shall be commenced within _____ calendar days after receipt of notice to proceed.

(b) The work shall be completed within _____ calendar days after receipt of notice to proceed.

(c) Failure to complete the work within the number of calendar days stated in this Article, including extension granted thereto as determined by Section 19 of the General Conditions, shall entitle the Owner to deduct from the moneys due to the Contractor as "Liquidated Damages" an amount equal to $_____ for each calendar day of delay in completion of the work.

(d) If the Contractor completes the work earlier than the date determined in accordance with Paragraph (b), and the Engineer shall so certify in writing, the Owner shall pay the Contractor an additional amount equal to $_____ for each calendar day by which the time of completion so determined has been reduced.

ARTICLE III — The Contract Sum

(a) Except for adjustments as provided herein, the Owner shall pay to the Contractor, for the performance of the work, the lump sum of $_____ which amount shall be known as the Contract Sum.

(b) The Contract Sum shall be equitably adjusted to cover changes in the work ordered by the Engineer, but not shown on the Drawings or required by the Specifications. Such increases or decreases in the Contract Sum shall be determined by agreement between the Owner, or the Engineer, as his representative, and the Contractor. If it is impracticable to arrive at a pre-agreed-upon amount, the work so ordered may be done under the provisions of Article V.

ARTICLE IV — Progress Payments

The Owner shall make payments on account of the Contract as follows:

(a) On not later than the fifth day of every month the Contractor shall present to the Engineer an invoice covering the percentage of the total amount of the Contract which has been completed from the start of the job up to and including the last day of the pre-

Lump Sum—11

ceding month, together with such supporting evidence as may be required by the Engineer. This invoice shall also include the cost of such material required in the permanent work as has been delivered to the site but not as yet incorporated in the work.* Where provision is made for payment for materials delivered to the site or elsewhere, evidence that the Contractor has paid suppliers should be required in order to establish that the Owner is paying for property to which the Contractor has clear title.

(b) On not later than the 15th of the month, the Owner shall pay to the Contractor 90 per cent of the amount of the invoice—less previous payments made. The 10 per cent retained percentage may be held by the Owner until the value of the work completed at the end of any month equals 50 per cent of the total amount of the Contract, after which if the Engineer finds that satisfactory progress is being made, he shall recommend that all of the remaining monthly payments be paid in full. Payments for work, under Subcontracts of the general Contractor, shall be subject to the above conditions applying to the general Contract after the work under a Subcontract has been 50 per cent completed.

(c) Final payment of all moneys due on the Contract shall be made within 30 days of completion and acceptance of the work.

(d) If the owner fails to make payment as herein provided, or as provided in Article V(d), in addition to those remedies available to the Contractor under Section 25 of the General Conditions, there shall be added to each such payment daily interest at the rate of 6 per cent per annum commencing on the first day after said payment is due and continuing until the payment is delivered or mailed to the Contractor.

ARTICLE V — Extra Work

If the Engineer orders, in writing, the performance of any work not covered by the Drawings or included in the Specifications, and for which no item in the Contract is provided, and for which no unit price or lump sum basis can be agreed upon, then such extra work shall be done on a Cost-Plus-Percentage basis of payment as follows:

(a) The Contractor shall be reimbursed for all costs incurred in doing the work, and shall receive an additional payment of ....% of all such cost to cover his indirect overhead costs, plus ....% of all cost, including indirect overhead, as his fee.

(b) The "Cost of the Work" shall be determined as the net sum of the following items:
1. Job Office and all necessary temporary facilities such as buildings, use of land not furnished by the Owner, access roads and utilities. The costs of these items include construction, furnishings and equipment, maintenance during the period that they are needed, demolition and removal. Salvage values agreed on or received by the Contractor shall be credited to the Owner.

---

* In addition to advance payment for materials delivered to the site, wording should indicate that, where applicable, advance payment may be in order for materials in storage away from the site, for field plant and equipment, access roads, etc.—details to be spelled out in the Special Conditions.

Lump Sum—12

2. All materials used on the work whether for temporary or permanent construction.

3. All small tools and supplies; all fuel, lubricants, power, light, water and telephone service.

4. All plant and equipment at specified rental rates and terms of use. If the rental rates do not include an allowance for running repairs and repair parts needed for ordinary maintenance of the plant and equipment, then such items of cost are to be included in the Cost of the Work.

5. All transportation costs on equipment, materials and men.

6. All labor for the project and including the salaries of superintendents, foremen, engineers, inspectors, clerks and other employees while engaged on the work but excluding salaries of general supervisory employees or officers, who do not devote their full time to the work.

7. All payroll charges such as Social Security payments, unemployment insurance, workmen's compensation insurance premiums, pension and retirement allowances, and social insurance premiums, vacation and sick-leave allowances applicable to wages or salaries paid to employees for work done in connection with the contract.

8. All premiums on fire, public liability, property damage or other insurance coverage authorized or required by the Engineer or the Owner, or regularly paid by the Contractor in the conduct of his business.

9. All sales, use, excise, privilege, business, occupation, gross receipt and all other taxes paid by the Contractor in connection with the work, but excluding state income taxes based solely on net income derived from this contract and Federal income taxes.

10. All travel or other related expense of general supervisory employees for necessary visits to the job excluding expenses of such employees incurred at the Home Office of the Contractor.

11. All Subcontracts approved by the Engineer or Owner.

12. (Insert other costs proper for inclusion in this Contract.)

    a. _____

    b. _____

    c. _____

13. Any other costs incurred by the Contractor as a direct result of executing the Order, subject to approval by the Engineer.

14. Credit to the Owner for the following items:

    a. Such discounts on invoices as may be obtainable provided that the Owner advances sufficient funds to pay the invoices within the discount period.

    b. The mutually agreed salvage value of materials, tools or equipment charged to the Owner and taken over by the Contractor for his use or sale at the completion of the work.

Lump Sum—13

  c. Any rebates, refunds, returned deposits or other allowances properly credited to the Cost of the Work.

(c) The cost of the work done each day shall be submitted to the Engineer in a satisfactory form on the succeeding day, and shall be approved by him or adjusted at once.

(d) Monthly payments of all charges for Extra Work in any one month shall be made in full on or before the 15th of the succeeding month. Those payments shall include the full amount of fee earned on the cost of the work done.

  IN WITNESS WHEREOF the parties hereto have executed this Agreement, the day and year first above written.

——————————————————— OWNER

WITNESS:

————————————————By: ————————————————
                   Title

——————————————— CONTRACTOR

WITNESS:

————————————————By: ————————————————
                   Title

Lump Sum—14

THE ASSOCIATED GENERAL CONTRACTORS

STANDARD SUBCONTRACT AGREEMENT
FOR BUILDING CONSTRUCTION

This Document has important legal and insurance consequences; consultation with an attorney and insurance consultants and carriers is encouraged with respect to its completion or modification.

THIS AGREEMENT made at

this   day of   , 19   , by

and between

hereinafter referred to as the Contractor, and

hereinafter referred to as the Subcontractor, to perform part of the Work on the following Project:

PROJECT:

OWNER:

ARCHITECT:

AGC DOCUMENT NO. 5   •   STANDARD SUBCONTRACT AGREEMENT FOR BUILDING CONSTRUCTION   •   APRIL 1980
© 1980 ASSOCIATED GENERAL CONTRACTORS OF AMERICA

ARTICLE 1

Scope of Work

1.1 The Contractor employs the Subcontractor as an independent contractor, to perform the following part of the Work which the Contractor has contracted with the Owner to provide on the Project:

The Subcontractor agrees to perform such part of the Work (hereinafter called "Subcontractor's Work") under the general direction of the Contractor and subject to the final approval of the Architect/Engineer or other specified representative of the Owner, in accordance with the Contract Documents. Subcontractor will furnish all of the labor and materials, along with competent supervision, shop drawings and samples, tools, equipment, scaffolding, and permits which are necessary for such performance.

1.2 The Contract Documents are:

The Subcontrator binds himself to the Contractor for the performance of Subcontractor's Work in the same manner as the Contractor is bound to the Owner for such performance under Contractor's contract with the Owner. The pertinent parts of such contract will be made available upon Subcontractor's request.

1.3 Should any question arise with respect to the interpretation of the drawings and specifications, such questions shall be submitted to the Architect/Engineer and his decision shall be final and binding. If there is no Architect/Engineer for this Project, the Contractor's decision shall be followed by the Subcontractor.

ARTICLE 2

Payments

2.1 The Contractor agrees to pay to the Subcontractor for the satisfactory completion of Subcontractor's Work the sum of _____ ($ _____) in monthly payments of _____ percent of the work performed in any preceding month, in accordance with estimates prepared by the Subcontractor and approved by the Contractor and _____.
Payments made on account of materials not incorporated in the work, but delivered and suitably stored at the site, or at some other location agreed upon in writing, shall be in accordance with the terms and conditions of the Contract Documents. Subcontractor will provide monthly completed lien waivers and supplier affidavit forms, in a form satisfactory to the Owner and Contractor. Payment of the approved portion of the Subcontractor's monthly estimate shall be conditioned upon receipt by the Contractor of his payment from the Owner. Approval and payment of Subcontractor's monthly estimate is specifically agreed not to constitute or imply acceptance by the Contractor or Owner of any portion of the Subcontractor's Work.

2.2 In the event the Subcontractor does not submit to the Contractor such monthly estimates by _____ then the Contractor may at his option include in his monthly estimate to the Owner for Work performed during the preceding month such amount as he may deem proper for the Work of the Subcontractor for the preceding month and the Subcontractor agrees to accept such approved portion thereof in lieu of monthly payment based upon the Subcontractor's estimate.

2.3 In the event it appears to the Contractor that the labor, material and other bills incurred in the performance of Subcontractor's Work are not being currently paid, the Contractor may take such steps as he deems necessary to insure that the money paid with any progress payment will be utilized to pay such bills.

2.4 Final payment shall be paid to the Subcontractor upon approval by the Owner, Architect and the Contractor of the Subcontractor's Work and, upon payment having been received by the Contractor for all of Subcontractor's Work and satisfactory evidence having been received by the Contractor that all labor, including customary fringe benefits and payments due under collective bargaining agreements, and all subcontractors and materialmen have been paid to date and are waiving their lien rights upon the final payment of a specific balance due.

2.5 The Contractor may deduct from any amounts due or to become due to the Subcontractor any sum or sums owing by the Subcontractor to the Contractor; and in the event of any breach by the Subcontractor of any provision or obligation of this Subcontract, or in the event of the assertion by other parties of any claim or lien against the Owner, the Contractor, Contractor's Surety, or the premises upon which the Work was performed, which claim or lien arises out of the Subcontractor's performance of this Agreement, the Contractor shall have the right, but is not required, to retain out of any payments due or to become due to the Subcontractor an amount sufficient to completely protect the Contractor from any and all loss, damage or expense therefrom, until the claim or lien has been adjusted by the Subcontractor to the satisfaction of the Contractor. This paragraph shall be applicable even though the Subcontractor has posted a full payment and performance bond.

ARTICLE 3

Prosecution of the Work

3.1 Time is of the essence for both parties, and they mutually agree to see to the performance of their Work and the Work of their subcontractors so that the entire project may be completed in accordance with the Contract Documents. The Subcontractor shall provide the Contractor with scheduling information and Subcontractor's proposed schedule for the Subcontractor's Work. The Contractor shall then prepare the Schedule of the Work and, as may be necessary, revise such schedule as the Work progresses. Subcontractor acknowledges that revisions may be made in such schedule and agrees to make no claim for acceleration or delay by reason of such revisions so long as such revisions are of the type normally experienced in Work of this scope and complexity.

3.2 The Subcontractor shall prosecute Subcontractor's Work in a prompt and diligent manner in accordance with the Schedule of Work without hindering the Work of the Contractor or any other subcontractor. If work of others is damaged by Subcontractor, the Subcontractor will cause such damage to be corrected to the satisfaction of and without cost to the Contractor and Owner. In the event Subcontractor fails to maintain his part of the Schedule of the Work, he shall, without additional compensation, work such overtime as the Contractor may direct until Subcontractor's Work is in accordance with such schedule.

3.3 The Subcontractor shall be responsible for and will prepare for performance of Subcontractor's Work, including without limitation thereto, the submission of shop drawings, samples, tests, field dimensions, determination of labor requirements and ordering of materials as required to meet the Schedule of Work. Subcontractor shall notify Contractor when portions of his Work are ready for inspection.

3.4 The Subcontractor will furnish periodic progress reports of the Subcontractor's Work as mutually agreed including the progress of materials or equipment to be provided under this Agreement that may be in the course of preparation or manufacture.

3.5 The Subcontractor shall cooperate with the Contractor and subcontractors whose work may interfere with the Subcontractor's Work and participate in the preparation of coordinated drawings and work schedules in areas of congestion, specifically noting and advising the Contractor of any interference by other contractors or subcontractors.

3.6 The Subcontractor shall keep the building and premises reasonably clean of debris resulting from the performance of Subcontractor's Work. If the Subcontractor fails to comply with this paragraph within 48 hours after receipt of notice of noncompliance from the Contractor, the Contractor may perform such necessary clean-up and deduct the cost from any amounts due to the Subcontractor.

3.7 The Subcontractor shall give adequate notices pertaining to the Work of the Subcontractor to proper authorities and secure and pay for all necessary licenses and permits to carry on Subcontractor's Work, the furnishing of which is required by the Contract Documents.

3.8 The Subcontractor shall comply with all Federal, State and local laws, Social Security Laws and Unemployment Compensation Laws, Workers' Compensation Laws and Safety Laws insofar as applicable to the performance of this Agreement. He shall pay all taxes applicable to the performance of Subcontractor's Work. He shall also maintain his own safety program for compliance with such laws.

3.9 The Subcontractor will not assign this subcontract nor subcontract the whole or any part of the Work to be performed hereunder without the prior written consent of the Contractor, with the exception of those subcontractors listed by the Subcontractor and furnished to the Contractor at the time this Agreement is executed.

ARTICLE 4

Changes in the Work

4.1 The Contractor and Subcontractor agree that the Contractor may add to or deduct from the amount of Work covered by this Agreement, and any changes so made in the amount of Work involved, or any other parts of this Agreement, shall be by a written amendment hereto setting forth in detail the changes involved and the value thereof which shall be mutually agreed upon between the Contractor and Subcontractor. The Subcontractor agrees to proceed with the Work as changed when so ordered in writing by the Contractor so as not to delay the progress of the Work, and pending any determination of the value thereof unless Contractor first requests a proposal of cost before the change is effected. If the Contractor requests a proposal of cost for a change, the Subcontractor shall promptly comply with such request.

4.2 Subcontractor shall be entitled to receive no extra compensation for extra Work or materials or changes of any kind regardless of whether the same was ordered by the Contractor or any of his representatives unless a Change Order therefor has been issued in writing by the Contractor. If extra work was ordered by the Contractor and the Subcontractor performed same but did not receive a written order therefor, the Subcontractor shall be deemed to have waived any claim for extra compensation therefor, regardless of any written or verbal protests or claims by the Subcontractor. The Subcontractor shall be responsible for any costs incurred by the Contractor for changes of any kind made by the Subcontractor that increase the cost of the work for either the Contractor or other subcontractors when the Subcontractor proceeds with such changes without a written order therefor.

4.3 The Subcontractor agrees that no claim for additional services rendered or materials furnished by the Subcontractor to the Contractor shall be valid unless notice is given to the Contractor prior to the furnishing of the services or material or unless written notice of the claim therefor is given by the Subcontractor to the Contractor not later than the last day of the calendar month following that in which the claim originated, with the amount of the claim to be given in writing by the Subcontractor as soon as practicable.

4.4 The Subcontractor will make all claims for extra compensation and for extension of time to the Contractor promptly in accordance with this Article and consistent with the Contract Documents.

4.5 Notwithstanding any other provision, if the Work for which the Subcontractor claims extra compensation is determined by the Owner or Architect not to entitle the Contractor to a Change Order or extra compensation, then the Contractor shall not be liable to the Subcontractor for any extra compensation for such Work, unless Contractor agreed in writing to such extra compensation.

ARTICLE 5

Insurance and Indemnity

5.1 Prior to starting Work the Subcontractor shall procure and maintain in force, Workers' Compensation Insurance, Employers Liability Insurance, Comprehensive General Liability Insurance with contractual coverage and Automobile Liability Insurance and such other insurance, to the extent required by the Contract Documents for the Subcontractor's Work.

5.2 The Subcontractor's Comprehensive General and Automobile Liability Insurance, as required by Paragraph 5.1 shall be written for not less than limits of liability as follows:

AGC DOCUMENT NO. 5 • STANDARD SUBCONTRACT AGREEMENT FOR BUILDING CONSTRUCTION • APRIL 1980

a. Comprehensive General Liability

1. Bodily Injury $_____ Each Occurrence
                                                          (Completed Operations)

                                $_____ Aggregate

2. Property Damage $_____ Each Occurrence

                                $_____ Aggregate

b. Comprehensive Automobile Liability

1. Bodily Injury $_____ Each Person

                                $_____ Each Occurrence

2. Property Damage $_____ Each Occurence

5.3 Comprehensive General Liability Insurance may be arranged under a single policy for the full limits required or by a combination of underlying policies with the balance provided by an Excess or Umbrella Liability policy.

5.4 The foregoing policies shall contain a provision that coverages afforded under the policies will not be cancelled or not renewed until at least thirty (30) days' prior written notice has been given to the Contractor. Certificates of Insurance acceptable to the Contractor shall be filed with the Contractor prior to the commencement of Work.

5.5 The Contractor and Subcontractor waive all rights against each other and against the Owner, the Architect/Engineer, separate contractors, and all other subcontractors for damages caused by fire or other perils to the extent covered by Builder's Risk or any other property insurance, except such rights as they may have to the proceeds of such insurance.

5.6 To the fullest extent permitted by law, the Subcontractor agrees to indemnify and hold harmless the Contractor, the Owner, the Architect/Engineer and all of their agents and employees from and against all claims, damages, losses and expenses, including but not limited to attorney's fees, arising out of or resulting from the performance, or failure in performance, of the Subcontractor's Work under this Subcontract, provided that any such claim, damage, loss or expense (1) is attributable to bodily injury, sickness, disease, or death, or to injury to or destruction of tangible property (other than the Work itself) including the loss of use resulting therefrom, and (2) is caused in whole or in part by any negligent act or omission of the Subcontractor or anyone directly or indirectly employed by him or anyone for whose acts he may be liable regardless of whether it is caused in part by a party indemnified hereunder. Such obligations shall not be construed to negate, abridge, or otherwise reduce any other right or obligation of indemnity which would otherwise exist as to any party or person described in this Paragraph 5.6.

5.6.1 In any and all claims against the Contractor or any of his agents or employees by any employee of the Subcontractor, anyone directly or indirectly employed by him or anyone for whose acts he may be liable, the indemnification obligation under this Paragraph 5.6 shall not be limited in any way by any limitation on the amount or type of damages, compensation or benefits payable by or for the Subcontractor under Workers' Compensation acts, disability benefit acts or other employee benefit acts.

5.6.2 The obligations of the Subcontractor under this Paragraph 5.6 shall not extend to the liability of the Architect/Engineer, his agents or employees, arising out of (a) the preparation or approval of maps, drawings, opinions, reports, surveys, Change Orders, designs or specifications, or (b) the giving of or failure to give directions or instructions by the Architect/Engineer, his agents or employees, providing such giving or failure to give is the primary cause of the injury or damage.

ARTICLE 6

Performance Bond and Labor and Material Payment Bond

A Performance Bond and a Labor and Material Payment Bond in a form satisfactory to the Contractor shall be furnished in the full amount of this Agreement, if required by the Contractor. This obligation shall continue throughout the agreement and may be required at any time during the performance of Subcontractor's Work by a change under Article 4.

ARTICLE 7

Warranty

The Subcontractor agrees to promptly make good without cost to the Owner or Contractor any and all defects due to faulty workmanship and/or materials which may appear within the guarantee or warranty period so established in the Contract Documents; and if no such period be stipulated in the Contract Documents, then such guarantee shall be for a period of one year from date of completion and acceptance of the project by the Owner. The Subcontractor further agrees to execute any special guarantees as provided by the terms of the Contract Documents, prior to final payment.

ARTICLE 8

Contractors' Obligations

8.1 The Contractor agrees to be bound to the Subcontractor by all the obligations that the Owner assumes to the Contractor under the Contract Documents and by all provisions thereof affording remedies and redress to the Contractor from the Owner insofar as applicable to this Agreement.

8.2 Upon request, the Contractor will give the Subcontractor written authorization to obtain direct from the Architect/Engineer or Owner's authorized agent, evidence of amount and percentages of completion certified on his account.

8.3 The Contractor shall not issue or give any instruction, order or directions directly to employees or workmen of the Subcontractor other than to the persons designated as the authorized representative(s) of the Subcontractor.

8.4 The Contractor shall make no demand for liquidated damages in any sum in excess of the amount specifically named in this Agreement or the Contract Documents. Liquidated damages shall not be assessed for delays not caused by the Subcontractor. Liquidated damages, when assessed, shall not exceed the Subcontractor's proportionate share of the responsibility for such delay. This provision does not preclude any claim the Contractor may have for direct damages under law.

8.5 The Subcontractor will furnish those temporary facilities and services required by the Subcontractor except for those to be provided by the Contractor set forth in the Attachment A to this Agreement. Adequate storage areas, if available, will be allocated by the Contractor for the Subcontractor's materials and equipment during the course of the Work.

8.6 The Contractor agrees that no claim for services rendered or materials furnished by the Contractor to the Subcontractor shall be valid unless notice is given to the Subcontractor prior to furnishing of the services or material or unless written notice of the claim therefor is given by the Contractor to the Subcontractor not later than the last day of the calendar month following that in which the claim originated, with the amount of the claim to be given in writing by the Contractor as soon as practicable.

ARTICLE 9

Termination

9.1 Should the Subcontractor fail at any time to supply a sufficient number of properly skilled workmen or sufficient materials and equipment of the proper quality, or fail in any respect to prosecute the Work with promptness and diligence, or fail to promptly correct defective Work or fail in the performance of any of the agreements herein contained; the Contractor may, at his option, provide such labor, materials and equipment and to deduct the cost thereof, together with all loss or damage occasioned thereby, from any money then due or thereafter to become due to the Subcontractor under this Agreement.

9.2 If the Subcontractor at any time shall refuse or neglect to supply sufficient properly skilled workmen, or materials or equipment of the proper quality and quantity, or fail in any respect to prosecute Subcontractor's Work with promptness and diligence, or cause by any action or omission the stoppage or interference with the work of the Contractor or other subcontractors, or fail in the performance of any of the covenants herein contained, or be unable to meet his debts as they mature, the Contractor may at his option at any time after serving written notice of such default with direction to cure in a specific period, but not less than two (2) working days, and the Subcontractor's failure to cure the default, terminate the Subcontractor's employment by delivering written notice of termination to the Subcontractor. Thereafter, the Contractor may take possession of the plant and work, materials, tools, appliances and equipment of the Subcontractor at the building site, and through himself or others provide labor, equipment and materials to prosecute Subcontractor's Work on such terms and conditions as shall be deemed necessary, and shall deduct the cost thereof, including without restriction thereto all charges, expenses, losses, costs, damages, and attorney's fees, incurred as a result of the Subcontractor's failure to perform, from any money then due or thereafter to become due to the Subcontractor under this Agreement.

9.3 If the Contrator so terminates the employment of the Subcontractor, the Subcontractor shall not be entitled to any further payments under this agreement until Subcontractor's Work has been completed and accepted by the Owner, and payment has been received by the Contractor from the Owner with respect thereto. In the event that the unpaid balance due exceeds the Contractor's cost of completion, the difference shall be paid to the Subcontractor; but if such expense exceeds the balance due, the Subcontractor agrees promptly to pay the difference to the Contractor.

ARTICLE 10

Claims

10.1 All claims, disputes and other matters in question arising out of, or relating to, this Subcontract or the breach thereof shall be decided by Arbitration in accordance with the Construction Industry Arbitration Rules of the American Arbitration Association then obtaining unless the parties mutually agree otherwise. This agreement to arbitrate shall be specifically enforceable under the prevailing arbitration law. The award rendered by the arbitrators shall be final, and judgment may be entered upon in accordance with applicable law in any court having jurisdiction thereof.

10.2 In the event the Contractor and Owner or others arbitrate matters relating to this Subcontract, it shall be the responsibility of the Subcontractor to prepare and present the Contractor's case, to the extent the proceedings are related to this Subcontract.

10.3 Should the Contractor enter into arbitration with the Owner or others regarding matters relating to this Agreement, the Subcontractor shall be bound by the result of the arbitration to the same degree as the Contractor.

10.4 The Subcontractor shall carry on Subcontractor's Work and maintain his progress during any arbitration proceedings.

ARTICLE 11

Prevailing Law

This Agreement shall be governed by the law in effect in _____

IN WITNESS WHEREOF the parties hereto have executed this Agreement under seal, the day and year first above written.

ATTEST:

_____

_____
Subcontractor

By _____
(Title)

ATTEST:

_____

_____
Contractor

By _____
(Title)

Appendix D

Uniform Construction Index Cost Analysis Format*

*Reproduced with the permission of the Construction Specifications Institute, 1150 17th Street, N.W., Washington, D.C. 20036

Uniform Construction Index	**Cost Analysis Format**

0 CONDITIONS OF THE CONTRACT

00000.-00099. unassigned

1 GENERAL REQUIREMENTS

01020. ALLOWANCES
01021.-01099. unassigned
01100. ALTERNATIVES
01101.-01199. unassigned
01200. PROJECT MEETINGS
01201.-01299. unassigned
01300. SUBMITTALS
01301.-01399. unassigned
01400. QUALITY CONTROL
01401.-01499. unassigned
01500. TEMPORARY FACILITIES AND CONTROLS
01501.-01599. unassigned
01600. MATERIAL AND EQUIPMENT
01601.-01699. unassigned
01700. PROJECT CLOSEOUT
01701.-01999. unassigned

2 SITE WORK

02000. ALTERNATIVES
02001.-02009. unassigned
02010. SUBSURFACE EXPLORATION
02011. Borings
02012. Core Drilling
02013. Standard Penetration Tests
02014. Seismic Exploration
02015.-02099. unassigned
02100. CLEARING
02101. Structure Moving
02102. Clearing and Grubbing
02103. Tree Pruning
02104. Shrub and Tree Relocation
02105.-02109. unassigned
02110. DEMOLITION
02111.-02199. unassigned
02200. EARTHWORK
02201.-02209. unassigned
02210. Site Grading
02211. Rock Removal
02212. Embankment
02213.-02219 unassigned
02220. Excavating and Backfilling
02221. Trenching
02222. Structure Excavation
02223. Roadway excavation
02224. Pipe Boring and Jacking
02225.-02226. unassigned
02227. Waste Material Disposal
02228.-02229. unassigned
02230. Soil Compaction Control
02231.-02239. unassigned
02240. Soil Stabilization
02241.-02249. unassigned
02250. SOIL TREATMENT
02251. Termite Control
02252. Vegetation Control
02253.-02299. unassigned
02300. PILE FOUNDATIONS
02301.-02349. unassigned
02350. CAISSONS
02351. Drilled Caissons
02352. Excavated Caissons
02353.-02399. unassigned
02400 SHORING
02401.-02419. unassigned
02420. Underpinning
02421. 02499. unassigned
02500. SITE DRAINAGE
02501.-02549. unassigned
02550. SITE UTILITIES
02551.-02599. unassigned
02600. PAVING & SURFACING
02601.-02609. unassigned
02610. Paving
02611.-02619. unassigned
02620. Curbs and Gutters
02621.-02629. unassigned
02630. Walks

02631.-02639. unassigned
02640. Synthetic Surfacing
02641.-02699. unassigned
02700. SITE IMPROVEMENTS
02701.-02709. unassigned
02710. Fences and Gates
02711.-02719. unassigned
02720. Road and Parking Appurtenances
02721.-02729. unassigned
02730. Playing Fields
02731.-02739. unassigned
02740. Fountains
02741.-02749. unassigned
02750. Irrigation System
02751.-02759. unassigned
02760. Site Furnishings
02761.-02799. unassigned
02800. LANDSCAPING
02801.-02809. unassigned
02810. Soil Preparation
02811.-02819. unassigned
02820. Lawns
02821.-02829. unassigned
02830. Trees, Shrubs, and Ground Cover
02831.-02849. unassigned
02850. RAILROAD WORK
02851. Trackwork
02852. Ballasting
02853.-02899. unassigned
02900. MARINE WORK
02901.-02909. unassigned
02910. Docks
02911.-02919. unassigned
02920. Boat Facilities
02921.-02929. unassigned
02930. Protective Marine Structures
02931. Fenders
02932. Seawalls
02933. Groins
02934. Jettys
02935.-02939. unassigned
02940. Dredging
02941.-02949. unassigned
02950. TUNNELING
02951.-02959. unassigned
02960. Tunnel Excavation
02961.-02969. unassigned
02970. Tunnel Grouting
02971.-02979. unassigned
02980. Support Systems
02981.-02999. unassigned

**Uniform
Construction
Index**

**Cost Analysis
Format**

---

3 CONCRETE

03000. ALTERNATIVES
03001.-03099. unassigned
03100. CONCRETE FORMWORK
03101.-03149. unassigned
03150. EXPANSION &
CONTRACTION JOINTS
03151.-03199. unassigned
03200. CONCRETE
REINFORCEMENT
03201.-03209. unassigned
03210. Steel Bar and Welded Wire
Fabric Reinforcing
03211.-03229. unassigned
03230. Stressing Tendons
03231.-03299. unassigned
03300. CAST-IN-PLACE CONCRETE
03301.-03304. unassigned
03305. Concrete Curing
03306.-03309. unassigned
03310. Concrete
03311.-03319. unassigned
03320. Lightweight Concrete
03321. Insulating Concrete
03322. Lightweight Structural
Concrete
03323.-03329. unassigned
03330. Heavyweight Concrete
03331.-03339. unassigned
03340. Prestressed Concrete
03341.-03349. unassigned
03350. SPECIALLY FINISHED
CONCRETE
03351. Exposed Aggregate Concrete
03352. Bushhammered Concrete
03353. Blasted Concrete
03354. Heavy-Duty Concrete Floor
Finishes
03355. Grooved-Surface Concrete
03356.-03359. unassigned
03360. SPECIALLY PLACED
CONCRETE
03361.-03369. unassigned
03370. Grout
03371.-03399. unassigned
03400. PRECAST CONCRETE
03401.-03409. unassigned
03410. Precast Concrete Panels
03411. Tilt-Up Wall Panels
03412.-03419. unassigned
03420. Precast Structural Concrete
03421.-03429. unassigned
03430. Precast Prestressed Concrete
03431.-03499. unassigned
03500. CEMENTITIOUS DECKS
03501.-03509. unassigned
03510. Gypsum Concrete
03511.-03519. unassigned
03520. Cementitious Wood Fiber
Deck
03521.-03999. unassigned

4 MASONRY

04000. ALTERNATIVES
04001.-04099. unassigned
04100. MORTAR
04101.-04149. unassigned
04150. MASONRY ACCESSORIES
04151.-04159. unassigned
04160. Joint Reinforcement
04161.-04169. unassigned
04170. Anchors and Tie Systems
04171.-04179. unassigned
04180. Control Joints
04181.-04199. unassigned
04200. UNIT MASONRY
04201.-04209. unassigned
04210. Brick Masonry
04211.-04219. unassigned
04220. Concrete Unit Masonry
04221.-04229. unassigned
04230. Reinforced Unit Masonry
04231.-04239. unassigned
04240. Clay Backing Tile
04241.-04244. unassigned
04245. Clay Facing Tile
04246.-04249. unassigned
04250. Ceramic Veneer
04251.-04269. unassigned
04270. Glass Unit Masonry
04271.-04279. unassigned
04280. Gypsum Unit Masonry
04281.-04399. unassigned
04400. STONE
04401.-04409. unassigned
04410. Rough Stone
04411.-04419. unassigned
04420. Cut Stone
04421. unassigned
04422. Marble
04423.-04429. unassigned
04430. Simulated Masonry
04431.-04434. unassigned
04435. Cast Stone
04436.-04439. unassigned
04440. Flagstone
04441.-04449. unassigned
04450. Natural Stone Veneer
04451.-04499. unassigned
04500 MASONRY RESTORATION &
CLEANING
04501.-04509. unassigned
04510. Masonry Cleaning
04511.-04549. unassigned
04550. REFRACTORIES
04551.-04999. unassigned

5 METALS

05000. ALTERNATIVES
05001.-05099. unassigned
05100. STRUCTURAL METAL
FRAMING
05101.-05119. unassigned
05120. Structural Steel
05121.-05129. unassigned
05130. Structural Aluminum
05131.-05199. unassigned
05200. METAL JOISTS
05201.-05299. unassigned
05300. METAL DECKING
05301.-05399. unassigned
05400. LIGHTGAGE METAL
FRAMING
05401.-05499. unassigned
05500. METAL FABRICATIONS
05501.-05509. unassigned
05510. Metal Stairs
05511.-05519. unassigned
05520. Handrails and Railings
05521. Pipe and Tube Railings
05522.-05529. unassigned
05530. Gratings
05531.-05539. unassigned
05540. Castings
05541.-05699. unassigned
05700. ORNAMENTAL METAL
05701.-05709. unassigned
05710. Ornamental Stairs
05711.-05719. unassigned
05720. Ornamental Handrails and
Railings
05721.-05729. unassigned
05730. Ornamental Sheet Metal
05731.-05799 unassigned
05800 **EXPANSION CONTROL**
05801.-05999 unassigned

Uniform Construction Index	Cost Analysis Format

6 WOOD AND PLASTICS

06000. ALTERNATIVES
06001.-06099. unassigned
06100. ROUGH CARPENTRY
06101.-06109. unassigned
06110. Framing and Sheathing
06111. Light Wooden Structures Framing
06112. Preassembled Components
06113. Sheathing
06114. Diaphragms
06115.-06129. unassigned
06130. HEAVY TIMBER CONSTRUCTION
06131. Timber Trusses
06132. Mill-Framed Structures
06133. Pole Construction
06134.-06149. unassigned
06150. TRESTLES
06151.-06169. unassigned
06170. PREFABRICATED STRUCTURAL WOOD
06171.-06179. unassigned
06180. Glued Laminated Construction
06181. Glue-Laminated Structural Units
06182. Glue-Laminated Decking
06183.-06189. unassigned
06190. Wood Trusses
06191.-06199. unassigned
06200. FINISH CARPENTRY
06201.-06219. unassigned
06220. Millwork
06221.-06239. unassigned
06240. Laminated Plastic
06241.-06299. unassigned
06300. WOOD TREATMENT
06301.-06399. unassigned
06400. ARCHITECTURAL WOODWORK
06401.-06409. unassigned
06410. Cabinetwork
06411. Wood Cabinets: Unfinished
06412.-06419. unassigned
06420. Paneling
06421. Architectural Hardwood Plywood Paneling
06422. Softwood Plywood Paneling
06423.-06429. unassigned
06430. Stairwork
06431. Wood Stairs and Railings
06432.-06499. unassigned
06500. PREFABRICATED STRUCTURAL PLASTICS
06501.-06599. unassigned
06600. PLASTIC FABRICATIONS
06601.-06999. unassigned

7 THERMAL & MOISTURE PROTECTION

07000. ALTERNATIVES
07001.-07099. unassigned
07100. WATERPROOFING
07101.-07109. unassigned
07110. Membrane Waterproofing
07111.-07119. unassigned
07120. Fluid Applied Waterproofing
07121. Liquid Waterproofing
07122.-07129. unassigned
07130. Bentonite Waterproofing
07131.-07139. unassigned
07140. Metal Oxide Waterproofing
07141.-07149. unassigned
07150. DAMPPROOFING
07151.-07159. unassigned
07160. Bituminous Dampproofing
07161.-07169. unassigned
07170. Silicone Dampproofing
07171.-07174. unassigned
07175. Water Repellent Coating
07176.-07179. unassigned
07180. Cementitious Dampproofing
07181.-07189. unassigned
07190. Vapor Barriers/Retardants
07191.-07199. unassigned
07200. INSULATION
07210. Building Insulation
07211. Loose Fill Insulation
07212. Rigid Insulation
07213. Fibrous and Reflective Insulation
07214. Foamed-in-Place Insulation
07215. Sprayed-On Insulation
07216.-07229. unassigned
07230. High and Low Temperature Insulation
07231.-07239. unassigned
07240. Roof and Deck Insulation
07241.-07249. unassigned
07250. Perimeter and Under-Slab Insulation
07251.-07299. unassigned
07300. SHINGLES & ROOFING TILES
07301.-07309. unassigned
07310. Shingles
07311.-07319. unassigned
07320. Roofing Tiles
07321.-07399. unassigned
07400. PREFORMED ROOFING & SIDING
07401.-07409. unassigned
07410. Preformed Wall and Roof Panels
07411. Preformed Metal Siding
07412.-07419. unassigned
07420. Composite Building Panels
07421.-07439. unassigned
07440. Preformed Plastic Panels

07441.-07459. unassigned
07460. Cladding/Siding
07461. Wood Siding
07462. Composition Siding
07463. Asbestos-Cement Siding
07464. Plastic Siding
07465.-07499. unassigned
07500. MEMBRANE ROOFING
07501.-07509. unassigned
07510. Built-Up Bituminous Roofing
07511.-07519. unassigned
07520. Prepared Roll Roofing
07521.-07529. unassigned
07530. Elastic Sheet Roofing
07531.-07539. unassigned
07540. Fluid Applied Roofing
07541.-07569. unassigned
07570. TRAFFIC TOPPING
07571.-07599. unassigned
07600. FLASHING & SHEET METAL
07601.-07609. unassigned
07610. Sheet Metal Roofing
07611.-07619. unassigned
07620. Flashing and Trim
07621.-07629. unassigned
07630. Roofing Specialties
07631. Gutters and Downspouts
07632.-07659. unassigned
07660. Gravel Stops
07661.-07699. unassigned
07700. Flashing
07701.-07799. unassigned
07800. ROOF ACCESSORIES
07801.-07809. unassigned
07810. Skylights
07811. Plastic Skylights
07812. Metal-Framed Skylights
07813.-07829. unassigned
07830. Hatches
07831.-07839. unassigned
07840. Gravity Ventilators
07841.-07849. unassigned
07850. Prefabricated Curbs
07851.-07859. unassigned
07860. Prefabricated Expansion Joints
07861.-07899. unassigned
07900. SEALANTS
07901.-07949. unassigned
07950. Gaskets
07951.-07999. unassigned

Uniform Construction Index

Cost Analysis Format

**Uniform
Construction
Index**

Cost Analysis
Format

09561.-09579. unassigned
09580. Plywood Block Flooring
09581.-09589. unassigned
09590. Resilient Wood Floor
System
09591.-09599. unassigned
09600. Wood Block Industrial
Flooring
09601.-09649. unassigned
09650. RESILIENT FLOORING
09651. Cementitious Underlayment
09660. Resilient Tile Flooring
09661.-09664. unassigned
09665. Resilient Sheet Flooring
09666.-09669. unassigned
09670. Fluid Applied Resilient
Flooring
09671.-09679. unassigned
09680. CARPETING
09681. Carpet Cushion
09682. Carpet
09683. Bonded Cushion Carpet
09684. Custom Carpet
09685.-09689. unassigned
09690. Carpet Tile
09691.-09699. unassigned
09700. SPECIAL FLOORING
09701.-09709. unassigned
09710. Magnesium Oxychloride
Floors
09711.-09719. unassigned
09720. Epoxy-Marble-Chip Flooring
09721.-09729. unassigned
09730. Elastomeric Liquid Flooring
09731. Conductive Elastomeric
Liquid Flooring
09732.-09739. unassigned
09740. Heavy-Duty Concrete
Toppings
09741. Armored Floors
09742.-09749. unassigned
09750. Brick Flooring
09751.-09759. unassigned
09760. FLOOR TREATMENT
09761.-09799. unassigned
09800. SPECIAL COATINGS
09801.-09809. unassigned
09810. Abrasion Resistant Coatings
09811.-09819. unassigned
09820. Cementitious Coatings
09821.-09829. unassigned
09830. Elastomeric Coatings
09831.-09839. unassigned
09840. Fire-Resistant Coatings
09841. Sprayed Fireproofing
09842.-09849. unassigned
09850. Aggregate Wall Coatings
09851.-09899. unassigned
09900. PAINTING
09901.-09949. unassigned
09950. WALL COVERING
09951. Vinyl-Coated Fabric Wall
Covering
09952. Vinyl Wall Covering
09953. Cork Wall Covering
09954. Wallpaper

09955. Wall Fabrics
09956.-09959. unassigned
09960. Flexible Wood Sheets
09961.-09969. unassigned
09970. **PREFINISHED PANELS**
09971.-09989. unassigned
09990. Adhesives
09991.-09999. unassigned

10 SPECIALTIES

10000. ALTERNATIVES
10001.-10099. unassigned
10100. CHALKBOARDS AND
TACKBOARDS
10101.-10149. unassigned
10150. COMPARTMENTS AND
CUBICLES
10151. Hospital Cubicles
10152.-10159. unassigned
10160. Toilet and Shower Partitions
10161. Laminated Plastic Toilet
Partitions
10162. Metal Toilet Partitions
10163. Stone Partitions
10164.-10169. unassigned
10170. Shower and Dressing
Compartments
10171.-10199. unassigned
10200. LOUVERS AND VENTS
10201.-10239. unassigned
10240. GRILLES AND SCREENS
10241.-10259. unassigned
10260. WALL AND CORNER
GUARDS
10261.-10269. unassigned
10270. ACCESS FLOORING
10271.-10279. unassigned
10280. SPECIALTY MODULES
10281.-10289. unassigned
10290. PEST CONTROL
10291.-10299. unassigned
10300. FIREPLACES
10301. Prefabricated Fireplaces
10302. Prefabricated Fireplace
Forms
10303.-10309. unassigned
10310. Fireplace Accessories
10311.-10349. unassigned
10350. FLAGPOLES
10351.-10399. unassigned
10400. IDENTIFYING DEVICES
10401.-10409. unassigned
10410. Directories and Bulletin
Boards
10411. Directories
10412.-10419. unassigned
10420. Plaques
10421.-10439. unassigned
10440. Signs
10441.-10449. unassigned
10450. PEDESTRIAN CONTROL
DEVICES
10451.-10499. unassigned
10500. LOCKERS
10501.-10529. unassigned
10530. PROTECTIVE COVERS
10531. Walkway Covers
10532. Car Shelters
10533.-10549. unassigned
10550. POSTAL SPECIALTIES
10551. Mail Chutes
10552. Mail Boxes

**Uniform
Construction
Index**

**Cost Analysis
Format**

11 **EQUIPMENT**

Uniform Construction Index

Cost Analysis Format

12 FURNISHINGS

12000. ALTERNATIVES
12001.-12099. unassigned
12100. ARTWORK
12101.-12109. unassigned
12110. Murals
12111.-12119. unassigned
12120. Photo Murals
12121.-12299. unassigned
12300. CABINETS AND STORAGE
12301.-12499. unassigned
12500. WINDOW TREATMENT
12501.-12549. unassigned
12550. FABRICS
12551.-12599. unassigned
12600. FURNITURE
12601.-12669. unassigned
12670. RUGS & MATS
12671.-12699. unassigned
12700. SEATING
12701.-12709. unassigned
12710. Auditorium Seating
12711.-12729. unassigned
12730. Stadium Seating
12731.-12734. unassigned
12735. Telescoping Bleachers
12736.-12799. unassigned
12800. FURNISHING ACCESSORIES
12801.-12999. unassigned

13 SPECIAL CONSTRUCTION

13000. ALTERNATIVES
13001.-13009. unassigned
13010. AIR-SUPPORTED STRUCTURES
13011.-13049. unassigned
13050. INTEGRATED ASSEMBLIES
13051.-13099. unassigned
13100. AUDIOMETRIC ROOM
13101.-13249. unassigned
13250. CLEAN ROOM
13251.-13349. unassigned
13350. HYPERBARIC ROOM
13351.-13399. unassigned
13400. INCINERATORS
13401.-13439. unassigned
13440. INSTRUMENTATION
13441.-13449. unassigned
13450. INSULATED ROOM
13451.-13499. unassigned
13500. INTEGRATED CEILINGS
13501.-13539. unassigned
13540. NUCLEAR REACTORS
13541.-13549. unassigned
13550. OBSERVATORY
13551.-13599. unassigned
13600. PREFABRICATED BUILDINGS
13601.-13699. unassigned
13700. SPECIAL PURPOSE ROOMS & BUILDINGS
13701.-13749. unassigned
13750. RADIATION PROTECTION
13751.-13769. unassigned
13770. SOUND & VIBRATION CONTROL
13771.-13799. unassigned
13800. VAULTS
13801.-13849. unassigned
13850. SWIMMING POOLS
13851.-13999. unassigned

14 CONVEYING SYSTEMS

14000. ALTERNATIVES
14001.-14099. unassigned
14100. DUMBWAITERS
14101.-14199. unassigned
14200. ELEVATORS
14201. Elevator Hoisting Equipment
14202. Elevator Operation
14203. Elevator Cars and Entrances
14204.-14299. unassigned
14300. HOISTS & CRANES
14301.-14399. unassigned
14400. LIFTS
14401.-14429. unassigned
14430. Platform and Stage Lifts
14431.-14499. unassigned
14500. MATERIAL HANDLING SYSTEMS
14501.-14549. unassigned
14550. CONVEYORS & CHUTES
14551.-14569. unassigned
14570. TURNTABLES
14571.-14599. unassigned
14600. MOVING STAIRS & WALKS
14601.-14609. unassigned
14610. Escalators
14611.-14699. unassigned
14700. PNEUMATIC TUBE SYSTEMS
14701.-14799. unassigned
14800. POWERED SCAFFOLDING
14801.-14999. unassigned

15 MECHANICAL

15000. ALTERNATIVES
15001.-15009. unassigned
15010. GENERAL PROVISIONS
15011.-15049. unassigned
15050. BASIC MATERIALS AND
  METHODS
15051.-15059. unassigned
15060. Pipe and Pipe Fittings
15061.-15074. unassigned
15075. Hose
15076.-15079. unassigned
15080. Piping Specialties
15081.-15099. unassigned
15100. Valves and Cocks (Manual)
15101.-15119. unassigned
15120. Control Valves
15121.-15139. unassigned
15140. Pumps
15141.-15159. unassigned
15160. Vibration Isolation
  & Expansion Compensation
15161.-15169. unassigned
15170. Meters and Gages
15171.-15174. unassigned
15175. Tanks
15176.-15179. unassigned
15180. INSULATION
15181.-15199. unassigned
15200. WATER SUPPLY &
  TREATMENT
15201.-15219. unassigned
15220. Pumps and Piping
15221.-15239. unassigned
15230 Booster Pumping Equipment
15231.-15239. unassigned
15240. Water Reservoirs and Tanks
15241.-15249. unassigned
15250. Water Treatment
15251.-15269. unassigned
15270. Distribution and Metering
  Systems
15271.-15299. unassigned
15300. WASTE WATER DISPOSAL &
  TREATMENT
15301.-15309. unassigned
15310. Sewage Ejectors
15311.-15319. unassigned
15320. Grease Interceptors
15321.-15329. unassigned
15330. Basins and Manholes
15331.-15339. unassigned
15340. Sewerage
15341.-15349. unassigned
15350. Lift Stations
15351.-15359. unassigned
15360. Septic Tank Systems
15361.-15379. unassigned
15380. Sewage Treatment
15381.-15399. unassigned
15400. PLUMBING
15401.-15419. unassigned
15420. Equipment

15421.-15439. unassigned
15440. Special System Accessories
15441.-15449. unassigned
15450. Plumbing Fixtures
15451. Special Fixtures and Trim
15452.-15454. unassigned
15455. Water Coolers
15456. Washfountains
15457.-15469. unassigned
15470. Pool Equipment
15471.-15499. unassigned
15500. FIRE PROTECTION
15501.-15509. unassigned
15510. Sprinkler Equipment
15511.-15519. unassigned
15520. CO_2 Extinguishing
  Equipment
15521.-15529. unassigned
15530. Standpipe and Fire Hose
  Equipment
15531.-15539. unassigned
15540. Pressurized Extinguishers
  and Fire Blankets
15541.-15549. unassigned
15550. Fire Extinguisher Cabinets
15551.-15559. unassigned
15560. Hood and Duct Fire
  Protection
15561.-15599. unassigned
15600. POWER OR HEAT
  GENERATION
15601.-15609. unassigned
15610. Fuel Handling Equipment
15611. Oil Storage Tanks, Controls,
  and Piping
15612. Bottled Gas Tanks, Controls,
  and Piping
15613. Oil Piping
15614. Gas Piping
15615. Stokers and Conveyors
15616. Ash Removal System
15617. Breechings
15618. Exhaust Equipment
15619. Draft Control Equipment
15620.-15629. unassigned
15630. Boilers
15631.-15639. unassigned
15640. Boiler Feedwater Equipment
15641.-15649. unassigned
15650. REFRIGERATION
15651.-15657. unassigned
15658. Refrigerant Piping System
15659. unassigned
15660. Compressors
15661.-15669. unassigned
15670. Condensing Units
15671.-15679. unassigned
15680. Chillers
15681.-15689. unassigned
15690. Evaporators
15691.-15697. unassigned
15698. Commercial Ice Making
  Equipment
15699. Refrigeration Accessories
15700. LIQUID HEAT TRANSFER
15701.-15709. unassigned

15710. Hot Water Specialties
15711.-15719. unassigned
15720. Steam Specialties
15721.-15729. unassigned
15730. Heat Exchangers
15731.-15739. unassigned
15740. Terminal Units
15741.-15759. unassigned
15760. Packaged Heat Pump
15761.-15769. unassigned
15770. Packaged Heating and
  Cooling
15771.-15779. unassigned
15780. Humidity Control
15781.-15799. unassigned
15800. AIR DISTRIBUTION
15801.-15809. unassigned
15810. Furnaces
15811.-15819 unassigned
15820. Fans
15821.-15834. unassigned
15835. Air Curtains
15836.-15839. unassigned
15840. Ductwork
15841.-15849. unassigned
15850. Special Ductwork Systems
  Equipment
15851.-15859. unassigned
15860. Duct Accessories
15861.-15869. unassigned
15870. Outlets
15871.-15879. unassigned
15880. Air Treatment Equipment
15881.-15889. unassigned
15890. Sound Attenuators
15891.-15899. unassigned
15900. CONTROLS &
  INSTRUMENTATION
15901.-15909. unassigned
15910. Control Piping, Tubing, and
  Wiring
15911.-15919. unassigned
15920. Control Panels
15921.-15929. unassigned
15930. Primary Control Devices
15931.-15949. unassigned
15950. Sequential Controls
15951.-15959. unassigned
15960. Recording Devices
15961.-15969. unassigned
15970. Alarm Devices
15971.-15979. unassigned
15980. Special Process Controls
15981.-15999. unassigned

Uniform Construction Index

Cost Analysis Format

16 ELECTRICAL

16000. ALTERNATIVES
16001.-16009. unassigned
16010. GENERAL PROVISIONS
16011.-16099. unassigned
16100. BASIC MATERIALS AND METHODS
16101.-16109. unassigned
16110. RACEWAYS
16111.-16119. unassigned
16120. CONDUCTORS
16121.-16129. unassigned
16130. Outlet Boxes
16131.-16132. unassigned
16133. Cabinets
16134. Panelboards
16135.-16139. unassigned
16140. Switches and Receptacles
16141.-16149. unassigned
16150. Motors
16151.-16159. unassigned
16160. Motor Starters
16161.-16169. unassigned
16170. Disconnects (Motor and Circuit)
16171.-16179. unassigned
16180. Overcurrent Protective Devices
16181.-16189. unassigned
16190. SUPPORTING DEVICES
16191.-16198. unassigned
16199. Electronic Devices
16200. POWER GENERATION
16201.-16209. unassigned
16210. Generator
16211.-16219. unassigned
16220. Engine
16221.-16229. unassigned
16230. Cooling Equipment
16231.-16239. unassigned
16240. Exhaust Equipment
16241.-16249. unassigned
16250. Starting Equipment
16251.-16259. unassigned
16260. Automatic Transfer Equipment
16261.-16299. unassigned
16300. POWER TRANSMISSION
16301.-16309. unassigned
16310. Substation
16311.-16319. unassigned
16320. Switchgear
16321.-16329. unassigned
16330. Transformer
16331.-16339. unassigned
16340. Vaults
16341.-16349. unassigned
16350. Manholes
16351.-16359. unassigned
16360. Rectifiers
16361.-16369. unassigned
16370. Converters
16371.-16379. unassigned

16380. Capacitors
16381.-16399. unassigned
16400. SERVICE & DISTRIBUTION
16401.-16409. unassigned
16410. Electric Service
16411. Underground Service
16412.-16419. unassigned
16420. Service Entrance
16421. Emergency Service
16422.-16429. unassigned
16430. Service Disconnect
16431.-16439. unassigned
16440. Metering
16441.-16449. unassigned
16450. Grounding
16451.-16459. unassigned
16460. Transformers
16461.-16469. unassigned
16470. Distribution Switchboards
16471.-16479. unassigned
16480. Feeder Circuit
16481.-16489. unassigned
16490. Converters
16491. Rectifiers
16492.-16499. unassigned
16500. LIGHTING
16501.-16509. unassigned
16510. Interior Lighting Fixtures
16511.-16514. unassigned
16515. Signal Lighting
16516.-16529. unassigned
16530. Exterior Lighting Fixtures
16531. Stadium Lighting
16532. Roadway Lighting
16533.-16549. unassigned
16550. Accessories
16551. Lamps
16552. Ballasts and Accessories
16553.-16569. unassigned
16570. Poles and Standards
16571.-16599. unassigned
16600. SPECIAL SYSTEMS
16601.-16609. unassigned
16610. Lightning Protection
16611.-16619. unassigned
16620. Emergency Light and Power
16621.-16639. unassigned
16640. Cathodic Protection
16641.-16699. unassigned
16700. COMMUNICATIONS
16701.-16709. unassigned
16710. Radio Transmission
16711.-16719. unassigned
16720. Alarm and Detection Equipment
16721.-16739. unassigned
16740. Clock and Program Equipment
16741.-16749. unassigned
16750. Telephone & Telegraph
16751.-16759. unassigned
16760. Intercommunication Equipment
16761.-16769. unassigned
16770. Public Address Equipment
16771.-16779. unassigned

16780. Television Systems
16781.-16849. unassigned
16850. HEATING & COOLING
16851.-16857. unassigned
16858. Snow Melting Cable and Mat
16859. Heating Cable
16860. Electric Heating Coil
16861.-16864. unassigned
16865. Electric Baseboard
16866.-16869. unassigned
16870. Packaged Room Air Conditioners
16871.-16879. unassigned
16880. Radiant Heaters
16881.-16889. unassigned
16890. Electric Heaters (Prop Fan Type)
16891.-16899. unassigned
16900. CONTROLS & INSTRUMENTATION
16901.-16909. unassigned
16910. Recording and Indicating Devices
16911.-16919. unassigned
16920. Motor Control Centers
16921.-16929. unassigned
16930. Lighting Control Equipment
16931.-16939. unassigned
16940. Electrical Interlock
16941.-16949. unassigned
16950. Control of Electric Heating
16951.-16959. unassigned
16960. Limit Switches
16961.-16999. unassigned

The Critical Path Method

BACKGROUND

The critical path method (CPM) is a graphical network-based scheduling technique that evolved from a research effort initiated in late 1956 by the Engineering Services Department of the E. I. Du Pont de Nemours Company. They were assisted in this effort by a computer group from Remington Rand UNIVAC. Their objective was to explore the use of computer-aided systems in planning, scheduling, monitoring, and controlling Du Pont's engineering projects. The research was coordinated by Morgan R. Walker of Du Pont and James E. Kelley, Jr., of Remington Rand.

Although the original technique was developed around the computer, the computer is by no means necessary for the successful implementation of CPM on many projects. Simplified graphical representations such as that developed by John Fondahl at Stanford University have made it possible to handle some fairly complex schedules manually. CPM has therefore been effectively employed by small as well as large firms in the construction industry. When applied intelligently, it has achieved considerable success.

CPM enables planners and managers to thoroughly analyze the timing and sequential logic of all operations required to complete a project before committing time, money, equipment, labor, and materials for engineering and construction. Key personnel discover in advance the conditions that may arise on the project and gain a deeper understanding of the complex interrelationships of the activities to be performed. Planning with CPM focuses expert attention on potential trouble spots and indicates where extra effort can best be applied to reduce costs and delays without wasting resources. Experience in construction has often shown that this systematic forethought in itself more than justifies the use of CPM. In addition, CPM is a scheduling method that permits relatively easy revision of the schedule and simulation and evaluation of the impact of changes. It thus becomes an excellent control tool during the execution of the project as well.

BASIC CONCEPTS AND DEFINITIONS

CPM is a project-oriented scheduling technique. The *project* has an intentionally limited life span and should consist of a well-defined collection of tasks or activities that, when completed, mark the end of the project. Examples of projects include the design and/or construction of dams, tunnels, ports, refineries, and buildings. Each may actually be a component of a larger project.

An *activity* is a task or closely related group of tasks whose performance contributes to the completion of the overall project. An activity should be so sufficiently well-integrated that it can be rescheduled as a unit. One example of an activity could be "Construct column footing." Most activities, including this one, can be further subdivided into component activities. The degree of breakdown depends upon the size and type of project, its requirements, and the purpose for which the schedule is intended. In this example, component activities could include: "Excavate," "Fabricate forms," "Assemble rebar cage," "Set forms," "Fine grade," "Set rebar cage," "Place and finish concrete," "Cure concrete," and "Strip forms." These activities consume both time and resources. In scheduling, activities might also be used to represent administrative procedures, such as "Client approval of plant layout;" to show delays that require time but no resources, such as "Winter shutdown" and "Spring floods;" and to allow for shipment and delivery of equipment and materials, such as "Order ready-mix."

In the arrow diagram form of the CPM, directed lines, called *arrows*, represent activities. The direction of the arrow indicates the direction of progress. Nodes are placed at the beginning and end of each arrow, and an alphabetic and/or numeric label is assigned to each node to symbolically identify the activity. Figure E-1 is an example activity using such notation.

Activities may be combined in a logical manner determined by the

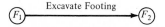

Figure E-1 Example arrow activity.

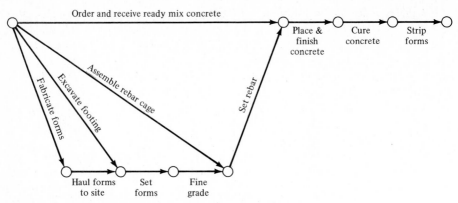

Figure E-2   Arrow diagram for concrete footing construction.

construction sequence of the operation being performed, the methods used, the time allowed, and the resources available. The combination of activities may be represented in a graphical form called a *network*. Figure E-2 is a possible arrow network for the concrete footing example. This network itself may be but a small *subnetwork* of the overall project network.

Precedence diagramming (sometimes called the "activity-on-node" or "circle and connecting line" method) is an alternative way of representing a critical path network and has a number of advantages. It is the opposite of arrow diagramming in that the nodes represent activities and the arrows or connecting lines show the logical relationships between them. Figure E-3 shows the activity "Excavate footing" in precedence notation. A major advantage of this system is that it eliminates the need for dummies to correctly represent the logic. Precedence diagrams are not nearly as strict in regard to the positioning of activities and are therefore much easier to construct and modify: One simply puts the nodes representing activities on paper and then draws the lines to connect them. Figure E-4 is a precedence diagram equivalent to the arrow network in Figure E-2.

Logical properties of networks include *precedence, succession,* and *concurrence.* The start of a particular activity is permitted by the completion of all preceding activities or by the start of the project. In the example, both "Order and receive ready-mix concrete" and "set rebar" precede or are *predecessors* of "Place and finish concrete." Both predecessors must be completed before "Place and finish concrete" can start. Similarly, the completion of an activity either permits the start of a following activity or marks the end of the project. In

Figure E-3   Example precedence activity.

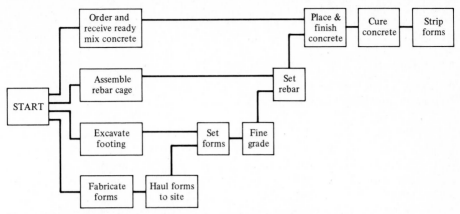

Figure E-4 Precedence diagram for concrete footing construction.

the example, completion of "Place and finish concrete" permits its direct *successor,* or *follower,* "Cure concrete," to commence. Other activities may logically proceed simultaneously, in which case they are logically *concurrent.* In the example, "Set forms" and "Assemble rebar cage" are logically concurrent activities. Planners must logically think through these relationships to construct a network. The process of constructing a network, in turn, is a strong aid in such logical thought processes.

CONSTRUCTING ARROW NETWORKS

Here and in the following section, a symbolic example illustrates basic procedures for constructing arrow networks and making CPM calculations. Table E-1 defines the sequential logic of the example project.

On an actual project, development of this logic would generally parallel initial rough drafting of the network. The full logic is defined here at the beginning to serve as a point of departure for explaining network construction techniques.

Table E-1 Example Network Logic Definition

Activity	Predecessors	Followers
A	—	D, E
B	—	G, H, K
C	—	F
D	A	L
E	A	G, H
F	C	K
G	B, E	L, M
H	B, E	L, M
K	B, F	—
L	D, G, H	—
M	G, H	—

Figure E-5 Beginning of arrow network.

To begin, note that activities A, B, and C have no predecessors. They may therefore share a common starting node. The starting node for an acitvity is commonly called its *i node*. Here the initial i node is labeled ①. A *j node* is placed at the end of each activity and labeled. Each j node, in turn, becomes the i node for activities immediately following. Each set of *i-j numbers* should uniquely define one and only one activity. The logic described thus far may be shown as in Figure E-5.

A node such as one, which serves as an i node for more than one activity, is sometimes called a *burst node*.

Referring to the Followers column in Table E-1, activity A is followed by D and E. Activity A, in turn, is the sole predecessor of D and E. Similarly, F follows C, and C is the sole predecessor of F. The partial network now appears as in Figure E-6.

Node numbers are shown a bit out of sequence here to be consistent with the final form of the network. Ordinarily, the only restriction is that each one be unique. So far, the i-j numbers for activities A to F are 1-2, 1-3, 1-4, 2-9, 2-5, and 4-6, respectively.

Activity G follows both B and E. For the moment, this logic may be shown by terminating, or *merging*, activities B and E at the same j node. This could be done by deleting node ③ and connecting B to node ⑤. A node such as ⑤, which is the end node to two or more activities, is sometimes called a *merge node*. Node ⑤, in turn, becomes the i node for activity G.

Note that G and H both have the same predecessors and the same followers. One might be inclined to show this parallel relationship as in Figure E-7.

It can be seen, however, that although the logic is correct, each activity is identified by the same i-j numbers. To uniquely identify each activity, an additional element, called a "dummy activity" or a "dummy arrow," is introduced. A *dummy* requires neither time nor resources, but is required to properly show the logic of an arrow network or to provide unique labeling. With

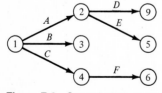

Figure E-6 Second stage of network construction.

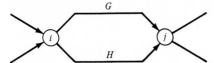

Figure E-7 Incorrect notation for concurrent activites.

a dummy, the logic of this section of the network may correctly be shown in one of the forms in Figure E-8.

In this case, where identification is the problem, the dummy requires an additional node. The partial network may now be sketched as in Figure E-9.

Referring back to the logic table, activity M follows both G and H, which in turn are the sole predecessors of M. Node ⑧ may therefore correctly be used as the i node for M. Referring again to the table, activity L follows G, H, and D. At first it might appear that this could be shown by also terminating activity D at node ⑧ and using this as the i node for L. This would indeed show the correct predecessors for activity L. However, it would also show that activity D precedes activity M, which is incorrect. This is a situation in which it is necessary to introduce a dummy to show the correct network logic. By putting a dummy from node ⑧ to node ⑨, the logic of this portion of the network may be correctly shown as in Figure E-10. Since neither L nor M has any followers, they are terminated at a common end node, labeled ⑩.

Activity K follows both B and F. One might try to show this logic by ending F at node ⑤ and starting K at node ⑤. This course would incorrectly show E as a predecessor of K and F as a predecessor of G and H, also incorrect. Apparently a dummy is needed, but where? Putting a dummy from node ⑤ to node ⑥ improves the situation by making F no longer preceding G and H, but it still leaves E incorrectly preceding K. To correctly show the logic in this case, two dummies are needed. Node ③ is reinstated as the j node for activity B. A dummy is then inserted from node ③ to node ⑤ to show B preceding G and H, and another dummy from node ③ to node ③ shows B preceding K. Node ⑥ is the i node for K. Since K has no followers, it is merged with L and M at j node

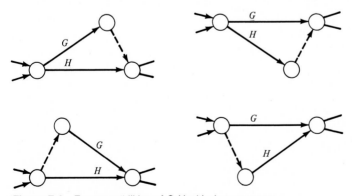

Figure E-8 Four possibilities of G-H with dummy arrow.

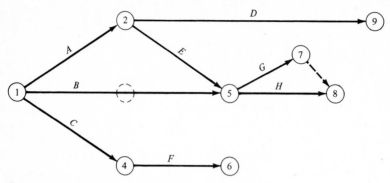

Figure E-9 Partial network including dummy activites.

(10), the last node in the network. The completed network in shown in Figure E-11.

This example illustrates most of the basic concepts in arrow network logic. One additional pitfall that should be pointed out is the unintentional creation of *loops* in the network. For example, if the direction of the arrow representing activity D were reversed, there would be one loop through activities 2-5, 5-8, 8-9, and 9-2 and another loop through 2-5, 5-7, 7-8, 8-9, and 9-2. Loops such as these have no logical beginning or end; their presence indicates an error in a CPM network. In this case, the error is easy to spot, but some fairly lengthy loops can creep into more complex networks and be fairly difficult to detect. Most CPM computer programs have routines to search out and trace any loops that may be present. Loops must be corrected before processing can continue.

CONSTRUCTING PRECEDENCE NETWORKS

Figure E-12 shows the logic of precedence network equivalent to Figure E-11. Although not mandatory except in some computer scheduling systems, common "start" and "end" activities have been shown to tie the logic together.

Since no special consideration need be given to dummy activities, all that really need be done to construct a draft of a precedence network is to put the

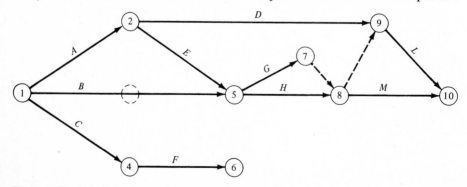

Figure E-10 Use of dummy 8-9 to preserve correct logic.

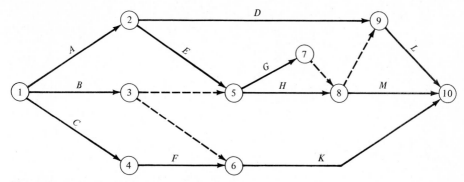

Figure E-11 Complete network.

activities down on paper and draw lines to show the precedence logic. However, for clarity, it is preferable that the logic flow left to right, so a second draft may be necessary. This of course is true also in arrow networks, although the arrow tips help clarify the logic also.

Another problem that occurs in both arrow and precedence diagrams is that sometimes the activity or logic lines unavoidably cross over each other. In this precedence diagram, B-G crosses A-E and H-L crosses G-M. Redrafting can minimize the number of crossing lines, but this criterion should not normally take priority over factors such as left-to-right logic flow, grouping of related activities, and so on. Rather, a small jump symbol ($\curvearrowright$), such as the two shown on B-G and G-M, is normally sufficient to preserve clear graphic communication.

CPM TIME CALCULATIONS

So far, only the logic element in CPM networks has been discussed. The second main element is time. In general, these schedule calculations involve the following steps:

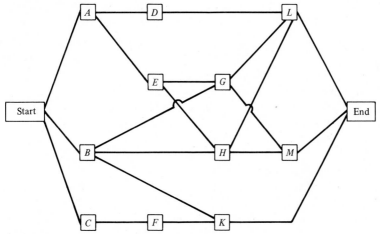

Figure E-12 Equivalent precedence network.

    1 Determination of the duration of each activity

    2 A "forward pass" calculation to determine the earliest allowable start and finish time for each activity

    3 The "backward pass" calculation to determine the latest allowable start and finish time for each activity

    4 "Total-float" calculations to determine how long each activity could be delayed without delaying the *project completion*

    5 "Free-float" calculations to determine how long each activity could be delayed without delaying *any other activities*

    6 Determination of the *critical path(s) for the network*

Each step is discussed for an arrow diagram since these usually are a bit more difficult. A summary of the calculation for an equivalent precedence diagram follows.

Estimating Durations

Once all activities in a project have been defined and organized into a logical CPM network, their durations must be estimated. An activity's *duration* is the expected amount of time, expressed in consistent time units, that will be required to complete the activity from start to finish. The time units may be days, weeks, or even hours or minutes, just so that all activities use the same units.

The importance of accurate estimates of durations cannot be overstated. On actual projects, these numbers are not just pulled out of the air; each duration estimate is the product of careful thinking involving the methods by which the activity will be accomplished, the resources (labor, equipment, material, financing) that are available, productivity, external constraints, and so forth. This process closely parallels that for making cost estimates.

For purposes of illustration, assume that duration estimates in weeks for the example from Figure E-11 have been carefully made. These durations are shown beneath the label for each activity on the network in Figure E-13.

Forward Pass[1]

The calculation procedure called the *forward pass* establishes the earliest expected start and finish times for each activity in the network. The following nomenclature is used in the discussion of the forward pass:

    D (x) = Estimate of *d*uration for activity x

    ES(x) = *E*arliest (expected) *s*tart time for activity x

    EF(x) = *E*arliest (expected) *f*inish time for activity x

    S   = Project *s*tart time

---

[1]The form of the notation used in this appendix and summarized in chap. 12 is based upon *A Management Guide to PERT/CPM,* Jerome D. Wiest and Ferdinand K. Levy, Prentice-Hall, Englewood Cliffs, N.J., 1969, p. 31.

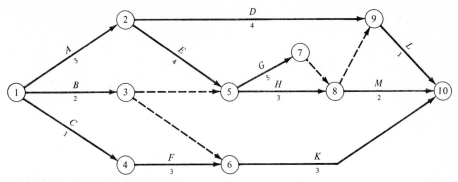

Figure E-13 Network with time units.

Initially, a convention must be established for S, the project start time. In this discussion, S will be 1; that is, the project commences at the start of time period 1. An alternative convention often used is to set S equal to 0; that is, the project is ready to go by the end of time period 0. Actually, any number may be used for S; it is merely a reference point for the schedule.

The set of rules that defines the procedure for the forward pass calculations is called an *algorithm*. Only three rules are required:

1. The early start (ES) of all activities with no predecessors is equal to the project start time (S).

2. No activity may commence until all its preceding activities have been completed. Therefore, the early start time of any activity other than starting activities is equal to the maximum of the early finish (EF) times of its predecessors.

3. The early finish (EF) of an activity is equal to its early start (ES) plus its duration (D).

In mathematical notation, these rules can be expressed as follows:

ES (initial activities) = S
ES(x) = Maximum (EF(all predecessors of x))
EF(x) = ES(x) + D(x)

To illustrate these rules with the example, Figure E-14 shows the diagram notation convention used.

To begin, the early start of activities A, B, and C is 1. The early finish for each activity is determined as follows:

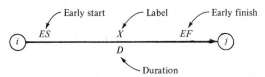

Figure E-14 Notation for arrow diagram forward pass calculations.

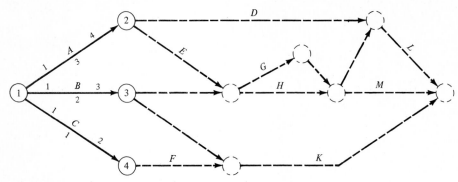

Figure E-15 Network with first step of forward pass calculations.

$$EF(A) = ES(A) + D(A) = 1 + 3 = 4$$
$$EF(B) = ES(B) + D(B) = 1 + 2 = 3$$
$$EF(C) = ES(C) + D(C) = 1 + 1 = 2$$

The early finish for A of 4 may be interpreted to mean that the activity is completed by the beginning of time period 4. On the network, the calculations appear as in Figure E-15.

The completion of A permits D and E to commence since they have no other predecessors. Their early starts are therefore set equal to 4. Similarly, F can commence once C is complete and thus has an early start of 2. The calculations for these activities in mathematical form and on the network (Figure E-16) are:

$$ES(D) = ES(E) = EF(A) = 4$$
$$EF(D) = ES(D) + D(D) = 4 + 4 = 8$$
$$EF(E) = ES(E) + D(E) = 4 + 4 = 8$$
$$ES(F) = EF(C) = 2$$
$$EF(F) = ES(F) + D(F) = 2 + 3 = 5$$

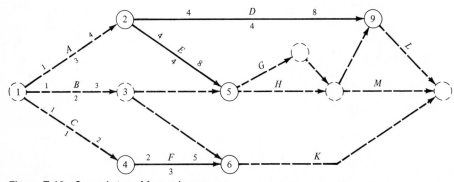

Figure E-16 Second step of forward pass.

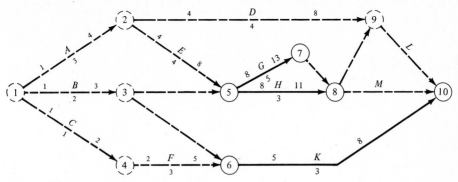

Figure E-17   Third step of forward pass.

The commencement of activity G requires that both B and E be complete. Therefore, the early start of G is the maximum of the early finishes of B and E:

$$ES(G) = Max(EF(B), = EF(E)) = Max(3, 8) = 8$$

The same applies to activity H:

$$ES(H) = Max(EF(B), = EF(E)) = Max(3, 8) = 8$$

Similarly, the commencement of K requires the completion of both B and F.

$$ES(K) = Max(EF(B), = EF(F)) = Max(3, 5) = 5$$

Now early finish values for G, H, and K can be computed.

$$EF(G) = ES(G) + D(G) = 8 + 5 = 13$$
$$EF(H) = ES(H) + D(H) = 8 + 3 = 11$$
$$EF(K) = ES(K) + D(K) = 5 + 3 = 8$$

The completion of D, G, and H enables L to commence, and the completion of G and H enables M to commence. The forward pass calculations may now be completed (Figure E-18) as follows:

$$ES(L) = Max(EF(D), EF(G), EF(H)) = Max (8, 13, 11) = 13$$
$$ES(M) = Max(EF(G), EF(H)) = Max(13, 11) = 13$$
$$EF(L) = ESL) + D(L) = 13 + 1 = 14$$
$$EF(M) = ES(M) + D(M) = 13 + 2 = 15$$

The early finish of M is the maximum early finish in the project and thus becomes the earliest completion date of the project. The total project duration is therefore calculated to be 14 time units. That is, project duration = Max(EF) − S = 15 − 1 = 14. This completes the forward pass calculations.

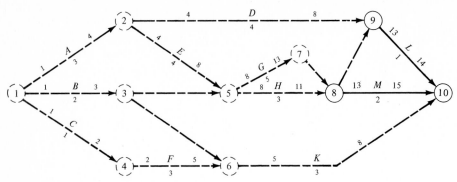

Figure E-18 Forward pass complete.

Backward Pass

The calculation procedure called the *backward pass* establishes the latest allowable start and finish times for each activity that will still permit the overall project to be completed without delaying beyond the scheduled completion date. The following nomenclature is used in the discussion of the backward pass:

$D(x)$ = Estimate of *D*uration for activity x
$LS(x)$ = *L*atest allowable *S*tart time for activity x
$LF(x)$ = *L*atest allowable *F*inish time for activity x
T = *T*arget project completion time

The project completion time T is generally taken as the early project completion time from the forward pass; this will be done here. However, any date may be taken as this reference point. For example, a contractual completion date could be used.

The following rules define the algorithm for the backward pass:

1. The latest allowable finish (LF) of all activities with no followers is equal to the target project completion time (T).
2. The latest allowable finish time (LF) for any other activity is equal to the earliest of the latest allowable start times of its successors.
3 The latest allowable start time (LS) for any activity is equal to its latest allowable finish (LF) minus its duration(D).

In mathematical notation these rules can be expressed as follows:

$$LF(\text{end activities}) = T$$
$$LF(x) = Min(LS(\text{all followers of } x))$$
$$LS(x) = LF(x) - D(x)$$

To illustrate these rules with the example, the notation in Figure E-19 is added to the forward pass diagram convention.

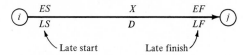

Figure E-19 Supplementary notation for backward pass.

To begin the calculations, the late finish of activities K, L, and M, which have no followers, may be taken as 15, the project completion time. The late start for each activity is determined as follows:

$$LS(K) = LF(K) - D(K) = 15 - 3 = 12$$
$$LS(L) = LF(L) - D(L) = 15 - 1 = 14$$
$$LS(M) = LF(M) - D(M) = 15 - 2 = 13$$

On the network, the calculations appear as in Figure E-20.

The late start for L, the only follower of D, becomes the late finish of D. The minimum of the late starts of L and M becomes the late finish for G and H. These calculations are:

$$LF(D) = LS(L) = 14$$
$$LF(G) = LF(H) = Min(LS(L),LS(M)) = Min(14, 13) = 13$$
$$LS(D) = LF(D) - D(D) = 14 - 4 = 10$$
$$LS(G) = LF(G) - D(G) = 13 - 5 = 8$$
$$LS(H) = LF(H) - D(H) = 13 - 3 = 10$$

The late finish of activity B is the minimum of the late starts of activities G, H, and K. Similarly, the late finish for activity E is the minimum of the late starts of activities G and H. The late start of activity K, the only follower of activity F, becomes the late finish for F. This stage of the backward pass is calculated as follows:

$$LF(B) = Min(LS(G), LS(H), LS(K)) = Min(8, 10, 12) = 8$$
$$LF(E) = Min(LS(G), LS(H)) = Min(8, 10) = 8$$

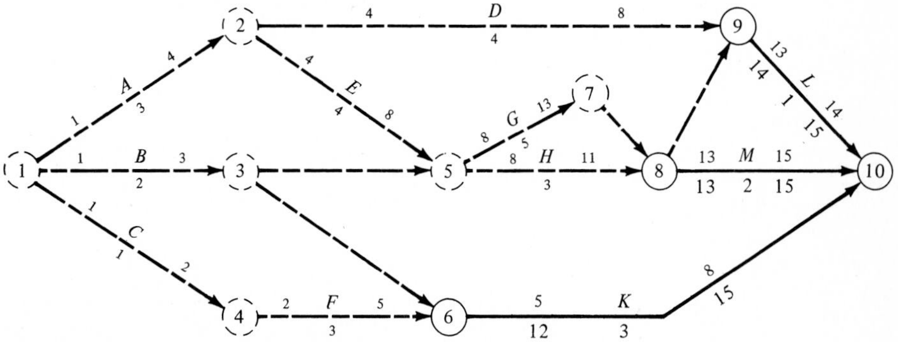

Figure E-20 First step of backward pass.

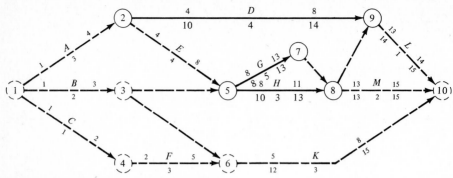

Figure E-21 Second step of backward pass.

$$LF(F) = LS(K) = 12$$
$$LS(B) = LF(B) - D(B) = 8 - 2 = 6$$
$$LS(E) = LF(E) - D(E) = 8 - 4 = 4$$
$$LS(F) = LF(F) - D(F) = 12 - 3 = 9$$

The minimum of the late starts of D and E becomes the late finish of A. The late start of F is the late finish of C. The backward pass calculations may now be completed:

$$LF(A) = Min (LS(D), LS(E)) = Min(10, 4) = 4$$
$$LF(C) = LS(F) = 9$$
$$LS(A) = LF(A) - D(A) = 4 - 3 = 1$$
$$LS(C) = LF(C) - D(C) = 9 - 1 = 8$$

Since this backward pass started with the completion time from the forward pass, the minimum late start of all the activities [that is, $LS(A) = 1$] should equal the start time S of the project. This serves as a check on the calculations and completes the backward pass. If another value of T were used, the minimum late start of all the activities would equal the difference between this and the completion time from the forward pass. For example, if 19 days were available for the project, the last day could be set at 20, and on the backward pass all late

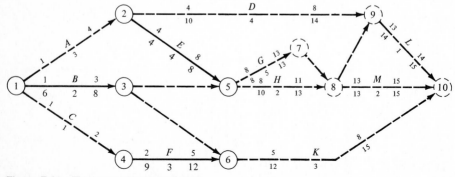

Figure E-22 Third step of backward pass.

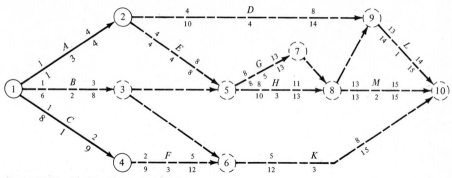

Figure E-23 Backward pass complete.

starts, late finishes, and total floats would be 5 days higher. The critical activities would have the minimum total float—5 days instead of 0.

Total Float

The *total float*[2] for an activity is the maximum amount of time that the activity can be delayed without extending the completion time of the overall project. However, such a delay might postpone the early start of one or more of its following activities. Once the forward and backward pass calculations have been completed, the total float for each activity may be calculated directly as the difference between the activity's late start and its early start, or as the difference between its late finish and its early finish. This may be expressed in mathematical notation as follows:

$$
\begin{aligned}
TF(x) &= \text{total float for activity x} \\
&= LS(x) - ES(x) \\
&= LF(x) - EF(x)
\end{aligned}
$$

It may be added to the diagram notation in either of the forms shown in Figure E-24.

On the example, total floats are calculated as in Figure E-25.

Free Float

Free float is the maximum amount of time an activity can be delayed without

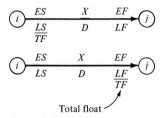

Figure E-24 Supplementary notation for total float.

[2]Float is sometimes called slack.

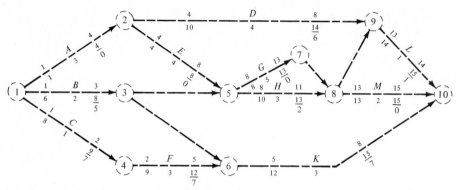

Figure E-25 Arrow network with total-float calculations.

delaying the early start of any of its followers. It also follows directly from the forward and backward pass calculations, and it may be determined as the minimum of the early starts of all the activity's immediate followers minus the activity's early finish. This may be expressed mathematically as follows:

FF(x) = Free float for activity x
       = Min (ES(all immediate followers of x)) − EF(x)

On the example, activities B and D have positive free float, which differs from their total float. The free floats for these activities are calculated:

FF(B) = Min(ES(G), ES(H), ES(K)) − EF(B)
      = Min(8, 8, 5) − 3 = 5 − 3 = 2
FF(D) = ES(L) − EF(D) = 13 − 8 = 5

The positive free float of activities H, K, and L equals their total float and is determined in a manner similar to that for B and D. Note that activity C has 7 units of total float but no free float. All the other activities are on the critical path and thus have zero float—total or free. Also note that the free float for any activity is always less than or equal to the total float.

Critical Path

A *critical path* is a continuous chain of activities from the beginning to the end of a network with the minimum float value. In the case where the target project completion time is set equal to the early project completion time, a critical path is a chain of activities with zero float. By summing activity durations, the critical path is the longest path through the network. The critical path for the example network is shown in Figure E-26 with a heavy line.

There may be more than one critical path in various parts of the network. For example, if the duration of activity D were increased to 10, there would be an additional path through activities D and L, as shown in Figure E-27.

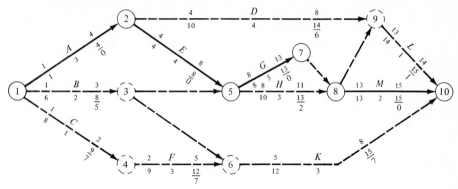

Figure E-26 Critical path.

Equivalent Calculations on a Precedence Diagram

The calculation procedure for a precedence network is identical to that for an arrow network, except that one need not consider dummies. One of the main issues in precedence networks, however, is the style in which the calculations and related activity information are shown. Two main alternatives are to put the calculations outside the activity symbol (Figure E-28a) and within the activity symbol (Figure E-28b). Using the style in Figure E-28a, the calculations for the network diagram would be as shown in Figure E-29.

Summary of Notation and Equations

Regardless of whether the logic is shown by arrow or precedence notation, the algorithms for network computations are the same. The following notation and formulas provide all that is required for standard CPM network calculations.

Notation

$D(x)$ = Estimate of *d*uration for activity x

$ES(x)$ = *E*arliest (expected) *s*tart time for activity x

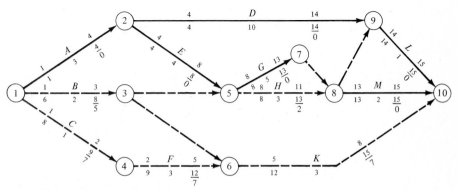

Figure E-27 Multiple critical paths.

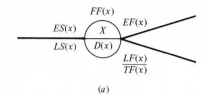

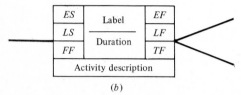

(b)

Figure E-28   Styles for precedence diagram calculations.

EF(x) = *E*arliest (expected) *f*inish time for activity x
LS(x) = *L*atest allowable *s*tart time for activity x
LF(x) = *L*atest allowable *f*inish time for activity x
TF(x) = *T*otal *f*loat for activity x
FF(x) = *F*ree *f*loat for activity x
S   = *P*roject *s*tart time
T   = *T*arget project completion time
Equations for calculating the CPM parameters
   Forward pass
   ES(x) = S for beginning activities, or

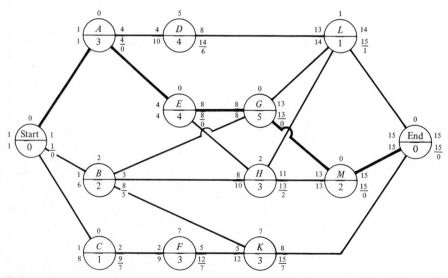

Figure E-29   Precedence network CPM calculations.

$$ES(x) = Max(EF(\text{all predecessors of activity } x))$$
$$EF(x) = ES(x) + D(x)$$
Backward pass
$$LF(x) = T \text{ for ending activities, or}$$
$$LF(x) = Min(LS(\text{all followers of activity } x))$$
$$LS(x) = LF(x) - D(x)$$
Floats
$$TF(x) = LS(x) - ES(x)$$
$$= LF(x) - EF(x)$$
$$FF(x) = Min(ES(\text{all immediate followers of activity } x)) - EF(x)$$
Critical Path

A critical path is a continuous chain of activities with the minimum total float value. By summing activity durations, it is the longest duration path through the network. There may be more than one critical path in various parts of the network.

ARROW VERSUS PRECEDENCE NETWORKS

A number of objections have been voiced against the precedence diagram. Some claim that the arrow better represents the flow of time and progress from start to finish of an activity while a circle, or box, gives a more static impression. This is largely a matter of individual preference. It could be claimed that the activity-on-node representation focuses more attention on the activity itself. Others feel that precedence diagramming is awkward and inefficient for computer processing, although subsequently developed programs, including IBM's Project Control System and Stanford's STANCI, have overcome this effect. Calendar-scaling is more difficult, although not impossible, with precedence diagramming. By and large, the primary disadvantage of precedence diagramming is that it was developed after arrow diagramming became firmly entrenched in industry and is therefore not as widely used.

Precedence networks are much to be preferred on projects that will rely exclusively on manual processing. Also, some people have found it easier to develop the original rough networks in precedence form and then let a skilled technician draft them into the corresponding arrow form, with dummies inserted when necessary to correctly represent the logic.

CALENDAR-SCALED DIAGRAMS

This section describes a method of constructing calendar-scaled CPM diagrams that are similar to the plotter-drawn networks produced by many computer systems. The basic unit of time for this purpose is 1 day.

To convert the *working-day schedule* to a *calendar-dated schedule,* the start day is designated on the calendar. Succeeding parts of the working-day schedule are then compared to the calendar on a day-by-day basis. Extra days are inserted for non-workdays, such as weekends and holidays. These non-workdays must be specified in advance. The overall procedure is quite straightforward and yields corresponding calendar dates for each workday in the schedule.

In the arrow type of calendar-scaled diagram, extra dummy arrows and nodes are inserted so that all time and resource-consuming activities can be shown horizontally and each has a unique i node. In this way the interpretation of the horizontal arrows is analogous to bars on a bar chart. The diagram has therefore been found to be easily understood in the field. Activities are generally shown scheduled at their early start times by a solid line, and a contrasting dashed line shows the remaining free float, if any.

To illustrate the construction of a calendar-scaled arrow diagram, assume that the example project from the previous sections is to be started on Monday, July 3, 1978. Assume also that a standard 40-hour, 5-day week will be worked. The calendar for July 1978 is as follows:

Sun.	Mon.	Tue.	Wed.	Thur.	Fri.	Sat.
						1
2	3	<4>	5	6	7	8
9	10	11	12	13	14	15
16	17	18	19	20	21	22
23	24	25	26	27	28	29
30	31					

A holiday is taken on the 4th. The 1st, 2d, 8th, 9th, 15th, 16th, 22d, 23d, 29th, and 30th fall on weekends. The remaining days are available for work

For arrow network construction, the line symbols in Figure E-30 are used. With this notation, the calendar-scaled network may be constructed. The general procedure is:

1. Lay out a calendar grid with a duration greater than that of the project.
2. Block out non-workdays.
3. Plot activities to the same scale.
   a. Show continuation through nonworkdays (e.g., activities A and B).
   b. Where an i node is common to two or more activities, such as node ② for D and E, insert a dummy, such as ②ₐ ------> ②ᵦ to

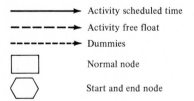

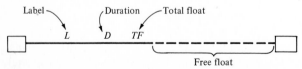

Figure E-30 Notation for calendar-scaled arrow diagram.

separate them vertically In the case of start nodes, use new
separate nodes for each starting activity: ⓐ , ⓑ , and ⓒ .

c. If another activity does not immediately follow, the interval until
the start of the earliest follower is filled with a dashed line
representing free float, as shown on activities D, H, and K in the
following example.

4. Label the activities.

The calendar-scaled CPM diagram may be drawn directly from the tabular
logic, or it may be converted from the conventional CPM diagram.

The CPM solution for the example network is repeated on Figure E-31a;
Figure E-31b shows its corresponding calendar-scaled arrow diagram. Readers

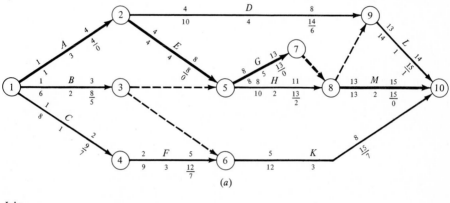

(a)

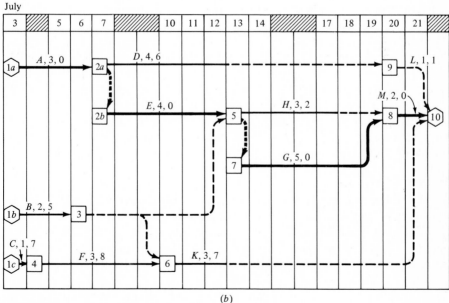

(b)

Figure E-31 Conversion to calendar-scaled arrow network.

familiar with precedence diagramming may be interested to note a number of similarities between the calendar-scaled diagram and a precedence network.

PRACTICAL CONSIDERATIONS

In addition to understanding the basic theory and network mechanics, a number of practical matters must be considered to most effectively put critical path scheduling into practice. This section considers a number of these topics.

Using Float Effectively

Both free float and total float can give management considerable flexibility in scheduling a project's activities. Judicious rescheduling of activities within their float ranges can effectively "level" resource usage and make a smoother, more efficient job. On the other hand, float is a valuable commodity that can be wasted if used indescriminately. Total float, especially when it is reflected through a series of activities in a chain, must be regarded as "community property" among those activities. If a superintendent or supervisor carelessly lets an early activity in the chain slip to its late start and finish times, thinking that there is plenty of leeway, the remaining activities in the chain will become critical. Considerable managerial flexibility is thus lost. For this reason, companies sometimes do not reveal float values, late start dates, and late finish dates to their supervisor and subcontractors, giving them only scheduled dates determined by project management. Management does have all the information from the schedule. This of course takes much of the responsibility and flexibility away from line supervision. There is no fixed answer to this problem; it is a matter of policy that must be resolved by management on each project.

Responsibility

Responsibilities for preparing CPM schedules should be clearly defined in company policies and procedures. As a general principle, however, it can be stated here that persons who will be responsible for carrying out a particular area of work in the project should substantially contribute to the corresponding part of the CPM schedule preperation. They will of course be assisted by a scheduler, and the scheduler will actually have the responsibility of converting the rough logic and preliminary network sketches into neatly drafted CPM diagrams.

Level of Detail

The level of detail to which to subdivide a network's activities depends upon a number of factors, including the schedule's intended purpose, the type of project, whether computer or manual processing will be used, and the preferences of management. Schedules may be prepared at several levels of detail. A. T. Armstrong-Wright's example in *Critical Path Method* illustrates this idea:

The network for a board of directors of a power company considering a new power station might contain activities such as:

Raise capital
Obtain land
Plan project
Construct stage I

The project manager might take the above activity Plan project and in his network break it down further:

Determine required output
Survey site
Design plant
Order plant
Design building
Project plan to Managing Director

while even greater detail would be required by the Chief Electrical Design Engineer; he might break down the activity Design plant as follows:

Select generator size and type
Prepare preliminary layout
Design wiring diagram
Design transmission lines
Preliminary plans to Project Manager

Similarly, the construction manager will require a detailed breakdown of the broad activity Construct Stage I. Whether or not these detailed networks are then combined into one comprehensive network will depend on the method of control and liason between departments (pp. 31–32).

Detailed planning is generally beneficial, but excessive detail in the network can overcomplicate the schedule and create unnecessary effort and cost in preparation and processing. For these reasons, selective detailing can be used to advantage. For example, different parts of a network might be prepared at different levels of detail. Starting with a fairly broad network, activities along the critical path, as well as other activities and areas that might be potential trouble spots, could be further subdivided for closer analysis. Another possibility is to take the general network and expand it into a progressive "wave" of detailed activities 1 to 3 months in advance of the commencement of the work in that interval.

In scope, activities should be defined and detailed so as to correspond to work items subject to cost control. Where possible, an activity should be contained entirely within one individual's responsibility. This requires a fairly high degree of homogeneity in resources—labor, materials, and equipment. Activity durations should be long enough to permit progress feedback to be reported in time for corrective action to be taken, if necessary.

Organization of the Network

Basic concepts of network organization were clearly expressed by A. T. Armstrong-Wright as follows:

In producing the fair diagrams of the network, careful attention must be given to the orderly arrangement of activities. The arrows should be drawn horizontally with only the ends turned to connect to events (nodes) so that descriptions can be easily written and read. The description of activities entered above each arrow should be clear and concise. Above all, the use of inexplicit abbreviations or codes should be avoided. Experience has shown that if constant and laborious reference to explanatory lists of abbreviations and codes is necessary, the network will soon fall into disuse and will be ignored from the start by all but the very enthusiastic.

By convention, networks are drawn with progress from left to right. This is, in fact, the normal method of indicating the passage of time on graphs, histograms and bar charts. There may be certain projects or processes where progress can best be indicated in some other direction, but these will generally be the exception. For example, the network for the construction of a skyscraper could be drawn with progress shown vertically upwards. One serious disadvantage of this is that arrows would be mainly vertical with descriptions either being written horizontally, thus taking much space, or written vertically, in which case the network would have to be read sideways. Inevitably the network would be turned on its side and hence any advantage of showing progress vertically would be lost.

The network should be divided into clear areas of responsibility so that it is not necessary to scan the whole network to locate activities or which one individual or works unit may be responsible. This is usually achieved by dividing the network into horizontal zones. This method is particularly suitable where the work of the individual units is for the most part independent, with only a few connecting activities.

Where there is much intermingling of the work of several teams or units, it may be better to divide the network into zones representing the location of the work rather than areas of responsibility. It is useful in this case to relate the network to a day plan (pp. 34–35).

Either type of organization described here is made possible by the use of "banding" in a computer system's plotter-drawn networks. Groupings could also be made by prime accounts or by other systems that would fit the needs of the project. In some computer systems, this grouping is specified by properly coding the nodes on the network diagram.

REFERENCES

Only the basic fundamentals of CPM have been discussed in this section. The following references are recommended for additional reading.

1. Antill, James M., and Ronald W. Woodhead, *Critical Path Methods in Construction Practice,* 2d ed., John Wiley & Sons, Inc., New York, 1970.

   This is a lengthy but thorough text on conventional critical path techniques.

It is heavily construction-oriented and contains a number of good construction examples. There is also a chapter on using CPM to document and justify claims and help estimate the cost impact of construction changes on the schedule.

2. Armstrong-Wright, A. T., *Critical Path Method,* Longman Group Ltd., London, 1969.

This inexpensive paperback text has clear and simple explanations of CPM and related techniques. The author also has included some very good discussion of the practical aspects of using the techniques.

3. Clough, Richard, and Glenn A. Sears, *Construction Project Management,* 2d ed., John Wiley & Sons, Inc., New York, 1979.

A very practical and well-written book, with an extensive series of applications to a realistic project.

4. Fondahl, John W., *A Non-Computer Approach to the Critical Path Method for the Construction Industry,* Technical Report No. 9, Stanford University, Dept. of Civil Engineering, The Construction Institute, Stanford, Calif., November 1961 (rev. 1962). Also, *Methods for Extending the Range of Non-Computer Critical Path Applications,* Technical Report No. 47, 1964.

Both manuals contain a thorough introduction to the precedence diagramming form of the critical path method, with numerous special techniques for processing the schedules manually. Regardless of the method used, there is a wealth of practical information about the applications and limitations of CPM and about implementing it in a construction organization.

5. Harris, Robert, *Precedence and Arrow Networking Techniques for Construction,* John Wiley & Sons, Inc., New York, 1978.

This book has considerable emphasis on the precedence approach, and is intended for use as an upperdivision college textbook as well as for practitioners.

6. Kelley, James E., Jr., and Morgan R. Walker, "Critical Path Planning and Scheduling," *Procedings of the Eastern Joint Computer Conference,* Boston, 1969, pp. 160–173.

This is the paper that originally introduced CPM.

7. Moder, Joseph J., and Cecil R. Phillips, *Project Management with CPM and PERT,* 2d ed., Van Nostrand Reinhold Co., New York, 1970.

This is a good, thorough text on CPM and related techniques. It has some good introductory material on computer applications.

8. Wiest, Jerome D., and Ferinand K. Levy, *A Managment Guide to PERT/ CPM,* 2d ed., Prentice-Hall, Englewood Cliffs, N.J., 1977.

A clear, concise yet thorough introduction to CPM and related techniques. It has some good comments on practical aspects of applications.

BIBLIOGRAPHY

The references in this bibliography have been grouped into general categories corresponding to some of the main topics in this book. The list is by no means exhaustive, but rather, is intended to provide supplementary reading for those who wish to study particular subjects in greater detail. Many of the references have also been chosen because they, in turn, have good bibliographies of their own.

General Construction Administration and Management

Barrie, Donald S., ed., *Directions in Managing Construction,* John Wiley and Sons, New York, 1981.

Bonny, John B., and Joseph P. Frein, *Handbook of Construction Management and Organization, 2nd ed.,* Van Nostrand Reinhold Co., New York, 1980.

Business Roundtable, *More Construction for the Money,* 2 Park Avenue, New York, New York, January, 1983.

Cassimatis, Peter J., *Econimics of the Construction Industry,* The National Industrial Conference Board, Studies in Business Economics No. 111, New York, 1969.

Clough, Richard H., *Construction Contracting, 4th ed., John Wiley & Sons, Inc., New York, 1981.*

Federal Laws Relating to Employment of Labor in Construction, The Associated General Contractors of America, Washington, D.C., revised 1977.

Fisk, Edward R., *Construction Project Administration,* John Wiley and Sons, New York, 1978.

Halpin, Daniel W., and Woodhead, Ronald W., *Consruction Management,* John Wiley and Sons, New York, 1980.

Havers, John A., and Frank W. Stubbs, Jr., *Handbook of Heavy Construction,* 2d ed., McGraw–Hill Book Company, New York, 1971.

Manual of The Associated General Contractors of America, Washington, D.C. (Contains a compilation of forms, contracts, procedures, etc.)

Merritt, Frederick S. (ed.), *Building Construction Handbook,* 3d ed., McGraw-Hill Book Company, New York, 1975.

O'Brien, James J., and Robert G. Zilly (eds.), *Contractor's Management Handbook,* McGraw-Hill Book Company, New York, 1971.

Paulson, Boyd C., Jr., *Goals for Basic Research in Construction,* Technical Report No. 202, Stanford University, Dept. of Civil Engineering, The Construction Institute, Stanford, Calif., July 1975.

———, "Education and Research in Construction," *Journal of the Construction Division,* ASCE, vol. 102, no. C03, proc. paper 12393, September 1976, pp. 479–495.

"Probing the Future," *Engineering News-Record,* Centennial Issue, vol. 192, no. 18, April 30, 1974.

Reiner, Lawrence E., *Handbook of Construction Management,* Prentice-Hall, Inc., Englewood Cliffs, N.J., 1972.

Rossow, Janet A. K., and Fred Moavenzadeh, *The Construction Industry, A Review of the Major Issues Facing the Industry in the United States,* Massachusetts Institute of Technology, Dept. of Civil Engineering, Cambridge, Mass., Summer 1974.

———, and ———, "Management Issues in the U.S. Construction Industry," *Journal of the Construction Division,* ASCE, vol. 102, no. C02, proc. paper 12184, June 1976, pp. 277–294.

Rubey, Harry, and Walker W. Milner, *Construction and Professional Management*, University of Oklahoma Press, Norman, Okla. 1971.

Ward, Jack W., *Construction Information Source and Reference Guide*, 3d ed., Construction Publications, Phoenix, Ariz., January 1973.

Wass, Alonzo, *Construction Management and Contracting*, Prentice-Hall, Inc., Englewood Cliffs, N.J., 1972.

Zehner, John R., *Builder's Guide to Contracting*, McGraw-Hill Book Company, New York, 1975.

Professional Construction Management

Allen, C. R., "The Construction Management Concept," *AACE Bulletin*, vol. 15, no. 6, December 1973, pp. 169–173.

Barrie, Donald S., "CM as Seen by an Engineer-Contractor," *Plant Engineering*, July 13, 1972, p. 85.

————, and Boyd C. Paulson, Jr., "Professional Construction Management," *Journal of the Construction Division*, ASCE, vol. 102, no. CO3, proc. paper 12394, September 1976, pp. 425-436.

Barrie, Donald S., "Guidelines for Successful Construction Management," *Journal of the Construction Division*, ASCE, vol. 106, no. CO3, September, 1980, pp. 237-245.

Bush, Vincent G., *Construction Management*, Reston Publishing Co., Inc., Reston, Va., 1973.

CM for the General Contractor: A Guide Manual for Construction Management, The Associated General Contractors of America, Washington, D.C., 1975.

Construction Contracting Systems: A Report on the Systems Used by PBS and Other Organizations, General Services Administration, Public Buildings Service, Washington, D.C., March 1970.

"Construction Division Newsletter," ASCE, issues of December 1974, March 1975, and June 1975.

"Construction Management Guidelines for Use by AGC Members," Attachment to Special Contracting Methods Committee Report, The Associated General Contractors of America, Washington, D.C., Feb. 15, 1972.

"Construction Management: Putting Professionalism into Contracting," *Construction Methods and Equipment*, vol. 54, no. 3, March 1972, pp. 69–75.

"Construction Management—Whirling in Evolution and in Ferment," *Engineering News-Record*, vol. 188, no. 18, May 4, 1972, pp. 14-19.

Dressler, Joachim, "Construction Management in West Germany," *Journal of the Construction Division*, ASCE, vol. 106, no. CO4, December, 1980, pp. 477-487.

Foxall, William B., *Professional Construction Management and Project Administration*, Architectural Record and The American Institute of Architects, New York, 1972.

The GSA System for Construction Management, General Services Administration, Public Buildings Service, Washington, D.C., April 1975.

Gerwick, Ben C., Jr., and John C. Wollery, *Construction and Engineering Marketing for Major Project Services*, John Wiley and Sons, New York, 1983.

Goldhaber, Stanley, Chandra K. Jha, and Manuel C. Macedu, Jr., *Construction Management Principles and Practices*, John Wiley and Sons, New York, 1977.

Gorman, James E., *Simplified Guide to Construction Management for Architects and Engineers*, Cahners Books International, Inc., Boston, 1976.

Heery, George T., *Time, Cost and Architecture*, McGraw-Hill Book Company, New York, 1975.

Jordan, Mark H., and Robert I. Carr, "Education for the Professional Construction Manager," *Journal of the Construction Division*, ASCE, vol. 102, no. C03, proc. paper 12392, September 1976, pp. 511–519.

Kettle, Kenath A., "Project Delivery Systems for Construction Projects," *Journal of the Construction Division*, ASCE, vol. 102, no. CO4, proc. paper 12594, December 1976, pp. 575-585.

Kettle, Kenath A., "Proposed Construction Management Specification," *Journal of the Construction Division*, ASCE, vol. 105, no. CO4, December, 1979, pp. 367-380.

"The Man Behind the Concept," *Construction Methods and Equipment*, vol. 54, no. 4, April 1972, pp. 110-118.

Murray, L. William, et al., "Marketing Construction Management Services," *Journal of the Constuction Division*, ASCE, vol. 107, no. CO4, December, 1981, pp. 665-677.

Paulson, Boyd C., and Tsuneo Aki, "Construction Management in Japan," *Journal of the Construction Division*, ASCE, vol. 106, No. CO3, September, 1980, pp. 281-296.

"Professional Construction Management Services," Subcommittee Report, *Journal of the Construction Division* , ASCE, vol. 105, no. CO2, June, 1979, pp. 139-156.

"Standard Form of Agreement Between Owner and Construction Manager," Document B-801, The American Institute of Architects, Washington, D.C., December 1973.

"Standard Form of Agreement Between Owner and Construction Manager," Document No. 8, The Associated General Contractors of America, Washington, D.C., June 1977.

"Study Committee Report on Construction Management," Consulting Engineers Council, Washington, D.C., January 1972.

Tatum, Clyde B., "Evaluating PCM Firm Potential and Performance," *Journal of the Construction Division*, ASCE, vol. 105, no. CO3, September, 1979, pp. 239-251.

Project Planning and Control, and Related Methodologies

General Background

Benjamin, Jack R., and C. Allin Cornell, *Probability, Statistics, and Decision for Civil Engineers*, McGraw-Hill Book Company, NewYork, 1970.

Borcherding, John D., and C. H. Oglesby, "Construction Productivity and Job Satisfaction," *Journal of the Construction Division*, ASCE, vol. 100, no. C03, proc. paper 10826, September 1974, pp. 413–431.

Bowker, Albert H., and Gerald J. Lieberman, *Engineering Statistics*, Prentice-Hall, Inc., Englewood Cliffs, N.J., 1972.

Clough, Richard H., and Glenn A. Sears. *Construction Project Management*, 2nd ed. John Wiley & Sons, Inc., New York, 1979.

Collins, Carroll J., "Impact—The Real Effect of Change Orders," *Transactions of the American Association of Cost Engineers*, Morgantown, W. Va., June 1970, pp. 188–191.

Coxe, Weld, *Marketing Architectural and Engineering Services*, Van Nostrand Reinhold, New York, 1971.

Crandall, Keith C., *The Design of a Limited Interactive Management System for Construction Project Control,* Technical Report No. 131, Stanford University, Dept. of Civil Engineering, The Construction Institute, Stanford, Calif., December 1970.

Derk, Walter T., *Insurance for Contractors,* 4th ed., Fred S. James & Co., Chicago, 1974.

Douglas, James, *Construction Equipment Policy,* McGraw-Hill Book Company, New York, 1975.

Dunham, Clarence W., Robert D. Young, and Joseph T. Bockrath, *Contracts Specifications and Law for Engineers,* 3rd ed., McGraw-Hill Book Company, New York, 1979.

Freund, John C., *Modern Elementary Statistics,* 4th ed., Prentice-Hall, Inc., Englewood Cliffs, N.J., 1973.

Grant, Eugene, L.W. Grant Ireson, and Richard S. Leavenworth, *Principles of Engineering Economy,* 7th ed., The Ronal Press Company, New York, 1982.

Halpin, Daniel W., "CONSTRUCTO—An Interactive Gaming Environment," *Journal of the Construction Division,* ASCE, vol. 102, no. C01, proc. paper 11969, March 1976, pp. 145–196.

———, and R. W. Woodhead, *CONSTRUCTO—A Heuristic Game for Construction Management,* University of Illinois Press, Urbana, Ill., 1973.

———, and ———, *Design of Construction and Process Operations,* John Wiley & Sons, Inc., New York, 1976.

Hillier, Frederick S., and Gerald J. Lieberman, *Introduction to Operations Research,* 2d ed., Holden-Day, Inc., San Francisco, 1974.

Hollander, G. L., "Integrated Project Control," Part I, *Project Management Quarterly,* vol. 4, no. 1, April 1973, pp. 6–13; Part II, vol. 4, no. 2, June 1973, pp. 6–14.

Jones, G. L., *How to Market Professional Design Services,* McGraw-Hill Book Company, New York, 1973.

Lichtenberg, Steen, *Project Planning—A Third Generation Approach,* Polyteknisk Forlag, Lyngby, Denmark, 1974.

Miller, I., and J. E. Freund, *Probability and Statistics for Engineers,* Prentice-Hall, Inc., Englewood Cliffs, N.J., 1965.

Parker, Henry W., and Clarkson H. Oglesby, *Methods Improvement for Construction Managers,* McGraw-Hill Book Company, New York, 1972.

Paulson, Boyd C., Jr., "Concepts of Project Planning and Control," *Journal of the Construction Division,* ASCE, vol. 102, no. C01, proc. paper 11984, March 1976, pp. 67–80.

———, "Designing to Reduce Construction Costs," *Journal of the Construction Division,* ASCE, vol. 102, no C04, proc. paper 12600, December 1976, pp. 587–592.

Proceedings of the Annual Seminar/Symposiums, The Project Management Institute, Drexel Hill, Pa. Published annually since 1969.

Project Management Quarterly, The Project Management Institute, Drexel Hill, Pa. Published quarterly since 1969.

Russo, J. A. Jr., *The Complete Money Saving Guide to Weather for Contractors,* Environmental Information Services Associates, Newington, Conn., September 1971.

Schrader, Charles R., "Motivation of Construction Craftsman," *Journal of the Construction Division,* ASCE, vol. 98, no. C02, September 1972, pp. 257–273.

————, "Boosting Construction Worker Productivity," *Civil Engineering*, vol. 42, no. 10, October 1972, pp. 61–63.

Sweet, Justin, *Legal Aspects of Architecture, Engineering and the Construction Process,* 2nd ed., West Publishing Co., St. Paul, Min., 1977.

Wagner, Harvey M., *Principles of Operations Research*, 2d ed., Prentice Hall, Inc., Englewood Cliffs, N. J., 1975.

Wilson, A., *The Marketing of Professional Services*, McGraw-Hill Book Company, New York, 1972.

Wilson, Woodrow W., "Model Form of 'Instructions to Bidders'," *Journal of the Construction Division*, ASCE, vol. 100, no. C01, proc. paper 10407, March 1974, pp. 27–31.

————, "Model Form of 'Notice to Bidders'," *Journal of the Construction Division,* ASCE, vol. 100, no. C03, proc. paper 10818, September 1974, pp. 373–375.

Estimating

Behrens, H. J., "The Learning Curve," in F. C. Jelen (ed.), *Cost and Optimization Engineering*, chap. 9, McGraw-Hill Book Company, New York, 1970, pp. 170–184.

Building Construction Cost Data, Robert Snow Means Co., Inc., Duxbury, Mass. Published annually.

Building Estimator's Reference Book, 18th ed., The Frank R. Walker Co., Chicago, 1973.

Construction Users Anti-Inflation Roundtable, "Effect of Scheduled Overtime on Construction Projects," *AACE Bulletin*, vol. 15, no. 5, October 1973, pp. 155–160.

Contractors Equipment Manual, 7th ed., The Associated General Contractors of America, Washington, D.C., 1974.

Cooper, George, and Stanley Badzinski, Jr., *Building Construction Estimating*, 3d ed., McGraw-Hill Book Company, New York, 1971.

Deatherage, George E., *Construction Estimating and Job Preplanning*, McGraw-Hill Book Company, New York, 1965.

Dodge Manual for Construction Pricing and Scheduling, McGraw-Hill Information Systems Co., New York. Published annually.

Erikson, Carl A., and Leroy T. Boyer, "Estimating-State-of-the-Art," *Journal of the Construction Division*, ASCE, vol. 102, no. C03, proc. paper 12382, September 1976, pp. 455–464.

Fondahl, John W., and Ricardo R. Bacarreza, *Construction Contract Markup Related to Forecasted Cash Flow*, Technical Report No. 161, Stanford University, Dept. of Civil Engineering, The Construction Institute, Stanford, Calif., November 1972.

Foster, Norman I., *Construction Estimates from Take-Off to Bid*, 2d ed., McGraw-Hill Book Company, New York, 1972.

Guthrie, Kenneth M., *Process Plant Estimating and Control*, Craftsman Book Company of America, Solana Beach, Calif., 1974.

Lichtenberg, Steen, "The Successive Principle—Procedures for a Minimum Degree of Detailing," *Proceedings of the Sixth Annual Seminar/Symposium of the Project Management Institute*, Washington, D.C., September 1974, pp. 570–578.

————, "Project Management Systems—Monsters or Assistants to the Manager?" *Proceedings of the Eighth Annual Seminar/Symposium of the Project Management Institute*, Montreal, October 1976.

Lowell, E. D., "Estimating Building Construction Costs," in Frederick S. Merritt (ed.), *Building Construction Handbook*, 3d ed., section 25, McGraw-Hill Book Company, New York, 1975.

McGlaun, Weldon, "Overtime in Construction," *AACE Bulletin*, vol. 15, no. 5, October 1973, pp. 141–143.

National Construction Estimator, G. Moselle (ed.), Craftsman Book Company, Los Angeles, 1975

Neil, Hames M., *Construction Cost Estimating for Project Control,* Prentice-Hall, Englewood Cliffs, New Jersey, 1982

Parker, Albert D., Donald S. Barrie, and Robert N. Snyder, *Planning and Estimating Heavy Construction*, McGraw–Hill Book Company, New York, 1984.

Paulson, Boyd C., Jr., "Estimating and Control of Construction Labor Costs," *Journal of the Construction Division*, ASCE, vol. 101, no. CO3, proc. paper 11579, September 1975, pp. 623-633.

Peurifoy, Robert L., *Estimating Construction Costs*, 3d ed., McGraw-Hill Book Company, New York, 1975.

Saylor, Lee, *Current Construction Costs*, Lee Saylor, Inc., Walnut Creek, Calif. Published annually.

Zimmerman, O. T., "Capital Investment Cost Estimating," in F. C. Jelen (ed.), *Cost and Optimization Engineering*, chap. 15, McGraw-Hill Book Company, New York, 1970, pp. 301–337.

Planning and Scheduling

Antill, James M., "Critical Path Evaluations of Construction Work Changes and Delays," *Australia Institution of Engineers, Civil Engineering Transactions*, vol. 77, no. 1, April 1969, pp. 31–39.

———, and Ronald W. Woodhead, *Critical Path Methods in Construction Practice*, 2d ed., John Wiley & Sons, Inc., New York, 1970.

Armstrong-Wright, A. T., *Critical Path Method*, Longman Group Ltd., London, 1969.

Battersby, A., *Network Analysis*, 3d. ed., The Macmillan Co., New York, 1970.

Burman, Peter J., *Precedence Networks for Project Planning and Control*, McGraw-Hill Book Company, London, 1972.

Carr, Robert I., and Walter L. Meyer, "Planning Construction of Repetitive Building Units," *Journal of the Construction Division*, ASCE, vol. 100, no. C03, proc. paper 10812, September 1974, pp. 403–412.

Cost Control and CPM in Construction, The Associated General Contractors of America, Washington, D.C., 1968.

CPM in Construction, A Manual for General Contractors, The Associated General Contractors of America, Washington, D.C., 1965.

Davis, Edward W., "CPM Use in Top 400 Construction Firms," *Journal of the Construction Division*, ASCE, vol. 100, no. C01, proc. paper 10395, March 1974, pp. 39–49.

Dressler, Joachim A., "Stochastic Scheduling of Linear Construction Sites," *Journal of the Construction Division*, ASCE, vol. 100, no. C04, proc. paper 11024, December 1974, pp. 571–587.

Fondahl, John W., *A Non-Computer Approach to the Critical Path Method for the*

Construction Industry, Technical Report No. 9, Stanford University, Dept. of Civil Engineering, The Construction Institute, Stanford, Calif., November 1961.

——, *Methods for Extending the Range of Non-Computer Critical Path Applications,* Technical Report No. 47, Stanford University, Dept. of Civil Engineering, The Construction Institute, Stanford, Calif., 1964.

——, *Some Problem Areas in Current Network Planning Practices and Related Comments on Legal Applications,* Technical Report 193, Stanford University, Dept. of Civil Engineering. The Construction Institute, Stanford, Calif., April 1975.

Harris, Robert B., *Precedence and Arrow Networking Techniques for Construction,* John Wiley and Sons, New York, 1978.

Moder, Joseph J., and Cecil R. Phillips, *Project Management with CPM and PERT,* 2d ed., Van Nostrand Reinhold Co., New York, 1970.

Naaman, Antoine E., "Networking Methods for Project Planning and Control," *Journal of the Construction Division,* ASCE, vol. 100, no. C03, proc. paper 10814, September 1974, pp. 357–372.

O'Brien, James J. (ed.), *Scheduling Handbook,* McGraw-Hill Book Company, New York, 1969.

——, *CPM in Construction Management,* 2d ed., McGraw-Hill Book Company, New York, 1971.

——, "VPM Scheduling for High-Rise Buildings," *Journal of the Construction Division,* ASCE, vol. 101, no. C04, proc. paper 11773, December 1975, pp. 895-905.

Paulson, Boyd C., Jr., "Man-Computer Concepts for Planning and Scheduling," *Journal of the Construction Division,* ASCE, vol. 98, no. C02, proc. paper 9204, September 1972, pp. 275–286.

Peer, Shlomo, "Network Analysis and Construction Planning," *Journal of the Construction Division,* ASCE, vol. 100, no. C03, proc. paper 10792, September 1974, pp. 203–210.

Priluck, H. M., and P. R. Hourihan, *Practical CPM for Construction,* Robert S. Means, Co., Inc., Duxbury, Mass., 1968.

Sears, Glenn A., *A CPM-Based Cost Control System,* Technical Report No. 199, Stanford University, Dept. of Civil Engineering, The Construction Institute, Stanford, Calif., August 1975.

Wiest, Jerome D., and Ferdinand K. Levy, *A Management Guide to PERT/CPM,* Prentice Hall, Inc., Englewood Cliffs, N.J., 1969.

Cost Engineering

AACE Bulletin, American Association of Cost Engineers, Morgantown, W. Va. Published bimonthly.

Ahuja, Hira N., *Successful Construction Cost Control,* John Wiley and Sons, New York, 1980.

Cost Engineers' Notebook, 1972 rev. ed., American Association of Cost Engineers, Morgantown, W. Va., 1972. Updated periodically.

Grant, Eugene L., and L. F. Bell, *Basic Accounting and Cost Accounting,* 2d ed., McGraw-Hill Book Company, New York, 1964.

Horngren, Charles T., *Cost Accounting: A Managerial Emphasis,* 3d ed., Prentice-Hall, Inc., Englewood Cliffs, N.J., 1972.

Jelen, F. C. and James H. Black, *Cost and Optimization Engineering,* 2nd ed., McGraw-Hill book Company, New York, 1983.

Kharbanda, O. P., E. A. Stallworthy, and L. F. Williams, Revised by James T. Stoms, *Project Cost Control in Action,* Prentice-Hall, Englewood Cliffs, New Jersey, 1981.

Park, William R., *Cost Engineering Analysis,* John Wiley & Sons, Inc., New York, 1973.

Popper, Herbert (ed.), *Modern Cost Engineering Techniques,* McGraw-Hill Book Company, New York, 1970.

Teicholz, Paul, "Requirements of a Construction Company Cost System," *Journal of the Construction Division,* ASCE, vol. 100, no. C03, proc. paper 10786, September 1974, pp. 255–263.

———, "Labor Cost Control," *Journal of the Construction Division,* ASCE, vol. 100, no. C04, proc. paper 11020, December 1974, pp. 561–570.

Transactions, American Association of Cost Engineers, Morgantown, W. Va. Published annually since 1956.

Uniform Construction Index, The Construction Specifications Institute, Washington, D.C., 1972.

Procurement

Ali, A. M., "Inventory Problems," in F. C. Jelen (ed.), *Cost and Optimization Engineering,* chap. 10, McGraw-Hill Book Company, New York, 1970, pp. 185–206.

Fabrycky, W. J., and J. Banks, *Procurement and Inventory Systems,* Reinhold Publishing Corporation, New York, 1967.

Kumar, A., and H. Leng, "A Material Control System for Large Construction Projects," in *Proceedings of the Fifth International Seminar/Symposium of the Project Management Institute,* Toronto, Canada, October 1973, pp. 601–623.

Lee, Lamar, Jr., and Donald W. Dobler, *Purchasing and Materials Managements,* 2d ed., McGraw-Hill Book Company, New York, 1971.

Value Engineering

Barrie, Donald S., and Gordon L. Mulch, "The Professional Construction Management Team Discovers Value Engineering," *Journal of the Construction Division,* ASCE, vol. 103, no. C02, Sept., 1977.

Dell'Isola, Alphonse J., "A Value Engineering Case Study," *Heating, Piping and Air Conditioning,* June 1970, pp. 50–54.

———, *Value Engineering in the Construction Industry,* Construction Publishing Company, Inc., New York, 1974. (now Van Nostrand Reinhold Company).

DOD Handbook (Value Engineering), 5010.8-H, U.S. Government Printing Office, Superintendent of Documents, Washington, D.C., Sept. 12, 1968.

Miles, L. D., *Techniques of Value Analysis and Engineering,* 2d ed., McGraw-Hill Book Company, New York, 1961.

O'Brien, James J., *Value Analysis in Design and Construction,* McGraw-Hill Book Company, New York, 1976.

Value Engineering (Handbook), PBS P 8000.1 (Jan. 12, 1972) and Change 0.1 (March 2, 1973), U.S. General Services Administration, Washington, D.C.

Value Engineering in Federal Construction Agencies, Symposium–Workshop Report No. 4, National Academy of Sciences, Federal Construction Council, Building Research Advisory Board, Washington, D.C., May 1969.

Quality Assurance

Publications of the American Society of Quality Control (ASQC):
> *Annual Technical Conference Transactions* (theory and applications)
> *Journal of Quality Technology* (theory and methodology)
> *Quality Progress* (applications and trade articles)

Cohen, Norman J., "Statistical Theory in Materials Sampling," *Journal of the Construction Division*, ASCE, vol. 97, no. C01, proc. paper 8005, March 1971, pp. 95-111.

Goldbloom, Joseph, "Recommended Standards for the Responsibility, Authority, and Behavior of the Inspector," *Journal of the Construction Division*, ASCE, vol. 101, no. C02, proc. paper 11384, June 1975, pp. 359–364.

Grant, Eugene L., and Richard S. Leavenworth, *Statistical Quality Control*, 4th ed., McGraw-Hill Book Company, New York, 1972.

Hester, Weston T., "Alternative Construction Quality Assurance Programs," *Journal of the Construction Division*, ASCE, vol. 105, no. CO3, September, 1979, pp. 187-199.

Juran, Joseph M., Frank M. Gryna, and Richard S. Burgham (eds.), *Quality Control Handbook*, 3d ed., McGraw-Hill Book Company, New York, 1975.

Kirkpatrick, Elwood G., *Quality Control for Managers and Engineers*, John Wiley & Sons, Inc., New York, 1970.

Knowler, Lloyd K., and others, *Quality Control by Statistical Methods*, McGraw-Hill Book Company, New York, 1969.

O'Brien, James J., *Construction Inspection Handbook*, Van Nostrand Reinhold Company, New York, 1974.

Parsons, Roland M., "System for Control of Construction Quality," *Journal of the Construction Division*, ASCE, vol. 98, no. C01, March 1972, pp. 21–36.

Samson, Charles, Philip Hart, and Charles Rubin, *Fundamentals of Statistical Quality Control*, Addison-Wesley Publishing Company, Reading, Mass., 1970.

Simmons, David A., *Practical Quality Control*, Addison-Wesley Publishing Company, Reading, Mass., 1970.

Willenbrock, Jack H., and Scott Shepard, "Construction QA/QC Systems: Comparative Analysis," *Journal of the Construction Division*, ASCE, vol. 106, no. CO3, September, 1980, pp. 371-387.

Computer Applications

Ashley, David B., *Construction Project Risk Sharing*, Technical Report 220, The Construction Institute, Department of Civil Engineering, Stanford University, Stanford, California, June, 1977.

Bacarreza, Ricardo, *The Construction Project Markup Decision Under Conditions of Uncertainty*, Technical Report 176, The Construction Institute, Department of Civil Engineering, Stanford University, Stanford, California, June, 1973.

Card, Stuart K., Thomas P. Morgan and Allen Newell, *Applied Information Processing Psychology: The Human-Computer Interface,* Lawrence Evlbaum Associates, Hillsdale, New Jersey, 1981.

Carota, James, *The Small Contractor and the Small Computer,* Technical Report 248, The Construction Institute, Department of Civil Engineering, Stanford University, Stanford, California, June, 1980.

Condon, Robert J., *Data Processing Systems Analysis & Design,* 2d ed., Reston Publishing Company, Reston, Virginia, 1978.

Davis, William S., *Computers and Business Information Processing,* Addison Wesley, Menlo Park, 1981.

Dressler, Joachim A., *Development of an Interactive Computer Program for Resource Allocation,* Technical Report 189, The Construction Institute, Department of Civil Engineering, Stanford University, Stanford, California, December, 1974.

Eckhouse, Richard H., Jr., *Minicomputer Systems: Organization and Programming (PDP-11),* Prentice-Hall, Inc., Englewood Cliffs, New Jersey, 1975

Fondahl, John W., and Ricardo Bacarreza, *Construction Contract Markup Related to Forecasted Cash Flow,* Technical Report Number 161, The Construction Institute, Department of Civil Engineering, Stanford University, Stanford, California, November, 1972.

Isaacs, Gerald L., *BASIC REVISITED: An Update to Interdialect Translatability of the BASIC Programming Language,* CONDUIT/Central, Iowa City, Iowa, 1976.

Kalk, Anthony, *INSIGHT—Interactive Simulation of Construction Operations Using Graphical Techniques,* Technical Report 238, The Construction Institute, Dept. of Civil Engineering, Stanford University, Stanford, California, July, 1980.

Knuth, Donald E., *The Art of Computer Programming, Vol. I Fundamental Algorithms,* Addison-Wesley, Inc., Menlo Park, California, 1973.

Ledgard, Henry F., and Louis J. Chmura, *FORTRAN with Style: Programming Proverbs,* Hayden Book Company, Inc., Rochelle Park, New Jersey, 1978.

——, John F. Hueras, and Paul A. Nagin, *PASCAL with Style: Programming Proverbs,* Hayden Book Company, Inc., Rochelle Park, New Jersey, 1979.

Libes, Sol, *Small Computer Systems Handbook,* Hayden Book Company, Inc., Rochelle Park, New Jersey, 1978.

Martin, J., *Design of Man-Computer Dialogues,* Prentice-Hall, Inc., Englewood, Cliffs, New Jersey, 1973.

Meadow, C. T., *Man-Machine Communications,* John Wiley and Sons, Inc., New York, 1970.

Nagin, Paul A., and Henry F. Ledgard, *BASIC with Style: Programming Proverbs,* Hayden Book Company, Inc., Rochelle Park, New Jersey, 1979.

Newman, William M. and Sproull, Robert F., *Principles of Interactive Computer Graphics,* McGraw-Hill Book Company, New York, 1973.

Paulson, Boyd C., *et al., Human-Computer Simulation and Analysis of Construction Operations,* Technical Report No. 250, The Construction Institute, Department of Civil Engineering, Stanford University, Stanford, California, July, 1980.

Ramsey, H. Rudy, and Atwood, Michael E., *Human Factors in Computer Systems: A Review of the Literature,* Technical Report SAI-79-111-DEN, Science Applications, Inc., Sept. 21, 1979.

Shah, J., *Engineering Simulation Using Small Scientific Computers,* Prentice-Hall, Inc., Englewood Cliffs, New Jersey, 1976.

Shneiderman, Ben, *Software Psychology,* Winthrop, Cambridge, Mass., 1980.

Soucek, B., *Minicomputers in Data Processing and Simulation,* John Wiley and Sons, Inc., New York, New York, 1972.

Thierauf, Robert J., and George W. Reynolds, *Systems Analysis and Design: A Case Study Approach,* Charles E. Merrill Publishing Co., Columbus, Ohio, 1980.

Weitzman, Cay, *Minicomputer Systems: Structure, Implementation, and Application,* Prentice-Hall, Inc., Englewood Cliffs, New Jersey, 1971.

Safety and Health

Business Roundtable, *Improving Construction Safety Performance,* Construction Industry Cost Effectiveness Project Report A-3, New York, January, 1982.

California Construction Safety Orders, Dept. of Industrial Relations, Division of Industrial Safety, San Francisco.

Construction Industry: OSHA Safety & Health Standards Digest, OSHA 2202, U.S. Government Printing Office, Superintendent of Documents, Washington, D.C. Revised June 1975.

Construction Safety and Health Regulations: Part 1926, OSHA 2207, U.S. Government Printing Office, Superintendent of Documents, Washington, D.C., June 1974.

Construction Safety and Health Training, General Services Administration, National Audiovisual Center, Washington, D.C. (Manuals and slides for 30-hour course.)

deStwolinski, Lance W., *Occupational Health in the Construction Industry,* Technical Report No. 105, Stanford University, Dept. of Civil Engineering, The Construction Institute, Stanford, Calif., May 1969.

———, *A Survey of the Safety Environment of the Construction Industry,* Technical Report No. 114, Stanford University, Dept. of Civil Engineering, The Construction Institute, Stanford, Calif., October 1969.

Gans, George M., Jr., "The Construction Manager and Safety," *Journal of the Construction Division,* ASCE, vol. 107, no. CO2, June, 1981, pp. 219-226.

General Safety Requirements, Manual EM 385-1-1, and Supplements 1 and 2, U.S. Army Corps of Engineers, Washington, D.C.

Hinze, Jimmie, *The Effect of Middle Management on Safety in Construction,* Technical Report No. 209, Stanford University, Dept. of Civil Engineering, The Construction Institute, Stanford, Calif., June 1976.

Hinze, Jimmie, "Human Aspects of Construction Safety," *Journal of the Construction Division,* ASCE, vol. 107, no. CO1, March, 1981, pp. 61-72.

Knox, H., "Construction Safety as it Relates to Insurance Costs," *AACE Bulletin,* vol. 16, no. 3, June 1974, pp. 71–73.

Levitt, Raymond E., *The Effect of Top Management on Safety in Construction,* Technical Report No. 196, Stanford University, Dept. of Civil Engineering, The Construction Institute, Stanford, Calif., July 1975.

———, and Henry W. Parker, "Reducing Construction Accidents—Top Management's Role," *Journal of the Construction Division,* ASCE, vol. 102, no. C03, proc. paper 12384, September 1976, pp. 465-478.

Levitt, Raymond E., Henry W. Parker, and Nancy M. Samelson, *Imrpoving Construction Safety Performance: The User's Role,* Technical Report 260, The Construction Institute, Department of Civil Engineering, Stanford University, Stanford, California, August, 1981.

Manual of Accident Prevention in Construction, 6th ed., The Associated General
Contractors of America, Washington, D.C., 1971.
"The Occupational Safety and Health Act of 1970," P.L. 91-596 (OSHA 2001), U.S.
Government Printing Office, Superintendent of Documents, Washington, D.C.,
December 1970.
OSHA Safety and Health Training Guidelines for Construction, (PB-239 312/AS), U.S.
Dept. of Commerce, National Technical Information Service, Springfield, Va.
Robinson, M.R., *Accident Cost Accounting as a Means of Improving Construction Safety,*
Technical Report 242, The Construction Institute, Department of Civil Engineer-
ing, Stanford University, Stanford, California, August, 1979.
Safety Requirements for Construction by Contract, U.S. Dept. of the Interior, Bureau of
Reclamation, Washington, D.C.
Samelson, Nancy Morse, *The Effect of Foremen on Safety in Construction,* Technical
Report No. 219, Stanford University, Dept. of Civil Engineering, The Construction
Institute, Stanford, Calif., June, 1977.

Industrial Relations

Anderson, Howard J., *Primer of Labor Relations,* Bureau of National Affairs, Washing-
ton, D.C., 1975.
Bonny, J. B. and J. P. Frein, eds., *Handbook of Construction Management and
Organization,* 2d, ed., chap. 24, L. E. Knack, "Labor Relations and their Effect on
Employment Procedures", Van Nostrand Reinhold, 1980.
Borcherding, John D., "Construction Labor Unions in the United States," chap: 10 in:
Directions in Managing Construction, by Donals S. Barrie, ed., John Wiley & Sons,
New York, 1981.
Bourdon, C., and R. E. Levitt, *Union and Open Shop Construction,* Lexington Books,
Lexington, Massachusetts, 1980.
Business Roundtable, *Construction Industry Cost Effectiveness Project, Reports on
Industrial Relations:* A-1 Construction Productivity Measurement: A-2 Construction
Labor Motivation; C-1 Exclusive Jurisdiction in Construction; C-2 Scheduled
Overtime Effect on Construction Projects; C-3 Contractor Supervision in Unionized
Construction; C-4 Constraints Imposed by Collective Bargaining Agreements; C-5
Local Labor Practices; C-6 Absenteeism and Turnover; C-7 Impact of Local Union
Politics; D-1 Use of Subjourneymen in the Union Sector; D-2 Government
Limitations on Training Innovations; Utilization of Vocational Education in Con-
struction Training; D-4 Training Problems in Open-Shop Construction; D-5 Labor
Supply Information; E-1 Administration and Enforcement of Building Codes and
Regulations, 1982, Park Avenue, New York, New York.
Christesen, R.J., and C. B. Tatum, "Labor Relations Considerations on PCM Projects,"
Journal of the Construction Division, ASCE, vol, 106, no. CO4, December 1980,
pp. 535-549.
Christie, R. A. *Empire in Wood: A History of the Carpenters Union,* Cornell University
Press, New York, 1956.
Construction Labor Report, Bureau of National Affairs, Inc., Washington, D.C. (weekly
subscription periodical providing extensive reporting on industrial relations in
construction).
Fondahl, John and Boyd Paulson, *The Impact of Exclusive Craft Jurisdiction in the*

Construction Industry, Technical Report 263, The Construction Institute, Department of Civil Engineering, Stanford University, Stanford, California, October, 1981.

Levitt, Raymond E., "Union vs. Non-Union Construction in the U.S.," *Journal of the Construction Division,* ASCE, vol. 105, no. CO4, December, 1979, pp. 289-303.

———, and Clinton C. Bourdon, "Cost Impacts of Prevailing Wage Laws in Construction," *Journal of the Construction Division,* ASCE, vol. 105, no. CO4, December, 1979, pp. 281-288.

———, and Donald S. Barrie, "Open Shop Movement," chap. 12 in: *Directions in Managing Construction,* by Donald S. Barrie, ed., John Wiley & Sons, New York, 1981.

———, and Joel B. Leighton, Employer and Owner Associations, chap. 11 in: *Directions in Managing Construction,* by Donald S. Barrie, ed., John Wiley & Sons, New York, 1981.

Mangum, G. L., *The Operating Engineers: Economic History of a Trade Union,* Harvard University Press, Cambridge, Mass., 1964.

Mills, Daniel Quinn, *Industrial Relations and Manpower in Construction,* MIT Press, Cambridge, Mass., 1972.

Monthly Labor Review, U.S. Dept. of Labor, Bureau of Labor Statistics.

Northrup, Herbert R., and Howard G. Foster, *Open Shop Construction,* University of Pennsylvania Press, Philadelphia, 1975.

O'Brian, J. J. and R. G. Zilly, eds., *Contractor's Management Handbook,* chap. 9, D. Q. Mills, "The Labor Force and Industrial Relations," McGraw-Hill, New York, 1971.

Segal, M., *The Rise of the United Association,* Harvard University Press, Cambridge, Massachusetts, 1969.

Index